ROUTLEDGE LIBRARY EDITIONS:
WOMEN IN SOCIETY

Volume 7

WOMEN AND
SYMBOLIC INTERACTION

WOMEN AND
SYMBOLIC INTERACTION

Edited by
MARY JO DEEGAN
AND
MICHAEL R. HILL

R Routledge
Taylor & Francis Group

LONDON AND NEW YORK

First published in 1987 by Allen & Unwin, Inc.

This edition first published in 2025
by Routledge
4 Park Square, Milton Park, Abingdon, Oxon OX14 4RN

and by Routledge
605 Third Avenue, New York, NY 10158

Routledge is an imprint of the Taylor & Francis Group, an informa business

© 1987 by Allen & Unwin, Inc.

British Library Cataloguing in Publication Data
A catalogue record for this book is available from the British Library

ISBN: 978-1-032-87216-2 (Set)
ISBN: 978-1-032-85096-2 (Volume 7) (hbk)
ISBN: 978-1-032-85139-6 (Volume 7) (pbk)
ISBN: 978-1-003-51673-6 (Volume 7) (ebk)

DOI: 10.4324/9781003516736

Publisher's Note
The publisher has gone to great lengths to ensure the quality of this reprint but points out that some imperfections in the original copies may be apparent.

Disclaimer
The publisher has made every effort to trace copyright holders and would welcome correspondence from those they have been unable to trace.

Women and ———— Symbolic Interaction

EDITED BY

Mary Jo Deegan
University of Nebraska–Lincoln

Michael R. Hill
Albion College

Boston
ALLEN & UNWIN Inc.
London • Wellington • Sydney

Allen & Unwin, Inc.
8 Winchester Place, Winchester, MA 01890, USA.

The U.S. Company of
Unwin Hyman Ltd,

P.O. Box 18, Park Lane, Hemel Hempstead, Herts HP2 4TE, UK
40 Museum Street, London WC1A 1LU, UK
37/39 Queen Elizabeth Street, London SE1 2QB, UK

Allen & Unwin Australia Pty Ltd,
8 Napier Street, North Sydney, NSW 2060, Australia

Allen & Unwin (New Zealand) Ltd, in association with the Port Nicholson Press Ltd
Private Bag, Wellington, New Zealand

First Published in 1987

Library of Congress Cataloging-in-Publication Data

Women and symbolic interaction.

Bibliography: p.
Includes index.
1. Symbolic interactionism. 2. Feminism–United
States. I. Deegan, Mary Jo, 1946-   . II. Hill,
Michael R.
    291.W539   1987   305.4'2'0973   87–17427
    ₁N 0-04-497006-4 (pbk. : alk. paper)

British Library Cataloguing in Publication Data

₋men and symbolic interaction.
    Women–Social conditions
  ₁. Deegan, Mary Jo II. Hill, Michael R.
  305.4'2'   HQ1154

ISBN 0-04-497006-4

To ALAN BOOTH
Friend, Mentor, and Colleague

Contents

Section VII
The Marketplace and Social Class: The Social Claim

Section VIII
Working Hypotheses as Problematic "Solutions"

Section IX ————————————————————————————————
Concluding and Beginning

A Tribute to Mary Jo Deegan
Recovering the Feminist Past of Sociology

Mary Jo Deegan was a pioneering feminist sociologist who dedicated her career to challenging discrimination against women in society and within the discipline of sociology itself. Her groundbreaking work brought to light the significant contributions of numerous forgotten women sociologists, gradually reshaping our understanding of the field's history.

Deegan's journey began in the late 1960s when, as a graduate student at the University of Chicago, she became interested in qualitative research and in feminist theory. Early on, she recognized her desire "to be a feminist, activist, and change agent" while many of her male counterparts sought academic prestige and power. This commitment would define her life's work.

Searching for materials on early women sociologists, Deegan was astonished to find a vast body of literature on women's labor, wages, and unions that had been largely overlooked. She asked herself, "Who were these early female sociologists, and why didn't anyone ever mention them or their writings in my so-called 'best' and advanced training?" This question sparked a decades-long research project to uncover and resurrect the critical history of women in sociology.

Her seminal book, *Jane Addams and the Men of the Chicago School, 1892–1918*, was a watershed moment for U.S. sociology. It revealed the influential role of Chicago's Jane Addams and numerous other women sociologists in developing early on the feminist pragmatism perspective, which emphasized qualitative research, cooperative ethics, liberal education, and democracy. Deegan showed how these early women sociologists contributed to the development of symbolic interactionism, a distinctively U.S. sociological perspective that views human behavior as socially constructed, highly interactive, and cooperatively changeable.

Deegan's historical and theoretical research work faced resistance from some major quarters of the discipline, but she persisted, driven by a belief in the liberatory potential of her critical scholarship, especially for women. As she once noted, women can create change, "but only if a large enough number want to do it, agree on definitions of what is desirable, and have access to the means to obtain these goals."

For me, Mary Jo was not only a pioneering social scientist but a dear colleague and friend. Her passion for uncovering the forgotten histories of women in sociology was infectious, and her commitment to challenging oppressive gender, racial, and class structures was unwavering. She lived, as she once put it, an "interesting life defined and expressed very differently than those bounded by traditional and narrowly defined careers in the discipline." One great satisfaction of doing this type of critical and liberation sociology is getting other people to see ideas and histories that they've never seen before and to read social research materials they have not read before.

In honoring Mary Jo's legacy, we must continue her work of recovering the significant feminist past of sociology and amplifying the many feminist and other voices of those who have been marginalized. Her scholarship has opened our eyes to the rich tapestry of women's major contributions, reminding us that the sociology discipline's history is far more diverse and radical than we once understood it to be. Mary Jo Deegan's life was a testament to the power of human persistence, courage, and a relentless pursuit of societal truth and justice.

Note:

For a longer version of my overview and analysis of Mary Jo Deegan's life and pathbreaking work, see Joe R. Feagin, Hernan Vera, and Kimberly Ducey, *Liberation Sociology*, 3rd Edn. (New York: Routledge, 2005), pp. 236–239.

Professor Joe R. Feagin

Preface

To us, as feminist professors, the structural inequality of women is obvious. To our nonfeminist students, however, this inequality is often invisible. They believe, optimistically, that all women's problems have been solved or will be by the time they complete their undergraduate education. They are firm believers that American society is egalitarian and radically different from the world of ten or twenty years ago. This book is oriented toward our students and our vision. We, too, believe that people are flexible and can change, and that the United States Constitution guarantees equality for all citizens. We know, however, that women's status is not radically different from its definition a century ago, let alone a mere decade or two.

Symbolic interaction unites our very different worldviews in the classroom, because it articulates a positive view of human potential and gives us the tool to show how social custom, patterns, institutions, and patterns of interaction make the rhetoric of women's equality compatible with our lived patterns of inequality. Symbolic interaction takes our everyday experiences and shows their underlying patterns of meaning.

Discrimination against women occurs in all our interactions, our language, and our daily situations. It is not something "out there" and foreign to daily life. Symbolic interaction gives us the language to discuss inequality based on the everyday experiences we share, instead of appearing to impose a radical and hostile interpretation of everyday life on students who believe that their everyday life is characterized by equality in action and opportunity.

This book is a communication bridge between feminists and nonfeminists, and it is oriented toward two particular audiences. One audience, as we have discussed, is college students. The other audience consists of apolitical symbolic interactionists. The radical intent of symbolic interaction to improve everyday life has been lost since this discipline's emergence around the turn of the twentieth century. In the intervening decades, symbolic interactionists have become increasingly silent on large social issues and actions. They have emphasized, instead, small groups and face-to-face interaction. This book speaks to the potential of symbolic interactionism to link the everyday, public actions of people with the hidden rules of social life. The study of women in the marketplace and the home has opened new theoretical doors in symbolic interactionism for professionals as well as nonprofessionals.

We hope this book is part of a larger effort to study political situations, particularly between women of different races, classes, bodily capacities, religions, sexual preferences, and ages. Only a small door to understanding inequality has been opened here; we hope it will be widened by our readers and colleagues who share our perspective.

A number of people helped make this book possible. The staff and reviewers at Allen and Unwin Publishers, particularly John Michel, have provided insightful critiques and access to their many resources as publishers. Howard E. Becker, Arlene Kaplan Daniels, Gary Fine, and John Johnson all suggested names of authors who had done outstanding work on women and symbolic interaction. The staff at the University of Minnesota–Duluth also gave us support, especially J. Clark Laundergan, Chair of the Department of Sociology, and Kathy Nelson, Assistant to Michael Hill. Grace Sheldrick of Wordsworth Associates provided excellent editorial advice.

Special thanks are due to the undergraduate students in Deegan's course, Women in Contemporary Society, who have challenged her for more than a decade to show them why they should believe that inequality exists. This tough audience has pushed her to articulate the connections between the individual and society in a way that would be impossible without their naïve optimism, hostility to feminism, and patience to endure a course in which they have enrolled. As a somewhat captive audience and captive professor, we have struggled to address our different visions of everyday life. We have been able to speak to one another, however, through the language of symbolic interactionism. We hope the same can be said of many other people.

MARY JO DEEGAN
University of Nebraska–Lincoln

MICHAEL R. HILL
Albion College

Section I

Beginning

Chapter 1

Symbolic Interaction and the Study of Women: An Introduction

Mary Jo Deegan
University of Nebraska – Lincoln

CHICAGO AND SYMBOLIC INTERACTION

S ymbolic interactionism arose in a distinctively American setting and era: in the city of Chicago at the turn of the century. Chicago was booming then, industrially and commercially, in the midst of the Midwestern prairie at the southern terminus of Lake Michigan. Immigrants from Europe poured into this exploding metropolis seeking new life, employment, and the promise of social equality. Chicago's social scientists were amazed and impressed by the city's dynamic growth. They became enthused by opportunities to create new communities and new definitions of behavior. These social scientists literal-ly saw human activity create new patterns in society. It appeared to them that people could build and do anything they wanted. These social scientists' obser-vations took the form of a theoretical proposition: although members of each generation have to be taught to be members of a society, as adults these members are capable of generating society itself. Chicago's early social scientists not only understood people to be surprisingly flexible, but also hypothesized that simply changing the definition of a given behavior could generate new patterns of behavior.

To explain the massive urban transformation occurring in their own backyard, the early Chicago scholars developed a revolutionary view of human beings as social products. Briefly stated, their thesis asserted that people are socially created and that people can create new societies in which to live. Earlier theories of biological and/or economic determinism were rejected. The Chicago social scientists started from the assumption that *people* generate other people. Consequently, they held that it must be people who control human action and behavior, and the mechanism of control resides in socially constructed meanings. This theory of human behavior is called *symbolic interaction,* and it forms the historical basis for the set of readings included in this book.[1]

Source: This chapter was written for inclusion in this volume.

SOCIAL INTERACTIONS AND EMERGING
DEFINITIONS OF WOMEN

Symbolic interaction provides a particular definition of what it means to be a woman in American society, because "being female" is a social definition that emerges from human action and meaning. Since symbolic interaction is our framework for interpreting women's lives in this book, an introduction to the central ideas of symbolic interaction is necessary. New students will find this introduction especially useful because symbolic interactionists frequently assign highly specific and technical meanings to words that are used much more generally and casually in everyday conversation. The definitions provided here are a quick and handy way to grasp accurately the special meanings of this terminology.

To symbolic interactionists, *gender* is learned social behavior associated with each anatomical sex. It is a social classification. Every person (or *actor*) is taught the meanings for gendered behavior. Each person, in turn, teaches it to others. Gender involves more than simply learning masculine or feminine behavior. It also involves the entire person in the process of *becoming human*. Being a man or a woman, moreover, is a social definition that is learned by individuals throughout their lives. Women and men are, therefore, social products. They emerge from a process of human interaction based on language and the human capacity to understand it.

Women, the focus of this book, develop into social beings in the following sequence. Initially copying others' gestures, the infant girl progresses through play and game stages until she forms a *mind* with the rational ability to understand symbolic gestures. This mind allows her to become an object to herself with the capacity to make moral judgments and decisions on courses of action. Each woman develops in this way a *self* that is reflective and capable of viewing actions from both her own point of view and that of *others*. She is historically located in the community through this learning process, called socialization (Mead, 1934).

Her *community*, like her "self," is socially generated and maintained. It exists as a product of collective selves. Considerable continuity therefore exists between the individual and social institutions. Individuals create and maintain *institutions*, or habitual ways of defining action and meaning through the use of symbolic gestures. Optimal development of the self involves the increasing capacity to understand larger and more complex groups of others, from the small group, to the community, and finally, to what G. H. Mead called *international-mindedness* (Mead, 1929, 1934).

Social disorganization occurs when the self and the community disagree about the meaning of behaviors and the definitions of situations. This disorganization can result in conflict on the level of the self, the small group, the community, or the general society. It can also be the location of social innovation and change as new perspectives and definitions of action emerge to resolve these

conflicts. In American society, the definitions of being a woman and of her appropriate place in the home, the family, the marketplace, politics, and everyday
life in general are in a state of change. Conflicting definitions of the meaning of
women's behavior abound, and efforts to try new definitions of the situation
thus emerge (Thomas, 1923; Thomas and Znaniecki, 1917-1918).

The process of being a woman in modern life is thus subject to considerable
stress and debate. Women are caught between changing definitions of their
behavior. Jane Addams, an early symbolic interactionist, articulated these conflicting definitions of women's status as struggles between the *family claims* and
social claims. For example, the family claim may define mothers as ideally
suited for primary responsibility for child care, while the social claim may define
women (including mothers) as economically productive adults who should be in
the marketplace. If "wage-earning women" leave paid employment to raise
children, they are defined as "dropping out" of the marketplace and as less
"serious" and "stable" workers than men. If they have children and do not leave
their work careers, however, they may be defined as "selfish" or "bad mothers"
who do not have a "good set of values" for socializing "their" children into human
society. Problematic behavior of "their" children is often attributed to their
"failure" in mothering because of their full-time employment in the public sphere.
This conflicting definition of the "appropriate" behavior for women is only one
example of many, but it is a major issue debated throughout society.[2]

Changing definitions, as noted, are also opportunities for expanded rights
and adventure. Too strong an emphasis on the negative aspects of change can
hide the benefits of disorganization. As flexible beings who act on the basis of
socially generated meanings, women have the capacity to be liberated people in
communities of equals. Changing definitions of women's behavior are particularly positive opportunities for women, because women have been defined traditionally as less capable human beings than men.

The social construction of female life has been predicated on the subjection
of women to men. In all aspects of public life, women have been expected to be
less powerful and less significant than men. In private life, women are defined as
more equal to men than in the public sphere. All private life in the United
States, however, is dependent on access to capital, and that is primarily obtained
through the marketplace. In plain words, private life is maintained through
spending money, and men earn more money than women in the public sphere. In
addition, since most of "women's work" in the home is unpaid labor, the private
lives of wives, mothers, and daughters depend on their access to money. This access is primarily gained through husbands, fathers, and sons, for women who are
working for a "family claim" are not defined as eligible for "paid labor." This inequality in access to capital for labor expended is based on the symbolic interpretation of the value of women's world and work. In fact, most of the labor that
women do as "women" (e.g., cooks, house cleaners, and child caretakers) is not
recognized as an "economic exchange." Women work for love whereas men work
for money (Bernard, 1981).

This situation of inequality conflicts with other nongendered rights of all Americans to be treated as "first-class" citizens and to receive equal pay for equal work. Thus, American women have struggled for centuries to be accepted as people with equal status to men. Certain women have, indeed, risen above the common lot of their sisters. Others have banded together to create communities with new definitions of women's social meaning and location. Over time, nonetheless, the status of women as a social group has remained more limited than that of men. Since Americans believe in "progress," it is often difficult to believe that women's place in the United States is not dramatically improving. However, the number of women who hold national political offices, the ratio between men's and women's salaries, and the segregation of the marketplace into male and female sectors has remained fairly constant over the past three decades, if not the entire century.[3]

Societies are capable of great change as well as stability. Definitions of gendered behavior are institutionalized through the actions and shared meanings of large groups of people. Symbolic interaction, however, with its assumption of human flexibility and creativeness, is one of the few social theories that point to ways in which the individual can change the group and the community.

This optimistic, and very American, view of the world was originally part of the "first wave" of the women's movement, which culminated in 1920 when women won the right to vote. The positive potential of symbolic interaction for interpreting women's status in society lost vitality during the years when the women's movement languished. With the appearance of the "second wave" of the women's movement in the mid-1960s, symbolic interaction reappeared as an innovative way to understand sex roles and gendered action. The readings included here reflect the original promise and its contemporary fulfillment. The organization for these readings is briefly presented below, and the major theoretical ties for each section are given.

THEORETICAL READINGS ON THE EMERGENCE OF WOMEN FROM SOCIAL INTERACTION

The first two readings elaborate on the theoretical perspective introduced here. Symbolic interaction's precise language, based on everyday words, is the major focus for Taft in Chapter 2 [hereafter the readings are referred to by chapter number; i.e., (#2) and Goffman (#3)].

The interplay between the general approach of symbolic interaction and the particular topics of interest to women is immediately clear in the chapter by Jessie Taft, "The Woman Movement and Social Consciousness." Taft was a student of two major founders of symbolic interaction, G. H. Mead and W. I. Thomas, and her work shows the historical continuity between the first and second waves of feminism. The selection is taken from her 1913 doctoral dissertation, but the problems she discusses continue to divide the lives of women today. Addams's ideas about the "family claim" and "social claim" also influence Taft's articulation of the "woman question."

More than half a century passed before our next major theoretical statement on women, "The Arrangement between the Sexes," was written. In 1977, Erving Goffman integrated the issue of the sexual division of social action with his particular form of symbolic interaction. His approach, called *dramaturgy*, discusses the self as a dramatic presentation with specific roles, scripts, teams, dress, and language. Goffman's work shifts the language of symbolic interaction in major ways. First, his dramatic metaphor to explicate behavior is innovative. Second, his focus on systematic rules of action placed less emphasis on individual decisions for action. Third, his interpretation of sex/class as the primary guide for action puts the study of gender at the forefront of symbolic interactionism.[4]

These two readings by Taft and Goffman unite the remaining selections. They raise fundamental questions about self-development, the potential to learn a range of actions, and the possibility of social change through individual action. When teaching the other chapters included in this reader, I continually reintroduce the concepts from these first readings. These abstract concepts and the more concrete studies are intimately linked in symbolic interaction because each self, institution, and society is historically located. There are no unchanging truths in symbolic interaction, only the world we create and maintain in our daily lives.

SOCIALIZATION: ESTABLISHING A MIND, SELF, AND IDENTITY

Many social scientists, particularly Freudians and developmental psychologists, emphasize the importance of childhood learning, called *early socialization* or *primary socialization*. They believe that all other behaviors are built on this foundation. Although symbolic interactionists think that early socialization is important, they differ from other social scientists in a number of crucial ways. Symbolic interactionists assume that (1) "secondary" or adult socialization is vital, (2) adolescents and adults can act in ways different from those established by their early socialization, (3) people tend to maintain learned ways of behavior, and (4) most of our ideas about gender and early socialization are learned and are not "determined" biological constraints.

Acquiring Gender: Childhood Socialization

Cahill (#4) elaborates on basic concepts of identity and the self by raising specific questions about the process of acquiring gender. By looking at children–especially children identified as acting inappropriately according to gender rules–Cahill stresses the need to focus on behavior and the learning process as observable events. He also defines the concepts of *gender identity*, *gender*, and *sex* using the assumptions of symbolic interaction. Following the ideas of

Mead once again, Cahill notes that play is a crucial stage in the development of self and consciousness.

Reeves and Boyette (#5) further establish Cahill's views by using children's art as indicators of gender learning. Art allows children to express their ideas in a way that their limited verbal skills cannot. In a very specific way, feelings and ideas about the self and others are visually created by children. The authors found that the content and form of children's art are gendered and based on traditional views of women and men.

Acquiring and Negotiating Gender: Adult Socialization

These same types of issues are addressed by Risman (#6 and #7), although she examines adults' gender learning instead of children's. In the first selection (#6), Risman critically evaluates models of gender learning other than symbolic interactionism. These models fail to explain the specific world and experiences of transsexuals, people who change their anatomical sex. Risman emphasizes the flexibility of gender and its potential to change throughout life. She expands Cahill's discussion (#4) of the differences between "anatomy," "gender identity," and "gender role," although she questions his findings on the stability of early gender learning.

Risman next shows (#7) how the college "Greek" system reinforces and amplifies early gender experiences so that college women in contemporary society learn to behave in traditional ways to "catch a man" and exhibit "coy sexuality." These traditional ways of being female interact with women's career choices and training, giving us a model of modern conflicts between family and social claims. In the college-based "Greek" system, however, a group outside of the nuclear family continues the "family claim" on a campus, where "social claims" are ostensibly being learned.

In a similar way but in a dissimilar context, Hammond (#8) finds that women medical students use "female" ways of acting as particular styles and strengths in their chosen profession. Women medical students sometimes stress their differences from their male cohorts to legitimize their entry into a competitive and prestigious male-dominated occupation. The justification that female doctors provide services that are distinct from those of male doctors perpetuates rather than changes present sex roles. This explanation also postpones students' confrontations with the shared work and qualifications of all physicians.

Dill's article (#9) powerfully pulls together a number of ideas presented in the previous chapters. By discussing "sisterhood" as an extension of the family claim into the social arena, she illustrates a radically different application of the concept of "sister" than that found in the "sorority sister." Dill elaborates on many points raised by Taft and Goffman but extends their analyses to a contemporary critique. She critically notes the tendency of many feminist theorists to ignore the vital significance of race and class in the female experience. She argues that the process of creating a female self varies by class and race. Because the articles by Risman (#7) and Hammond (#8) examine the lives of women of privilege, Dill provides a needed dimension for the study of women and symbolic interaction.

MARRIAGE AND THE HOME: THE FAMILY CLAIM

The family claim is usually learned first in the home during childhood. This claim continues throughout women's lives, especially if they become wives and mothers. The number of women who do become wives and mothers has dramatically increased since the turn of the century, although the popular image suggests the opposite. Fewer than 4 percent of American women never marry, and only a slightly higher percentage never become mothers. Thus, the roles of wives and mothers are major issues in the construction of the female experience; each of these "family claims" is examined next.

The Family Claim for Wives

Learning gender roles continues throughout women's adult lives, particularly for wives and workers in the home. Corporate wives, Andersen (#10) tells us, have a class status allowing them to enjoy traditional women's roles. Their power in the community and access to capital make the wife, mother, and homemaker roles highly rewarding. Taft's (#2) earlier explanation of change and support of the women's movement arises from an examination of all women, particularly women who want and need to work in the marketplace. Dill (#9) discusses the failure of traditional women's roles to provide economic power and security, particularly for women of color. Andersen shows, in contrast, a specific privileged group of women, corporate wives, who work at being powerful wives in the community. Their access to power explains why corporate wives cherish and defend images of women as needing men's protection and support, particularly financial support. Such women of privilege are frequently "sorority sisters" during their college years, similar to the women discussed by Risman.

Gillespie (#11) continues to look at unusual wives with power, the wives of public figures. The public wife is expected to be loyal to her husband's career and personality; she must move and dress in a manner that is both demure and on display; and she must represent the highest moral expectations as a force for "human interest" in her husband's life. Each of these expectations structures the way these women present themselves to others. Public wives generate "ideal models" for other women to emulate. Gillespie directly extends Goffman's dramaturgical theory (#3). Goffman's general assumption that sex/class is the most fundamental division in society is supported by Gillespie's specific analysis.

Despite these traditional family models, Gross (#12) has found that some wives are changing their lives through commuter marriages. Women in the past often stayed home while their husbands were away for extended periods, but women who establish homes separate from their husbands' violate traditional definitions of marriage. Gross discusses concretely how conflicts between family and social claims can be resolved in this situation. Establishing and maintaining a commuter marriage is a difficult process, albeit a rewarding one, for the couples studied.

The Family Claim for Mothers

The process of becoming a mother and mothering has been subject to considerable mythmaking, but little analysis by women. The topic of miscarriage, in particular, has been consistently ignored. Reinharz (#13) wrote her selection on miscarriage specifically for this volume to begin to fill this gap in symbolic interaction literature. She amply documents the importance of language in establishing both the role of mother-to-be and the relation to the baby conceived. Methodologically, Reinharz has filled another gap by analyzing a "life history," or a participant's account of his or her actions. This technique was finely tuned by W. I. Thomas and Florian Znaniecki in 1917, but it has fallen into disuse during the intervening decades.

Women who do become mothers are traditionally expected to be married, although the relation between marriage and motherhood has always been complex. Horowitz (#14) shows how ethnicity and class influence the definition of this status in a particular population, inner-city Chicanas. She provides a theoretically complex discussion of the multidimensional patterns that may emerge. She also examines the connection between sexuality, identity, and action in a context different from Cahill (#3), who discusses similar topics for children, or Risman (#6), who analyzes the variety of normal behaviors and their interaction with narrower cultural definitions.

Although motherhood has been a traditional role for most women, some women are not encouraged to be mothers. Thus, disabled women who are mothers represent another group breaking traditional expectations. Shaul, Dowling, and Laden (#15) interviewed disabled mothers and learned how becoming a mother can be a nontraditional choice for this population. Since some people see disabled women as incapable of fulfilling sexual, adult roles, disabled mothers are innovative in a number of ways. The development of new parenting models, physical equipment for child care, and expectations of obedience reveals the flexibility not only of the mothers but of their children as well.

THE MARKETPLACE AND SOCIAL CLASS:
THE SOCIAL CLAIM

Women of all ages are increasingly entering the marketplace, working for more years, and expecting to work for money during at least part of their lifetimes. Mothers of young children are also becoming paid laborers with in-creasing frequency. Despite these major changes in the social claim for women, the salaries that women earn are approximately 60 percent of what men earn. Women work in sex segregated jobs, and they are paid less for the same work that men do. Thus, women are congregated in low paying and low status jobs.

Kanter (#16) provides a groundbreaking analysis of the difficulty of being in the numerical minority for any worker, regardless of sex, class, or race. Every action, gesture, idea, and decision comes under special scrutiny in this situation. By looking at group processes first and then at gender, she shows that the number of women proportionate to the number of men in any given occupation structures entry, promotion, and performance. With a sex-segregated labor market, women in male-dominated jobs face a peculiar social definition of their behavior that systematically restricts their actions and opportunities.

Working-class women in male-dominated jobs – police officers, construction workers, truckers, garbage collectors – experience additional problems to those discussed by Kanter. Along with being numerical minorities, these women must prove that they are capable of doing "masculine" labor associated with physical skills. Martin's study of police officers (#17) documents the gendered nature of these jobs. She shows that the language used in these settings is integral to deep structural divisions between the sexes. Martin links interpersonal interaction with organizational structure, thereby revealing the connections between spon-taneous daily interactions and long-term patterns.

Despite the similar experiences of women in the same occupations and classes, other important factors exist, such as the particular individuals involved in a situation, and their race. In other words, both common and separate in-terests vary in importance in a specific analysis or interaction, and an under-standing of both general and specific behaviors is needed. Jones (#18) emphasizes the unique experiences of a group of black female tobacco workers in Durham, North Carolina, from 1920 to 1940. In her study of a particular group, she un-folds the general process of developing female consciousness. These black women document women's struggles throughout this century and between the "waves" of feminist activities. Fights for equality have occurred across race and sex lines, but the work of white women and black men have been more publicly recognized than that of black women.

Even an examination of these factors does not exhaust the array of in-fluences on women's work in the marketplace. The impact of gender on work varies considerably according to the definition of the task, women's roles in the work situation, and training. Thus, Easterday, Papademas, Schorr, and Valen-tine (#19) analyze how gender expectations are important issues for symbolic in-teractionists. These authors' thesis is that gender in the marketplace can be a variable status, and training for these changing situations should account for this reality.

CONTEMPORARY EFFORTS TO INCREASE WOMEN'S OPPORTUNITIES: WORKING HYPOTHESES AS PROBLEMATIC "SOLUTIONS"

All of the readings mentioned thus far examine the complex and problematic nature of women's lives. Most authors discussed a number of ways to redefine the situation of women in a specific context or group. The last group of readings, however, focus on the change process itself. They analyze the intricacies of defining new goals, implementing changing definitions, and enacting new behaviors.

Although symbolic interactionists believe that people create their own lives, this does not mean that women can change society without resistance, trial and error, and ambiguity. The last readings, on "solutions" to women's problems, show that long-range changes in women's lives require massive changes throughout the society as well as in individual lives. Thousands of American women are living nontraditional lives, fighting for equality and protection under the law, and finding out that such changes are difficult to institutionalize, enact, and define.

Barriers to action are poignantly revealed in Abel's (#20) chapter examining the process of legal action initiated by women faculty. Discrimination against women as intellectuals and university employees is well documented. The way to end such oppression, however, has been severely limited by a system of arbitration, requiring each woman to face the institution as an individual, often for a number of years and in a hostile environment. Recent budgetary constraints on federal agencies supporting such lawsuits and other "supportive" governmental legislation have made implementation of legal options even more problematic. Abel stresses the need for women to respond as a group with a similar problem instead of as individuals who are in a unique situation of discrimination.

In a different argument, Ferraro (#21) shows that institutions ostensibly designed by women to help women may blame women for being victims. Social agencies for rape victims and battered women want to serve "worthy" clients who present the "correct" self-presentation. The process of testing the victim instead of responding to the crime is an important issue for victimized women, because the public institutions become another instrument for punishing wounded women.

As Ferraro documents, however, battered women need services that are often difficult to provide. Solutions to problems are often difficult to define, implement, and sustain. An ongoing network of agencies and funding exists in society, and feminists must find ways of defining their work so that the everyday order is challenged and the new agency (or institution) can survive. Ferraro provides an important example of *working hypotheses*, or attempts to apply knowledge about a problem and then evaluate how well the response decreases, increases, or eliminates the problem. Battered women's shelters have not reduced battering, so new solutions must be sought.

The mass media also offer both possibilities and barriers to new roles for women. Frequently, novels have provided more control for feminists than the "hotter," more powerful media of films and television. Womens' differential access to the mass media is beautifully documented by Blum (#22). She begins by demonstrating that feminist popular culture can capture the public's imagination. In this case, Marilyn French's book, *The Women's Room*, is a creative and poignant novel about one woman's attempt to gain control over her life and choices. The protagonist's failure to obtain all of her goals is something she confronts with dignity in the book, but not in the televised version. By minutely examining the shift in language, images, roles and decisions, Blum shows how feminist visions and language in a written medium can be subverted by a more powerful medium, television.

Finally, an innovative social experiment is incisively analyzed by Weston and Rofel (#23). These authors minutely examine how a "liberated" workplace becomes problematic. They begin by showing that a garage controlled and owned by lesbians creates an environment in which workers are free to express their sexual preferences and lifestyle. This context is exciting and different from a patriarchal and sexist one, but the issues of control over labor, capital, and the means of production ultimately create new barriers. To the owners' and workers' dismay, they discover that class relations need to be more formalized and structured in order to be more "fair." Clearly, this workshop is a step toward more freedom for women, but the effect of capital and the larger society must be taken into account in the process of creating a new, living society. Weston and Rofel have taken a step beyond the original "working hypothesis" to generate a new vision of how to implement greater freedom for women. They remind us that social change must be flexible, reflexive, and renewed.

CONCLUSION: WORKING HYPOTHESES FOR THE FUTURE

Symbolic interactionists optimistically support the possibility of individual will and action. It is people who create human behavior, and it is people who can change it. Women have a very limited role in public life in this society, however, and their roles in the home and family are dependent on capital and power found in that public realm. Changing the inequality permeating this society requires that women gain more power, legitimacy, and control. Women can do this, but only if a large enough number want to do it, agree on definitions of what is desirable, and have access to the means to obtain these goals. Clearly these are big "ifs."

Women of the 1980s, like women who lived a century ago, vary greatly in their vision of the ideal future. Some women want major changes, some want a few changes, some like traditional gender roles, and a few would like women to have even fewer freedoms than they now have. The social movement to improve women's opportunities needs to be lived, led, and defined by women, however, despite this great variation in views and vested interests.

These changes require a redistribution of power, making the issue of men's roles in women's liberation particularly problematic. Despite these difficulties in defining action, all people, men and women, create society. And all people are needed to fulfill the dreams of a new society. Symbolic interactionism gives us hope that new societies are possible. It lets us see how the present society appears to be "given" or "natural," and how it is supported by a web of ideas and actions that are woven into complex patterns. Symbolic interactionism gives a realistic view of possibility and a pragmatic way to become who we want to be.

Each chapter in this book shows a specific way to improve women's lives, and the accumulation of these working hypotheses is a small step toward a concrete new future for women. These authors do not promise a revolution in one step but in a series of steps that need to be enacted throughout our communities and daily lives. In the concluding chapter (#24), I summarize and review the working hypotheses found in the separate chapters to show that particular changes need to be accomplished for all women, regardless of race, class, sexual preference, age, religion, bodily capacities, or ethnicity. These working hypotheses are pragmatic suggestions for a revolution in language, ideology, and distribution of material power throughout society. The continual pressure to change all situations by all members of society is needed to liberate women. Anything less than this total involvement creates only small pockets of social change that are easily accommodated by a sexist society.

NOTES

1. The Chicago School of Symbolic Interaction is a particular type of theory generally attributed to men who worked at the University of Chicago, including George Herbert Mead, William Issac Thomas, Robert E. Park, and Louis Wirth. The Chicago School is also a very complex and encompassing group, including people in other cities. Thus, Charles H. Cooley, who worked at the University of Michigan, is still considered part of the Chicago School. Chicago women, moreover, have often been excluded from the list of founders. Jane Addams was never a full faculty member of the University of Chicago, but I consider her a major figure in the Chicago School. Sophonisba Breckinridge is another woman whom I, but not many other contemporary scholars, include in this school.

The early situation is clearer, however, than the contemporary one. A later school based on the Chicago School that used quantitative measures (instead of qualitative or descriptive data) of the self is called the Iowa School of Symbolic Interactionism. In the 1960s, many symbolic interactionists were located in California making Chicago sociology more national. An Illinois School is now emerging, with fundamental criticisms of qualitative Chicago sociology and a new emphasis on quantitative measures and behavioral experiments. The dominant approach, found in this book, is the Chicago School work that is qualitative and emphasizes the writings of Mead, Thomas, and Addams.

2. See Jane Addams, *Twenty Years at Hull-House* (New York: Macmillan, 1910) for a discussion of these concepts and many more. She also vividly described the chaotic and exciting world of Chicago during the founding years of symbolic interaction. An analysis of Addams's relation to the work of Mead and Thomas is found in Deegan (*in press*).

3. This reader is not intended statistically to document women's status in the public sphere. Two excellent readers who provide this type of information are Glazer and Waehrer (1977) and Freeman (1985). Because these data need to be continually updated for skeptics who believe that women's status is dramatically changing today, the best information is always found in the latest U.S. Census reports.

4. Despite the power of Goffman's work to interpret and analyze women's status, the language he uses is often subject to the same discriminatory limitations he is critiquing. Wedel's (1978) criticism of the sexist language used in this chapter is well taken, although these flaws do not negate the total argument.

We strongly considered including Wedel's criticisms in this anthology, but Wedel uses sexist language, too. For example, the title of her comment, "Ladies, We've Been Framed!" indicates some of the difficulties here. Many women find the word *ladies* unacceptable, and Wedel, like Goffman, plays with words. The temptation to be humorous and clever weakens the writings of both Goffman and Wedel.

REFERENCES

Addams, Jane 1910 *Twenty Years at Hull-House*. New York: Macmillan.

Bernard, Jessie 1981 *The Female World*. New York: The Free Press.

Deegan, Mary Jo In Press *Jane Addams and the Men of the Chicago School: 1890–1918*. New Brunswick, New Jersey: Transaction Press.

Freeman, Jo, ed. 1985 *Women: A Feminist Perspective*, Third Edition. Palo Alto, California: Mayfield Publishing Co.

Glazer, Nona and Helen Y. Waehrer, eds. 1977 *Women in a Man-Made World*, Second Edition. Chicago: Rand McNally.

Mead, George H. 1934 *Mind, Self, and Society: From the Standpoint of a Social Behaviorist*. Edited by Charles W. Morris. Chicago: University of Chicago Press.

———1929 "National Mindedness and International-Mindedness," *International Journal of Ethics* 39 (November): 392–407.

Thomas, William I. 1923 *The Unadjusted Girl: With Cases and Statements for Behavior Analysis*. Boston: Little, Brown and Co.

——— and Florian Znaniecki 1917–1918 *The Polish Peasant in Europe and America*. Five vols. Boston: Badger Press.

Wedel, Janet 1978 "Ladies, We've Been Framed!" *Theory and Society* 5 (Spring): 113–25.

Section II ─────────────────────────────

The Emergence of Women from Social Interaction

Chapter 2 ────────────────────────────

The Woman Movement and Social Consciousness

Jessie Taft

INTRODUCTION

For the last twenty-five years or more, women, their position and function in the scheme of things, their biological superiority or inferiority, their mental and physical characteristics, their achievements and failures, have been discussed and rediscussed with unflagging interest. Every nook and corner of feminine nature has been brought to light and examined as if woman were a newly discovered species. Yet out of this endless controversy only a very general agreement has been reached. It is fair to say that the majority of intelligent people today are agreed on at least two points: the necessity of improving motherhood and the need of some form of useful work for every woman. But here the agreement ends. As to exactly what conduces to improved motherhood or constitutes the proper kind of useful labor, both masculine and feminine authorities disagree.

In the meantime, while the controversy continues, despite the approval or disapproval of the theorists, women, whether they wish it or no, are necessarily affected by all the changes in education, industry, and government that are in the process of remaking society. Women find themselves as a matter of hard fact in the equivocal position of being neither one thing nor the other, neither in the home nor out of it, neither wholly mediaeval nor wholly modern. The world to which women have been accustomed for centuries and to whose patterns their minds have been shaped is not for the most part the world of the modern man. His world is not only different, it is even hostile and antagonistic in many respects to the world of the woman; so much so that women who attempt to conform to both worlds, as many are compelled to do, find themselves face to face with conflicts so serious and apparently irreconcilable that satisfactory adjustment is often quite impossible on the part of the individual woman. The world outside the home has proved itself so ill suited to women and children,

Source: Jessie Taft, "The Woman Movement and Social Consciousness." In *The Woman Movement and Social Consciousness.* Chicago: University of Chicago Press, 1915. Pp. ix–11, 36–57.

even to the extent of being positively injurious, and the home in its present form has seemed to be so little adapted to the larger world's ideals of trained motherhood, scientific domestic economy, and socialized ethics, that the problems arising from the clashing of the two spheres have grown into great social questions to be handled by society as a whole.

An unprejudiced examination of the actual conditions which the average middle class woman has to meet in adjusting her life to the home and to the man's world gives sufficient evidence of the reality of the problems which are back of the so-called "woman question" and reveals their intimate connection with every other great social movement of our day. The cry of the uneasy woman[1] is not merely the reprehensible expression of her own personal restlessness. Consciously or unconsciously it voices her share in the protest of the age against the impossible situation in which humanity finds itself today, and her struggles, even though they seem to be a vain beating against the righteous and inevitable order of things, are a real part of that larger conflict which society as a whole is waging in its effort to combine modern industry and modern individualism.

It is the purpose of this thesis to determine just what are the problems represented by the woman movement, to trace their connection with the larger, more inclusive social problems, and to indicate in a general way the direction from which a solution may be expected.

I. THE PROBLEM

1. Personal and Social Aspects

The problems which justify the woman movement appear and may be handled under two aspects: first, as they break out in the life of the individual woman as personal difficulties demanding some kind of personal adjustment; second, as they take on the guise of public questions assuming such proportions as openly to threaten the welfare of society. The following section is an attempt to treat them very briefly from both points of view. None of this material is new, but it is well worth presenting as a whole in condensed form that its very bulk may convince us of the reality of what is so often regarded as an illusion due to the restless and unstable character of women always longing for that which they have not and failing to make use of that which they have.

From the standpoint of the individual woman the most hopeless problem, and one which carries with it a long train of lesser difficulties, lies in the economic field. Here she faces what appears to be under our present system an almost insoluble dualism. Shall the young girl of today prepare for marriage or for wage-earning, for neither, or for both? The women of the laboring classes can indulge in little preparation either for marriage or for earning a living, yet for them economic independence is usually necessary before marriage and frequently after. The women of the wealthier classes, on the other hand, have the advantage of being able to make their own situation to a large extent and may prepare for both, either, or neither, as they choose. On the middle class woman, however, this uncertainty of training presses heavily.

An examination of all the factors involved shows a heavy balance on the side of the advisibility of preparing to earn a living. Marriage, housekeeping, childbearing, as commonly understood and practised, do not, if one has average intelligence, necessarily require any special training beyond that which is picked up at home or can be acquired when the time comes by actual doing. It is possible and customary to get along as most people do without scientific preparation for marriage. Moreover, marriage is not a certainty upon which one may depend as a sure or even probable means of support. Nor is marriage for the sake of livelihood any longer considered morally justifiable and, with that avenue cut off, the probability of marriage is greatly lessened. To find a husband one loves is not so easy as finding merely a husband. Widowhood, too, is a possibility that must be reckoned with. But, even granted the certainty of marriage, there are still a considerable number of years during which the young woman may find economic independence essential. Modern economic conditions tend both to defer marriage and so to deplete the amount of work done in the home that in many cases the daughter's share is not of sufficient economic value to enable her father to support her. Even when the father is quite able to support his daughter indefinitely or until her marriage, the work which falls to her in the home is seldom of such a nature as to keep her interest or bring out and develop all her unused resources and powers. As long as the mother is at the helm, very little authority or responsibility is likely to rest upon the daughter, and the modern girl usually feels that, however wealthy her parents, she is not justified in living unless she is engaged in responsible work and is giving value received to society. On the whole, therefore, even when there is no economic necessity, self-support or preparation for it appears to be the part of prudence and good judgment.

As a result of this training for work in the world rather than for homemaking, the desire of the normal woman for a husband, children, and a home inevitably clashes with other desires developed in connection with her work in the world or in her preparation for such work. She naturally wishes to continue to do that for which she has been trained and for which she may have a natural aptitude. She clings to her economic freedom. The heterogeneous, unsystematized work of housekeeping has little attraction for one accustomed to regular hours and specialized, standardized work whose dignity as a trade or profession is universally recognized. She may realize that she has not merely a disinclination but a deep-rooted distaste for household tasks and a positive lack of ability to perform them well. Knowing this, she must face the possibility that, if she forces herself to assume duties to which she brings neither liking nor training, there may arise a discontent with life so great as to endanger the success of her marriage.

If she is a woman with a socially trained conscience she may even feel that, if she accepts the home under its present conditions and allows her husband to support her, she owes it to society to take the time before marriage to make herself as fit as possible for her duties as consumer, food preparer, housekeeper, childbearer, and trainer. Yet she knows that this, if taken seriously, means a second profession or group of professions.

Furthermore, to the gifted and ambitious woman, the woman who has found growth and freedom and happiness in her work, comes the fear which is almost certainty, that, she too, like so many others, if she marries, will find her talents and her ambitions hopelessly swamped by the infinite detail, the wear and tear of domestic duties, and that middle age will see her contented, settled down, all her possibilities for growth gone forever, even the desire to do, dead. Should her zest for life and work persist to that period when her family duties no longer absorb her, will it be possible for her after the long years of absence to resume the work for which she was trained? For the alert modern woman, conscious to her finger tips, knowing in her heart that she could give a lifetime of happy associations to the man she loved, and to society, healthy, normal children, the deadlock into which the present social order forces her is a cruel, blighting thing—a choice between a crippled life in the home or an unfulfilled one out of it.

We are not attempting in this discussion of difficulties arising on the economic side to justify any of the conditions or attitudes presented, but merely to state them as real problems actually appearing in the lives of many women. While none of the conflicting impulses above described may result in the giving up of marriage in a concrete case, yet they tend to restrain the woman from making any effort in the direction of matrimony and they make married life more difficult, more easily shipwrecked.

Turning from the economic to the ethical field, we find that there also women encounter a dualism. The values which they have put first—life, love, children—are not the values most emphasized by men outside the home. The fact that women are forced to subordinate these values if they enter the man's world as it is, involves constant emotional strain. Their sense of relative values is continually violated. Equipped with only a family ethics, women as they go into the larger world often seem to lack the loyalty, the ethical consciousness which men consider essential for such social institutions as law, government, or business. Men feel that honor as they understand it is quite impossible for women, because women are so often unable to see wrong in what men condemn when it does not violate the closer relations and loyalties to which their code applies; whereas the women fail equally to comprehend the man's disregard of the duties to the immediate family and the weakness of his allegiance to that which is for them supreme.

This mutual incompatibility of ethical standards due to the difference in the worlds to which they were meant to apply and the corresponding difference in the emphasis placed on values is a favorite theme of Ibsen and is brought out with unusual clearness in the drama *John Gabriel Borkman*. Borkman who has spent years in prison for the dishonest use of other people's money in the making of his own fortune is reproached bitterly by his former sweetheart for his crime, which, for her, is found to consist, not in the fact that he has broken the law of the land, but solely in this, that he voluntarily gave up his love for her and their mutual happiness for the sake of business advancement, that he killed the love life in her soul. When a woman with such standards of life burnt deep into her soul attempts conscientiously to reconcile them with what the world demands as honorable, she faces a herculean task which is likely to crush or harden her and which she can never accomplish as an individual.

The man also, it is true, in so far as he too lives in both the home and the world has just as overwhelming a discrepancy in standards and, as an individual, is just as unequal to the task of dealing with them; the strain, however, is usually not so great because he lives much less completely than the woman in both worlds and therefore feels much less keenly the need of harmonization. The woman is never allowed to forget that, whatever her work, the home and all that it stands for must be her deepest interest; she cannot throw off its standards lightly. Yet, if she is to succeed in the world without, she cannot afford to ignore the rules as she finds them there, whereas the man has long treated the home as a place where he can and does cast off the rules and standards of his workaday world. Nobody expects him to carry the ideals of the home back to his business and he has grown accustomed to keeping them shut off in an air tight compartment of his personality.

A part of this ethical conflict, but so large and prominent a part that it looms up as a separate problem, is the double standard in sex. A standard of absolute physical chastity for the woman is confronted by a world where almost unlimited license is taken for granted. This fact, reinforced by the ordinary training of the home to the effect that sex, especially in all its physical manifestations, is inherently and mysteriously evil and is allowable only when the evil is counteracted by the charm of the marriage ceremony, that the flesh and the devil are one, may lead the woman to revolt in disgust against sex in general, to such an extent that the natural impulse to marry is actually checked by her intense horror of the physical relationship involved and by her belief that all men are brutes in so far as they seek sex satisfaction.[2] The antagonism between her bringing up in the home and the world of sex as she finds it beyond the home, makes for every thinking woman a problem that may last over years of her life – the task of building up an idea of sex that is consistent with the facts and yet leaves a universe in which she can live comfortably, of escaping from her own barren chastity while avoiding the man's meaningless license, of creating a new appreciation and expression of the most fundamental human instinct.

In the political field, the suffrage movement is the expression of a conflict of demands on the part of society and of impulses on the part of the individual woman. Society expects women to be good and useful citizens. It holds them responsible for the welfare of homes and children and is ready to criticize them

for failures within their own province. At the same time, it makes direct responsibility impossible for women by forbidding the use of the instrument through
which for the most part civic control is acquired. The woman, on the other hand,
must reconcile her own inertia and the natural inclination to dodge responsibility
reinforced as it is by the extreme effort required to exercise indirect influence, by
public acquiescence, and even by legal prohibition, with a conscience awakened
by a larger worldly experience which insists that she is already morally responsible and ought never to rest until she is legally so.

Even within the apparently unimportant realm of clothes, there runs the
same inevitable dualism of conflicting demands and impulses. The home,
especially the home of today, permits a style of dress which is impracticable for
the woman who works in the world. Men like and demand so-called fashionable
clothes for their women folk and every normal woman desires her apparel to be
pleasing in the eyes of at least one man; yet women know that the ultra feminine
clothes imposed on them by fashion and masculine taste are disastrous for real
work and make them appear ridiculous to the sober workaday world. They must
choose, therefore, between lessened sex attraction and increased respect on the
part of the men with whom they work. If the woman has succeeded in suppressing her own yearning for fluffy, frivolous clothes which she realizes make her appear more desirable to men of her acquaintance, she has still to face the practical
difficulties of obtaining any other kind. Women's clothes, in accordance with the
desires of men and the economic changes in women's work, have evolved along
the line of adaptation to a class which does no serious work, whose chief end in
life is to attract attention and elicit admiration, and which has no responsibility
for paying the bills.

This type of dress is suitable only for the very wealthy leisure class and for
the prostitute. When the professional or business woman attempts to keep
herself clothed in simple durable garments that are appropriate to her work and
her income, she finds that she is not free to follow the dictates of common sense.
In order to get what she wants she must expend time, money, and thought quite
out of proportion to the value of clothes in her life. For the working girl in store
or factory, the problem is almost insoluble. For the average working girl, a good
appearance is essential to keeping a job; yet the only clothes within her means
are the most extreme, the most unsuitable for her work, and the least durable.
She cannot afford to buy such clothing, yet she can never afford to dress sen-
sibly unless she has unusual advantages in the way of skill in dressmaking or a
home where clothes can be made. A woman wants to be beautiful in the eyes of
men; she also wants to be sensible – sometimes. Men themselves demand of her
both beauty and sense; yet the world in which she is forced to live at present
makes the combination a difficult one.

We now turn back to consider these same problems, but this time from the
standpoint of society as a whole rather than from the point of view of the individual woman.

On the economic side, the dilemma in which woman as an individual finds herself is expressed socially on a large scale both within the home and without it in conditions unfavorable, to the welfare of the community.

Under the present organization of the home, society must suffer the consequences of an institution carried on almost entirely by unskilled labor. Women have fallen into their new role of consumers without knowledge and without any sense of responsibility.

Consumption as carried on by the home is still a relatively unconscious performance.[3] Society must carry the burden of badly nourished families resulting in large part from women's ignorance of food values, of poorly clothed families due to women's ignorance of textiles, and of families that are sickly and diseased because the mothers know nothing of sanitation, hygiene or eugenics.[4]

That society recognizes the weakness of its homes is seen in the fact that it is attempting to correct evils connected therewith by various laws and institutions. Rash consumption is met by such organizations as the Consumers' League and by all sorts of newspaper and magazine campaigns calculated to educate women buyers. Pure food laws are designed to protect families from the ignorant mother as well as from the corrupt dealer. To check the increasing amount of child delinquency, due in large measure to poor home conditions, society offers the juvenile court. The social settlement, the associated charities with visiting nurse and housekeeper, child welfare and household exhibits on a gigantic scale, baby health contests, schools for mothers, are society's attempts to remedy the ignorance and unfitness of the mother in the poorer home. Preventive methods also are being worked out in schemes for an educational system which shall insure some training in home making to every girl who attends public school. The difficulty is, of course, to contrive some method of giving her two preparations, one in general housekeeping and child training and another in some vocation by which she may earn her living, if necessary.

Outside the home, likewise, society feels the results of untrained or half trained workers. The occupations entered by women are lowered by the lack of a professional attitude on their part. Women do not take their jobs seriously enough because they expect to marry. Usually they are not well trained for their work; but neither are they thoroughly trained for home making and society loses all around.[5] There is great waste involved in training thoroughly women who will drop their work in a few years; there is also waste in not training them; but the greatest waste of all, if society expects the home to continue to be efficient on its present basis, is in allowing them to marry, not only unprepared, but also frequently unfitted for home work by their experience in the shop or office.[6]

The addition of a large number of unskilled and unorganized women to the industrial world has tended to render certain labor problems more acute and more conscious. Conditions which were bad enough for men come out more sharply when applied to women. The effect of long hours, of night work, of standing all day, of bad sanitary conditions, is more serious in the case of women, and the results for their children, if they are married, or for their future motherhood, are serious enough to force the state to protect them in a measure. If women must or will work outside of the home, society cannot afford to suffer because of conditions not essential to the work itself. Therefore, we see society's consciousness of the woman's problem expressed in the struggle for the shorter day,[7] in laws allowing time off and part pay before and after the birth of a child,[8] and providing means for nursing the child during working hours,[9] in various regulations obliging employers to furnish seats, better sanitary conditions, and forbidding night work and certain dangerous trades. Only recently there came up before the school authorities of New York City as a live and burning issue the question of what was to be done with women teachers who asked for leave of absence to become mothers. That this situation, which was once merely a personal problem for some women, has now become a bona fide public question is made evident by the general interest on the part of the community and by the amount of time and space given to its serious discussion both in newspapers and in public meetings. The lack of solidarity characteristic of women brought up in the individualistic home, the habit of many of them of living partly on the home and partly on their own earnings, their lack of skill, and the over supply of labor which they cause, have all combined to increase the wage cutting that has forced society to face the problem of a living wage and the necessity of getting working women to organize and become conscious of themselves as constituting a class. The efforts of the Woman's Trade Union League to increase the trade schools for girls and the agitation for a minimum wage law indicate the lines of attack.[10] Unequal pay for men and women is something that exists all along the line except perhaps on the stage. The most conspicuous effort to relieve the situation has been the legislation in New York City equalizing the pay of men and women teachers.

In the ethical field, too, the woman who is in modern society and yet not of it, is forcing upon society the need for reconstruction along finer and subtler lines than can be reached by legislation. The woman whose social consciousness is formed still on the pattern of the isolated family is out of place and a stumbling block to a society that is struggling for a more inclusive, more highly socialized consciousness, and whose working machinery is already social on a huge scale. Society finds its ends obstructed by the women who do not understand that they are responsible as members of a larger social order as well as of the family. Ibsen, over and over again, presents this conflict. In *An Enemy of the People*, when Dr. Stockman decides to do his duty to the public at any cost, the reaction of the wife is, "But towards your family, Thomas. Towards us at home. Do you think *that* is doing your duty towards those that are dependent on you?" The woman tends not to recognize the claim of those beyond the family circle.[11] Society gets concrete evidence of this in the difficulty of making women understand that their families cannot be made exceptions in cases of quarantine laws, other health regulations, or rules of the public schools. The attitude of the mother is likely to be, "My child must have this or that advantage," rather than,

"All the children in the school should benefit by a given improvement." Her child must have good light and a seat that is comfortable even though the others do not. Brieux brings out a very extreme case of this kind in *Damaged Goods* when he makes Madame DuPont quite willing to break the laws, to bribe, to lie, to sacrifice the health, perhaps the life of a wet-nurse and her family, that her diseased grandchild may have every chance of recovery. This woman's sense of social responsibility, far from including a lower social class, hardly extends beyond the limits of her own immediate family. The lack of respect for law when it conflicts with her ends, and the preponderance of the personal over the impersonal in the traditional homebred woman, also come home to society when she shows a tendency to cheat the impersonal corporations such as the street car, railroad, or telephone companies, to defraud the government through the customs house or the tax collector, or to express her sympathy for criminals in foolish gifts.

On the other hand, the invasion of women into the regions beyond the home has very naturally forced into prominence the interests for which women stand and has brought into sharp relief the incompatibility of business for money only and municipal government for politicians, with the ends which women hold essential – the welfare of children and the health and happiness of human beings. The presence of women therefore, in new and manifold places is a mighty influence in compelling society to consider how the values of the home can be reconciled with money making, power, and ambition as ends in themselves.

The new activity of women is also an agent in the great movement against prostitution, one of the means by which society has become more and more conscious that prostitution must be dealt with scientifically as one deals with the great destructive forces of nature. Prostitution is interrelated with almost every problem that concerns women. (a) The lack of eugenic consciousness and conscience, together with ignorance on the part of women concerning venereal diseases and the facts of sex, has increased the production of the unfit, the subnormal, the neurotic, on whom prostitution depends so largely for its supply. This alone forms a great social problem which can be reached only through slow educational processes and is being so reached. Men are, of course, just as responsible as women, but women must be instructed, or there can be no relief. (b) As women come to consciousness, they make it very plain to society that one standard for men and an outlawed class of women, with another for all the rest of women, is an impossible situation. If men are not able or willing to accept the code of physical purity which they have exacted of women, society as a whole must work out a new standard for both. (c) The conditions under which women work, the barbarous state of domestic service, the fatigue of the long working day and unsanitary surroundings, the less than living wage, all tend to make prostitution a more pressing problem and the question of prostitution reacts again to send home the need of better conditions for working women. (d) There is dawning upon the more enlightened the thought that after all prostitution may possibly be the logical corollary of a marriage system, based not on sexual selection, but on economic motives, and that sexual selection must be given freer play if prostitution is to be wiped out and eugenic mating encouraged. This means a recognition of the immediate relation between prostitution and the economic dependence of women and a realization that, in some way, for the sake of women, marriage, and the home, the economically independent woman must be made compatible with a form of home and of marriage which is also approved of by society.[12]

(e) Prostitution is influenced in some degree by a number of factors which tend to make marriage later or more difficult, such as hard economic conditions, the greater effort required to support a comparatively nonproductive family, as well as the increasing inclination of women for education, economic independence, and specialized work with the accompanying disinclination to take on the restrictions of matrimony. Life without marriage and children has been rendered more tolerable to women, thus enabling them to hold out against their own normal desires, by their discovery that home and companionship are still possible for them. Everywhere we find the unmarried woman turning to other women, building up with them a real home, finding in them the sympathy and understanding, the bond of similar standards and values, as well as the same aesthetic and intellectual interests, that are often difficult of realization in a husband, especially here in America, where business so frequently crowds out culture. The man who comes within her circle of possibilities is too often a man who has no form of self expression beyond his business and who, therefore, fails to meet her ideal of companionship in marriage. Thus prostitution is strengthened by the ease with which women are able to satisfy in part their needs for love and home while still retaining independence and to feel that a full life is to be lived even without marriage. One has only to know professional women, teachers, social workers, doctors, nurses, and librarians to realize how common and how satisfactory is this substitute for marriage. They have worked out a partial solution to their problem in that they have contrived to combine a real home based on love and community of interests with work in the world, but they have solved it at the expense of men and children.[13]

(f) Another aid to prostitution results from trying to combine in marriage two people, one of whom has been brought up on the principle of absolute suppression of sex and horror of the physical; the other of whom has been accustomed from childhood to take sex and the right to its physical expression as a matter of course.[14] To the man of such a marriage, where he is incapable of bringing the woman to his attitude or of working out a new one acceptable to both, the prostitute will offer real temptation or a natural solution of the problem.[15]

Bound up with the problem of prostitution, as well as with every other phase of the woman problem, is the question of divorce,[16] which is being agitated form one end of the country to the other. Law makers are urged to place fresh restrictions on the dissolution of marriage, with utter disregard of the complexity of the influences bringing about the increase of divorce. All the strains and tensions which meet in marriage today are part of the divorce problem.[17] All the stirrings and awakenings of the feminine mind, all the difficulties of adjusting the new order to the old, all the economic problems in which women are involved, the revolt against a double standard in morals, the growth of a finer, higher standard for married life on the part of both men and women, and the feeling of the need for nicer adaptations, greater unity of interest, occupation, view of life, ethical theory—all these growing demands on marriage render divorce an inevitable phenomenon symptomatic of other conflicts and struggles for development.

III. A SOCIAL THEORY OF THE SELF AS THE GROUND OF THE WOMAN MOVEMENT

The clash of home and outer world which so disturbs the feminine mind today, as well as the struggle of labor and capital, might be avoided to a large extent by mere change in the external working conditions, by a lessening of the hours of labor, by a minimum wage, by improved housing and sanitation, by a scientific cooperative housekeeping. But in the last analysis, the basic conflict on whose solution even the improvement of external conditions depends, the conflict between the narrow self and the wide social environment, can be adjusted only on the supposition that personality or selfhood is made, not born, and that a less conscious form of personality may evolve into a more conscious form under conditions which are neither mysterious nor absolute but can be understood and made use of. The criticisms and analyses of the modern woman which we have examined all point to a personality inadequate to the life into which social and economic changes have plunged her. If the crux of the matter lies here, the fundamental purpose of the woman movement must be to correct this state of affairs by helping to bring into being a more conscious womanhood and by arousing society to an awareness of its need for such a womanhood. To believe that this is possible is to imply certain things about the nature of selves, personality, or self-consciousness (the terms are used interchangeably in this discussion). If we conceive of the self as something which is given, static, present from the beginning both in the individual and the race, or, what is practically the same thing, as something which develops absolutely, reaching its full growth regardless of any known conditions, then we have put the self outside of our own world, have made it mysterious and unknowable, and by so doing have given up the hope of social reconstruction, for there is no reconstruction of society without a reconstruction of selves. We can get no hold on a self that is static nor on one that develops absolutely. If social problems are ever to be solved like other problems in our world, selves must be thought of as existing in grades and degrees, evolving gradually in the individual and in the race, with certain definite conditions of growth which can be discovered and used. When we understand how consciousness develops into more and more adequate forms, then we have turned our once mysterious and unknown phenomenon into yielding, pliable material for a genuine social science. Control of physical objects was impossible as long as physical facts were accepted as fixed, mysterious, or absolute. Just so, social control is impossible as long as the self remains an unknown quantity.

If the knowability of the self is assumed, there follows the necessity of indicating at least the type of condition which determines its appearance and growth as we should do in the case of the physical fact.[18] There would seem to be a clue in the very general tendency of modern thought to conceive of the self as social in character.[19] The relation between ego and alter is quite generally recognized as essential by philosophers, sociologists, and psychologists alike, yet, even such thinkers as Royce and Baldwin, who have done so much to show the dependence of the self on other selves, assume a consciousness of self arising, first of its own accord, i.e., absolutely, and then projecting itself into others who thereupon are perceived as selves likewise.

This is to make the self social in name only. It remains just as mysterious and unapproachable as before. There is no real interdependence of self and other. To escape from the absolute self, to make the self genuinely social and thus to keep it within the range of possible social control, we are convinced that we must take the final step proposed by Professor Mead of conceiving the self to appear and develop as the *result* of its relations to other selves. We must postulate a social environment as an absolute prerequisite for consciousness of self and assume that the self thus developed continues to take on more highly conscious forms according to the increasing extent and complexity of the social relations which it actively maintains.[20] According to such a theory, it is the necessity of dealing with a social environment that brings the normal human being to a consciousness of himself as over against other selves. The self which he acquires must, in the nature of the case, be no richer nor more complex than the other selves in relation to which it is formed and developed. Physical environment alone is incapable of supplying the kind of stimulus requisite for calling out the social reaction and it is just through the social attitude that the human being finally becomes aware of himself. In dealing with inanimate objects attention can safely confine itself to the object; there is no necessity of the agent's being aware of his own attitude towards it. Attention is naturally at home with the stimulus and unless it is compelled by something in the situation to turn in upon the subject it tends to remain there. The necessity on the part of the subject of becoming aware of his own responses as such, arises in dealing with the social object. Only when one human being is acting as stimulus to another have we a situation where the behavior of the *agent* must in time become as important for the attention as the changes in the *social object* to which he is reacting, for only in such a case does his own act determine the stimulus to which he will have to respond. The man who survives in a social group must attend to the form of his act sufficiently to know what effect it will have on the person towards whom it is directed; that is, his own act must take on for him a meaning in terms of the sort of reaction it is likely to call out in the other and he must be able to interpret and anticipate the response of the other in the earliest stages, while it is still mere gesture or attitude, in terms of the action he must make in reply.

In just this sort of interaction of selves are found the common roots of self-consciousness and consciousness of meaning. Both require a situation in which attention is forced to one side of the response and in which two attitudes are necessarily held in suspense within one mind, a proposed action of the agent and the probable response of another or others into whose place the agent is able to put himself in imagination. It is this necessity for playing many parts, for building up and taking over the selves of others, that gives the individual the basis for his own consciousness of self and it is the connecting of his own suspended act with the attitude of the other by means of some gesture which represents it that he gets his first grip on meaning.

The earliest and most imperative demand for the child is that he shall adjust himself to social objects. His knowledge of himself is not nearly as important for him as his knowledge of the adults around him on whom he depends for survival. He must be able to put himself in their places, to take on their attitudes, to play their parts, to get enough of an idea of them as persons that he may in a measure anticipate their responses to his own acts. All this necessarily precedes his discovery of himself and conditions it. Take as an illustration the case of a child who reaches for the largest piece of cake at a party. The action is a perfectly natural one and there is no innate reason why it should be restrained. But the child is not an isolated being, he has been brought up within a family circle where father and mother have taught him that taking the largest piece is wrong and selfish. As the child instinctively starts to take the cake, there may come a check in the sudden realization of what his mother's attitude would be. This may be symbolized in his own mind by a visual image of her frown or by words of reproof that she has used. Whatever the content of consciousness, it serves as a symbol for his inhibited action; that is, he gets a consciousness of meaning and momentarily he takes on the self of his mother and feels her disapproval of the act he was about to perform. If he had rushed into action with no inhibition, there would have been no chance for consciousness of meaning or awareness of self, but in holding on to the two attitudes, his own instinctive one and the opposing attitude of his mother, he experiences the sort of tension and contrast that leads him to feel one of the attitudes as *his*. The emotion aroused by the thwarted desire has time to be felt as *his* emotion and the very fact that he has a symbol which enables him to keep his action in the attitude stage gives him the prerequisites for the meaning relation. He may feel that he is one with his impulsive tendency and in that case the self of his mother will be set over against him as an other, but if he is a very well trained child he may identify himself with the mother attitude. In the latter case, he becomes a new self looking with scorn upon that other self which would have been guilty of such an act. In either case, his sense of self is constituted and enlarged by this taking on of the ideally constructed self of another.

Consciousness of meaning, then, and consciousness of self are possible only as one first builds up a consciousness of the meaning and selves of others to whom one must respond relevantly in order to maintain existence. To become conscious of self is to become conscious of one's attitudes, that is of the meaning of the act one does not carry out and of the emotion that accompanies it as one's own. The individual is enabled to do this only by first becoming aware of the at- titudes of those about him and transferring them in turn to himself as interpreta- tions of his own actions and their probable effect on others. The meaning of his own acts comes to him in terms of the social reactions they call out. The condi- tion of attaining to self-consciousness is, therefore, a social environment, and the degree of complexity or the completeness of self consciousness attained will vary with the complexity of the social organization of which it is a part. A simple form of society with simple problems in which necessary attitudes are comparatively few, unorganized, and simple, will build up undifferentiated, narrow, selves whose meanings and emotions are limited to a narrow range of objects and which are not highly conscious of those meanings as peculiarly a part of the self.

Out of this background of social interaction and dependent upon it, reflec- tive consciousness is evolved, from the first grasp on meaning that comes with the use of symbols, through the gradually acquired skill in the analysis of the static nonpersonal object, to the point where analysis is turned upon the think- ing process itself. At this point, thought recognizes the part it has played in con- structing the very object which thus far it had only analyzed. Now, con- sciousness not only reflects, it understands the method of its reflection and thereby gains its control over the physical environment. But all this appears to be an abstract process and is so considered. Its social character and its relation to concrete personality are for the most part ignored. Here we have a purely in- tellectual form with a perfectly definite though unacknowledged social content; a process that is constituted by the relations between human beings and that is *one* with the very process whereby personality is built up. As long as the in- tellectual side of the self remains in this abstract form, control of the nonpersonal object may be perfected; but the final goal will be reached only when, through recognition of the social character of these seemingly abstract, intellectual systems, the process by means of which the self comes into being and develops is also recognized and personality takes its place in the mobile, reconstructable world. What really happens is, not so much that we gain a new control over the social object as distinct from the physical, as that all objects are seen to be social and subject to the same sort of control that hitherto has been limited to physical, or at least to nonpersonal objects and systems.

The discovery of the social character of even the intellectual processes and the relation of these processes to the building up of a self gives a breadth and comprehensiveness to personality that it has never before attained in history. At a very early period it is possible for consciousness to take on the form of a self through building up the selves around it and playing various parts without having reached the point where it is capable of subjecting to analysis the self thus attained. It is also possible for consciousness to advance to the stage where it can turn in upon itself and dissect the self in a highly sophisticated way without even then realizing that it is a part of a social process and that its intelliectual activities, however expressed, are just as much a part of the personality and just as social as the feelings or the will. The final step of seeing the self as a process whose law can be stated and of finding in the self and in all social relations material that admits of reconstruction and scientific handling, just as in the case of supposedly nonsocial objects and relations, marks the highest point of growth in self-consciousness as yet developed in our experience.

All this is not to deny that the human mind supplies an element which must always be an unknown quantity, that after all it is the potentiality which is capable of developing self-consciousness, but it is to say that the material which this potentiality requires for its unfolding is social in character. When external conditions change the sweep and nature of social relations so rapidly that the social character of many of them is obscured for the time being, it will be possible to get a situation such as we have outlined in the preceeding section, where the individual has not yet caught up with his enlarged environment, is using social relationships in a purely mechanical way, and is not constituted a self by them, and where the only cure for the disorder and unrest thus produced lies in the possibility of the individual's finally waking up to the social character of the new connections and building up another and more perfectly conscious self to correspond. Reform, even of external conditions, must receive its impulse from selves that have become reflectively self-conscious to the point of realizing the social nature of the apparently abstract relations which are crushing the individuals at the other end of them and of deliberately assuming towards these relations a personal attitude.

It is evident that such a theory of self-consciousness implies a positive difference in the type of personality that it is possible to develop at different periods in history. Not that great personalities are not to be found in every period, but it nevertheless remains true that the individual or the society that is conscious of the method by which personality is built up and is aware of the social content of all activities and all systems has the power to go farther in realizing all the possibilities of personality than the individual or the society which is unconscious of these implications. With the former, the process is controlled and voluntary; with the latter, it is necessarily haphazard because it is only partially conscious.[21] Just how far the individual shall go, then, in the direction of reflectively conscious personality cannot rest entirely with him or his own genius but must depend to a large extent on the period in which he lives.

The process in time, which through increasingly complex social conditions and accumulated experiences finally forces the individual into the center of the stage yet ultimately connects him once more with his fellows, is a very gradual and prolonged affair, but whoever is born in the later stages gets the benefit of all that has preceded. The introspective attitude which was slowly and painfully acquired by the race, the power to analyze process and method as well as objects, which came only after centuries of conflict and effort at adjustment, can be gained easily today in part of the individual's lifetime because he is born into a world where scientific method is an established habit. In the attainment of personality as in the pursuit of science, the individual stands today on the shoulders of past generations and may begin where they left off.

Only on such a basis is there any happy outcome to be looked for in the conflicts between the individual and society which are overwhelming us today. If the Greek philosopher, or the mediaeval lord, or even the thinker of the Kantian period reached the limit of human development in the direction of self-consciousness, then there can be no salvation for us. Nothing short of the birth of a new man with a higher type of personality can offer a solution for the social evil, the woman problem, child labor, and industrial slavery. History shows that this is not only possible but actual. We are, in fact, seeing the birth of a new type of consciousness as far in advance of the consciousness of the period of the French Revolution as that was in advance of Greek consciousness at its best.

It is, of course, not possible to indicate perfectly differentiated and isolated levels of consciousness in history. One period melts into another. The later development is foreshadowed in the earlier and the earlier is present in and alongside of the later, but it is possible to point out in a general way, at least, three fairly distinct and characteristic stages in the development of consciousness of self appearing within the historical period. There is first the type of consciousness which we shall designate by the term *objective consciousness of self*, which colors Greek life and thought, although with the Greeks and through the Middle Ages it is already in the process of evolving into the second stage, which may be labeled *subjective consciousness of self*, and reaches it climax in Kant and the personalities of the French Revolution. Lastly comes what we have termed the period of reflective or social consciousness of self which is just now making its appearance and is indicated in the tremendous increase of social responsibility and awakening of social consciousness in all classes and countries. Although a great European war is still a possibility for our civilization, the attitude of public opinion towards such a war, at least in this country and Britain, could hardly have been comprehended a century ago, so greatly have our feelings of common brotherhood and interdependence increased and extended.

Greek consciousness, even at its best, illustrates the object character of the earlier forms of self. It deals marvelously well with the world of objects and ideas. It is at ease with universals, with truth, reality, beauty, virtue, all located in an external world, but it is never quite fully aware of itself and its own importance. The Greek thinker was eternally seeking truth, wisdom, and reality but he seldom thought of looking for them within. Their validity would necessarily lie in their independence and objectivity. So strong is this tendency of earlier Greek thinkers to find truth only in the objective that when they did begin to turn analysis towards the subjective and to discover the relation of the individual mind to the objective world, they felt themselves to be destroying objective validity, for recognizing the part played by the private experience of the person usually meant for them a giving up of the universal, hence the real, and ended in scepticism. The bottom seemed to drop out of reality for the Greeks when they were forced to admit the part taken by the particular mind in knowledge. To prevent this fatal result, they often removed the stigma of particularity and reinstated the universal by making the rational element in the individual not a personal or private affair but part of the world reason. The Greek type of self, therefore, tended to become a split up metaphysical object, made up of the various absolute qualities in which it shared, and valued for their sake. Personality was not a supreme category for the Greeks as it is for us, nor was the individual necessarily conceived of as having certain inherent rights and value just because he was a human being.

It was possible in consequence for the Greeks to present as ideal the high-minded man of Aristotle[22] who not only may but even must ignore entire classes of people because they are supposed to have no share, or a very small share, in the universal qualities which give the self its worth and reality. Despite the fact that Aristotle calls man "a political animal" and recognizes in a measure his innate social impulses, his state leaves mechanics, artisans, husbandmen, slaves,[23] children, and even women,[24] as alien, unassimilated elements, lacking in virtue almost entirely or else possessing a subordinate variety quite different from that of the real citizens. "The only parts of the state in the strict sense are the soldiery and the deliberative class." "The citizens ought not to lead a mechanical or commercial life; for such a life is ignoble and opposed to virtue." With such a theory and such a state it is made impossible from the start that the finest and most highly developed person in it could ever become conscious of more than a very limited number of social relations, for his relations to all the working clases are held to be abstract, necessary, it is true, but not implying any social connection. Ability to put himself in the place of the artisan, to feel sympathy for his ends, would imply a lowering of his own standard of virtue. There could never be, by any possibility, real community or feeling of social dependence between them. Likewise, with his domestic relations. There is no reciprocity of relationship between him and his wife and children. It is a one-sided affair, dependence on the one side, authority on the other. They are formed by him but he is not formed by them. They depend on him, he is independent of them. We cannot conceive of him as attempting to look at any question from the child's or the wife's point of view, however much it concerned them, or of feeling that it was as important for him to be able to put himself in their places as for them to understand him, because to do so would be to assume a less rational, less virtuous attitude with which he could have nothing in common as long as he maintained his own superior character.

Plato, on the other hand, one would say at first thought, surely was a modern. There are very few of our up-to-date theories that are not suggested in the *Dialogues*. Plato's treatment of the position of women is startlingly advanced. He makes very little sex distinction in work and education. Women stand on an equal footing with men in the Republic as far as their innate abilities permit. Plato, nevertheless, illustrates the failure of the Greek mind to appreciate the meaning and value of personality, to estimate properly the innate worth of the individual, much less to comprehend the essential character of social relationships. Women, as a sex, it is true, are not slighted in the scheme of Plato, but human beings, men and women alike, are disregarded. The citizen, first of all, exists for the republic not the republic for the citizen. Again the reality lies in the universal, the idea of the state. Beyond Greece, moreover, are only the barbarians. The essential connection with other races is not yet felt or understood. They are merely *not* Hellenes and exist chiefly for purposes of war. So with the lower classes. While Plato does not explicitly exclude them from citizenship as does Aristotle, he ignores them. They form no part in the consciousness of the guardian or warrior class. Social divisions are cut and dried, classes are distinct. Relations are external and artificial and not based on mutual interests and understanding of each other's attitudes and desires. The socialized person would have been an impossibility in Plato's Republic, nor, had he existed, would he have been considered a desirable citizen. Jowett sums it all up when he says of the Republic: "The citizens, as in other Hellenic states, democratic as well as aristocratic, are really an upper class, for although no mention is made of slaves, the lower classes are allowed to fade away into the distance and are represented in the individual by the passions. Plato has no idea either of a social state in which all classes are harmonized, or of a federation of the world in which all nations have a place.[25] A personality developed under such conditions could never come up to our ideal of the wise man whose ability to take on the attitude of many people and classes of people enables him to bring together within one consciousness all the various points of view, all the impulses and tendencies that have to be considered if a satisfactory solution for social problems is to be reached, and furnishes him with the background requisite for a real judgment on the problem in question; the man for whom no social relation, however familiar or habitual, is without need of perpetual reflection and reconstruction; the man whose self includes so many and such varied "others," and who is so aware of his dependence on these "others," that it is impossible for him to act without reference to them.

At a period of history where the first level of consciousness predominates, where truth, reality, and order, so far as valid, lie outside the consciousness of the individual, where the individual's thinking has no power over the real, and ideals and standards are of no value unless given apart from human agency, control must of necessity be external. Authority comes from without, as in the case of the child, in the shape of custom, law, ideas, religion, the Logos. If this extraneous authority breaks down under criticism and there is nothing at hand to substitute, chaos ensues. All human beings must have gone through this stage, phylogenetically and ontogenetically. But at any level of racial history there will always be found some individuals who never pass beyond the childlike condition, for whom authority must always be external, and to whom complete self-consciousness never comes. Moreover, women as a class are likely to remain at this level longer than men, since they are subject to a twofold restraint: that by which men are bound, and the authority of husbands and fathers as well. Their activities and social relations in consequence are doubly restricted.

Transition from the first to the second level of consciousness begins to be very apparent in Greek life when the breaking down of the social fabric turns the attention of men from the state, which no longer offers a refuge and an ideal, to the individual himself as the source of his own happiness and salvation. Reason and philosophy fail to satisfy the spiritual needs of the people and eventually religion in some sort is sought as a salvation and guide. Christianity reinforces this emphasis on the individual as the center of experience. The entire universe becomes simply the means whereby mankind works out salvation. If God may reveal himself to the humblest, then every individual is potentially a channel of revelation and his experiences may attain to objective validity. Emotion and feeling, the most essentially subjective in character of all mental faculties, are for the first time conceived of as having worth in themselves. True, the formalizing of Christianity into the dogmas of the church and the preservation of the authority of the church tended to confine revelation to an historic period, but personality has been recognized, the possibility of the reconstruction of the self and of society acknowledged in the doctrine of the new birth, and the external authority of the church condemned by the very theory on which it is built.

The increase of commerce and industry, the discovery of new countries, the sudden advance of science, and the dissatisfaction with the barrenness of scholastic thought, all indicate the steady movement away from the dogmatic authority of the objective to the claiming of objective validity for the experience of the individual as such. The revival of learning, the Reformation, new theories of the state advanced by Hobbes and Locke, the philosophies of Descartes, Leibnitz, Locke, Hume, and finally Kant and Hegel, the French Revolution, all mark the individual's discovery of himself and of his supreme importance in the universe. Kant takes the last step of carrying the entire world of objects over into the subject which becomes the constructive center of the world, the seat of law and order. The tendency is, therefore, to rob external authority of all claim to validity since nothing is valid which does not spring from the very nature of the self. But, as each self is equally the touchstone of validity, and as there is no essential bond uniting any one self to any other, there seems to be no way of bringing together this world of atomistic individuals unless authority be vested in some external source and the selves be voluntarily limited for the sake of harmony and the safe enjoyment of partial freedom. Typical was the difficulty which Hobbes faced. There is no natural basis for the state when individuals are all laws unto themselves and exist originally as independent atoms. It is easy to perceive that each atom has rights, but its rights will be obtained only at the expense of another atom's rights. Rights of individuals are as antagonistic as they are inherent and valid, and satisfaction for one individual's rights must needs mean suppression for the equally valid rights of the next one. Rights are thought of as independent entities, as hard and fixed as the individual himself, and they are treated as if they enjoyed some kind of absolute existence apart from their exercise in the actual social institutions of the time. Their dependence for reality on a social order and concrete social organization is overlooked to a large extent.

About the time of the French Revolution, the contagion begins to reach women and following in the steps of the men a few groups here and there demand the rights that inhere in every human being for women also. The leaders of the Revolution give them no encouragement. Special limitation by God and Nature is the ground on which women are forbidden to appeal to the doctrines on which men base their claims. Nevertheless, the appeal is made by women like Olympia de Gouges and Mary Wollstonecraft, and is supported by such men as Condorcet and John Stuart Mill. It is not strange that the woman movement in its first stages followed the general line of development in philosophical and social doctrine and voiced the same cry for abstract rights inhering in women as individuals apart from their relations as mothers, wives, and daughters. Theoretical recognition of their equality with men and of their natural rights similar in every particular to those possessed by men seems to be the goal of their efforts. The fact that rights to be real and actual involve the concrete freedom of realizing to the utmost their fundamental relations to society, that they mean not bare, abstract assent but definite social channels through which they become effective and thus real, that the supreme right is the right to function normally as an organic part of the social whole, is not yet conscious with the majority of the progressive women any more than it is with the men. Emphasis on bare rights apart from obligations and responsibilities leads us to a species of anti-social, man-hating individualism on the part of the pioneers in the woman movement. The satisfaction they demand for their own rights seems to involve taking away from others. If women gain rights, men must lose them. There arises an atmosphere of hostility; every woman for herself against every man. This finds expression in declarations of rights such as the one given out by the first Women's Rights Convention in the United States, in 1848, beginning, "The history of mankind is a history of repeated injuries and usurpations on the part of man towards woman, having in direct object the establishment of an absolute tyranny over her." All of this only reflects the principle of such a theory as that of Hobbes in which there is no basis for the union of individuals except through external authority and in which common ends are inconceivable because each man can seek only his own satisfaction. Just this conception of the individual was used to oppose the entrance of women into the wider fields of activity long after it had ceased to be applied to men. The interests of women and of men were assumed to be mutually hostile and exclusive. If society were to be maintained in harmony, women must voluntarily submit to having their rights curtailed.

The third level of consciousness which is but now being glimpsed by the advance guard of civilization is that of the recognition of the social character of all experience, cognitive as well as emotional and affective. Methods of control have been worked out in the realm of the sciences, but they were supposed to concern objects quite different from those involved in social interaction in the obvious sense. Now that abstract intellectual processes of science are seen to be built up like the rest of the self through social consciousness, the entire social organization and the selves within it are perceived to be equally objective and real, and to offer problems that can in time be solved by a reflective process which is not alien but flesh of their flesh.[26] It is beginning to dawn on humanity that selves are made, not born, and that it is possible to exert some control over the conditions which determine personality since they can in a measure be stated. People are realizing that the kind of selves that are found in the slum districts of big cities make undesirable citizens and will continue to do so; that punishment as such does not change the criminal; that prostitution is in fact a social evil and that its existence under any regulations, however strict, is a direct influence on the formation of the selves of the community and that it cannot be isolated because, so long as it affects part, the whole is formed with reference to that part.

The third level sees that there was no basis for the state in the conception of humanity as composed of atomistic individuals; that if we start with separate units we can never hope to put them together. The foundation of the state is the inherent social impulses and organization of the individuals that compose it. There need be no contradiction in the seeking of a common end by many individuals. When ends are conceived of as objective and real, not as mere subjective states of satisfaction, it is evident that they must be sought in common if they are to be completely realized. Individuals are so interrelated and dependent that each one depends on the rest for obtaining his own ends. No person can seek his own health as his object excluding all reference to the health of his neighbors. Unless health is a common object of desire in a community and is sought for by each person with regard to all others, no one individual is safe from infection. The same is true with reference to protection and education of children. No one can be sure of gaining for his own family any advantages which conditions do not make secure for the majority. If my neighbor is not safe, I am in danger; if his children can grow up in ignorance, mine also run a risk for individual fortunes come and go. Rights, too, are recognized as concrete functions in an organized society dependent for existence upon that society and are no longer thought of as absolute entities inhabiting an absolute self. My rights, unless realized along with those of other people through the forms of a social order, are nothing but abstractions.

There is no doubt that humanity is actually seeing the birth of the third stage of consciousness, but men are very slow to realize the full import of its social character. They continue to accept their social relations unreflectively, as they always have. They are conscious of the more obvious ones in a way, but many that are not so apparent they fail to recognize as social at all. What a comparatively modern movement is the study of the child and his relationships to parents and teachers from his own point of view! Here was one of the fundamental social relations, taken as a matter of course for ages, and only in our own times subjected to reflection and brought to consciousness. The habitual, automatic character of sex relations is only now being shown up in the efforts to spread information regarding the most ordinary, normal phenomena of sex life and in the blind resistance such efforts are meeting in many quarters. Eugenics marks the birth of sex conscience with regard to the unreflective exercise of a basic social impulse. The beginnings of organized efforts to understand the social evil are likewise the result of this attempt to comprehend and bring to light all the hidden meanings and far-reaching influence of the sex instinct. All this is far from being conscious with the mass of people and still further removed is any adequate consciousness of those far-reaching social connections which are obscured by distance, lack of direct personal contact, and the abstract character of the economic interests involved. But even here awakening is promised in such phenomena as labor unions, the Consumers' League, the Trade Union League, laws for factory inspection and the protection of women and children who labor, workmen's compensation acts, and the birth of a new political party which tries to represent this consciousness.

Full self-consciousness will never be approached, however, until all social relationships are recognized and understood in all their bearings and the self of the individual is consciously built up with reference to them. A father is only nominally such if he has not a personality which corresponds to and is formed by his relation to his children and consciously so. A man may have begotten many children, but if he does not know them, never sees them nor has any connection with them, he is not a father for he possesses no father self. Just so, when our consciousness of social relations becomes more sensitive and complex, we shall not know what it is to treat any social relation abstractly. The man to whom we sell or from whom we buy, the man who works in our factory or for whom we work, although we are removed from direct personal contact and the relation seems to be purely economic, will be for us an "other" and our relationship to him will be known for what it is, a truly social affair, and will correspond to and constitute a phase of our self-consciousness.

In the meantime, partially unconscious social relations or relations whose social character is not perceived, continue to affect the individual and society whose responses to them are entirely inadequate. Where an individual is treating a social situation abstractly as if it were purely economic for example, he is bringing about certain results which he does not foresee, which are not part of his conscious purpose, and which are therefore entirely uncontrolled in their reaction upon himself and upon society at large. Since the social factors in the situation are overlooked, since there is no social self corresponding to them, no evaluation of them, the self and society are being determined in a purely accidental and external way with regard to them. Internal control will be possible only when the self that reacts to the situation is conscious of the real nature of all the relations involved and presents a self organized with reference to them.

On the first level of consciousness, control is bound to be from the outside in the form of arbitrary authority. Thought is not sufficiently aware of its own method to feel any assurance even over against the physical object which it still accepts as something given. In all social institutions, government, the church, the family, authority is the key note. It is the period of unquestioning obedience on the part of the subject to the lord, wife to husband, children to parents, apprentice to master, slave to owner. Lack of freedom is softened by the social impulses which act as a check on egoistic tendencies and which cannot fail to be aroused when social life is so simple, direct, and personal.

In the second stage, when society flies apart into hostile individuals, thought recognizes its own power in handling the physical world, but social control must still be an external affair although it is no longer a matter of arbitrary authority. Instead there arise the theories of competition and contract. Control will be chiefly such as results from the natural friction among the atoms, a mechanical pull and haul. Each individual is to be left to get what he can for himself with only enough interference to make organized society possible. Each atom retains all the abstract freedom which was not sacrificed to the government as essential to orderly living.

Our age is witnessing the disappearance of the isolated individual and the growth of an internal control based on the recognition of the dependence of the individual on social relations and his actual interest in social goods and in the discovery that thought is social in origin and can be used to advantage in the social as well as in the physical world. The freedom that was supposed to reside in the individual is seen to be realized only through society. The individual is not economically or morally free except when he is able to express himself, to realize his ends through the common life.[27] As an individual, he is powerless to determine his own actions beyond a certain point. He must think with society and make his thought effective through social media or he has no control. Moreover, the hypotheses which he offers as solutions to social problems must include as part of the data to be considered the impulses and interests, the point of view, of all classes of people, if they are to be successful. In other words, not only is thought social in origin, but it keeps a social content and character. The individual must think as a social being, must take over the points of view of all his social "others" if his thinking is to be true in a social order, that is, the value of his thought in handling social questions is tested just as it is in handling physical problems, by the adequacy with which it covers all the data involved. Hypotheses which ignore the interests of entire classes of people, which fail to recognize existing social relations, will not work in the long run. The hard and unyielding individual with his boundless, empty freedom is compensated for the loss of his abstract rights by the discovery that concrete freedom, an actual realizing of his own powers, is possible through a social order and through a selfhood that grows in an intelligible way and is, therefore, subject to reconstruction by the same methods that are continually changing the physical world in accordance with human desires.

There is no field in which this attitude is not making itself felt and nowhere more clearly than in the change that has taken place in the character of the woman movement within the last ten years. Even militancy, which seems in its later phases to be a purely hostile manifestation, can hardly be classed with the type of opposition characteristic of the beginning of the woman movement. In its origin, at least, violent and hostile demonstrations were taken up purely as a methodology which was thought necessary to success. It was not in the minds of the originators a blind outbreak of hatred but a carefully thought out plan based on a theory of the useful and peaceful relation which women should bear to the social order. If the suffragettes themselves have come to the point where their acts truly express hostile emotions, then they have lost control of their method and thereby also the end in view. Their tactics must be judged pragmatically and, in so far as they cease to be merely tactics, have on the very face of things failed and have become expressions of an earlier and more limited consciousness. Militant methods are open to criticism not so much because of their militancy, but because of their apparent futility when carried beyond a certain point. In any case, the militant movement represents only a small proportion of the advanced womanhood of today and it still remains true that to clamor for rights, to inveigh against men as the oppressors of the sex, is not only bad taste but beside the mark. What the thinking of women of the western civilization, consciously or unconsciously, are asking of society today is not the vote, not economic independence, nor any given right or privilege, but a real hearing, a genuine and thoughtful consideration of their difficulties from the standpoint of the woman herself and an attempt on the part of society at a reasonable adjustment of those difficulties resulting in a reconstruction of the feudal ideal of womanhood such that the modern woman will once more be brought into active working relationship with the modern world.

IV. CONCLUSION

We are now in a position to take a final survey of the woman movement in its relation to the larger stream of social evolution. The course of the preceding argument has been very briefly as follows: first, the woman movement is the ex-pression of very genuine problems both for the individual woman and for society as a whole; second, those problems are the result of an unavoidable conflict of impulses and habits, values and standards, due to the effort of trying to combine, without deliberate and conscious adjustment on the part of society itself, two dissimilar worlds; third, such conflicts are, as a matter of fact, equally real for men and for women as the labor movement testifies, and give evidence of a real dualism of self and social environment, of a genuine inequality between the kind of consciousness actually developed and the type of consciousness required to deal with the complexities of modern social relations; and finally, the restoration of equality between self and environment depends on the possibility of develop-ing a higher type of self-consciousness whose perfect comprehension of its rela-tions to other selves would make possible a controlled adjustment of those rela-tions from the point of view of all concerned. We endeavored to show that such a conception rests upon a social and dynamic theory of personality and pointed out an actual development in personality throughout history up to the present moment when the wished-for type is not only desired but is being actualized. In this concluding section, the attempt will be to leave an impression of the woman movement stripped bare of the detail of argument as it appears in perspective to one who looks at it from the point of view indicated in the preceding discussion.

The woman movement, viewed not as an isolated phenomenon but as in in-tegral part of the vaster social evolution, is seen to be only the woman's side of what from the man's angle is called the labor movement. It is a reaction against the same conditions and a demand for changes in the social order such that life will once more become harmonious. The accident of modern civilization has brought about inevitable conflict in the fundamental human impulses for both men and women. It has apparently allowed for complete, almost overt expression of one set of impulses, at the expense of a partial or sometimes complete repres-sion of the other. This has meant, of course, that the set of impulses which was allowed to develop unchecked by the other set was as abnormal and as far from a well-balanced rounded fulfilment as were the unexpressed impulses. The in-dustrial and economic system of today, which has come into being more or less unconsciously and accidentally, has so divorced the economic and the social that it is only with a tremendous struggle for more inclusive forms of consciousness that we shall be able to recognize that the split is only apparent and that a system which not only believes in, but insists on, such a separation results in ir-reconcilable dualism in the lives of the men and women involved, persisting to the point of gigantic social problems, agitations, and movements. Thus the labor movement symbolizes the impossibility of choosing between the fulfillment of the economic impulse and the fulfilment of the impulse to live. Men are granted

unlimited opportunities to work, but no provision is made by the system for intelligent parenthood, for good citizenship, for a thoughtful development and use
of the sex impulse. A man's parental expression is limited to caring for the
economic welfare of his family. His own growth as a person must be sacrificed to
the necessity of supporting himself and family. Work must be combined with life,
but our system makes little provision for such a combination, hence, forcing into
opposition fundamental impulses clamoring for expression. The labor movement
demands a new society in which creative, sexual, parental and other social impulses will have an unquestioned right to fulfillment.

With women, on the other hand, social impulses are the only ones which
are overtly recognized. Women are constantly forced into the economic world,
but the system ignores that fact and provides in no way for combining the
peculiar social function of women with any economic function which they may
find desirable or necessary. Such economic expression as has been conceded to
them is confined to the home. Likewise, the other impulses, even the maternal,
have no recognized place outside the limits of the individual home. For the
woman, the system has no avenues of fulfilment foreseen and provided
beforehand for any impulse whatsoever outside the home itself. Everything
which has opened up has been at best, even after long and patient effort, only
makeshift and haphazard. Society is always emphasizing the obligation of the
woman to carry out the sex and maternal impulses at all costs and minimizing the
need or value of the economic so far as she is concerned. In the conditions of living which are forced upon her, she is compelled to make the sorry choice of a
limited sex and maternal expression or a doubtful and hazardous attempt on the
economic side. In either case, she loses so far as society's aid or prevision is concerned. Only by the extraordinary force of a powerful personality will she make
a signal success at either venture. Society no more makes a thoughtful attempt to
give the maternal interests the most complete development and employment
possible than it makes any pretense at all of using intelligently the natural impulse of the woman to be of economic value in the world. Much less does it offer
a rational scheme for combining both motives within a possible form of living for
the average normal woman. Thus the woman, even more than the man, faces a
perfectly hopeless alternative. Neither side at the present moment is overwhelmingly attractive in itself even apart from the sacrifice of other impulses
which its choice involves. What woman would willingly abandon love and
children? What normal woman would accept a life in which she gave up all effort
at serious work of genuine economic value to society? What woman would attempt without shrinking the almost impossible task of combining the two as affairs stand today? Above all, what woman would undertake wifehood and
motherhood with the limitations placed on it by our present social system and
feel that those two fundamental parts of herself could ever reach a satisfactory
and adequate fulfillment?

That the peculiarly unhappy position of the woman is a reality and not an illusion can be detected in the arguments used to convince woman of her obligation to bear and rear. The element of sacrifice is so obvious that it is even seized
upon and treated as a virtue, an added glory for the crown of the wife and
mother. Moreover, this notion of necessary sacrifice on the part of the woman
and the bare fact of motherhood itself have grown into a sort of fetish. The experiences of motherhood are exalted to the point where they are assumed to be a
sufficient compensation for any and all sacrifices. To silence our own doubts and
justify our procedure, we have come to believe in the inherent and absolute
value to the woman of the mere fact of giving birth to a child even though the
emotions and purposes thus originated are never carried past the instinctive or
intuitive level to a rationalized and socialized expression. We are afraid to face
the fact that the home in its present unrelated, individual form does demand of
women, and men too for that matter, a sacrifice so great as to have lost a large
part of its value for spiritual growth, an overwhelming and crushing sacrifice of
the possibilities of motherhood and fatherhood that defeats its own end.

All of this hopeless conflict among impulses which the woman feels she has
legitimate right, even a moral obligation, to express, all of the rebellion against
stupid, meaningless sacrifice of powers that ought to be used by society, constitutes the force, conscious or unconscious, which motivates the woman movement and will continue to vitalize it until some adjustment is made.

The labor movement and the woman movement do not understand always
how close is their relationship, nor do they see clearly that the reason why the
obviously stupid and unsuitable social conditions which they combat are so difficult to alter is because human beings have not yet arrived at the stage where
they know how to attack and solve social problems. The real goal of both
movements is a society whose consciousness shall have reached the social stage
and hence is capable of dealing scientifically with social as well as physical problems, a society which no longer leaves the social forms and relationships whereby human impulses are expressed to chance or physical force, but subjects them
to rational control.

In the physical world we have at least become conscious of our method and
hence have acquired a control over physical conditions which promises to
become more and more complete. If the desire arises in a community to do
something for which present physical conditions make no allowance, it becomes
instantly a problem for the experts and it is only a question of time when a way
will be found for the gratification of the felt need. The very basis of the physical
problem is the thwarted desire of human beings to do something and the method
of obtaining the end is, of course, a full and free admission of the inherent right
and value of the desire, a deliberate searching for every element involved in the
physical conditions of the problem, and a careful experimental attempt to find
the combination which will satisfy all the conditions. We should not consider our

problem solved if the scientist said to us, "You do not really want this thing, you only imagine it, and in any case it would be bad for you to have it. You have managed to live all these years without it, why complain now?" Imagine such an answer to the determination to fly in the air. But, supposing, if we persisted in our wish to fly and began to talk about it and clamor for a way to be opened, the authorities were to turn on us, demand silence on pain of arrest and imprison- ment, label us socialists or anarchists, and tell us we were rebelling against the fixed and righteous order of things as they are. Should we consider that any at- tempt had been made at solving our problem of how to make a machine that would fly in the air? Yet, impossible as it may seem, that is thus far the favorite method of dealing with any unsatisfied, insufficiently expressed set of human wants, whose fulfilment would mean change of the social order. First, deny the existence of the want; second, call it wicked, foolish, or injurious to individual and society; third, suppress it by force—and you have dealt with it adequately.[28]

The chief task of all social movements, then, must be at first to impress upon the rest of society the right of unsatisfied and unexpressed human impulses to constitute a real problem worthy of the same amount of expert attention whether they demand a new way of crossing the Atlantic Ocean or a new com- bination of work and social expression in the lives of men and women. This they will never bring about until there is a sufficient number of people who are so socially sensitive and adaptable that they feel within themselves as their own the impulses and points of view of all classes and both sexes. Such individuals will be the social scientists who will offer solutions to our social problems because they are able to place themselves at the very heart of these problems and thus to comprehend the conditions, the unsatisfied, conflicting impulses, upon the harmonization and fulfilment of which any solution that has the right to the name must be based. The fundamental purpose of the woman movement, therefore, as of any great social movement, is bound to be the producing of social scientists who will be capable of offering hypotheses that are based on the actual data constituting the problems, and the bringing about of an increasing social consciousness among all people such that they too will become sufficiently aware of the real content of social relationships to be willing to undergo the ad- justments of the social order necessary to make actual the theories which prom- ise salvation.

NOTES

1. Tarbell, *The Business of Being a Woman.*
2. Havelock Ellis, *Sex in Relation to Society*, II, p. 77.

3. Ida Tarbell, *The Business of Being a Woman*, chap. III.

4. Charlotte Perkins Gilman, *Women and Economics*, p. 192.

5. David Snedden, *The Problem of Vocational Education*.

6. C. P. Gilman, *Women and Economics*, p. 245.

7. Louis Brandeis, *Women in Industry*.

8. H. Ellis, *Sex in Relation to Society*, I, p. 21.

9. *Ibid.*, p. 27.

10. Adams and Sumner, *Labor Problems*, Bk. I, 11; Louise Bosworth, *The Living Wage of Women Workers*, pp. 4–7.

11. W. I. Thomas, *Sex and Society*, pp. 223–234.

12. Havelock, Ellis, *Sex in Relation to Society*, VII, p. 254–Pt. III, p. 316; IV, pp. 363, 409, 410; W. I. Thomas, *Sex and Society*, p. 245; Edward Carpenter, *Love's Coming of Age*, p. 8; Walter Lippmann, *A Preface to Politics*, chap. iv.

13. Edward Carpenter, *The Intermediate Sex*.

14. M. R. Coolidge, *Why Women Are So*, pp. 31, 329, 330.

15. Havelock Ellis, *Sex in Relation to Society*, VII, pp. 295, 296, 299, 300; May Sinclair, *The Helpmate*.

16. Special Reports of the Census Office: 1867–1906, *Marriage and Divorce*, Part I, pp. 11 ff.

17. Havelock Ellis, *Sex in Relation to Society*, X, pp. 461, 462, 464; C. D. Wright, *Increase of Divorce in the United States*; Dewey and Tufts, *Ethics*, chap. XXVI, 6; 2. p. 603.

18. No attempt is made in this thesis to present a theory of personality. The writer merely wishes to indicate the type of theory that seems to her to be essential for a solution of the existing conflicts. For a consistent and detailed statement of such a theory see later references to articles by Professor George H. Mead.

19. William James, *Psychology*, chapter on Self; J. M. Baldwin, *Mental Development*; C. H. Cooley, *Human Nature and the Social Order*; Josiah Royce, *Psychology*, chap. xii; *Studies in Good and Evil*, chaps. vi, vii, viii.

20. George Mead, "What Social Objects Must Psychology Presuppose?" *Journal of Philosophy, Psychology and Scientific Methods*, 1910, Vol. VII, pp. 170–180; "The Mechanism of the Social Consciousness," *ibid.*, Vol. IX, No. 15, 1912, "Social Consciousness and the Consciousness of Meaning," *Psychological Bulletin*, Vol. VII, pp. 397–405.

21. Dewey and Tufts, *Ethics*, chap. xviii.

22. *The Nicomachean Ethics*, Bk. IV.

23. *Politics*, Bk. IV, chap. ix.

24. *Politics*, Bk. I, chap. xiii.

25. *Dialogue of Plato*, Jowett, 3d ed., Vol. III, p. clxxii.

26. C. H. Cooley, *Human Nature and the Social Order*, chaps. v, vi; Josiah Royce, *Psychology*, chap. xii; J. M. Baldwin, *Mental Development*, Vol. II, Bk. I; Josiah Royce, *Studies in Good and Evil*, chaps. vi, vii, viii.

27. Dewey and Tufts, *Ethics*, chap. xx.

28. For a complete presentation of this failure of our civilization to handle its social problems see Walter Lippmann's *Preface to Politics*.

BIBLIOGRAPHY*

HISTORICAL MATERIAL

Legal

Abbott, Grace. *Legal Position of Married Women in the United States*, Master's Thesis, University of Chicago, 1909.

Blackstone. *Commentaries*, Vol. I, chap. xv.

Bryce. *Studies in History and Jurisprudence*, Essay on Marriage and Divorce, 1901.

Cleveland, A. R. *Women under the English Law*, 1896.

Holdsworth. *History of English Law*, Vol. II, pp. 75-87; Vol. III, pp. 153-165. 1908-09.

Howard, G. E. *History of Matrimonial Institutions*, 1904.

Pollock and Maitland. *History of English Law*, 1899, Vol. I, pp. 263, 305, 320-325, 433-438, 482-485; Vol. II, pp. 147, 259 ff., 364 ff., 382, 404 ff., 432 ff.

Schouler, James. *Law of Domestic Relations*, 1905.

General

Paston Letters, The, 1909.

Boulting, Wm. *Women in Italy*, 1910.

Clavière, R. de Maulde la. *The Women of the Renaissance*, 2d ed., 1905.

Cornish, F. W. *Chivalry*, 1901.

Eckenstein, Lina. *Woman under Monasticism*, 1896.

Gautier, Leon. *Chivalry*, 1891.

Hill Georgiana. *Women in English Life*, 1896.

Knox, J. *First Blast of the Trumpet against the Monstrous Regiment of Women*, 1558.

Lecky. *History of European Morals*, 1869.

Paston, Geo. *Lady Mary Montagu and Her Times*, 1907.

Putnam, Emily J. *The Lady*, 1910.

Reich, Emil. *Woman through the Ages*, 1909.

Rowbotham, J. F. *The Troubadours and the Courts of Love*, 1895.

Staars, David. *The English Woman*, 1909.

Swift, J. *A Letter to a Very Young Lady on Her Marriage*.

Synge, M. B. *Social Life in England*, 1906.

Traill, H. D. *Social England*, 1894-1905.

Weinhold, Karl. *Die deutschen Frauen im Mittelalter*, 1851.

Wright, Thos. *Womankind from the earliest times to 17th C.*, 1869.

BIOLOGICAL

Castle, W. E. *Heredity in Relation to Evolution and Animal Breeding*, 1911.

---

*This bibliography includes background materials as well as works cited in the notes (MJD).

Coulter, J. M. *Heredity and Eugenics*, 1912.
Davenport, C. B. *Heredity in Relation to Eugenics*, 1911.
Dinsmore, Emmet. *Sex Equality*, 1907.
Ellis, Havelock. *Man and Woman*, 1904.
Geddes and Thompson. *Evolution of Sex*, 1889.
Letourneau. *The Evolution of Marriage*, 1911.
Saleeby, C. W. *Parenthood and Race Culture*, 1909.
Thomas, W. I. *Sex and Society*, 1907.
Thompson, J. A. *Heredity*, 1908.
Weininger, Otto. *Sex and Character*, 1906.

SOCIOLOGICAL AND ECONOMIC

Academy of Political Science, Vol. I, No. 1, Economic Position of Women.
Marriage and Divorce: Special Reports of Census Office, 1867-1906.
Abbott, Edith. *Women in Industry*, 1910.
Adams and Sumner. *Labor Problems*, Bk. I, chap. ii, pp. 29, 48 ff., 1905.
Barnes, Earle. *Woman in Modern Society*, 1912.
Bosanquet, Helen. *The Family*, 1906.
Bosworth, Louise M. *The Living Wage of Women Workers*, 1911.
Brandeis, Louis. *Women in Industry*, 1908.
Braun, Lily. *Die Frauenfrage*, 1901.
Carpenter, Edward. *Love's Coming of Age*, 1911. *The Intermediate Sex*, 1912.
Coolidge, Mrs. M. R. *Why Women Are So*, 1912.
Dock, Lavinia. *Hygiene and Morality*, 1910.
Dorr, Rheta C. *What Eight Million Women Want*, 1910.
Ellis, Havelock. *Sex in Relation to Society,* Studies in the Psychology of Sex, Vol. VI, chapter on Prostitution; chapter on Art of Love, 1910.
Flexner, A. *Prostitution in Europe*, 1914.
Gilman, Mrs. Charlotte P. *Women and Economics. Our Andro-centric Culture*, 1898.
Hard, Wm. Series of Articles in *Everybody's*, 1910.
Key, Ellen. *The Woman Movement*, 1911. *Love and Marriage*, 1911.
Kneeland, Geo. J. *Commercialized Prostitution in N.Y. City*, Century, 1913.
Chicago Vice Commission Report, 1911.
Lippmann, Walter. *Preface to Politics*, chapters on Chicago Vice Report, and on possibilities of applying science to social problems, 1913. *Drift and Mastery*, chap. iv on Woman Movement, 1914.
Parsons, Elsie Clews. *The Family*, 1906.
Pearson, Karl. Essay on Women and Labor in *The Chances of Death*, 1897. *The Ethic of Free Thought*, chap. ix, 1901.
Schreiner, Olive. *Woman and Labor*, 1911.
Snedden, David. *Problems of Vocational Education*, 1910.
Trabell, Ida. *The Business of Being a Woman*, 1912.
Veblen, T. B. *Theory of the Leisure Class*, chap. xiv, 1899.
Wright, C. D. *Increase of Divorce in the United States.*

POLITICAL

Hecker, E. A. *A Short History of Woman's Rights*, 1914.
Ostrogorskii, M. *The Rights of Women*, 1893.
Mill, J. S. *The Subjection of Women*, Holt, 1882.
Sumner, Helen. *Equal Suffrage*, 1909.
Schirmacher, Dr. Kathe. *The Modern Woman's Rights Movement*, 1912.
Wollstonecraft, Mary. *Vindication of the Rights of Women*, 1792.

PSYCHOLOGICAL AND PHILOSOPHICAL

Aristotle. *Nichomachean Ethics*, trans. by Welldon. *Politics*, trans. by Welldon.
Baldwin, J. M. *Mental Development*, Part II, 1895. *The Individual and Society*, 1911.
Cooley, C. H. *Human Nature and the Social Order*, 1902. *Social Organization*, 1909.
Dewey, John. "A Theory of Emotion," *Psychol. Review*, Vol. I, No. 6; Vol. II, No. 1. *How We Think*, 1910.
Dewey and Tufts. *Ethics*, 1908.
Fite, Warner. "The Feminist Mind," *The Nation*, Feb. 6, 1913.
Heymans, G. *Die Psychologie der Frauen*, 1910.
James, William. *Psychology*, chap. xxv, on "Emotion," 1890.
Jowett. *Diaglogues of Plato*, 3d ed., Vol. III.
Mead, G. H. "Social Consciousness and the Consciousness of Meaning," *Psychol. Bulletin*, 1910, Vol. VII, pp. 397–403; "What Social Objects Must Psychology Presuppose?" *Journal of Philosophy, Psychology and Scientific Methods*, 1910, Vol. VII, pp. 174–180; "The Psychology of Social Consciousness Implied in Instruction," *Science, N. S.* 1910, Vol. 31, pp. 688–693; "Fite's 'Individualism'," *Psychol. Bulletin*, Vol. VIII, No. 9; "Self-consciousness, Social Consciousness and Nature," *Philos. Review*, Vol. IV, 1895.
Royce, Josiah. *Psychology*, chap. xii, 1903. *Studies in Good and Evil*, 1898.
Thompson, H. B. *Psychological Norms in Men and Women*, University of Chicago Contributions to Philosophy, 1907.

Chapter 3

The Arrangement between the Sexes

Erving Goffman

1.

In modern industrial society, as apparently in all others, sex is at the base of a fundamental code in accordance with which social interactions and social structures are built up, a code which also establishes the conceptions individuals have concerning their fundamental human nature. This is an oft stated proposition, but until recently its awesomely ramified significance escaped us. The traditional sociological position that sex is "learned, diffuse, role behavior" – fair enough in itself – seemed to have inoculated previous generations of social scientists against understanding instead of allowing the disease to spread. More even than in the matter of social class, these students simply acted like everyone else, blindly supporting in their personal conduct exactly what some at least should have been studying. As usual in recent years, we have had to rely on the discontented to remind us of our subject matter.

It is these issues I want to try to approach, doing so from the perspective of social situations and the public order sustained within them. (I define a social situation as a physical arena anywhere within which an entering person finds himself exposed to the immediate presence of one or more others; and a gathering, all persons present, even if only bound together by the norms of civil inattention, or less still, mutual vulnerability.)

2.

Women do and men don't gestate, breast-feed infants, and menstruate as a part of their biological character. So, too, women on the whole are smaller and lighter boned and muscled than are men. For these physical facts of life to have no appreciable social consequence would take a little organizing, but, at least by

Source: Erving Goffman, "The Arrangement Between the Sexes." From "Theory and Society," 4,3 (Fall, 1977): 301–331, Elsevier, Amsterdam, by permission of Martinus Nijhoff Publishers, Dordrecht, Holland.

modern standards, not much. Industrial society can absorb new ethnic groups
bearing raw cultural differences, a year or so of isolating military service for
young men, vast differences in educational level, business and employment
cycles, the wartime absence of its adult males every generation, appreciable annual vacations, and countless other embarrassments to orderliness. That our
form of social organization has any necessary features is, I take it, rather questionable. More to the point, for these very slight biological differences–compared to all other differences–to be identified as the grounds for the kind of
social consequences felt to follow understandably from them requires a vast, integrated body of social beliefs and practices, sufficiently cohesive and all-
embracing to warrant for its analysis the resurrection of unfashionable functional
paradigms. (Perhaps traditional Durkheimian notions work here because in this
business we are all priests and nuns and need but be together and a hallowed
ground for worship comes to hand.) It is not, then, the social consequences of innate sex differences that must be explained, but the way in which these differences were (and are) put forward as a warrant for our social arrangements,
and, most important of all, the way in which the institutional workings of society
ensured that this accounting would seem sound. (Indeed, one might argue that
the chief consequence of the women's movement is not the direct improvement
of the lot of women but the weakening of the doctrinal beliefs that heretofore
have underpinned the sexual division of deserts and labor.) In all, one is faced
with what might be thought of as "institutional reflexivity"–a newish phrase for
an old social anthropological doctrine.

3.

   In all societies, all infants at birth are placed in one or in the other of two sex
classes, the placement accomplished by inspection of the infant's naked person,
specifically its genitalia, these being visibly dimorphic–a placement practice not
dissimilar to that employed in regard to domestic animals. This placement by
physical configuration allows a sex-linked label of identification. (In English, for
example, man-woman, male-female, boy-girl, he-she.) The sorting is confirmed at
various stages of the individual's growth by still other biological signs, some
recognized in the common lore, some (at least in modern society) an elaboration
of science, as described, for example, in chromosomal, gonadal, and hormonal
findings. In any case, sex-class placement is almost without exception exhaustive
of the population and life-long,[1] providing an exemplary instance, if not a prototype, of social classification. Further, in modern society we feel that male-
female is one social division that works in full and realistic harmony with our
"biological inheritance" and is something which can never be denied, a unique
agreement between the immediate understanding of the man in the street and
the findings in laboratories. (Thus the layman may be willing to grant Margaret

Mead's famous argument about temperament being culturally, not biologically, determined, and moreover that women can quite competently function as dentists, even as firemen, and still further, that (in English) literary bias is present in the convention which establishes "he" before "she," "man" before "woman," "his" before "hers," in phrases which couple the two, allows "man" to stand for humankind, and employs "his" as the proper relative pronoun for semi-indefinite terms such as "individual," male designations clearly being the "unmarked" form; but in making these concessions, he, like Margaret Mead (and myself apparently), sees no reason to deny that the terms "he" and "she" are still entirely adequate as designations of the individuals under discussion.) It should be repeated, then, that by the term "sex-class" I mean to use a category that is purely sociological, that draws on that discipline alone and not on the biological sciences.

In all societies, initial sex-class placement stands at the beginning of a sustained sorting process whereby members of the two classes are subject to different socialization. From the start, persons who are sorted into the male class and persons who are sorted into the other are given different treatment, acquire different experience, enjoy and suffer different expectations. In response there is objectively overlayed on a biological grid – extending it, neglecting it, countering it – a sex-class-specific way of appearing, acting, feeling. Every society elaborates sex-class in this way, although every society does this after its own fashion. Viewed by the student as a way of characterizing society, this complex can be called *gender*; viewed as a way of characterizing a society, it can be called *sexual subculture*. Observe that although gender is almost wholly a social, not biological consequence of the workings of society, these consequences are objective. An entire population can certainly be unknowing of a particular gender difference, or even falsely opinioned regarding it, yet the difference can still be there, and again, chiefly not because of biology but because of the social experience common to the members of each of the classes.

Every society seems to develop its own conception of what is "essential" to, and characteristic of, the two sex classes, this conception embracing both praised and dispraised attributes. Here are ideals of masculinity and femininity, understandings about ultimate human nature which provide grounds (at least in Western society) for identifying the whole of the person, and provide also a source of accounts that can be drawn on in a million ways to excuse, justify, explain, or disapprove the behavior of an individual or the arrangement under which he lives, these accounts being given both by the individual who is accounted for and by such others as have found reason to account for him. Norms of masculinity and femininity also bear on objective (albeit mainly socially acquired) differences between the sex-classes, but, as suggested, do not coincide with these differences, failing to cover some, misattributing others, and, of course, accounting for a considerable number by means of a questionable doctrine – in our society, a doctrine of biological influence.

Insofar as the individual builds up a sense of who and what he is by referring to his sex class and judging himself in terms of the ideals of masculinity (or femininity), one may speak of *gender identity*. It seems that this source of self-identification is one of the most profound our society provides, perhaps even more so than age-grade, and never is its disturbance or change to be anticipated as an easy matter.

By "sexuality" I will refer to patterns of activity involving sexual stimulation, sexual experience, and the adumbration of inducement to these activities taking a culture-specific form of appearance, dress, style, gesture, and the like. Obviously, much of this sexual practice is sex-class correlated and therefore part of gender. But presumably not all sexuality distinguishes between the sex-classes, being similarly manifest by both. More important, sexuality appears to have a biological life cycle, presumably being very little marked in infancy, very marked in young adulthood, and once again quiescent in later years. This cycle is, of course, manifest through the development and atrophy of the so-called secondary sexual characteristics, of interest here because social ideals regarding masculinity and femininity are often linked to these manifestations. Gender as such, however, has little of a developmental character, except for the pattern in some societies of treating young males as part of the women's group in certain matters; sex-class linked behavior changes through the life of the individual, and in a sequential, patterned way, but not necessarily in response to some unitary inner development. In any case, it should be perfectly clear that gender and sexuality are not the same thing; by my understanding, at least, a seven-year-old boy who manfully volunteers to help his grandmother with her heavy packages is not trying to make out with her.

It seems that *beliefs* about gender, about masculinity-femininity, and about sexuality are in close interaction with actual gender behavior, and that here popular social science plays a part. Discoveries about gender and about sexuality, whether well or badly grounded, are selectively assimilated to normative understandings regarding masculinity-femininity—sometimes quite rapidly—and thus empowered can have a self-fulfilling effect on objective gender behavior. Nonetheless, *beliefs* about gender, about masculinity-femininity, and about sexuality are themselves not a part of gender, except to the extent—which can be considerable—that they are differentially espoused as between the sex-classes.

Each of the two sex-classes supports its own patterns of in-class social relationships, giving rise to such infrastructures as old boy nets [networks], buddy formations, female support systems,[2] and the like.

Two concluding comments of caution. In referring to an attribute of gender, it is easy to speak of matters that are "sex-linked" (or "sex-correlated") in order to avoid the more cumbersome locution, "sex-class linked." And, of course, it is very natural to speak of "the sexes," "cross-sex," "the other sex" and so forth. And so I shall. But this is a dangerous economy, especially so since such glossing fits perfectly with our cultural stereotypes. One should think of sex as a property of organisms, not as a class of them. Thus "secondary sexual charateristics"

are attributes associated with sexuality, but it is misleading to speak of these attributes as sex-linked if, in so doing, one means to imply the existence of a class
of persons fundamentally defined and definable by matters biological. As suggested, secondary sexual characteristics are indeed, by and large, linkable to sex-
class; but each of the two human categories involved has many non-biological attributes and behavioral practices differentially linked to it, too. Underlying this
issue, of course, is an even more troublesome one. Given a definition of a
category of persons, in this case sex-class, it would seem that any apt label we
employ to refer to its members – in this case, "men," "women," "male," "female,"
"he," "she" – can easily come to function as a characterization, symbol, and
overall image of the class, a way of constituting one attribute into the jug while
other attributes merely fill it.

Second, there is the matter of "traits," "attributes," and "practices." For example, on traditional middle-class playgrounds in America, boys roughhouse
more than girls, and roughhousing can be considered as perhaps a practice of the
male sex-class. To say here "of the male sex-class" implies that the behavior is
somehow not merely encompassed by male bodies severally but also motivated
and styled by something from within these several bodies and not, therefore,
merely the response of individuals to a formally established ruling. One might
want to refer here to a genderism, namely, a sex-class linked individual
behavioral practice. But take the practice found on school grounds a generation
ago of lining up the students outside the doorway in two sex-segregated files
before re-entering the school after a recess, presumably so that entrance would
be orderly and respectful. Now although such an arrangement certainly "expressed" beliefs about the differences between the sex-classes and was certainly
made up of sex-class linked behavior, still, lines formed with one's sex mates cannot easily be treated as a personally encompassed and generated bit of
behavior, a generism. If anything, what one has here is an institutional
genderism, a behavioral property of an organization, not a person. Lining up
behavior might be seen as individually encompassed, but as such ceases to be
gender specific, being something that the two classes equally engage in. The
lines themselves, it might be added, are a simple – nay, geometric – example of
parallel organization, an arrangement in which similar efforts or services, similar
rights or obligations, are organized in a segregated manner. However, as in the
case of the parallel organization which occurs with respect to other binary social
divisions – white/black, adult/child, officer/enlisted man, etc. – parallel
organization based on sex provides a ready base for the elaboration of differential
treatment, these adumbrative elaborations to be seen as consonant and suitable
given the claimed difference in character between the two categories. Thus, to
revert to the simple example, once children are made to form sex-segregated files,
it is a simple matter to rule that the female file enters before the male file,
presumably because the "gentler" sex should be given preference in the matter of
getting out of the raw outdoors first, and both sexes should be given little
lessons on proper regard for gender.[3]

4.

In almost all known societies it seems that sleeping, child-raising, and (to a lesser degree) eating tend to be centered in small establishments, these functions – especially in modern societies – organized around a married breeding pair; that broadly speaking the social roles of men and women are markedly differentiated, this, incidentally, giving to women the lesser rank and power, restricting her use of public space, excluding her from warfare and hunting, and often from religious and political office; and that more than the male, the female finds her life centered around household duties. This complex of arrangements is a central theme in human social organization, embarrassing the distinction between savage societies and civilized ones. The reason for these facts would be interesting to know, if, in fact, anyone is ever able to uncover them. (Perhaps a factor is that the segmentation that can be built on sex and procreative lines immensely simplifies social organization.) More interesting still is the ideological use to which these facts have been put. For this patterning in societies in general has allowed us to try to account for what occurs in our own industrial world by referring back to what occurs in small, nonliterate societies – indeed gives us some warrant for using the concept of "a society" in the first place – and from there encourages us to keep on going all the way to nonhuman primates and a fundamentally biological view of human nature. My position will be that the lesson that other societies – let alone other species – teach us has not yet been formulated soundly enough to provide us a warranted text to use for instructional purposes, and I propose to restrict myself to the here and now.

If one thinks of women – as I suppose one should – as just another disadvantaged category of persons in modern society, then comparisons with other such categories recommends itself along with a statement of where women fit on the scale of being treated unfairly. The answer to the latter question sometimes is: not very far down. Women in American society are more or less equal to men in the question of ethnic and social class; whatever these latter properties confer by way of social gain or loss upon men, they do so, too, upon women. So, too, there is considerable equality between the sexes in regard to inheritance, educational opportunity (at least undergraduate), personal consumption of goods, most rights before the law, and the love and respect of their children. Women are disadvantaged in regard to payment for work and grade of work attained, access to certain occupations and certain credit resources, legal practice with respect to name, claims on the use of public streets and places. (Some of these disadvantages diminish in the face of modernization and population control policies.) And it might even be claimed that women are advantaged in certain ways: they have generally enjoyed freedom from military conscription, whole or partial exemption from certain kinds of heavy work, preferential courtesies of various kinds – these too, perhaps diminishing with increased modernization.

This view of the situation of women has some utility in regard to social policy and political action, but for our purposes is too blunt. (The sociologically interesting thing about a disadvantaged category is not the painfulness of the disadvantage, but the bearing of the social structure on its generation and stability.) The issue, then, is not that women get less, but under what arrangement this occurs and what symbolic reading is given to the arrangement.

Given that a basic unit or our society is the domestic establishment with its nuclear family, ideal or fragmented, the whole embedded in a community somewhat homogeneous with respect to class, color, and ethnicity, and omitting incarcerative institutions, one has reason to distinguish two kinds of disadvantaged categories: those that can and tend to be sequestered off into entire families and neighborhoods and those that do not. Blacks are an example of the first; the physically handicapped, the second. Among those disadvantaged categories which are not segregated, women stand rather apart. Other unsegregated categories, such as the blind, the obese, the ex-mental patient, are scattered somewhat haphazardly throughout the social structure. (Relative concentration may occur in a particular ethnic group, age grade, economic level, or sex class, but incidence is still low.) Women are anything but that: they are allocated distributively to households in the form of female children, and then later, but still distributively, to other households in the form of wives. In the first, nature averages out the matter between the two sexes; in the second, law and custom allow only one to a household but strongly encourage the presence of that one.

Women as a disadvantaged group are, then, like maids (and like house servants), somewhat cut off ecologically from congress with their kind. Unlike household staff, however, women are also separated from one another by the stake they acquire in the very organization which divides them. For instead of an employer or master, a woman is likely to have (through the course of her life) a father, a husband, and sons. And these males transmit to her enough of what they themselves possess or acquire to give her a vested interest in the corporation. Defined as deeply different from men, each is yet linked to particular men through fundamental social bonds, placing her in a coalition with her menfolk against the whole of the rest of the world, a coalition, incidentally, which leads her to participate together with a connected male in in many social situations. For plainly, here the disadvantaged and the advantaged comprise two perfectly divided halves of the whole society, with similarity in expectations organized within sex-class and bondedness organized across the sexes. (A pretty support for this arrangement is "complementary ritual": a show of affiliation that one spouse extends to a particular female or male will be echoed in what the other spouse displays to the same person; thus the peculiar character of the cross-sex bond can be preserved in the face of third parties.) It is this sort of patterning, as if designed by some juvenile geometer who had read Radcliffe-Brown at too early an age, that presents the sociologically interesting phenomenon—and a remarkable phenomenon it is.

Furthermore, through one ritualized gesture or another, males are very likely to express, albeit fitfully, that they define females as fragile and valuable, to be protected from the harsher things of life and shown both love and respect.[4] Women may be defined as being less than men, but they are nonetheless ideal-ized, mythologized, in a serious way through such values as motherhood, in-nocence, gentleness, sexual attractiveness, and so forth–a lesser pantheon, perhaps, but a pantheon nonetheless. Moreover, many women–perhaps the vast majority in America even today–are profoundly convinced that however baleful their place in society, the official view concerning the natural characterological differences between themselves and men is correct, eternally and naturally so.

It is these special factors associated with the position of women that make our modern equalitarian world considerably like the most patriarchal you can im-agine–a chip off a very old block. And what makes industrial society special is not that our form of economic production little depends on the natural dif-ferences between the sexes–it might be very hard to find a society anywhere at any time that actually did–but rather that some of our citizenry no longer believe that women's traditional place is a natural expression of their natural capacities. And without that belief, the whole arrangement between the sex-classes ceases to make much sense. I do not claim that skepticism here will fun-damentally alter the arrangement between the sexes, only that if the traditional pattern is sustained, it will be sustained less comfortably.

5.

I have mentioned the obvious fact that women, unlike other disadvantaged groups, are held in high regard. Consider now two basic expressions of this con-dition: the courtship complex and the courtesy system.

1. In our society courtship tends to occur when potential partners are in their late teens and early twenties, this, incidentally, being a time when, on biological grounds, the female maximally fits commercial ideals regarding sexual attractiveness. The female adorns herself in terms of received notions of sexual attractiveness and makes herself available for review in public, semi-public, and restricted places. Males who are present show broadcast attention to females held to be desirable, and await some fugitive sign that can be taken as encourage-ment of their interest.[5] Routinely, courtship will mean that a male who was on distant terms comes to be on closer ones, which means that the male's assessing act–his obliging–constitutes the first move in the courtship process. And also that decorum will play an important role; for both male and female will act as if she is unaware that she has incurred an assessment (and, if favorable, that she has aroused sexual interest) and that she is not to be importuned if she does not respond with an encouraging act, the male presumably suppressing or displacing his desire. This is not to deny that successful suitors are likely to be those males who did not quite restrict their address to decorous distance-keeping.

The strategic advantage of the male in courtship derives from his ability and right to withdraw interest at any point save perhaps the last ones, that of the female from control of access to her favors, such sequential access being in our society expressive evidence of pair formation. (Power is another matter, deriving from extendable rights in property, social class, and so forth.) The advantages here are not quite balanced because the man also defines such access as evidence of his capacity as a male, and so he has reasons to submit to a female's gatekeeping apart from courtship considerations. (Women get confirmation, too, but the initial show of interest will often do.) But whether the male is interested in courtship or mere seduction, he must pursue the female with attentions and she has the power to lengthen or shorten the pursuit.

Observe that in traditional terms the female's discretion over bestowal can only remain a right insofar as she is successfully secretive about occasions for its use, or is chary about the numbers whom she so honors and the rapidity with which, in the case of any particular successful candidate, she does so. Traditional logic dictates that she bestow her final favors on only one person, and upon him only in response to his having committed himself to supporting her. This practice in turn permits, or at least is very consonant with, two others.

First, she can allow herself to be assessed in terms of nubility because the period for mate selection is geared into her very temporary qualification in this regard. (Thus the harsh fact that she will for many later years be disqualified, and increasingly so, from what she is supposed to be, will be correlated with, and mitigated by, her withdrawal from competition into domesticity, where presumably she will be able to enjoy what she has been able to win during her biologically supported period at play in the courtship game.[6])

Second, one traditional means of encouraging females to keep up the side and not bestow sexual favors too easily, which if done generally might debase the coin, was to define sexuality as dirty and bad, something that is contaminating, something only men want, something, therefore, that destroys good women and creates loose ones. However, the contract to mate was sealed by the female bestowing access rights, a frame for the act which hopefully transformed it into evidence of relationship formation, not easy virtue. She became a mate, not a lay, someone intrinsically pure who had proven vulnerable to but one special man, and this–he could think–because of his own special worthiness. The affirmation of masculinity the male thereby obtained was patently paradoxical; only virginally spirited women desirable as mates could bestow it, but the gift tended to destroy what had been given. In any case, we have here the traditional, standard formula of the respectable classes: he obtains exclusive rights of access and she gets a social place. Of course, for increasing numbers of our population sexual access has ceased to function in quite this way. Sexual license before marriage with someone not destined to be one's spouse is becoming quite routine, and what betrothal brings in these cases, ideally, is exclusive claim, not first claim.

As oft remarked, the courtship system implies that the two sexes will be differently situated in regard to norms of sexual attractiveness. On the face of it, the job of the male is to be attracted and of the female to attract, and similarly, on the face of it, in deciding whom to encourage from among those men who have shown interest, she is likely – it is said – to take into consideration broader matters than mere good looks and youthfulness. As already suggested, the implication is that she (more than he) will be committed to standards of appearance from which age will soon and increasingly cause her to deviate. Note that more so than with men, what a woman inherits socially from her parents cannot prevent her social position becoming precarious should she remain unmarried, in consequence of which she has an added reason to treat unsuitable suitors more and more seriously.

2. As courtship practices provide one expression of the high value placed on women, so the courtesy system provides another. In terms of what interpersonal rituals convey, the belief (in Western society) is that women are precious, ornamental, and fragile, uninstructed in, and ill-suited for, anything requiring muscular exertion or mechanical or electrical training or physical risk; further, that they are easily subject to contamination and defilement and to blanching when faced with harsh words and cruel facts, being labile as well as delicate. It follows then, that males will have the obligation of stepping in and helping (or protecting) whenever it appears that a female is threatened or taxed in any way, shielding her from gory, grisly sights, from squeamish-making things like spiders and worms, from noise, and from rain, wind, cold, and other inclemencies. Intercession can be extended even to the point of mediating her contacts with officals, strangers, and service personnel. And some of these obligations on the part of the male will extend not merely to females to whom he is personally related, but to any female who comes in sight, that is, to any female in the gathering in which he happens to find himself, especially is it appears that she is otherwise unattended by a male. This extension to the category as a whole is nicely confirmed by the fact that the manner in which a male proffers a courtesy to his wife can take an impersonal form, one perfectly suited to be shown to any female, and by the fact that minor coutesies can provide males with a defensible reason for involving themselves with attended females not known to them, as when a man momentarily turns from his course of action to light a woman's cigarette, exhibiting through a self-effacing manner that he has no designs on her time or attention and is not to be seen as ambitious, even by her male companion. Another confirmation, pretty as an example but ugly as a fact, is reported in the rape literature;[7] faced with forced attentions from strangers or persons known, and with the failure of other dissuasions, victims tend to beg and plead for mercy, employing the term "please" – a term that presupposes a claim of some sort that one's plight is to be given consideration, a claim that any woman ought to be able to invoke in regard to any man.

3. There appears to be a fundamental interweaving in our public life of courtship and courtesy, with consequences that are important. Obviously the obligation of a male to offer help of one kind and another, to volunteer his own

effort as a substitute for that of any neighboring female, is not merely an obligation but also a license. For he can use this obligation selectively as a cover under
which to focus his attentions upon attractive women, thus considerably increasing the means available to him to press his pursuit beyond what mere co-
participation in a gathering might otherwise provide; for example, she may find
herself obliged to convey gratitude, signs of relief, and so forth. He thus
facilitates and encourages the female's show of interest in him, should she be of
that mind, and may even oblige her somewhat in that direction. Note, courtesies
shown by males to desirable females may be profered with no great expectation
or hope that something beyond the contact can come of them; the interaction
itself, laced with such joking allusions as the male can muster, provides him a
small nibble of sexuality and a small confirmation of his masculinity.

One consequence of this link between courtship and courtesy is the provision of a benign basis for managing those social contacts which might otherwise
be competitive or even hostile. Another consequence is that although the standard courtesies accorded females by males tend to be applied fully and with
pleasure to the young and pretty, they tend to be applied with increasing reser-
vation as these two properties are wanting. The old and the ugly are thus
nature their sex-class is supposed to have conferred upon them. And they will
have cause to respond by being very careful not to press their case, or demand or
intrude to the point where such niceties as are shown them might be
withdrawn. (Thus it turns out that "well-dressed," young, attractive females
must be very circumspect in public places for one reason, the unattractive for
another.)

Another consequence of the mingling of courtship and courtesy bears on the
manner in which a female is constrained to conduct herself in mixed gatherings.
By acting in a retiring manner, by projecting shyness, reserve, and a display of
frailty, fear, and incompetence, she can constitute herself into the sort of object
to which a male can properly extend his helping hand, suppressing coarseness in
his speech and behavior while doing so. But observe that when the gathering
contains men other than her husband, another reason encourages her in this un-
forthcomingness. Given that males will be watching for encouragement, looking
to some lapse in the female's wonted reserve as a sign of this, it follows that any
forwardness on her part, any initiative, insobriety, aggressiveness, or direction-
giving, can be seen as sexually inviting, a sign, in short, of accessibility.[8] Thus,
specific legal or moral sanctions are not ordinarily needed to restrain women in
public, only self-interest, but this self-regulation can be seen as a functional consequence, a by-product, of the interworkings of other social definitions.

6.

Now the heart of the matter. It is common to conceive of the differences between the sexes as showing up against the demands and contraints of the environment, the environment itself being taken as a harsh given, present before

the matter of sex differences arose. Or, differently put, that sex differences are a biological given, an external constraint upon any form of social organization that humans might devise. There is another way of viewing the question, however. Speculatively one can reverse the equation and ask what could be sought out from the environment or put into it so that such innate differences between the sexes as there are could count–in fact or in appearance–for something. The issue, then, is institutional reflexivity. Consider some examples.

1. Clearly on biological grounds, mother is in a position to breast-feed baby and father is not. Given that recalcitrant fact, it is meet that father temporarily but exclusively takes on such tasks as may involve considerable separation from the household. But this quite temporary biologically-grounded constraint turns out to be extended culturally. A whole range of domestic duties come (for whatever reason) to be defined as inappropriate for a male to perform; and a whole range of occupations away from the household come to be defined as inappropriate for the female. Given these social definitions, coalition formulation is a natural response to the harsh facts of the world, for only in this way will one be able to acquire what one needs and yet not have to engage in labor that is unsuitable for someone of one's kind. Nor is couple formation required only because of gender constraints on task performance. In public life in general women will find that there are things that should be done for them, and men will find that there are things that they should be doing for others, so once again they find they need each other. (So that just as a man may take a wife to save himself from labor that is uncongenial to him, so she can seek him so as to have the company she needs if she is to make full use of public places.) Thus, the human nature imputed to the male causes him to be dependent on a female connection, and the reciprocal condition prevails for women. Who a male finds he needs if he is to act according to his nature is just who needs him so that she can act according to hers. Persons as such do not need one another in these ways, they do so only as gender-based identities.

2. Consider the household as a socialization depot. Take as a paradigm a middle-class pair of cross-sexed sibs. The home training of the two sexes will differ, beginning to orient the girl to taking a domestic, supportive role, and the boy to a more widely based competitive one. This difference in orientation will be superimposed on a fundamental quality in many matters that are felt to count. So from the start, then, there will be two basic principles to appeal to in making claims and warranting allocations. One is the equality of sibs and beyond this of participating members–the share and share alike theme realized in its strongest form in many wills and in its most prevalent form in turn-taking systems. The other is the accounting by sex, as when the larger portion at mealtime is given to the male "because he's a boy" or the softer of two beds is allocated to the female "because she's a girl," or a male is accorded harsher negative sanctions than a female because his is the coarser nature and it will take more to get through to

him. And these accountings by appeal to gender will never cease to be used as a handy device to rationalize an allocation whose basis is otherwise determined, to exclude a basis of allocation that might cause disgruntlement, and, even more, to explain away various failures to live up to expectations. All of this is perfectly well known in principle, although not adequately explored in detail. What is not well appreciated is that differently sexed children coming under the jurisdiction of the same parental authority and living much of their early lives in one another's presence in the same set of rooms produce thereby an ideal setting for role differentiation. For family life ensures that most of what each sex does is done in the full sight of the other sex and with full mutual appreciation of the differential treatment that obtains. Thus, whatever the economic or class-level and however well or badly off a female sees she is when compared to children in other families, she can hardly fail to see that her male sib, equal to her when compared to children in other families and often equal, too, in regard to ultimate claims upon the family resources, is yet judged differently and accorded different treatment from herself by their parents. So, too, a male sib. Thus from the beginning males and females acquire a way of judging deserts and treatment that muffles (by cross-cutting) differences in class and economic power. However superior the social position of a family may be, its female children will be able to learn that they are different from (and somewhat subordinate to) males; and however inferior the social position of a family may be, its male children will be able to learn that they are different from (and somewhat superordinate to) females. It is as if society planted a brother with sisters so women could from the beginning learn their place, and a sister with brothers so men could learn their place. Each sex becomes a training device for the other, a device that is brought right into the house; and what will serve to structure wider social life is thus given its shape and its impetus in a very small and very cozy circle. And it also follows that the deepest sense of what one is—one's gender identity—is something that is given its initial character from ingredients that do not bear on ethnicity or socio-economic stratification, in consequences of which we all acquire a deep capacity to shield ourselves from what we gain and lose by virtue of our placement in the overall social hierarchy. Brothers will have a way of defining themselves in terms of their differences from persons like their sisters, and sisters will have a way of defining themselves in terms of their differences from persons like their brothers, in both cases turning perception away from how it is the sibs in one family are socially situated in a fundamentally different way from the sibs of another family. Gender, not religion, is the opiate of the masses. In any case, we have here a remarkable organizational device. A man may spend his day suffering under those who have power over him, suffer this situation at almost any level of society, and yet on returning home each night regain a sphere in which he dominates. And wherever he goes beyond the household, women can be there to prop up his show of competence. It is not merely that your male executive has a female secretary, but (as now often remarked) his drop-out son who moves up the hierarchy of alternative publishing or protest politics will have female help, too; and had he been disaffected enough to join a rural commune, an appropriate division of labor would have awaited him. And should we leave the real world for something set up as its fictional alternative, a science fiction cosmos, we would find that here, too, males engage in the executive action and have females to help out in the manner of their sex. Wherever the male goes, apparently, he can carry a sexual division of labor with him.

3. In modern times, mating pairs appear naked to each other and are even likely to employ a bathroom at the same time. But beyond this, the mature genitalia of one sex is not supposed to be exposed to the eyes of the other sex. Furthermore, although it is recognized that persons of both sexes are somewhat similar in the question of waste products and their elimination, the environment in which females engage in this act ought (we in America apparently feel) to be more refined, extensive, and elaborate than that required for males. Presumably out of consideration for the arrangement between the sexes in general, and the female sex-class in particular, it has come to pass, then, that almost all places of work and congregation are equipped with two sets of toilet facilities (a case of parallel organization), differentiated with respect to quality. A case of separate and unequal. Therefore, in very nearly every industrial and commercial establishment, women will be able to break off being exposed to males and their company and retire into an all-female enclave, often in the company of a female friend, and there spend time in toiletry, a longer time presumably, and perhaps more frequently, than males spend in their segregated toilet, and under more genteel environmental conditions. A resting room that is sex-segregated (as many are) may extend this divided realm. There is thus established a sort of with-then-apart rhythm, with a period of the sexes being immersed together followed by a short period of separation, and so on. (Bars, gyms, locker rooms, pool rooms, etc., accomplish the same sort of periodic segregation, but from the male side, the difference being that whereas female redoubts tend to be furnished more genteely than the surrounding scene, male redoubts [at least in the U.S.] are often furnished less prepossessingly than the surround.) This same pattern seems to be extended outward from toilets and resting rooms to larger domains. Large stores have floors which merge the sexes but also smaller zones which offer one-sex merchandise patronized very largely by that sex alone. Schools provide coeducational classes, punctuated by gym, sports, and a few other activities that are sex-segregated.[9]

All in all, then, one does not so much deal with segregation as with segregative punctuation of the day's round, this ensuring that subcultural differences can be reaffirmed and reestablished in the face of contact between the sexes. It is as if the joining of the sexes were tolerable providing periodic escape is possible; it is as if equality and sameness were a masquerade that was to be periodically dropped. And all of this is done in the name of nicety, of civilization, of the respect owed females, or of the "natural" need of men to be by themselves. Observe that since by and large public places are designed for males (the big exception being large department stores), female facilities have had to be added to ones already established. Predictably, it has been an argument against hiring females that an extra complement of toilet facilities would be necessary and is not available.

Now clearly, if ogling and sexual access is to play the role it does in pair formation in our society, then sequestering of toilet functions by sex would seem to be indicated. And even more clearly, what is thus sequestered is a biological matter in terms of which the sex-classes biologically and markedly differ. But the sequestering arrangement as such cannot be tied to matters biological, only to folk conceptions about biological matters. The *functioning* of sex-differentiated organs is involved, but there is nothing in this functioning that *biologically* recommends segregation; *that* arrangement is totally a cultural matter. And what one has is a case of institutional reflexivity: toilet segregation is presented as a natural consequence of the difference between the sex-classes, when in fact it is rather a means of honoring, if not producing, this difference.

4. Consider now selective job placement. Traditionally in industrial society women have gravitated to, or have been gravitated to, jobs which sustain the note established for them in households – the garment industry, domestic labor, commercial cleaning, and personal servicing such as teaching, innkeeping, nursing, food handling.[10] In these latter scenes, presumably, it will be easy for us to fall into treating the server as someone to help us in a semi-mothering way, not someone to subordinate coldly or be subordinated by. In service matters closely associated with the body and the self, we are thus able to play down the harshness that male servers might be thought to bring.

Women, especially young, middle-class ones, have also, of course, been much employed in clerical and secretarial labor, which work is often defined as a dead-end job to be filled by someone who dresses well and doesn't expect or want to make a career out of the labor. Presumably secretaries are merely marking time until marriage, preferably in a place where opportunity to "meet" men is to be found. In any case, the age and sex difference between secretary and employer allows for some styling in avuncular terms. By removing the relationship from the strict world of business, the superior can suffer being intimately viewed by a subordinate without feeling that he has lost rank by the association. He can also make minor demands beyond the core of the contract, expecting to be seen as someone whose needs should be attended to however varied these might be – as a child would be attended by a mother. In return he can extend family feeling, using a personal term of address (of course asymmetrically), please-and-thank-you brackets around each of the minor discrete services called for, and gallantry in the matter of opening doors and moving heavy typewriters. He can also allow her to use the telephone for personal calls and can respond to pleas for special time off to accomplish the business of her sex.

So, too, one finds in jobs where women "meet the public" – ticket-takers, receptionists, airhostesses, salespersons – that standards of youthful "attractiveness" apply in employee selection. Which practice is, of course, even more marked in selecting women for advertising displays and the dramatic arts. The consequence is that when a male has business contacts with a female, she is more than otherwise likely to be someone whom he might take pleasure in associating with. Again, the courtesy he here extends and receives can carry a dash of sexual interest. (It appears that the higher the male reaches in the hierarchies within business, government, or the professions, the classier will be the women he is required to have incidental dealings with, a sign and symbol of success.)

Finally, note that in almost all work settings established as places for thoroughly masculine labor, one or two women can be found engaged in some sort of ancillary work. It turns out, then, that there are few social settings where males will not be in a position to enact courtesies due to the female sex.

In all, then, one can see that selective employment comes to ensure that males are likely to find themselves rather frequently in the presence of females, and that these women will not only tend to allow a personalization of the contact, but will be relatively young and attractive beyond what random selection ought to allow. In that sense, the world that men are in is a social construct, drawing them daily from their conjugal milieu to what appear to be all-male settings; but these environments turn out to be strategically stocked with relatively attractive females, there to serve in a specialized way as passing targets for sexually alusive banter and for diffuse considerateness extended in both directions. The principle is that of less for more, the effect is that of establishing the world beyond the household as a faintly red-light district where men can easily find and safely enjoy interactional favors. Observe that the more a male contents himself with gender pleasantries – systematically available yet intermittent and brief – the more widely can a preferential category of females be shared by males in general.[11] (Indeed, the traditional dating game can be seen not merely as a means of getting the sexes paired, but as a means of giving a large number of men a little of the company of exemplary women.)

5. Among all the means by which differentiation along sex-class lines is fostered in modern society, one stands out as having a special and an especially powerful influence: I refer to our *identification system*, this involving two related matters, our means of discovering "who" it is that has come into our ken, that is, our placement practices, and our means of labeling what it is we have thus placed.

On the placement side, it is clear that the appearance established as appropriate to the two sexes allows for sex typing at a distance. Although recently this arrangement has developed some potential for error, still the system is remarkably effective at any angle and from almost any distance, saving only that viewing be close enough to allow perception of a figure. Effectiveness of place-ment by sight is matched by sound; tone of voice alone – as on the phone – is suf-ficient by and large for sexual identification. Indeed, handwriting is effective, too, although perhaps not as fully as appearance and voice. (Only appreciable differences in age are as effectively betrayed through all three channels; race in America is conveyed through sight and, by and large, through voice but not through handwriting.)

On the naming side, we have a system of terms including proper personal names, titles, and pronouns. These devices are used for giving deference (whether respect, distance, or affection), for specifying who we are addressing or who among those present we are referring to, and for making attributions in written and spoken statements. And in European languages, by and large, ex-cept for second-person pronouns, these naming practices inform at least about sex-class, this often being the only matter they do inform about.

Now our placement practices and naming practices, taken together as a single system, serve to define who we are to have dealings with and enable these dealings to proceed; and both sets of practices very strongly encourage categorization along sex-class lines. Right from the very start of an interaction, then, there is a bias in favor of formulating matters in sex-relevant terms, such that sex-class provides the overall profile or container, and particularizing prop-erties are then attributed to the outline by way of specification. This is not a small bias. And note that this identification-naming system is overwhelmingly accounted for by the doctrine that consequent discriminations are only natural, something not to be seen as a product of personal or social engineering but rather as a natural phenomenon.

7.

I have touched on five examples of institutional reflexivity, five features of social organization which have the effect of confirming our gender stereotypes and the prevailing arrangement between the sexes: the sex-class division of labor, siblings as socializers, toilet practices, looks and job selection, our iden-tification system. In all of this an underlying issue has been the biological dif-ferences between the sexes. It is that issue to which I return now, especially in the matter of differences in size, strength, and combat potential.

My argument throughout has been the now standard one that the physical differences between the sexes are in themselves very little relevant to the human capacities required in most of our undertakings. The interesting question then becomes: How in modern society do such irrelevant biological differences between the sexes come to seem of vast social importance? How, without biological warrant, are these biological differences elaborated socially? Again the answer will argue for institutionalized reflexivity.

1. Clearly if hand-to-hand combat could be arranged on every occasion of human contact, the biological difference between the sex-classes would signify, for in such combat the weaker would have to extend himself to the full to try for a win or to flee for safety, and overwhelmingly in cross-sex contacts, the himself would be a herself. In much of adult life, these trials are ruled out. But they are not ruled out as a source of guiding imagery. Among young males – and males only – training and practice in boxing and wrestling are fairly widespread, if spread shallow. Thus, instead of spluttering on the occasion of a physical challenge, males learn to do something in a somewhat concerted fashion. In any case, one has here a key source of metaphor, the dueling or punch-out format. Men, even middle-class ones, hold themselves ready to have to defend themselves physically (as a defense of self) or attack another (as a defense of loved ones, property, or principles). For middle-class males, at least, this does not mean actual combat, merely a sizing up of situations in terms of this possibility. Before a male becomes openly aggressive, he thus judges the possible outcome in terms of "having it out" and whether he could "handle" the other. (Of course, he will also be concerned about creating a "scene," with its attendant ill fame, entanglements with the police and the courts, cosmetic disarray, etc.) This judgment produces a great deal of circumspection and carefulness and often the erroneous outward appearance that fighting has ceased to be a relevant possibility. But, in fact, the issue is not that the model has ceased to function as a guide, rather that it functions very well.

Corresponding to the role of combat as a source of imagery and style in dealings between men, one finds an image of sexual imposition or force in dealings across sexes. Relationship formation is seen to come from aggressive initiatory activity on the part of males, a breaking down of boundaries and barriers, a pursuit, a pressing of one's suit. (Indeed, fiction affirms a remarkable version – a mythic encapsulation, as it were – portrayed through hands that start by unsuccessfully fighting off a rapist and end by caressing a lover; and it turns out that some actual rapists look, albeit unsuccessfully, to have the fantasy realized.[12]) Thus, the courtship scene, held to express the ultimate nature of the beasts, turns out to be one of the few available contexts in which myths concerning the differences between the sexes can be realized. Basic social facts, then, are not much carried into this realm as carried out of it.

2. Consider now dimorphism and social situations. Males, being bigger and stronger than females, can, if of a mind, help women out in social situations in regard, say, to things that are heavy or out of reach. Males on the same count can physically threaten present females, as well as come to their aid should others threaten. In all of this, males will have an opportunity of doing and females of showing respect, if not gratitude, for what is done. But observe how social practice has made it possible for men and women to stage these self-confirming scenes.

Men, of course, are trained from childhood in outdoor competencies, mechanical, electrical, automotive, and so forth, just as they very often are given some rudimentary practice in the arts of self-defense. They come then, to social situations with these advantages, just as women come to social situations without them.

Differential size and strength similarly has a social element. Although men on the whole are larger and stronger than women, there is appreciable overlap in the two normal curves. Thus, if present conventions were reversed and if care were taken, a very evident number of couples could contain males shorter than or equal in height to their female companions. But in fact, selective mating ensures that with almost no exceptions husbands are bigger than wives and boyfriends are bigger than their girlfriends. (One has here a prime example of a norm sustained without official or specific social sanction, diffuse unsatisfactory consequences apparently serving to ensure utter uniformity.) Now since our Western society is very considerably organized in terms of couples, in the sense that the two members are often to be found in each other's company (most constantly, of course, in the recreational and domestic spheres), it will be that displays by men to women of physical help and physical threat will be widely possible. The marital bond – whatever else it is – can be seen as having the consequence of more or less permanently attaching an audience directly to each performer, so that wherever the male or female goes, an appropriate other will be alongside to reciprocate the enactment of gender expressions. Pair formation creates a mutually captive audience. Nor does the matter stop with the marital and dating pair. Even temporary clusters at sociable occasions are likely to be recruited so once again the male is in a position to do his show without being embarrassed by the presence of a female who (it appears) is physically endowed to do it better. Observe, too, that the customary age differential between the pairing sexes ensures that, by and large, the male will be more experienced and moneyed than the female, this, too, supporting the show of control he exhibits in social situations.

In sum, early training reinforces what selection by age and height differential establishes, namely, social situations in which men and women can effectively play out the differential human nature claimed for them. Thus, the image can be sustained that all women are muscularly less developed than all men in all respects, a binary division alien to the biological facts; for in fact, physical forcefulness involves several variables which are incompletely correlated, and a line cleanly dividing the two sex-classes cannot be drawn. Yet the patterning of sex-class behavior is such that puny men and robust women mainly suffer the assaultive contingencies associated with their sex-class, not their size.

3. An important feature of the life of the young, especially the male young, in our society is competitive sports and games. This organized vying is presented by adults as a desirable thing, a scene in which youths can work off their animal energies, learn fairness, perseverance, and team spirit, obtain exercise, and sharpen a desire to fight against the odds for a win; in short, a training ground for

the game of life. (Thus when boys are given instruction in fighting, the teaching tends to be in a fair contest frame, with rules and referees to see that nothing gets out of hand.) But indeed, one might just as well see these vying frames as the only discoverable way of establishing the world as we claim it to be. So, one could argue, it is not that sports are but another expression of our human (specifically male) nature, but rather that sports are the only expression of male human nature – an arrangement specifically designed to allow males to manifest the qualities claimed as basic to them: strengths of various kinds, stamina, endurance, and the like. In consequence of this early training in sports, individuals can carry through life a framework of arrangement and response, a referencing system, which provides evidence, perhaps *the* evidence, of our having a certain nature. Adult spectator sports, live and transmitted, ensure a continuous reminder of this contesting perspective.

There is an important point to be made about contests. Fairness is achieved not only by obedience to the rules of the sport, but also by selecting evenly matched opponents or by handicapping superior ones. This ensures that the outcome will be unpredictable and therefore suspenseful. But for an understanding of biological differences, the issue is that even in the put-together world of sports, only very careful selectivity provides the circumstances in which marginal effort will be determinative, when, that is, the full exercise of physical skill, endurance, and strength is necessary. And in sports, circumstances are also presented in which weight, reach, and height are crucial. *It is here, then, that the sort of biological differences that exist between males and females would tell.* But for these differences to tell, these are the arrangements that must be established. Now what one finds increasingly in civil life is that extremely few jobs call on this marginal performance, this stretching of physical capacity. Yet it is just this marginal difference between the strong and the weak, the sturdy and the slight, the tall and the short, that is employed in the doctrine we have concerning work and sex.

4.   Another matter to examine is playfulness. In many social circles, the occasions when physical coercion is threatened or applied may be rare indeed. But although the social environment is thus uncooperative in allowing for a show of gender, forcing the use of sporting scenes designed for the purpose, the ad hoc use of playfulness can compensate, ensuring that opportunity for mock moves of physical dominance will abound. Thus between males one finds various forms of horseplay – shoving, pushing, punching, withholding – along with mock contests such as Indian wrestling, spur of the moment races, hand-squeeze trials, and the like. Across sex, males engage in lift-off bear hugs, mock chasing after, coercive holding in one position, grasping of the two small wrists in one big hand, playful rocking of the boat, dunking, throwing or pushing into the water, spraying with water, making as if to push off a cliff, throwing small stones at the body, approaching with snake, dead rat, squid, and other loathsome objects, threatening with electrical shocks of an order they themselves can bear, and other delights.[13] Observe that by unseriously introducing just those threats and pains that he

might protect a woman from, a male can encourage her to provide a full-voiced rendition of the plight to which her sex is presumably prone. And, of course, she herself can create the unserious circumstances in which her display of gender will be possible, as when she pummels he who holds her, as if out of hopelessness at having any effect upon the giant that has captured her, or hids her eyes from the terrible things that are being shown on the silver screen while he laughingly watches on, or squeals and turns away from the overexciting finish of a horse race, or runs across the street with her head down and her arms flailing in mock terror over the oncoming traffic, or unsuccessfully attempts to open a jar with a play at straining all her muscular reserve, or gestures abject fear when the phone rings and signals a call that is unwelcome, or gesticulates that walking over the stones to get to the water is destroying her tender feet, or that the cold is making her shiver like unto little Liza on the ice floe.

5. I have argued that genderisms are not generated by the impact of an unrelenting environment itself, but by an environment in some sense designed for the purpose of this evocation. Observe now that individuals need not wait for the environment to produce those circumstances for which the display of a genderism will provide a usable response. Individuals can apply a format that automatically transforms an environment into one which induces such a display, guaranteeing that something suitable will be found for ritual management. We tend to think of a chivalrous man helping a woman – unacquainted or merely ac-quainted – to manage a load that is heavy or messy or precariously placed, and therefore we can see him as someone who stands by parentally in case of trouble; but indeed, a male, bent on this sort of gallantry, can search a women-connected scene for the heaviest or messiest or most precarious concern she happens to have, and then volunteer help with what is thus found. This action on his part is then likely to be confirmed by the gratitude she shows for the consideration given her. But, of course, in *every* social situation involving a female (or anyone else) there will be a heaviest, a messiest, and a most precarious concern, even though by the standards set in other settings, this may involve something that is light, clean and safe. (There is a symmetry here; a female can similarly search the scene for whatever is best adapted to release her from an indication of weakness, fear, mechanical incompetence, or, on the other side, give evidence of her capaci-ty to provide minor domestic-like services.)

6. I have suggested that every physical surround, every room, every box for social gatherings, necessarily provides materials that can be used in the display of gender and the affirmation of gender identity. But, of course, the social interaction occurring in these places can be read as supplying these materials also. Participants in any gathering must take up some sort of microecological position relative to one another, and these positions will provide ready metaphors for social distance and relatedness, just as they will provide sign vehicles for conveying relative rank.

More important, the management of talk will itself make available a swarm of events usable as signs. Who is brought or brings himself into the immediate orbit of another; who initiates talk, who is selected as the addressed recipient, who self-selects in turn-taking, who establishes and changes topics, whose statements are given attention and weight, and so forth. As with verbal interaction, so also with joint participation in silent projects such as walking together, arranging objects, and the like. For here, too, organization requires that someone make the decisions and coordinate the activity; and again the opportunity is available, often apparently unavoidably so, for someone to emerge as dominant, albeit in regard to trivial matters.

An interactional field, then, provides a considerable expressive resource, and it is, of course, upon this field that there is projected the training and beliefs of the participants. It is here that sex-class makes itself felt, here in the organization of face-to-face interaction, for here understandings about sex-based dominance can be employed as a means of deciding who decides, who leads, and who follows. Again, these scenes do not so much allow for the expression of natural differences between the sexes as for the production of that difference itself.

May I recommend that the capacity to work social situations for what can inevitably be found in them is of considerable importance. When boys and girls are socialized, one of the basic things they learn is this capacity to size up a social situation for what can be expressively wrung from it. This capacity in turn depends upon the culture's idiom of expression, itself fed from several sources, such as – in Western culture – training in the ideally expressive environments of games and contests, imagery drawn from animal lore, residues from military training, and so forth. In consequence, men and women are able to scan any ongoing social activity for means through which to express gender. And, of course, these means do considerable organizational work; as suggested, what becomes involved in the question of who makes the decisions in regard to a multitude of small doings which, pieced together, allow for smooth collaborative activity. Some of this organizational work need not be done. Much of it could be done by celebrating other statuses. But given that this work is presently done by an appeal to sex-class, and given that various institutional practices ensure the copresence of men and women, then the question becomes moot as to whether these rituals ought to be seen as a means of celebrating the social structure, or whether the importance of the social structure, at least in its relevant aspects, ought to be seen as that of providing a template for expressive displays which help to organize social situations. (Which is not to say that social structure is somehow a construct or real only as it affects what occurs in face-to-face interaction.)

8.

I have argued that females are a distinctive disadvantaged category in that they alone among these – save only children – are idealized, in Western society

as pure, fragile, valued objects, the givers and receivers of love and care, this giving and receiving being, in a way, their office. And I have also pressed a kind of
institutional reflexivity, the argument that deep-seated institutional practices
have the effect of transforming social situations into scenes for the performance
of genderisms by both sexes, many of these performances taking a ritual form
which affirms beliefs about the differential human nature of the two sexes even
while indications are provided as to how behavior between the two can be expected to be intermeshed. Now consider the politics of these rituals.

First note that the traditional ideals of femininity and the ideals of
masculinity are alike in that both sets tend to be supported for the relevant sex
by both sexes. At the same time, the ideals are complementary in that the ones
held for women are differentiated from the ones held for men and yet the two fit
together. Frailty is fitted to strength, gentleness to sternness, diffuse serving to
project orientation, mechanical unknowingness to mechanical competencies,
delicacy relative to contamination vs. insensitivity to contamination, and so
forth. It turns out, then, that a woman could only realize the ideals of femininity
by holding herself away from the heat, grime, and competition of the world
beyond the household. So these ideals have, then, a political consequence, that
of relieving persons who are males from half the competition they would otherwise face. (A similar consequence can be attributed to age-grading and late
schooling.) This in no way implies, of course, that a woman has no ability to
make her suitors compete for her hand, or make the one to whom she is inclined
dance at her attendance to further his suit, but only that this female power is sequestered from the main show. As she herself is. Even those females who are
able and willing to trade some of their favors in exchange for special consideration in the work world will find themselves quite differently related to the contingencies of employment than are males, a difference that then continues to
mark at least middle-class women off as belonging essentially to a work-alien,
private-sphere.

But this sequestering itself is of a special kind. For, as already considered,
social organization ensures that men and women will be in one another's
presence, women being a disadvantaged group that is not (in modern society)
hidden away in bad neighborhoods or in barracks on the outskirts of town. So
the difference between the sex-classes will very commonly be something that
can be given ritual expression.

Apologists can, then, interpret the high value placed on femininity as a
balance and compensation for the substantive work that women find they must
do in the domestic sphere and for their subordination in, if not exclusion from,
public spheres. And the courtesies performed for and to women during social occasions can be seen as redress for the retiring role they are obliged to play at
these times. What could be thought good about their situation, then, seems
always to enter as a means of cloaking what could be thought bad about it. And
every indulgence society shows to women can be seen as a mixed blessing.

9.

Surely the argument that ours is a sexist society is valid–as it is for societies in general. A considerable amount of what persons who are men do in affirmation of their sense of identity requires their doing something that can be seen as what a woman by her nature could not do, or at least could not do well; and the reverse can be said about persons who are women. Furthermore, some of these doings the individual does in the company of the other sex, an arrangement facilitated by diverse institutional practices, allowing for the dialogic performance of identity–ritual statements by one party receiving ritual answers from the other party, both displays being necessary for the full portrayal of the human nature of the individuals involved. But, of course, in the case of persons who are women, the issue is not merely that they are in a complementary position to persons who are men; the issue is that for women this complementarity also means vulnerability and, in the feelings of some, oppression. In this light, and as an illustration, consider public life.

Wherever an individual is or goes he must bring his body along with him. That means that whatever harm bodies can do, or be vulnerable to, goes along, too. As for vulnerabilities, their source allows us to distinguish two kinds. First, impersonal risks as lodged in a setting and not specifically intended for the recipient: physical risks–fire, falling objects, accidental collision, etc.; medical risks due to contagion, poisons, etc.; contamination of body by smell and grime. Second (and our concern here), social risks, those seen as a product of a malefactor's intention. Here central matters are physical assault, robbery, sexual molestation, kidnapping, blocking of passage, breaching of conversational preserves, verbal insult delivered in conversation already established, importunement. Whomsoever an individual is in the presence of, he makes them vulnerable in these ways and they make him vulnerable similarly.

Now the standard feature of all public life–especially that occurring whenever unacquainted individuals come into one another's immediate presence–is that the inclination to exploit the immediate vulnerability of others is suppressed, if not repressed. A folk theory is maintained that indeed persons can be physically close and be of no interest whatsoever to one another, that, for example, not even evaluative assessment of social attributes is occurring. Among the unacquainted, the symbol of this arrangement is civil inattention, the process of glancing at an other to express that one has no untoward intent nor expects to be an object of it, and then turning the glance away, in a combination of trust, respect, and apparent unconcern.

The arrangement under which an individual causes no difficulty and is given none, when both prospects are eminently feasible, is felt to be ensured by devices of social control. The law is one factor (at least it used to be so thought); another, disapproval and moral condemnation by witnesses to the act–in effect, the threat of defaming. In the case of attack on males (or on females by other females) there is also the issue of physical and verbal counterattack, the possibility of getting back in return what had theretofore been suppressed, and getting as good as one gives or better.

It is known, of course, that conventional standards of social control in public places can prove inadequate; if not that, then certainly that individuals can come to believe that this is the case. The consequence is felt insecurity in public places. What I want to consider here, however, is the special relation of females to these circumstances.

As suggested, women are not trained in fighting and moreover are encouraged to employ quite passive means of avoiding fights and to withdraw from such as have begun. Therefore, relative to men under attack, women are less capable and felt to be so. (I suppose it might be said that men must fear being shown up as unwilling to fight, and that women have less to fear in this matter.) It seems also the case that a woman is at a disadvantage in giving insult back in response to attack. She is faced with the dilemma that any remonstrance becomes itself a form of self-exposure, ratifying a connection that theretofore had merely been improperly attempted. (Surely an insidious trick on the part of social organization.) Also, not socialized into the fighting frame, she can find herself blithely returning an insult – when a man, mindful of possible escalation, might be leery of doing so – which, in turn, evokes a response that cannot be managed by either party. The male recipient of female insult can feel, for example, that his readiness to abjure the use of physical force with females presupposed that females would not press quarrels to the point where a fight would ordinarily be required; finding that this tacit contract has been breached, he may not know what to do, and whatever he does, do it in a troubled and confused way.[14]

But the difference between the sexes in the matter of being vulnerable in public places goes deeper still.

Consider again what an individual can suffer at another's hands in public. There is loss of life, an equal value as between the sexes except perhaps in time of war. There is injury to limbs, presumably also an equal matter, except that bodily disfigurement is perhaps a greater contingency for females than for males. (More important, perhaps, life and limb, being thought to have ultimate value, can be used in coercive exchange, as in "Your money or your life.") There is the disarray of personal front (clothing and appearance), likely in any physical altercation, and here the standards women are obliged to maintain are considerably more strict than those required of men. (After all, for a woman to appear in public with her costume disarrayed can be taken as a sign of accessibility and looseness of morals.) There is expropriation of cash and valuables, men probably having somewhat more to lose of the first, woman of the second.

From this point, the situation of the two sexes sharply differs. Except in prison, men in modern society can't be much threatened by sexual violence nor threatened by physical harm if sexual access is not allowed; women can be. But there is a more subtle and more important difference. As suggested, the court-ship process leads the male to press his pursuit, first in finding some reason for opening up a state of talk, and second, in overcoming the social distance initially maintained therein. Breaching of existing distance, partly on speculation, is, then, a standard part of the male's contribution to cross-sex dealings, at least as far as the male is concerned. And it is in the nature of his view of these dealings that they know no season or place; any occasion will do. All good-looking females wherever found are worth a moment's ogling, and this attention also allows for discernment of possible signs of encouragement or (if not that) signs that discouragement is not complete. And men can be easily confirmed in this approach because they know that many of the relationships they do end up hav-ing with women began in this way and were not likely to have begun at all had no breaching occurred. Note that women themselves do not take a consistent line here, for just as some will be offended by these overreachings, so others (even as they discourage the interest shown their person) can be inwardly pleased by the delict, seeing in it an indication of their rating, a measure of their "attractiveness."[15]

It follows, then, that females are somewhat vulnerable in a chronic way to being "hassled;" for what a male can improperly press upon them by way of drawing them into talk or by way of improperly extending talk already initiated stands to gain him (and indeed her) a lot, namely, a relationship, and if not this, then at least confirmation of *gender* identity.[16]

In this context, rebuffs on the part of the female carry special contingencies. The issue appears in starkest form, perhaps, in robbery itself, apart from matters of sex. For it turns out that once the robber has broken cover and revealed himself as a wrongdoer, as a culprit committing an indictable offense, such ag-gressive feelings as he might otherwise have had but supressed become something he might as well express, having already paid most of the price for such expression. His "wantonly" injuring his victim may, then, be a sign not of special sadistic impulse but rather of what we all might inflict were no penalty (at least no further penalty) to be incurred. Something similar can occur in the case of salutations some men feel impelled to extend to women with whom they are unacquainted. When such overtures are rebuffed, the male finds not only that he is exposed as desiring what he is now judged unworthy of receiving, but also that he has established himself as someone who has attempted to improperly force or extend a communicative contact. Not uncommonly, then, he uses this channel to redefine what he has not been able to obtain, openly conveying in-sults to she who has denied him.

And one can see why men are not reciprocally subject to molestation by women; for in general, were a woman to press her favors, there would be men who could only stand to gain by accepting. Takers could always be found. And one can see that women have a power men do not much have, that of allowing access to themselves. A wife can thus betray her husband more easily than the reverse, even though he has greater mobility, implying access to a larger number of pastures.

So it is apparent that men and women find themselves quite differently related to public life, its contingencies being very much greater for females than for males, and for reasons that are structurally deep-seated. This difference cuts sharply and cleanly along sex-class lines in spite of the fact that physical potential for assault and for self-defense is by no means so clearly divisible into non-overlapping classes. Plainly, it is for membership sorting that biology provides a neat and tidy device; the contingencies and response that seem so naturally to follow along the same lines are a consequence of social organization.

NOTES

1. It is apparent, of course, that there are cases of temporary misassignment at birth, cases of mixed biological signs (intersexing), and, recently, surgical and social "reassignment." It should be just as apparent that these three classes of cases are exceptional, that they take their significance from the fact that they are exceptional, and that sex-class placement is, relative to all other placements, rigorously achieved.

2. See Carroll Smith-Rosenberg, "The Female World of Love and Ritual: Relations between Women in Nineteenth-Century America," *Signs* 1, 1 (1975), pp. 1–30, especially p. 9ff.

3. The history of parallel arrangements for the sexes in American society has never been written.

4. Jessie Bernard in *Women and the Public Interest* (Chicago, 1971), pp. 26, 28, provides a version: ascription; diffuseness; particularism; collectivity-orientation; affectivity; passivity in love-making; obedience, submissiveness to commands and rules, dependence, fearfulness, modesty, chastity, bashfulness, maidenly reserve, love of home, restricted outside interests, monogamic inclination, interest in bodily adornment, love of finery, care for babies.

5. "Civil inattention" allows male and female a quick mutual glance. Her *second* quick look can serve as a signal of encouragement to him. Some men have much experience with second looks; other men, practically none. For experimental and field evidence, see Mark S. Carey, "Nonverbal Openings to Conversation," paper presented at the Eastern Psychological Association Meetings, April 18, 1974, Philadelphia, Pennsylvania, and "Talk? Do You Want to Talk?: Negotiation for the Initiation of Conversation between the Unacquainted," Ph.D. dissertation, Department of Psychology, University of Pennsylvania, 1975.

6. Current tendencies in the direction of no-fault, no alimony divorce, defined as liberalization, override this compensatory arrangement, ensuring that at least some women will get the worst of both worlds.

7. For example, Diana Russell, *The Politics of Rape* (New York, 1975). pp. 28, 38, 99, 132, 201, 223.

8. This accounts for some paradoxical facts. Given that men are defined as desiring access to women and women as holding them in check, it would seem that men would have less license to be familiar with women, in the sense of touching, than have women with men. But, I believe, among nonintimates, men touch women more than the reverse. For men have the right, apparently, to have their reachings seen as protective or joking or undemandingly affectionate; the same act performed by a woman to a man could too easily be read as an invitation, an open movement outward, and thus tends to be suppressed. (Here see Nancy Henley, "The Politics of Touch," in *Radical Psychology*, Phil Brown, ed. [New York, 1973], pp. 421–433.) Between men and women who have a socially ratified intimacy, women seem to have the greater license.

The matter extends beyond obvious reachings out like touch to quite passive ways of being exposed. Thus, a woman who carries on or with her a camera, a dog, a book, or almost any object, is providing reasons strangers can use as a basis for initiating a comment to her and is thus in effect exposing herself.

9. Recently, of course, in the U.S.A. there has been public protest against sex segregation of facilities and activities, feminists taking the lead.

10. Harold L. Wilensky, "Women's Work: Economic Growth, Ideology, Structure," *Industrial Relations*, 7, 3 (1968), p. 244: "If they do go on [to graduate school] they overwhelmingly head toward traditionally 'feminine' fields such as art, nursing, education, social work, biochemistry, English, languages, and the humanities."

11. In noting the special functions of sprinkling women selectively in the work scene, one ought to take note also of a parallel process, the placement of large, sleek white men in highly visible executive and political roles where they can serve as representatives of organizations and in its name meet its specialized public.

12. Russell, *op.cit.*

13. In rural settlements, square dancing used to provide a nicely patterned opportunity for males to swing their partners off their feet, to the accompaniment of squeals of pleasurable fear, all this under the eye of the whole community. Children, of course, are even more subject to playful assaults, such as being thrown into the air and caught, swung by the hands, and so forth. Observe, too, that there are special play environments, such as swimming pools, hay stacks, and the like, which allow a whole cosmos of unserious playful acts, that being one of their functions.

14. The traditional solution was for a male companion of the threatened female to do the fighting for her, constituting himself her champion. In liberated circles this recourse is sometimes disapproved.

15. Some relevant evocations are provided by Doris Lessing, *The Summer Before the Dark* (New York, 1973), pp. 180–207.

16. A useful informal literature is available on hassling. See, for example, Gwenda Linda Blair, "Standing on the Corner," *Liberation* 18, 9 (July–August 1974) pp. 6–8; Barbara Damrosch, "The Sex Ray: One Woman's Theory of Street Hassling," *Village Voice*, April 7, 1975, p. 7.

Section III

Acquiring Gender: Childhood Socialization

Chapter 4 ——————————————————————————————————

Directions for an Interactionist Study of Gender Development

Spencer E. Cahill

Harold Garfinkel and Erving Goffman have demonstrated the utility of the
interactionist approach for the study of sex and gender. This paper proposes
some hypotheses and research strategies for complementary interactionist
studies of the gender development process. A review of previous research
and clinical data concerning feminized boys that patterns of caregiver-infant
interaction and caregivers' use of sex designating verbal labels provide the
basis for gender identity formation. The child then actively seeks to confirm
this identity through social interaction and, thereby, learns to express gender.
Some prominent theories of gender development and some important aspects
of the child's learning of gender expression are briefly reviewed. A
hypothesized sequence of gender development and suggestions for its empirical investigation are offered in conclusion.

D espite the recent surge of sociological interest in the topic of sex and
gender, systematic research into the gender development process has
been noticeably lacking. My intention in this article is to help fill this void by
suggesting directions for an interactionist study of gender development. The interactionist perspective is particularly suited for this task because it provides
both a systematic theory of self development and methodological guidance.
George Herbert Mead's (1934:140) observation that "the self . . . is essentially a
social structure, and it arises in social experience" provides both the theoretical
and methodological focus for this discussion.

Clearly, gender development is one aspect of self development. The interactionist perspective implies, therefore, that gender identity, like other social identities, emerges out of social interaction and is incorporated into the individual's
transsituational self. Moreover, because the self is subject to constant empirical

Source: Spencer E. Cahill, "Directions for an Interactionist Study of Gender Development,"
SYMBOLIC INTERACTION 3 (Spring, 1980): 123-38. Reprinted by permission of JAI Press, Inc.,
Greenwich, Conn.

tests, this identity, if it is to remain stable, must be continually confirmed across varying interactional situations. The interactionist perspective suggests, therefore, two general research questions concerning the gender development process. How does gender identity emerge out of the process of social interaction? And, how does the child learn to indicate that identity to others and to his or her self?

The interactionist perspective also implies that attention must be focused on naturally occurring interactions and social experience for answers to these questions. Systematic observations of interactions between children and their caregivers,[1] other significant adults, and peers is required. Moreover, because interactionism recognizes the importance of meanings to social interaction, investigation of individuals' definitions and understandings of sex and gender is also required.

However, in order to suggest specific hypotheses and research strategies for their empirical investigations it is necessary to review some existing social scientific theory and research on this topic. Harold Garfinkel (1967:116–185) and Erving Goffman's (1977; 1979) work on sex and gender will be reviewed in order to introduce some important concepts and provide a warrant for the suggested direction of study. Existing research evidence concerning sexually differential parental conceptions of infants and patterns of caregiver-infant interaction will then be reviewed. Some prominent theories of gender development and some major issues concerning the learning of sex-related "behavioral repertoires" (Denzin, 1972:302) will also be briefly examined. This discussion will provide a basis for the proposed research program outlined in conclusion.

Special attention will be given throughout this discussion to clinical data concerning cases of atypical gender development.[2] Examination of this data is particularly useful in this exploratory context. These cases can be treated as "demonstration experiments" (Garfinkel, 1967:38) which make apparent some of the "taken-for-granted" and "out-of-awareness" features of the gender development process. When viewed in this manner, these cases provide useful insights into typical processes of gender development. Notably, Harold Garfinkel's (1967:116–185) case study of the "transsexual" Agnes was the first study of sex and gender with an affinity to interactionism and, after twelve years, still one of the most informative.

PRELIMINARY CONCEPTIONS

The major conclusion of Garfinkel's (1967:181) study of Agnes was that "members' practices . . . produce the observable and tellable normal sexuality of persons." Although Garfinkel focused attention on the more obvious practices of sex – specific dress and household activities, evidence of more subtle and "out-of-awareness" sex-related practices has been accumulating. Research suggests that language use (Lakoff, 1975), patterns of conversation (West and Zimmerman, 1977; Fishman, 1978), gaze behavior (Exline, *et. al.*, 1965), touch (Henley, 1970), and spacing (Harnett, *et. al.*, 1970) are all involved in the achievement of sexual differences in social interaction. Although such practices "are so much a part of . . . everyday life that they are done automatically" (Hall, 1967:74), they are, to borrow from Goffman (1979:7), "socially learned and socially patterned; it is a socially defined category which employs a particular expression."

The point of departure for interactionist studies of sex and gender is, therefore, the recognition that sex is an instance of social classification. As Goff- man (1977:302) notes, sex is exemplary, if not prototypical, of social classifica- tion for it is "almost without exception exhaustive of the population and life- long." Individuals in this society are "rigorously dichotomized into the 'natural,' i.e., *moral* entities of male and female" (Garfinkel, 1967:116). This rigorous dichotomization is accomplished at birth by "inspection of the infant's naked per- son, specifically the genitalia" (Goffman, 1977:302). As Garfinkel (1967:123) points out, "the possession of a penis by a male and a vagina by a female are essential insignia" of sex class incumbency. Moreover, because sexual classifica- tion is life-long, individuals are continually being classified on the basis of secon- dary sexual characteristics and what Ray Birdwhistell (1972:53) terms "tertiary sexual characteristics," learned and situationally produced social behaviors. However, despite the immediate criterion, sexual classification is, "for the most part, genital attribution" (Kessler and McKenna, 1978:153).

The use of behaviors as criteria for sexual classification and, therefore, genital attribution is accounted for by reference to "the doctrine of natural sexual expression." Goffman (1979:7) has noted that there is a commonly held belief in this society that signs can be read to ascertain the "essential nature of objects," especially human beings. A prototype of essential expresion is what has been termed gender (Goffman, 1979:7). Gender refers to "sex-specific ways of appear- ing, acting and feeling" (Goffman, 1977:303). "The proper terms for sex are 'male' and 'female'; the corresponding terms for gender are 'masculine' and 'feminine'" (Stoller, 1968:9). The rule of correspondence between sex and gender is the doc- trine of natural sexual expression. Although gender is something "that can be conveyed fleetingly in any social situation," it strikes "at the most basic characterization of the individual," his or her sexual nature (Goffman, 1979:7).

Beliefs concerning normal sexuality are sustained not only through gender based sexual classification of others but also through a similar self-classification. An important component of the individual's relatively stable sense "of the 'real'—I myself as I really am" (Turner, 1968:94) is an awareness, "whether con- scious or unconscious," that he or she belongs to "one sex and not the other" (Stroller, 1968:9).

> In so far as the individual builds up a sense of who and what he is by referring to his sex class and judging himself in terms of the ideals of masculinity (or femininity), one

may speak of *gender identity.* (Goffman, 1977:304, emphasis in original)

As Ralph Turner (1968:97) notes, self-conception is a special case of person-conception. The individual interprets both the behavior of others and his or her own behavior as indications of essential sexual nature.

It must be stressed that while biology provides a neat and tidy sorting device for sexual classification it does not determine gender identity or gender expression. For example, Money and Ehrhardt (1974:174) conducted three in-depth comparative studies of matched pairs of hermaphrodites (individuals with ambiguous genitalia) who were similar on a number of demographic variables and concordant for diagnosis but discordant for gender identity. They concluded that these cases, "and many more like them, wreck the assumption that gender identity . . . is preordained by the sex chromosomes" and "prohibit the assumption that gender identity is . . . preordained by prenatal hormonal history."

Moreover, the very existence of the condition known as transsexualism prohibits any such assumptions. Transsexualism is a condition of incongruent gender identity and biologically determined sex. As Garfinkel's (1967:116–185) study of Agnes and Thomas Kando's (1973) study of seventeen similar cases have indicated, transsexuals have little difficulty in expressing the gender with which they identify and, in fact, consider that expression "less strenuous" than exhibiting the behaviors associated with their biological sex (Kando, 1973:131). These studies suggest, as Goffman (1977:330) has argued, that "the contingencies and responses that seem to so naturally follow" from sexual classification are the consequence of social influences. In order to understand the process of gender development, therefore, including the initial formation of gender identity, attention must be turned to the child's social experience.

GENDER IDENTITY

Because gender identity emerges so early in individuals' biographies, the study of gender identity formation must focus on the first few months of life. Robert Stoller (1968:62–63) has observed that gender identity is often apparent by the time the child begins to walk. Moreover, on the basis of clinical experience medical practitioners involved in sex reassignment procedures advise against imposing "a sex reassignment on a child in contradiction of a gender identity already well advanced in its differentiation – which means that the age ceiling for an imposed reassignment is, in the majority of cases, around eighteen months" (Money and Ehrhardt, 1974:13). Although this early appearance of gender identity is often treated as evidence of its biological determination, children have had considerable social experience by this age. Not only have they experienced considerable nonverbal interaction but have also typically developed through interactional experience some competency in the use of ver-

bal labels. As the interactionist perspective suggests, it is these early interac'
tional experiences and their consequences that must be examined in order to
discover the roots of gender identity.
Fortunately, information concerning these early interactional experiences is
available. Previous research has investigated caregivers' sexually differential
conceptions of and interactions with infants and the effects of such differences
on the child's subsequent behavior. Although this research was not, in most
cases, directly concerned with gender identity formation, when reviewed in
comparison with information concerning feminized boys the findings of this
research are suggestive of research hypotheses for future interactionist studies of
gender identity formation. Available clinical interviews with feminized boys and
their parents will provide indications of the centrality of certain interactional ex'
periences to the emergence of typical gender identity.
      Notably, one of the first, if not the first, descriptions given a newborn is a
sex class label. Research indicates that such labels affect caregivers' conception
of the infant, and, by implication, their interactions with him or her. Jeffrey
Rubin and his associates (1976:185) have found that even before parents have
had physical contact with their newborns they rate male and female infants
significantly different on a number of descriptive adjective pairs, especially those
referring to "physical and constitutional factors."
      Rubin and his associates (1976:181–182) administered a questionnaire com'
posed of 18 objective pairs to primiparous parents (15 with daughters, 15 with
sons) within the first 24 hours postpartum. Parents were asked to describe their
newborn by placing a check on a Likert-type scale for each adjective pair. Among
the 18 pairs were such gender typical descriptions as firm-soft, strong-weak, and
hardy-delicate. Although mothers were less differentiating than fathers, both
agreed on a gender typical direction of sex differences (Rubin, et. al., 1976:185).
This finding is notable because the male and female infants did not differ in
regard to weight, length, or Apgar score[3] (Rubin, et. al., 1976:185). Rubin and
his associates (1976:186) concluded that sex labels "may well affect subsequent
expectations about the manner in which . . . infants ought to behave, as well as
parental behavior itself."
      The importance of caregivers' intial conception of infants is underlined by
clinical data concerning feminized boys. Richard Green (1974:239) reports that
of 38 feminized boys referred to the UCLA Gender Identity Clinic one-third
were perceived by parents as "unusually attractive." Green provides the follow'
ing fragment from an interview with the parents of monozygotic twin boys, one
of which is feminized the other typically masculine.

DOCTOR: Did they look different at birth?
FATHER: Paul (feminine) looked a great deal heavier and rounder, a good looking
    baby. The other was like a spider monkey.
MOTHER: Frank (masculine) was very badly mutilated. Oh, he looked like a

drowned baby bird. He was a very ugly infant. Paul had big eyes and was a pound heavier, so his face was fuller. (Green, 1974:206)

Although not conclusive, this evidence does suggest that caregivers' conceptions of infants affect caregiver-infant interactions in ways that contribute to the formation of gender identity.

Research conducted by Michael Lewis and his associates over the past fifteen years also provides support for this suggestion. In one such project observers were sent into the homes of 32 three month old infants (16 female, 16 male) of differing racial and socio-economic backgrounds (Lewis, 1972a:99). The behaviors of both mother and infant were classified in terms of predetermined categories and note was taken of whether the behavior was in response to a behavior of the other. Observations were recorded for each ten second interval over the course of an hour (Lewis, 1972a:101). Analysis of the observations indicated that, "at this age, boys receive more proximal stimulation – touching and holding – while girls receive more distal stimulation – looking and vocalization" (Lewis, 1972a:106). Mothers of male and female infants did "not differ in amounts of responsiveness but rather in the nature . . . of responsiveness" (Lewis, 1972a:120). Notably, this difference in the nature of responsiveness was not a function of the infant's *behavior* but of the infant's sex (Lewis, 1972a:110).

These sexually differential caregiver responses to infants become even more pronounced as the child grows. Lewis and Susan Goldberg observed interactions between another 64 mother-infant pairs (32 female infants, 32 male) at both six and thirteen months of age. When the infants were six months of age Lewis and Goldberg (1969:22) observed a variety of behavioral responses in the home. The results indicated that "when the children were 6 months old, mothers touched, talked to, and handled their daughters more than their sons" (Lewis and Goldberg, 1969:29). On the basis of these and the previously discussed observations, Lewis offers the following summary of caregiver-infant interaction during the first six months of life.

> These studies show that from the earliest age, girl infants are looked at and talked to more than boy infants. For the first six months or so, boy infants have more physical contact than girl infants, but by the time boys are six months old, this reverses and girls get more physical contact and more nontouching contact. (Lewis, 1972b:56)

If, as the interactionist perspective suggests, the individual responds to his or her self as others respond to him or her then these sexually differential patterns of caregiver-infant interaction would be expected to result in sex differences in the infants' emerging self-conceptions.

Lewis and Goldberg's subsequent observation of the above mentioned 64 mother-infant pairs is suggestive of the validity of this expectation. When the infants were thirteen months of age each pair was left alone for fifteen minutes in an observation room filled with a variety of toys. Mothers were instructed to watch their child and respond in any way they wished. Types of behavior and their frequencies as well as how far and for how long the children stayed away from their mothers were recorded (Lewis and Goldberg, 1969:22–23). The results indicated that the girls touched, vocalized to, looked at, and stayed closer to their mothers significantly more than the boys (Lewis and Goldberg, 1969:25). Lewis (1972b:56) concluded, in another context, that "what the parent does to the infant, the infant is likely to do back." In other words, children respond to themselves as significant others respond to them.

Clinical data concerning feminized boys is indicative of the importance of this processural pattern of sexually differential caregiver-infant interaction for the formation of typical gender identity. As noted earlier, many feminized boys are perceived as unusually attractive. For this and, as the following interview fragments with parents of feminized boys illustrate, many other reasons, these boys had received a considerable amount of attention and physical contact.

> MOTHER: . . . Gee, most of the time I would spend holding him because my other two – they were big already and they didn't need my attention that much.
> MOTHER: I think he preferred being held more. I held him more . . . I had this little toy (sic). And, I lavished my emotion I guess on him by cuddling him. It would be something to do.
> FATHER: The trouble started when he was born a boy, because a boy had never been born in my wife's family and he was spoiled rotten.
> DOCTOR: How's that?
> FATHER: Oh, picked up everytime he opened his mouth to cry or do something. Every time I saw him he was being held by my wife's sister or mother. (Green, 1974:220–221)

Moreover, Robert Stoller (1968:98) reports that in the three cases of boyhood transsexualism he observed "there had been a delay in permitting the boys to be free of their mothers' bodies, of their constant cuddling and following eyes." These accounts are particularly striking in view of Lewis's findings. The reported pattern of interaction between caregivers and feminized boys corresponds to what Lewis found to be typical for girls. This correspondence suggests that sexually differential patterns of caregiver-infant interaction are central to the formation of gender identity.

Probably of equal importance to the formation of gender identity is caregivers' use of sex labels when interacting with the child. Norman Denzin (1972:306–307) has proposed "a naming or labeling hypothesis for self-development" because identification involves naming. During the first year of life the child often hears expressions like "Oh, are you a pretty girl" or "That's a big boy." Ruth Hartley argues that such sex-designating terms "serve as signs leading to self-identity, much as a name does, and are comprehended syncretic-aly as reprsenting whatever complex of sensation and emotion is experienced at the time of its use" (Hartley, 1964:5). Because gender identity emerges as the child begins to develop competency in the use of verbal labels, significant others' sex-designating references to the child would also seem to play a role in the formation of gender identity.

Clinical data concerning feminized boys supports this suggestion. Green (1974:225) reports that comments "by adults such as: 'he's so pretty, he should have been a girl,' or adults mistaking boys for girls . . . appear to be more frequently reported by mothers of feminine boys than mothers of masculine boys." Green provides the following illustrative fragments from interviews with mothers of feminized boys.

> MOTHER: When he was younger, people would mistake him for a girl . . . Up until the time he was about three, people kept mistaking him for a girl, and I was kind of proud.
>
> MOTHER: Even the other day, my aunt stated that she gets him and the oldest daughter mixed up . . . everyone has always commented like that, even I have at times.

Gender identity formation seems to depend then on others' use of sex-designating labels when interacting with the child.

However, as Hartley suggests, it is the association of these sex-designating labels with sexually differential interactional experiences which is responsible for gender identity formation. As the interactionist perspective suggests, sexually differential patterns of caregiver-infant interaction result in sex-related differences in self-conception. Because these sex differences in interactional experience also tend to to associated with sex-designating labels, the child identifies these sex-specific complexes of responses to his or her self with sex-specific verbal labels. Even before the child forms a concept of sex as a stable category, he or she may identify his or her self with these sex-designating labels. It is hypothesized, therefore, that as the child associates sex-designating self-labels with the sexually differential responses to his or her self which result from sexually differential patterns of caregiver-infant interaction gender identity emerges.

This hypothesis, it should be noted, challenges the Freudian theory of sexual identification. Freud (1925:186ff.) argued that the entire process of gender development depended on the child's identification with a same sexed parent figure during the phallic stage of psychosexual development between three and six years of age. Freud considered this identification with same sexed parent figure synonymous with sexual identification. However, as already noted, gender identity is apparent well before this age. Freud would seem to have the process of gender development standing on its head. It is because the child has a well-formed gender identity that he or she identifies with the same sexed parent. First the child identifies his or her self by sex and then may model the same sexed parent in learning to express gender. Freud confused the causal direction of this relationship. Same sexed parental identification is the effect not the cause of gender identity.

LEARNING TO EXPRESS GENDER

As the interactionist perspective suggests, once gender identity emerges the child becomes an active agent in his or her own gender development. Ralph Turner (1968:97) has pointed out that "the self-conception is subject to recurring empirical test." The child's gender identity, an aspect of his or her self-conception, will need to be confirmed in various interactional situations if it is to remain stable. The child must, in short, learn to express his or her gender, to behave in ways that will be interpreted as indicative of a normal sexual nature. By behaving in such ways, the child will elicit gender identity confirming responses from others.

In learning to express gender the child may imitate or model same sexed adults and come to positively value those adults with whom he or she shares a common gender identity. However, such modeling is neither the basis of gender identity formation nor do such models need be parent figures. The child's environment is, in most cases, adequately stocked, if nowhere else than on television, with same sexed adult models. It is hardly surprising then that "research findings comparing . . . boys from father absent and father present households . . . find little difference in masculinity-femininity attitudes" (Kohlberg, 1966:157). Modeling of same sexed adults may play a role in gender development but not necessarily a crucial one.

What does seem to be crucial to gender development is the responses of significant others, regardless of sex, to the child's early gender expression. Green's data on feminized boys illustrates the importance of these responses.

> Whatever the circumstances that promotes boyhood femininity, what comes closest so far to being a *necessary* variable is that, as any feminine behavior begins to emerge, there is *no* discouragement of that behavior by the child's principal caretaker. This has been true so far, in nearly every family. (Green, 1974:238, emphasis in original)

Notably, the treatment of feminized boys at the UCLA Gender Identity Clinic, which has had preliminary success, is based on encouraging "appropriate" gender expression (Green, et. al., 1972). Although gender identity emerges early in the child's biography, its expression and stability depends on subsequent interactional experiences.

Gender development is not, however, the *passive* product of social learning. Social learning studies of "sex-role socialization" have stressed the importance of the consequences of sex-related behaviors for their subsequent performance (Mischel, 1966:59) but have failed to recognize the child's active role in this process.[4] The child does not randomly exhibit behavior but actively seeks to confirm his or her gender identity through social interaction. As cognitive development theorists point out, the process of gender development depends on the "child's active structuring of his (sic) experience" (Kohlberg, 1966:85), and the "basic organizer" of this experience is the child's gender identity (Kohlberg, 1966:164).

Unlike interactionism, however, cognitive development theory views the child as structuring his or her experience in terms of "basic universal sex-role stereotypes" (Kohlberg, 1966:164). Both the cultural variability of gender ideals (Martin and Voorhies, 1975) and observations of children's use of sexual classification challenges this position. Carol Joffe (1973:112) reports the following observation of children's sexual classification of activities.

K and two other girls are playing on top of a large structure in the yard. A (male) comes over and K screams, "Girls only!" to which A screams back, "No, boys only!"

As this example illustrates, children's sex labeling of activities seems to "have no relation whatsoever to the matter at hand, or even to the traditionally accepted notions of what is appropriate for boys and girls" (Joffe, 1973:111). Although children organize their activities and experience in terms of gender, they do not do so in basic universal ways.

Cultural gender ideals do, of course, influence the typical process of gender development. These ideals serve as rough guidelines for the child in confirming his or her gender identity and for others in responding to the child's gender expression. However, gender ideals must be interpretively applied across varying situations. As Goffman (1979:8) points out, what "characterizes persons as sex-class members is their competence and willingness to sustain an appropriate schedule of displays" and the appropriateness of displays is situationally specific. In order to confirm his or her gender identity the child must gain an increasingly sophisticated battery of behavioral repertoires and interpretive skills in determining their situational appropriateness. The development of such behavioral and interpretive sophistication is not explicable solely in terms of eliciting stimulus and subsequent response nor in terms of basic universal sex-role stereotypes.

Moreover, as suggested earlier, the process of gender development can not be explained by reference to anatomical differences between the sexes. Freud (1925:190ff.), his followers (Ferenczi, 1938), and others (Kohlberg, 1966:165) have implied that anatomical features are intrinsically meaningful. However, as John Dewey (1926:155) noted, the meaning of objects, including the body, depends on human use and interpretation. As both Stoller's (1968:3–88) and Money and Ehrhardt's (1974:123–130, 159–174) reports concerning children with ambiguous genitalia indicate, the most important factor to these children's typical gender development is their parent's unquestioned acceptance of the assigned sex, not the nature of the child's genitalia.

This is not meant to suggest, however, that interactionists should ignore the influence of anatomy on gender development. As essential insignia of sex-class membership, genital configuration may well affect the process of gender development.

> Castration anxiety . . . might then mean that one does not so much fear losing his organ as that by losing the organ that is usually the only truly distinguishing feature of maleness in a boy, he might lose his sense of maleness, his identity. (Stoller, 1968:153)

Moreover, as Mead (1938:44) noted, "physical things resist our action." Ambiguous genitalia will affect the child's gender development if the condition interferes with the child's gender expression. An obvious example of such interference would be if an assigned male was unable to urinate while standing. As interactionism suggests, the influence of anatomical factors on gender development depends on their definition as indicators of sex class membership and their use in gender expression. And, such interpretation and use must be learned.

Furthermore, traditional approaches to gender development have overlooked the central importance of self and peer stimulation to this process. Competence in gender expression depends on an "increased situational awareness and an expanding breadth or range of interactional others" (Denzin, 1972:309). As Norman Denzin (1975:475) points out, "play constitutes the most important interactional experiences of the young child." As such, play, both solitary and conjoint, is the most important mechanism in the learning of gender expression. In play children learn to express gender by taking sex-specific roles, by presenting and defending their gender identity, and by constructing social worlds around sexual classification. By viewing the child as a reflexive self, interactionism recognizes that the child is the primary agent in his or her own gender development.

Information concerning feminized boys underlines the importance of the child's self-stimulation in play to gender development. Green (1974:145) reports that when playing house "half the feminine boys play the role of mother, and an additional quarter portray some other female" while among a comparable group of "masculine" boys "none typically plays the mother or another female." Treatment of feminized boys at the Gender Identity Clinic includes an emphasis on noncompetitive "masculine activities" such as hiking, outdoor cooking, and handicrafts (Green, et. al., 1972:217). Because play "assumes a dominant position in the cycle of activities of the young child" (Denzin, 1975:475), it becomes the primary arena of gender identity confirmation and, therefore, of the learning of gender expression.

Another important factor in the child's confirmation of gender identity is gender specific dress. Gender specific clothing provides an immediate and easily interpretable indication of sexual nature. Because of this, it may be a more important insignia of sex class membership for children than genital configuration. Green (1974:143) reports that all 38 of the feminized boys he studied began cross-dressing before their sixth birthday, three-fourths by their fourth birthday, and most between the ages of two and three. Such cross-dressing was either promoted, approved or at the very least, not disapproved by the child's significant others (Green, 1974:218–219). An important way that both the child and caregivers attempt to control the child's situated gender image is by gender specific dress.

Besides eliciting gender identity confirming responses, gender specific clothing subtly influences gender expression. Virginia Woolf has poetically described the indirect influence of clothing on gender expression in her novel *Orlando*.

> It is clothes that wear us and not us them, we may make them take the mould of arm or breast, but they mould our hearts, our brains, our tongues . . . The man has his hand free to seize his sword; the woman must use hers to keep the satins from slipping from her shoulders. (Woolf, 1956:188)

Gender specific clothing promotes certain postures and body movements which are interpreted as gender expressive. Such subtle influencing of gender expression may also take place because of the objects the child chooses and is encouraged to play with. In any case, gender expression is learned not only through interaction with others but also through interaction with physical objects.

SUMMARY

The foregoing discussion suggests the following sequence of gender development. From the very first day of life the child is responded to by caregivers in terms of his or her sex. Caregivers' sexually differential responsiveness is associated with their use of sex-designating terms. By the second year of life the child has incorporated these complexes of responses to his or her self and their association with sex-specific verbal labels into his or her self-conception. The child then attempts to actively confirm his or her gender identity and is influenced in these attempts by the responses of others. Through imitation, playing at gender specific roles, selection of dress and objects of play, and increased interactional experience the child becomes increasingly competent in the subtleties of gender expression. During this same period the child learns the importance of anatomical features to the confirmation of gender identity. Of course, the content of this process is dependent on cultural definitions and common sense understandings of sex and gender. This depiction of the process of gender development is offered as a set of research hypotheses which require empirical verification.

However, the utility of an interactionist approach to gender development is indicated by more than its fruitfulness in supplying research hypotheses. As the preceding discussion indicated, interactionism accounts more fully for the available data then other popular approaches to gender development. The importance of developing interactionist explanations of gender development is indicated by the fact that those most familiar with both typical (Lewis, 1972a) and atypical (Stoller, 1968; Green, 1974) gender development have been moved by their data closer to an interactionist position than even they realize. In order to develop such explanations, however, studies of the gender development process which are more directly informed by interactionism will be necessary.

STUDYING GENDER DEVELOPMENT

These studies must necessarily be multifarious, reflecting the complex nature of the development process. A number of varied research projects will, therefore, be suggested. However, the following suggestions are neither detailed nor exhaustive of the relevant research possibilities. The purpose of this discussion is to suggest directions for the interactionist study of gender development, not to offer detailed methodological advice. Before offering specific research suggestions, however, some general methodological comments are necessary.

Interactionist studies of the gender development process must place primary reliance on behavioral observation of naturally occurring interactions. Because social interaction is situated, contextually embedded, observation of interactions in artificial laboratory situations or analysis of interactions in isolation from their context of occurrence can lead to serious misunderstandings. Because the goal of study is an understanding of the typical process of gender development, the interactional events that constitute this process must be observed when and where they occur. Moreover, observation must take precedence over verbal techniques of data collection. The use of interviewing in isolation from behavioral observation caries with it the assumption that individuals are aware of their sex-specific behaviors and sexually differential responses to others. Clearly, such an assumption is inadvisable.

This is not meant to suggest, however, that interviewing is never appropriate in interactionist studies of gender development. On the contrary, interviews may supply important supplementary data. Interviewing could be used to sensitize the behavioral observation to important issues, to gather information concerning subjects' interpretations of observed events, and, thereby, to check the validity of researchers' emerging interpretations of these events (Denzin, 1971:169). Practical constraints may also require reliance on subjects verbal accounts. In such cases strategies for determining the accuracy of these accounts will be necessary. These general points might be better illustrated by outlining more specific research suggestions.

For example, Michael Lewis (1972a; 1972b) and his associates' (Lewis and Goldberg, 1969) previously discussed research provides methodological inspiration for the empirical investigation of the hypothesized sequence of gender identity formation. In general, such an investigation would involve a comparative analysis of the typical pattern of male and female infants' interactions with caregivers. This analysis would focus on detailing differences between caregivers' nonverbal responses to male and female infants and the association of these sexually differential responses with sex-designating verbal labels.

Although the hypothesized sequence of gender identity formation suggests that attention be focused on these behaviors, other sampling decisions will be necessary. If the process of gender identity formation is to be fully investigated, observation of children of different ages or at different points in specific children's biographies will be necessary. However, the preceding discussion suggests that such a cross-sectional or longitudinal study could be limited to the first two years of life. Sampling decisions will also be necessary in selecting particular interactions for observation and analysis. Denzin's (1971:175) advice concerning the construction of representational maps of subjects' interactional worlds should be heeded. Such a "map" would enable the informed selection of representative caregiver-infant interactions for analysis.

Whenever possible tape and video recordings of the selected interactions should be obtained. These recordings will facilitate systematic analysis and allow for tests of intersubjective reliability. However, if the practical problems of recording such interactions can not be surmounted, existing recordings of similar interactions (e.g., Brazelton, et al., 1974) should be analyzed. The nonverbal and verbal behaviors of both the caregiver and infant should be transcribed in order to provide a behavioral topography of the interaction (Scheflen, 1973). This behavioral topography will enable detailed examination of the sequential pattern of the interaction and, therefore, determination of the extent to which caregivers' sexually differential responses are a function of differences in male and female infants' behavior. The results of this analysis could then sensitize observation of interactions which can not be recorded.

Systematic "demonstration experiments" may also prove useful in identifying and examining the role of specific factors and events in the gender development process. For example, one such "demonstration experiment" is suggested by Money and Ehrhardt's (1974) matched hermaphrodite studies. Access to children with ambiguous genitalia could be gained through clinicians specialized in this area and then these subjects matched with normal children who are similar in all important respects except this one. Observations of the children with ambiguous genitalia could then be compared to similar observations of the matched normal children. Because the normal children would, in some sense, provide a control group, comparative analysis of the social experiences of the two groups would demonstrate the meanings and relative influence of anatomical features in the gender development process.

A number of more limited research projects could be designed to investigate specific aspects of the process by which gender expression is learned. Observation and recording of children's social interactions could be used to investigate the ways in which specific gender expressions are elicited and reinforced. Comparative analysis of observations of children from single and two parent homes could be used to more closely investigate the effect of parental identification and modeling on the gender development process. Attention could also be focused on the child and others' responses to sex-specific clothing and objects of play and the subtle effects of these objects on the child's expressive style. However, such studies should not be limited to observation of the child's interactions with family members.

Because the child is considered the primary agent in his or her own gender development, there is a great need for systematic descriptions of young children's use of sexual classification and gender expectations when not in the presence of adults. Observation might best be conducted in settings of unsupervised play. The resulting descriptions would not only provide insights into the active role of children in their own gender development, but comparison of children's use of sexual classification and gender ideals with that of adults could provide an indication of the extent to which children use sexual stereotypes in "basic universal ways." Interviews with the subjects could be used to sensitize the observation and to determine the extent of correspondence between children's accounts of sex and gender and their behavior. Of course, special vigilance would be necessary to avoid interpreting the children's behaviors and verbal responses in terms of adult definitions of sex and gender. The point of such a study would be to gain, with a control on preconception, a more complete description of the role of sex in children's culture. Until the consequences of the early gender development process are fully described the study of these processes will lack clear direction.

CONCLUSION

The suggested research program has been offered in the hope of stimulating interest in the topic of gender development from an interactionist perspective. What needs to be investigated, to paraphrase Goffman (1979:7), is not the process through which people learn how and when to express gender, but the process through which individuals learn to be normally sexed persons, persons for whom this expression is only natural. Such a process can best be understood from a perspective which focuses on the interrelationships between selves, language, joint acts, social settings, objects, and relationships (Denzin, 1971:171). What is needed, in short are interactionist studies of gender development.

NOTES

1. The term "caregiver" refers to the person(s) primarily responsible for giving care to, rather than taking care of, an infant. "The neuter quality of this term pays heed to the fact that males may well be just as capable of giving care as females, and fail to do so, in humans at least, only because of societal pressures." (Lewis and Rosenblum, 1974:xv, fn. 1)

2. The data examined here is necessarily limited to feminized boys. Because "masculinity" or tomboyishness in girls is more common and less likely to result in gender identity conflict in adulthood, such girls seldom come to the attention of clinicians (Green, 1974:142).

3. "Apgar scores are assigned at five and ten minutes postpartum, and reflect physician's ratings of color, muscle tonicity, reflex irritability, and heart and respiratory rates" (Rubin, et al., 1976:185).

4. It must be noted that this is a characterization of previous social learning studies. Recent behaviorist theory emphasizes the importance of self-stimulation and self-control in social learning processes and is, therefore, compatible with the direction of study being suggested here (Baldwin and Baldwin 1980).

REFERENCES

Baldwin, John and Janice Baldwin 1981 Behavioral Principles in Everyday Life. Englewood Cliffs, NJ: Prentice-Hall.

Birdwhistell, Ray 1972 Kinesics and Context. New York: Ballantine.

Brazelton, T. Berry, Barbara Koslowski, and Mary Main 1974 "The origins of reciprocity: The early mother-infant interaction." Pp. 49–76 in Michael Lewis and Leonard Rosemblum (eds.), The Effect of the Infant on its Caregiver. New York: John Wiley and Sons.

Denzin, Norman 1971 "The logic of naturalistic inquiry." Social Forces 50 (December):166–182.

1972 "The genesis of self in early childhood." Sociological Quarterly 13 (Summer):291–314.

1975 "Play, games, and interaction: the context of childhood socialization." Sociological Quarterly 16 (Autumn):458–478.

Dewey, John (1926) 1958 Experience and Nature. Lasalle, IL: Open Court Publ.

Exline, Ralph, David Gray and Dorothy Schuette 1965 "Visual behavior in a dyad as affected by interview content and sex of respondent." Journal of Personality and Social Psychology 1 (March):201–209.

Ferenczi, Sandor (1938) 1968 Thalassa: A Theory of Genitality. Translated by Henry Bunker, New York: Norton.

Fishman, Pamela 1978 "Interaction: the work women do." Social Problems 25 (April):397–406.

Freud, Sigmund (1925) "Some psychological consequences of the anatomical distinction between the sexes" Pp. 186–197 in James Strachey (ed.), Collected Papers Volume V. New York: Basic Books.

Garfinkel, Harold 1967 Studies in Ethnomethodology. Englewood Cliffs, NJ: Prentice-Hall.

Goffman, Erving 1977 "The arrangement between the sexes." Theory and Society 4 (Fall) 301–331.

1979 Gender Advertisements. New York: Harper Colophon.

Green, Richard 1974 Sexual Identity Conflict in Children and Adults. New York: Basic Books.

Green, Richard, Lawrence Newman, and Robert Stoller 1972 "Treatment of boyhood 'transsexualism.'" Archives of General Psychiatry 26 (March):213–217.

Hall, Edward T. 1967 The Silent Language. New York: Fawcett.

Hartley, Ruth 1964 "A developmental view of female sex-role definition and identification." Merrill Palmer Quarterly 10 (January):3–16.

Hartnett, John, Kent Bailey, and Frank Gibson, Jr. 1970 "Personal space as influenced by sex and type of movement." Journal of psychology 76 (November):139–144.

Henley, Nancy 1970 "The politics of touch." Paper presented at the annual meetings of the American Psychological Association.

Joffe, Carol 1973 "Taking young children seriously." Pp. 101–116 in Norman Denzin (ed.) Children and Their Caretakers. New Brunswick, NJ: Transaction Books.

Kando, Thomas 1973 Sex Change. Springfield, IL: Charles Thomas Publ.

Kessler, Suzanne and Wendy McKenna 1978 Gender: An Ethnomethodological Approach. New York: John Wiley and Sons.

Kohlberg, Lawrence 1966 "A cognitive-developmental analysis of children's sex-role concepts and attitudes." Pp. 82–173 in Eleanor Maccoby (ed.), The Development of Sex Differences. Stanford, CA: Standford Univ. Press.

Lakoff, Robin 1975 Language and Woman's Place. New York: Harper Colophon.

Lewis, Michael 1972a "State as an infant-environment interaction: an analysis of mother-infant interaction as a function of sex." Merrill-Palmer Quarterly 18 (April):97–121.

1972b "There's no unisex in the nursery." Psychology Today 5 (May):54–57.

Lewis, Michael and Susan Goldberg 1969 "Play behavior in the year-old infant: early sex differences." Child Development 40 (March):21–31.

Lewis, Michael and Leonard Rosenblum 1974 "Introduction." Pp. xv–xxiv in M. Lewis and L. Rosenblum (eds.), The Effect of the Infant on its Caregiver. New York: John Wiley and Sons.

Martin, M. Kay and Barbara Voorhies 1975 Female of the Species. New York: Columbia Univ. Press.

Mead, George Herbert (1934) 1962 Mind, Self and Society. Edited by Charles Morris. Chicago: Univ. of Chicago Press.

1938 The Philosophy of the Act. Edited by Charles Morris. Chicago: Univ. of Chicago Press.

Mischel, Walter 1966 "A social learning view of sex differences in behavior." Pp. 56–81 in Eleanor Maccoby (ed.), The Development of Sex Differences. Stanford, CA: Stanford Univ. Press.

Money, John and Anke Ehrhardt 1974 Man and Woman: Boy and Girl. New York: New American Library.

Rubin, Jeffrey, Frank Provenzano, and Zelda Luria 1976 "The eye of the beholder: parents' views on sex of newborn." Pp. 174–181 in A. Kaplan and J. Bean (eds.), Beyond Sex-Role Stereotypes: Readings Toward a Psychology of Androgyny. Boston: Little Brown.

Scheflen, Albert   1973   Communicational Structure: Analysis of a Psychotherapy Transaction. Bloomington, IN: Indiana Univ. Press.

Stoller, Robert   1968   Sex and Gender. New York: Science House.

Turner, Ralph   1968   "The self-conception in social interaction." Pp. 93–106 in C. Gordon and K. Gergen (eds.), The Self in Social Interaction. New York: John Wiley and Sons.

West, Candance and Don Zimmerman   1977   "Women's place in everyday talk: reflections on parent child interaction." Social Problems 24 (June):521–529.

Woolf, Virginia   1956   Orlando. New York: Harcourt, Brace and Jovanovich.

Chapter 5

What Does Children's Art Work Tell Us about Gender?

Joy B. Reeves
Nydia Boyette

Abstract

If art is an authentic expression of the self, a sociologist should be able to examine children's art work to see what effect various social agents have had
on gender socialization. Inferences could be made from the art work about
the socialization process. In this study, the authors examined children's art
work to investigate the implicit sex role perceptions of children. The population included 110 students between the ages of 9 and 12 in three elementary
schools in Texas. 126 pieces of art were examined and 500 independent
ratings were made. Results of the study indicated that the content and form
of children's art work differ significantly by sex. A gender role perspective
was used to explain the pattern.

I t is a widely accepted fact that men and women inhabit different social-
psychological worlds (Whitehurst, Booth and Mohammand, 1979; Bernard, 1981). Gender socialization helps to explain this fact. Although gender
socialization is a continous process, the norms and values internalized by young
children are very influential in shaping their gender-based world. The people
who surround the child and with whom the child interacts regularly are the
teachers of gender identity and gender role (Davidson and Gordon, 1979: 13).
According to Kohlberg (1966), children actively search for coherent explanations
of how their social worlds operate. They soon learn that teachers and friends
reward behavior that conforms to and punish behavior that deviates from their
own definitions of gender roles. They learn that gender is a relevant basis for
classifying people (Davidson and Gordon, 1979: 22). Long before boys and girls
reach the age of puberty (when the effect of biological hormones is at its

Source: Joy B. Reeves and Nydia Boyette, "What Does Children's Art Work Tell Us about
Gender?" Qualitative Sociology 6 (Winter 1983). Published by Human Sciences Press, Inc., 72 Fifth
Ave., New York, N.Y. 10011. Copyright 1983. Used by permission.

greatest), they recognize clear differences in appropriate gender behavior (Weitz-man, 1979).

The play activities of children appear to be especially important in gender socialization. For example, researchers have observed differences in the material contents of the rooms of boys and girls. Compared to girls' rooms, boys' rooms contain toys of more classes (educational, sports, animals, spatial-temporal ob-jects, railroad depots, military equipment, machines and vehicles). The toys used by boys tend to encourage activities outside the home whereas girls' toys are less varied in type and encourage play within the home (Rheingold and Cook, 1975). Content analyses of children's books indicate that females are underrepresented in the titles, pictures, character roles and plots of children's literature and that most books deal with males and their adventures (Weitzman, et al., 1972). The study of children's play patterns also reveals significant gender differences (Lever, 1978). For example, girls tend to play out social scenarios and cooperate, whereas boys interact through games and are more competitive. Girls' games have fewer rules compared to boys' games. Finally, when girls play games with rules, they tend to ignore the rules. The opposite situation holds for boys (Lever, 1978).

If it is true that boys and girls inhabit different social worlds then it should be possible to see these worlds reflected in their art work. Art is a way of ex-pressing one's values, beliefs and attitudes about one's environment. When a child draws a picture he/she is trying to put this environment into proper perspective. Once this is done the child has a better idea of where to place herself/himself in a vast and complex social system (Goodnow, 1977).

A review of sociological literature indicates that children's art work is an un-tapped data source. Specifically, no sociologists have researched children's art work for the express purpose of demonstrating the effect of gender role socializa-tion. By contrast, art professionals and child development specialists have noted gender differences in art work but these have been a peripheral concern (Feldman, 1970; Kellogg, 1969; Dennis, 1966; Gardner, 1973; Klepsh and Logle, 1982; Machover, 1974; Goodenough, 1926; DiLeo, 1970; and Kellogg and O'Dell, 1967). The purpose of this paper is to report and discuss the results and implications of an empirical study designed to test the hypothesis that the art work of children differs by gender. We contend that art work taps the child's reality in a direct way and avoids the problems of other methods, such as the child feeling intimidated by direct questions or wanting to please the researcher. Of course, the art work remains to be interpreted by the researcher and thus the interpretation could be faulted by the researcher's preconceptions.

RESEARCH METHODS

The population for this study included 110 students between the ages of nine and twelve from four classrooms in three elementary schools, and siblings of these students if they were the same age. This specific age range was selected because social ties to peers of the same sex are strongest at this age (Lowenfeld and Brittain, 1970). Second, sex role identification is supposed to be more obvious for this age group than for younger children (Kellogg, 1969). Thus gender differences in art work could be expected to be very blatant at this age.

One school was located in a large city (Houston, Texas) and the other schools were located in a small East Texas town with a population of 27,000. The sample was simply one of convenience since this study was defined as exploratory. Most children in the study were anglos and came from varied social class backgrounds. The total number of drawings examined was 126 (a few children submitted more than one drawing) and the total number of independent observations was 500. The number of observations was greater than the number of drawings because each piece of art work contained more than one observable item of interest to the researchers.

Teachers in four classrooms were instructed to ask their students to draw anything they wanted using the media of pen, pencil, or crayons. They were told that their pictures could be used in a study being conducted by university teachers. Some of the students asked if their brothers and sisters could participate in the study. The teacher said yes if they were between the ages of nine and twelve. Thirty minutes was allocated by the teachers for the student to draw a picture. The teachers were told the drawings would be analyzed for gender differences. A content analysis was performed of each art product, using a specially designed classification instrument built on ideas from a literature review and personal observation. Three independent observers (one male; two females) were given 15 empty 2 x 2 tables with the variable under scrutiny identified and operationalized. Each observer reviewed separately individual pieces of work and recorded the results on the blank tables. Comparisons among observers were made later to ascertain the degree of consensus. A few variables were dropped due to lack of consensus.

RESULTS AND DISCUSSION

Literature on children's play behavior, children's books, gender socialization and personal observation led the researchers to believe that boys' pictures would disproportionately contain the following *content*: buildings, violence, nondomestic scenes, activity, mechanical structures and teeth (Lever, 1978; Rheingold and Cook, 1975; Key, 1971; U'ren 1971; Walstedt, 1975; Machover, 1974; Gardner, 1973; Klepsch and Logle, 1982). If it is true that one dimension of the male gender role includes an anti-feminine aspect as David and Brannon (1976) suggest, then it is reasonable to conclude that males would not draw what they perceived to be feminine content. Feminine content included houses, nonexposed teeth, nonviolent scenes, domestic scenes, non-activity and non-

FIGURE 5.1

mechanical structures. Conversely, it excluded characteristically masculine content.

The researchers also predicted that the *form* of art work would vary by gender. Masculine form would include non-detailed eyes, disproportionately large hands, a human profile and predominating angular shapes. Feminine form would include detailed eyes, hands, frontal position of human figures and round shapes (Goodenough, 1926; Bascow, 1980; Machover, 1974; Klepsh and Logle, 1982). The specific statistical results and detailed research procedures of this study have been reported elsewhere (Boyette and Reeves, 1982). Here the authors will describe the content of the art and interpret its sociological meaning.

The content analysis revealed that both the content and the form of children's art work vary by gender. More specifically, boys are *less* likely to depict domestic scenes than are girls, and they are *more* likely to depict activity, angular shapes, humans in profile, and violent scenes than are girls. Lastly, girls are more likely to pay attention to the eye than are boys. This is not to say that boys did not draw feminine content or that girls did not draw masculine content. There were deviations from what the researchers expected but the pattern was quite clear. Note the various photographs of children's art work for gender differences in Figures 5.1–5.6. (The art work is illustrative rather than representative of the study sample.)

Figure 5.1 was drawn by a nine year-old girl. The landscape is a peaceful, bucolic scene. No activity is present. Note the roundness of the hills, mountain tops, sun and clouds.

The cover drawing was drawn by a nine year-old girl. Note the conversation. The male is requesting marriage; the girl isn't quite sure but replies in the

FIGURE 5.2

affirmative when she finds out her suitor plans to live on a farm. The roundness is also depicted in these figures. Note the detailed eyes and cosmetics used for the female and the non-detailed eyes for the male. Both figures are frontal. The

FIGURE 5.3

male is distinguished by a hat and beard stubble. The female has a cross around her neck symbolizing religious orientation and possibly morality. Her counterpart has a necklace but no cross.

Figure 5.2 was drawn by a ten year-old girl. A housewife is depicted in a domestic scene. The girl is indicating cynicism by depicting a "sad" housewife who wears a "smile" symbol on her dress. The cynical attitude may reflect the attitude of the child's mother whom the researchers know to be a feminist who is nondomestic.

Figure 5.3 was drawn by a nine year-old boy. Note the excitement. An airplane is having trouble as indicated by the flopped over propeller. People are being carried into the hospital (far left of picture). Geometric forms pervade the picture. Strokes are harsh and strong.

Figure 5.4 was drawn by a ten year-old boy. Race cars are commonly drawn by boys. Note the action . . . it is a race and the driver seeks the championship. Note the swaying of the crowd and the action lines of the car.

Figure 5.5 was drawn by a nine year-old boy. The human figure is not frontal but not quite profile either. The pressure of the strokes on the figure is quite different from that on the guitar. Evidently, the artist was not sure of himself when drawing the man singing. Note the man is not just sitting . . . he is doing something. He is singing and playing the guitar. The fact that the instrument is a guitar rather than a piano or harp suggests the artist thinks this instrument is appropriate for a male to play. Also note the sideburns, heavy moustache and male-type neckline.

Figure 5.6 was drawn by an 11 year-old boy. The war scene is blatantly aggressive and violent.

FIGURE 5.4

FIGURE 5.5

It is not surprising to see that girls prefer domestic scenes because domestici-ty is associated with the female gender role. This finding suggests that girls are still being trained to identify with the home and that their primary role is thought to be that of homemaker, regardless of their mothers' occupations.

FIGURE 5.6

Absence of domesticity for males suggests domesticity is not valued as appropriate for males. Rather, success seems to be an important component of boys' pictures and the male sex role.

That boys depict more activity than girls is also not surprising. These pictures reveal that girls perceive themselves as passive people who have things done to them and for them. Boys "do" whereas girls are involved in "being." The few active drawings done by girls depicted feminine scenes such as skipping rope (Lever, 1978) or women using vacuum cleaners. The domestic scenes depicted by males were often drawings of their mothers performing the usual female household tasks. One male child showed his mother reprimanding him harshly for making a dirty mess in the house. Boys favored adventure scenes where exciting things were going on: a sea diver exploring treasure at the bottom of the ocean; an astronaut checking out outer space; a skier zipping down a hill; or a race car driver deftly negotiating a curve in a stadium.

Why did we predict correctly that girls prefer round shapes and boys angular shapes? The basis for this distinction came from the literature on children's play; however, there may be more to it than revealed in the literature. For example, the female body contains more fat than the male body, and curves certainly are more associated with females than males. The attire of boys and girls also reflects different shapes: girls wear ruffles which are round in shape whereas boys tend to wear more tailored clothes. The decor of a child's bedroom may reflect sex differences in terms of round or angular shapes. An examination of the 1982 Sear's, Penny's and Montgomery Ward catalogs reveals that boys' rooms are more likely to be streamlined (bunk beds; tailored bedspreads and drapes) than are girls' rooms. Feminine bedroom decor includes such things as flowers, French Provincial furniture, round decorator pillows and round canopies. In short, little girls' environments appear to be full of softness and curves, while boys' environments contain hard geometric designs.

Human profile is associated with action (Machover, 1974) and thus we can understand that boys depicted more humans in profile and girls depicted them frontally. No females portrayed violence in their pictures. Violence continues to be a dimension of the male sex role (David and Brannon, 1976); its absence among the girls' drawings indicates that it is not culturally sanctioned for females in our society to express violence or aggression. A large portion of the violent scenes were concerned with war, a disconcerting though not surprising finding which deserves further study. Why do boys who have never experienced war draw pictures about it? Perhaps it is because war games are popular with boys, and survival games are popular with male adults. The idea that war can be a testing ground for demonstrating masculinity is well entrenched in our culture.

Why do girls pay closer attention to eyes than do boys? From a gender role perspective, girls are taught to value the input they can get from observing the human eye (Henley, 1973). This is one reason why women prefer men to look at them when they are talking. In our culture girls are encouraged to be socially competent, that is, popular (Lowenfield and Brittain, 1970). A girl learns early that a message communicated through eye contact can enhance her social competence; she learns when to approach and when not to approach the object of her attention, and what pupil dilation could mean (Henley, 1973). The multitude of beauty aids for the female eye as advertised in the media appears not to have gone unnoticed by the children in the study. The message that females must use cosmetics to be physically attractive was very apparent in the girls' art work.

CONCLUSIONS AND IMPLICATIONS

Three inferences may be drawn from the data; 1) boys and girls experience differenct social-psychological worlds; 2) since boys and girls prefer to draw different kinds of things, different subjects must be important or enjoyable to them; and 3) children perceive and express gender in stereotyped ways. These perceptions may be attributed to differential gender role socialization.

The implications of this study are numerous. Despite massive efforts by feminists to alter the general perceptions of gender roles, this group of Texan anglo children in the 9-12 age group still express traditional gender roles, at least in their art work. Although Sweden is twenty years ahead of the United States in terms of gender equality, Swedish children also continue to perceive gender role differences (Safilios-Rothschild, 1972). One cannot help but question if children can experience gender role transcendence; perhaps this transcendence can only occur after one has matured psychologically.

There are also several interesting methodological implications of this study. First, like diaries, children's art work can be used as a research tool for understanding and predicting behavior. Second, children's art work can also be used to gauge changes in attitudes and behavior in a single culture, and differences across cultures. For example, one could ask if the art work of contemporary Swedish children contains the same differences between boys and girls as were found in the American sample. Third, children's art could be used, along with other measures, to evaluate the effectiveness of specific policies such as sex desegregation programs in public schools. The utility for sociologists of using children's art work to assess the consequences of prejudice, social class, urban life and different familial arrangements also holds promise. Fourth, it is possible to study children at different ages and see when they start showing gender differentiation in their drawings. According to Kellogg (1967), there is no observable gender differentiation in drawings by toddlers. Finally, there are implications for teaching. Through the use of children's art work, one can easily and effectively demonstrate the socialization process, cultural change and the consequences of social stratification. Best of all, children's art work is readily available for study. Children love to show off their work. The authors of this paper hope others will be as excited as they are about the varied potential of children's art work in sociology.

REFERENCES

Bascow, S.   1980   Sex-Role Stereotypes. Monterey, California: Brooks/Cole.

Bernard, J.   1981   The Female World. New York: Free Press.

Boyette, N. and J. Reeves   1982   "What does children's art work tell us about society?" Presented to Mid-South Sociological Association, Jackson, Mississippi, Oct. 27–30.

David, D. and Brannon, R.   1976   The Forty-Nine Percent Majority: The Male Sex Role. Reading, Massachusetts: Addison-Wesley.

Davidson, L. and L. Gordon   1979   The Sociology of Gender. Chicago: Rand McNally.

Dennis, W.   1966   Group Values Through Children's Drawings. New York: Wiley.

Di Leo, J.H.   1970   Young Children and Their Drawings. New York: Brunner/Mazel.

Feldman, E.G.   1970   Becoming Human Through Art. Englewood Cliffs: Prentice-Hall.

Gardner, H.   1973   The Arts and Human Development. New York: Wiley.

Goodenough, F.L.   1926   Measurement of Intelligence by Drawing. New York: World Book.

Goodnow, J.   1977   Children Drawing. Cambridge, Massachusetts: Harvard University Press.

Henley, N.M.   1973   "Power, sex, and non-verbal communication." Berkeley Journal of Sociology 18: 1–26.

Kellogg, R.   1969   Analyzing Children's Art. Palo Alto: National Press Books.

Kellogg, R. and S. O'Dell   1967   The Psychology of Children's Art. New York: Random House.

Key, M.R.   1971   "The role of male and female in children's books dispelling all doubt." Pp. 56–70 in R. Unger and F. Denmark (eds.), Women: Dependent or Independent Variable? New York: Psychological Dimensions.

Klepsh, M. and L. Logie   1982   Children Draw and Tell. New York: Brunner/Mazel.

Kohlberg, L.   1966   "A cognitive development analysis of children's sex role concepts and attitudes." Pp. 82–92 in E.E. Macoby (ed.), The Development of Sex Differences. Stanford: Stanford University Press.

Lever, J.   1978   "Sex differences in the complexity of children's play and games." The American Psychological Review 43: 471–483.

Lowenfield, V. and W.L. Brittain   1970   Creative and Mental Growth. New York: Macmillan.

Machover, K.   1974   Personality Projection in the Drawing of the Human Figure. Springfield, Illinois: Charles C. Thomas.

Rheingold, H.L. and Cook, K.V.   1975   "The contents of boys' and girls' rooms as an index of parent's behavior." Child Development 46: 459–463.

Safilios-Rothchild, C.   1972   Toward a Sociology of Women. Lexington: Xerox College Publishing.

U'ren, M.B. 1971 "The image of women in textbooks." Pp. 318-34 in V. Gornick and B. Moran (eds.), Women in a Sexist Society: Studies in Power and Powerlessness. New York: Basic Books.

Walstead, J.J. 1975 "A content analysis of sexual discrimination in children's literature." Pp. 36-38 in R. Unger (ed.), Sex Role Stereotypes Revisited: Psychological Approaches to Women's Studies. New York: Harper and Row.

Weitzman, L. 1979 Sex Role Socialization: A Focus on Women. Palo Alto: Mayfield.

Weitzman, L., D. Eifler, E. Hakada, and C. Ross 1972 "Sex role socialization in picture books for preschool children." American Journal of Psychology 77: 1125-1150.

Whitehurst, R.N., G. Booth, and H. Mohammand 1979 "Factors in marital breakup." Pp. 121-126 in L. Cargen and J. Ballantine (eds.), Sociological Footprints. Boston: Houghton Mifflin.

Section IV

Acquiring and Negotiating Gender: Adult Socialization

Chapter 6 _____

The (Mis)Acquisition of Gender Identity among Transsexuals

Barbara J. Risman

Abstract

Transsexualism suggests questions for sociologists who study gender. Is gender identity always a precursor to role behavior or might it result from the social reactions to deviant behavior? This article considers several theoretical explanations for the (mis)acquisition of gender identity among transsexuals: biological hypotheses, psychoanalytic theories, social learning, and role theory. The author concludes that gender role and gender identity are confounded in past research and that the issue of inflexibility of identities needs to be treated more systematically.

T here are at least two possible approaches to the study of transsexuals. The first is a descriptive account of the phenomenon as a curious anomaly within the human condition. The second approach involves in-vestigating the unusual to learn more about general theoretical principles that contribute to both normative and deviant behavior. This article attempts the lat-ter, a critical review of the literature focusing on the process of gender identity acquisition among transsexuals.

Although the study of gender identity acquisition among transsexuals might be interesting in and of itself, it is also important for sociological theory more generally. The process of learning one's gender identity, and the corresponding social role, are ubiquitous aspects of every human society. To understand how persons came to perceive themselves as men when they are biologically female,

The author wishes to thank Philip Blumstein and Pepper Schwartz and anonymous reviewers at *Qualitative Sociology* for their helpful comments on earlier drafts of this paper. Requests for reprints should be sent to Barbara Risman, Dept. of Sociology, DK-40. University of Washington, Seattle, Washington, 98195.

Source: Barbara J. Risman, "The (Mis)Acquisition of Gender Identity among Transsexuals," *Qualitative Sociology* 5 (Winter 1982). Published by Human Sciences Press, Inc., 72 Fifth Ave., New York, N.Y. 10011. Copyright 1982. Used by permission.

or women when they are biologically male, may shed light on the general processes involved in gender identity acquisition.

The research focusing on cross-gender identity acquisition can be organized
into four working paradigms: biological, psychoanalytic, social psychological, and
role theory. Each paradigm will be discussed, and then the methodological problems common to all the research on transsexualism shall be addressed. This article suggests that present theoretical explanations of transsexualism may be
inadequate because they fail to clearly differentiate between social reaction to
gender role deviation and acquisition of inappropriate gender identity.[1]

The analytic difference between gender identity and gender role has been
addressed by researchers working within various theoretical paradigms
(Kohlberg, 1966; Money and Ehrhardt, 1972; Laws and Schwartz 1977; Davidson and Gordon, 1979). Although there is little agreement on the process by
which gender identity and gender role are acquired, there is consensus on definitional distinctions between the two concepts. Kohlberg (1966) suggests that
gender identity exists when a child consistently and correctly identifies his or
her sex. Money and Ehrhardt (1972:300–301) explain that gender identity is
"the sameness, unity and persistence of one's individuality as male or female . . .
especially as it is experienced in self awareness . . . gender identity is the private
experience of gender role." Davidson and Gordon (1979) suggest that gender
identity is the awareness that one is a boy or a girl. Although authors phrase
their definitions differently, a common thread links each definition. Identity is
the private experience of gender, the awareness that one is male or female.
Gender role refers to culturally specific normative expectations associated with
gender. Despite these well recognized conceptual differences between identity
and role, they have often been confused in research on transsexuals. The problem is exacerbated by the glossing over of gender role issues in etiological discussion of transsexualism.

The process by which transsexuals develop inappropriate gender indentities
is the focus of this article. Transsexuals raise central questions for the sociology
of gender: Is gender identity always a precursor to role behavior? Or is gender
identity more flexible than previously assumed, perhaps affected by social reactions to deviant behavior?

THEORETICAL EXPLANATIONS FOR MISACQUISITION OF GENDER IDENTITY AMONG TRANSSEXUALS

Harry Benjamin (1966) in his pioneering treatise on transsexualism proposed
three possible causes for the phenomenon: inborn genetic tendencies, neuro-
endocrinological abnormalities, and psychological damage based on early
childhood conditioning. Benjamin suggests that social learning triggers transsexualism only if there is a constitutional, biological predisposition.

Biological Hypotheses

The research attempting to identify biological predispositions toward transsexualism, as suggested by Benjamin (1966), has consistently reported null results. In a literature review, Matto (1972) reports that male transsexuals are physiologically normal in all physical criteria used to determine sex: chromosomes, gonads, external genitalia, internal reproductive capabilities, and hormone levels. Pauly (1947b) reports that all of the female transsexuals in his review of individual case studies were genotypically normal, and that 95% were free of any, even nonsexual, physical abnormalities. In medical studies of transsexuals, rather than reviews of the medical literature, Philbert (1971) reports that male transsexuals are not distinguishable from normals *vis à vis* endocrine levels, and Jones (1973) reports that female transsexuals are genetically normal females.

Contrary to Benjamin's hypothesis, the data do not support a biological explanation for the acquisition of inappropriate gender identity. Therefore, most of the research has focused on the psychological and social causes of the phenomenon. Reports of psychological distress during childhood have been as consistent as the lack of evidence for biological predispositions. Various theories have been suggested to explain transsexuals' gender identity acquisition. These include psychoanalytic, social learning, development and role theories.

Psychoanalytic Theories

In general, psychoanalytic theorists argue that an awareness of genital similarity leads to identification with same sex parent. This identification prompts imitation of "appropriate" role behavior. The process of gender identity acquisition is not directly addressed because the awareness of similar genitals implicitly presupposes an already established gender identity. Graphically, this can be presented as in Figure 6.1.

Green (1974) and Matto (1972) both discuss the application of traditional psychoanalytic thought to transsexuals. Green suggests that Freudian psychologists presume both sexes to have similar psychic bisexuality before birth, and that the ascendant psychological component depends primarily on early experiences with parents. Feminity in boys is explained by the assumption that because early caretakers are female, all children tend toward femaleness, and that without strong male figures, boys may become transsexuals (Matto, 1972). Such boys show identification with their mother, often because they have

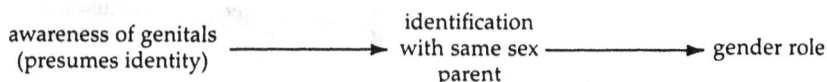

awareness of genitals ⟶ identification with same sex ⟶ gender role
(presumes identity)   parent

FIGURE 6.1

physically or emotionally absent fathers. The lack of identification, and subsequent role conformity, is implicitly blamed upon incorrect gender identity. Why and how the process occurs is not clear within this paradigm.

Psychoanalytic theories focus on the unfolding of instinctual needs during childhood, although including the importance of social factors. The assumption that gender conflict is a result of a problematic transference of identity modeling from the initial caretaker may help explain male transsexualism, but since girls' caretakers are female, this cannot explain transsexualism among women.

Psychological Theories: Social Learning and Developmental Perspectives

By far the most common perspectives in the past literature are developmental and social learning theories. Both psychological theories share the general assumption that differential reinforcement and other's awareness and labelling of genitals are causally related to gender identity and role. The models differ in time ordering of variables (see Figure 6.2).

These theories differ in significant ways, particularly concerning whether role or identity is acquired first. Yet, social learning theory and developmental theory share a basic and central assumption. These processes occur during early childhood, and identity remains relatively inflexible thereafter. This assumption of identity permanence is responsible for many researchers and clinicians uncritically accepting transsexuals' accounts of "having always known they were caught in the wrong body."

Green (1974) suggests that developmental theories are concerned with both reinforcement behavior and gender identification. A role model must be perceived as nurturant, must be in command of desired goals such as love, and must reinforce appropriate gender-typic behavior. If any aspect of this chain is weak, gender identity confusion may result.

Stoller (1969) implicitly depends on social learning theory, focusing primarily on the early family situation. Stoller identifies a family pattern that exists both

Social Learning Theory　　　　　identification with same-sex parent

Others' awareness of genitals → differential reinforcement → gender role → gender identity

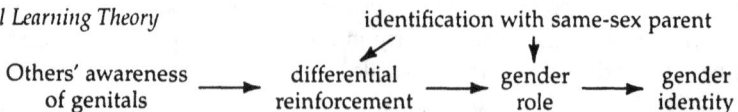

Developmental Theory

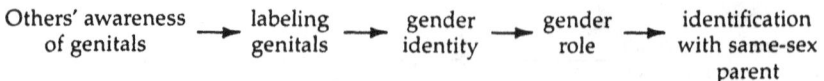

Others' awareness of genitals → labeling genitals → gender identity → gender role → identification with same-sex parent

FIGURE 6.2

in the recollection of male transsexuals and the current family situations of boys with gender identity conflicts. First, the mother displays gender identity problems of her own. She was often unusually boyish in adolescence and continues to be "masculine" as an adult. That is, she is aggressive, competitive and enjoys team sports. Stroller describes such "masculine" mothers as "bisexual," blurring the distinction between sex object preference and gender role behavior. The second characteristic of such families is the unusual amount of physical contact between mother and son in the first two years of family life. Finally, the mother has "too much" power in the family due to the psychological withdrawal or physical absence of the father. Presumably, the mother reinforces cute, feminine, docile behavior while discouraging aggressive male behavior. Stroller does not distinguish between gender role behavior and gender identity conflict for mother or son.

Much less research has focused on female transsexuals. Pauly (1974a) suggests this lack of attention may be both due to the fewer identified cases of female transsexualism and to researchers' "gender centricity." Male researchers may have simply been more interested and concerned about gender conflict in males. The few studies addressing the psychological development of female transsexuals agree that the etiology differs from that of male transsexuals.

Stoller (1972) argues that female transsexuals are more like homosexuals than are their male counterparts. Female transsexuals are harder to diagnose because of less clear clinical boundaries. Perhaps the diagnostic boundaries are less clear because women in this society are allowed more gender-role flexibility than are men. Stoller suggests that while male transsexuals acquire their identity in a nonconflictual learning process, female transsexualism is a defense against trauma in childhood. Both Stoller and Pauly focus on early family situations finding the following patterns: (1) parents who do not think their baby girl is beautiful, (2) a depressed, fragile, psychologically-removed mother who withdraws nurturance while her daughter is very young; (3) a father who does not support his wife in her psychological suffering, instead often being alcoholic and abusive; (4) encouragement for the female child to step in and support the mother in a "husbandly" fashion, the child is reinforced because her family needs her in this function; and (5) finally, masculine behavior is encouraged and feminine behavior discouraged until the masculine qualities coalesce into a cohesive identity.

Role Theory

Role theorists lack a precise theoretical model to explain the acquisition of gender identity. Perhaps this can be attributed to the belief that "identity" is a psychological construct, and not appropriate for sociological analysis. The research which has approached the study of transsexualism from a uniquely sociological perspective (Garfinkel, 1967; Matto, 1972; Feinbloom, 1976) often relates only tangentially to the acquisition of gender identity. Levine and colleagues (1975) are an exception to this generalization. They describe 12 men who became transsexuals through a series of role transformations, rather than the more usual pattern of "having always known." The role transformations reported were due largely to the negative responses of significant others, throughout the life cycle. As reactors reinforce the individuals sense of role failure, the individual moves through a sequence of role changes: from ambivalence toward gender role during childhood and primary school; to homosexuality in adolescence and beyond; to experimental cross-dressing, sometimes as a drag queen; and finally, to permanent cross-dressing with the ever present desire for sex-change surgery.

Common Methodological Issue

The question arises as to the possibility of differential interpretation of the data dependent upon the researchers' conceptual schema. Levine et al. (1975), mention their respondents' reports of dominant mothers, while developmental psychologists who focus on the first years of life report the trauma of school years and adolescent homosexuality. It may be that the identical recollection (biased as it may be) is created into a shared definition differently by the psychologist, the sociologist, the psychoanalyst and the patient. Intellectually, this may be acceptable – and even necessary – if the assumption that reality is socially constructed and therefore multiple realities may coexist is seriously entertained. Such a stance, however, is of little benefit to those faced with the diagnostic decision, or understanding the process of gender identity acquisition.

The research findings within the various theoretical perspectives share common methodological problems. First, nearly all past research (with the exception of Levine et al., 1975; and Feinbloom, 1976) on adult transsexuals have studied only those persons who have sought out clinicians in hopes of acquiring a sex-change operation (Benjamin, 1966, 1967, 1979; Garfinkel, 1967; Baker, 1969; Stoller, 1969; Philbert, 1971; Pauly, 1974a, 1974b; Bentler, 1976). Such samples have not been conceived as a limitation because of the assumption that all "true" (Benjamin, 1966) transsexuals desire to surgically change their sex. In fact, one characteristic used to distinguish transsexuals from transvestites is the overwhelming desire for sex change. There are two problems with such a restricted research population. First, some persons may desire to change their sex, yet for various reasons do not appear in a psychiatrist's office. Such reason may include class status, family obligations, religious values, availability of medical or psychiatric facilities; the assumption that those who do not voluntarily seek clinicians are not transsexuals seems problematic, even if convenient for research. This definitional problem leads to the second concern with diagnosing transsexualism as the desire for surgical change of sex. By such a definition, transsexualism could not have existed before the technological advances of modern science. Perhaps the definition of transsexualism as cross-gender identity would be less historically ethnocentric.

It is clear that however transsexualism is defined, only those who identify themselves as such shall be available for intensive study. Yet, to circularly conceptualize the phenomenon to justify the available research population as all-inclusive seems unwise, if not intellectually deceitful.

Although the samples are small, descriptions of symptoms and family histories are fairly consistent across studies (discussed below). The problem, however, remains as to the generalizability of small self-selected samples to other transsexuals who may exist more covertly in the population at large.

Reliability of the data is also a serious problem, particularly when discussing the apparent consistency of findings. Distortion may enter the analysis either through retrospective interpretation or conscious misrepresentation. Edwin Schurr (1971) defines retrospective interpretation as a facet of the labelling process whereby reactors come to view deviators "in a totally new light." For instance, relatives of transsexuals may begin to remember and/or manufacture past biographies consistent with the new information regarding their child or sibling's identity preference. The past is reinterpreted dependent on the knowledge of present deviance. The concept of retrospective interpretation might be extended to include the deviant's reinterpretation of the past also. Once the label of transsexual is incorporated into the self-concept, the individual may begin to recreate his or her past congruent with the new self. Selective memory aids the reinterpretation of childhood problems and role ambiguities as the *now* obvious manifestation of the current self-identity.

Another source of bias in the data is the possibility that adult transsexuals consciously misrepresent their present and past histories to clinicians (Blumstein, 1979). Data about transsexuals are often collected by persons who are both researchers and diagnosticians. It is conceivable that the two purposes are incompatible. The transsexual has a great deal at stake in his or her attempt to receive the sex-change surgery. It is likely that transsexuals will present themselves in whatever manner they believe will further their chances for success. Transsexuals live within their own subculture (Feinbloom, 1976; Levine et al., 1975) and presumably share information about which strategies are most successful when dealing with medical and psychological diagnosticians, the gatekeepers to medical aid. In addition, it is possible that transsexuals read the medical and popular information regarding their condition. This might lead both to conscious distortion of truth in the quest for sex change, and also to the more subtle process of self-initiated retrospective interpretation.

Ira Pauly (1974a) argues that selective recall (and by implication conscious distortion) is not an overwhelming burden for psychiatric researchers. Pauly presumes that an absolute and objective reality exists waiting only for the psychiatrist to assess it. Scheff (1968) has suggested, however, that since reality is socially constructed, multiple realities may coexist. Instead of a reality existing to be assessed, Scheff postulates that the emergent shared definition of reality is a function of the relationship between interactants. In a psychiatric interview (the setting for most data discussed in this article), patients offer their symptoms and the psychiatrist responds by accepting and/or reinforcing particular offers and rejecting others. The interrogator, as confident professional, has more power in determining the creation of a shared reality, despite the patient's experiential knowledge. Analyzing the psychiatric diagnostic process sociologically supports the contention that the reliability of the research findings on transsexuals may be problematic. Transsexuals, perhaps more than most research subjects, are eager to please their interrogators; willing to cede all power to the psychiatrist (alias researcher) to define the shared reality, hoping that such cooperation may increase their chances to be selected for sex-change surgery. This "cooperation" also leads, clearly, to biased research.

SUMMARY AND THEORETICAL CRITIQUE

Gender Role and Identity: Theoretical and Operational Confusion

There seems to be a general confusion within the literature on transsexualism; the distinction between gender role and gender identity is often ignored, or treated superficially. This is most clearly illustrated by the studies of therapeutic intervention with effeminate boys. Lebovitz (1972), Zuger (1966), and Green et al. (1972) make no distinction between role and identity: they all assume that behavior is a manifestation of underlying identity. Therapy involves providing male role models, and the conscious reinforcement of aggression and competitiveness as expressions of masculinity. The following quote (Green et al., 1972:215) typifies the attitude towards the encouragement of appropriate gender identity by reinforcing stereotypically masculine behaviors. In this case history, the mother's behavior has been judged as promoting her son's cross-gender identity:

> The boy was in front of his home, dancing about a water hose in a style reminiscent of a water sprite, all the while shrieking in a girlish manner. A neighbor riding past on his bicycle . . . called him "sissy." The patient turned the hose on the boy, knocking him from his bicycle, perhaps the most "phallic" gesture to that time. The mother . . . emerged from the house and chastized her son for knocking the boy from his bicycle (not for the feminine behavior).

Such intertwined conceptions of gender identity and role are pervasive in nearly all the literature on male transsexuals. The presumption that to be male is to be macho, aggressive, and "rough and tumble" is integrated into much of the scientific literature uncritically. Rosen et al. (1977), however, are an exception. They argue that gender behavior disturbance and cross-gender identity are two distinct continuum, which often co-vary. They suggest that efforts to construct a single, unidimensional scale is a reflection of assumptions based on sex and gender stereotypes unrelated to reality.

Male and Female Difference

It is interesting that the distinction between gender role and identity, though rarely drawn in discussions of male transsexuals, is always drawn in discussion of female transsexuals (Green, 1969, 1974; Pauly, 1974a). Authors assume that there are aspects of boyhood that girls are naturally jealous of; and therefore girls should be expected to occasionally display cross-gender behavior. For instance, Green (1969:27) writes:

> Boys lead more adventurous and autonomous lives than girls. Girls are aware of the more privileged status of roles in the culture. That cross-gender role behavior is not synonymous with cross-gender identity is revealed by the fact that most of these tomboys abandon or modify such behavior with the emergence of adolescence and the dating age.

No similar argument is suggested by any author to explain the desire for doll-playing and nurturant activities among boys.

Benjamin (1966) and Pauly (1974a) discuss the differential rates of transsexualism by anatomical sex. Estimates of the ratio vary from 1:1 to 8:1, male to female. In Sweden, equal numbers of men and women have applied for legal change of sex. Requests for sex-change surgery average 2.4:1, male to female, at Johns Hopkins University Hospital. Benjamin (1966) has seen eight times as many males as females who desire sex-change operations. It may be that some of the reported differential rates are due to more publicity surrounding the male to female operation. While the ratio is hard to determine, it seems safe to conclude there is some preponderance of males who desire to change their sex.

Psychologically oriented theorists find the predominance of anatomically male transsexuals rather surprising. Pauly (1974a:495–496) hypothesizes that since women receive fewer negative sanctions for cross-gender behavior, it might be expected more female tomboys than male sissies would grow into adult transsexuals.

> In spite of a more permissive attitude toward cross-gender behavior in little girls, most of these tomboys seem to outgrow their masculine interests and preferences as adults. At least fewer of them want totally to reject their female sex and gender role.
> On the other hand, effeminate boys are ridiculed by their peers and usually admonished by their parents, and despite this negative social reinforcement they too have more frequent and serious gender identity problems as adults than do their female counterparts.

Perhaps the differential social treatment of tomboys and sissies might help explain the preponderance of male transsexuals. Sissy is a much more negative label than tomboy. Boys who deviate from their gender role are reacted to swiftly and negatively by significant others. Girls who deviate from their gender role prescriptions are not nearly as severely punished, and may even be encouraged. Erich Goode (1978) suggests that unanticipated deviant consequences are possible outcomes of interactional settings where one actor is reacted to negatively by others. The deviator begins to think of him or herself negatively. Once the label of sissy is applied, the little boy no longer thinks of himself as a person who likes doll-play, but as the kind of boy who is a sissy, the kind of boy who is like a girl. Perhaps through such a process, boys who deviate from gender behavior prescriptions begin to redefine the self as a deviator. The stereotype which aligns doll-playing with feminine identity is incorporated into their conceptions of self.

I am suggesting that the primary deviance of cross-gender behavior may lead to a label, which when incorporated into the self-concept prompts the secondary, far more serious, deviance of a cross-gender identity. Perhaps the greater gender-role flexibility for girls allows them to escape this process of labeling and secondary deviance.

Past research has assumed that gender-role deviance is merely a manifestation of cross-gender identity. It is possible that the causality may flow in the opposite direction: the societal reaction to gender role deviance may lead to a stereotype which involves self-labeling as a transsexual.

There is no obvious justification for the assumption that these processes, whatever direction the causality, function only during childhood. Social reactions to nonconformity continue throughout the life cycle. Future research ought to investigate how individuals decide they are transsexuals. Studies need to focus on when individuals (mis)acquire their identities, as well as etiology.

The answers to such questions may shed light on the general process by which "normals" acquire their gender identities. Are identities inflexible after they coalesce in early childhood? If transsexuals do (mis)acquire their identities at various stages of their development, then the data would suggest otherwise. Studies of transsexuals address the issue of the malleability of individuals' self-concepts, including gender identities. Are identities fixed in childhood, or do individuals renegotiate their self-concepts throughout life?

NOTES

1. Recently, two works which address parallel concerns have been brought to my attention: Janice G. Raymond (1979) discusses transsexualism as a feminist ethicist in her book *The Transsexual Empire*. Suzanne J. Kessler and Wendy McKenna (1978) interviewed transsexuals in an ethnomethodological framework for their book entitled *Gender*. Both works address the questions raised in this article.

2. The models used in the article were first suggested to me by Charles Hill in a graduate student seminar. Similar models are also used by Kessler and McKenna (1978).

REFERENCES

Baker, Lt. H. J. 1969 "Transsexualism-Problems in Treatment." American Journal of Psychiatry 125(10):118-124.

Benjamin, H. 1966 The Transsexual Phenomenon. New York: The Julian Press.

———1967 "Transvestism and Transsexualism in the Male and Female." Journal of Sex Research 3(2):107-127.

———1969 "Newer Aspects of the Transsexual Phenomenon." Journal of Sex Research 5(2):135-144.

Bentler, Peter M. 1976 "A Typology of Transsexualism: Gender Identity, Theory and Data." Archives of Sexual Behavior 5(6):567-584.

Davidson, Laurie and Laura Kramer Gordon 1979 The Sociology of Gender. Chicago: Rand McNally College Publishing Company.

Feinbloom, Deborah Heller 1976 Transvestites and Transsexuals. New York: Delacorte Press.

Garfinkel, Harold 1967 Studies in Ethnomethodology. New Jersey: Prentice Hall, Inc.

Goode, Erich 1978 Deviant Behavior: An Interactionist Perspective. New Jersey: Prentice Hall, Inc.

Green, Richard 1969 "Childhood Cross-Gender Identification." in R. Green and J. Money (eds.) Transsexualism and Sex Reassignment. Baltimore: Johns Hopkins Press, pp. 23-35.

———1971 "Diagnosis and Treatment of Gender Identity Disorders During Childhood," Archives of Sexual Behavior 1(2):167-173.

1974 Sexual Identity Conflict in Children and Adults. New York: Basic Books.

Green, Richard, Lawrence, Newman and Robert J. Stoller 1971 "Two Monozygotic (Identical) Twin Pairs Discordant for Gender Identity," Archives of Sexual Behavior 1(4):321-327.

Green, Richard, Lawrence, Neroma and Robert J. Stoller 1972 "Treatment of Boyhood 'Transsexualism'" Archives of Sexual Behavior 26:213-217.

Hoenig, J. and J.C. Kenna 1974 "The Nosological Position of Transsexualism," Archives of Sexual Behavior 3(3):273-287.

Jones, James R. and Jean Samimy 1973 "Plasma Testosterone Levels and Female Transsexualism, Archives of Sexual Behavior 2(3):251-256.

Kessler, Suzanne J. and Wendy McKenna 1978 Gender: An Ethnomethodological Approach. New York: John Wiley and Sons.

Kohlberg, Lawrence 1966 "A Cognitive-Developmental Analysis of Children's Sex-Role Concepts and Attitudes." In Eleanor Maccoby (ed.); The Development of Sex Differences. Stanford, California: Stanford University Press.

Laws, Judith and Pepper Schwartz 1977 Sexual Scripts: The Social Construction of Female Sexuality. Hinsdale, Illinois: The Dryden Press.

Lebovitz, Phil S. 1972 "Feminine Behavior in Boys: Aspects of Its Outcome." American Journal of Psychiatry 138(10):103-109.

Levine, Edward, Charles Shaicva, and F.M. Mihailovic 1975 "Male to Female: The Role Transformation of Transsexuals." Archives of Sexual Behavior 4(2):176-185.

Matto, Michelle S. 1972 "The Transsexual in Society." Criminology 10(1):85-109.

Money, John and Anke Ehrhardt 1972 Man and Woman, Boy and Girl. New York: Mentor Books.

Pauly, Ira B. 1974a "Female Transsexualism: Part I." Archives of Sexual Behavior 3(6):487–508.

————1974b "Female Transsexualism: Part II." Archives of Sexual Behavior 3(6):509–526.

Philbert, M. 1971 "Male Transsexualism: An Endocrine Study." Archives of Sexual Behavior 1(1):91–93.

Raymond, Janice C. 1979 The Transsexual Empire: The Making of the She-Male. Boston: Beacon Press.

Reekers, George A. 1975 "Stimulus Control Over Sex-Typed Play in Cross-Gender Identified Boys." Journal of Experimental Child Psychology 20(1):136–148.

Rosen, A.C., G.A. Rekers and L.R. Friars 1977 "Theoretical and Diagnostic Issues in Child Gender Disturbances." Journal of Sex Research 13(2):89–103.

Scheff, Thomas J. 1968 "Negotiating Reality: Notes on Power in the Assessment of Responsibility." Social Problems 16(1):3–17.

Schur, Edwin M. 1971 Labelling Deviant Behavior. New York: Harper and Row Publishers.

Socarides, Charles W. 1969 "The Desire for Sexual Transformation: A Psychiatric Evaluation of Transsexualism." American Journal of Psychiatry 125(10):1419–1425.

Stoller, Robert J. 1967 "It's Only a Phase." Journal of the American Medical Association 201(5):314–315.

————1969 "Parental Influences in Male Transsexualism." in R. Green and J. Money (eds.); Transsexualism and Sex Reassignment. Baltimore: Johns Hopkins Press, pp. 153–169.

———— 1972 "Etiological Factors in Female Transsexualism: A First Approxima-tion," Archives of Sexual Behavior 2(1):47–64.

Zuger, Bernard 1966 "Effeminate Behavior Present in Boys From Early Childhood, I. The Clinical Syndrome and Follow-up Studies." Journal of Pediatrics 69(6):1098–2107.

Chapter 7 ——————————————————————————————

College Women and Sororities: The Social Construction and Reaffirmation of Gender Roles

Barbara J. Risman

Gender socialization in urban societies is acknowledged to occur primarily in adolescence. Risman's analysis of one college sorority displays additional ways in which women adopt role-specific behaviors that are formally encouraged by both social regulations and informally shaped by cultural norms. Her data suggest that the socialization processes and the consequent roles may in fact be inappropriate to facilitating women's adaptation to a changing social environment.

A self, then, virtually awaits the individual entering a position; he need only conform to the pressures on him and he will find a "me" ready-made for him . . . doing is being. — Goffman (1961: 87-88)

I am learning to be a woman. — Sorority member, 1979

A basic assumption in social psychology has always been that individuals learn who they are and how they ought to behave in interaction with those around them. As Shibutani (1955) suggests, it matters little if the influential group is labeled a "reference group" or is discussed in the context of the

Barbara J. Risman is currently a Ph.D. candidate in the Department of Sociology at the Unversity of Washington, in Seattle. She teaches courses for both the Sociology and Women Studies' Departments. Her research interests focus on the social creation of gender and sex differences in parenting.

Author's Note: I would like to thank Philip Blumstein, Arlene Kaplan Daniels, and the anonymous readers at Urban Life for their thoughtful reviews of earlier drafts of this article. I would also like to thank Pepper Schwartz for her help, both with the analysis of data and with earlier revisions of this article.

Source: Barbara J. Risman, "College Women and Sororities: The Social Construction and Reaffirmation of Gender Roles," Urban Life, Vol. 11 (July 1982), pp. 231-252. Copyright © 1982 by Urban Life. Reprinted by permission of Sage Publications, Inc.

"generalized other." The salient issue is that each of us approaches the world and orders our perceptions from the standpoint of our group's culture. Through direct or vicarious group participation, we internalize the group's perspective, as well as external phenomena, to define ourselves.

Sororities provide an interesting setting to observe the relationship between institutionalized social norms and individual members' self-development. This study will analyze the day-to-day operation of the sorority system as it affects each member's ideas about herself and her perspective on the world around her. Female college students are in the process of learning what it means to be women. It is my hypothesis that the Greek system functions effectively as a mechanism for traditional gender role socialization. Whether or not these sorority members are being prepared for roles that actually exist within contemporary society is not clear. In a society where women marry into their standard of living (e.g., Bernard, 1972) traditional gender role socialization may be effective training for adolescent females. In a world where women spend much of their lives in the paid labor force, such training may be anachronistic.

There has been little past research on sororities from this perspective. Waller (1937) discussed the "rating and dating" system on campus, but did not address the relationship between courtship patterns and gender roles. Scott (1965) and Reiss (1965) both focus on the "Greek" system of fraternities and sororities as mechanisms through which economically elite ascriptive groups maintain control over courtship. Control over courtship, however, includes a dimension not discussed by past researchers; control over courtship has traditionally extended not merely to the regulation of partners, but to behavioral patterns as well. Institutionally regulated courtship patterns are central to the study of gender role behavior. Traditionally, courtship has been an asymmetrical process; what is appropriate behavior for men is inappropriate for women and vice versa. When such interaction patterns are organizationally regulated – as in the Greek system – individuals can be observed as they participate in group culture, and through such behavior learn what is proper for themselves and for others.

Many theorists (e.g., Gerth and Mills, 1953; Turner, 1978; Hewitt, 1979) have suggested that institutional opportunity and reward structures function to limit the possible identities people can assume. Identities are only in part a matter of choice in that ascribed characteristics, such as sex, clearly influence how others react to an individual. This is particularly relevant for a study of sororities and gender role; in the Greek system formal regulations are different for males and females. Institutional patterns can also limit the identities people may assume by restricting the significant others by whose standards the self shall be appraised. Peasants cannot learn to think themselves elegant from the society of kings; girls in low-status sororities do not mix with high-status fraternity boys. These institutional limitations, ascribed characteristics, and social distance between groups will be analyzed to help understand how the Greek world influences sorority members' self-concepts.

This study will concentrate on values underlying both official regulations and informal cultural norms currently in vogue in the college Greek world. Just as academic institutions involve anticipatory socialization for adult work roles, so too, voluntary organizations – the Greek system – function as anticipatory socialization for adult social roles. The process by which rituals, courtesies, and priorities are learned, expressed, and accepted by female students as they become sorority girls[1] is the focus of this research.

The interaction within a sorority is highly effective in shaping a girl's self-image. Although there are certainly no physical barriers to what the girls themselves call the "outside," sorority members report that nearly all their time is spent with other Greeks. The girls in this study sleep, eat, play, and work within the same closed group of significant others. The Greek system provides them with one audience for every aspect of life. Greeks do, of course, mix with non-Greek students, instructors, and parents, but most daily interaction is confined to one highly organized, rational, and normatively conservative audience. If one's self-concept is developed through interaction with others, and all significant others belong to one cohesive social group, that group's norms and values become singularly influential for the individuals involved.

METHODOLOGY

The data were collected between 1976 and 1979 at a large state university on the West coast using both participant observation and in-depth interview techniques. The focus of observations changed over the three years. The first year was devoted almost exclusively to access attempts by approaching organizations that differed according to prestige ranking within the Greek system.[2] Over half the sororities on campus were contacted. Although the girls themselves were usually willing, and occasionally eager, to participate in this study, in all but one organization the alumni refused to allow them to do so. For example, alumni serve gatekeeping functions by discouraging interaction with outsiders.

The research design was modified to focus on individuals within the Greek system in order to avoid the problems inherent in the more formal organizational study first envisioned. As individuals, girls in every sorority were free to discuss their experiences. Far too many girls volunteered from sororities at every level within the Greek hierarchy. Twenty-two girls were chosen at random from those willing to be interviewed. An interview schedule was followed that covered all facets of each girl's life: family background, reasons for "going Greek," female friendships, social life, and future plans. These interviews provided initial access and prompted invitations to Greek functions, introduction to other sorority members, and relationships that ensured recurring contact throughout the next two years. Observations included attendance at sorority dinners, preparation for "rush," fraternity parties, "Greek week" for high school recruitment, and a fashion show advising potential members how to dress for "rush." Other observations were more informal: conversations with sorority members over coffee, drinks after work, and discussions in class. In addition, approximately 25 undergraduate papers that discussed sorority life were analyzed.

The respondents in this study represent a significant portion of contemporary college students. On this campus approximately 10% of the undergraduates belong to fraternities and sororities (there are over 4000 Greeks on campus). Nor are the respondents in this study atypical among those in the Greek system. The validity of these findings is supported by the remarkable consistency between data collected using different measurement strategies. The indepth interviews corroborated the participant observation, and both these strategies were corroborated by the student papers analyzed. In addition, the results have since been discussed with other sorority girls who recognize the world described, although many claim that the picture painted fits everyone except their particular organization.

CRITERIA FOR MEMBERSHIP: PRIORITIES AND GROUP EVALUATIONS

Most everyone reports "going Greek" to ensure a good social life, usually phrased as wanting to "meet people." Girls join sororities to belong to a closeknit community in an otherwise overwhelming and alienating university. Girls going through the membership selection process often mentioned the desire to have a "home away from home." Joining a sorority assures the first-year undergraduate of instant friends of both sexes. Spared, somewhat, the loneliness that accompanies the initial search for acceptance in a new environment, she foregoes the search for a pool of acquaintances from whom she will later choose her friends. Nearly every respondent indicated that most of her friends were in sororities. That large circle of friends, and the ease of their acquisition, is an oftcited benefit of Greek life.

The process by which girls choose, and are chosen, to join specific sororities is called "rush." No one in the sorority system likes rush, but most agree it is a necessary evil. A common complaint is that girls are forced to choose new members with very little information. This perception is quite accurate; data upon which to choose sisters is indeed scarce. Discussion during the rush parties (approximately four hours in total) were by regulation confined to small talk; discussing politics, morality, religion, or sexuality was usually forbidden.

When asked why certain girls were chosen, the most common answer was that they "fit in." When pressed for a definition of the term, the bottom line was primarily physical attractiveness integrated with social skills and, secondarily family status. One girl stated succinctly what others implied:

Most important, you'd be looking for pretty girls, that is what is going to attract the frats.

Judging each other in terms of male approval is a theme that recurs in discussions with sorority girls.

It is certainly not the case that all sororities pledge only attractive girls. Each house "knew against whom they competed," and concentrated their efforts to rush only those girls who might possibly join. Each sorority did select as attractive pledges as possible. The "top" house pledged only very attractive and, often, wealthy girls. As one member in a "status" house explained:

> To put it bluntly, we've got the best girls! You know, the smartest, the best looking, the most popular, stuff like that. I know it sounds conceited, but that is, you know, the way it is. . . . I was really honored to be invited into this house. And I enjoy all the prestige the name gives me, you know.

A pledge from another "status" house, as tall and blonde as most of her sisters, explained what made her house different from others:

> Money, for one thing. In my house everyone is from middle upper-middle class backgrounds.

She explained that they could control class background through their strong system of alumni recommendations. Alumni contacted acquaintances in potential member's communities and prepared a folder on each girl, including information on father's occupation, religious affiliation, and high school activities. Such alumni involvement varied widely, and was directly related to the sororities' national status. In "top" houses recommendations were essential. "Midrange" houses still required "recs" but were more willing to find an alumna to meet with unknown, but desired, potential members. The lowest status houses did not require alumni recommendations at all.

A member of a less prestigious, but middle-range sorority assessed her situation:

> If a girl is looking for a glamour house, she isn't going to be happy here. . . . We don't have any raving beauties in this house, but we don't have any really homely girls either.

One officer in a relatively low-status house distinguished her sorority from one at the "bottom of the barrel."[3]

> "AAA" has really big girls (she made a gesture indicating robust hips). They get the "rejects." Isn't that a terrible word, but that is what they're called.

What each sorority girl learns through this rush process is that the important ingredients for a woman's success, *for her own success*, are physical attractiveness, social skills, and social class.

GOING GREEK: IMPLICATIONS FOR SELF-IDENTITY

The sorority pledged during rush determines the group of girls and boys with which each individual will spend the next four years of her life. "Status" fraternities intermingle with "status" sororities, and rarely with middle-range sororities. The status differences between sororities are obvious, known to potential members, and nationally consistent. A "top" sorority is one with national recognition, and not coincidentally, the members are either pretty or wealthy, and preferably both. Sororities maintain their status by expending considerable time, effort, and money to stage a "successful" rush. For a "successful" rush a sorority must attract the "best" (e.g., most attractive) pledges available to them. Each house must present an image attractive to the members they desire.

Thus, image projection is the essence of rush. And the image that sells sororities to potential members is sexual attractiveness to men. The skits sororities perform during rush parties are often overtly sexual, scantily dressed girls sing "let us entertain you" with pelvic thrusting in cadence to music. The projection of sexuality is consciously designed but so is the limit to such an image. During a rehearsal for rush, a sorority president and impromptu choreographer remarked about a skit:

> It comes across as too much sex, especially after the last act; sexy is okay, it's good, but we are not running a whorehouse.

There is a conscious desire to portray coy sexuality – attractiveness – without suggesting "cheapness." Sexy mannerisms are used as bait, assuring the green first-year student that she too, will become cool, hip, and sexually attractive to men if she pledges their sorority.

The sorority a girl joins has serious consequences for her self-image. One pledge described how rush had affected many of her friends and, implicitly, herself.

> If they don't make it into a top house they are devastated. Away from home for the first time, and being alone. To have someone or some group you respect tell you you're not good enough for them can be devastating if you don't have any well formed self-identity . . . you kind of look at a skit and say, "Am I like that?"

One pledge graphically described this scene, reported by nearly every respondent:

> There was a lot of pain involved. . . . Girls that didn't get asked back to a house they
> wanted would go around crying and screaming.

Neither of these girls had been invited to join the sorority of her choice. Rush can be painful, especially for girls not invited to join the sorority they desire. New members are correct in their assumption that the sorority they pledge will delineate their future opportunities. Placement in the Greek status hierarchy effectively defines the significant others with whom each individual will interact while in college. Just as surely as labels and self-fulfilling stereotypes are attached to deviant actors (e.g., Schur, 1971), they are attached to the "kind of girls" in different sororities. These labels are an integral part of the Greek social fabric, believed by those around each girl, and consequently, by herself. Schur discusses how a "deviator" tends to get "caught up" in his deviant role; change the pronouns and this description is equally applicable to the sorority stereotypes. Individuals begin

> to find that it (i.e., the role or label) has become highly salient in his overall personal
> identity, that his behavior is increasingly organized "around" the role, and that
> cultural expectations attached to the role have come to have precedence, or increased
> salience relative to other expectations in the organization of his activities and general
> way of life [Schur, 1971: 69].

Sorority girls are treated as typifications of their organizations: "glamour girls, ice boxes, prudes, or nice but ordinary." They begin to see themselves as truly "fitting in" to their sororities. From this process of internalizing group expectations there emerges a modified self.

An illustration of organizational prestige setting parameters for personal interaction—and subsequently self-image—involves two sophomores who transferred to the university as a couple after spending their first year at a small college nearby. The respondent and her boyfriend went through rush and she recalled their experiences.

> He pledged a really top fraternity. He was really upset when he found out I'd pledged
> BBB. He even told me he was embarrassed to come pick me up at the house, because
> his brothers would see him. He didn't tell me, but I know, his brothers started asking
> him why he was going out with a BBB when he could get a CCC or DDD, like they
> all dated. With that much social pressure, he probably started wondering why he
> was dating a BBB. I thought we were above that kind of thing (she wiped a tear
> away discreetly, pretending it was dust).

This girl's worth had been reevaluated based upon her organizational affiliation. When asked how the relationship was doing, she quickly added, "We broke up." The respondent, at the time of this interview, was dating someone from a middle-range fraternity.

The consolation for girls in low-status sororities, particularly those labeled "rejects," is that their group has its own account of reality. People in status houses are considered to be "snobs" and foolishly preoccupied with fashion. Despite pejorative accounts of "status" houses, girls date up whenever possible. Individuals and sororities as collectives seek to improve their status ranking by attracting higher status boys. The example above demonstrates, however, the limitations to this strategy; low-status girls rarely date "top" boys, but they may have more success with midrange fraternity boys.

Girls are ranked initially by their sorority affiliation, which depends to a large extent on attractiveness to men. Their second opportunity to raise personal status also depends on attractiveness to boys, this time more directly. These girls are learning that their success depends not upon personal achievement in school or sports, but upon their relationship to boys.

COURTSHIP PATTERNS: ASYMMETRIC GENDER ROLES

The dating system, however, accomplished more that status ranking or mate seeking. Courtship patterns teach individuals what is appropriate during cross-sex interaction. Dating game rules are clearly different for each sex. The underlying norms and official rules for male-female interaction within the Greek social world are consistent: sororities act *in loco parentis*: fraternities do not. Different rules for boys and girls are accepted by all as both natural and inevitable. The regulations put forth by alumni, but enforced by peer pressure and monetary fines, are based on a traditional ideology of gender roles. Under the *formal* rules, it is the male's place to invite the female. He is the aggressor, she the pursued.

The girls exchange the right to be guests for the right to initiate interactions. Fraternity-sorority exchanges – organized mixers – are always held in fraternities and usually paid for by the boys. Sorority girls give many accounts for this: Sorority houses are elegant and might be damaged during a rowdy party; liquor is not allowed in sorority houses and is ever-present at Greek social occasions despite most members being under age; and, couples cannot find privacy in a sorority since boys are not allowed above the first floor, while girls are always welcome in fraternity rooms.

Sorority girls also reliquish control over their situation. For example, alumni control the physical setting, and thus, they "manage the props" used in everyday interpersonal interaction. One high status sorority was redecorating and the girls desired some input. A student representative was allowed to attend the decorating committee's meetings, but students and alumni agreed that since the alumni had raised the money, they would decide its use. In addition, the girls currently living in the house would be gone within four years while the house itself would remain. This particular house was slightly more extravagant than others, although all were plush. Typically, the first floor of a sorority house is decorated elegantly with a baby grand piano in the main living room, thick, light-ly colored carpets, and framed watercolors, not a good place for rowdy students. The props—furniture, color scheme, ambience—are designed for quiet, neat, polite "young ladies." In contrast, fraternity houses have linoleum floors or wall-to-wall carpets and sturdy furniture easily removed for parties; the props here are arranged for young men who become wild, rowdy, and knock things over when drunk.

Although boys overtly control exchanges, girls are able to use the leverage available to them through their social chairman.[4] Her most important task is to subtly suggest exchanges to appropriate boys. The social chairman of a small house consciously trying to raise its reputation by having exchanges with higher status fraternities explained her duties this way:

> If I know someone in a house I particularly want to have an exchange with I nudge him . . . to have his social chairman call me.

Although this social chairman had never considered calling a fraternity herself, at least one social chairman from another sorority had made such advances. The general consensus was that only girls in very low status houses would need to "resort" to calling fraternities.

One pledge not pleased with her sororities' social chairman had set her sights on the job. And she had strong ideas about the post.

> A good social chairman will get around. She'll go to different parties and have dates with guys from good frats, and subtly mention that they should get together sometime in an exchange. There are subtle ways, the way women always have power.

The president of this pledge's house explained that it was only "natural" to wait for the boys to call because "the guys pay for everything, after all." The boy's monetary expenditures give them power with its accompanying privileges. They have bought control over the very occurrence of every organized encounter.

The official rules governing male-female interaction reflect assumptions for traditional sex-specific gender roles. What is appropriate for boys, freedom to ful-ly participate and to make their own decisions concerning alcohol consumption and sex, is totally inappropriate for girls. It is obvious that both girls and boys are involved in drinking and sex. The difference is that girls shroud such ac-tivities in "discretion" and concern for reputation. Within the Greek world view this makes sense. A woman's looks and reputation are keys to her success.

This dual system of norms for exchanges, officially endorsed by the Greek system, permeates all facets of male-female interactions, even outside the institutional setting. The sentiment was similar whether the hypothetical situation involved the social chairman initiating an exchange or an individual girl initiating a date:

> The girls feel they'd rather not go out than to have to ask to be taken . . . it is really scorned.

The idea of taking someone out themselves is beyond these girls' perception of the possible; going out, but not being taken is a paradox not befitting their role as desirable sorority "coeds."

The appearance of "being taken out," even if the reality is different, often is important. One pledge recounted a conversation in the women's room of a downtown restaurant. Each of four girls had invited a date to the "pledge dance," an institutionalized girl-ask-boy evening.[5] Before the dance, the four couples went to dinner. In true Sadie Hawkins Day fashion, the girls were responsible for the tab. The following is a conversation recounted by the one girl who felt comfortable paying for her date.

> The [other] girls asked me if I gave my date money for the dinner. I said, "Of course not." It was my money, and I was going to pay for the dinner. They said they had all given their dates the thirty dollars for dinner on the way over in the car telling them that they weren't that liberated.

There was absolute consensus that under normal circumstances girls did not pay for dates, although couples going steady might occasionally go "dutch treat." Likewise, female initiated dates were not considered appropriate. One girl suggested that although females sometimes initiate dates:

> It isn't direct. I mean you've got to be subtle or else it scares the guys. Plus it's always better when the guy makes the first move. . . . It's just more proper. I think the other girls look down on girls who, oh, let's say, ask guys out on dates. They kind of look desperate. I guess, I mean, it just doesn't look very good, not only for the girls but for the sorority too.

This concern about personal and collective reputation was a predominant theme in discussions of dating and sexuality.

The regulations and informal norms of the Greek system institutionalize traditional gender role values. The girls trade the luxury of being guests for the right to initiate or direct cross-sex interaction. Girls learn the more subtle "feminine" ways to exert power over their lives, and they learn these are the "proper" strategies to use. The sorority girls internalize the values explicitly endorsed in the formal rituals. They believe it "only natural" to want males to lead and to depend on boys for personal status and self-esteem.

If it is an organizational goal to train girls to be wives whose access to power is subtle and indirect, and to train boys to be heads of households, then the organizations' regulations are both relevant and effective. If the girls' collective or individual goals differ from this implicit organizational ideology, then these regulations may be dysfunctional.

INSTITUTIONALIZED FRIENDSHIP: PRIORITIES AND SISTERHOOD

Numerous sorority rituals are designed to encourage solidarity among members. Rush is used as an opportunity to "pull the house together," as well as to select new members. First year "pledge" classes often have a weekend retreat to get to know one another. In many sororities all the pledges live in one large room filled with bunk beds. Although this arrangement is a direct result of over-crowding, the ideological rationalization involves increasing solidarity among pledges.

The quality of friendships that develop in sororities was a source of disagreement among respondents. Some girls were quite satisfied with their female friendships; others were openly disappointed. For many girls, female friendships were not important enough to merit much discussion. Although the satisfaction levels vary tremendously, the descriptive accounts of relationships between girls were remarkably similar.

One officer, very involved with her sorority and quite satisfied with her friendships, expressed "love" for all her sisters, and explained the substance of these relationships in detail after some probing.

> I mean that whenever I don't have a date with my boyfriend, or anyone else, then I am likely to ask my sisters to do something before I bother calling someone else.

Another respondent described the situation similarly, but with bitter and con-scious disillusionment:

> Around here no one makes plans together, of course, until the last minute if no date has turned up. You should watch the Friday night scene here between 7:00 and 9:00 o'clock. The girls left around at the end decide to do something together or stay in their rooms. Whereas I make plans to see my close friends, for most of these girls their friends are around them all the time. They walk to classes together, talk about what classes they are going to take, meet here or there to walk between classes together. They do things together in that sense all the time, but they don't make plans together.

Not surprisingly, this girl moved out of her sorority during the course of this research. She was concerned not with the actual time sorority sisters spend together, but the priority given to that time. Two other respondents, both of whom remained active in their sororities, actually scheduled time with female friends. Both recognized that they were atypical.

There is general agreement among those satisfied and disillusioned with the situation that female friendships are less important than relationships with boys. Descriptions of girl-to-girl relationships were remarkably similar, although respondents suggest the description was true for everyone but themselves. The adjective consistently used to describe one another is "catty." The vice-president of a small house went so far as to suggest that backstabbing and cattiness were the definitive:

> I am not into the sorority part of it. The finding of a husband, stabbing each other in the back for boyfriends, all the cattiness.

There seemed to be widespread dissatisfaction with this facet of sorority life, but no sign of attempts to change these interaction patterns.

Despite the term sorority meaning "sisterhood," neither the phrase itself nor the concept holds much appeal for today's sorority girl. The women's movement emphasis on sisterhood and female solidarity is not central to sorority members' world view.

The low priority assigned to female friendship and the acceptance of "catty" behavior as unavoidable lends credence to Giallombardo's (1966) argument that woman-to-woman relationships are based on "calculated solidarity." In her study of female-female relationships in a federal penitentiary, Giallombardo suggests that, because a woman's future is determined by her success in the marriage market female companions are seen primarily as rivals, even in single-sex institutions. Giallombardo (1966: 15) defined "calculated solidarity" as

> a social unity based not on automatic conformity to a set of common social norms perceived to be morally binding, but rather a unity which is subject to constant reinterpretation . . . as she perceives each situation from the point of view of her own interest.

This analysis seems particularly appropriate to the Greek world, where the girls vie against each other for what they perceive as a finite set of high-status fraternity boys. The "cattiness" and "back-stabbing" described by sorority girls indicates the precariousness of female bonds within sororities. Unity is desired and expected, unless it interferes with the more salient process of dating, in which case each actor calculates her best interests.

DISCUSSION

The official regulations and unofficial norms that determine male-female interactions in the Greek system function to "create" women with traditional goals and desires. As one respondent suggested, sorority girls are in the process of learning to be women. The Greek system serves as their primary reference group for the first few years that they are free from direct parental control. The behavioral patterns encouraged in this setting function effectively as mechanisms for traditional gender role socialization. One senior described her criteria for a spouse when questioned about her *own* future plans:

> Let me see, a professional college grad with a good job. You know security is important. He doesn't have to be fantastic looking, but tall, dark, and handsome wouldn't hurt . . . two cars, a boat, a lake cabin. You know, your basic upper-middle class life.

Most girls desire to have a career, before and after raising children. There was universal agreement that mothers ought to stay home with their children, that women's careers must be designed so as not to interfere with homemaking responsibilities. This girl's discussion of her own hopes represents the general consensus.

> I hope I won't have to work before all my kids are in school. . . . Little kids need a mother and I'd like to center my attention on being a good mother, instead of a part-time one. I mean, if you have to work then, you know, what can you do? Nothing. But like I said, I hope I won't have to. I'll let my husband handle the income part.

The two respondents with less traditional desires were quite discouraged about alternative possibilities. One junior, an officer in a large and prestigious sorority who had taken a women's studies course, suggested that an egalitarian, dual career marriage was merely a utopian dream. She knew no boys who would consider sharing homemaking and child rearing responsibilities. This dream, which she admitted was *her* dream, might be an option for her daughters or granddaughters. This girl had accepted the reality that if she wanted a family, and she did, she must become a homemaker.

It is entirely another question as to whether sororities are creating women to fill positions that actually exist in contemporary society, the upper-middle class homemaker, or whether such roles are becoming anachronistic. As Bernard (1972) has noted, women have traditionally married into a standard of living. These girls are acutely aware that marriage is a means of upward mobility, or of retaining their class status. If these girls' lives do, indeed, depend on their success in the marriage market, then calculated solidarity (disloyalty to women in rivalry for husbands) may be for them a rational strategy. It seems unlikely, however, that contemporary sorority girls emerge from college with the social or psychological skills necessary for active participation in the competitive, professional, contemporary labor force for which they are presumably being trained while at the university.

This is not to suggest that none of these young women will become surgeons, lawyers, or executives; only that the selves they have nurtured while

in college will need considerable reorganization if and when they enter demanding occupational social worlds. Without longitudinal data it is impossible to
determine the long-term effects of sorority life.

More than thirty years ago Mirra Komarovsky (1946) identified contradictions in female gender roles that remain descriptive of the respondents in this
study. During times of social change, cultural norms may deter individuals from
courses of action that would serve their own and society's best interests. According to Komarovsky, college women in the 1940s were presented with two
mutually exclusive roles: the "feminine" role and the "modern" model. This latter
role was essentially the "career woman" model. Komarovsky (1946: 184) writes:

> The goals set by each role are mutually exclusive and the fundamental personality
> traits each evokes are at points diametrically opposed, so that what were assets for
> one become liabilities for the other, and the full realization of one role threatens
> defeat in the other.

It seems that the Greek system assures that these roles remain in conflict. The
Greek system functions to ensure that boys and girls leave college with different
and complementary social skills, goals, and gender roles.

Not every respondent was the "prototypical" sorority girl described in this
study: a few planned time with female friends, one dated a non-Greek boy, two
considered lifetime careers, and one secretly lived with her boyfriend. These exceptions, however, illustrate the strength of the Greek normative system by
displaying the counternormative nature of these "abnormal" behaviors. The
woman living with her boyfriend, for example, once discovered, was asked to
resign her office on "moral" grounds and did so, agreeing with the legitimate need
for her sorority to protect its good reputation.

The question of causality arises when discussing the creation of traditional
gender roles. It may be that traditionally oriented girls seek sorority life because
it is consistent with their normative ideologies. Although this is certainly the
case for some, it is not applicable to many of the girls in this study. Most had
joined sororities for a place to belong in a large and often frightening university.
All sought the comfort of a *gemeinschaft* community, especially one with a
guaranteed social life and approved by their parents. Even more to the point,
however, is that people change as they move into new circumstances. College
students are often exposed to ideas and life-styles they would not have encountered at home. An eighteen-year-old girl is not imprinted "traditional" for
life; the experiences she has and the people with whom she interacts will contribute to her continuously evolving sense of self. What happens to sorority girls
however, is that they are shielded from alternative perspectives by the comfortable, conservative Greek world. The two respondents who considered combining demanding careers with motherhood felt that their desires were "incompatible" in today's world, that world organized from within their Greek perspective.

Finally, there is an interesting issue yet to be addressed. How is it that the Greek world remains relatively insulated from the changes in women's roles that have been heralded over the last two decades? The sororities discussed in this article exist in an era in which books and movies concerning gender role changes are nationally acclaimed, and women have begun to enter professional ranks in business and academia. An explanation for this apparent continuity can perhaps be found by closely analyzing the types of interaction that dominate life in the Greek social world.

In a discussion of social change, Hewitt (1979) suggests that interaction can be described as either routine or problematic. To the extent that behavior is problematic and conduct is thus impeded, self-conscious reflectiveness arises leading to the negotiation of new behavioral patterns. To the extent, however, that behavior is institutionalized routinely and all participants share identical perspectives and expectations, interaction flows smoothly and change is more rare.

The abundance of institutionalized routine behavior in the Greek social world may help to account for the continuance of traditional gender role patterns. The Greek system successfully retards change by routinizing and institutionalizing male-female interaction and by restricting participants to those individuals who accept Greek social norms. Those that do not, resign, thus ensuring the smoothness of expected interaction. Although even routine interaction always includes some problematic components, the Greek social structure seems to minimize the nonroutine and thus to discourage social change.

What the future holds for these girls is not evident. Most want traditional lives, to be mothers and homemakers, to have careers when and if that is convenient. Yet, the world they must enter after graduation is changing. How many of their spouses will be able to afford, on one young professional's income, the lifestyle these girls expect? For many of these girls, working outside the home will be an economic necessity. Others may decide they desire to work outside their homes, once they have spent some time in them. In either case, the priorities these girls have set, and the selves they have nurtured while in the Greek system, may prove quite inappropriate in the world they must enter when they grow up.

NOTES

1. "Girl" is used advisedly. Sorority members refer to themselves as "girls, sorority girls." "Sorority women" is used to indicate alumni. College-aged sorority members perceive themselves as girls, legitimately subjected to quasi-parental supervision.

2. In order to rank each organization's institutional prestige within the Greek system, questionnaires were distributed to sociology classes. The questionnaires merely listed every sorority and students were asked to indicate the "top three and bottom three

houses." The consensus was quite high at both ends of the spectrum. The prestige rank-ings were also consistent with alumni reports.

3. Fraternity and sorority initials are entirely fictitious. Each time a different organization is referred to in a quotation it has been named alphabetically. Hence, the first sorority is referred to as "AAA," the second as "BBB," and so on. Any resemblance bet-ween these fictitious names and real organizations is entirely accidental.

4. The word "chairman" is the term used by sorority members themselves.

5. The very existence of an institutionalized girl-ask-boy evening is strong, supporting data for the hypothesis that courtship is an asymmetrical process in the Greek system. Boys asking girls for dates is so taken-for-granted that girls need a formal, organizationally approved justification for initiating dates, which under other circumstances would clearly be counternormative behavior.

REFERENCES

Bernard, J. (1972) The Future of Marriage. New York: Bantam.

Gerth, H. and C. Wright Mills (1953) "Institutions and persons," in Jerome G. Manis and Bernard N. Metlzer (eds.) Symbolic Interaction: A Reader in Social Psychology. Boston: Allyn & Bacon.

Giallombardo, R. (1966) Society of Women: A Study of Women's Prisons. New York: John Wiley.

Goffman, E. (1961a) Encounters. Indianapolis: Bobbs-Merrill.

———(1961b) Asylums. Garden City, NY: Doubleday.

Hewitt, J. (1979) Self and Society. A Symbolic Interactionist Social Psychology. Boston: Allyn & Bacon.

Komarovsky, M. (1946) "Cultural contradictions and sex roles."Amer. J. of Sociology 52, 3: 184.

Reiss, I. (1965) "Social class and campus dating." Social Problems 13 (Fall).

Schur, E.M. (1971) Labeling Deviant Behavior. New York: Harper & Row.

Scott, J.F. (1965) "The American college sorority: its role in class and ethnic en-dogamy." Amer. Soc. Rev.

Shibutani, T. (1955) "Reference groups as perspectives." Amer. J. of Sociology 60: 562-569.

Turner, J.H. (1978) "Symbolic interactionism and social organization," in Jerome G. Manis and Bernard N. Meltzer (eds.) Symbolic Interaction: A Reader in Social Psychology. Boston: Allyn & Bacon.

Waller, W. (1937) "The rating and dating complex." Amer. Soc. Rev. 2 (October): 727-734).

Chapter 8

Biography Building to Insure the Future: Women's Negotiation of Gender Relevancy in Medical School*

Judith M. Hammond

In this paper I focus on how women in their first year of medical school build biographies of fitness as a means of negotiating the status of peer in a male-dominated group. Their goal is to negotiate a master status and primary identity as medical student. They do this by making gender, a key characteristic, both irrelevant and relevant. I also discuss the technique of using interview data to provide a particular perspective on the medical students' situation and their use of the interview as a vehicle for identity building. I conclude that women's apparent status in maintaining identities as successful people and in negotiating barriers to the collegial status stem both from their numbers and from using situationally appropriate vocabularies of motives to build past and future biographies of fitness.

INTRODUCTION

Male professions have been organized by and for men. When females enter the scene, men are not used to relating to women as colleagues. Hughes (1945) has discussed the dilemmas that status contradictions create for members of a profession when women and blacks seek admission to such collegial fraternities. Blacks and females are anomalies. They are people who, even though they have the credentials for membership, are the wrong

*This is a revised version of a paper presented at the American Sociological Association Meetings, San Francisco, California, September 1978. Lawrence Radine provided invaluable stimuli to my thinking in developing the argument. I thank him, Barrie Thorne, Muriel Berkeley, Lillian Bauder, Ted Borhek, and Jerry L.L. Miller for their criticisms. Data collection was supported in part by the Health Studies Program at Syracuse University. Support while writing this paper was provided by NIMH Training Grant No. 2T 32-14598-03SS and the Center for Research on Social Organization of the University of Michigan.

Source: Judith M. Hammond, "Biography Building to Insure the Future: Women's Negotiation of Gender Relevancy in Medical School." Symbolic Interaction 3 (Fall, 1980): 35-50. Reprinted by permission of JAI Press, Inc., Greenwich, Conn.

social type. Such social types are not easily fitted into the society of colleagues who relate to one another with similar background assumptions and a host of largely taken-for-granted and mutually familiar ways.

The problem, however, is not only that these social types are new and unusual, but that their traits are defined by the professional membership as a hinderance: race and gender indicate qualities or characteristics which make them unfit for doing professional work. Notions of fitness or appropriateness are used as criteria for admission and to support standards of work performance. These notions of fitness support the exclusion of women and racial and ethnic minorities from training in white male professions.[1]

In the case of medicine, based on the profession's notions of gender fitness, women's exclusion leaves more than mere remnants of those official notions with which today's women must contend. Notions of gender fitness and the organiza-tion of work in which they are intermeshed create a situation in which the burden of proof remains on women's shoulders to convince their male counter-parts of their ability and right to be colleagues. Kanter (1977), following Simmel (1950), points out that pressures to act in certain ways to compensate for the dynamics of tokenism become less necessary as the ratio of minority social types increases. The proportion will affect interaction, and integration into the group may be enhanced as the ratio of minority types increases beyond tokenism.

But more than relative numbers affect interaction. When large numbers of women enter a male domain, the participants must determine appropriate ac-tions (deeds and language) with which and through which they will develop and maintain a relationship. They must close a kind of credibility gap by determining past and present conditions for a joint future. They come to an agreement on proffered biographies.

The language or vocabulary of motives used in building one's biography is a vehicle through which people seek to develop or maintain their public identities and statuses. Vocabularies of motives in Mills' (1940) terms serve to support current and future actions. At the same time, the language used gives private and personal support to a person's own self-image or identity.

How people, both tellers and listeners, use and understand vocabularies of motives in maintaining or negotiating a relationship, has been the focus of a number of conceptual formulations regarding language use. Scott and Lyman (1968) discuss the use of the form account by those who have done something inappropriate and who must create a biography which repairs a fractured rela-tionship. Stokes and Hewitt (1976) discuss aligning actions in which people in problematic situations attempt to align their actions with cultural norms or the perceived relevance of those norms. What is important in these formulations is the agreed-upon acceptability of the language in use and of the identities or rela-tionships for which the negotiators are aiming. The situation must be rather routine for a situated-regularized-agreed-upon vocabulary to have developed.[2]

In this paper I focus on a situation in which there is disagreement as to the desired relationship. I focus on how women build biographies of fitness to negotiate the relationship of peers in the first year of medical school. I then discuss the technique of using interview data to provide a particular perspective on the students' situation and their use of the interview as a vehicle for identity building. After presenting a situation in which women's admission to a collegial status is questionable, I present the way in which women go about biography building to negotiate the status they want. I conclude that women's apparent success in this class stems from using situationally appropriate vocabularies of motives to build past and future biographies, and that the ratio of women to men is a necessary condition for success. I conclude, in addition, that women's acts of biography building serve both to change and to maintain official notions of gender fitness.

SUBJECTS, SITUATION, AND METHODOLOGICAL PERSPECTIVE

Medical students in this study attended a northeastern state university which I call a common name: Medical Center. Forty-eight of the 120 students in the first-year class participated; 28 of the 35 women agreed to be interviewed; a random sample of the men (N = 20) was included. Women made up approximately 30 percent of the class. This proportion was above the national figure (27 percent) in 1974–75 when the students began school. The ratio of women to men (30:70) in the Medical Center class approximated what Kanter (1977) has termed a tilted ratio (35:65) of minority to dominant social types. All students were in the basic sciences curriculum in which they took en masse the same course sequence and laboratory work. The data are from 100 hours of conversation with students in open-ended interviews. Taped interviews generated 2,000 pages of typed manuscript. For more detail see Hammond (1977).

In open-ended interviews people have freedom to bring into the discussion important issues in their lives. As they talk about their situation, the themes of their lives together emerge. For the Medical Center students the themes revolved around solving a common set of problems. The common problems were defined as the necessities which must be satisfied to survive successfully the first year of medical school. Students were concerned with the solutions to the problem of becoming what they called "capable, serious medical students."[3] Such students are acceptable as "colleagues" and are potentially "good physicians." In addition, necessity was defined as the need to maintain some resemblance of being a "normal human being." The content of the collective set of data is an information set about the way one group of students defined necessity and constructed biographies which served to build public and personal identities supporting their courses of action.

Students viewed me as a sympathetic listener. In this interview situation I became a part of the audience for identity building. With few exceptions the students were willing participants who frequently thanked *me* for talking with them. Students' expressions of their experience of the passage from college student to medical student varied in intensity. Some expressed relief at having had a chance to talk with an outsider about their experiences, and all viewed the situation as one in which they could present "my point of view" or the "way I see things." The data are corroborated by both sexes. Both men and women were able to report the men's actions and language vis-a-vis the women; both men and women reported the women's actions and language vis-a-vis the men.

THE SITUATION IN SCHOOL

All new medical students believe they must present appropriate characteristics (credentials, motivation, skills) in the form of appropriate biographies to become accepted as members-in-training. These characteristics are expressed through appropriate past and future biographies which students (male and female) define as crucial for gaining admission to medical school. In addition, these biographies are crucial for gaining acceptance as peers among class members and in maintaining one's personal identity as both a capable student and "a normal human being."

Claims and credentials for competency as a medical student must include *past actions* and *future prospects*. Peer acceptance is negotiated among students not only by presenting credentials, scores, and skills, but by building biographies of past and future motives which are acceptable in supporting claims to the "capable, serious medical student" status. Past and future motives become important keys to interpreting others' present actions and supporting one's own identity in the medical school context of enormous threats to self-concept.

Even though women have backgrounds, skills, and motivation to gain admission, women's past and future biographies are perceived as different by their male counterparts. Men, using gender as one criterion to peer acceptance, qualify their relationship to the women, who desire a "collegial" or equal status.

THE MEDICAL SCHOOL RITE OF PASSAGE

The intensive medical school program is a leveling out process in which one identity becomes paramount for new initiates (Dornbusch, 1955). Successful initiates become "capable, serious medical students." Becoming such a student requires closing a credibility gap which determines how willing students are to accept another as a "serious student." The acceptance as a "serious student" provides peer support and strengthens self-concept in the intensely threatening first few weeks and months of school. Becoming a good student, however, involves developing a strategy of action. This process begins *before* the profession's official socialization process begins. Medical school applicants learn as undergraduates the appropriate strategy of acts and appropriate language with which they negotiate with admissions committees. The strategy used to get into school is to build biographies of past performance and future intentions which show they are exceptional candidates for the profession. This includes, in the words of one student,

> Studying hard and getting good grades, and making sure you get to know your professors so you can get good recommendations, and getting some outside activities so you'll look well-rounded. And writing a good essay.

The strategy is to use a language that builds a biography showing an inordinately high level of motivation and potential as a physician. If the applicant is a woman, the strategy in biography building must also include "making sure you know, as a woman, how you're going to conduct your life as a woman once you get into medical school."

ENCOUNTERING COLLEGIAL DISBELIEF

Men students have a number of basic strategies, based on notions of gender fitness, of doubting the competency and motives of women. By questioning women students' biographies, their pasts and futures, men attempt to cast[4] them into a less-than-typical-medical-student-because-you-are-female status. By doubting women's histories of skills, activities, and motives and by doubting their future potential, men classmates make gender salient to current status. Through men's language an historical key to admission into the medical profession, gender, becomes a key in everyday interaction to women's desired collegial status.

Among men students there are five typical ways in which women are cast into identities based on presumptions about gender. These are: 1) expressing no understanding of why a woman would want to be a physician; 2) questioning women's skills, experiences, credentials; 3) casting women into specific feminine roles such as husband-hunter, potential sex partner, cute girl; 4) expecting women to enter fields traditionally appropriate for women; and 5) questioning women's practical potential. This complex of questions adds up to what the women students called "not being taken seriously."

No Understanding
Men doubt women's commitment to medicine and question their interest in medicine and science. By expressing no understanding of why a woman would

want to be a physician, men are signaling that women are not as motivated as the typical medical student ought to be.

> It seems that their interests, naturally, are different [from the guys] . . . in general the girls can be more interested in things other than medicine.
>
> Nick

The questioning of women's motivation often takes the form of questioning women's career choice. This is done by asking women why they chose medicine instead of some less demanding profession. Judy A.'s comments below are typical of the conversations reported by the women:

> I think most of the men students in the class don't think women should go into medicine," Judy A. said about this. "I've found very few . . . guys that were liberated. . . . They . . . find it very hard to understand why any woman would want to be in medicine. . . . It bothers me that somebody would wonder why you want to be a doctor if they want to be a doctor. I mean, like couldn't you have the same motivations that they do? I had one friend that I got into a big argument with one night, and he said, 'Why don't you just be a dentist? Like you'll have more time to yourself.' And I said, 'Would you want to be a dentist?' And he'd go, 'No,' and then I said, 'Then why should I want to be a dentist? . . . I'm going to be a doctor!' They can't understand that, you know. . . . This guy had this theory . . . if you're a woman, obviously you're going to be the one to bring up the kids. . . . You know, maternal instinct and all that? Like you shouldn't spend all your time being a doctor. You can't do both. Well, that's what most of them think: you can't do both.

Skills and Credentials

A second strategy used in doubting women's fitness is to question their histories of skills, credentials, and experiences. Men use these doubts to interpret women's present performance as inadequate. Men such as Paul reported,

> The girls in the class don't have the science background that the man has . . . and they are having a harder time than a lot of the guys. In anatomy seven people failed and all seven were girls.

Or as Jim R. said,

> I think the admissions committee loused it up. . . . I know of five girls in our class that graduated from college with under a 3.0 average.

Feminine Roles

A third strategy is to attempt to cast women into some type of social or sexual relationship:

A lot of the men think of women as sex symbols and not as very effective people. . . .
The guys in the class approach the girls . . . joking and making fun of the girls. . . .
Take, for example, like, a girl will be wearing a new pair of pants. There will always
be some . . . remark.

Paul

"'Oh she's a cute girl . . . isn't she nice,'" reported Meg about this type of interaction, "and I can't stand it, I hate it." Meg goes on to describe how the men
first attempted to relate to the women: socially, rather than as serious medical
students.

. . . I think a lot of them . . . with another man can sit down and do serious work.
With a woman they can have a nice time and study, if you can sort of see the difference. Like you know, I have guy friends that I study with . . . but I think we just
had a nice time together. He likes me because I'm charming and I can talk about other
things besides medicine . . . but he, you know, wouldn't study with me because I had
something to offer him. It's not like I can help him with physiology. And I think that's
how it is with a lot of women.

Appropriate Fields
A fourth way of not treating women as serious medical students is to act as
if their feminine qualities may allow them a "special role" "appropriate" to some
types of patients.

I think women might have a sensitivity, let's say, towards female patients, that a male
physician wouldn't.

Phil

Laura S., who is interested in opthalmology reported:

I'm not interested in just only being a pediatrician, which is the first thing that people
ask me.

Practice Potential
And a fifth strategy is to question women's practice potential.

The only problem with the women being in medicine is that, if she wants to raise a
family and becomes pregnant, then she has to take time out. . . .

Dave

They are awfully limited, said Nick.
Could you describe what you mean by a limited role, I asked.
I mean not so demanding a specialty. A specialty that isn't as time
consuming . . . a faculty member said women have no place in medicine, as well as

diabetics, people with cerebral palsy [or] anyone with a shorter life expectance . . .
before they get to medical school.
Women have a long life expectancy, I put in.
No, but women take out time for childbirth. So their medical life is shortened by
children.
Is that the faculty members' opinion, or yours? I asked.
It's my opinion.

"Wanting to be taken seriously," the women did not accept being cast by
men classmates as less-than-serious students, or as people who will be limited in
their medical careers by family obligations and/or women's interests. The effect
of men's questioning is to cast women into a marginal status, perpetuating
gender as a barrier for women by casting them into a double-bind position. If
women accept the identity of "girl-in-school" or "liberated career woman," then
there is something abnormal about them for not wanting a traditional family life.
If they are normal enough to want a traditional home life, they are cast as potential dropouts from the profession. In either case they have usurped some man's
rightful place in school. An ambivalent status is not an equal one. And either of
the two statuses finds women unfit as colleagues. How do the women deal with
this potential no-win situation?

First, they refuse to be cast into an identity, or status, which is less than
"the rest of the class" (the men). When men cast women into a particular identity as unfit for medical pursuits, men assume identities for themselves as those
who are fit. Women refuse the relationship offered based on gender fitness and
offer another one instead.

A woman medical student, for example, when requested by a male medical
student to explain to him, "why a girl would want to go into medicine," refuses
to be cast as a "girl in medical school" and uses language in which she assumes
the identity of a "medical student like every other medical student." She refuses
the question and casts her classmate into the identity of student relating to student. If she wants to be a colleague, she will insist that he take on the identity of
one and she will assume that identity for herself.

> "It's definitely a professional type of air about them," Izzy said about this part of the
> women's strategy. "And that's definitely the kind of person that a doctor should be,
> you know? Very professional in everything. Everything! . . . You know, so that as far
> as other men in the class are concerned, the women treat them as professional col-
> leagues. I mean . . . anything else beyond that the girls turn off to. . . . I know of a few
> men who wish that the female medical students were more responsive to them as
> women. . . . But I don't know of any girls who wished the men would be more respon-
> sive as men . . . I think they just want to be treated as equals."

At issue here is under what circumstances can this process actually be
turned around by people who do not agree with the identities offered by others?

The questions of male classmates are attempts to impute motives and biographies. The questions require responses from the women, but circumstances do not permit the women to say "bug off." Such a strategy is not yet an acceptable one to men in competitive professional settings, and to say "bug off" is not yet acceptable to most women in such settings either. The motive and work options for being successful in such a competitive program are very narrowly defined by the students. Taking on the *acceptable* medical student identity is to use *language* which enables others to grant that identity and confer peer status. The correct vocabulary of motives is a major requisite of peer acceptance. This acceptance, in addition, is an important aspect of being able to see oneself as a successful achiever. Achievement-oriented, ambitious young women who want to be seen and to see themselves as successful, work toward the peer relations they define as part of being successful. They respond to the men as peers, as medical students.

WOMEN'S BIOGRAPHIES

The complex of claims in a medical student's biography is important for acceptance among peers. Through their biographies medical students negotiate peer acceptance and build the self-confidence needed to continue in the rite of passage into the profession. For women there is, in addition, the work of having to make gender irrelevant in inter-personal relationships. They must work to prevent interactions which exclude them from full membership in the class or which chip away at their identities as ambitious and capable people. They use the language that all entering students have learned or are learning to use. Making the case that they are "no different from any other student," they refuse to be cast into a less than equal status by their male counterparts. At the same time women use language which makes their gender salient for their success, especially as practitioners. They develop a theme of their biographies as *women* and how being women assists success.

This dual strategy means that women use the agreed-upon language of medical students for biography building making themselves "no different:" 1) they present their skills and credentials; 2) they assert their motivation and desire for a challenging career; and in addition 3) they assert their right to be in school. Women also develop strategies for how "they will do it" *as women*: 1) if going into medicine is a challenge, then entering a male domain is also a challenge for them as women; 2) they point out women's special qualities, now needed in medicine, which they can contribute to patient care; and 3) they agree that men have a right to question their practice potential, but put off to the future the solution to combining career and marriage.

WOMEN USE THE AGREED-UPON
BIOGRAPHICAL STRATEGIES OF MEDICAL
STUDENTS: WOMEN ARE "NO DIFFERENT"

When women talk about their motivation and desire to become physicians and present their credentials in the form of grades and scores and experiences, they are acting and speaking in ways typical of first-year medical students. There is little difference from men in the biographies they build. Both women and men tell how they got interested in medicine, what they did to prepare themselves for admission, and the major reasons for wanting to become doctors.[5] They emphasize their experiences and *high* level of motivation. In fact, when women talk about being "no different" and that standards were not lowered for their admission, they have a strong case (Johnson and Dube, 1975).

Rights

In building biographies women insist they have "a right to become a physician" and a right to enter any specialty they wish. Women students do not see themselves as having a "place" in medicine or a "limited role" because they are female.

In claiming their right to become doctors, women begin to build biographies which demonstrate that they are "equal to men." *Their* interests and competencies will "determine" what they do. "I've never thought of myself as a woman applying . . . And I don't think of my role as a woman in medicine. I think women can do very well as physicians," said Judy M., who wants to go into family practice. "There is not a 'role' for me," stated Lynn, who hopes to go into administration, do research, and teach surgery. Irrespective of the kind of doctors they want to be, no one sees herself as "a woman in medicine." To negotiate an equal status with their male classmates, their claim to the right to be a doctor puts them on an equal footing with the men. It is hard to deny a claim to a woman's *right* to want to be a physician, even if her reasons or interests are perceived as different from men's.

Credentials

But the right to claim equality as a medical student can only be offered if the claim is supported by the requisite academic and experiential credentials. Men do not deny the right to want to be a physician, but men offer challenges to women's credentials at the beginning of the school year.

'The women were resented,' Meg's comments are typical, 'because the guys felt . . . there's sort of a reverse discrimination being practiced. That they're taking more women just because they're women. Guys *hate* that! You know, a lot of guys have said to me, 'I have a lot of friends who didn't get in with the same credentials as you. They took you 'cause you're a woman.' I was really pissed off . . . There are so many factors that go into it, you know? I went to a prestigious university. I just didn't go to Podunk U., you know!?'

In presenting their credentials, women work to make apparent differences unimportant. They claim the same credentials as men or, if they have fewer science courses or work-related experiences, they work to make credentials equivalent as Meg does above.

Motivation and Desire

To present themselves as highly motivated and motivated for the right reasons means to medical students that they *will* be good doctors and that they deserve to be in school. Part of the agreed-upon strategy in building their biographies is to build in the right kind of motivation.

Any person who deserves acceptance as a "capable, serious medical student" has to want to be one for the *right* reasons. Students want to "help people" or like "working with people." They want work that is "challenging" and "demanding," "not boring" but "full of variety," which provides "immediate rewards," and "immediate gratification." For them, the medical student who will become the good physician combines "a liking for science with a liking for people." And the personal motivation is strong; he or she, alone, made the decision to enter medicine for these reasons; parents "didn't push."

Students build biographies as altruistic, humanistic, and highly-motivated initiates, demonstrating a desire to acquire the skills and knowledge, and to take on the job of the physician. In addition, they also must want the authority. Their personalities are "not suited" to being "subordinates." For these students becoming physicians is "the best" they could do with their lives. It is "at the top" in service to others, personal rewards, complexity of skills, and in autonomy.

Added to the strength of their motivation is their willingness to undergo "sacrifices," that no one who has "not experienced it can understand." Howard makes this clear in the following comments:

> I thought I worked hard as an undergraduate. . . . I recently spoke with a fellow that's applying and I told him that I never would want to discourage him, but he'll have to experience how much he will sacrifice. Actually there's no telling anybody to the point where they really understand the amount of work in the next few years. . . . That's appalling. . . .

The sacrifices now are ones people are willing to make for future gain, as Laura G. points out:

> . . . you know, I'm normal. I'd love to go out. I'd love to go to the movies all of the time. You just can't do that. And, if you sacrifice, you might as well be sacrificing for something you really like. There's just so much work you have to get done for an ex-

am. . . . And I love what I'm doing. I mean, it's a love-hate relationship for sure, but in the end I love what I'm doing, so it makes it all worth it.

That they are motivated enough to make the sacrifices to meet the challenge, and even to like what they are doing, is a part of building biographies to gain confirmation from others and to support their own self-images.

When students build biographies they are building resources for getting through the program. These resources include membership in a collegial group and a positive self-concept. The highly-motivated medical student is one about whom classmates have no doubt that he or she will eventually become a good physician. Since one's public image and one's self-image are important for success as medical student, to be able to build a biography in which one has the right combination of skills and abilities, work experiences, courses, grades, board scores, and interests which make one "well-rounded," is routinely expected and accepted. Through the identity built, students garner peer and public support as well as the inner strength for "making it through."

WOMEN BUILD BIOGRAPHIES FOR HOW "THEY WILL DO IT" AS WOMEN

On the one hand, women see themselves as "no different from anyone else in medicine." They act and talk as medical students and future physicians. On the other hand, they advocate appreciation of women's special qualities. Women use these qualities as an additional basis for their acceptance. Their primary goal is to make gender less relevant in the medical school context. They do this by transforming the issue of women's fitness and transferring it to the interactional setting of physician and patient.

A Challenge as Women

The strategy of refusing to be cast by male classmates as potential dropouts from the profession is to build biographies which show them as "up to the challenge" of entering "a male domain that is opening up to women." If medical students desire challenge, then women *are* challenged to enter a domain from which they have arbitrarily been excluded, especially if "it may close up to women again." Cheryl's comments are representative of her classmates who want to enter what they term "high-powered" specialty areas where women have formerly been denied admission:

I feel that there are many more women in medical school now . . . it's just going to open up. Not like a knock on the door and they will let you in. But it will be a knock two or three times to get in. Which is why I really wanted to get into something very highly specialized, because there really haven't been very many women there before.

For some the challenge of entering medicine is an opportunity to use the ambition and achievement orientation that girls in high school and college develop, but for which they often have found no outlet when their schooling is over. As Kay tells it, the women's movement provided her with the confidence to try:

> I started to read the books . . . and I just devoured them. I was a senior in high school, and I was getting tired of high school, and I didn't know where I was going, and I was ambitious but didn't know how to channel it into anything. And then I read them, and I just – oh, I was completely sold! And especially . . . if you really want a career and family, you can go ahead and do it. And women should be able to do whatever they want to.

The challenge is one for which women have had the capabilities but not the supports and opportunities necessary for continued achievement.

Women's Special Qualities

Women in the class also emphasized the contributions that they can make in the quality of care they give. These women emphasized their potential contributions of "understanding and time" to the doctor-patient relationship and to patients' families. Laura S.'s comments are representative of those that women make about a "woman's point of view:"

> I think medicine would, number one, become less glorified. . . . Just because the whole idea of the white coat and the black bag and the whole thing from way back seem so stereotyped. . . . It's like somebody proclaiming, "Here we are and, look, we're all male and we're all doctors." And it's like they're calling the shots and everybody's got to follow them. I think there's a lot to be understood from the women's point of view. About treating, like, the families of patients. . . . And I hope that by the time I'm done with this training routine . . . that they pump you through, I won't have lost that kind of attitude.

Some women talked about the contributions they could make in terms of their ability to empathize with and understand certain types of patients. They referred to the women and children who make up the majority of patients in obstetrics, gynecology, pediatrics, and family practice. Four entering women had interests in the women's health care movement, in educating women about their own bodies, birth control, and child bearing.

> I thought it would be particularly good to do this, Judy B. reported, in a field like gynecology. That could be just very important in terms of supplying the kind of health care that's not there now. And supplying other needs than those specifically medical. I mean a woman gynecologist could do more than a man . . . just like the psychiatric aspects may be, and empathy aspects.

Other women felt they would be well accepted by children and their parents.

". . . I think, as a woman pediatrician," Sarah's comments are representative, "I would be very well accepted by patients. By their mothers, their children."

In other words, "women have a lot to offer. I think *I* have a lot to offer," as Meg put it.

> A lot of women can be more empathetic, more understanding, make things more per-sonal, rather than "business-like." Although I think for a long time a lot of the women who were in medicine were very business-like, because those . . . types of women, who could survive the competition, were really "manly" sorts of women, if I must use that term. Now they're taking ordinary women, you know? Women. Normal women. Women that can be feminine and that can also succeed . . . I don't think you have to sacrifice femininity or being gentle or understanding in favor of being educated and a physician. . . . It seemed to me that there for a while, you had to sacrifice one or the other.

According to these women, they have a lot to offer a profession which wants humane and altruistic candidates. They have particular needed qualities, "which men are often not permitted to express" in our society. And, as Meg points out, the women feel they do not have to become the stereotype of the manly woman.

One result is that the women continue to make gender relevant to their ac-ceptance by presenting themselves as special. There were eight women in this study (29 percent) who did not refer to women's special contributions. Five of these will go into surgical specialties (other than obstetrics) or specialties where such qualities are devalued by members of that specialty. These specialties are typified by students as those in which physicians do not "get too emotionally in-volved with patients."

It's an Important Question, but Medicine Is More Important Now

Women face the question from men in their class of how they will combine career and marriage. The questions, of course, imply that women will practice less than men, and/or lose acquired skills.

> A practicing physician is the best type of physician, is the policy around here, accord-ing to Cheryl and her classmates. It really is. They hate to see someone getting out of the practice just to have kids . . . and so you can tell that there's a little bit of the pressure on you. Some of the people would . . . rather not see you get married at all and just continue practicing just like a male, but . . . you can't compromise your own beliefs and the way you feel . . .

But to be "competitive and highly motivated" . . . is sometimes "irritating" . . . and makes them "not normal women."

Medical women, past and present, appear to have to support being both women (translation: good mothers) and physicians to be acceptable to members of the profession (Walsh, 1977; Weichert, 1977). In the past men members used both professional competency and feminine competency as criteria for accep' tance. By definition to do both was not to do either well. Few women could work their way out of the double bind.[6]

Women in the class studied here put off the dilemma of such a double bind. They built biographies which support their being different women for the time being. They built biographies as women who will postpone marrying and having children until after training, and yet who will not waste their training. "I could never think about getting married while I was in med school." "It probably would not be until after my residency," are typical ways they talk about it. The basic tactic is to agree that they aspire to the traditional role and that the ques' tion of combining career and motherhood is an important one. They argue that "being a physician is a major responsibility" and "being a mother is a major responsibility," but they are into "medicine now." The question of combining career and family is put off to the future. They are not sure how they will do both, but as Laura G. points out,

I definitely want a family. It's not right now . . . to tell the truth . . . I really am not sure how I'm going to do it, but somehow, someway.

Only one woman in the class refused to agree with male classmates that the question of how she will combine career and marriage is a legitimate one: "I'll call the shots in my personal life." She refused to accept the premise that what she does with her personal life should affect her standing in the profession. The rest dealt with the question but were able to get agreement that it is a future concern by equivocating about having families. They built biographies in which there are long complex accounts of the problems of combining career and parenthood. They do not like to say whether or not they want children and they leaned towards putting career first. "I will just have to play it by ear" for the time being because "I don't know whether I'll marry or have children or not." Others plan to have children. They plan to "do both, even though it may be hard," but one woman plans to adopt children.

SUMMARY AND CONCLUSIONS

Barriers to women's participation in the professions are mediated at the in' terpersonal level in part by the language used in the interactions between men members and women seeking collegial acceptance. The organization of work along gender lines, supported by notions of gender fitness, is perpetuated through everyday interaction. In medical school, men students use language to make gender a criterion for acceptance in the developing collegial structure of work and study. Women medical students build past and future biographies with which they respond to their male classmates' attempts to cast them into identities that make women inappropriate candidates for physicians and/or as abnormal women. Through their speech and acts the women negotiate acceptance as "capable, serious medical students like anyone else."

Cast by the men as usurpers of some man's "rightful place in school" and/or as "potential part-timers" women build past and future biographies to overcome their threatening position and potential. The women's negotiation of the question of their fitness is predicated upon three major elements of the situation. One is the ready availability to women and acceptability by others of the student identity and status.[7] The women's task is to remind men that academic ability, ambition, competitiveness, energy and drive are *normal* for many women, especially in the student role. As each woman develops her biography, she draws on the student identity and makes it her primary status vis-a-vis men students.

A second element assisting women's claims has to do with changes in the official notions of fitness or appropriateness. For at least the past decade the medical profession has been seeking candidates with more nurturant personalities. That is, candidates who are less interested in the "high-powered specialties" and more interested in primary patient care. The women use this focus on altruistic and nurturant qualities to turn notions of female unfitness around. Nurturant feminine qualitities which have been associated with motherhood, low practice time potential, and certain specialties are made by these women appropriate for patient care in any specialty.

A third element makes their negotiations both possible and necessary. This is the ratio of women to men. The relative proportion of women in the class assists them in their working to prevent being cast into some type of marginal status. Token women, or very small proportions of women, would not have enough contact with men classmates, as either visible participants or through interaction, to assist men in developing relationships which are not based on preconceptions, misconceptions, or prejudices about women. In this class there were enough women to refute stereotypes of female unfitness and to make such notions as inappropriate bases for interaction.

On the other hand, with such a large proportion of women in the class, the men needed reasons to accept the *fait accompli*. Men can neither ostracize one-third of their class nor make women so uncomfortable they leave or accept some marginal status. Women's biographies enable men to grant the medical student identity and confer peer status.

By building biographies that "women are no different than any other medical student," the women do not derogate by their presence the image of the *medical student* as one who relies on skills and a high level of motivation to enter and successfully endure the rigors of medical school. In building biographies which emphasize the special qualities women can contribute to *patient care*, they diffuse their threatening potential to the image of the *physician*. The heroics and the charisma – those qualities needed beyond intellect in meeting the *challenge* of a demanding career – are left to the men. Women can handle and desire such challenging careers. But future standards of work performance based on heroism and time commitment are realigned with the student ideal and the professional concern of quality of care.

Through the women's biographies runs the theme that being a normal woman and being a capable medical student are not mutually exclusive categories. Future femininity is claimed by accepting marriage as inevitable for a woman, and by accepting the ideal and desirability of motherhood. By equivocating about its inevitability they push the negotiation of this barrier to the future.

1. Racial and ethnic minorities underrepresented in American medicine are not included in this paper. There are similarities and differences in notions of racial and gender fitness, but in this paper I will discuss only the relevance of gender.

2. Or there must be agreement that a particular language strategy may be generalized to a wide variety of action, as when all sorts of actions are explained, supported, or justified by a Freudian vocabulary or a Born-Again Christian vocabulary.

3. All words and phrases in quotes are those of the medical students in the study unless otherwise noted.

4. This is called altercasting. See Eugene A. Weinstein and Paul Deutschberger, "Tasks, bargains, and identities in social interaction," Social Forces 42 (May 1964):451–452.

5. Women medical students, however, are somewhat more likely than men to say they seek individuality and to mention altruistic reasons more frequently (Cartwright, 1972; Hammond, 1977).

6. The accusation that women do not measure up to standards of practicetime has recently received heavy attack. Women physicians work about ten hours per week less than men (Carol E. Weichert, "Women in medicine: an indigenous view." Journal of American Medical Women's Association 3 (1977):90–91) and yet are overrepresented in full-time salaried nine-to-five positions (requiring fewer hours work to report). Women physicians also deliver more than their share of direct patient care (Center for Women in Medicine, "Women in medicine: action planning for the 1970's," Resource Booklet, Philadelphia, 1974.) A recent study (Marilyn Heins, Sue Smock, Jennifer Jacobs, and Margaret Stein, "Productivity of women physicians," Journal of the American Medical Association 236 (October 25, 1976): 1961–1964) found 76 percent of women physicians in the sample worked full time. Since the average life expectancy of women is seven years longer than men, and 84.6 percent of male physicians are retired after age 60 and only 60 percent of women physicians are retired (Walsh, 1977), the perspective that women's practice potential is less than men's is being questioned. The male students in this class felt they too face the dilemma of combining career and family responsibilities, when physicians are known to spend so much time at their work that home-life, wives, and children are neglected. But as men, they do not have an acceptable public explanation as a condition of equal status among their peers.

7. Becker, Geer, Hughes, and Strauss (1961) discuss how medical students in Boys in White drew on a latent identity, their middle-classness, in developing solutions to the problems of being medical students.

REFERENCES

Becker, Howard S., Blanche Geer, Everett C. Hughes, and Anselm Strauss (1961) Boys in White. Chicago: University of Chicago Press.

Cartwright, Lillian Kaufman (1972) "Conscious and unconscious factors entering into the decision of women to study medicine." Journal of Social Issues 28 (Spring): 201–215.

Dornbusch, Sanford (1955) "Military academy as an assimilation institution." Social Forces 33 (May): 316–321.

Hammond, Judith M. (1977) Women in Medicine: The Management of Status by Women in a Male-Dominated Insititution. Unpublished doctoral thesis, Syracuse University.

Hughes, Everett C. (1945) "Dilemmas and contradictions of status." The American Journal of Sociology 50 (March): 353–359.

Johnson, Davis G. and W.F. Dube (1975) Descriptive Study of Medical School Applicants. Washington, D.C.: Association of American Medical Colleges.

Kanter, Rosabeth Moss (1977) "Some effects of proportion on group life: skewed sex ratios and responses to token women." American Journal of Sociology 82 (March): 965–990.

Mills, C. Wright (1940) "Situated actions and vocabularies of motive." American Sociological Review 5 (December): 904–913.

Scott, Marvin B. and Stanford M. Lyman (1968) "Accounts." American Sociological Review 33 (December): 46–62.

Simmel, Georg (1950) The Sociology of Georg Simmel. Translated by Kurt H. Wolff. Glencoe, Ill.: Free Press.

Stokes, Randall and John P. Hewitt (1976) "Aligning actions." American Sociological Review 41 (October): 838–849.

Walsh, Mary Roth (1977) Doctors Wanted: No Women Need Apply: Sexual Barriers to the Medical Profession 1835–1975. New Haven: Yale University Press.

Weichert, Carol E. (1977) "Women in medicine: an indigenous view." Journal of the American Medical Women's Association 32 (March): 90–91.

Chapter 9

Race, Class and Gender: Prospects for an All-Inclusive Sisterhood

Bonnie Thornton Dill

T he concept of sisterhood has been an important unifying force in the
contemporary women's movement. By stressing the similarities of
women's secondary social and economic positions in all societies and in the family, this concept has been a binding force in the struggle against male chauvinism
and patriarchy. However, as we review the past decade, it becomes apparent
that the cry "Sisterhood is powerful!" has engaged only a few segments of the
female population in the United States. Black, Hispanic, Native American, and
Asian American women of all classes, as well as many working-class women,
have not readily identified themselves as sisters of the white middle-class
women who have been in the forefront of the movement.

This article examines the applications of the concept of sisterhood and some
of the reasons for the limited participation of racially and ethnically distinct
women in the women's movement, with particular reference to the experience
and consciousness of Afro-American women. The first section presents a critique of sisterhood as a binding force for all women and examines the limitations
of the concept for both theory and practice when applied to women who are
neither white nor middle class. In the second section, the importance of women's
perception of themselves and their place in society is explored as a way of understanding the differences and similarities between Black and white women. Data
from two studies, one of college-educated Black women and the other of Black
female household workers, are presented to illuminate both the ways in which
the structures of race, gender, and class intersect in the lives of Black women
and the women's perceptions of the impact of these structures on their lives.
This article concludes with a discussion of the prospects for sisterhood and suggests political strategies that may provide a first step toward a more inclusive
women's movement.

Source: Bonnie Thorton Dill, "Race, Class, and Gender: Prospects for an All-Inclusive
Sisterhood." This article is reprinted from FEMINIST STUDIES, Volume 9, no. 1 (1983):131–150,
by permission of the publisher, FEMINIST STUDIES, INC., c/o Women's Studies Program, University of Maryland, College Park, MD 20742.

THE LIMITATIONS OF SISTERHOOD

In a recent article, historian Elizabeth Fox-Genovese provided a political critique of the concept of sisterhood.[1] Her analysis identifies some of the current
limitations of this concept as a rallying point for women across the boundaries of
race and class. Sisterhood is generally understood as a nurturant, supportive
feeling of attachment and loyalty to other women which grows out of a shared
experience of oppression. A term reminiscent of familial relationships, it tends to
focus upon the particular nurturant and reproductive roles of women and, more
recently, upon commonalities of personal experience. Fox-Genovese suggests
that sisterhood has taken two different political directions. In one women have
been treated as unique, and sisterhood was used as a basis for seeking to maintain a separation between the competitive values of the world of men (the
public-political sphere) and the nurturant values of the world of women (the
private domestic sphere). A second, more recent and progressive expression of
the concept views sisterhood as an element of the feminist movement which
serves as a means for political and economic action based upon the shared needs
and experiences of women. Both conceptualizations of sisterhood have limitations in encompassing the racial and class differences among women. These
limitations have important implications for the prospects of an all-inclusive
sisterhood.

Fox-Genovese argues that the former conceptualization, which she labels
bourgeois individualism, resulted in "the passage of a few middle class women into the public sphere," but sharpened the class and racial divisions between them
and lower-class minority women.[2] In the latter conceptualization, called the
politics of personal experience, sisterhood is restricted by the experiential differences that result from the racial and class divisions of society.

> Sisterhood has helped us, as it helped so many of our predecessors, to form ourselves
> as political beings. Sisterhood has mobilized our loyalty to each other and hence to
> ourselves. It has given form to a dream of genuine equality for women. But without a
> broader politics directed toward the kind of social transformation that will provide
> social justice for all human beings it will be a poignant irony, result in our dropping
> each other by the wayside as we compete with rising desperation for crumbs.[3]

These two notions of sisterhood, as expressed in the current women's movement, offer some insights into the alienation many Black women have expressed
about the movement itself.

The bourgeois individualistic theme present in the contemporary women's
movement led many Black women to express the belief that the movement existed merely to satisfy needs for personal self-fulfillment on the part of white
middle-class women.[4] The emphasis on participation in the paid labor force and
escape from the confines of the home, seemed foreign to many Black women.
After all, as a group they had had higher rates of paid labor force participation

than their white counterparts for centuries, and many would have readily accepted what they saw as the "luxury" of being a housewife. At the same time, they expressed concern that white women's gains would be made at the expense of Blacks and/or that having achieved their personal goals, these so-called sisters would ignore or abandon the cause of racial discrimination. Finally, and perhaps most important, the experiences of racial oppression made Black women strongly aware of their group identity and consequently more suspicious of women who, initially at least, defined much of their feminism in personal and individualistic terms.

Angela Davis, in "Reflections on the Black Woman's Role in the Community of Slaves," stresses the importance of group identity for black women. "Under the impact of racism the black woman has been continually constrained to inject herself into the desperate struggle for existence. . . . As a result, black women have made significant contributions to struggles against racism and the dehumanizing exploitation of a wrongly organized society. In fact, it would appear that the intense levels of resistance historically maintained by black people and thus the historical function of the Black liberation struggle as harbinger of change throughout the society are due in part to the greater objective equality between the black man and the black woman."[5] The sense of being part of a collective movement toward liberation has been a continuing theme in the autobiographies of contemporary black women.

> Views and experiences vary, but Shirley Chisholm, Gwendolyn Brooks, Angela Davis and other Black women who wrote autobiographies during the seventies offer similar . . . visions of the black woman's role in the struggle for Black liberation. The idea of collective liberation . . . says that society is not a protective arena in which an individual black can work out her own destiny and gain a share of America's benefits by her own efforts. . . . Accordingly, survival, not to mention freedom, is dependent on the values and actions of the groups as a whole, and if indeed one succeeds or triumphs it is due less to individual talent than to the group's belief in and adherence to the idea that freedom from oppression must be acted out and shared by all.[6]

Sisterhood is not new to Black women. It has been institutionalized in churches. In many black churches, for example, membership in the church entitles one to address the women as "sisters" and the men as "brothers." Becoming a sister is an important rite of passage which permits young women full participation in certain church rituals and women's clubs where these nurturant relationships among women are reinforced.[7] Sisterhood was also a basis for organization in the club movements that began in the late 1800s.[8] Finally, it is clearly exemplified in Black extended family groupings that frequently place great importance on female kinship ties. Research on kinship patterns among urban Blacks identifies the nuturant and supportive feelings existing among female kin as a key element in family stability and survival.[9]

While Black women have fostered and encouraged sisterhood, we have not used it as the anvil to forge our political identities. This contrasts sharply with the experiences of many middle-class white women who have participated in the current women's movement. The political identities of Afro-American women have largely been formed around issues of race. National organizations of Black women, many of which were first organized on the heels of the nineteenth century movement for women's rights, "were (and still are) decidedly feminist in the values expressed in their literature and in many of the concerns which they addressed, yet they also always focused upon issues which resulted from the racial oppression affecting all black people."[10] This commitment to the improvement of the race has often led Black women to see feminist issues quite differently from their white sisters. And, racial animosity and mistrust have too often undermined the potential for coalition between Black and white women since the women's suffrage campaigns.

Many contemporary white feminists would like to believe that relations between black and white women in the early stages of the women's movement were characterized by the beliefs and actions of Susan B. Anthony, Angelina Grimke, and some others. The historical record suggests however, that these women were more exceptional than normative. Rosalyn Terborg-Penn argues that "discrimination against Afro-American women reformers was the rule rather than the exception within the woman's rights movement from the 1830's to 1920."[11] Although it is beyond the scope of this article to provide a detailed discussion of the incidents that created mistrust and ill-feeling between black and white women, the historical record provides an important legacy that still haunts us.

The movement's early emphasis upon the oppression of women within the institution of marriage and the family, and upon educational and professional discrimination, reflected the concerns of middle-class white women. During that period, Black women were engaged in a struggle for survival and a fight for freedom. Among their immediate concerns were lynching and economic viability. Working-class white women were concerned about labor conditions, the length of the working day, wages, and so forth. The statements of early women's rights groups do not reflect these concerns, and "as a rigorous consummation of the consciousness of white middle-class women's dilemma, the (Seneca Falls) Declaration all but ignored the predicament of white working-class women, as it ignored the condition of Black women in the South and North alike."[12]

Political expediency drove white feminists to accept principles that were directly opposed to the survival and well-being of Blacks in order to seek to achieve more limited advances for women. "Besides the color bar which existed in many white women's organizations, black women were infuriated by white women's accommodation to the principle of lynch law in order to gain support in the South (Walker, 1973) and the attacks of well-known feminists against anti-lynching crusader, Ida Wells Burnett."[13]

The failure of the suffrage movement to sustain its commitment to the democratic ideal of enfranchisement for all citizens is one of the most frequently cited instances of white women's fragile commitment to racial equality. "After the Civil War, the suffrage movement was deeply impaired by the split over the issue of whether black males should receive the vote before white and black women . . . in the heated pressures over whether black men or white and black women should be enfranchised first, a classist, racist, and even xenophobic rhetoric rept in."[14] The historical and continued abandonment of universalistic principles in order to benefit a privileged few on the part of white women is, I think, one of the reasons why Black women today have been reluctant to see themselves as part of a sisterhood that does not extend beyond racial boundaries. Even for those Black women who are unaware of the specific history, there is the recognition that under pressure from the white men with whom they live and upon whom they are economically dependent, many white women will abandon their "sisters of color" in favor of self-preservation. The feeling that the movement would benefit white women and abandon Blacks, or benefit whites at the expense of Blacks, is a recurrent theme. Terborg-Penn concludes, "The black feminist movement in the United States during the mid 1970's is a continuation of a trend that began over 150 years ago. Institutionalized discrimination against black women by white women has traditionally led to the development of racially separate groups that address themselves to race determined problems as well as the common plight of women in America."[15]

Historically, as well as currently, Black women have felt called upon to choose between their commitments to feminism and to the struggle against racial injustice. Clearly they are victims of both forms of oppression and are most in need of encouragement and support in waging battles on both fronts. However, insistence on such a choice continues largely as a result of the tendency of groups of Blacks and groups of women to battle over the dubious distinction of being the "most" oppressed. The insistence of radical feminists upon the historical priority, universality, and overriding importance of patriarchy in effect necessitates acceptance of a concept of sisterhood that places one's womanhood over and above one's race. At the same time, Blacks are accustomed to labeling discriminatory treatment as racism and therefore may tend to view sexism only within the bounds of the Black community rather than see it as a systemic pattern.[16] On the one hand, the choice between identifying as black or female is a product of the "patriarchal strategy of divide-and-conquer"[17] and therefore, a false choice. Yet, the historical success of this strategy and the continued importance of class, patriarchal, and racial divisions, perpetuate such choices both within our consciousness and within the concrete realities of our daily lives.

Race, of course, is only one of the factors that differentiate women. It is the most salient in discussions of Black and white women, but it is perhaps no more important, even in discussions of race and gender, than is the factor of class. Inclusion of the concept of class permits a broader perspective on the similarities and differences between Black and white women than does a purely racial analysis. Marxist feminism has focused primarily upon the relationship between class exploitation and patriarchy. While this literature has yielded several useful frameworks for beginning to examine the dialectics of gender and class, the role of race, though acknowledged, is not explicated.

Just as the gender-class literature tends to omit race, the race-class literature gives little attention to women. Recently, this area of inquiry has been dominated by a debate over the relative importance of race or class in explaining the historical and contemporary status of Blacks in this country. A number of scholars writing on this issue have argued that the racial division of labor in the United States began as a form of class exploitation which was shrouded in an ideology of racial inferiority. Through the course of U.S. history, racial structures began to take on a life of their own and cannot now be considered merely reflections of class structure.[18] A theoretical understanding of the current conditions of Blacks in this country must therefore take account of both race and class factors. It is not my intention to enter into this debate, but instead to point out that any serious study of Black women must be informed by this growing theoretical discussion. Analysis of the interaction of race, gender, and class fall squarely between these two developing bodies of theoretical literature.

Black women experience class, race, and sex exploitation simultaneously, yet these structures must be separated analytically so that we may better understand the ways in which they shape and differentiate women's lives. Davis, in her previously cited article, provides one of the best analyses to date of the intersection of gender, race, and class under a plantation economy.[19] One of the reasons this analysis is so important is because she presents a model that can be expanded to other historical periods. However, we must be careful not to take the particular historical reality which she illuminated and read it into the present as if the experiences of Black women followed some sort of linear progression out of slavery. Instead, we must look carefully at the lives of Black women throughout history in order to define the peculiar interactions of race, class, and gender at particular historical moments.

In answer to the question: Where do Black women fit into the current analytical frameworks for race and class and gender and class? I would ask: How might these frameworks be revised if they took full account of black women's position in the home, family, and marketplace at various historical moments? In other words, the analysis of the interaction of race, gender, and class must not be stretched to fit the proscrustean bed of any other burgeoning set of theories. It is my contention that it must begin with an analysis of the ways in which Black people have been used in the process of capital accumulation in the United States. Within the contexts of class exploitation and racial oppression, women's lives and work are most clearly illuminated. Davis's article illustrates this. Increasingly, new research is being presented which grapples with the complex interconnectedness of these three issues in the lives of Black women and other women of color.[20]

PERCEPTIONS OF SELF IN SOCIETY

For Black women and other women of color an examination of the ways in which racial oppression, class exploitation, and patriarchy intersect in their lives must be studied in relation to their perceptions of the impact these structures have upon them. Through studying the lives of particular women and searching for patterns in the ways in which they describe themselves and their relationship to society, we will gain important insights into the differences and similarities between Black and white women.

The structures of race and class generate important economic, ideological, and experiential cleavages among women. These lead to differences in perception of self and their place in society. At the same time, commonalities of class or gender may cut across racial lines providing the conditions for shared understanding. Studying these interactions through an examination of women's self perceptions is complicated by the fact that most people view their lives as a whole and do not explain their daily experiences or world view in terms of the differential effects of their racial group, class position, or gender. Thus, we must examine on an analytical level the ways in which the structures of class, race, and gender intersect in any woman's or group of women's lives in order to grasp the concrete set of social relations that influence their behavior. At the same time, we must study individual and group perceptions, descriptions, and conceptualizations of their lives so that we may understand the ways in which different women perceive the same and different sets of social structural constraints.

Concretely, and from a research perspective, this suggests the importance of looking at both the structures which shape women's lives and their selfpresentations. This would provide us, not only with a means of gaining insight into the ways in which racial, class, and gender oppression are viewed, but also with a means of generating conceptual categories that will aid us in extending our knowledge of their situation. At the same time, this new knowledge will broaden and even reform our conceptualization of women's situations.

For example, how would our notions of mothering, and particularly motherdaughter relationships, be revised if we considered the particular experiences and perceptions of Black women on this topic? Gloria I. Joseph argues for, and presents a distinctive approach to the study of black mother-daughter relationships, asserting that

> to engage in a discussion of Black mothers and daughters which focused on specific psychological mechanisms operating between the two, the dynamics of the crucial bond, and explanations for the explicit role of patriarchy, without also including the important relevancy of racial oppression . . . would necessitate forcing Black mother/daughter relationships into pigeonholes designed for understanding white models.
>
> In discussing Black mothers and daughters, it is more realistic, useful, and intellectually astute to speak in terms of their roles, positions, and functions within the Black society and that society's relationship to the broader (White) society in America.[21]

Unfortunately, there have been very few attempts in the social sciences to systematically investigate the relationship between social structure and self perceptions of Black women. The profiles of Black women that have been appearing in magazines like *Essence*, the historical studies of Black women, fiction and poetry by and about Black women, and some recent sociological and anthropological studies provide important data for beginning such an analysis. However, the question of how Black women perceive themselves with regard to the structures of race, gender, and class is still open for systematic investigation.

Elizabeth Higginbotham, in a study of Black women who graduated from college between 1968 and 1970, explored the impact of class origins upon strategies for educational attainment. She found that class differences within the Black community led not only to different sets of educational experiences, but also to different personal priorities and views of the Black experience.[22] According to Higginbotham, the Black women from middle-class backgrounds who participated in her study had access to better schools and more positive schooling experiences than did their working-class sisters. Because their parents did not have the economic resources to purchase the better educational opportunities offered in an integrated suburb or a private school, the working-class women credited their parents' willingness to struggle within the public school system as a key component in their own educational achievement. Social class also affected college selections and experience. Working-class women were primarily concerned with finances in selecting a college and spent most of their time adjusting to the work load and the new middle-class environment once they had arrived. Middle-class women, on the other hand, were freer to select a college that would meet their personal, as well as their academic, needs and abilities. Once there, they were better able to balance their work and social lives and to think about integrating future careers and family lives.

Among her sample, Higginbotham found that a larger proportion of women from working-class backgrounds were single. She explained this finding in terms of class differences in socialization and mobility strategies. She found that the parents of women from working-class backgrounds stressed educational achievement over and above other personal goals.[23] These women never viewed marriage as a means of mobility and focused primarily upon education, postponing interest in, and decisions about, marriage. In contrast, women from middle-class backgrounds were expected to marry and were encouraged to integrate family and educational goals throughout their schooling.

My own research on household workers demonstrates the ways in which class origins, racial discrimination, and social conceptions of women and women's work came together during the first half of the twentieth century to limit work options and affect family roles and the self perceptions of one group of Afro-American women born between 1896 and 1915.[24] Most of them were born in the South and migrated North between 1922 and 1955. Like the majority of black working women of this period, they worked as household workers in private homes. (During the first half of the twentieth century, labor force participation rates of Black women ranged from about 37 percent to 50 percent. Approximately 60 percent of black women workers were employed in private household work up until 1960.)[25]

The women who participated in this study came from working-class families. Their fathers were laborers and farmers, their mothers were housewives or did paid domestic work of some kind (cooking, cleaning, taking in washing, and so forth). As a result, the women not only had limited opportunities for education, but also often began working when they were quite young to help support their families. Jewell Prieleau (names are pseudonyms used to protect the identity of the subjects), one of eight children, described her entrance into work as follows: "When I was eight years old, I decided I wanted a job and I just got up early in the morning and I would go from house to house and ring doorbells and ask for jobs and I would get it. I think I really wanted to work because in a big family like that, they was able to feed you, but you had to earn your shoes. They couldn't buy shoes although shoes was very cheap at that time. I would rather my mother give it to the younger children and I would earn my way."

Queenie Watkins lived with her mother, aunt, and five cousins and began working in grammar school. She described her childhood jobs in detail.

> When I went to grammar school, the white ladies used to come down and say "Do you have a girl who can wash dishes?" That was how I got the job with the doctor and his wife. I would go up there at six o'clock in the morning and wash the breakfast dishes and bring in scuttles of coal to burn on the fireplace. I would go back in the afternoon and take the little girl down on the sidewalk and if there were any leaves to be raked on the yard, I'd rake the leaves up and burn them and sweep the sidewalk. I swept off the front porch and washed it off with the hose and washed dishes again — for one dollar a week.

While class position limited the economic resources and educational opportunities of most of these women, racial discrimination constricted work options for Black women in such a way as to seriously undercut the benefits of education. The comments of the following women are reflective of the feelings expressed by many of those in this sample:

> When I came out of school, the black man naturally had very few chances of doing certain things and even persons that I know myself who had finished four years of college were doing the same type of work because they couldn't get any other kind of work in New York.
> In my home in Virginia, education, I don't think was stressed. The best you could do was be a school teacher. It wasn't something people impressed upon you you

could get. I had an aunt and cousin who were trained nurses and the best they could do was nursing somebody at home or something. They couldn't get a job in a hospital. I didn't pay education any mind really until I came to New York. I'd gotten to a certain stage in domestic work in the country and I didn't see the need for it.

Years ago there was no such thing as a black typist. I remember girls who were taking typing when I was going to school. They were never able to get a job at it. In my day and time you could have been the greatest typist in the world but you would never have gotten a job. There was no such thing as getting a job as a bank teller. The blacks weren't even sweeping the banks.

For Black women in the United States, their high concentration in household work was a result of racial discrimination and a direct carry-over from slavery. Black women were in essence "a permanent service caste in nineteenth and twentieth century America."[26] Arnold Anderson and Mary Jean Bowman argue that the distinguishing feature of domestic service in the United States is that "the frequency of servants is correlated with the availability of Negroes in local populations."[27] By the time most of the women in this sample entered the occupation a racial caste pattern was firmly established. The occupation was dominated by foreign-born white women in the North, and Black freedwomen in the South, a pattern which was modified somewhat as southern Blacks migrated north. Nevertheless, most research indicates that Black women fared far worse than their white immigrant sisters, even in the North. "It is commonly asserted that the immigrant woman has been the northern substitute for the Negro servant. In 1930, when one can separate white servants by nativity, about twice as large a percentage of foreign as of native women were domestics. . . . As against this 2:1 ratio between immigrants and natives, the ratio of Negro to white servants ranged upward from 10:1 to 50:1. The immigrant was not the northerner's Negro."[28]

Two major differences distinguished the experiences of Black domestics from that of their immigrant sisters. First, Black women had few other employment options. Second, Black household workers were older and more likely to be married. Thus, while private household work cross-culturally, and for white women in the United States, was often used as a steppingstone to other working-class occupations, or as a way station before marriage, for Black American women it was neither. This pattern did not begin to change substantially until World War II.

Table 9.1 indicates that between 1900 and 1940 the percentage of Black women in domestic service actually increased, relative to the percentage of immigrant women which decreased. The data support the contention that Black women were even more confined to the occupation than their immigrant sisters. At the turn of the century, large numbers of immigrants entered domestic service. Their children, however, were much less likely to become household workers. Similarly, many Black women entered domestic service at that time, but their children tended to remain in the occupation. It was the daughters and

TABLE 9.1

Percentage of females of each nativity in U.S. labor force who were servants, by decades, 1900–1940

	1900	1910	1920	1930	1940
Native white	22.3	15.0	9.6	10.4⎤	11.0
Foreign-born white	42.5	34.0	23.8	26.8⎦	
Negro	41.9	39.5	44.4	54.9	54.4
Other	24.8	22.9	22.9	19.4	16.0
Total	30.5	24.0	17.9	19.8	17.2
(N, in thousands)	(1,439)	(1,761)	(1,386)	(1,906)	(1,931)
(Percent of all domestic servants)	(95.4)	(94.4)	(93.3)	(94.1)	(92.0)

Source: George J. Stigler, *Domestic Servants in the United States: 1900–1940*. Occasional Paper no. 24 (New York: National Bureau of Economic Research, 1946), p.7.

granddaughters of the women who participated in this study that were among the first generation of Black women to benefit from the relaxation of racial restrictions which began to occur after World War II.

Finally, Black women were household workers because they were women. Private household work is women's work. It is a working-class occupation, has low social status, low pay, and few guaranteed fringe benefits. Like the housewife who employs her, the private household worker's low social status and pay is tied to the work itself, to her class, gender, and the complex interaction of the three within the family. In other words, housework, both paid and unpaid, is structured around the particular place of women in the family. It is considered unskilled labor because it requires no training, degrees, or licenses, and because it has traditionally been assumed that any woman could or should be able to do housework.

The women themselves had a very clear sense that the social inequities which relegated them and many of their peers to household service labor were based upon their race, class, and gender. Yet different women, depending upon their jobs, family situations, and overall outlooks on life, handled this knowledge in different ways. One woman described the relationship between her family and her employer's as follows: "Well for *their* children, I imagine they wanted them to become like they were, educators or something that-like [sic]. But what they had in for my children, they saw in me that I wasn't able to make all of that mark but raised my children in the best method I could. Because I wouldn't have the means to put *my* children through like they could for their children." When asked what she liked most about her work, she answered, "Well what I like most about it, the things that I weren't able to go to school to do for my children. I could kinda pattern from the families that I worked for, so that I could give my children the best of my abilities." A second woman expressed much more anger and bitterness about the social differences which distinguished her life from that of her female employer. "They don't know nothing about a hard life. The only hard life will come if they getting a divorce or going through a problem with their children. But their husband has to provide for them because they're not soft. And if they leave and they separate for any reason or (are) divorced, they have to put the money down. But we have no luck like that. We have to leave our children; sometime leave the children alone. There's times when I have asked winos to look after my children. It was just a terrible life and I really thank God that the children grow up to be nice." Yet while she acknowledged her position as an oppressed person, she used her knowledge of the anomalies in her employers' lives – particularly the woman and her female friends – to aid her in maintaining her sense of self-respect and determination and to overcome feelings of despair and immobilization. When asked if she would like to switch places with her employers, she replied, "I don't think I would want to change, but I would like to live differently. I would like to have my own nice little apartment with my husband and have my grandchildren for dinner and my daughter and just live comfortable. But I would always want to work. . . . But, if I was to change life with them, I would like to have just a little bit of they money, that's all." While the women who participated in this study adopted different personal styles of coping with these inequities, they were all clearly aware that being black, poor, and female placed them at the bottom of the social structure, and they used the resources at their disposal to make the best of what they recognized as a bad situation.

Contemporary scholarship on women of color suggests that the barriers to an all-inclusive sisterhood are deeply rooted in the histories of oppression and exploitation that Blacks and other groups encountered upon incorporation into the American political economy.[29] These histories affect the social positions of these groups today, and racial ethnic women[30] in every social class express anger and distress about the forms of discrimination and insensitivity which they encounter in their interactions with white feminists. Audre Lorde has argued that the inability of women to confront anger is one of the important forces dividing women of color from white women in the feminist movement. She cites several examples from her own experiences which resonate loudly with the experiences of most women of color who have been engaged in the women's movement.[31]

After fifteen years of a women's movement which professes to address the life concerns and possible futures of all women, I still hear, on campus after campus, "How can we address the issues of racism? No women of color attended." Or, the other side of that statement, "We have no one in our department equipped to teach their work." In other words, racism is a Black women's problem, a problem of women of color, and only we can discuss it.

White women are beginning to examine their relationships to Black women, yet often I hear you wanting only to deal with the little colored children across the roads of childhood, the beloved nursemaid, the occasional second-grade classmate. . . . You avoid the childhood assumptions formed by the raucous laughter at Rastus and Oatmeal . . . the indelible and dehumanizing portraits of Amos and Andy and your daddy's humorous bedtime stories.

Bell Hooks points to both the racial and class myopia of white feminists as a major barrier to sisterhood.

When white women's liberationists emphasized work as a path to liberation, they did not concentrate their attention on those women who are most exploited in the American labor force. Had they emphasized the plight of working class women, attention would have shifted away from the college-educated suburban housewife who wanted entrance into the middle and upper class work force. Had attention been focused on women who were already working and who were exploited as cheap surplus labor in American society, it would have de-romanticized the middle class white woman's quest for "meaningful" employment. While it does not in any way diminish the importance of women resisting sexist oppression by entering the labor force, work has not been a liberating force for masses of American women.[32]

As a beginning point for understanding the potential linkages and barriers to an all-inclusive sisterhood, Lorde concludes that "the strength of women lies in recognizing differences between us as creative, and in standing to those distortions which we inherited without blame but which are now ours to alter. The angers of women can transform differences through insight into power. For anger between peers births change, not destruction, and the discomfort and sense of loss it often causes is not fatal, but a sign of growth."[33]

PROSPECTS FOR AN ALL-INCLUSIVE SISTERHOOD

Given the differences in experiences among Black women, the differences between Black and white women, between working-class and middle-class women, between all of us, what then are the prospects for sisterhood? While this article has sought to emphasize the need to study and explicate these differences, it is based upon the assumption that the knowledge we gain in this process will also help enlighten us as to our similarities. Thus, I would argue for the abandonment of the concept of sisterhood as a global construct based on unexamined assumptions about our similarities, and I would substitute a more pluralistic approach that recognizes and accepts the objective differences between women. Such an approach requires that we concentrate our political energies on building coalitions around particular issues of shared interest.

Through joint work on specific issues, we may come to a better understanding of one another's needs and perceptions and begin to overcome some of the suspicions and mistrust that continue to haunt us. The limitations of a sisterhood based on bourgeois individualism or on the politics of personal experience presently pose a very real threat to combined political action.

For example, in the field of household employment, interest in the needs of a growing number of middle-class women to participate in the work force and thus find adequate assistance with their domestic duties (a form of bourgeois individualism) could all too easily become support for a proposal such as the one made by writer Anne Colamosca in a recent article in the *New Republic*.[34] She proposed solving the problems of a limited supply of household help with a government training program for unemployed alien women to help them become "good household workers." While this may help middle-class women pursue their careers, it will do so while continuing to maintain and exploit a poorly paid, unprotected, lower class and will leave the problem of domestic responsibility virtually unaddressed for the majority of mothers in the work force who cannot afford to hire personal household help. A socialist feminist perspective requires an examination of the exploitation inherent in the household labor as it is currently organized for both the paid and unpaid worker. The question is, what can we do to upgrade the status of domestic labor for ALL women, to facilitate the adjustment and productivity of immigrant women, and to insure that those who choose to engage in paid private household work do so because it represents a potentially interesting, viable and economically rewarding option for them?

At the same time, the women's movement may need to move beyond a limited focus on "women's issues" to ally with groups of women and men who are addressing other aspects of race and class oppression. One example is school desegregation, an issue which is engaging the time and energies of many urban Black women today. The struggles over school desegregation are rapidly moving beyond the issues of busing and racial balance. In many large cities, where school districts are between 60 percent and 85 percent Black, Hispanic, or Third World, racial balance is becoming less of a concern. Instead, questions are being raised about the overall quality of the educational experiences low-income children of all racial and ethnic groups are receiving in the public schools. This is an issue of vital concern to many racially and ethnically distinct women because they see their children's future ability to survive in this society as largely dependent upon the current direction of public education. In what ways should feminists involve themselves in this issue? First, by recognizing that feminist questions are only one group of questions among many others that are being raised about public education. To the extent that Blacks, Hispanics, Native Americans, and Asian Americans are miseducated, so are women. Feminist activists must work to expand their conceptualization of the problem beyond the narrow confines of sexism. For example, efforts to develop and include nonsexist literature in the school curriculum are important. Yet this work cannot exist in a vacuum, ignoring the fact that schoolchildren *observe* a gender-based division of labor in which authority and responsibility are held primarily by men while women are concentrated in nurturant roles; or that schools with middle-class students have more funds, better facilities, and better teachers than schools serving working class populations. The problems of education must be addressed as structural ones. We must examine not only the kinds of discrimination that occur within institutions, but also the ways in which discrimination becomes a fundamental part of the institution's organization and implementation of its overall purpose. Such an analysis would make the linkages between different forms of structural inequality, like sexism and racism, more readily apparent.

While analytically we must carefully examine the structures that differentiate us, politically we must fight the segmentation of oppression into categories such as "racial issues," "feminist issues," and "class issues." This is, of course, a task of almost overwhelming magnitude, and yet it seems to me the only viable way to avoid the errors of the past and to move forward to make sisterhood a meaningful feminist concept for all women, across the boundaries of race and class. For it is through first seeking to understand struggles that are not particularly shaped by one's own immediate personal priorities that we will begin to experience and understand the needs and priorities of our sisters – be they black, brown, white, poor, or rich. When we have reached a point where the differences between us ENRICH our political and social action rather than divide it, we will have gone beyond the personal and will, in fact, be "political enough."

NOTES

The author wishes to acknowledge the comments of Lynn Weber Cannon and Elizabeth Higginbotham on an earlier version of this article.
1. Elizabeth Fox-Genovese, "The Personal is not Political Enough," *Marxist Perspectives* (Winter 1979-80): 94-113.
2. Ibid., 97-98.
3. Ibid., 112.
4. For discussions of black women's attitudes toward the women's movement see Linda LaRue, "The Black Movement and Women's Liberation." *Black Scholar* 1 (May 1970): 36-42; Renee Ferguson "Women's Liberation has a Different Meaning for Blacks," in *Black Women in White America: A Documentary History*, ed. Gerda Lerner (New York: Pantheon, 1972); Inez Smith Reid, "*Together*" *Black Women* (New York: Emerson-Hall, 1972); Cheryl Townsend Gilkes, "Black Women's Work as Deviance: Social Sources of Racial Antagonism within Contemporary Feminism" (Paper presented at the Seventy-fourth Annual Meeting of the American Sociological Association, Boston, August 1979).
5. Angela Davis, "Reflections on the Black Woman's Role in the Community of Slaves," *Black Scholar* 2 (December 1971): 15.
6. Mary Burgher, "Images of Self and Race," in *Sturdy Black Bridges*, ed. Roseann P. Bell, Bettye J. Parker, and Beverly Guy-Sheftall (Garden City, N.Y.: Anchor Books, 1979), 118.

7. For a related discussion of black women's roles in the church, see Cheryl Townsend Gilkes, "Institutional Motherhood in Black Churches and Communities: Ambivalent Sexism or Fragmented Familyhood" (published paper).

8. For a discussion of the club movement among black women, see, in addition to Lerner's book, Alfreda Duster, ed., *Ida Barnett, Crusade for Justice: The Autobiography of Ida B. Wells* (Chicago: University of Chicago Press, 1970); Rackham Holt, *Mary McLeod Bethune: A Biography* (Garden City, N.Y.: Doubleday & Co., 1964); Jeanne L. Noble, *Beautiful, Also, Are the Souls of My Black Sisters: A History of the Black Woman in America* (Englewood Cliffs, N.J.: Prentice-Hall, 1978); Mary Church Terrell, *A Colored Woman in a White World* (Washington, D.C.: Ransdell Publishing Company, 1940).

9. Carol Stack, *All Our Kin* (New York: Harper & Row, 1970); and Elmer P. Martin and Joan Martin, *The Black Extended Family* (Chicago: University of Chicago Press, 1977).

10. Gilkes, "Black Women's Work as Deviance," 21.

11. Rosalyn Terborg-Penn, "Discrimination Against Afro-American Women in the Woman's Movement, 1830–1920," in *The Afro-American Woman: Struggles and Images,* ed. Sharon Harley and Rosalyn Terborg-Penn (Port Washington, N.Y.: Kennikat Press, 1978), 17.

12. Angela Davis, *Women, Race, and Class* (New York: Random House, 1981), 54.

13. Gilkes, "Black Women's Work as Deviance," 19. In this quotation Gilkes cites Jay S. Walker, "Frederick Douglass and Woman Suffrage," *Black Scholar* 4 (7 June 1973).

14. Adrienne Rich, "'Disloyal to Civilization': Feminism, Racism, and Gynephobia," *Chrysalis,* no. 7 (1978): 14.

15. Terborg-Penn, 27.

16. Elizabeth Higginbotham, "Issues in Contemporary Sociological Work on Black Women," *Humanity and Society* 4 (November 1980): 226–42.

17. Rich, 15.

18. This argument has been suggested by Robert Blauner in *Racial Oppression in America* (New York: Harper & Row, 1972); and William J. Wilson in *The Declining Significance of Race: Blacks and Changing American Institutions* (Chicago: University of Chicago Press, 1978).

19. Davis, "Reflections on the Black Woman's Role."

20. See Cheryl Townsend Gilkes, "Living and Working in a World of Trouble: The Emergent Career of the Black Woman Community Worker" (Ph.D. diss., Northeastern University, 1979); and Elizabeth Higginbotham, "Educated Black Women: An Exploration in Life Chances and Choices" (Ph.D. diss., Brandeis University, 1980).

21. Gloria I. Joseph and Jill Lewis, *Common Differences: Conflicts in Black and White Feminist Perspectives* (Garden City, N.Y.: Anchor Books, 1981), 75–76.

22. Higginbotham, "Educated Black Women."

23. Elizabeth Higginbotham, "Is Marriage a Priority? Class Differences in Marital Options of Educated Black Women" in *Single Life,* ed. Peter Stein (New York: St. Martin's Press, 1981), 262.

24. Bonnie Thornton Dill, "Across the Boundaries of Race and Class: An Exploration of the Relationship between Work and Family among Black Female Domestic Servants," (Ph.D. diss., New York University, 1979).

25. For detailed data on the occupational distribution of black women during the twentieth century, see U.S. Bureau of the Census, *Historical Statistics of the United States: Colonial Times to 1970.* H. Doc. 83–88, (Washington, D.C.: GPO, 1973).

26. David Katzman, *Seven Days a Week: Women and Domestic Service in Industrializing America* (New York: Oxford University Press, 1978), 85.

27. Arnold Anderson and Mary Jean Bowman, "The Vanishing Servant and the Contemporary Status System of the American South," *American Journal of Sociology* 59 (November 1953): 216.

28. Ibid., 220.

29. Elizabeth Higginbotham, "Laid Bare by the System: Work and Survival for Black and Hispanic Women," forthcoming in Amy Swerdlow and Hannah Lessinger, *Race, Class, and Gender: The Dynamics of Control* (Boston: G.K. Hall); and Bonnie Thornton Dill "Survival as a Form of Resistance: Minority Women and the Maintenance of Families" (Working Paper no. 7, Inter University Group on Gender and Race, Memphis State University, 1982).

30. The term "racial ethnic women" is meant as an alternative to either "minority," which is disparaging; "Third World," which has an international connotation; or "women of color," which lacks any sense of cultural identity. In contrast to "ethnic," which usually refers to groups that are culturally distinct but members of the dominant white society, "racial ethnic" refers to groups that are both culturally and racially distinct, and in the United States have historically shared certain common conditions as oppressed and internally colonized peoples.

31. Audre Lorde, "The Uses of Anger," *Women's Studies Quarterly* 9 (Fall 1981): 7.

32. Bell Hooks, *Ain't I a Woman: Black Women and Feminism* (Boston: South End Press, 1981), 146.

33. Lorde, 9.

34. Ann Colamosca, "Capitalism and Housework," *New Republic*, 29 March 1980, 18–20.

Section V ————————————————

Marriage and the Home:
The Family Claim for Wives

Chapter 10 ———————————————————————————

Corporate Wives: Longing for Liberation or Satisfied with the Status Quo?

Margaret L. Andersen

HAPPY HOUSEWIVES OR WOMEN WITH THE BLUES?

P opular literature and public opinion polls have, of late, created the impression that there is widespread and growing support in American society for the liberation of women from traditional roles (Gallup, 1976; Harris Survey, 1976; Washington Post, 1976). Yet, in spite of these optimistic messages, many women remain in these roles and some even claim to be content with their situation. This is in direct contrast to the wealth of research and testimony emerging from the feminist movement which has debunked the conventional image of contentment among traditional wives. This literature documents the extent of depression, abuse, and violence in the American home (Weissman and Paykel, 1972; Seidenberg, 1973; Steinmetz and Straus, 1974); it reports the ambivalence and trauma that women experience as mothers (Bart, 1970; Lazarre, 1976; Rich, 1976); it reveals a high incidence of drug and alcohol abuse among middle-class housewives (Chambers, 1971; Tessler, Stokes and

Author's note: The author wishes to thank the readers who carefully read and made suggestions on an earlier copy of this manuscript: Sally Bould, William Chambliss, Arlene Kaplan Daniels, Jan DeAmicis, Sandra Harding, Michael Lewis, Randall Stokes, and Gerald Turkel. Research for the article was supported by a Grant-in-Aid from the Office of Research, University of Delaware. This was originally presented as a paper at the Eastern Sociological Society, New York City, 1979.

Editor's note: Margaret Andersen examines the support by middle-class women of traditional gender roles in marriage. She examines women who follow their husbands transferred by corporate employers. These "corporate gypsies" generally support women's rights, but nonetheless retain a strong personal sense of role distinction. Andersen examines this contradiction in the context of its relevance to the concept of false consciousness and inequality of women.

Margaret L. Andersen is Assistant Professor of Sociology at the University of Delaware. Her research and teaching interests include sex roles/women's studies, race relations, and social theory. She is the author of a forthcoming book, Thinking about Women: Sociological and Feminist Perspectives (Macmillan).

Source: Margaret L. Andersen, "Corporate Wives: Longing for Liberation or Satisfied with the Status Quo?" Urban Life, Vol. 10 (October 1981), pp. 311–327. Copyright © 1981 by Urban Life. Reprinted by permission of Sage Publications, Inc.

Pietras, 1978); and it suggests that "mid-life crises" are an ordinary and expected aspect of maturing as an American adult (Sheehy, 1974). In fact, by now, most people are probably familiar with the feminist position that no man is so exceptional that he justifies a woman's sacrificed career, never-ending housework, and total absorption in the lives of others.

How then do we explain the continuing support for traditional roles in the beliefs and behaviors of some groups of women? Feminists have often described the beliefs of such women as false consciousness; that explanation has gone largely unchallenged in the sociological literature. This research studies corporate wives who say they are happy with their lives as women and who support feminism only as it addresses the issues of employment discrimination. Their beliefs are explored, not as a question of false consciousness, but as stemming from the actual material conditions of their lives.

Unlike women who are discontent with traditional sex roles, these women are not frustrated by their situations, nor do they experience the personal malaise suggested by the scholarly and feminist literature on the topic. Quite the contrary, the women report great happiness with themselves and their situation and they say they would not want things any other way. They support changes that would give women equal opportunity to work if they want to, but in their own case, they prefer to remain as housewives. They think that feminism does not appreciate the contribution that they make and they dissociate themselves from those women who they see as too radical. As they say,

> I'm fanatical that a woman who wants to, can raise children and work at the same time. But I'm not a great women's libber. I love being Mrs. Harry Thomas[1] and I have loved every minute of it. What I fight for, in essence, is to know me for me. Great steps are being made, but I think a lot of the real strong women's lib movement hurts, I really do, because it turns the men off.

Another says,

> Feminists have stirred up the happy housewife. They've said, "something is the matter with you because you are home."

And another,

> Oh, yeah, I feel sympathetic to the goals. But I don't feel sympathetic to a lot of the shouters. I feel we should pass the Equal Rights Amendment. It's only a simple statement against discrimination. It's hard to believe anybody could be against that. But feminists make a lot of dumb statements like having to go to the same rest room.

The mixed character of their feminist beliefs corrects those generalizations made about support for feminism which do not adequately describe the specific character of support and resistance to certain feminist issues. Moreover, their beliefs about themselves pose a challenge to sociologists and feminists who have not adequately explained the source of the women's contentment. There is a contradiction in the life the women say they have and the way that life has been described by others. This contradiction has not, of yet, been adequately explained. Feminists usually would explain it as a question of false consciousness. According to this argument, if the women only say their true conditions, they would raise their consciousness and embrace the total ideology of feminism. One feminist writes:

> That people are unaware of the oppression of women is a serious problem, but one that will be resolved as our movement grows and makes its presence felt. The problem of false consciousness, however, is harder to solve, and ultimately more dangerous, since our consciousness will determine our goals and strategy. . . . Surely one important task of our movement is to make it clear to ourselves and to all women that our low social, economic, and sexual status results not from any natural inferiority but from actual, recognizable, analyzable oppression, however subtle in form [Gardner, 1970: 82–83].

Thus, the argument of false consciousness assumes that the women's actual condition is different from what they claim. It assumes that their situation is oppressive and that denial of that oppression is proof of its existence. Thus, underlying the false consciousness explanation is an assumption that the women's claims to happiness are insincere. A perspective on how the real conditions of their lives might create the contentment they report is understated, if not ignored, by the false consciousness argument. Moreover, if researchers assume that the women's claims are insincere, then they are put in the untenable position of being unable to believe what their subjects report. A more appropriate research strategy is to look, not for the falsehoods of their claims, but to the actual conditions of the women's lives and the way those conditions might generate the contentment the women express.

In so doing, we study the character of social relationships as they are defined by the subjects themselves. This approach assumes that the women are situated as social actors in a context that encourages their complacence, rather than assuming that the women are misled in preferring the current status of their lives. There is no defense of the sexist conditions in which their lives are nested intended here. But a question is pursued which asks how the women's situation encourages the beliefs that they have. It is assumed here that human actors make choices and establish beliefs in the context of the material and social resources available to them. For these women, these resources are not slight; they establish their beliefs, not out of passive resignation to their situation in life, but out of an active commitment to the systems in which their lives are imbedded. Their beliefs about feminism, thus, support those themes in feminist ideology which do not significantly alter the class structure, but only make new opportunities available to individual women who at least have the resources to pursue them. Before looking further at their beliefs about feminism, we need some description of the situation in which the women live.

THE CASE OF THE CORPORATE GYPSIES

Research for this article uses a case study interview method in which twenty women, all of them corporate wives and members of a newcomers' club in a small southern city, were interviewed in their homes during January 1977. The women are generally young (most were between 25 and 40); they are well-educated and politically liberal, and most do not work. All but one of them had children and they are active as civic volunteers.

The label "corporate gypsies" was used by one of the women to describe the central pattern in their lives – that, like other corporate families, the women frequently move as their husbands are transferred from one job to another. For this particular group, the families move on an average of once every three years; frequent relocation has become a way of life for them. One woman reports having moved a total of eighteen times in the twenty-five years of her marriage. Although her case is the extreme, it symbolizes the frequent disruption which characterizes the family life of all of them. Their moves are most often to distant places where they have no family or friends.

Their continual mobility creates uncertain environments for the women. It also encourages financial dependence on their husbands, for with such frequent moving, it would be difficult for the women to maintain careers of their own. Most have decided that they do not want to work, even though, on the whole, they are well-educated and hold some professional or technical skill. All but two of them have completed at least one year of college and one-third have completed bachelor's degrees. One also holds a master's degree and has worked as a college instructor. With the exception of only two who have never worked and three who have held clerical jobs, the women have, at one time, been employed in professional and technical work. Among them are several teachers, medical technologists, a draftswoman, an artist, a nurse, two merchandise buyers and one self-employed business entrepreneur. But, in each case, their careers have become secondary to their marriage and most had quit their jobs early in their marriages or when their first child was born. Currently, only one of them works full-time and three work part-time. Two of them expressed a concern that, if they had to return to work, they would no longer have the skill required. But since only one of the twenty wanted to work in the future, this was of little concern to most.

They are economically secure, as their husbands are among the more prosperous in this city; their income brackets place them in the top 14% of the city's population (U.S. census, 1970). Nine of the women report their family income in the $15,000-$25,000 bracket; eight, $25,000-$50,000; and two,

$50,000–$100,000. (One did not respond, but based on her husband's position, it is likely she would fall in the upper category.)

For each of them, the newcomers' club is a focal point for volunteering and they speak of volunteering as an activity that gives them a feeling of belongingness and service. The newcomers' club was founded to help women establish friendships when they arrived, but it also organizes weekly volunteering in local nursing homes. Most of the women are also active in other volunteer groups. The women say that their volunteer service benefits their community and, as a result, it enhances their own status as outsiders in a new environment. But, primarily, they attribute their volunteer activity to the chance it provides to meet other women. The women remember feeling lost and alone when they first moved to town. They went to the newcomers' club to meet other women. Its volunteer activities were central to the group, but still secondary to the association the group provides. One of the founders reports,

> This is a hard town to move into and women get lost in the shuffle. If the club does nothing else but, once a month, give them a basis and a core, then it is worthwhile. It's a place for them to belong. Thus we're doing more of a community service.

Another member says,

> I have always been involved in volunteer work and I guess the basic motivation is service to the community. But I have, very frankly, just enjoyed working with the people and that is my selfish motivation.

One woman who has been active in newcomers' clubs for over fifteen years says,

> In the beginning of our marriage, my husband traveled for five years, Monday through Friday, and I felt like I had just been dumped. If it hadn't been for the newcomers' club getting me busy and active, I don't think I could have made it – simply because we didn't have a good family life.

No doubt there are other corporate wives who do not fare so well when they move and for whom volunteering and newcomers' clubs do not touch the experience of their isolation. But, for the women studied here, volunteering provides the chance for affiliation with others, community leadership, and self-expression. While volunteering does not cause their contentment, it does give them a feeling of accomplishment and belonging with others, as well as providing a place where their skills can be used. In a collective letter to the author, they write of the contribution they make to their community and to their family:

> We are making substantial contributions to society, not only by our family orientation, but also by our involvement in civic and volunteer activities. The need for these volunteers is great and will not be fulfilled by job-seekers who disdain work for which

they are not paid. It is also possible that, in our quiet way, and by working within the system, we will continue to be responsible for introducing progressive and innovative change in our community.

Their self-proclaimed liberalism makes their reaction to feminism all the more interesting. They have exactly the characteristics which research identifies as conducive to feminist support – they are young, middle-class, well-educated, and politically liberal (Welsh, 1975; Tarvis, 1973). But, although they think of themselves as a new generation of women and they support feminism on a limited basis, they are quick to dissociate themselves from feminists and they do not support the more far-reaching goals of feminist thought.

FEMINISM: WOMEN'S RIGHTS AND WOMEN'S LIBERATION

Public discussions about feminism seldom make the distinctions in feminist ideology which exist within the movement itself. Consequently, generalizations which are made about widespread support for feminism are misleading indica-tions of the actual character of support unless they delineate particular issues and the support and resistance they encourage. It is clear in the case of the cor-porage gypsies, that, even though they support equal rights for working women, they do not support more radical changes in traditional sex role relations or in the traditional division of labor. They see little relevance of feminist issues to their own lives and when they speak of women's liberation, they ridicule feminists and are quick to distance themselves from the feminist movement. When they are asked if they support the women's liberation movement, they reply,

> I do go along with a lot of their thoughts – for instance, equal pay for equal work. I think some of the rules and regulations of industries and different companies, as far as women are concerned, are ridiculous. But I don't consider myself a women's libber.
> I can't go along with the very radical. They're leaning a bit too far.
> My husband's always been the one who took care of me and always opened and shut the doors. I like this sort of thing. I love to be taken care of. I have nothing against someone who doesn't want it that way. I feel that, if women are capable, they should be paid the same as a man – if they have the training. But when these ex-tremists go the other way – no way! They have such a downgrading look on a man. Like I say, I've always been taken care of and they seem to want no part of it.

It is important to emphasize that these corporate wives are not overtly resis-tant to the women's liberation movement. Their replies to the question about whether they support women's liberation affirm what other sociological studies have shown – that even when women support women's rights to equal employ-ment opportunity, they continue to support the traditional division of labor by gender (Mason and Bumpass, 1975) and that they are more likely to support specific proposals for reform than they are to support the general idea of women's liberation (Welsh, 1975). The corporate gypsies state,

> I think a woman, if she is qualified to have a job, should be given as much money as a man. I'm definitely for women's lib in that way. However, as for the leaders of the women's movement, they are just interested in promoting themselves and their little bandwagon because they want to do whatever they want to do.
>
> I support women's liberation to a certain extent. In the beginning I thought it was kind of crackpot. And like the other day, I saw some lady on television and I wanted to say, "Oh, why are you dressing like a man?" because she just looked ridiculous. I feel like you should get the pay, but I don't want women to run the world. I still want somebody to open the doors, pay the bills.
>
> Some of their ideas, I'm sympathetic for. Some of their others, I think they've carried to the extreme. But, basically, I'm for the movement – especially equal wages for women. But making the man feel the woman is his equal is going to the extreme.

The women cannot be characterized as antifeminist, at least in the sense represented by conservative groups like Schafly's anti-ERA movement, the Total Woman movement, or the Right-to-Life movement. Their reaction to feminism is more ambivalent, in that they support wage reform and access to opportunity, but they resist those feminist changes which would alter the conditions of their own lives.

In their eyes, only working women encounter the problems of sexism. Thus, they support changes that would benefit women who work but they claim feminism has no relevance to their own lives. Although none opposed feminism outright, some are simply disinterested and say that the women's movement just doesn't relate to them. They say,

> I haven't given it much thought. I'm a homebody.
>
> I'm not interested at all in women's liberation. I don't believe in it. I mean, what's the big deal?

They all agree that women's liberation has little relevance to their own life and that they prefer things the way they are. When asked if they have ever felt they were at a disadvantage because they are a woman, each responds that she is not at a disadvantage. A few say that there were times in the past that were personally stressful, but that all that had passed:

> There were periods of time when I wanted to be important. That meant most everything – to be recognized – and now that's not important to me. I've never had any big things happen in my life. I'm just a regular person who is happy. I've got a marvelous, most beautiful husband and two great children. Everything just could not be any better.

Her words are similar to those of others who report satisfaction with their lives and also say they had never been at a disadvantage as a woman:

> I have never been at a disadvantage. I love being a woman and I wouldn't want to be a man. Men have it harder – they have to go out in the world and work everyday.
> Every person has to be fulfilled, but feminists put women in a position they don't want to be in. Most of my friends don't work and are happy. I am satisfied and I always have been. I think a lot depends on your life with your husband.
> I suppose every woman has felt like she's had an advantage – like when they drive into a service station and they really need something done. If you talk real sweet to the guy, you know, they'll take you first. The disadvantage is, you know, in wages, but I can't say I was treated unfairly as a secretary because I didn't have that much education background. I just went in there – I typed, I filed. I don't think I was taken advantage of. I don't think I was paid less than what I was worth. It was very boring. I don't care to do anything like that again. I hate shorthand. I hate all these secretarial things.

Most of them want to maintain even the symbols of traditional sex roles and they believe in the traditions of chivalry and femininity:

> I think it takes away from a woman's femininity when she's too aggressive.
> I go along with a lot of their ideas, like equal pay for equal work. But I don't think I'd want to stop having all the niceties that a gentleman does for a lady – like opening doors and taking them out to dinner.
> I wonder what it will be like ten years from now? How will a man feel about a woman? Will he feel about her as someone to be protected and very feminine or will he think of her as an equal – just someone to live with and share expenses with?

Their ideas indicate two different orientations in the feminist movement which have been defined as the women's rights perspective and the women's liberation perspective (Freeman, 1973; Goldstein, 1980; Welsh, 1975; Hole and Levin, 1971). The corporate gypsies generally support the women's rights perspective of the movement – that which seeks to remove discriminatory rules from the public sphere of women's activity. The more broadly defined women's liberation perspective argues that discrimination alone is not the source of women's inequality. While they may agree that removal of the formal barriers of sex discrimination is an important feminist goal, they also want more far-reaching changes and patriarchy (Jaggar and Struhl, 1978). It is these changes which the corporate gypsies resist and it is also these changes which would most transform their immediate situations. Since they are content with their situation, it is not surprising that this is the aspect of feminism which they denounce. In the end, they resist feminist change that alters their own conditions, although they support the rights of women who want to compete in a man's world.

When they speak about their support for feminism, they emphasize that it is all right for other women, but not for themselves. They argue they do not need liberation, although they can see why some women would:

Not being a career person, I don't feel any disadvantage.
I can't say that I've felt at a disadvantage. Maybe if I were out working, I'd have more definite opinions on that.
I have no desire to work. I'm very happy the way things are. I'm just not one of those people who feels nonliberated.

Their own lives are happy because, as they put it, they are married to good men who give them emotional support as well as the material things they enjoy:

If I ever do get a feeling of inferiority, my husband has been a booster.
I really have enjoyed the fact that I have been in a household of boys. And I have enjoyed the fact that I have a husband who certainly has been able to provide the things that we enjoy.

In each interview, the women report that they have no complaints about their lives. Their satisfaction with their lives stands in contradiction to other reports of the distress in such households. An earlier paper on these women suggested the possibility that their accounts are insincere (Andersen, 1979) but, in response to that suggestion, the women organized a collective rebuttal to the author. In their letter, they adamantly defend their place and they strongly argue that women like themselves can, in spite of what sociologists say, find fulfillment in the roles of wife, mother and volunteer. Their letter contains several of the clues which help explain the source of their satisfaction. They write:

(We deny) that personal fulfillment for women can be found only in the active pursuit of a career. Well-educated women can find contentment and fulfillment in nurturing their families, in involvement in the life of their communities, in participation in charitable activities, and in happy association with others. We do not consider all working women to be child-neglecting, emasculating, selfish vipers. In return, we should not be regarded as mercenary status seekers, interested only in appearance and possessions. There is no one right way to live. We know who we are – true believers in free people who decide for themselves what their responsibilities are. We believe that we need to create a world where everyone can peacefully live the life they choose (Source: personal correspondence with the author, September 1978).

Throughout, the women insist that their situation is a good one. In another part of the letter they claim the author is jealous of their economic resources, thus underscoring the material basis of their situations. Their happiness as wives, mothers, and community volunteers cannot be seen in isolation from this fact. Lest it sound that an image of the happy slave is being adopted here, the obvious point should be made that there are doubtless scores of women who, in exactly the same situations, are unhappy and depressed. But, these corporate wives would laugh at the very idea that they are like slaves and they may well be right that their current situations are the best they can imagine. No doubt, future security and well-being depends on the continuing support and prosperity of their husbands. But, particularly in relation to the majority of women in the paid labor force (Blau, 1978), these women currently receive many of the benefits of a system of unequal privilege and economic inequality. For most women in the paid labor force, work has meant low wages, low prestige, and little in the way of work satisfaction, autonomy or creativity. As long as these conditions remain, it is little wonder that women who believe they are economically secure will prefer the traditional roles of homemaker and volunteer. When these roles are also nested in a system of class inequality which brings economic and social resources to a few women, then it is unlikely that those women will challenge their satisfaction with the status quo and seek changes which would disrupt their own well-being.

This perspective on their beliefs situates corporate wives within the context of the material and social resources available to them. In the absence of any personal crisis which might disrupt their contentment, we can see that their beliefs about feminism and about themselves reflect their interest in the system that delivers resources to them.

CONCLUSION

This argument turns the perspective of false consciousness on its head. Where false consciousness would depict the women as unaware of their true and oppressive conditions, this article suggests that they are keenly aware of their real situation and it is not experienced as oppressive. In typing their beliefs to the context of their experience, belief is seen as emerging from the dynamic interaction of the person and his or her actual environment. Women can be differentiated by their class difference (Middleton, 1974) and that experience shapes the character of their beliefs. Admittedly, corporate wives benefit from that class system through their attachment to men. Still, they are indirectly among the benefactors of a system which feminists argue is one of the primary bases for gender inequality (Mitchell, 1971; Hartmann, 1977; Eisenstein, 1979; Zaretsky, 1976). The contentment of the corporate gypsies should be seen within the context of their commitment to that system. When we consider this, it is little wonder that their only criticism of the system is that more women should be admitted to it. To ask them to do more than change the entrance requirements, so that resources and power could be redistributed, is asking them to challenge the fundamental basis of their current experience. In conclusion, we must discard the assumption that most women will become feminists once they "see the light." This research shows that some women have actively chosen a life which makes economic affluence, personal autonomy, and community influence a possibility for them.

This article is not intended to defend the status quo or the system of inequality for women. But it does clarify some issues about who is most likely to support feminist change in the complete structure of gender relations. Those who believe that liberal reform alone can eliminate inequality between men and women can take heart in the fact that these women will likely support such changes. But, if we understand that women's inequality is the result of a more complex interplay between capitalism and patriarchal relations, then those who optimistically assume the eventual support of such women are likely to be sadly disappointed. There are signs everywhere – from the increased use of the "liberated woman" in corporate advertising to the adoption of feminist rhetoric by self-help movements – that feminism can be used to legitimate the continuation of economic inequality. Rather than merely accepting these signals as evidence of widespread feminist change, we have to ask the harder questions about how the persistence of women's inequality and its acceptance among some women is tied to the class relations in which women find themselves.

NOTE

1. The name used in the text is a pseudonym. Research subjects were promised anonymity as one of the conditions of their participation in the research.

REFERENCES

Andersen, M. (1979) "Affluence, contentment, and resistance to feminism: the case of the corporate gypsies" in M. Lewis (ed.) Research in Social Problems and Public Policy. Greenwich, CT: Johnson Assoc.

Bart, P. (1970) "Mother Portnoy's complaint." Transaction 8 (November–December): 69–74.

Blau, F. (1978) "The data on women workers, past, present and future," pp. 29–62 in A. Stromberg and S. Harkness (eds.) Women Working. Palo Alto, CA: Mayfield.

Chambers, C. (1971) Differential Drug Use Within the New York State Labor Force. New York: New York State Narcotic Addiction Control Commission.

Daniels, A.K. (1978) "Invisible careers: the professional volunteers." Paper prepared for the Feminist Scholarship Conference. University of Illinois at Urbana-Champagne (February 27–March 4).

Eisenstein, Z.R. (1979) Capitalist Patriarchy and the Need for Socialist Feminism. New York: Monthly Review Press.

Freeman, J. (1973) "The origins of the women's liberation movement." Amer. J. of Sociology 79 (January).

Friedan, B. (1963) The Feminine Mystique. New York: Norton.

Gallup Poll (1976) Field Enterprises.

Gardner, J. (1970) "False Consciousness." Notes from the Second Year: Women's Liberation. New York: Radical Feminism.

Gold, D.B. (1971) "Woman and voluntarism," pp. 533–554 in V. Gornick and S. Moran (eds.) Woman in Sexist Society. New York: Basic Books.

Goldstein, L. (1980) "Mill, Marx and women's liberation." J. of History and Philosophy (July).

Gunther, M. (1975) "Female alcoholism: the drinker in the party." Today's Health (June).

Harris Survey (1976) Louis Harris and Assoc. (Spring).

Hartmann, H. (1977) "Capitalism, patriarchy and job segregation by sex." Signs 1 (Spring).

Hole, J. and E. Levine (1971) Rebirth of Feminism. New York: Quadrangle.

Jaggar, A. and P. Struhl (1978) Feminist Frameworks. New York: McGraw-Hill.

Lazarre, J. (1976) The Mother Knot. New York: Dell.

Mason, K.O. and L.L. Bumpass (1975) "U.S. women's sex role ideology, 1970." Amer. J. of Sociology 80 (March): 1212–1219.

Middleton, C. (1974) "Sexual inequality and stratification theory," in F. Parkin (ed.) The Social Analysis of Class Structure. London: Tavistock.

Mitchell, J. (1971) Women's Estate. New York: Pantheon.

Rich, A. (1976) Of Woman Born. New York: Norton.

Roper Organization (1974) The Virginia Slims American Women's Opinion Poll, Volume III.

Seidenberg, R. (1973) Corporate Wives – Corporate Casualties? New York: American Management Association.

Sheehy, G. (1974) Passages. New York: E.P. Dutton.

Steinmetz, S. and M. Straus (1974) Violence in the Family. New York: Harper & Row.

Tavris, C. (1973) "Who likes women's liberation and why: the case of the unliberated liberals." J. of Social Issues 29: 175–198.

Tessler, R., Stokes, R., and M. Pietras (1978) "Consumer response to Valium." Drug Therapy (February): 178 ff.

Washington Post (1976): September 28.

U.S. Department of Commerce, Bureau of the Census (1970) 1970 Census of the Population, Volume 1. Washington, D.C.: U.S. Government Printing Office.

Weissman, M.M. and E. Paykel (1972) "Moving and depression in women." Transaction/Society 9 (July–August): 24–28.

Welsh, S. (1975) "Support among women for the issues of the women's movement." Soc. Q. 16 (Spring): 216–227.

Zaretzsky, E. (1976) Capitalism, The Family and Personal Life. New York: Harper & Row.

Chapter 11 ─────────────────────────────────────

The Phenomenon of the Public Wife: An Exercise in Goffman's Impression Management*

Joanna B. Gillespie

──

Approaching the topic of American leader-image from the perspective of politics-as-theater (political communication as exchange of symbols), this paper examines a taken-for-granted visual symbol which a national political leader is invariably expected to present: a wife. Her contributions to her husband's "impression management" techniques (Goffman, 1959) are studied in Goffman's "defensive" categories of dramaturgical loyalty, dramaturgical discipline, and dramaturgical circumspection.

This analysis suggests that the visible presence of a wife in public leadership rituals offers the public voter or viewer important reassurances or symbolic guarantees about her husband's "morality" – and, therefore, his appropriateness for public trust. She has become a necessary part of his public performance because of our everyday need for "cultural absolutes" (Furay, 1977) in the image of our leadership figures.

F ascination with wives of public men in America is a peculiar and enduring phenomenon. The cheering for Mrs. Washington when she arrived in Philadelphia too late for her husband's inaugural was reported to have exceeded that given the first President of the United States (Means, 1963). And "poor Mrs. Madison was almost pressed to death . . . everyone crowded round her, those behind pressing on those before, and peering over their shoulders to have a peep of her . . ." at the first inaugural ball (Hunt, 1906:61).[1]

With the development of newspaper technology,[2] the public idolization of First Ladies (a term not employed until 1877) developed to the point of making a

*I thank my colleagues Suzanne Vromen, Robert Perinbanayagam, the editor, and various reviewers for their suggestions during the evolution of this paper, as well as Robert Bellah's seminar on Civil Religion which provoked its original conceptualization.

Source: Joanna B. Gillespie, "The Phenomenon of the Public Wife: An Exercise in Goffman's Impression Management." Symbolic Interaction 3 (Fall, 1980): 109–126. Reprinted by permission of JAI Press, Inc., Greenwich, Conn.

president's wife's inaugural ball gown a public icon. It was news when Rosalynn Carter donated her gown to the Smithsonian, an event greeted by the head of that organization with this remark: "This marvelous unbroken collection (of inaugural gowns of First Ladies) at the Smithsonian has become a popular symbol of the history of our country" (New York Times, July 21, 1978, p. 11).

Today it is still largely taken for granted that a public official will appear with a wife at his side for certain ceremonial events. If he is a political aspirant, she will be part of the scene at his announcement of candidacy. She will be at the voting-booth with him and at the victory or defeat announcement. Local newspapers publish pictures of wives holding the Bible for the oath-taking of husbands at all levels of municipal government. A popular journalistic metaphor for the importance of a civil occasion is the presence of the wife; the unexpected appearance of the supreme Court Justices' wives in their husbands' official arena signalled to reporters that an unusually important ruling – the Bakke decision – was to be announced.[3]

In any of these wife-appearances, the question arises as to why she is there? What does her presence have to do with the way her husband is perceived? What does her presence have to do with his job? What sort of information about him is her image presumed to impart?

The thesis of this paper is that the wife has long been a crucial, if unacknowledged, sociological component of a leader's "political self-presentation" (Duncan, 1968), and this may be analyzed by examining her role in the husband's impression-management strategies (Goffman, 1959). The broader theoretical context for this Goffmanian interpretation is a symbolic-interactionist view of American politics (Hall, 1972) in which the social order is seen as negotiated and political authority as a process of emerging consensus, collective goals, and manipulation of symbols (Edelman, 1977; Cohen, 1974).

A brief theoretical statement is followed by an historical context for the emergence of the public wife as "morality" symbol and the connection of this with a family/father image. Examination of the wife's contribution to the politician's impression-management will be through Goffman's categories of dramaturgical discipline, dramaturgical loyalty, and dramaturgical circumspection. The concluding discussion raises the issue of social change in the expectations and effectiveness of the wife-symbol.

LEADER SELF-PRESENTATION IN POLITICAL SOCIODRAMA

Our collective consciousness about leadership selection and legitimation relies heavily on certain kinds of non-verbal or dramaturgical assurances about a contender – his normality, his respectability, his trustworthiness – which must be read from a distance. The public figure must appear to personify the principles of the society – to be the guardian of the social order (Duncan, 1968) – and to create an impression of "almost sacred compatibility between the man and his job" (Goffman, 1959:46).

In the process of negotiating leader-impressions – of "courting" the general public through the staging of images and events – the leader surrounds himself with symbols which purport to give off "facts" about his necessary but intangible personal traits. Goffman's analytic approach – looking at the everyday interactions and cues which people use to define a situation and create a shared perception of the social order – has been transposed to the larger canvass of political interaction by Hall (1972).[4] His two major concepts, symbolic mobilization of support, and control of the flow of information, illuminate some of the practices around the wife-symbol. She can be read as a major component of the first concept, and thus sociologically relevant to the American political myth-system (Edelman, 1977) – the theater of politics (Mount, 1973). The public wife becomes a vehicle for imparting to her husband's public image legitimacy for leadership deriving from a primary source of societal authority and power: the family.

Family as a symbol of stability and validity taps a very deep vein in American civil life. The belief that a leader will have father-like concern and be responsible for the maintenance of the social order was expressed in the first models of civil government in this country. The Puritan elders (literally, village fathers) exercised authority over both family and community, and assumed responsibility for enforcing standards of public behavior and morality in both (Morgan, 1966). Public standards for the *appearance* of morality and civic conventionality persist in modern times, in the "prudish" conduct expected of public officials (although the average citizen allows himself more latitude as evidenced by the fact that a congressman's misbehavior is "news"). The image of a banker as "stuffy" may be amusing but is also apparently experienced as comforting, or at least appropriate (Klapp, 1964). Our national "fathers" have always had to seem above reporach, in general moralistic terms – a practice which began with the engineering of a "flawless founding father" image for George Washington in the decades after his death (Friedman, 1975, Ch. 2).

The sociodrama of leadership sets in motion a type of morality play (Klapp, 1964; Novak, 1974; Keller, 1963). The public man must create a political self – become a "merchant of morality" (Goffman, 1959:291) – which fits a generalized image of our national self-definition, sometimes referred to as our civil religion.[5] At its most basic, this tradition holds that Americans want to believe that they, and their representatives or leaders, are basically good (or at least not "bad").[6] In our need for this kind of reassurance, the wife seems to have become a widely recognized and taken-for-granted factor. As Goffman (1959:27) says, a

given social front tends to become institutionalized in terms of the abstract stereotyped expectations to which it gives rise, and tends to take on a meaning and stability
apart from the specific tasks which happen . . . to be performed in its name. The front
becomes a 'collective representation' in its own right.

Political leadership image, in this view, is a reflector of social realities rather
than a primary expression of or agent for social change (Mount, 1973). The process of negotiating it – for example, the office of the presidency (Hall, 1979) –
through symbolic mobilization of support,[7] serves as a significant form of social
integration and bargaining (Duncan, 1968). That the wife of a public man has
been, and continues to be associated symbolically with these rituals of the collective consciousness is curious and problematic, considering the diversity of the
publics which comprise the American social fabric.

Duncan (1968:81) defines types of audience which may be intended in a
symbolic-interactionist interpretation: the "they" of general publics; the "we"
who are perceived as leaders or guardians of the community; the significant
others who are as near as friends or confidants, the "thou"; the self-addressed inwardly, the "I" and "me"; or an ideal audience whom we think of and address as
an ultimate source of the social order – "it" (p. 81).

It may be that the last, almost metaphysical, category is the closest we can
come to a definition of "audience" in this type of analysis, since the actual
responses of people to a political scene or performance may be attributed to
many different things, most of which can only be inferred or interpreted by
analysts, commentators, and political impression-managers themselves. One can
only speculate about how much or to what degree a given sociological fact about
a public person will specifically motivate or influence actual voting behavior –
and of which groups or sub-groups within the total society.

The larger theoretical point is that political interaction consists of exchang-
ing symbolic "information," the meanings and readings of which change as the
society changes, and that the general public generally (never totally) identifies
with the various public figures which they (varying parts of the "mass" audience)
see as personifying general societal principles they themselves hold. In this sense
leader-image becomes a reification of a basic but often-unconscious traditional
value system.

The next section takes a brief evolutionary look at the leader's wife emerging as a public symbol, and some aspects of our understanding of morality for
which her public appearance serves as a kind of visual shorthand.

THE WIFE AS MRS. MORALITY

Women have always played a part in the ceremonial life of societies, and apparently have also been viewed as morally different from men. In pre-history and
again in medieval times, this difference was negative: woman seen as powerful

avenging mother-goddess (Boulding, 1976; Taylor, 1970) or as corrupter, blocking man's path to eternal salvation (Bullough and Bullough, 1977; O'Faolain and
Martines, 1973). After the Reformation, and during the Victorian idealization of
asexual woman, it was positive; moral superiority became attached to the
middle-class married woman.

> Challenging the traditional vaunted moral (and intellectual) superiority of men,
> authors increasingly celebrated examples of female piety . . . and benevolence (during
> the early 1800's). . . . Women came to be depicted as not only virtuous in themselves,
> but as more virtuous than men, indeed, as the main 'conservators of morals' in society
> (because of their pervasive influence on both men and children) (Bloch, 1978:116).

A change in family authority and interaction patterns accompanied the industrialization and beginnings of urbanization in the United States. The mother
– in Godey's Lady's Book,[8] in novels, in child-rearing advice books and sermons –
emerged as a glorified agent for spirituality, as "priestess" of the hearth (Bunkle,
1974; Cott, 1977; Welter, 1976; Wishy, 1968). Women were recognized as the
dominant consumers of organized religion and the moral arbiters within the
home, replacing the Puritan patriarch. The cult of true womanhood (Welter,
1976) made women responsible for both domestic and public morality in the
Jacksonian period. The nation "would be as great or weak, good or bad, as the
character of its citizens – raised by true American women in true American
families" (Cott, 1977:200).

Only a slight expansion of the middle-class woman's social space accompanied the feminization of family – and religious-authority.[9] Some activist
women enlisted in a moral crusade, "housecleaning society," which justified their
being out in public (Pivar, 1973; Thomas, 1965; Finley, 1931). The basic norm
for wifehood, however, remained that the home should be her major sphere of influence.

In the post–Civil War period, however, an acceptable public role began to
emerge for the wives of prominent business (and society) leaders – that of
hostess, symbol of home and family, at significant public events.[10] Women began
being seen in new places. With the growth of newspapers and photographic
technology, these wives offered a new public focus which was fed with lavish
detail. Interest in the wife and family – in the visual biography – of any public
figure became a major activity for journalists, and an obsession with consumers,
"Legitimate public exhibitionism" (Hall, 1972:63) characterized the political
strategies of public figures. A public man's private life assumed a new visual importance, of which the wife was most often the symbol.

Expanding interest in wives' public appearance may have been part of the
general social response to the conditions of rapid industrialization and urbanization, with the accompanying negative effect on family authority (Sennett, 1977;
Slater, 1977, Zaretsky, 1976). A definite shift in political interaction – the rise
of personality politics – seems to have emerged at this time. The typical cultural

evaluation of a public official's authenticity began to require a superimposing of his private life on his public appearances (Sennett, 1977:173). "Personality" became a social category in the public realm, and "sincerity" emerged as a dominant impression which leaders had to create (Zaretsky, 1976). The "self" – creation of a political character – became a product to be presented and managed.

In an increasingly complex society, wife-symbolism seemed to become analagous to another form of morality-certification analyzed by Weber in his essay "Protestant Sects and the Spirit of Capitalism" – the guarantee of good citizenship and credit-worthiness associated with the fact of membership in the Methodist or Baptist sects (Gerth and Mills, 1958). The sectarian label and what it represented opened instant community to a stranger in mobile American society. The name itself carried an impression of character, morality, and trustworthiness. The wife's public appearance at her husband's side similarly seems to convey answers to a range of unarticulated questions about him and to cover a set of assumptions which communicate non-verbal assurance to an audience.

The persistence of this symbolic message, up to very recent times, may in part be a function of the essentially conservative character of political interaction. "Voters exercise a strong, continuous pressure in favor of the familiar, the comprehensible, the conventional" (Mount, 1973:197–198). It was customary, and in certain sections is still, to note a single politician's unmarried status by accounting for it: the bachelor Governor of California, the divorced candidate Adlai Stevenson. Obviously, the concerns about morality and married-state are related to the issue of a man's sexual normality, in addition to such character traits as honesty, integrity, and dependability.

A sexuality dimension of public morality-image was not overtly acknowledged until very recently. If excuses or rationalization about a man's unmarried state were offered, any underlying causes for the anxiety were not often publicly verbalized. However, in the most recent mayoral election in New York City, the unmarried candidate, Edward Koch, was presented photographically and in televised advertisement with an attractive wife-substitute, a fellow-politician and friend, Bess Myerson. His political strategists admitted in a news story that his victory – narrow as it was – might well be attributed to his careful impression-management (not their phrase) with a highly photogenic surrogate public-wife.[11]

However, the larger value-issue for a public man's morality-impression is undoubtedly familial: the father image. Family symbolism seems related to the social order in a basic and primordial way, and is itself a kind of certification for citizenship. A member-in-good-standing of a family unit appears already to have basic knowledge of how to relate to other human beings. Identification with a man's "familyness" suggests that he can manage larger groups. One who is worthy of the respect of a family is to be trusted in other spheres.

But embedded in the father-image is a more problematic concern, namely potency. Our male leaders must strike us as holding a secured mid-position between appearing sexually powerful (the man is a normal male because he has a wife and children) and sexually controlled and channeled (he can't be a libertine or a pervert because he has a wife and children). Family symbolism has to carry many interwoven reassurances – and the images invoked are varied:

1. family = order – The wife of New Jersey Governor Byrne is quoted as saying, "Family and society are based on certain guidelines and rules in which we are supposed to function" (*Newark Star Ledger*, Sept. 12, 1978, pp. 1, 29);
2. family = model – Joan Mondale is quoted as saying, "The kind of family we have is an influence, a model, an ideal, a pattern – and a neat family" (*New York Times*, Oct. 14, 1976, p. 32);
3. family = a familiar and comforting locus of feeling – Clare Boothe Luce, quoted about Eisenhower: "to older women, he was like a son, to middle-aged women, a husband; and to young women, a father." Comparing his opponent, Stevenson, with Eisenhower, she used the image "brother-in-law" (*New York Times*, July 28, 1960, p. 12);
4. family = respectability – "Senator John Tower changed his negative image to a positive one in the 1966 campaign by prominently being featured with his wife and attractive family" (Nimmo, 1970:138);
5. family = universal point of human identification– "(Candidate) Robert Wagner . . . emphasizes he is a family man, appearing on television with his wife and two sons; it is because he 'believes he can help other families improve their situation that he is running,' he said." (*New York Times*, Oct. 17, 1953, p. 17);
6. family = bedrock of American virtue – Sargent Shriver, quoted about his wife during the 1972 presidential campaign, "First of all she is a great wife and mother, and if she were incompetent as either, neither she nor I would be any good as campaigners. For the solid basis for any campaign, or for any society, is a happy, loving, dedicated home front" (*Newark Star Ledger*, Oct. 15, 1972, "Parade" Section, p. 1).

To see a wife holding a Bible at an oath-taking or an official's wife and children "on display as living passports validating the humanity" (Edmondson and Cohen, 1976:87) of the public man reassures onlookers of the man's sexual normality, and thus his morality. As a culture we have so romanticized the myth of the All-American Happy Political Family that the short-hand symbol for it, the public wife, thus appears for some parts of the general public to be a kind of moral and cultural absolute. Even for a corporation executive or a clergyman, being a family man is most often a requirement, a sign of stability and maturity, and certainly taken into account in promotion decisions (Kanter, 1977:105). The strength of the morality, married man myth can be illustrated by its negative effect. During a Rockefeller bid for presidential nomination, a political advisor worried about his recently-acquired second wife, Happy, having become pregnant.

"This can open up all the old wounds. This can remind voters of the question of morality in Nelson's divorce and remarriage" (Wyckoff, 1968:189).

An advisor to President Nixon wrote

> We have to be very clear that the response (of the voters) is to the image, not to the man, since 99% of the voters have no contact with the man. It's not what's there that counts, it's what is projected . . . and carrying it one step further, it's not what he pro-jects but what the voter receives . . . It's not the man we have to change, but rather the received impression . . . (quoted in Novak, 1974:49).

Given this acknowledgement of impression-management techniques as means by which those with power can exploit dominant belief and value systems (Rogers, 1977), it is not surprising to discover that "the Nixon administration was filled with picture-book families" (Edmondson and Cohen 1976:49).

The impetus to produce a "robot wife programmed to smile or listen intently as if hearing him for the first time" (MacPherson, 1975:26) becomes one of the leader's public necessities and a tribute to impressions of morality as shaped by our cultural norms and dramaturgical modes. Specific ways in which the wife as morality-symbol may function in her husband's impression-management will be cast in Goffman's defensive categories of dramaturgical loyalty, dramaturgical discipline, and dramaturgical circumspection.

THE WIFE AND DRAMATURGICAL LOYALTY

The most conspicuously required public-wife characteristic is that she ap-pears as if there is nothing in the world she would rather be or do. All members of a political team who help to establish a public man's image must seem to have accepted, along with him, "certain moral obligations" (Goffman, 1959:121) – they must seem willing and pleased to participate with him in the signals and rituals which at least some observers will be reading as guarantees of his future performance.

Dramaturgical loyalty also assures the mass audience that a public person has nothing to hide, no dark secrets to reveal. It is the essence of political-wife loyalty to present an image of such grass-roots conventionality so as to forestall any questions. The concerns about a man's character appear to be soothed when the wife "looks as if she is a good cook, can darn socks, and speak in public modestly, but not too much . . . and dance sedately with an ambassador"[12] (Time, April 26, 1943, p.34).

From Mrs. Polk, standing loyally beside her husband in a downpour (Means, 1963:79) and Mrs. Harding, campaigning among women in the first election after women's suffrage but refusing to talk politics because that was her husband's role (Means, 1963:187), through the 1950's to the archetypal wifely loyalty of Patricia Nixon, the image and message persist. The present vice-president's wife expresses it succinctly. "It's in your own self-interest to promote your husband. What you say reflects on your husband all the time. You hope you present a good side" (MacPherson, 1975:54).

What makes the wife's loyalty convincing is a willingness not to exploit her own role in the public appearances of her husband. She gracefully accepts being part of the backdrop:

> When the Arms Control Agreement was signed in Moscow, the wives of the participants were not included . . . But Pat, with her great sense of history, refused to miss this momentous occasion. She arranged to stand in a dark corner of the hall, behind a pillar *where no one could see her* (emphasis added) but where she could witness the event with her own eyes (Richard Nixon, quoted in an article in the *Newark Star Ledger*, October 15, 1972, "Parade" Section, p. 1).

The Truman "family act" during his campaign is credited by political writers as a key factor in his victory.

> Mr. Truman would introduce his wife as 'the boss' and his daughter as 'the boss who bosses the boss'. . . . Mrs. Truman and Margaret never said a word, but they were sensational . . . you could almost hear the crowds thinking: what a nice family, just like the folks next door (Means, 1963:229).

In the same feminine-mystique era, New York Mayor Impelliteri's victory was saluted with the same images: "Look at the lovely couple (pictured above) . . . they could be your own family, or the family next door. You can see their clean, decent, wholesome character in their faces. . . . He is your Mayor, she is his only Boss" (*New York Daily News*, Nov. 3, 1950, p. 44).

Goffman's description of this dramaturgical technique is defensive. He focuses on the function of the "supportive players" to obviate questions, to maintain a facade which prevents negative impressions from arising. The wife, perhaps more than any of the other satellites of a public figure, seems responsible for motivating viewers to be comfortable with the man – to reassure them that their loyalty to her husband will be a safe investment. Journalistic fascination with the disloyal wife demonstrates the obverse of this dramaturgical stance. When a wife publicly attacks a former spouse, an almost automatic defensive tone appears in the stories – e.g., Senator Herman Talmadge and his wife's accusations; former San Francisco Mayor Joseph Alioto, and his wife.

A contemporary concern among Ted Kennedy's impression managers is about the dramaturgical loyalty of his wife: the newspapers have explicitly assured the public that she will fulfill that demand. A national syndicated columnist has raised the question as to whether she can be counted on not to reveal anything which would mar the image of her husband as a would-be guardian of the social order (McGrory, *San Francisco Chronicle*, July 12, 1979, p. 55).

THE WIFE AND DRAMATURGICAL DISCIPLINE

Physical self-control, management of face and voice, is the primary characteristic of this stance. This aspect of the wife's dramaturgy requires the most basic acting. She must appear immersed in the activity of doing nothing except gazing adoringly at her husband, as if unaware that it is a performance. At President Wilson's first inaugural, reporters wrote approvingly, "Mrs. Wilson seemed entirely unconscious of the fact that the eyes of the multitudes were constantly turned toward her" (New York Times, March 5, 1913, p. 5). A personal letter from Washington in 1801 describes the citizen perception of disciplined demeanor presented by the outgoing Adams administration: "(The defeated) all with one consent do what . . . dignity and self-respect require; everything . . . to conceal the natural feelings excited by disappointment and to assume the appearance not only of indifference but of satisfaction . . ." (Hunt, 1906:248).

The particular contribution of the wife to the husband's image of discipline is read by journalists in eye focus, body position, and stillness. Joan Kennedy "sitting with her hands folded in her lap, smiling and controlled, is the style Americans have come to respect in their political wives" (MacPherson, 1975:68). Rosalynn Carter, "her hands neatly disposed, sitting upright, ankles crossed, listening to herself being described as a representative of the 'American dream'" (New York Times, Nov. 6, 1977, p. 1), and Betty Ford, "irreverent but not too irreverent" (Drew, 1976:40–44) convey a sense of ease in the midst of the seering publicness of their husbands' lives, by seeming not to notice the focus on themselves.

This stance requires a balance between appreciation of peoples' intense focus and disclaiming any personal credit for it. An example of the first is Dolley Madison, reported to be fresh even after having been on her feet all day, and "the more she has round her the happier she appears to be; . . . really she makes everyone so happy . . . I think she is a very suitable person for the station she fills . . ." (Sung, 1977:181). An example of the second is Governor Rockefeller's second wife, during his New Hampshire campaign:

> She sat, the only seated person in the hall, as if in a witness chair; the townspeople gathered in a semi-circle somewhat apart from the candidate and the seated woman as if they were a jury. While her husband spoke eloquently and well, whether or not they were listening to him I cannot say, but their eyes were all staring unnervingly at the handsome woman with bowed head and curled legs who sat in the spot of light. They might have been a gathering of Puritans come to examine the accused (White, 1965:108).

In some ways the quintessential example of wifely discipline may have been Eleanor Roosevelt's early public wifehood. Her extraordinary sense of duty helped overcome her natural shyness. She developed into her husband's emissary and in many ways became an equal public figure. In her later life she was too independent in mind, too determined to do things for herself, to be circumscribed by the standard rituals of public wifery (Lash, 1971; also Ayres, 1979:39, in which Eleanor Roosevelt's independence is contrasted with Rosalynn Carter's "deliberate supplementary stance").

The message of dramaturgical discipline is most vivid at moments of tension: defeat, victory, awe during oath-taking. Pictures of brave smiles or controlled tears play a part in the public assimilation of the cyclical processes of leadership. It appears however that newspaper photographs mostly reflect the victorious moment. Few newspapers carried the only moment in Mrs. Nixon's incredibly disciplined public career when, in spite of obviously super-human effort, she could not suppress her emotions. Her husband's bitter concession to John F. Kennedy in November, 1960, was dramatized by her distorted and crumbling face during the pitiless televised announcement.

The dramaturgical discipline required of the wife seems to be part of a generalized cultural norm about power, a "Protestant stance" which maintains a cool distance from the enjoyment of one's power – one should never look powerful (Novak, 1974:281). Duncan (1968) suggests similarly that the mass audience legitimates a public person who presents himself as offering "service." Claims to leadership must balance an appearance of willingness and authoritarian self-confidence. The wife tags along, a hostage to this discipline, as stated by the wife of New York Senator Jacob Javits: "The wife who accompanies the man who shakes the hand knows what 'impersonal' means better than anyone. She is completely left out" (MacPherson, 1975:40). Being at once peripheral and yet essential to her husband's image was learned painfully by Mrs. Javits. Her professional activities were subject to dramaturgical circumspection in 1976.[13]

The public wife's contribution in this impression-strategy must assure viewers that the private life of her husband is "in control;" his public persona will not suddenly crack and allow an embarrassing "scene" to emerge. An unpredictable or too-flamboyant wife would be perceived as a dangerous lack of control in the flow of information and imagery which characterize the political interaction around leadership.

THE WIFE AND DRAMATURGICAL CIRCUMSPECTION

The third and most far-reaching aspect of impression management, for the wife, encompasses extended aspects of her behavior, clothing, and grooming. It is evidenced in her generalized awareness of being "on stage" much of the time and reaches into what for the average person would be private areas. Essentially

the technique of being dramaturgically circumspect is that of guarded boundaries, of always being seen as conventional. Naturally this becomes onerous to
the wife. Even Martha Washington

> felt like a state prisoner more than anything else; there is (sic) certain bounds set for
> me which I must not depart from, and as I cannot do as I like, I am obstinate and stay
> home a great deal (Means, 1963:14).

Dolley Madison also trimmed her sails a bit after her husband's election.

> She is more . . . dignified in her deportment . . . indulges less in her favorite amuse-
> ment of cards, a most fitting change since her husband is about to be exalted to the
> highest and most honorable station . . . (Sung, 1977:179).

The image of maximum civic piety has seemed, at least until the very recent
times, to feed on "Victorian-family" pictures. A *Life* pictorial essay on Mrs. Kennedy and Mrs. Nixon during the 1960 campaign showed Jackie in such homey
shots as dressing her child and Pat sewing a dress or petting the cat (*Life*, Oct.
10, 1960, pp. 150–157). The journalistic attention to daily life details of President Carter's youngest child is a current example. Occasionally, an explicit
guideline may be published for a political wife's circumspection image. A recent
one from a major political party warns that the wife, if she cares for her
husband's success, will not be photographed wearing glasses, or with a cigarette
or drink in her hand. She must remove her name tag when being photographed,
never express her own views on any issue if they differ even slightly from her
husband's, and never mention her own work or interests (MacPherson,
1975:118). Wives must be on-stage even when they are off; a favorite stereotype among political campaign managers is of how wife-meddling has hurt campaigns – e.g., a recent syndicated column (*San Francisco Chronicle*, May 23,
1979, p. A6) is titled "Keeping the Candidates' Wives at Bay."
     The public wife's clothing is supposed to be circumspect, to escape notice. It
is rarely mentioned, except on the women's pages in newspapers. However,
acute television-watchers may have observed a telling change in the style and
appearance of Senator Robert Dole's wife as he became a contender for
Republican Presidential nomination. During the 1976 campaign when he was
running for Vice President, Mrs. Dole had been the very stereotype of the
smartly-dressed career woman. As he began to maneuver toward the presidency
itself, she began to appear in the innocuous public-wife "uniform" – pastel-
colored, sleeved, round-collared dresses.
     Mrs. Nixon is the exemplar of dramaturgical circumspection and idealized
conventionality. Her only flaw, some analysts contend, is her flawlessness. She
has embodied the essence of this strategy. She is careful to do nothing which
would dislodge the impression of his being in charge of his household or of the
nation. During the 1973 inauguration, she verbalized it. She planned indeed to

hold the Bible for his oath, but it is her job "to keep the spotlight on him, where it belongs" (*New York Times*, Jan. 21, 1973, p. 40).

A particularly acute example of a wife's dramaturgical circumspection is the sensitivity of Daniel Ellsberg's wife to his image in photographs. Though as tall as he, she is described as knowing "instinctively" when a camera was focused on them; "at the precise moment when the shutter clicked, she bent her knees, tilted her head, and smiled at him" (Edmondson and Cohen, 1976:145).

An example dramatizing these three dramaturgical stances is the former wife of former San Francisco Mayor Joseph Alioto, who "ran away" (MacPherson, 1975). For many years of public-wifehood Mrs. Alioto had conformed. When suddenly she found herself outraged at the omission of the customary public acknowledgment ("this is my wife") at a routine political dinner, she left without explanation. After three weeks her husband was forced to confess to the press that he had no idea where she was. By putting him in that position, Mrs. Alioto violated both dramaturgical discipline and loyalty. When she returned and called a news conference of her own, she violated circumspection. A reporter, reading these actions dramaturgically, asked her, "If your husband can't manage you, how can he run a city?" (MacPherson, 1975:93). By playing out *her* personal needs on the public stage, Angelina Alioto focused the classic anxiety for the stability of the social order: what will become of us if the political "father" is troubled in this way, cannot manage for us, represents not man-in-charge but beleaguered manhood?

Perhaps the dramaturgical defenses Goffman has identified remain effective, to the degree that we still experience them in political symbolic-exchange, because of cultural and sociological validities we choose not to acknowledge, but which still persist.

DISCUSSION AND SUMMARY

Though undeniably our societal mores for male public figures are in transition,[14] it is also clear that the kind of Victorian family iconography decried by intellectuals and denounced by feminists is still with us. The need to typify wives in dependent and depersonalized images appears to persist as an important component of the exercise and maintenance of public power. There is little question that Patricia Nixon's image of constancy sustained one kind of belief in Richard Nixon's fitness for office, deep into the denouement of Watergate. The Gallup polls still reflect higher ratings for the "most admired woman" who is the satellite of a famous man than for women who achieve public notice "on their own" (Lang, 1978).[15]

Obviously this paper has focused on the wives of men in political office because the implications of their dramaturgical roles are more visible, and more evidently far-reaching, than wives of men in other places on the public spectrum.[16] And also obviously, certain evolutionary changes in the impression-management regarding wives are also beginning to be visible. On May 27, 1979, a journalistic recording of this, in the *New York Times* (p. 48), was the appearance, at her husband's side, of the wife of the then-victorious candidate for Canadian Prime Minister (now since defeated) who planned to retain her "own" name. The essential symbol was traditional: she was there, and smiling, looking up at him as a wife should. It was also new: she presented herself as a professional, and intended to maintain that identity.

At the deeper level of symbolic interaction, a small but revolutionary gesture which was added to the canon of public ceremonial raises other interesting and provocative issues. A basic principle governing the cultural function of public wifery seems to be that the higher the occasion, the closer to those civil-religion traditions surrounding moments of "sacred" public ritual, the more important the wife's visibility. This rule locks her into a passive ceremonial role. When the real business of state or organization is being conducted, wars declared, treaties negotiated, her on-stage presence would be seen as not only superfluous but distracting; it would diminish the seriousness of it (Mrs. Carter's presence at the signing of the Panama Canal Treaty in June 1979 and in other "hard" news events shows an evolution in this practice).

Because of the convention that the public wife's place is in the human-interest, or non-business, side of public appearances, Mrs. Lyndon Johnson's inserting herself at the most solemn moment of the inauguration drama, the taking of the oath of office, was truly revolutionary. She seized the Bible from a Supreme Court Clerk and held it herself for her husband. It was a radical act, in however small a way. She dramatized a new relationship between the wife symbol and our most exalted civil liturgy by putting herself in the very center of it.

The significance of that act is now visible at all levels of officeholders. The reverberations of it were nationally apparent in a January 24, 1977, *New York Times* (page 16) photograph of the Carter cabinet swearing-in. There were fourteen couples, not just appointees alone and each had a spouse holding a Bible for the oath of the mate. This also included two husbands for Cabinet-member's wives. The wives in the picture, however, has assumed the dramaturgically correct stance of looking up at their husbands with tilted head and adoring eyes.

Does this innovation in public ceremonial presage a gradual diminishing of our cultural preoccupation with public men's private lives or is it an expanding ritual affirmation of family-symbolism? Is it the public wife's acknowledgment that she accepts and shares the public demands of impression-management or that she is violating the principle of dramaturgical circumspection by wanting to be a part of the public sacrament herself?

Goffman suggests that the intersection of a dramaturgical perspective on human interaction with a cultural perspective is most clearly seen in actions relating to the maintenance of moral standards, since cultural values determine the ways in which we assign meaning to what is seen and experienced, and shape the framework of appearances which need to be maintained.

When a man enters the public arena, the mass audience must discover "facts" about him which are almost never fully transmissable. Instead, we rely on image and theatrical information – cues, hints, gestures, impressions. Goffman identifies the paradox which characterizes politics-as-theater: the more dependent an audience is on realities which are not available to perception, the more dependent people are on impressions and appearances. Hence the basic dialectic of political image management: as performers giving off impressions of public morality and fitness for office, public figures try to maintain the idea that they are indeed fulfilling the standards for civic conventionality by which they are to be judged. At the same time, the activity of "engineering" convincing impressions of these standards makes them "merchants of morality." "The very obligation and profitability of appearing always in a steady moral light . . . forces one to be the sort of person who is practiced in the ways of the stage" (Goffman, 1959:251). The public wife appears on that stage, in the past and still to a large extent in most national political symbol-interactions, to nurture impressions of that "steady moral light."

NOTES

1. An anonymous Government Printing Office bulletin is titled "Wives of the U.S. Presidents" (1954) and belabors the point that every U.S. President was married, or had a surrogate public wife: Jefferson's daughter, Jackson's wife's niece (married to his private secretary), Van Buren's daughter-in-law, Harrison's daughter-in-law, Tyler's daughter-in-law (until he remarried), Taylor's daughter, Fillmore's daughter, Buchanan's niece, Johnson's daughter, and Arthur's sister. Obviously, at least at that period, identifying the wife-symbol of the First Family was important; "with the progress of the years, the attention of the public has come more and more to center about the wife of the President, almost as much as on the Chief Executive himself" (1954:50). The question of whether this emphasis shifts, or lessens in given eras, will be speculatively raised in the summary of this paper.

2. Rosemblum (1978) demonstrates that news-photography "conventions" or codes result from an interaction of technological, organizational, and institutional factors. The American public was apparently ready to have photographic confirmation of the familyness of the President newly-elected in the fall of 1908; the very first Pictorial section in the *New York Times* (Jan. 1, 1909, p. 1), for example, featured "the first complete group photograph of the newly elected presidential *family*," (emphasis mine) followed in succeeding weeks by pictures of Mrs. Taft as public-hostess, greeting foreign dignitaries at President Taft's side, entertaining with him at State dinners.

3. "The first hint came when Mrs. William Brennan and Mrs. Thurgood Marshall arrived. Wives of Justices rarely drop in at the Supreme Court on hot, muggy Washington mornings unless something momentous is about to occur" (*Newsweek*, July 10, 1978, p. 19). "A traditional clue to the import of a ruling about to be handed down is the appearance of the Justices' wives, so there was a rustle of anticipation in the crowded courtroom, just before ten, at the sight of Cecelia Marshall, Marjorie Brennan, and Elizabeth Stevens. The wives had arrived" (*Time*, July 10, 1978, p. 9).

4. George Herbert Mead's symbolic interactionism is the foundation of Goffman's analysis of interaction patterns (Dreitzel, 1970). Application of Goffman to a sociology-of-power schema is possible, according to Rogers, (1977) because "he pays analytic attention to the function of intentionality in social life." An essay on charismatic leadership (Perinbanayagam, 1971) provides a model of symbolic interaction analysis of other than face-to-face encounters, demonstrating "the convergence between dialectical processes . . . and Mead's definition of meaning" as socially constructed.

5. Civil religion has been variously defined as a "transcendant universal religion of the Republic standing in judgment over the folk-ways of Americans," a form of Protestant civic piety, and a democratic faith (Jones and Richey, 1974:16). It encompasses a shared collective perspective on our national history and myths, and a set of values, symbols and rituals which have become institutionalized (Novak, 1974).

6. An analysis of our national hero symbolism traces an evolution from the image of the Scholar and the Gentleman, including the "seal of being a Christian," (Green, 1970:49) during our nation's first century, to that of Daring Adventurer. The hero "moved from the atmosphere of the gentleman's club to the market place" (Green, 1970:59). Character traits of aggressiveness, vitality and endurance gradually replaced the former ideals of cultivation and service to country and fellow-men. This image, in turn, gradually moved toward the Teddy Roosevelt hero as political magnate. In the 1940's, as bureaucratic modes of organization and influence expanded, the Hero-as-Businessman emerged, along with values of efficiency, stability, moderation, and consistency (Green, 1970).

7. Symbolic devices used by Presidential candidates as reflected in their campaign biographies combine "wish-fulfillment" with "traditions" such as hereditary stock, achievement, fathers as civic models, mothers epitomizing Christian virtue, idealized (probably rural) childhood setting, occupational experience, etc. (Brown, 1960).

8. "The lady's role as spiritual exemplar to her competitive-minded husband is clearly more vital in (Editor Sarah Josepha) Hale's mind than her function as his helpmate" (Douglas, 1977:57).

9. Undoubtedly some of the very earliest public wives were those of traveling evangelists who are reported to have sat on the platform with their husbands, e.g., Mrs. Charles Grandison Finney (McLoughlin, 1959).

10. An interesting social history of wifehood associates the emerging public-wife-role with the 18th and 19th century in which women "wore their husbands' titles": Mrs. John Jones, Mrs. Dr. Thomas Tyler, The Reverend Mrs. John Gillespie. "The wife of John Tyler delighted in the appellation 'Mrs. Presidentess' and after the expiration of her husband's term and his death, she insisted on being called Mrs. Ex-President Tyler" (Stannard, 1977:17). The author's thesis is that the wife's use of her husband's title gave the impression of enlarged status without upsetting the traditional circumscriptions of the middle-class wife.

11. "None of Koch's friends have ever thought that the relationship between him and Miss Myerson has been even remotely close to a romance, and they seem to feel a respectful amusement when they see pictures of the two of them holding hands. Miss Myerson is a formidable political talent, and her affection for Koch is genuine, but one of her functions is to dispel rumors that he is a homosexual. . . . It is not too much to suggest that without her, Koch might not have won." (*New York Times Magazine*, October 30, 1977, "The Koch Story" by John Corry, p.82).

This technique may indeed have helped. Some analysts attribute Koch's rather narrow victory to the issue of homosexuality in the campaign. Koch's opponent, Mario

Cuomo, had an attractive wife and family and used them frequently in his public appearances, so much so that Koch supporters demanded that he stop exploiting his family image because he was unfairly "using it 'as a means of pointing to his heterosexuality' — surely a new charge in local political life" (Andy Logan, *New Yorker*, November 21, 1977, "Around City Hall," p. 209). Aside from illustrating the greater freedom with which implications of homosexuality of political figures may be handled today, this report supports the interpretation of the use of family imagery to symbolize channeled and normal sexuality.

12. A *Time* magazine in 1943 summed this belief in a list of "ten presidential commandments": he must have solid American background, as humble as possible, and poorbut-honest parents; he must look good but not too good, and not have too much dramatism in his gestures; he should be healthy and vigorous; he should have an attractive wife and children; he should be successful, but not so much so as to set him apart from his fellow citizens; he must identify with a popular issue; must let someone else make him a candidate (best to be drafted!); must be acceptable to old-line party leaders as well as to well-heeled backers; and last, must let the voters see him, "as often and auspiciously as possible" (*Time*, April 26, 1943, p. 18).

13. After a brief flurry of criticism, Mrs. Javits gave up her public-relations job for Iran. Her husband said, "My position in public life has placed limits on the use by my wife of her talents in her chosen professional field . . . But we both take pride in serving the public and we have to be prepared to meet its requirements." In the same article, Mrs. Javits says, "I recognize that the family of a public official has some — as yet I believe unclear — accountability to his or her constituency" (*New York Times*, January 28, 1976, pp. 1, 6), a graceful acknowledgment of some of the structural discipline in her public wife role.

14. In the present climate of expanding roles for women, and in the sudden increase of political activity among women, the question arises about whether the same kind of symbolic importance attaches to the husbands of public women, few as they have been in number. There is no evidence to support this concern. In Western culture, women come from an entirely different moral tradition than men, and the necessity, therefore, of a woman public figure presenting a referential symbol has simply never developed. Also the sexual normality of women is of less societal concern than that of men. If a woman is single, it is less threatening to the social order. One of the very few recent studies of public women shows that the public cares mainly that their families "support" their publicness, and that a husband, if there is one, must be seen to agree to ("give permission for") the woman's "deviant" social role (Kirkpatrick, 1974).

The question may occur as to whether there is any substantive difference between public-wife requirements for national-public figure, and a corporation wife, an academic wife, a minister's wife. At first glance it might appear so, but in analytic terms they all draw upon the same moral tradition, woman as secondary, subservient, the other, and therefore differ primarily in quantitative terms such as size of public community, or degree of publicness.

15. Evidence of a grass-roots investment in public wifehood's martyrdom (Lang, 1978) can be found in popular women's magazines, e.g., *Ladies Home Journal*, July 1978 had a special feature "The Painful Price Our First Ladies Pay" and nearly every month one or another of the homemaker periodicals has something similar. Of course the recent books of revelation by Margaret Trudeau, the divorced wife of the former Canadian Prime Minister and Joan Kennedy tap this same theme.

208   THE PHENOMENON OF THE PUBLIC WIFE

16. Diplomats' wives also find themselves in tension regarding dramaturgical loyalty. They seem to be expected to exhibit loyalty not only to their husbands but to their husband's jobs. This is manifested in the informal censure a wife in a diplomatic colony may draw upon herself if she fails to restrict her social conversation to trivialities (rather than engaging in serious political exchanges with others) or if she insists on accepting employment outside the embassy itself. Both choices, falling, as they appear to do outside the unwritten code of acceptable actions for wives, make her "difficult" or suspect of "not showing enough consideration, and loyalty, to her husband's occupational needs and bonds" (Callan, 1975:96–98. See also Hochschild, 1969).

REFERENCES

Ayres, C. Drummond, Jr. (1979) "The importance of being Rosalynn." New York Times Magazine (June 3).

Bloch, Ruth H. (1978) "American feminine ideals in transition: the rise of the moral mother, 1785–1815." Feminist Studies 4 (June): 100–126.

Boulding, Elise (1976) The Underside of History: A View of Women Through Time, Boulder, Colorado: Westview Press.

Brown, William B. (1960) The People's Choice: The Presidential Image in Campaign Biography. Baton Rouge, Louisiana: Louisiana State University Press.

Bullough, Vern and Bonnie Bullough (1977) Sin, Sickness and Sanity: A History of Sexual Attitudes. New York: New American Library.

Bunkle, Phillida (1974) "Sentimental womanhood and domestic education, 1830–1870." History of Education Quarterly XIV (Spring): 13–31.

Callan, Hilary (1975) "The premise of dedication: notes toward an ethnography of diplomats' wives." Pp. 87–104 in Shirley Ardener (ed.), Perceiving Women. New York: Halsted Press.

Cohen, Abner (1974) Two-Dimensional Man: An Essay on the Anthropology of Power and Symbolism in Complex Society. Berkeley, California: University of California Press.

Cott, Nancy (1977) The Bonds of Womanhood: Woman's Sphere in New England, 1780–1835. New Haven, Connecticut: Yale University Press.

Douglas, Ann (1977) The Feminization of American Culture. New York: A.A. Knopf.

Dreitzel, Hans Peter, (ed.) (1970) Recent Sociology #2. New York: Macmillan Company.

Drew, Elizabeth (1976) "Reporter in Washington." New Yorker (October 25).

Duncan, Hugh Dalziel (1968) Symbols in Society. New York: Oxford University Press.

Edelman, Murray (1977) The Symbolic Uses of Politics. Urbana, Illinois: University of Illinois Press.

Edmondson, Madeleine and Allen Cohen (1976) The Women of Watergate. New York: Simon and Schuster.

Finley, Ruth E. (1931) The Lady of Godey's: Sarah Josepha Hale. Philadelphia: J.B. Lippincott.

Friedman, Lawrence T. (1975) Inventors of the Promised Land. New York: A.A. Knopf.

Furay, Conal (1977) The Grass-Roots Mind in America: The American Sense of Absolutes. New York: Franklin Watts.

Gerth, H.H. and C. Wright Mills (1958) From Max Weber: Essays in Sociology. New York: Oxford University Press.

Goffman, Erving (1959) The Presentation of Self in Everyday Life. Garden City, New York: Doubleday and Company.

Green, Theodore P. (1970) America's Heroes: Changing Models of Success in American Magazines. New York: Oxford University Press.

Hall, Peter M. (1979) "The presidency and impression management." Pp. 283-305 in Norman K. Denzin (ed.), Studies in Symbolic Interaction II. Greenwich, Connecticut: JAI Press, Inc.

(1972) "A symbolic interactionist analysis of politics." Sociological Inquiry 42:35-75.

Hochschild, Arlie R. (1969) "The role of the ambassador's wife: an exploratory study." Journal of Marriage and the Family 31 (February): 73-87.

Hunt, Gailliard (1906) The First Forty Years of Washington Society. New York: Charles Scribner's Sons, Inc.

Jones, Donald and Russell Richey, (eds.) (1974) American Civil Religion. New York: Harper and Row.

Kanter, Rosabeth (1977) Men and Women of the Corporation. New York: Basic Books.

Keller, Suzanne (1963) Beyond the Ruling Class. New York: Random House.

Kirkpatrick, Jeanne J. (1974) Political Woman. New York: Basic Books.

Klapp, Orrin (1964) Symbolic Leaders: Public Dramas and Public Men. Chicago: Aldine Publishing Company.

Lang, Gladys Engel (1978) "The most admired woman: image making in the news." Pp. 147-168 in Gaye Tuchman. Arlene Kaplan Daniels and James Benet (eds.). Hearth and Home: Images of Women in the Mass Media. New York: Oxford University Press.

Lash, Joseph P. (1971) Eleanor and Franklin. New York: New American Library.

Logan, Andy (1977) "Around City Hall." New Yorker (November 21): 209.

MacPherson, Myra (1975) The Power Lovers: An Intimate Look at Politicians and Their Marriages. New York: G.P. Putnam and Sons.

McLoughlin, William G. (1959) Modern Revivalism: Charles Grandison Finney to Billy Graham. New York: The Ronald Press Company.

Means, Marianne (1963) Women in the White House. New York: Random House.

Morgan, Edmund (1966) The Puritan Family. New York: Harper and Row.

Mount, Ferdinand (1973) The Theater of Politics. New York: Schocken Books.

Nimmo, Dan (1970) The Political Persuaders: The Techniques of Modern Election Campaigns. Englewood Cliffs, New Jersey: Prentice-Hall.

Novak, Michael (1974) Choosing Our King. New York: Macmillan.

O'Faolain Julia and Laura Martines, (eds.) (1973) Not in God's Image. New York: Harper and Row.

Perinbanayagam, Robert S. (1971) "The dialects of charisma." The Sociological Quarterly (Summer): 387-402.

Pivard, David J. (1973) The Purity Crusade: Sexual Morality and Social Control, 1868-1900. Westport, Connecticut: Greenwood Press.

Rogers, Mary F. (1977) "Goffman on power." American Sociologist 12 (April): 88–95.

Rosenblum, Barbara (1978) "Style as social process." American Sociological Review 43 (June): 422–439.

Sennett, Richard (1977) The Fall of Public Man. New York: A.A. Knopf.

Slater, Philip (1977) Footholds: Understanding the Shifting Sexual and Family Tensions in Our Culture. New York: E.P. Dutton and Company.

Stannard, Una (1977) Mrs. Man. San Francisco: Germain Books.

Sung, Carolyn Hoover (1977) "Catherine Mitchell's letters from Washington, 1806–1812." Quarterly Journal of the Library of Congress 34 (July):171–189.

Taylor, G. Rattray (1970) Sex in History. New York: Harper and Row.

Thomas, John (1965) "Romantic reform in America, 1815–1865." American Quarterly XVII (Winter):656–681.

U.S. Government Printing Office (1954) Wives of the U.S. Presidents. Washington, D.C.: U.S. Government.

Welter, Barbara (1976) Dimity Convictions: The American Woman in the 19th Century. Athens, Ohio: Ohio University Press.

White, Theodore H. (1965) The Making of the President, 1964. New York: Atheneum.

Wishy, Bernard (1968) The Child and the Republic. Philadelphia: University of Pennsylvania Press.

Wyckoff, Gene (1968) The Image Candidates: American Politics in the Age of Television. New York: Macmillan.

Zaretsky, Eli (1976) Capitalism, the Family, and Personal Life. New York: Harper and Row.

Chapter 12

Couples Who Live Apart: Time/Place Disjunctions and Their Consequences

Harriet Engel Gross

Couples who live apart present a unique opportunity to study the consequences of tampering with our culture's marital co-residence norm. Interviews
with 37 spouses, representing members of 21 couples who are legally married
and who live apart in service to career demands of both, suggest that time
and place discontinuities result from two residence living. Two residences
mean that spouses are not able to mesh and coordinate time schedules, nor
do they share the common base of their co-resident counterparts. The
time/place disjunctions that result threaten these marriages' ability to "make
sense" to the partners of such unions. This paper examines the sense-
jeopardizing consequence of living apart and suggest that this marital form's
inherent strains make it a difficult lifestyle.

T he cultural premium on voluntarism coupled with the presumed
uniqueness of intimate interpersonal relations prevents most people
from reflecting upon ways in which larger social forces permeate such relationships. Social scientists, to be sure, enjoy a corrective to this popular view in the
heritage from Simmel (1950, 1971) to Goffman (e.g., 1967) which affirms the
social structural undergirding of even our seemingly most subjective personal
responses. Among our theoretical forefathers it was Simmel particularly, who
underscored the ways in which time and space coordinates of social interaction
create and maintain subjective realities. His analysis of the stranger, for example,
illustrates this spatial/social focus. The stranger, he said, is both physically
among us, "near," and yet "far" in that he is socially remote – a conflation which

Support for this research was provided in part by research scholarships from the Australian National University and the Department of Education (Australia). I want to thank Blanche Geer, Jean
Martin and Jerzy Zubrzycki for their help, suggestions and support throughout the research period. I
am also grateful to Fred Davis and anonymous reviewers who provided comments on drafts of this
material, but I retain the responsibility for interpretations and conclusions drawn here.

Source: Harriet Engel Gross, "Couples Who Live Apart: Time/Place Disjunctions and Their
Consequences." SYMBOLIC INTERACTION 3 (Fall, 1980):69–82. Reprinted by permission of JAI
Press, Inc., Greenwich, Conn.

renders problematic his incorporation into the social fabric (Simmel, 1950:402–408).

What happens to the relationship of couples who live apart – the focus of the research to be reported here – also speaks to the significance of space and time as constitutive elements of social relations. In departing from the marital norm dictating co-residence, these couples alter typical time and place patterns of marriage in our culture. (See Leibowitz, 1978, for cross-cultural examples of marriages which do not presume co-residence and for the implications of defining marriage in terms of co-residence.) By doing so they render problematic what co-resident couples "take for granted" and probably assume to be inherent features of married life. As we shall see, the decision to maintain separate residences, challenges the taken-for-granted quality of intimate interaction. The subjective registration of this challenge – the sense that ensuing marital interaction feels somehow "wrong," "inappropriate" or "strange" alerts us to the problematic quality of the social structural scaffolding of relationships. Vary the temporal and spatial dimensions of relationships and the subjective sense of their "reality" responds in turn. Our discussion, then, will show how the lifestyle of couples who live apart allows us to analyze the subjective side of the structural basis of marriage. This will show that what marriage "means" in our culture depends upon the way we fashion its temporal and spatial organization.

SAMPLE

The data reported here are based on open-ended interviews (about 1½ hours) with 43 respondents (26 wives and 17 husbands) representing 28 dual career marriages (15 couples, 11 wife-only and 2 husband-only). Interviews were conducted from the Spring of 1977 through the Spring of 1979. At least one of the spouses lived in or within driving distance (3 hours) of the Chicago Metropolitan Area. Couples were legally married and had been living apart (residing separately for at least 4 days at a time) for at least three months.

We used these criteria because we reasoned first that the perceived permanence of the relationship would be different for legally cemented relationships and that the subjective difference might confound our analysis of the effects of separation. Secondly, we accepted (somewhat arbitrarily) a three month mimimum separation on the assumption that the effect on the separation would have to endure through time before consistent effects would show up. Couples were identified through referrals from colleagues, students and associates who were told the intent of the research. One respondent (husband) answered an advertisement asking for volunteers for a university-sponsored research project on the topic.

The following demographic profile is based on 43 respondents who are members of dual-career variants of such couples. (As a second stage of this research we are now interviewing non-dual-career spouses who live apart in an attempt to isolate independent effects of separate residences from dual career contingencies.) The mean age for husbands is 38; for wives it is 36. Consistent with Gerstel's (1977) findings, these are relatively affluent couples, with family income greater than $35,000 for one-third of the men and 46% of the women. This high family income reflects the high educational and occupational attainment of these individuals: 94% of husbands and 85% of wives have completed some graduate work. All but one husband and four wives are either executives or professionals or are currently completing advanced degrees to enable them to become such.

Not surprisingly, the expenses (e.g., travel, two-households) associated with the lifestyle make relative affluence (or potential for it in the form of professional orientations of those currently living on graduate school loans) a virtual precondition. Yet it is not income level per se that distinguishes these couples' arrangements from those of other marriages which call for some spousal separation. Examples of marriages in which the husband routinely leaves the household exist for both higher and lower income levels (e.g., truck drivers and traveling salesmen, at lower income levels, and business executives and politicians at upper income levels). What is different about the later variant of separated married couples however, is that typically (a) the husband is the spouse who leaves the home base; (b) he does not set up a separate household away from the family home; and (c) these arrangements represent a more normatively accommodated, established pattern. Several of our sample respondents addressed the difference between their own lifestyle and this more familiar husband-traveling pattern:

> When the husband leaves to work on a job and the wife stays home with the child, no one thinks anything about it.

The reference to children in this account may indicate another dimension of difference between the older and newer patterns. Anecdotal impressions about traveling-husband families suggest that children would be, at least as likely, in such families as the national average. Yet there are no data to this author's knowledge that speak to whether or not children are more routinely present in families of the older as compared with the newer type. In this sample, about half of the couples do have children and their presence does influence the delicate balance between costs and benefits, sometimes making living apart "worse" and sometimes "better" depending principally upon which spouse remains with the children and their ages (see Gross, 1979).

To return then to our newer variant of separated couples in this sample, let us look at the variables – length of marriage and length of separation. For the most part, these couples are not newlyweds: husbands have been married an average of 13 years and wives for 12 years. Typically, they have maintained two residences for a relatively short period: 59% of the men and 61% of the women have lived apart less than 18 months (14% have lived apart for 3 years or longer). The frequency with which they see each other seems to be bimodal: about one-half (husbands and wives) are apart less than one week (i.e., they are together on weekends), about 10% from one week to a month and about two-fifths for longer than a month. This suggests that the lifestyle is adopted under two sets of conditions: the spouses will see each other often enough (i.e., within a week) to make the separation reasonably tolerable, or the fact of being too far apart to regroup frequently is accepted as a necessary consequence of an unavoidable obstacle (e.g., only one medical school accepted the wife, and it is 1,000 miles from the husband's job location).

OF TIME AND PLACE

Berger and Kellner (1964) have called attention to the order-bestowing function of marriage – to the fact that marriage is a relationship that creates for the individual. ". . . the sort of order in which he can experience his life as making sense." Since, as these authors argue, the reality-making force of social relationships like marriage hinges on the proximity of partners to the relationship, we should expect marriages which separate spouses to render this reality or sense-making function more problematic. Gerstel's (1977) findings and Kirschner (1976), as well as our own, confirm this point, since we all find among these couples a sense that something is missing when they are apart. A wife's response put it this way:

> I miss the opportunity to share everyday things like "What did you have for lunch to-day?"

A husband said that he missed:

> The lack of interpersonal communication – that sharing of little things, like trying to tell some of the neat little things that happened since you last talked to her, but after twenty-four hours, they're more trivial than they were to start with. There was a loss of that facet of our relationship.

What they call attention to, as they amplify this point, is not a substantive interest in such minutae, but rather that such exchanges between spouses cement their intimacy, their sense of involvement with each other. Small talk, like the more weighty exchanges (what Gerstel calls "real" communication, 1977:360) between partners in intimate relationships, provides confirmation of – indeed, constructs the familiar web of meanings – which helps produce the ordered (and ordering) world that is their relationship. Since costly long-distance telephone conversation constrains against such small talk (visual cues are missing as well),

there is no easy way to replace or compensate for this marital interaction component (Gerstel, 1977:361).

I would suggest, however, that it is more than such face-to-face communication that builds the shared experience based on which marriage's sense-making
function depends; and that, therefore, the marriages of couples who live apart
lack something beyond Berger's and Kellner's (1964:3) point about the diminution of meaning-sustaining conversation. In co-residence marriages, couples have
a common base (*their* home) and coordinated time schedules around which they
join their ordered worlds. Such time and place commonalities are constitutive
dimensions of social relationships which ground or situate the partners to such
relationships. Couples who live apart, by contrast, do not build their daily
schedules around each other's time constraints to the same degree, nor do they
have one common base which is theirs together and their only "home." To the
extent that two-resident marriages alter the time and space dimensions of traditional marriage, they dislocate the partners in such relationships. The time and
place dislocations that result from these two features of living apart are experienced as time/place dissonance that jeopardizes the sense-making function of
their marriage over and above the threat that conversational diminution produces. I will begin the discussion of these issues with ways in which time
dislocations undermine the order-providing function of these marriages.

TIME

Time Apart

Co-resident couples who typically separate each workday morning to
regroup each evening have a daily regimen obviously different from these couples
who live apart. For two-resident couples, one consequence of not needing to fit
one's daily schedule and work periods around a mate's schedule is the freedom
from constraint that such dovetailing of schedules imposes. This freedom is a
decided advantage, the benefits of which both spouses, but particularly wives,
articulate. For career-committed individuals, the increased productivity that
follows from concentrated, uninterrupted work is highly valued (Gerstel, 1977:
363).

I have so much more time, I am able to do what I want, when I want.

Yet there is a concomitant response, usually subjectively unconnected to this
one, a response that notices a diminished capacity to work as concertedly or purposefully as they might like.

"I find I waste a lot of time."
"I don't get down to business the way I'd like to."

"I'm not as focused as I'd like to be all the time."

Our analysis of such responses indicates that they occur most often in the con-text of discussions about how time is spent when mates would normally be together. One husband told how he noticed that he had completed only four pages of a report he was reading during the whole evening. He could not concen-trate and his mind kept wandering away from what he was reading. I think of these statements about diminished concentration capacity as evidence for a feel-ing of being unmoored in a meaning-giving relationship. The fact that members of such couples are not around to sustain realities for each other results in a kind of unhinging, as if they literally felt detached from a meaning-giving unit.

Such responses seem to confirm the thesis that intimate relationships pro-vide the moorings that facilitate purposeful action. It is not surprising then that such purposefulness might be particularly jeopardized at those times when mates would be together as intimates. However, there is also some suggestion that separation influences capacity to focus attention and work productively during regular working hours. Especially for those couples who do not come together on a regular basis, e.g., every weekend, an awareness develops that "it is time" to get back together. One husband, whose work depended on what he called creative bursts, said he knew it was time to visit his wife when his creativity seemed to be waning.

After about four weeks of this sort of pagan lifestyle, I get less motivated.

For professionals, whose careers demand heavy intellectual and emotional outlays, any such threat to ability to concentrate or work concertedly could become prohibitively costly. The increased productivity that these spouses con-nect to their freedom from the constraints of their mates' schedules could be counteracted by this diminished capacity to work purposefully.

What such responses about inability to work productively may mean is that a partner to an intimate relationship may be missing the feeling of being situated in a relationship that gives meaning and purpose to one's life, precisely because one spends an important life-ordering commodity – time – in that relationship. "Being situated" here means being time-bounded, which is to say – having one's own time expenditures connected into the time expenditures of someone else with whom, as a consequence of this coordination, one builds a common sense of purpose and meaning. Joined-time then would be a constitutive dimension of the relationship – a quality that defines the relationship and allows it to provide the sense of ordering that it does.

Duration and Pattern of Separation
If joined time is a dimension of relationship that, when missing threatens the meaning-giving potential of that relationship, the question becomes – how much

and what kind of time must be spent in the relationship in order for it to provide its benefits? Though we cannot answer the questions about amount of time definitely, these couples' responses do suggest that the pattern of their separation and regrouping affects the quality of the relationship. Irregular regrouping, that is getting together when either one's schedule permits them to do so, challenges the relationship's taken-for-granted quality in ways that a regular regrouping pattern (e.g., every weekend) does not. Couples who see each other every weekend have the obvious advantage of being separated for shorter time periods compared to couples who cannot get together every weekend. They also have a pattern of separating and regrouping that roughly parallels the workleisure pattern for most of the culture. That is, they are away from each other when others are working and together for the weekend which they, like other couples, are then able to devote to activities they can do together. The "weekends-together" pattern, then, is least discrepant from the work-leisure rhythm of their co-resident dual-career counterparts. It is the pattern of separation relative to other patterns that is least likely to threaten their sense of what marriage "is." Spouses who spend weekends together do not report feeling "awkward" when they come together, but spouses separated for longer periods do use this and similar terms. The latter says such things as the situation feels "unreal" when they get back together or "artificial." One woman reported feeling that she was having an affair when she visited her husband.

> When I get there it takes a day or so to decide that nothing has changed and to feel comfortable about it. There's always that worry when you first get back together.

Another put it this way.

> It's usually sort of strange. There's a 'What do we talk about first?' – a distance. It's weird.

There is also significance to meeting every weekend consistently because a weekend visit after a longer separation may be too short and too compressed a period to accomplish everything their expectations build up for their time together.

> If you are together for a short time, say a weekend, the first day revolves around arriving, the second day is sandwiched in between with shopping and stuff that needs to be done, and the third day focuses on leaving.

Several spouses registered complaints similar to the one quoted below – acknowledging that the time together was not what they had hoped for. They seemed perplexed by this fact, as if they could not quite understand how something they had so looked forward to could disappoint them.

I've noticed with my husband now, there's a period of strangeness. We're glad to see one another, but we haven't got anything to say. It takes several days for that to break down and for us to begin chattering in detail – to really feel comfortable. And when you have only a couple of days, you never get it, so there's that strangeness, that let-down like – "Why aren't I enjoying this more?"

Again:

Our expectation level was so high because it was so important that every minute count and everything be perfect and it just wasn't. The pressure was always on and it was a real strain and we both felt it.

By contrast, couples who are together each weekend seem to accommodate themselves to the routine of this pattern and take comfort in its regularity. They tell of taking a specific train, arriving at a fixed time and a schedule of events throughout the weekend which seems to function as a new joined time that somewhat fortifies their relationship.

Time Together

Yet, even for couples who meet each weekend and who seem to have reconstituted their relationship around their new time together, there are strains related to time management. Couples who live apart are very much aware of their need to use their time together constructively (Kirschner and Wallum, 1978). In this respect, they are like other dual-career couples (Rapoport and Rapoport 1976:302) but time considerations are even more vital to them because the separation increases their time apart. They tell how they protect their time together from potential depletion and incursion of visits from friends and relatives. They allocate their time together in recognition of the fact they must spend what they have together wisely if the relationship is to withstand the injury to it that limited and non-normative time periods together impose. Though regularity of contact can mitigate the disappointments referred to above (when the visit is not all they had hoped for), such disappointment is not uncommon. Even for those who see each other relatively often, such unfulfilled expectations mar the satisfaction of coming together. Because time together is so clearly bracketed off from "other time," this very distinctiveness makes their period together more vulnerable. They are cognizant of "spoiled time" together in ways, I suspect, co-resident couples are not.

A husband of a wife who is away for three or four days a week during the legislative session (she holds a political office in the state capital) pointed this out in the context of talking about whether he missed her when she was away. No, he said, the effect of her absence on their time together bothered him more. This is because although she was physically present, she brought the demands of her job home with her – which kept her psychologically invested – i.e., "away."

She's pretty busy when she's home and I guess I find that more trying than her being away partly because since she is away a substantial part of the time – then it seems more important that we be together during the few days that she's here. It seems less understandable sometimes why that's not possible. When a person is away, of course, you're not with them. But when she comes home, "Why is it so important to have that political conversation right now? Why don't you talk to me?" So there is some friction.

In effect then, time together gets colored by his view of the expected effect of time apart. Just because they had been separated, they should, in his view, spend their time together in a more subjectively focused manner.

Because of feelings like these, for many of these spouses, the period together suffers from overload. Since time together is a limited commodity, there is an urgency to their respective needs to draw from it the sustenance that this very urgency undermines. They need more from their relationship at the same time that they can draw less from it.

Recognition that time together is not as comforting or satisfying as anticipated demonstrates the fragility of the constructed substance of intimate interaction. What is apparently necessary is some consistency of physically and emotionally close contact, that is, for a time span "long enough" to allow the nonconspicuous, effortless interaction that reestablishes the bonds of an intimate relation. When both the length of the time apart and the pattern of regrouping constrain against such rebonding, disappointment is particularly keen. The wife of a couple who have been living apart for a relatively long time, over five years, (recall that only 14% of the sample have been apart longer than three years) with separations lasting up to two and three months at a time, tells how these disappointments undermine the relationship's reality for her.

We met in Portland for a whole week just a few weeks ago, but it was not good. I know he feels too that we were not connecting well. When I go back this summer, we'll both really have to work on reestablishing our relationship. It does worry me.

Duration and pattern of separation, then, are important contingencies that affect the degree to which such marriages are able to provide the personal mooring expected from marriage in our culture, and, in turn, this capability is rerelated to the degree of strain experienced while together and apart. No doubt the effect of any of these variables (e.g., pattern of separation) interacts with others (e.g., duration of separation) to lessen or increase the challenge to the marriage's capacity to order their lives.

PLACE

"His," "Hers," and "Their" Place: Space Dislocations
The discussion of time dislocations centered on ways in which not spending

time together on a routine, joined basis, jeopardizes the taken-for-granted quality of the relationship so that it does not feel right or make sense. This is what terms such as "artificial," "awkward," and "weird" signifiy. In similar and intercon- nected ways (difficult to distinguish because time and place variations occur simultaneously) the place irregularities of these marriages contribute to the awareness that something is awry – out of order. These mates report reactions they recognize to be inappropriate, and they are puzzled by these responses. The puzzlement, I would argue, indicates that the taken-for-granted quality of the relationship is challenged and the challenge is unsettling, unhinging. A husband reported that his wife felt as if they were doing something illicit when he stayed with her in the dormitory room in which she lived.

> She kind of felt, at least early in the year, kind of immoral when she had a man staying in her room. It was a weird situation.

Despite the fact that her own moral view did not condemn sexual liaisons among others who lived in the dorm and, though it was co-educational residence, she felt "nervous" with her own husband in that place. Another husband said that he had to consciously avoid the feeling that he should "play host" when his wife visited him in his apartment. He knew the response was inappropriate, but it was something he apparently associated with someone "visiting" his place. Inap- propriate reactions like these are evidence of the disturbed nomos (Berger's and Kellner's [1964] term for sense of order) that variation from co-residence pro- duces. The "nervousness" and "weirdness" they associated with these situations are the strain they feel as a consequence of having the sense-making function of their relationship undermined.

A wife of a state legislator made the spatially interconnected loss quite ob- vious in her response to a question about how she felt when he was away – three nights a week when the legislature was in session.

> I wouldn't say I feel lonely as much as disconnected. It could be a redirected form of loneliness because if he were there, everything would just fall back into place.

These spouses use terms such as "turf" and "re-entry problems" to com- municate their place-related incongruities. Not unexpectedly, the place disloca- tions are most obvious for the partner who sets up a new residence and for both of them when they are together in that residence, away from their shared base. As the following excerpt indicates, "a new place" can add novelty to their rela- tionship but it is not "their place" ('this isn't my place, my turf'). The passage is in response to a question about different reactions when this wife and her husband come together in their previous home (where he remains) as compared to when he visits her, in her apartment.

> Oh yes, it's not nearly so good here because he's not so comfortable here. This isn't

my beat, this isn't my turf. And that's O.K., we do things together, we explore. It's
fun, it's an adventure, but what I like for total relaxation and happiness is to go home.

Here, "total relaxation," that is, feeling more comfortable, attests to the order-
sustaining value that shared space produces.

The re-entry problems they talk about are evidence that they miss the
familiarity, the sense of being "in place" that living together provides. Feeling ill
at ease in "his" or "her" place is further indication that the sense-making function
of relationships inheres in spatial interconnectedness. To the extent that they
feel "out of place," they are acknowledging that feeling "in place" gives the relationship the order-constructing quality they expect from it. Feeling like a guest
in the company of the mate, seeming to intrude, are additional reactions that
bespeak the dislocation they feel. That such feelings attach to the awareness of
not being a part of, not sharing the space that is identified as "his" or "hers" (as
distinct from "theirs") comes through in the following quote.

> She had her own little world here that I was definitely not a part of. I got the feeling
> that she kind of − resented is perhaps too strong − but thought, I was intruding into
> her sphere.

"Not Having Our Place": Loss of a Shared Base

The dislocations of space coordination are especially pronounced when both
move into new residences as a result of the decision to live apart. This can occur
for a variety of reasons: because they may want to reduce expenses and,
therefore, each takes a less costly apartment, or because the job changes put
them in two new locations. In such instances, neither one of them has a shared
base to retreat to and they both have "turfs" alien to the other. A husband
recognized his awareness, but thought it affected his wife more than it did him.

> It's kind of interesting, the fact that I moved out of what had been our apartment
> gave her a greater sense of being cut-off. She didn't have a home to go to, she never
> really felt at home here.

Not having a real "home" is definitely a part of place awareness. A wife for
whom separation began only five months after marriage felt this place-lack very
strongly. When asked what she considered "home," she said:

> What's really home is my parents' home still. I always talk about going home and
> that's Rockford to me. Going to Idaho is going to see Henry (her husband) and that's
> not really "going home." Part of it is not liking it there. I do feel pretty unsettled in
> terms of having a place to call home.

This same wife connected her husband's worries about the tenuousness of their
sense of coupleness to the fact that they were separated so shortly after their

marriage. She felt he had been very conscious of having wanted to "be married," and he worried about how being apart was going to make it more difficult to feel "as married" as a couple who had not had to separate so soon after their wedding.

> He sees himself reverting back to his single ways and he realizes we're going to have to do all the adjusting again with a baby thrown in besides. So there's a certain amount of anxiety I think.

Significantly she used several space-related figures of speech when she responded to whether she would ever want to live apart again. Note how the terms "settling down" and "torn apart" in her response suggest the dislocations, she feels have resulted from the fact of having been separated.

> I wouldn't do it without awfully good reasons. I'd never want to do it again, if we could avoid it. We went into it pretty naively and sure, we're going to get through it now – we're on the home stretch – but it's been an awful strain. We look forward to settling down and enjoying a relationship instead of having to work at it and being emotionally torn apart all the time.

COPING WITH STRAIN

Having made the point that time/place disjunctions render marital relations and the meaning one can draw from them more problematic, I should not leave the impression that there are no supports to counteract the considerable strains besieging these marriages. First, mitigating factors, especially length of marriage, do make the lifestyle less difficult for some couples. Secondly, these spouses perceive some advantages from living apart which they see as compensations if not strong sources of satisfaction. Thirdly, these partners' deep emotional investment in their relationship fortifies their efforts to cope with the lifestyle's challenges and makes their success at doing so a valued effort in itself.

LENGTH OF MARRIAGE

Having an account calibrated in years together is as important as a bank account on which to draw to pay for the emotional as well as considerable ensuing financial costs (e.g., telephone bills, traveling and two-household expenses. See also Kirschner and Wallum, 1978 and Gerstel, 1977).

Understandably, the longer they have been married, the greater their ability to withstand the ravages of missed time together. One younger husband, with access to a WATS line (such access so frequently figures into this lifestyle as to constitute an enabling condition), spoke to his wife every night, yet he reported that neither of them felt this was satisfactory. He stressed how they both missed the ability to talk to each other regularly. He readily agreed to the term "corrosive" when I used it to summarize what he had been saying about the effect of separation on their relationship. But an older wife, married more than fifteen years who was less negative about the effects of separation, said in response to my question about how often she and her husband kept in touch:

> Oh, we get a chance to speak to each other quite often, as often as we like. We talk on the phone about once a week.

The ability to cope with and manage the threat to their sense of the marriages' stability, the "intactness" of their relationship, then, is sensitive not only to how much time they now spend together, but how much time together they have behind them as well. To be sure, time together does not insure meaningfulness – witness the many psychologically distant couples who live together – but a certain irreducible minimum seems to be fundamental to the feeling that there is "enough time together" for there to be a meaningful relationship.

SEPARATION CONSEQUENCES

As we have seen, for these highly motivated, career-committed individuals, freedom to work as hard and as long as they choose – without concern for a spouse's schedule – is a valued outcome of being separated. In another paper (Gross, 1979) I discuss how this and other factors (e.g., age, sex, state of career, presence of children) affect the degree of strain couples perceive. In terms of the time perceptions on which this paper dwells, it is worth noting that a few spouses did recognize a heightened appreciation of their relationship because their time together was so scarce.

> When you do get together, it's something special. I prefer always to have not enough time. Our relationship has become more efficient in the use of time.

There is also the compensating novelty that nonroutine interaction brings – the feeling of adventure from having new places to explore – mentioned by the wife quoted above. But my impression of the interviews as a whole suggests that for the majority of these spouses such responses are viewed as island benefits in a sea of costs. For the most part these "benefits" are compensatory afterthoughts, much more than dominant reactions.

Furthermore, the positive quality of the perceived benefits have a precarious quality, suggesting a complex relationship between spatial separation and perceived advantages and disadvantages. A wife who said that the best thing about living apart was "personal space for myself and for him" noted that this same benefit could become a serious disadvantage.

Right now the worst is when the space is there at a time when I don't want it. That's only happened three times.

She was talking about a separation of just a little more than six months and conveyed real hesitancy about the benefits she had identified as she began to think and speak more about them.

This wife's hesitancy was echoed many times throughout the interviews. Benefits were rarely discussed zestfully. Rather the subject of benefits required some reflection – considered thoughts more than spontaneous, primary reactions. The fact that living apart allows these spouses to serve career goals while maintaining marital ties is its "self-evident" benefit. But the very need to alter so radically what they had thought married life presumed, i.e., co-residence, diminishes the value of any benefit they conjured up. This is a taxing arrangement to survive on a day-to-day basis. It follows an emotionally-churning, tough decision-making process in the first place. The compromise it represents for meeting career and familial needs simultaneously is a costly compromise. The interviews register the effort it takes to manage its constraints. A large part of such effort is made possible by the value they put on their relationship – a value which for some seems to increase as they see themselves successfully accomplishing what they know is difficult to do.

MUTUAL EMOTIONAL INVESTMENT

As a group, these couples exhibit a high degree of investment in the quality of their emotional relationship. They accept a view of marital interaction as intimate and emotionally close. They want to preserve this quality of their relationship and are mindful of the threats their current lifestyle imposes to some basic tie they felt they had before they began to live apart. One husband made this especially clear in telling me how annoyed he gets by imputations that there may be something wrong with a marital relationship willing to endure separation. On the contrary, he argued,

> Our relationship is like a potlatch. We're going through all this just because we want to keep what we have together.

His use of the term "potlatch" refers to a North American Indian tribal ritual which involves the purposeful destruction of property (burning of beads and blankets, etc.) to express status and thereby "earn" leadership positions in this community through such "conspicuous consumption" of wealth. What he meant was the expense and energy it took to keep their marriage going – a marriage that involves two households – was to him testimony for the importance of the relationship to him and his wife.

In general, then, the descriptions these spouses provide support a subjective view of their marriages as emotionally valuable and significant to them. Because of this premium on the relationship, it becomes worth their intentional, purposeful efforts to maintain it. They recognize the significance of the relationship to their own individual sense of well-being and this recognition helps them endure the lifestyle's challenge.

The intensity of the personal salience of their marriages, then, may be the key to what enables them to withstand the difficulties this lifestyle imposes (in the sense that their career needs require the decision to live apart). Here I would emphasize the similar finding of other researchers (e.g., Rapoport and Rapoport, 1976) that dual career couples as a group are very consciously aware of the marriage's value to them as individuals. In the case of dual career couples who live apart, it may be just such strong marital premium that shores up their considerable efforts to accommodate to the threats to the relationship that such a lifestyle imposes.

The fact that this premium on the marriage is conveyed in the context of a real sense of accomplishment at "pulling off" this lifestyle strengthens my impression that this may be the case. Making an advantage out of a disadvantage is a clear theme in these interviews. These partners take pride (and comfort) in their ability to cope with this arrangement, "to get through it." The sense of accomplishment they get from their joint effort – the marriages' continuing endurance – is comforting and rewarding. It is one of the few benefits they attach to the lifestyle.

We are patting ourselves on the back for being able to do this and pull it off successfully.

As this analysis has shown, it is a tough lifestyle involving painful trade-offs and recognizable "emotional work." That they acknowledge the effort it takes is clear from the interviews.

We look forward to settling down and enjoying a relationship instead of having to work at it and being emotionally torn apart all the time.

My judgment is that the intentional commitment to the marriage that so many of these couples exhibit makes its complexity bearable, providing motive power for the work it takes to cope with its pitfalls.

REFERENCES

Becker, H. S. 1963 Outsiders. New York: Free Press.
Berger, P. L., B. Berger and H. Kellner 1974 The Homeless Mind. Harmondsworth: Penguin.

COUPLES WHO LIVE APART

Berger, P. L. and H. Kellner 1964 "Marriage and the construction of reality." Diogenes 46 (Summer):1–25.

Cooley, C. H. 1962 (1922) Human Nature and the Social Order. New York: Scribners.

1967 "Looking-glass self." Pp. 231–3 in J. G. Manis and B. N. Meltzer (eds.), Symbolic Interaction. Boston: Allyn and Bacon.

Glaser, B. G. 1967 The Discovery of Grounded Theory. Chicago: Aldine.

Goffman, E. 1963 Stigma. Harmondsworth: Penguin.

Jones, W. L. 1978 Getting Settled. Unpublished Ph.D. Thesis. Canberra: The Australian National University.

Laing, R. D., H. Phillipson and A. R. Lee 1966 Interpersonal Perception. London: Tavistock.

Lindesmith, A. R. 1968 Addiction and Opiates. Chicago: Aldine.

Mead, G. H. 1932 The Philosopy of the Present. A. E. Murphy (ed.). London: Open Court.

1934 Mind, Self and Society. C. W. Morris (ed.). Chicago: University of Chicago.

1936 Movements of Thought in the Nineteenth Century. M. H. Moore (ed.). Chicago: University of Chicago.

1938 The Philosophy of the Act. C. W. Morris (ed.). Chicago: University of Chicago.

Schutz, A. 1971a Collected Papers I, The Problem of Social Reality. The Hague: Martinus Nijhoff.

1971b Collected Papers II, Studies in Social Theory. The Hague: Martinus Nijhoff.

Simmel, G. 1950 The Sociology of Georg Simmel. Trans. by K. Wolff, New York: Free Press.

Znaniecki, F. 1934 The Method of Sociology. New York: Rinehart.

Marriage and the Home: The Family Claim for Mothers

Chapter 13 ————————————————————————————

The Social Psychology of a Miscarriage: An Application of Symbolic Interaction Theory and Method

Shulamit Reinharz

Abstract
This chapter consists of three sections. The first offers an overview of the work of W. I. Thomas on the definition of the situation and the life-history method. The second applies his concepts and technique to analyze a single case of miscarriage. The third and final part briefly discusses how this document increases our understanding of W. I. Thomas's work and the need to look at institutional and historical forces influencing the definition of the situation. Throughout the chapter, societal implications are drawn to offset the current, rapidly expanding medical and legal intervention in reproduction that proceeds without any consideration of women's definition of the situation.

T his study analyzes a personal document in the manner of W. I. Thomas. My purpose is to understand how a woman continually defined, redefined, and negotiated a situation, how definitions affected the actions she wished to undertake, and how these definitions became social objects for her and affected both her identity and her emotions. Robert Stebbins (1986) has provided a useful overview of the history of research that drew on Thomas's concept. My approach in this chapter coincides with his view that social behavior is a product of three elements:

> The meaning or definition of a situation must be established before goal-directed behavior can occur. That meaning is a subjective state of mind; it intervenes between perception of what is happening and purpose action (or inaction) carried out with reference to what is perceived. (Stebbins, 1986: 134).

Source: This chapter was written for inclusion in this volume. Shulamit Reinharz teaches in the Department of Sociology at Brandeis University.

During the 1920s, University of Chicago sociologists used personal documents and interviews to construct life histories for the purpose of creating "a faithful rendering of the subject's experience and interpretation of the world he lives in" (Becker, 1966: vi). Although the method was widely used at first, it later fell into disuse and was replaced by research based on surveys and other quantitative methods. Nevertheless, the life-history method periodically reappears among qualitative researchers for two major reasons. First, it is useful when charting new territory and looking for "new variables, new questions, and new processes" (Becker, 1966: xii). Second, it is useful when attempting to examine social processes in contrast to structure. This method was particularly applicable in concert with the major social theory developed at Chicago that defined social process as symbolic interaction.

As Howard Becker noted in his discussion of the life history, the study of symbolic interaction "requires an intimate understanding of the lives of others" (1966: xiii). This understanding can be abetted by the use of Charles Cooley's method of sympathetic introspection. In this study of miscarriage, I interpret a woman's experience as if it were my own, in the manner of sympathetic introspection. My ability to do so is strengthened by personal experiences similar to hers and also by my familiarity with other personal documents concerning miscarriage (Reinharz, forthcoming a, b).

Thomas used personal documents such as letters and autobiographical statements not only to create a life history but also in a more circumscribed way to uncover a "definition of the situation." That is my purpose as well. On the basis of his studies, Thomas concluded that the family's and society's "definition of the situation" plays a large part in determining the behavior of an individual (Burgess and Locke, 1945). Thomas wrote about the "definition of the situation" in the following way:

> The child is always born into a group of people among whom all the general types of situation which may arise have already been defined and corresponding rules of conduct developed, and where he has not the slightest chance of making his definitions and following his wishes without interference. (Thomas, 1923: 42–43)

Definitions of the situation are important in part because they produce the labels that are applied to acts and people and thus describe the social world we produce and that in turn produces us. Acts are not

> single, isolated, muscular movement[s] but a highly complex and organized pattern of behavior, and each has been assigned a *name*. The name we give an act is, of course, a symbol, which has been designated by people through shared agreement. By assigning a name these people have isolated the act and given it importance. What constitutes an act, then, is convention, agreement. (Charon, 1985: 114).

Acts are not simply behaviors but are the product of mind and intention.

Acts are viewed as performed in situations, beginning with the individual's defining goals, immediate or distant, then defining objects in the situation around these goals. Humans are goal-directed; we establish and work for goals in every situation we enter. Each act, in a sense, can be said to begin with a goal that we establish for ourselves in the situation. We are planners; we plan our acts around these goals. (Charon, 1985: 115).

Personal documents are less frequently used in contemporary symbolic interaction research than are interviews and field notes. Although this use may reflect a methodological preference for larger samples, it may also be influenced by publishing practices. The reprinting of documents and their analyses are space-consuming. In this study, however, I return to the tradition of analyzing personal documents, using a published account of a woman's (Chris) miscarriage experience (Pizer and Palinski, 1981).** The personal document represents a form of unobtrusive data (Webb et al., 1966; Berman, 1985) not created for the purpose of this study and therefore not plagued by problems of reactivity. It does represent, of course, a particular rendition of this woman's miscarriage experience, one that is suited, in her view, to publication in a book about miscarriage. Context-free accounts are a logical impossibility.

I have inserted asterisks throughout this personal document to highlight words and phrases on which I comment. Following each paragraph of the personal document, I offer a symbolic interactionist interpretation based on an examination of Chris's particular use of words. In addition, I extricate a range of meanings behind the particular words by integrating other literature on reproduction.

AN AMERICAN MIDDLE-CLASS MARRIED MOTHER'S PERSONAL DOCUMENT OF MISCARRIAGE IN THE 1980s

It was a little over three years ago that *my husband, Mark, and I *decided (*rather naively) *to have a second *child. We had had one child without any real difficulties. *My pregnancy had been *normal, and I had *worked through *most of it.

When a woman recounts her miscarriage, she typically (Berezin, 1982; Borg and Lasker, 1981; Friedman and Gradstein, 1982; Jimenez, 1982; Paunthos and Romeo, 1985; Peppers and Knapp, 1980; Reinharz, 1987a, b) uses as a starting point the *decision* to have a child. Before the widespread use of birth control, pregnancy was more likely to be experienced as inevitable, a result of good or bad luck, divine intervention, or an accident of birth control. Between 1650 and 1750, for example, "ministers stressed the folly of presuming that any birth occurred independently of divine will." Women were told to "welcome pregnancy as a 'merciful visit' of the Lord, a sign of his blessing, and an opportunity to cooperate in their own redemption" (Scholten, 1985: 12–13). Now that women believe they can control contraception to a large extent, they also believe that they can control conception. This belief is reinforced by the claims of reproductive technologists (Dooley, 1985; Rowland, 1985).[1] Nevertheless, it should be understood that this sense of control exists only on the individual level; women as a group do not control conception, contraception, the right to abortion, or reproductive technologies.

A decision to become pregnant represents a new, perhaps momentous, definition of one's situation. This definition can result from private contemplation or social interaction. Whatever its source, it becomes a social object in the sense of being a springboard for action. Chris reconstructs the history of her miscarriage in terms of having redefined her situation as wanting to become pregnant, or wanting to have another child. Women deciding to become pregnant think in terms of a child, not a fetus. The decision to become pregnant is a turning point in a woman's identity or social role. The decision changes a woman's relation to her body, to sexuality, to time, to her partner(s), and to her future. From the moment of decision, she becomes an "about to be pregnant person" or "mother to be," an identity that can be lost (and frequently is) when a miscarriage occurs. Because her self changes, the woman can engage in new social relationships, e.g., with medical professionals and with her family who may or may not want her to become pregnant.

From the point of view of the woman who has miscarried, desired pregnancies (and miscarriages) begin at the moment of decision, not the moment of conception or a later stage of pregnancy. For many women thinking retrospectively about pregnancy and childbirth, the child begins when the decision is made to bear it.[2] When a woman decides to become pregnant, her child, which hitherto had been only a potentially wanted thing, is transformed into an actually wanted thing. The child begins to exist: it will have to be given up, or born, or continuously sought. In the excerpt above, the decision to have a child has action consequences; i.e., this couple decides to engage in unprotected intercourse.

After her miscarriage, Chris thinks she was naïve to believe that children are produced when one decides to produce them. Her body gave her feedback. She has suffered cognitive dissonance and changes her definition of the situation. Her old self (which made the decision) becomes an object she rejects in favor of a new, realistic self (which emerged when her actions failed to produce the intended consequences). The physical environment (i.e., her body) impinges on her definition of the situation and on her identity. The failure of her actions to produce the intended consequences alters her understanding of how children are obtained. This change has a socializing influence on her in the sense that it produces a new identity. She has changed, although "nothing" has happened.

The decision to have a second child was made by the husband and wife. The decision is not attributed to God, not participated in by their existing child, their physician, or others. Nor was the decision *imposed* on her by her husband or by theological views. (Her subsequent decisions will be shared by her physician.) The form that Chris's decision-making takes is typical of the contemporary American married couple.

Although the decision to have a child is a joint one between husband and wife, the pregnancy that ensues is the woman's: *my* pregnancy. Thus if it "fails," the woman has failed, until it can be proven otherwise. The pregnancy and the baby are two separate objects. Women "have pregnancies," then they "have babies"; thus, a miscarriage is a loss of both a pregnancy and a potential baby.

Chris divides pregnancies into "normal" and "abnormal." She calls her previous pregnancy "normal" because she was able to carry on *her* normal activities, such as work. In other words, the pregnancy was part of her both in terms of her body and her activities. She worked throughout most, not all, of her previous pregnancy, indicating that a slight modification of one's nonpregnant life does not force one to redefine a "normal" pregnancy as an "abnormal" one.

> *Our daughter Suze was nearly four years of age at the time and would be closer to five when her *sibling arrived, which *seemed all right. It was *a good time for us. Mark was finishing his physician's-assistant *training, and I was *working as a high-school counselor. We *planned the birth to coincide with the end of the school year and *joyfully announced my pregnancy to our families and friends, and of course, Suze, as I entered my *third month.

The pregnancy is a woman's, but the child is the couple's. People not only decide to become pregnant, but they also carefully decide *when* to become pregnant. Information concerning the presumed psychological effects on children of different spacings and of the timing of the birth on the parents' work are involved. The control of timing follows from and enhances the sense that pregnancy is a controlled phenomenon. The timing of pregnancy is a function of "industrial time" (Kahn, forthcoming) in the sense that an upcoming child's arrival is planned to be convenient for the working parents. Just as pregnancies are normal if they do not detract from work, so, too, babies are welcome in part in terms of how much they disrupt work. Interestingly, Chris does not seem to consider how her work could accommodate to the birth, but only how the birth would fit in with work demands.

Chris's writing reveals that she was designing her family in terms of her beliefs about its appropriate size and structure. The child that was being planned already existed as a family member, a sibling, and a work impediment. The wife defined the individual members of the family as ready to receive the new member who was not yet conceived. The child's father would be ready in nine months because his long-term work training would then be complete. The mother would be ready because she would have a particular type of work load at that time. The family was being rationally constructed in line with its values of being well organized, psychologically responsible, and efficient. Planning was organized for a pregnancy duration of nine months because pregnancy was defined as something that lasted nine months.

When appropriate planning is done and action follows with the intended consequences, the couple experiences joy. Their sense of control over pregnancy has been confirmed. Nevertheless, the couple does not share the news that the woman is pregnant (i.e., self-disclose her new identity) for at least two months. This is an interesting example of avoiding anticipatory socialization (i.e., into the role of pregnant woman) and of hiding potential stigma (i.e., the stigma of having miscarried). The fact that Chris mentions *not* informing friends and family until she entered her third month suggests that this is another decision. Sharing the news that one is pregnant is a significant social act, since this announcement of a new identity changes one's relationships and others' definitions of oneself. A couple rationally decides when it is appropriate to share this news. Again, planning, timing, deciding, acting, and weighing are the subjective experiences of pregnancy, at least for middle-class married women with desired pregnancies.

Chris does not reveal her reasons for waiting or her reasons for telling after two months, but one can imagine that she did so because of her own unconscious or conscious knowledge of the risks of miscarriage in the early period of pregnancy. If this is so, then she must have believed that it is not good to inform significant others until one has passed the high-risk period for miscarriage. Although Chris was pregnant, she was not ready to take the role of a pregnant woman (see George Herbert Mead, 1934) until she had passed a date when she thought she could no longer lose the role. Although I doubt women are instructed about this custom of withholding information, I am impressed with the ubiquity of the practice. When the couple told others, the planned baby became a social object known to wider circles. It became a potential person in many people's minds.

> Only a few weeks later we were *stunned by my miscarriage. I noticed some *slight spotting one Saturday but at the time wasn't at all alarmed. I'd never considered the possibility of any difficulty with the pregnancy and *didn't know anyone my age who had miscarried. When the spotting continued through Monday, I called my obstetrician's office, still not concerned that there was any major problem. The nurse I spoke with told me to come right in. When I said that I was working and couldn't come immediately, she told me that *they wouldn't be responsible for my condition unless I came right over. That was when I began to be alarmed.

Stunned is the word frequently used by women describing their immediate reaction to a first miscarriage. Being stunned suggests the shock following news of an unexpected death; it also connotes a physical blow. Dictionary definitions focus on suddenness and violence. The shock is brought about because it violates Chris's previous action context surrounding the pregnancy: careful decision-making and precise timing. It also violates her belief that "I'd never considered the possibilitiy of any difficulty with the pregnancy." Her not telling until she entered the third month, however, belies her "never having considered the possibility of any difficulty." How can these two statements be reconciled? Perhaps the key is that the miscarriage occurred in the third month, after she had "passed through the period of vulnerability." Perhaps "never" refers to "starting with the third month." This is a private scientific scheme that has no validity; that is, miscarriages do occur after the second month. Thus, part of her shock results from having her "private knowledge" invalidated.

Chris's comment that she did not know anyone who had miscarried is frequently mentioned by women writing about their miscarriages. This absence of experiential knowledge of many aspects of childbearing provides the groundwork for being shocked. Geographic mobility, the weakening of social ties, and the removal of pregnancy/delivery from the control of women contribute to the absence of shared information about women's reproductive lives. We turn instead to the media but do not always find the information we need. (This theme is developed in a later section of Chris's statement.) Ironically, in this scientific age, women's knowledge about how our bodies function is so meager that we can be shocked if we undergo something as common as miscarriage. This fact suggests a wide range of questions that could be generated under the rubric of "the sociology of ignorance."

> Up to about 1780, medical treatises and public ordinances viewed childbirth as women's domain. The cessation of the menses, the suspicion of pregnancy, the swelling of the body, miscarriage, abortion, birth, lactation were no less women's affair than infanticide or the rearing of the in-fant (in Latin, literally, the non-speaker). (Illich, 1982: 123)

Previously, women had been responsible for birth as mothers and as midwives. They therefore had to know what to expect and what to do. (I do not mean to imply that what they knew was always accurate or useful.)

Chris's miscarriage shocked her perhaps because modern women believe that we can control everything and because women are under the care of physicians who are thought to be scientists and thus able to control nature. Women tend to define miscarriages as failures rather than recognizing that pregnancy cannot be completely controlled. (See Chris's paragraph below.) Women's rediscovery of their bodies is slowly beginning to take place through the women's health movement. Self-help sessions, for example, teach a woman to view her own cervix, and books such as *Our Bodies, Ourselves* make women's bodily experiences available to other women despite their mutual isolation.

Barker-Benfield described the contrasting circumstances when male physicians first saw a cervix:

> At his own expense, Dr. Sims kept a stable of black slaves in order to conduct ex-
> perimental operations on their vaginal fistulae. In 1845, he had the idea of placing a
> Mrs. Merril on all fours − a position since then termed 'Sim's position' − and adapted
> a spoon handle for holding the vagina open. He reports in his diary: 'Introducing the
> bent handle, I saw everything as no man had ever seen before . . . the speculum made
> it perfectly clear from the beginning . . . I felt like an explorer in medicine who first
> views a new and important territory.' A colleague, Dr. Baldwin, commented on this:
> 'Sim's speculum has been to the diseases of the womb . . . what the compass is to the
> mariner.' The vagina became the entrance to new territory for the exploration of
> nature. (Barker-Benfield, 1976, cited in Illich, 1982: 110)

Apparently, Sims did not inform Mrs. Merril of what he saw.

Chris's response to continued spotting, which she interpreted as a problem
but not an alarming one, was to "call my obstetrician's office." Interestingly, she
reveals that one calls an office, not even expecting direct access to the obstetrician. In addition, her response to her "not a major problem" was to call a professional rather than draw on her own knowledge of what to do. She had no such
knowledge. Further, she was not yet willing to interfere with her "industrial
time." The nurse responded by emphasizing the contexts of fiscal and legal
responsibility. This response forced Chris to redefine the situation as "major."
Only then did she experience "alarm" and become willing to violate her "industrial time."

> I *left my office at school and went directly to his office. Unfortunately *my own
> physician wasn't there, so I *had to see one of his associates. He examined me and
> said, *Mrs. Palinski, you are aborting. Go home and rest. Call if cramps start, other-
> wise come back tomorrow.' No ifs, no maybes, just the flat statement that I was
> 'aborting,' and *then he left the room.

By redefining the situation as an emergency, she actively interrupted her
work. At the obstetrician's office, she again recognized her minimal control of the
situation, for she cannot see "her own physician" and thus "had to see" one of his
(presumably numerous) associates. The rotation of physicians is done for physician convenience even though the rapport between a particular physician and a
pregnant woman is thereby undermined. This rotation system underpins the
whole reproductive process, particularly labor and delivery. In addition, I interpret the word *see* as indicating the lack of touching, caring, and sharing
characteristic of contemporary doctor/patient relations.

The doctor addressed Chris formally, since he had no personal relation with
her. He used a medical term, *aborting*, to define her situation, implying that this
was the sole significant definition. By imposing his language, he strengthened his

control over her. He then told her what to do. Symbolically and literally, he in-sured that there would be no discussion or negotiation of meaning; he left. In ad-dition, he acted as if no other care was needed beyond his instructions. His departure was contingent on this definition. Because he left, Chris was unable to argue that a different response might be appropriate, given her emerging defini-tion of "losing my baby." On the basis of that definition, his behavior could be labeled abandonment, callousness, or even abuse.

Finally, his use of the word *cramps* implied menstruation, whereas if he had used the word *contractions*, she might have understood and begun preparing for the labor she would soon experience. His use of *cramps* rather than *contractions* derives from his defining what was in her body as tissue rather than something on its way to becoming a baby. This begins the process of undermining her definition of her pregnancy as a baby.

> I was *shocked, frightened and terribly sad. I sat on the examining table *crying for a while. Then a *sympathetic nurse came in to help me on with my clothes, and I left. I *sobbed all the way home and sat in my *kitchen all afternoon with a *dear friend, who is a nurse and women's health specialist and who was mercifully nearby. She *held my hand and *cried with me, *explaining things and *generally took care of me that day, a *shared experience which will *bond us forever. She told me *what to ex-pect — the cramping and the bleeding — which would increase until I passed the *fetus. When *I was talked out, she left.

Because of the doctor's interaction with her, Chris underwent her second shock. In addition, she experienced a range of emotions and physical responses, such as crying. Chris was so overcome by these emotions that she could not perform even simple tasks such as getting dressed. Because no one was helping her, the nurse who did come was labeled "sympathetic," even though her assistance was not elaborate.

Chris continued to cry even in public. Her feelings were so strong that they overcame her knowledge of behavioral norms in public spaces. Fortunately, Chris was able to call on "social support" in the person of someone who had the additional attribute of being well-informed. Sitting in her kitchen, in space where she could control the definition of the situation, appropriate emotions, and behavior, she experienced the opposite of medical abandonment. Her friend touched her body, explained rather than labeled, and spent a great deal of time with Chris. Chris explained that her friend took care of "me," presumably the in-tegrated body, mind, and emotions. The friend was willing to experience the emotions herself, unlike the physician, who is expected to ward off shared emo-tions since such emotions are ubiquitous, time-consuming, and potentially over-whelming.

The satisfying sharing between Chris and her friend became an object Chris called "a shared experience." It was as if this new object was used to replace the bonding that was expected to occur with the baby had it been born. We can see in Chris's language that at this point the baby turned into a fetus. Only when Chris defined her needs as having been met did the friend leave.

> *Later that night I had twenty minutes of very uncomfortable cramping, like contractions during birthing, and heavy bleeding. By morning it was obviously all over. I saw my physician that morning, and he told me very quickly that I had 'aborted.' I remember his use of that term in place of *miscarriage* was a bit unsettling.

In this passage, Chris labeled her physical sensations as both cramps and contractions. She mentions the speed with which her physician labeled her situation and the discomfort caused by his use of a medical term that implied an induced abortion.

> The doctor *talked with me a while about the probable cause, about *my feelings and about *the D and C (dilation and curettage) that he recommended as *our next step. He arranged to meet me at the hospital an hour later. I called Mark, who met us there and stayed with me while I was prepped and examined and through the D and C. Two hours later it was over, and I was riding home groggy and spent. In just over twenty-four hours *everything* had changed.

The doctor talked about the probable cause; he did not define the situation as requiring serious investigation. He acknowledged her feelings and recommended an operation. (Although all obstetrics books recommend this operation following miscarriage, the necessity of this procedure is hotly debated among critics of contemporary medical practice.) The operation was defined as a shared activity, although it is unclear if Chris meant shared by her and her doctor or her and her husband. After the operation, Chris defined her entire life as "changed," probably implying that she had changed from expecting a child to losing a pregnant identity, a pregnancy, and a potential child.

> I was quite depressed and withdrawn for several days afterward. I had found a new and frightening *mistrust for my body, which was extremely unpleasant. However, as *I am basically as survivor and a positive person, I threw myself into the task of *'solving' the problem. In the next few months *I looked into everything I could for information about miscarriage. I found very little. There weren't *any* books available even in the most extensive libraries. A few short paragraphs in books on pregnancy was the best that I could do.

Chris experienced more strong emotions and changed her definition of her body to something she could not trust. This new definition filled her with unpleasant emotions. At the same time, she drew on another, separate identity – a survivor and a positive person. By drawing on this past identity, she found a basis for new action. She now defined her experience as a solvable problem, not as a misfortune or an injustice. As a consequence, she created a new job for herself, beginning with a literature search. She found the literature woefully inadequate.

This definition provided grounds for further searches (and later, creation of her own literature).

> Even Mark's and my friends in the medical field found little in the medical libraries. Their message, and that of my doctor, was *to accept the miscarriage as a kind of pro-tective natural intervention which occurs in 15 to 20 percent of all pregnancies. I ac-cepted this and looked forward to the next pregnancy, which would erase this misery.

Significant others concurred in her definition of the available literature as inade-quate. She accepted the action they suggested, (to minimize the situation, to develop an attitude of acceptance, and even to adopt the belief that her miscar-riage prevented a birth anomaly). Essentially, they suggested she redefine this miscarriage as insignificant because miscarriage is so commonplace. Finally, they thought she should consider this miscarriage as related only to this particular pregnancy and not as an indicator of infertility. Given this definition, Chris could contemplate a new pregnancy. She also believed that a pregnancy brought to term would "erase" a pregnancy resulting in miscarriage, that a joy erases a misery.

> I became pregnant a few months after the first miscarriage, as *the doctor had ad-vised. At that time I was only *cautiously optimistic. We *didn't tell Suze or many other people, and during this *pregnancy I tried to do *all the right things for my body. I was *careful about my diet; I didn't smoke or drink. I cut back on my activity, got lots of rest, and even cut my working days from five to three. I had been living with some guilt and fear that *something I had done during the earlier pregnancy had caused *the failure, so I tried to be especially careful.

After a miscarriage, a doctor becomes an integral component in the decision making and timing of pregnancy. In addition, after a miscarriage, the pregnancy is defined differently. A particular set of attitudes, actions, and emotions are matched to this definition of the situation. Chris experienced the postmiscarriage pregnancy more as pregnancy than as "having a child." Her dominant emotion was caution, stemming from her new relation with her body – mistrust. The ac-tion consequences were 'not telling' significant others and modifying her behavior in accordance with her definition of what was right. Her body was almost a patient, a separate thing for which one did "the right things." Chris's behavior reflected a previously unexpressed belief that it was not "nature" but her own behavior that caused her miscarriage; thus, even though earlier she stated that she accepted others' definition, she also harbored another definition. Her depression might be interpreted as a consequence of feeling guilt for her failure to protect her child.

Given that Chris also defined herself as having *caused* her own miscarriage, she changed many aspects of her behavior-during-pregnancy to protect this child from her previously errant ways. Her diet, smoking, drinking, activity level, rest,

and work changed. It is unclear if these changes imply that her whole definition
of normal behavior during pregnancy changed or if she considered this an abnormal pregnancy (because it was occurring in an untrustworthy body) requiring
special treatment. She did not know which specific action caused her miscarriage. After all, her physician had not tried to determine the actual cause. Thus,
any and all of Chris's behavior might have caused it.

It is evident that Chris assumes responsibility for her previous miscarriage;
she does not blame her husband, natural processes, or her physician. She calls it
a failure, her failure. This definition demands specific actions to ensure success in
pregnancy.

> *In spite of all the special treatment that I was giving myself, the pregnancy only
> lasted twelve weeks. As soon as I started spotting *I knew I would miscarry, but I
> spent nearly a week in bed waiting. Eventually the cramps began – much more
> severe this time – and I went to the hospital. I spent approximately twelve hours in
> labor, passing lots of blood and feeling a lot of pain, before I actually took any medica-
> tion. I have vivid memories of the pain.

Chris had no control over her situation. Her extensive efforts to eliminate
her actions that might have caused the first miscarriage were unavailing. Her
definitions of the situation (i.e., that she could protect her baby by changing her
behavior) and her competence were again undermined. She had some new
knowledge, however, that prevented shock. Specifically, she redefined
"spotting" to mean the 'start of miscarriage.'

This miscarriage, however, did not proceed like her first one, so her frustration and pain increased. Belief in her own culpability prevented her from questioning her physician and made her willing to undergo hospital treatment again.
In fact, this time she used more treatment, going to the hospital to 'have the
miscarriage.' Again, her experience produced the blended definition of pain:
cramps and labor.

> I *had to wait another twelve hours before getting a D and C again. I didn't know it
> then, but *the Roman Catholic hospital I went to required a negative pregnancy test
> before they would perform the D and C (regardless of other symptoms). The *wait
> was very upsetting, and I decided not to return to a Catholic hospital if I was ever
> faced with a miscarriage again. This second miscarriage in less than six months left me
> more depressed and *more frightened about my chances of having another child.

The frustration of "having to wait" stemmed from three causes: Chris did
not control her situation and was inconvenienced; she was repulsed by having
the pregnancy remains in her longer than necessary; and she disagreed with the
Roman Catholic hospital's policy requiring evidence of death before scraping her
uterus. The hospital policy defined pregnancies as existing until tests show they
do not. Even though Chris knew experientially that she had miscarried, her experience was discounted.

The action resulting from her frustration was a decision not to use Roman Catholic hospitals for miscarriage treatment. Finally, on the basis of two miscarriages, Chris began to think that she would not be able to have another child. She thus had to reconfront the loss of several selves she had developed. The previous miscarriage became redefined not as a freak accident of nature or a consequence of 'not taking care of myself,' but as part of a pattern of infertility. Chris's new emotion was fright.

*I am not sure why Mark and I did not immediately have a series of tests done to find out right then what was wrong. We both wanted to have another child very much, and we did want answers. *Our obstetrician's point of view was that *since we had one normal child already, the available testing wouldn't offer us much information. Testing is often oriented toward the problems of couples who have not been able to reproduce at all. The medical advice we were given was generally encouraging; our doctor told us that we were still in a *good range statistically to produce a normal pregnancy. Our decision was to wait for a few months and then *try again.

Chris became confused about whether to look for a cause. On one hand, that course of action would be scientific. On the other hand, her obstetrician imposed his definition that the information received would be useless. Her determination to have another child remained strong, but she feared she was infertile (with respect to a second child). Her obstetrician defined her as fertile because she has already had a child. Her definition of herself as infertile reflected her future orientation; his definition of her as fertile reflected his past orientation.

The obstetrician defined her chances of becoming pregnant statistically, rather than in terms relative to her having had two miscarriages. Chris claimed they made a joint decision to continue the strategy of waiting and attempting to get pregnar.t. She was unable to convince the obstetrician of her definition that a serious investigation should take place. She was more interested in investigation and intervention than he, since it was her life, and time was slipping by. His motivation for defining her miscarriages as unserious and unworthy of investigating is unknown, but typical, according to other women's reports.

When I became pregnant about six months later, optimism was hard to come by. I hadn't really found any *tangible scientific information that helped me with my feelings. By then *every little ripple in my pregnant body *frightened me. I was even *superstitious about repeating experiences I associated with earlier miscarriages.

On the basis of inadequate information, Chris was frightened by her next pregnancy. She no longer talked about decisions to conceive or have a child. She focused entirely on her body and was frightened by it. Fear, a lack of information, and an intensely desired situation led to superstitious acts to ward off danger.

This *fourth pregnancy lasted four months. The familiar spotting, waiting, and contractions were followed, quickly this time, by a D and C. Once again it was all over.
The process this time took seven days.

This miscarriage is collapsed into a brief set of events. It has no personality of its
own except that in this case Chris had a quick, rather than a delayed, D and C.
Because she had no hope, she experienced little loss or emotion. By this time,
after repeated pregnancies and miscarriages, after a loss of optimism, Chris spoke
about her pregnancy as a pregnancy, not as a baby. The repetition began to
dehumanize, minimize, and medicalize her experience. The process is referred to
as an "it," described only quantitatively – seven days.

I knew then that I would not *risk another replay of those events without a *serious
medical evaluation. *We stayed with our obstetrician because we both liked and
*trusted him, and we began a *series of tests *immediately. While I was still in the
hospital after the D and C, they drew blood samples for hydroid testing. *The next
day I had a glucose-tolerance test for diabetes.

Now that she was using a medical paradigm, Chris thought of pregnancy in
terms of risks of miscarriage. Her medical (rather than self-blame) perspective led
her to think that medical testing might uncover the cause of her multiple miscarriages. Given this risk model, she redefined her previous professional treatment
as less than serious. She nevertheless retained her obstetrician, claiming to like
and trust him, despite her dissatisfaction expressed in previous paragraphs.
Chris's and her husband's trust may have been restored when the obstetrician
accepted her definition of the situation as 'worthy of investigation.' The consequence of this definition was his ordering of tests. For this reason, she did not
have to search for a different obstetrician. He agreed to become her ally in the
search for causes even though previously he had said that testing would offer little information. As if to corroborate her success in having the situation redefined
as serious, Chris remarked that the tests started immediately, while she was in
the hospital for the D and C following her latest miscarriage.

Over the next few months *both Mark and I went through several other tests, including genetic analysis and a urological evaluation. All along the way the
*specialists warned me *not to hope for any answers. By then I was hostile toward
all of them. 'Why don't they know anything?' I thought. 'And why isn't any research
being done?' I felt that *my future was in very detached, uninterested hands. It was
an extremely *tense period for me and for Mark.

Now that a medical new definition was in place and confirmed by action,
Chris felt less guilt. She considered the idea that 'the cause' could lie in either
her or her husband's body rather than in her behavior. Chris embarked on a
crusade to determine what was terminating her pregnancies. The more she was

disappointed in research, the more she believed in it. Because each new test could bring the answer she sought, each inconclusive result motivated her to seek new testing.

Chris expected the people who were searching with her to share her definition of the situation – a crusade to find the culprit. She defined the search as "my future," her life. The tests were literally a matter of life and death. However, the specialists did not appear interested. Their definitions and behaviors made Chris and her husband tense.

To Chris, bearing a child involved teamwork, and Chris expected all the specialists to share her commitment. Having this child became a career, a journey with markers and people giving messages. Specialists instructed Chris how to feel – "do not have hope." They defined the situation as beyond the reach of science and thus advised her to relinquish her journey. What she previously defined as "a serious medical evaluation" and "answers" were now recognized as stressful. Given the weightiness of these tests, in her view, it is not surprising that she saw the technicians as "detached" and "uninterested."

> The last step in the whole series of tests involved the culturing of *tissue from my cervix and uterus to examine for infectious diseases. The results came back from the state health department – *positive!* They had identified the T-strain mycoplasma – something like a virus – in my uterus. My obstetrician called to explain to me that this T-strain mycoplasma had only recently been associated with both infertility and miscarriage.

Now that she defined her situation as medical, Chris spoke of her body as parts. Her search for a rational answer to her repeated abortions is fruitful; a viable hypothesis is formulated and confirmed. In this context, it is understandable that Chris would define the test results that she was sick as good news.

Much psychological literature defines repeated abortions as the product of the woman's psyche (Reinharz, forthcoming b) and therefore not worthy of medical testing. This reluctance to test can be found even among physicians who do not blame women for single or repeated miscarriages:

> . . . because it is usually not possible to find a treatable cause for a miscarriage, there is seldom any point in a couple who have had less than three consecutive miscarriages having any investigations performed, or having any treatment, unless there appears to be a clear-cut reason for the miscarriages, such as an incompetent cervix, or there is some reason to believe that the woman has, for example, a relevant medical disorder. Even after three consecutive miscarriages it is unlikely that any specific abnormality will be detected (Lachelin, 1985: 55)

Lachelin recommends searching for causes only when the cause is nearly known!

We sent new cervical smears from me and urine from both Mark and me to the *lab for treatment determination. The *report indicated that one of the tetracyclines

would cure my infection. Although there was no indication that Mark was also
*infected, he and I both took the course of antibiotics and were 'cured.'

The lab is personified and received body tissues. Chris accepted the fact that she
was infected. Nevertheless, her husband also takes the treatment. This over-
cautiousness, similar to her behavior in the pregnancy following the first miscarriage, is another form of superstitious behavior that helped her retain her definition of the situation as "we tried everything we could." Doing "everything we
could" also strengthened her belief that she would succeed in having another
child. Mark's unnecessary taking of drugs indicated too that this couple feared
not taking medication more than taking it and suffering possible iatrogenic effects. Finally, doing something that was not medically necessary might also symbolize that Chris had taken control of the situation.

Naturally we were *overjoyed to have identified *any problem that could be treated,
although the doctor was careful to say that *we couldn't be sure that the
mycoplasma was the source of the problem. He was *encouraged; we were encouraged and very much relieved. We decided to risk another try, in spite of *the lack of
certainty about the mycoplasma issue. By that time we were speculating about the
possibility of doing this book, and we were already reading and researching the subject extensively. The more information Hank unearthed, the more we realized that
this mycoplasma business was anything but definite.

Again, joy stemmed from making a decision and gaining control. The doctor
began to feel hopeful, although he also wanted to limit the couple's optimism.
Getting pregnant was redefined as risk-taking, working within a range of odds,
dealing with uncertainty. Gone was the idea that pregnancy would yield a child;
gone was the sense of decision making. Now she 'took chances'; pregnancy had
become a gamble.

Chris had also adopted a new identity as a person with an important story
to share, a book to write. She tried to enhance her knowledge of science but
recognized that the more one learns, the more nebulous the information
becomes.

I found that I was pregnant in the fall of 1978 and spent a very *anxious winter. It
wasn't until Christmas time, when I was *too large to fit into my own clothes and
*people on the street were noticing my pregnancy, that I began *to feel that this one
was going to continue. As had been the case in the *the last two pregnancies, I was
very careful about diet, rest, and exertion. The one factor that I was *not able to control was my anxiety, which thankfully began to subside in the early spring. The
pregnancy was completely normal – no spotting, no cramps. *The baby became
noticeably active in early December and continued to be extremely physical throughout my pregnancy, including the day of delivery. The later part of the pregnancy was
a very happy, close time for Mark, Suze, and me, in spite of my increasing bulk and
discomfort.

Chris experienced this medicalized pregnancy as a time of anxiety. She was unwilling to define herself as having a pregnancy she could bring to term until forced to by her body (her clothes did not fit) and the generalized other (people on the street). She considered herself responsible for the outcome of her pregnancy and so acted cautiously. She was forthright about her desire to control the situation; she was unable, however, to control her anxiety. Her anxiety had a life of its own.

In this pregnancy, unlike the pregnancy that resulted in her first miscarriage, Chris defined normalcy in terms of physical symptoms. Also, for the first time since the initial miscarriage, Chris spoke of the baby. She defined the baby as very physical, very alive. She probably noticed its physicality because she was so concerned about the baby's viability. Chris returned to some of her initial emotions connected with pregnancy – happiness and closeness – regardless of any physical discomfort. Her body could no longer define any aspect of pregnancy as bad.

> On April 29, the exact due date, at 10:36 P.M., our *son, John William, was born. My labor was *short and hard – less than three hours of noticeable contractions. The last hour moved so quickly that John beat our obstetrician to the delivery. *Our plans for a Leboyer birth (low lights, silence, a gentle bath for the newborn immediately after birth) were scrapped when a rather surprised obstetrics resident was hurriedly summoned to 'catch' the baby! It was, of course, exciting and wonderful. *My only disappointment was that our obstetrician, Fred Storm, who had seen us through the past two years, wasn't there for those special moments.

The baby is now gendered. Labor is manageable; the baby's efficiency is emphasized. He becomes an actor and redefines the situation, disrupting his parents' plans for a particular type of delivery. He even changes the cast of characters. Lively John surprises the resident, but physicians are still needed to 'catch babies.' Chris would have liked to compensate her physician for his teamwork by sharing the birth of the child he helped her create. Her physician was not always there when she needed him, but she defined this particular time as *his* loss.

> Our son was healthy and active from the first seconds. He roomed in with me at the hospital and was pleasant to care for right away. A bout with jaundice a few days after we came home has been the only blot on his *perfect record, and he seems to have recovered from that *common though frightening problem. He is six weeks old now; as I type these words I'm listening with the proverbial 'one ear' for him to awaken from his afternoon nap.

Chris produced a baby she defines as "perfect." Perhaps she needs to convince herself of this definition since she had such trouble producing him. When she is frightened, she reminds herself that some problems are common. She is in the role of mother-of-infant, waiting for her child to awake. The identity of her wanted child and herself as the mother of an infant have been realized.

In subsequent paragraphs not reprinted here, Chris summarized her experiences beginning with the decision to have a second child and ending with his birth two and a half years later. The dominant feeling was physical and psychological pain, the latter stemming from feeling misunderstood, uninformed, and alone. The whole experience could have been less painful with public awareness that women who miscarry need support and services. Chris felt little support as a member of the group "women who miscarry."

She characterized her obstetrician as kind and able to communicate. These personal qualities, however, were insufficient to the task because he was unwilling, at first, to treat her miscarriages as worthy of investigation. In addition, the doctor's role did not include availability for grieving and daily care. Chris was expected to use other resources for these needs. Her primary source of support was other women, Chris explains, not her husband, who was grieving himself. Chris would have liked to find age peers who had miscarriage experience and would understand her pain and loss, but she found only women of her mother's generation. Many of her friends had not yet had children, let alone miscarriages; some had undergone elective abortion. The older women were helpful to her, but they did not assuage her sense that she was unusual, that is, deviant. Nor was she able to use their experience to evaluate the quality of her treatment. The lack of people to talk to about miscarriage also made her think this was a stigmatized experience. The more she searched for peers, the less she believed that fully 20 percent of pregnancies terminate in spontaneous abortion.

Perhaps her lack of peers also helps explain why Chris sought literature on miscarriage. In the literature, she hoped to find information about miscarriage, language to explain what she had experienced, and support. Appropriate language ostensibly would make her feel understood. Sources of information she consulted were women who had miscarried, popular literature, medical books, and women's magazines. However, the kind of information she wanted was unavailable, instead, all she found were physicians' definitions of the situation. These she defined as limited and frustrating. She also sought medical answers for why people miscarry and recognized that these answers do not exist. The lack of information about women's experiences and the technical information made Chris feel alone, without her baby, without her pregnancy, without her identity as a woman who would become a mother of a second child, without optimism, without understanding, and without a reference group who could share her definitions of the situation. Her miscarriage experiences were only resolved, therefore, when she both had the baby and wrote her book.

CONCLUDING THOUGHTS ON SYMBOLIC INTERACTION AND PERSONAL DOCUMENTS

This personal document demonstrates vividly that definitions of situation are important for defining action, as W. I. Thomas argued. It also demonstrates that definitions are in continuous flux, that contradictory definitions may coexist within a single person, and that definitions may be temporarily dropped and then revived. Definitions are not only negotiated with others, but also with oneself in self-conversations and reflection, in interaction with one's body, and in interactions with others. That an unborn child or an other noninteracting being can be a "loved other" and a "social object" is also suggested by this personal document of an experience common among women. These are significant confirmations and extensions of symbolic interaction theory.

On the other hand, because the process of becoming social and developing a self was analyzed here in terms of childhood, this study suggests that Mead and Cooley may have overemphasized social control rather than conflict and creativity in the shaping of the self. Chris's personal document thus may expose the middle-class or male-centered bias in symbolic interaction theory in the sense that actions are presumed to stem from intentions rather than from factors beyond people's control. Furthermore, this document suggests that because of the emphasis on ideas and roles, symbolic interaction may underestimate the extent to which physical properties and the biological self affect behavior and are experienced as uncontrolled. The concept of *defining a situation* implies that people have the ability to define and control. Studying women's lives (and the lives of other groups) reveals that women have little control over their lives and struggle continuously to gain some control. More often than not, women review their experiences with disappointment at not being supported or understood and at lacking needed information.

Symbolic interactionists' emphasis on interaction may also underestimate the extent to which social institutions shape human behavior (see Schwartz and Kahne, 1983). In the studies of the Chicago School, particularly in Thomas and Znaniecki's *The Polish Peasant* (1918–20) such institutions as the village, community, family, religion, and press were analyzed in terms of their formation of the selves of the Polish immigrants. Clifford Shaw stressed this use: "By means of personal documents it is possible to study not only the traditions, customs, and moral standards of neighborhoods, institutions, families, gangs and play groups, but the manner in which these cultural factors become incorporated into the behavior trends of the child" (Shaw, 1966: 10). Over time, this framework has been neglected and symbolic interaction theory has been used to explain processes primarily within dyads, small groups, or limited settings. To a large extent, sociology has become compartmentalized into macro- and microsociology. Because some of Chris's actions are framed by historical forces that define the relation between professional and lay persons and between men and women, I had to draw on contexts larger than individual interaction to understand her document. I conclude, therefore, that an adequate theory of social behavior must integrate symbolic interaction theory of social processes with macrosociological theory of institutions in historical perspective.

NOTES

1. Women who use reproductive technology frequently do not know that the success rates of these new techniques are extremely low, that they are participating in a medical situation in which they will have very little, if any, control, and that these procedures are stressful and expensive.

2. If we lived in a world in which women could act according to their own definitions of the situation, we would be able to understand that a woman can grieve the death of a child (e.g., in miscarriage) without being compelled to treat each pregnancy as a legal life.

REFERENCES

Barker-Benfield, G. J. (1976) *The Horrors of the Half-Known Life: Male Attitudes towards Women and Sexuality in Nineteenth-Century America.* New York: Harper and Row.

Becker, Howard (1966) "Introduction" in Clifford Shaw, *The Jack-Roller.* Chicago: University of Chicago Press.

Berezin, Nancy (1982) *After a Loss in Pregnancy: Help for Families Affected by a Miscarriage, a Stillbirth, or the Loss of a Newborn.* New York: Fireside/Simon and Schuster.

Berman, Harry (November 1985) "Admissable Evidence: Geropsychology and the Intimate Journal," paper presented at the Gerontological Society of America Meetings.

Borg, Susan and Judith Lasker (1981) *When Pregnancy Fails: Families Coping with Miscarriage, Stillbirth and Infant Death.* Boston: Beacon Press.

Burgess, Ernest and Harvey J. Locke (1945) *The Family: From Institution to Companionship.* New York: American Book Co.

Charon, Joel (1985) *Symbolic Interactionism: An Introduction, Interpretation, and Integration.* Englewood Cliffs, N.J.: Prentice-Hall.

Dooley, Meg (1985) "Helping Mother Nature." *Columbia* (October): 20–28.

Friedman, Rochelle and Bonnie Gradstein (1982) *Surviving Pregnancy Loss.* Boston: Little, Brown and Co.

Hewitt, John P. (1984) *Self and Society: A Symbolic Interactionist Social Psychology,* Third Edition. Boston: Allyn and Bacon.

Illich, Ivan (1982) *Gender.* New York: Pantheon Books.

Jimenez, Sherry Lynn Mims (1982) *The Other Side of Pregnancy: Coping with Miscarriage and Stillbirth.* Englewood Cliffs, N.J.: Prentice-Hall.

Kahn, Robbie Pfeuffer (forthcoming) "The Language of Birth: Repossessing Birth in Theory and Practice," unpublished doctoral dissertation, Brandeis University, Department of Sociology.

Lachelin, Gillian, M.D. (1985) *Miscarriage: The Facts.* London: Oxford University Press.

Mead, George Herbert (1934) *Mind, Self and Society: From the Standpoint of a Social Behaviorist.* Ed. and intro. by Charles W. Morris. Chicago: University of Chicago Press.

Panuthos, Claudia and Catherine Romeo (1985) *Ended Beginnings: Healing Childbearing Losses.* South Hadley, Mass.: Bergin & Garvey Publishers.

Peppers, Larry and Ronald Knapp (1980) *Motherhood and Mourning: Perinatal Death.* New York: Praeger.

Pizer, Hank and Christine Palinski (1981) *Coping with a Miscarriage: Why It Happens and How to Deal with Its Impact on You and Your Family.* New York: New American Library. (Plume paperback edition, 1981 printing)

Reinharz, Shulamit (1987a) "Miscarriage: A Cross-Cultural Study of Women's Experiences" in Dorothy Wertz (ed.), *Research in the Sociology of Health Care*, volume 7. Greenwich, Conn.: JAI Press.

Reinharz, Shulamit (1987b) "What's Missing in Miscarriage?" *Journal of Community Psychology.*

Rowland, Robyn (1985) "A child at any price? An overview of issues in the use of the new reproductive technologies, and the threat to women." *Women's Studies International Forum* 8: 539–546.

Scholten, Catherine M. (1985) *Childbearing in American Society: 1650–1850.* New York: New York University Press.

Schwartz, Charlotte Green and Merton J. Kahne (1983) "Medical help as negotiated achievement." *Psychiatry* 46: 333–350.

Shaw, Clifford (1966) (1930) *The Jack-Roller.* Chicago: University of Chicago Press.

Stebbins, Robert A. (1986) "The Definition of the Situation: A Review." In Furnham, Adrian (ed.), *Social Behavior in Context.* Boston: Allyn and Bacon, pp. 134–154.

Thomas, William I. (1923) *The Unadjusted Girl.* Boston: Little, Brown and Co.

Thomas, William I. and Florian Znaniecki (1918–20) *The Polish Peasant in Europe and America.* Boston: Badger Press.

Webb, Eugene J., Donald T. Campbell, Richard D. Schwartz, and Lee Sechrest (1966) *Unobstrusive Measures: Nonreactive Research in the Social Sciences.* Chicago: Rand McNally & Co.

Chapter 14 ──────────────────────────────────────

Passion, Submission and Motherhood: The Negotiation of Identity by Unmarried Innercity Chicanas*

Ruth Horowitz
University of Delaware

This paper examines the negotiation of young unmarried women's sexual identities in the cultural context of an innercity Chicano community. Previous work often views the unmarried mother status as unproblematic, that is, as deviant or as equal to a married mother. Values are assumed to determine directly the evaluation of the status of unwed mother, and motherhood is viewed as an instrumental action. This analysis of premarital sex and motherhood suggests that motherhood plays an expressive role and that the evaluation of a young woman's sexual identity is not directly determined by her becoming premaritally pregnant and an unwed mother, but her identity is negotiated. In this negotiation process traditional values are blurred and changed. Here nonuse of birth control cannot be explained by lack of information or irrationality but must be understood as part of the process of developing a sexual identity within a particular cultural context. The relationship between behavior and identity is viewed as problematic and the construction and symbolization of this relationship in a public dialogue is the concern of this analysis.

T he relationship between giving birth to an illegitimate child and evaluation received is perceived by many as unproblematic: culture is conceptualized as a fixed hierarchy of values and norms to which people orient their behavior. Values provide affective meaning to social relationships and to

*The research for this paper was supported by an LEAA grant, no. 76-JN-99-0004. I thank Steven Bossert and Gary Schwartz for their valuable insights and criticisms of several drafts of this paper and Margaret Andersen, Sally Bould, Carl Couch, Jane Davidson and Peter Manning for many helpful suggestions on later drafts. Ruth Horowitz's address is: Department of Sociology, University of Delaware, Newark, Delaware 19711.

Source: Ruth Horowitz, "Passion, Submission and Motherhood: The Negotiation of Identity by Unmarried Innercity Chicanas." *Sociological Quarterly* 22 (Spring, 1981): 241-253. Reprinted by permission of JAI Press, Inc., Greenwich, Conn.

role performances and control choices by indicating the relative merit of particular courses of action. Many studies of illegitimacy view becoming an unwed
mother as failing to achieve motherhood in the socially approved manner
(Goode, 1960 and 1961; Vincent, 1961), some as a means that is as good as marriage (Henriques, 1953; Stycos, 1955), and still others as a means almost as good
as marriage (Rodman, 1963). In all those studies, culture is perceived as a static
entity that encompasses social activity.

In this paper the relationship between sexual activities and unwed motherhood on the one hand and evaluations of those actions on the other is viewed as
problematic. Evaluation is viewed as a dialectical relationship between a system
of objectified meanings (Berger and Luckmann, 1967) and the group as a creative
unit both reaffirming and changing culture. Actions are interpreted by referring
to objectified values and in using the meanings embodied to make sense of a
situation. In the process people may extend the meaning of an objectified element. The dialectical interface of the objectified and emerging aspects of culture
occurs in communication. Culture acquires meaning from talk about an event,
and events only become collectively understood to the interactants through this
communication. Agreements and disagreements are forged and actions are experienced as part of the reality of the situation. Some elements are fluid and
unstable; other elements remain relatively stable.

This paper analyzes premarital conception, unwed motherhood, and nonuse
of birth control as part of the process of negotiating a sexual identity in an inner-
city Chicano community. Identities are not directly determined by the individual's actions but emerge and become more stabilized as self and others attempt to make sense out of sets of actions. Three values, virginity, male domination and motherhood, are operative for women within the context of family life
on 32nd Street and in other honor subcultures (Pitt-Rivers, 1966). These values,
which are congruous on the cultural level, can lead to conflicting expectations in
some situations when an attempt is made to follow all simultaneously. Accepted
resolutions to these dilemmas must be negotiated.

The data for this study were collected during three years of field work
among Chicano youth in the 32nd Street community of 44,500 residents with an
average family income of $8,560 in 1970. It ranks among the lowest of all
Chicago communities on an overall socio-economic index. Close to 70 percent of
the residents are of Mexican heritage. I talked with, interviewed and observed
well over one hundred and fifty young women, aged thirteen to twenty, in a
variety of situations and places: in public parks, in their homes, on the streets, at
dances, on shopping trips downtown, in groups, alone, and with and without
males present.

While I am not a Chicana and was slightly older than the young women in
this study, I became very close to many of them. Some asked for my advice,
which I gave infrequently, and introduced me to their families. As an outsider I
was able to move between the different groups and to have many intimate

discussions because I was not in a position to gain from spreading rumors and I presented them with little competition for their men. They attributed my failure to dress nicely, wear make-up and fix my hair as having no desire to "catch a man." These attributes allowed me to move easily between social settings and to be acceptable to the girls and their parents who were impressed with my ability to speak Spanish and thought of me largely as some kind of social worker.

AVAILABLE EXPLANATIONS OF ILLEGITIMATE BIRTHS

"Anomie," "cultural relativism," "value stretch," and lack of birth control information are the principal sociological explanations offered for the high rate of illegitimate childbirth in some societies or subcultures. Each perspective holds a conception of culture which provides a specific hierarchy of values for the evaluation of actions and is static. Each also regards unwed motherhood as an instrumental act, as a means for obtaining or holding on to a man.

Anomie theory predicts high rates of deviant behavior when there are few means to achieve the culturally specified goals of a society (Merton, 1938). Goode (1960, 1961) found high rates of illegitimate births in societies that lacked the culturally prescribed means of obtaining dowries to achieve the culturally prescribed goals of marriage. With the breakdown of old cultural traditions through poverty, mobility and modernization, cultural prescriptions no longer directed behavior. As fathers had little to offer as a dowry, there was little incentive for young men to marry; consequently, women had to negotiate their own marriages. Many had few resources and would intentionally become pregnant in hopes of marrying the father of the child. Anomie theory views illegitimacy as both a deviant, implying an unchanging hierarchy of values, and an *instrumental* form of behavior, a means to obtain a husband. The data from 32nd Street cannot be reconciled with anomie theory. An unwed mother is not necessarily seen as deviant. Her actions are expressive of a woman's sexual identity – not an act calculated to obtain a husband.

In opposition to anomie theories, the cultural relativists claim that the lower classes have a distinct hierarchy of values from the middle classes (Henriques, 1953; Stycos, 1955). Several studies of Caribbean cultures have argued that some classes accept the respectability of unwed motherhood and consensual unions. Unwed motherhood is accepted as an alternative to marriage for young women. On 32nd Street illegitimate childbirth is not *necessarily* perceived as a positive attribute outside of marriage, but may be so perceived depending upon both a young woman's actions surrounding her sexual activities and others' evaluations of these actions.

Rodman's (1963) notion of "value stretch" reconciles these two explanations. There is ample ethnographic evidence, even in the studies of the "cultural relativists," to demonstrate that unwed motherhood is not as highly valued as motherhood within marriage. Rodman views the residents in most lower class communities as holding largely middle class values; however, because of pervasive poverty, attainment of these middle class values is frequently frustrated. A wider range of values and behaviors becomes acceptable to the members of that society resulting in value stretch. In the context where not all men feel that they have the financial resources to marry, the bearing of illegitimate children is considered acceptable. This explanation also views the evaluation of unwed motherhood as a *given* within a particular subculture.

The anomie, cultural relativity, and value stretch explanations of illegitimacy imply that social roles are restraining and provide restricted opportunities so that young women organize their lives according to the opportunities available at the time. Values are seen as orienting and restricting behavior so that any "socialized" person would follow them, given the opportunity. This is an oversocialized view of man (Wrong, 1961). Moreover, illegitimacy is regarded as purely an instrumental act. That is, if a society provided the proper options (husbands) for becoming a mother (or the technology to prevent conception if undesired), there would be little reason for illegitimacy. These explanations are unable to clarify the situation among the young women on 32nd Street who not only have opportunities to marry without engaging in premarital sex (the approved set of actions), but who also know about birth control. Many conversations with young women made it clear that birth control was available to unmarried women and they knew about it. Moreover, the same women who became premaritally pregnant began to use it *after* marriage. To understand this behavior we must first examine the way three cultural symbols, virginity, motherhood and male domination, in the context of the 32nd Street Chicano community, have been objectified.

Virginity
The general feeling expressed by members of the 32nd Street community is that a woman should remain a virgin until marriage. While virginity seems to have less importance to young women in most groups today, it remains a salient value for them. For example, according to Reiss (1967) and Vincent (1961) there are increasing messages in society that "sex is fun" and sexual permissiveness is acceptable.

On 32nd Street, virginity is discussed and used in evaluating a young woman. Virginity is not only linked to a young woman's honor, but also the honor of her family. As Pitt-Rivers (1966: 45) describes the situation in Spain, the defense of honor of the women in a family is the duty of the males: "The honour of a man is involved therefore in the sexual purity of his mother, wife and daughters, and sisters, not in his own."

Virginity is publicly affirmed and emphasized in the traditional *quinceniera* (cotillion), a religious ceremony which celebrates a fifteen year old's birthday, her virginity and her passage to the new status of a woman ready for marriage. These are often large festive occasions. Not all young women have cotillions and speculation about a young woman's "state of virginity" increases at this age whether or not she has one. If she does not, it is sometimes said that she could not, because she was no longer a virgin. If a young woman does have a cotillion, then it is sometimes said that she is trying to prove that she is a virgin.

Today, like in modern Greece (Safililos-Rothschild, 1969), the family is more likely to try to maintain the secrecy of her dishonor or to persuade the couple to get married. For example, when Alicia became pregnant at fifteen she was sent to relatives in Mexico. Returning against the wishes of her parents prior to the birth of her child, she was forced to hide when guests arrived. Her parents took primary responsibility for the child, claiming him as a dependent and speaking of him as "our son."

Male Domination

The male domination of women is valued on 32nd Street. Fathers make decisions, are served within the home by their daughters and wives, punish the children, and decide if the woman may work outside the home. Male youth are also served by women. If the sons come in late, their mothers or sisters prepare their dinner and when clothing needs ironing, the young men demand that one of their sisters do it. Young women learn to expect this from men. While many women submit readily to male wishes, others do so only reluctantly. At a party one young woman asked:

> Please tell me if you see my brother because I can't drink with him around, he'll beat me. . . . You know we go to dances across town. We got to sneak 'cause if he ever found out he would follow us around and we'd never get to go anywhere.

When this young woman's brother later thought she had had enough to drink, he forced her to go home with him. He later returned to the party alone.

Motherhood

Becoming a mother has remained one of the salient dimensions of the development of a young woman's identity on 32nd Street. As a mother a woman receives special esteem and if anyone attempts to demean the importance of motherhood, the speaker is immediately challenged. One seventeen year old who had helped to bring up her six younger siblings told of an argument with her mother: "One time I told her I wasn't going to have any kids. She really got angry and said 'God will punish me. It was up to Him, not me.' She didn't speak to me for a week."

Although respect for both mothers and fathers is strong, youth remain more loyal to their mothers, returning frequently for her help even after they are grown and married. Mothers bring their children into the world and remain with them, while a father is a more distant figure, spending less time with his children as they get older. An example of a son's loyalty is illustrated by a young heroin addict's comment about stealing from his mother.

> I used to steal all the time from my brothers and sisters and went through my old man's coat pockets many times . . . even stole his watch once and pawned it, but you know when I took some "bread" [money] from my old lady then I knew I had to do something. Taking from your old lady's real bad.

Though respect for both parents is generally strong, mothers receive more sup-port, willing respect and loyalty than do fathers.

MAINTAINING AN IDENTITY AS A VIRGIN

Virginity, female subordination to males, and motherhood are important cultural values which are taken into account in the role expectations for women. A woman should remain a virgin until she becomes a loyal and submissive wife, then she should have children. If it is believed that these expectations have been followed, then the young woman will be highly valued by her peers of both sexes and by her family. It is difficult in the context of this community, however, to maintain one's identity as a virgin. Even if a young woman remains a virgin, others are apt to be suspicious. Men demand sexual encounters and, as there are no longer chaperones to keep couples apart, young women frequently submit.

A young woman's identity is continually discussed: her biography is checked with others to make known her actions. Incongruities between her self presentation and others' characterizations of her sexual activities are a common topic of conversation. Even a young woman who rarely goes out must be ex-ceedingly careful in her dealings with men to maintain her identity as a virgin. There are always people who may try to discredit her sexual identity as a virgin.

Some of the girls remain "pure" or are able to maintain the image of being pure by rarely being seen in public. Sonya, for example, is afraid of males and feels she does not know what to say to them or how to act if they speak to her first. During her senior year in high school she approached me almost in tears and asked what she should do when a male (a friend of her brother's) smiled at her. She had looked away quickly and run home. Sonya felt incapable of handling such situations and avoided any situation when she might have to interact with a male. Rarely seen in public, no one questioned her identity as a virgin.

In contrast, others go out, yet they are able to maintain their identities as virgins. Rita, at seventeen, was still closely watched and permitted very few dates, which made it relatively easy to maintain her identity as a virgin, although she "went out with" young men. She had a number of opportunities to become involved in a "loving" relationship and to engage in sexual relations, yet she kept her distance. At dances she danced, rather than slipping out to "neck." Two of her pregnant ninth grade friends claimed that Rita was different from them. "She doesn't seem to let dudes push her around at all and laughs them off. But all the dudes kept following her around. She ain't like us." It was not inferred from her activities that she had engaged in any intimate sexual activity. These girls who are perceived as virgins are said to make the best wives. Though this may be the ideal status, it is reality for only a minority.

CONFLICT: CHASTITY AND SUBMISSION

Managing the appearance of virginity becomes markedly more difficult once a young woman falls in love or is seen by others as doing so. Not only does she experience the tensions between remaining a virgin and submitting to the sexual demands of her boyfriend, but others view submission to the demands of men as the inevitable result of falling in love. The meaning of her actions is interpreted within that framework.

The process of becoming involved to the point of falling in love occurs in socially defined stages. At each stage there is greater risk of others viewing her as having engaged in sexual intercourse. The first step used in building a relationship is usually informal and is concerned with letting the other party know that there is some interest in starting a relationship. If they both agree then they meet informally in public. It must always seem as though the young man makes the first move, otherwise she will be regarded as attempting to dominate him. As they have no real link yet, she need not obey his wishes.

The second or "seeing" stage is usually reached when both agree to meet in the usual "hangout" but there are few obligations at this stage. Any girl can "see" more than one boy at the same time; however, "seeing" several increases the risk that others might question her virginity. Elena, a welldressed and attractive fifteen year old, explained:

> If you're seeing someone, you can't blame him if he has some hickies (or love bites) 'cause he can see anyone else he likes but it really hurts if you start to really dig him. You can have hickies too, but some dudes get real mad. They think they own you when you are seeing them. Sometimes a dude will ask you right away to go out with him. That's your downfall. Both of you are tied then – no more hickies except from him. If a dude comes with hickies, you got to let him know you know he is not supposed to be seeing other chicks.

The third stage, going out, is accepted by young women when they begin to fall in love. They perceive the nature of their relationship while going out as

their own potential "downfall." One afternoon I was walking with six girls when
a boyfriend of one approached the group. He stood in front of his girlfriend and
twisted her arm demanding to know where she was going. She replied that we
were going to listen to records. He pulled her around and told her that she was
going with him. She did not resist and none of the other young women paid any
attention. I asked her sister why she, herself, did not put up with that kind of
behavior. She replied that she was not in love with her boyfriend, and,
therefore, did not have to do everything he wanted. Another girl then stated
that it was "just a fact of life" and the rest agreed. Over the next eight months,
the older sister's behavior began to match that of her sister. She began to agree
to almost everything her boyfriend asked, which was frequently against what
she claimed was correct. Several times she had wanted to obey her parents'
curfew, but she stayed out late in accordance with her boyfriend's wishes. At
times the "chaste" identities of both sisters were questioned; however, no one
had specific evidence of their lack of chastity until each became pregnant.

Young men gain status among their peers from engaging in sexual encounters and place increasing pressure on their girlfriends to give in to their sexual demands. Here the young woman is faced with a dilemma whether to maintain her virginity or to give in to her boyfriend's demands. The dilemma is acute:
either choice will satisfy one value, but negate the other. Should the young
woman elect to submit, releasing her passion, she heightens the risk of
discrediting her identity as a virgin. Even if she does not become pregnant as a
result of her "passion" she still risks others' perceiving that she has had intercourse but prevented pregnancy through use of birth control.

MANAGING A SOCIAL IDENTITY AS A NON-VIRGIN

Though some women marry before they lose their virginity, many young
women do engage in premarital sex, the majority without the use of birth control. It is not only the act of premarital intercourse upon which their sexual identities are evaluated but the manner in which a woman handles a non-virgin identity. There are two factors which are frequently salient in negotiating her sexual
identity: the type of account (Scott and Lyman, 1968: 46) used to explain her
loss of virginity, and her public behavior relative to men and motherhood.
Should she successfully meet the criteria set by her peers in these two areas, her
sexuality remains "bounded" (restricted) even if she engages in premarital sex or
becomes pregnant. If she fails to meet the criteria developed by her peers, her
sexuality is viewed as "unbounded" and she is perceived of as a "loose woman."

Bounding Sexuality
"A Moment of Passion" and Subtle Pursuit of Men
The estimation of a young woman's intention to engage in premarital sex
forms the basis for evaluating sexual attributes. Demonstrating one's lack of in-

tention to engage in premarital sex can bound one's sexuality in the eyes of peers. To demonstrate to peers her lack of intention, she must account for her actions in terms of "being in love" and giving in to the sexual demands of her boyfriend in a "moment of passion." She is seen as having no control over her passion and can account for giving in to his advances in terms of the spontaneity of the situation and the need to submit. This account allows others to perceive the meanings of the acts in terms of her continued respect for virginity. Her action remains largely consistent with the values of virginity and male domination and thus her sexuality remains bounded in the eyes of her peers.

To avoid taking public action that might discredit their respect for virginity, women frequently develop complicated maneuvers designed to permit them not to seem "too forward." Women often refuse to call a man, because it might be interpreted as pursuing him. Several techniques are employed for communicating with men without seeming forward: gathering a group of female friends to pass "just by chance" by the place where favored young men spend time; finding a friend of the boyfriend and casually mentioning to the friend what they want the boyfriend to hear; and trying to appear sexy without being explicit, that is, wearing well-fitting but never tight pants and low-cut blouses which reveal little. Much careful work goes into trying to "give off" the appearance of bounded sexuality.

It is not the public knowledge of a young woman's premarital sexual activities that determines the boundedness of a woman's sexual identity, but the perceived meaning of her public activity. Ramona had been "going out" with Enrique for more than two years when she became pregnant. There was no public expression of her sexuality as she refrained from seeing him much in public without others around and was not seen talking with other men. Ramona, to his knowledge and his friends', neither chased him openly nor saw anyone else during their relationship. They were in love and, therefore, she had acted according to Enrique's wishes when she succumbed to his advances. Enrique perceived her actions as being faithful to him unlike some of his previous girlfriends. Her sexuality was perceived by others as remaining bounded even when she became pregnant. Enrique married her as soon as she told him of her pregnancy.

Unbounding Sexuality:
The Public Expression of Passion

Some of the young women do not interact with young men in a manner which might establish the bounded nature of their sexuality. This discredits their identities as sexually bounded young women. They begin to be perceived as "loose women" and to obtain identities as women who openly display their passion. For example, Alicia frequently acted in what seemed to be a bashful manner with men; at other times she appeared flirtatious. She claimed that she was not going to get involved again, and she wishes Gilberto (the father of her son) would keep his hands off her and leave her alone. Sometimes, when they

were both in the park, Gilberto would grab and strike her. When he had finished, she would walk away. Her interactions with him at a party, however,
would be perceived as flirtations and she was described as a "flirtatious bitch"
who caused most of her own problems. Some saw her throwing herself on men
and trying to "capture" (their word) a man. They expressed disgust at her "two
faces" while others viewed her as pathetic. A gang member remarked, "She's
OK, she helps us carry the 'heats' (guns), sneaks them into dances, and she'll
take them off you if the cops are coming. Remember the times she hid that .45 in
her kid's carriage with him asleep?"

Another man fathered her second child. She had tried very hard to develop
a good relationship with him; however, she complained publicly if she could not
find him and followed him around. To maintain some semblance of bounded sexuality, publicly she should have obeyed his wishes and not acted as though she
were attempting to control his actions. He began to ignore her; yet, she continued to come to the park, talk about him and ask for him. Already two months
pregnant with his child, she broke up with him. She could have continued the
relationship and perhaps received a marriage proposal only by *not* pursuing him.
For sexuality to remain bounded, the man must be perceived as being in control
of the relationship. When she was twenty-five she married a seventeen year old
and it was said that he married her because he was naive. He was too young to
understand or have knowledge of the unbounded nature of her sexuality. Men
evaluate a woman's worth as a wife in terms of the boundedness of her sexuality
and open pursuit, public flirtation, or engaging in sex "too soon" are illustrative
of unbounded sexuality. By overtly and aggressively attempting to lead a man into marriage, the meaning of a woman's sexual activity is altered and her worth is
minimized. Only by exceedingly veiled and subtle pursuit of a man is it possible
for sexuality to be seen as bounded from the perspective of all audiences.

UNBOUNDED SEXUALITY: THE DENIAL OF
MOTHERHOOD BY THE USE OF BIRTH CONTROL

Use of birth control by a single woman is an explicit indication of intention
to engage in sexual intercourse; it therefore precludes her from explaining such
action in terms of a "moment of passion." It is an open expression of uncontrolled
passion which allows a woman to engage in sex with whom and when she
pleases. It is viewed as the archetypical instance of unbounded sexuality. Moreover, she is explicitly negating the importance of motherhood.

There are young women on 32nd Street who choose this path. They accept
"the responsibility for the action in question, but den[y] the pejorative quality
associated with it" (Scott and Lyman, 1968: 47). These young women declare
that sex is fun and there is nothing wrong with enjoying themselves and
avoiding pregnancy. These young women experience the consequences of this

stance when thinking about marrying and settling down. Several young women expressed a desire to enjoy themselves and did not worry excessively about the predominant community morals. They were not completely immune to gossip about their reputations, however, and were upset to find that one of the gangs with whom they had spent time had spread rumors about them throughout the community. They went to another community for their social life where their actual social identities were unknown but there are few such opportunities to meet young men outside the community. They know they would not be viewed in the 32nd Street community as "good" wives. Sally said:

> Most of the dudes around here don't appreciate us too much. They think they're too good for us but there are some fine dudes in this world that haven't met us yet. When some of the dudes find that their little "virgin" ol' ladies are screwing around, they'll want someone like us 'cause they'll know what they're getting.

Although willing to risk being seen as undesirable marriage partners, these women are not fully convinced that the benefits outweigh the risks.

The public evaluation of unbounded sexuality allows unmarried women few options for marriage within the community. Unlike the women who are perceived as attempting to bound their sexuality, these women are viewed as having made no such attempt. Consequently, they are seen as impure.

MOTHERHOOD: THE POTENTIAL FOR THE TRANSFORMATION OF IDENTITY

For many of the young women on 32nd Street, unwed motherhood becomes an important aspect of their identity. Motherhood allows a young woman an additional opportunity to negotiate an identity of bounded sexuality. Within this cultural context, unwed motherhood is not a completely socially approved route to motherhood as a young woman is expected to remain a virgin prior to marriage. Yet, motherhood even as a result of premarital sex is a valid and esteemed role. In other words, in a culture where virginity, submission to men and motherhood are all held to be important values, achieving the revered role of motherhood resolves both symbolically and existentially the dilemma between passion (unbounded sexuality) and virginity (bounded sexuality).

By not pursuing men and by accounting for her lack of virginity in a culturally approved manner, a young woman may begin to transform her identity from potentially that of a "loose woman" to that of a "good mother." The transformation of identity is more than new attributes being added to the former identity; others see the individual as a different person (Garfinkel, 1956:421). Old interpretations of activities and motives are replaced by new ones.

In order to transform completely her identity in the eyes of community members to that of a woman whose sexuality is bounded, she must be perceived as concentrating her activities around the role of mother, as not openly pursuing men, and as explaining her non-virginity in terms of "being in love" and "a moment of passion." By attempting to negotiate her identity in this manner, her sexuality may be seen as bounded: limited to and by the role of mother. Her past actions are reinterpreted in light of her new status as mother. It must be made publicly clear, however, that motherhood is central to her life.

The reevaluation of an unwed mother's sexual identity is more than an individual's rationalization of a deviant act. It is a social reinterpretation and agreed to by others and there is a collective reinterpretation of her sexual nature. The act of becoming a mother does not in and of itself effect the resolution of a woman's identity. If others view the mother as attempting to explain her loss of virginity as a result of her lack of sexual knowledge (no one would believe her), as failing to take an active role in "mothering" and as continuing an active sex life, then her sexuality will not be bounded by motherhood.

Laura, for example, became pregnant at seventeen, but did not marry the father of her child. She stopped going to the park when her pregnancy became obvious. After the birth of her baby she would take the baby to the park for an hour after work and talk to her female friends. She rarely went to public dances and never flirted with males publicly. Whenever anyone would mention her name, they would refer to her as a "good mother." Ivy, on the other hand, played a dangerous game. Several of the young men began to claim that she was flirting too much in public. They agreed with one who said, "She's already got one kid now and she'll probably have another if she doesn't get married soon or stay inside. She's been fooling around a lot and people are beginning to talk." Although she did bring her child with her when she came to the park, she flirted while there. She was viewed as a borderline case. Several of the Lions thought that it was a "good move" on the part of her new boyfriend (not the father of her child) to forbid her from going to the park once they started "going out." He married her a year later and she stopped going to the park altogether. Her sexuality remained bounded.

When others view a young married mother as not demonstrating responsibility and devotion toward the child, her salient identity characteristic as a mother is disallowed. Elena failed to demonstrate the necessary responsibility of motherhood to others. When she brought her daughter to the park she would leave her baby with others and would sniff glue with her friends. The Lions gang, who liked having company, claimed behind her back that she was not a responsible mother and might hurt her daughter by her foolhardy behavior. Failure to be seen as a good mother gives a woman an image of unbounded sexuality, which makes it difficult to find a husband. Only marriage could successfully bound sexuality in such circumstances, because such women are not perceived as "good mothers" but few men in this community want wives whose sexuality is evaluated as unbounded.

DISCUSSION

The transformation of an unwed mother's sexual identity from potentially that of a disapproved woman with unbounded expression of passion to that of an approved identity as a "mother" whose sexuality is regarded as bounded is negotiated by the young woman and her audience. Motherhood, wed or unwed, is viewed as an expressive symbol, as conveying evidence of the kind of person she is, not as an instrumental act and is perceived as resolving the dilemma both symbolically and existentially between virginity and passion. Though this may not be the "correct" route to motherhood according to the traditional value orientations, it is a socially accepted cultural resolution as it is collectively agreed upon as bounding all other aspects of her sexuality.

While motherhood can resolve the dilemma between passion and virginity, it does not necessarily. Paradigms which regard culture as static with values specifying why one prefers one thing to another and endowing the actors' orientations to social objects with cultural significance view unmarried motherhood as either a positive or negative attribute rather than a negotiated identity. The sexual identity attributed to her depends upon how she manages to play on the ambiguities of the situation and what others think of her. The relationship between sexual identity and activity is "fuzzy" and is dependent upon the interaction between others' evaluations and her public behavior concerning the "goodness" of her mothering, her continuing relationship to men and her explanations of her pregnancy. Her sexual identity is constructed in a public dialogue that includes the activity of the target person.

In the analysis of the social process of how and in what terms young women attempt to negotiate their sexual identities as they move through the stages of a relationship with a young man, it becomes clear that the meaning and evaluation of a young woman's unwed motherhood is based on more than the status of motherhood itself. The issue of "boundedness" of sexuality occurs because of the cultural emphasis on virginity and the conception of women in Mediterranean style cultures; and the impact of the new cultural and social setting is to blur and change old values. As a result "boundedness" remains a public standard to be used to label offenders, to maintain a public dialogue and to rationalize marriage. In contrast, lack of chaperonage and submission to men are conducive to "getting pregnant" or at least taking that risk. These young women neither "give in" nor "hold out." They do both and neither. With this notion of boundedness it becomes clear why birth control used prior to marriage is viewed negatively as its use indicates both a complete disregard for virginity and the devaluation of motherhood. Passion rules and sexuality is unbounded. In identity negotiations, cultural traditions are reevaluated and transformed. New values arise out of what we say when we are choosing between courses of action; it is not static and regulative. Motherhood and male dominance become more salient than virginity in determining the boundedness of a woman's sexuality after she loses her virginity.

264 PASSION, SUBMISSION AND MOTHERHOOD

In this paper I have shown that motherhood, male domination and virginity all acquire meaning from interaction, from the symbols' capacity to transform what is said about an action, event or person to what is understood collectively. Identity formation is not a passive process, a response to a hierarchy of values. Not only do values give meaning to social relationships but also individuals are active participants in the negotiating of their identity; and in doing so, they reshape the traditional culture giving new meaning to old sexual identities. In conclusion, this analysis of identity and unwed motherhood has attempted to demonstrate the dialectical relationship between objectified systems of meaning and the actors as creative agents in the persistence and change of cultural traditions.

REFERENCES

Berger, Peter and Thomas Luckmann. (1967). The Social Construction of Reality. New York: Anchor Books.

Garfinkel, Harold (1956) "Conditions of successful degradation ceremonies." American Journal of Sociology 61:420–24.

Goode, William (1960) "A deviant case: Illegitimacy in the Caribbean." American Sociological Review 25:21–30.

———(1961) "Illegitimacy, anomie and cultural penetration." American Sociological Review 26:910–25.

Henriques, Fernando (1953) Family and Colour in Jamaica. London: Eyre Spottiswoode.

Merton, Robert K. (1938) "Social structure and anomie." American Sociological Review 3:672–82.

Pitt-Rivers, Julian (1966) "Honour and social status." Pp. 19–78 in J. G. Peristiany (ed.), Honor and Shame. Chicago: University of Chicago Press.

Reiss, Ira (1967) The Social Context of Premarital Sexual Permissiveness. New York: Holt, Rinehart and Winston.

Rodman, Hyman (1963) "Lower class value stretch." Social Forces 42:205–15.

Safilios-Rothschild, Constantina (1969) "'Honour' crimes in contemporary Greece." British Journal of Sociology 20:205–18.

Scott, Marvin B. and Stanford M. Lyman (1968) "Accounts." American Sociological Review 33:46–62.

Stycos, J. Mayonne (1955) Family and Fertility in Puerto Rico. New York: Columbia University Press.

Vincent, Clark (1961) Unmarried Mothers. New York: Free Press.

Wrong, Dennis (1961) "The oversocialized conception of man in modern sociology." American Sociological Review 26:183–93.

Chapter 15 ——————————————————————————————

Like Other Women: Perspectives of Mothers with Physical Disabilities

Susan Shaul
Pamela J. Dowling
Bernice F. Laden

This article is based on interviews with 10 mothers, ranging in age from 19 to 45 and living in the Puget Sound area of Washington State. These women have neuromuscular or musculoskeletal disabilities, and their children range in age from 11 months to adulthood. The article focuses on specific issues and concerns regarding early childhood management, and includes some discussion of prenatal and obstetrical care. Common misconceptions concerning motherhood and disability are also discussed. Men with disabilities also have special concerns as parents. Although their concerns are not addressed in this article, they are not seen as any less important or less deserving of attention.

INTRODUCTION

U ntil recently there has been a cultural bias that women with disabilities cannot and should not bear and raise children. Consequently, family planning services, obstetrical care, and early childhood guidance have often neglected the needs of women with disabilities. Mainstreaming, implementation of Section 503 and 504 of the National Rehabilitation Act of 1973, and other new state and federal legislation have begun to have an impact on service delivery to the disabled population, providing greater opportunities and increasingly complex choices. While many disabled women choose to pursue careers, others want to direct their energies toward raising children, or combining career and family. However, society's attitude toward women with disabilities has been slow to change.

Source: Susan Shaul, Pamela J. Dowling, and Bernice F. Laden, "Like Other Women: Perspectives of Mothers with Physical Disabilities," in *Women and Disability*, Mary Jo Deegan and Nancy Brooks, pp. 133–142. Reprinted by permission of Transaction Press, New Brunswick, N.J.

This resistance has been reflected in the lack of literature available to parents with disabilities. May (1974) discusses minor architectural adaptations and recreational activities which mothers with physical disabilities might accomplish. Otherwise, American society, as reflected in the literature, has denied the existence of any special needs. This denial reflects the larger attitudinal barriers faced by people with disabilities.

The stigma of being disabled is difficult to erase. A disabled woman's capacity to be a partner in an intimate, sexual relationship and her physical ability to conceive and bear a child may be doubted by even her own family. Bogle and Shaul (1979) point out, "Many congenitally disabled women report that their parents programmed them to be 'super career' women in the belief that they would never be considered marriage material" (p. 39).

Societal resistance to viewing women with disabilities as potential parents comes from several different pervasive cultural myths:

Physically disabled women are extraordinarily dependent on other people. Many nondisabled people mistakenly assume that individuals with disabilities are unable to do basic maintenance for themselves, let alone a child. In reality, most physically disabled people lead independent, productive lives.

Physical disability is somehow contagious or inherited. This is a remnant of the belief that people with disabilities are sick or unhealthy. Only a small percentage of disabilities are genetically based.

Physically disabled people are asexual. Many nondisabled people often view sex as an acrobatic activity. This causes difficulty in understanding that physically disabled people are capable of enjoying warm, intimate relationships and being sexually active.

Being disabled is such a depressing and dreary existence that a disabled individual should not bring a child into that world. Few disabled people spend time dwelling on their disability. They are involved in working, homemaking, and the same activities that the general population enjoys.

Physical mobility is essential to child-rearing. Because disabled women have not been portrayed as mothers, it is difficult for the general population to understand how a child can be raised by a woman with mobility restrictions.

This study was therefore undertaken as a pilot project to investigate the needs of mothers with disabilities. Ten women in the Seattle area agreed to be interviewed. They were contacted through a previous research project (Shaul et al., 1978) and informal networking in the community. The women had chosen to become parents after they were disabled. Their disabilities included spinal cord injury, multiple sclerosis, post-polio and spina bifida. At the time of the interviews, their children ranged in age from 11 months to mid-30's. While clearly not representative of all women with disabilities who choose to become pregnant, these women were able to indicate potential areas of concern and needs from service providers.

PRE-PREGNANCY

When deciding whether they want to become pregnant, most women with disabilities want to speak with a woman who has a similar disability. Many able-bodied women have relied on their mothers or friends to share what pregnancy and child-rearing are like, but disabled women often need more information and advice that is related to their specific disability.

> I really wanted to talk to another disabled woman who had gone through a pregnancy to find out what sort of things to anticipate during my pregnancy and after the baby was born. . . . I couldn't find anyone. . . . I think that networking among disabled women is just now beginning to grow. (paraplegic)

There are legitimate concerns as to how the physical stress of pregnancy may affect a disabled woman. For example, mobility, respiration, or elimination, perhaps not working at "normal" levels, will have the extra burden of the developing fetus.

At this point, many of these questions can be answered only by conjecture, as pregnant women with specific disabilities have not been studied. Health care professionals are not able to provide women with consistent answers. A woman with spina bifida told us:

> I talked to my doctor about becoming pregnant and he said absolutely not; so I talked to an obstetrician and he said I should have no problem. Confused, I talked to a third doctor and he told me I should get another opinion.

With expanded research, there will be increased professional awareness in the future, avoiding scenes that are still too common:

> The nurse looked at me, amazed. She said, laughing, "I guess I was just surprised you were really here for a pregnancy test." (quadriplegic)

Given the wide variety of attitudes found among health care providers, and inadequate information on pregnancy and disability, what are the experiences of mothers with disabilities really like?

PREGNANCY, LABOR, AND DELIVERY

It is common for health providers to expect that pregnancy, being a somewhat disabling condition for many nondisabled women, will cause tremendous inconvenience for disabled women. Many of the women in our study had very few problems with mobility and self-care. One post-polio woman in our study, who is paraplegic and uses a wheelchair, worked until two weeks before her delivery; a woman with spina bifida stayed ambulatory (using crutches) until the delivery. Another woman (post-polio) who uses a wheelchair told us:

> As I got bigger and bigger, it became harder to get up on my knees to get my pants on . . . so I just started wearing long dresses and no underwear.

Experiences with labor and delivery were similar to those of nondisabled women. One of the 10 had a premature infant, two had deliveries by Caesarean section, and the others had relatively uncomplicated vaginal deliveries. The three complications mentioned related specifically to the pregnancy, and not to the women's disabilities.

The women interviewed found the support systems available to nondisabled expectant and newly delivered women valuable. For example, one woman with spina bifida benefited enormously from Lamaze classes. The woman who had a premature baby participated in a neonatal intensive care unit parents' support group.

EARLY YEARS

One of the most difficult periods for child management is the first few years of the child's life. During this time, physically caring for the baby or young child usually requires some environmental modifications. The mothers found few resources that were commercially available. One woman said that pre- and postnatally she had a physical therapist, social worker, and interested nursing student all looking for different mechanical aids to ease child care. They came back empty-handed.

Over time, each woman found various devices to ease transporting her child. For one woman with spina bifida it was an "Umbroller", a lightweight stroller that is easily collapsible and portable.

> The Umbroller was helpful because the baby doesn't have to be able to sit up. I'd walk a step, take my hand away from the crutch, push the stroller down the hall a few feet, walk a few more steps, and push it a little further.

Another woman's father came up with some physical modifications:

> My dad built a tray that snapped onto the arms of my wheelchair. The baby could be inside the tray and my arms would be free to push my chair. I also used a portable bassinet with wheels that allowed me to push the baby from room to room. For a changing table, we took the short legs off an old coffee table and replaced them with long legs that raised the baby to just the right height. (paraplegic)

Going out alone is somewhat difficult for many new mothers, but it is aggravated by the encumbrance of disability. For a woman who uses a wheelchair, an infant can mark a temporary end to being able to travel around independently. It is difficult to push a wheelchair around shopping centers while holding onto an active child in your lap.

Getting a baby in and out of a car can be another major obstacle to going out.

> The biggest restriction I found during that time was the difficulty in taking him somewhere by myself. I have been driving since I was 16 and it was the first time my driving . . . independence had been restricted. I enter the car on the passenger side and slide over to the driver's seat. It was difficult to manage baby, car seat, and wheel chair. So until he learned to walk, I usually had a family member or friend accompany us on our outings. (paraplegic)

It is likely, too, that daily child management requires more energy from disabled women, which can lead to exhaustion. This period seemed to end for the women when relieved of a share of the responsibility. For one family in our study, the pediatrician recommended a "24-hour break for Mom, once a week," when the child would go to his grandparents. In other families, it was pre-school that enabled the mother to think about her own goals again, contact friends, and rebuild intimacy with her husband. All of the husbands had provided significant help with household chores, as well as child management. Several worked evenings, giving a handy break to the mothers during the day by helping out with dinner, dishes, calming temper tantrums, and organizing playtime activities.

DISCIPLINE

In the area of discipline, the families had adapted to the "givens" in the situation and had found ingenious solutions. Primary for everyone was the understanding that verbal commands are law. This was not always easy to do, but families had various ways of enforcing verbal authority.

> I depend a lot on voice control. She has to come to my commands. I can't pick her up every time she falls because maybe the chair isn't positioned right. Once she fell off her trike on the ramp and there was no way I could come out and get her untangled. She realized that and got herself untangled. She's just more aware of voice control. She has to be able to understand. (woman with multiple sclerosis)

One woman said that the best advice she had received was from her pediatrician, who recommended that she only make demands that she could enforce and be much more selective about what she was demanding of the child.

Developing authority behind verbal commands is often difficult for the parent with a disability because of the intermittent reinforcement of limit-testing with the nondisabled parent or other nondisabled people. For instance, one mother had very few discipline problems until her daughter went to a preschool where the teachers were very physical in restraining the children and often did things for the little girl she was capable of doing herself. Similarly, relatives or other interested people would pick her up when she was misbehaving. Then she came home and started testing already determined limits.

> I'd say to my friends, "I have to rely on voice commands and when you walk over and do something for her or pick her up, you're really putting a crunch on me, because then she expects me to do it." (quadriplegic)

The choice is made very early whether to keep the child confined within reach (which none of the parents had chosen) or give the child reasonable freedom while trusting in their survival skills. The children's adaptive capabilities are dramatic: they learn to climb on Mom's lap when hurt, reach up to be lifted out of a crib, or hold onto a wheelchair when crossing the street as if it were Mom's hand.

> I emphasized early how important it was to listen to what I said because there would be times I might not be able to get to him to help him out of a jam. He seemed to understand that. He is very good at listening to me about not going into the street, straying away in stores, or going someplace I may not be able to get to. But when it comes time for dinner, bedtime, or bath, he is like any other child and heads in the opposite direction! (paraplegic)

Some problems were eased by environmental revisions. Homes with disabled adults often have fewer pieces of furniture, as they restrict mobility. This cuts down on the number of obstacles for a toddler. Traditional environment revisions included safety plugs in sockets, glassware put away, dead-bolt locks (so the child could not get in and out to the street independently), fenced-in yards, and other toddler proofing mechanisms.

As mentioned earlier, child-rearing is far from a fait accompli for the able-bodied population. All mothers have questions regarding appropriate discipline techniques.

> You have to remind yourself that your disability really has nothing to do with whatever the problem is at hand . . . you know, it's a parent-child thing, not a disabled parent-child thing. (woman with multiple sclerosis)

Unfortunately, women with disabilities are placed in a double-bind. On the one hand they are told "you couldn't possibly raise children and discipline them well," and on the other, when everything turns out all right, they hear, "Well, dear, your child *had* to be good."

Boy, does that make me mad! It's baloney! Kids aren't good because they have to be. They're good because of the effort and love you put into them . . . if you're lucky. (quadriplegic)

ADVANTAGES AND DISADVANTAGES

At one point during the interview, we asked each woman, "Can you think of any advantages to being a disabled parent?" Most stressed that their children had an increased sense of independence because the child knew that some things wouldn't be done for him/her. Mothers mentioned that their children were getting dressed by themselves earlier, learning about keys and locks, getting food for themselves, and genuinely being helpful before their peers in nondisabled households. Most were concerned that this not be too oppressive:

I don't like kids to have to help their parents because of their disability. I don't want him waiting on me. I don't need that. I don't want him to think he has to do that for me. (woman with spina bifida)

Disability was often the stimulus to encourage independence in children for philosophical, as well as practical, reasons:

We were always very strict with the kids. We thought, "What if something happened to my husband or maybe we'd both die!" The polio brought it closer to you that you might die, so we tried to get the kids to be very responsible for themselves, and I think they were quite adult for their ages. (paraplegic)

Another advantage that the women cited was their children's increased sensitivity to other stigmatized individuals. Sometimes this took the form of defending or befriending "picked-on" children who were classmates, or not caring if someone "looked a little different." Most of the mothers had had the experience of being "defended" by their child to the world at large:

One time we were in a cafteria-type place and this woman kept staring and staring at me. Finally, my daughter (aged 20) needed to walk by this stranger and my daughter said, "You know, it's not nice to stare!" When she told me, I said, "You didn't!", and she said, "I sure did!" and we laughed and laughed. (quadriplegic)

The women were also able to cite some disadvantages to being disabled and a parent. The most significant disadvantage seemed to be that various family activities were difficult or impossible to participate in. One mother talked about not being able to attend a school play one of her children was in because the school was not accessible and she couldn't find any help that day. For a quadriplegic woman, there was the sadness of not being able to teach her daughter how to use scissors or a hammer. One of the paraplegic women said,

"How can I teach him how to play hopscotch or swim?" Most of the mothers acknowledged other people are available to help with these activities (father, grandparents, friends, aunts or uncles), but that they nonetheless feel a sense of loss.

Extended absences from their children because of medical needs were also disadvantages. This varies with the nature of the disability, being more of a concern with progressive disabilities.

> My daughter is constantly afraid I'm going to leave her and go back to the hospital for some complication or another of the multiple sclerosis. (woman with multiple sclerosis)

For those women injured after their children are already born, there is often a long readjustment period when they re-enter the home – a readjustment to Mom being back and then another to her being "different".

As children of mothers with disabilities come into contact with their peers, there may be an initial tension with the other children from having a mother who is different. One woman related an incident where her first-grader came home in tears. When he was able to tell her what had happened, he told her that he didn't want her to come to school anymore because all the kids made fun of the way she walked and he was the only kid with a Mom who was "different". After comforting him, she spoke to his teacher and made arrangements to come to school and do a little "inservice" with the kids, allowing them to ask questions and get to know her as Joey's Mom, instead of only as the "woman who walks funny."

RECOMMENDATIONS

Through this survey of women, many unmet needs became obvious. The following recommendations are based on concerns expressed by women with disabilities.

Pre-pregnancy counseling. Compiling experiences of mothers who are disabled and making the information available would be beneficial to women with disabilities contemplating motherhood. Peer groups or individual peer counselors could be made available for disabled women.

Human service professionals need additional training in the area of disability and pregnancy so they will be better equipped to answer questions posed by disabled women. Institutions of higher education and health care education programs could incorporate a module on sexuality, pregnancy and disability. Perhaps having a disabled mother visit classes to share experiences would be helpful to potential health care providers.

Prenatal/obstetrical care. More training and information on pregnancy and disability needs to be available in medical school curriculum so there will be more physicians available to give obstetrical care to women with disabilities in a comfortable and knowledgeable manner. Lamaze and other childbirth preparation classes should be held in accessible meeting places and be made available to disabled women.

Child management. Resource listings of adaptive devices or suggestions which would make child management easier should be developed and updated in a central clearinghouse. A support group of disabled mothers would foster sharing resources.

Research. Too much in the areas of female sexuality, reproduction, and parenting, at this point, is conjecture. Further research on medical implications of pregnancy and social implications of disabled parents is needed.

The technology of rehabilitation needs to catch up with the technology of obstetrics. There must be ways to make child care easier for disabled parents. As one woman said, "They invented the wheelchair. Surely they can invent an attachment to transport a child." Such "convenience" devices would have a tremendous positive impact for parents with disabilities.

SUMMARY

The traditional role of women as mothers is one of sole caretaker and nurturer of her children (i.e., feeding, dressing, chauffeuring, nursing, and disciplining). Although this image is in the process of changing, it is still one which society uses as its reference point. Since disabled persons are often seen as "sick," and in need of being taken care of, it is difficult for society to understand how a mother with a disability can fit the active nurturer/caretaker role. The majority of people have a hard time imagining how people with disabilities function and take care of themselves, let alone their children. As more and more disabled people enter the mainstream of life through employment, recreation, education and media representation, the myths surrounding disability will begin to lessen.

The strengths and capabilities of the women we spoke with were striking. They, like able-bodied parents, felt that children dramatically change one's life and that frustrations can result. They more often experienced limitations as to how much they could participate in their children's activities. But, like most parents, they said they were glad children were part of their lives.

As society's expectations for mothers change, women in general are finding more parenting and support system options available to them (i.e., shared responsibility for child-rearing with partner or extended family, daycare centers, single parenting). Not only does the disabled mother benefit from these options, but she has a wealth of information and expertise to add to the spectrum of parenting. Although there are unique concerns that merit special attention for mothers with disabilities, once these concerns are successfully addressed, more women with disabilities will be able to enjoy the option of motherhood. As one woman reflected:

> You don't need a body that is physically "perfect" to be a good mother . . . environments need to be modified and support systems worked out, but the most important qualification for parenting has nothing to do with physical perfection. It has to do with love, warmth, and a willingness to share that with a child. It has to do with being human and that is something we all share.

NOTE

Work on this article was made possible under Grant #10H530081032 from the Department of Health and Human Services, Bureau of Community Health Services, Family Planning Program, 1980.

REFERENCES

Bogle, J. and S. Shaul (1979) "Still a Woman, Still a Man." *Journal of Current Social Issues* (Spring): 39–41.

Goffman, E. (1963) *Stigma: Notes on the Management of Spoiled Identity.* Englewood Cliffs, N.J.: Prentice-Hall.

May, E. E., Neva R. Waggoner, and Eleanor Boettke (1974) *Independent Living for the Handicapped and the Elderly.* Boston: Houghton Mifflin Company.

Shaul, S., J. Bogle, A. Norman, and J. Hale-Harbaugh (1978) *Toward Intimacy: Family Planning and Sexuality Concerns of Physically Disabled Women.* New York: Human Sciences Press.

Section VII

The Marketplace and Social Class: The Social Claim

Some Effects of Proportions on Group Life: Skewed Sex Ratios and Responses to Token Women[1]

Rosabeth Moss Kanter

Proportions, that is, *relative* numbers of socially and culturally different people in a group, are seen as critical in shaping interaction dynamics, and four group types are identified on the basis of varying proportional compositions. "Skewed" groups contain a large preponderance of one type (the numerical "dominants") over another (the rare "tokens"). A framework is developed for conceptualizing the processes that occur between dominants and tokens. Three perceptual phenomena are associated with tokens: visibility (tokens capture a disproportionate awareness share), polarization (differences between tokens and dominants are exaggerated), and assimilation (tokens' attributes are distorted to fit preexisting generalizations about their social type). Visibility generates performance pressures; polarization leads dominants to heighten their group boundaries; and assimilation leads to the tokens' role entrapment. Illustrations are drawn from a field study in a large industrial corporation. Concepts are extended to tokens of all kinds, and research issues are identified.

I n his classic analysis of the significance of numbers in social life, Georg Simmel (1950) argued persuasively that numerical modifications effect qualitative transformations in group interaction. Simmel dealt almost exclusively with the impact of absolute numbers, however, with group size as determinant of form and process. The matter of relative numbers, of proportion of interacting social types, was left unexamined. But this feature of collectivities has an impact on behavior. Its neglect has sometimes led to inappropriate or misleading conclusions.

Source: Rosabeth Moss Kanter, "Some Effects of Proportions on Group Life: Skewed Sex Ratios and Responses to Token Women," *American Journal of Sociology*, Vol. 82, #5, (March 1977): 965–990. Copyright © 1977 by The University of Chicago. All rights reserved. Reprinted by permission of the publisher, The University of Chicago Press, and the author.

This paper defines the issues that need to be explored. It addresses itself to proportion as a significant aspect of social life, particularly important for understanding interactions in groups composed of people of different cultural categories or statuses. It argues that groups with varying proportions of people of different social types differ qualitatively in dynamics and process. This difference is not merely a function of cultural diversity or "status incongruence" (Zaleznick, Christensen, and Roethlisberger 1958, pp. 56–68); it reflects the effects of contact across categories as a function of their proportional representation in the system.

Four group types can be identified on the basis of various proportional representations of kinds of people. *Uniform* groups have only one kind of person, one significant social type. The group may develop its own differentiations, of course, but groups considered uniform are homogeneous with respect to salient external master statuses such as sex, race, or ethnicity. Uniform groups have a "typological ratio" of 100:0. *Skewed* groups are those in which there is a large preponderance of one type over another, up to a ratio of perhaps 85:15. The numerically dominant types also control the group and its culture in enough ways to be labeled "dominants." The few of another type in a skewed group can appropriately be called "tokens," because they are often treated as representatives of their category, as symbols rather than individuals. If the absolute size of the skewed group is small, tokens can also be solitary individuals or "solos," the only one of their kind present. But even if there are two tokens in a skewed group, it is difficult for them to generate an alliance that can become powerful in the group. Next, *tilted* groups begin to move toward less extreme distributions and less exaggerated effects. In this situation, with a ratio of perhaps 65:35, dominants are just a majority and tokens a minority. Minority members are potentially allies, can form coalitions, and can affect the culture of the group. They begin to become individuals differentiated from each other as well as a type differentiated from the majority. Finally, at a typological ratio of about 60:40 down to 50:50, the group becomes *balanced*. Culture and interaction reflect this balance. Majority and minority turn into potential subgroups which may or may not generate actual type-based identifications. Outcomes for individuals in such a balanced peer group, regardless of type, will depend on other structural and personal factors, including formation of subgroups or differentiated roles and abilities. Figure 16.1 schematizes the four group types.

The characteristics of the second type, the skewed group, provide a relevant starting point for this examination of the effects of proportion, for although this group represents an extreme instance of the phenomenon, it is one encountered by large numbers of women in groups and organizations in which numerical distributions have traditionally favored men.

At the same time, this paper is oriented toward enlarging our understanding of male-female interaction and the situations facing women in organizations by introducing structural and contextual effects. Most analyses to date locate male-female interaction issues either in broad cultural traditions and the sexual division of labor in society or in the psychology of men and women whether based on biology or socialization (Kanter 1976c). In both macroscopic and microscopic analysis, sex and gender components are sometimes confounded by situational and structural effects. For example, successful women executives are almost always numerically rare in their organizations, whereas working women are disproportionately concentrated in low-opportunity occupations. Conclusions about "women's behavior" or "male attitudes" drawn from such situations may sometimes confuse the effect of situation with the effect of sex roles; indeed such variables as position in opportunity and power structures account for a large number of phenomena related to work behavior that have been labeled "sex differences" (Kanter 1975, 1976a, 1976d, and [1977]). Therefore this paper focuses on an intermediate-level analysis: how group structures shape interaction contexts and influence particular patterns of male-female interaction. One advantage of such an approach is that it is then possible to generalize beyond

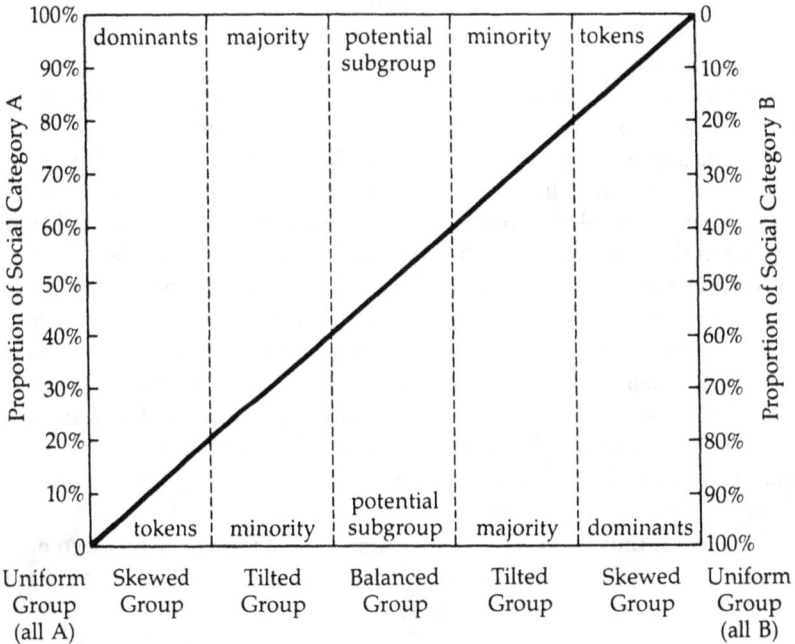

FIGURE 16.1
Group types as defined by proportional representation of two social categories in a membership.

male-female relations to persons-of-one-kind and person-of-another-kind interaction in various contexts, also making possible the untangling of what exactly is unique about the male-female case.

The study of particular proportions of women in predominantly male groups is thus relevant to a concern with social organization and group process as well as with male-female interaction. The analysis presented here deals with interaction in face-to-face groups with highly skewed sex ratios. More specifically, the focus is upon what happens to women who occupy token statuses and are alone or nearly alone in a peer group of men. This situation is commonly faced by women in management and the professions, and it is increasingly faced by women entering formerly all-male fields at every level of organizations. But proportional scarcity is not unique to women. Men can also find themselves alone among women, blacks among whites, very old people among the young, straight people among gays, the blind among the sighted. The dynamics of interaction (the process) is likely to be very similar in all such cases, even though the content of interaction may reflect the special culture and traditional roles of both token and members of the numerically dominant category.

Use of the term "token" for the minority member rather than "solo," "solitary," or "lone" highlights some special characteristics associated with that position. Tokens are not merely deviants or people who differ from other group members along any one dimension. They are people identified by ascribed characteristics (master statuses such as sex, race, religion, ethnic group, age, etc.) or other characteristics that carry with them a set of assumptions about culture, status, and behavior highly salient for majority category members. They bring these "auxiliary traits," in Hughes's (1944) term, into situations in which they differ from other people not in ability to do a task or in acceptance of work norms but only in terms of these secondary and informal assumptions. The importance of these auxiliary traits is heightened if members of the majority group have a history of interacting with the token's category in ways that are quite different from the demands of task accomplishment in the present situation – as is true of men with women. Furthermore, because tokens are by definition alone or virtually alone, they are in the position of representing their ascribed category to the group, whether they choose to do so or not. They can never be just another member while their category is so rare; they will always be a hyphenated member, as in "woman-engineer" or "male-nurse" or "black-physician."

People can thus be in the token position even if they have not been placed there deliberately for display by officials of an organization. It is sufficient to be in a place where others of that category are not usually found, to be the first of one's kind to enter a new group, or to represent a very different culture and set of interactional capacities to members of the numerically dominant category. The term "token" reflects one's status as a symbol of one's kind. However, lone people of one type among members of another are not necessarily tokens if their presence is taken for granted in the group or organization and incorporated into the dominant culture, so that their loneliness is merely the accidental result of random distributions rather than a reflection of the rarity of their type in that system.[2]

While the dynamics of tokenism are likely to operate in some form whenever proportional representation in a collectivity is highly skewed, even if the dominant group does not intend to put the token at a disadvantage, two conditions can heighten and dramatize the effects, making them more visible to the analyst: (1) the token's social category (master status) is physically obvious, as in the case of sex, and (2) the token's social type is not only rare but also new to the setting of the dominants. The latter situation may or may not be conceptually distinct from rarity, although it allows us to see the development of patterns of adjustment as well as the perception of and response to tokens. Subsequent tokens have less surprise value and may be thrust into token roles with less disruption to the system.

With only a few exceptions, the effects of differences in proportional representation within collectivities have received little previous attention. Hughes (1944, 1946, 1958) described the dynamics of white work groups entered by a few blacks, pointing out the dilemmas posed by status contradictions and illuminating the sources of group discomfort as they put pressures on the rare blacks. There are a few studies of other kinds of tokens such as Segal's (1962) observations of male nurses in a largely female colleague group. Reports of professional women in male-dominated fields (e.g., Epstein 1970; Hennig 1970; Lynch 1973; Cussler 1958) mention some special issues raised by numerical rarity. More recently, Laws (1975) has developed a framework for defining the induction of a woman into token status through interaction with a sponsor representing the numerically dominant group. Wolman and Frank (1975) reported observations of solo women in professional-training groups; Taylor and Fiske (1976) have developed experimental data on the perception of token blacks in a white male group. The material in all of these studies still needs a theoretical framework.

With the exceptions noted, research has generally failed to take into account the effects of relative numbers on interaction. Yet such effects could critically change the interpretation of familiar findings. The research of Strodtbeck and his colleagues (Strodtbeck and Mann 1956; Strodtbeck, James, and Hawkins 1957) on mock jury deliberations is often cited as evidence that men tend to play initiating, task-oriented roles in small groups, whereas women tend to play reactive, socioemotional roles. Yet a reexamination of these investigations indicates that men far outnumbered women as research subjects. There were more than twice as many men as women (86 to 41) in the 12 small groups in which women were found to play stereotypical expressive roles.[3] The actual sex composition of each of the small groups is not reported, although it could have important implications for the results. Perhaps it was women's scarcity in skewed groups that pushed them into classical positions and men's numerical

superiority that gave them an edge in task performance. Similarly, in the early
kibbutzim, collective villages in Israel that theoretically espoused equality of the
sexes but were unable fully to implement it, women could be pushed into traditional service positions (see Tiger and Shepher 1975) because there were often
more than twice as many men as women in a kibbutz. Again, relative numbers in-
terfered with a fair test of what men or women can "naturally" do (Kanter
1976b).

Thus systematic analysis of the dynamics of systems with skewed distributions of social types – tokens in the midst of numerical dominants – is overdue.
This paper begins to define a framework for understanding the dynamics of
tokenism, illustrated by field observations of female tokens among male
dominants.

THE FIELD STUDY

The forms of interaction in the presence of token women were identified in a
field study of a large industrial corporation, one of the *Fortune 500* firms (see
Kanter [1977] for a description of the setting). The sales force of one division
was investigated in detail because women were entering it for the first time. The
first saleswoman was hired in 1972; by the end of 1974, there had been about 20
in training or on assignment (several had left the company) out of a sales force of
over 300 men. The geographically decentralized nature of sales meant, however,
that in training programs or in field offices women were likely to be one of 10 or
12 sales workers: in a few cases, two women were together in a group of a dozen
sales personnel. Studying women who were selling industrial goods had particular advantages: (1) sales is a field with strong cultural traditions and folklore
and one in which interpersonal skills rather than expertise count heavily, thus
making informal and cultural aspects of group interaction salient and visible even
for members themselves; and (2) sales workers have to manage relations not only
with work peers but with customers as well, thus giving the women two sets of
majority groups with which to interact. Sixteen women in sales and distribution
were interviewed in depth. Over 40 male peers and managers were also interviewed. Sales-training groups were observed both in session and at informal
social gatherings for approximately 100 hours. Additional units of the organization were studied for other research purposes.

THEORETICAL FRAMEWORK

The framework set forth here proceeds from the Simmelian assumption that
form determines process, narrowing the universe of interaction possibilities. The
form of a group with a skewed distribution of social types generates certain

perceptions of the tokens by the dominants. These perceptions determine the interaction dynamics between tokens and dominants and create the pressures dominants impose on tokens. In turn, there are typical token responses to these pressures.

The proportional rarity of tokens is associated with three perceptual phenomena: visibility, polarization, and assimilation. First, tokens, one by one, have higher visibility than dominants looked at alone: they capture a larger awareness share. A group member's awareness share, averaged over shares of other individuals of the same social type, declines as the proportion of total membership occupied by the category increases, because each individual becomes less and less surprising, unique, or note-worthy; in Gestalt terms, they more easily become "ground" rather than "figure." But for tokens there is a "law of increasing returns": as individuals of their type come to represent a *smaller* numerical proportion of the group, they potentially capture a *larger* share of the group members' awareness.

Polarization or exaggeration of differences is the second perceptual tendency. The presence of a person bearing a different set of social characteristics makes members of a numerically dominant group more aware both of their commonalities with and their differences from the token. There is a tendency to exaggerate the extent of the differences, especially because tokens are by definition too few in number to prevent the application of familiar generalizations or stereotypes. It is thus easier for the commonalities of dominants to be defined in contrast to the token than it would be in a more numerically equal situation. One person can also be perceptually isolated and seen as cut off from the group more easily than many, who begin to represent a significant proportion of the group itself.

Assimilation, the third perceptual tendency, involves the use of stereotypes or familiar generalizations about a person's social type. The characteristics of a token tend to be distorted to fit the generalization. If there are enough people of the token's type to let discrepant examples occur, it is possible that the generalization will change to accommodate the accumulated cases. But if individuals of that type are only a small proportion of the group, it is easier to retain the generalization and distort the perception of the token.

Taylor and Fiske's (1976; Taylor 1975) laboratory experiments provide supportive evidence for these propositions. They played a tape of a group discussion to subjects while showing them pictures of the group and then asked them for their impressions of group members on a number of dimensions. The tape was the same for all subjects, but the purported composition of the group varied. The pictures illustrated either an otherwise all-white male group with one black man (the token condition) or a mixed black-white male group. In the token condition, the subjects paid disproportionate attention to the token, overemphasized his prominence in the group, and exaggerated his attributes. Similarly, the token was perceived as playing special roles in the group, often highly stereotypical ones. By contrast, in the integrated condition, subjects recalled no more about blacks than whites and evaluated their attributes in about the same way.

Visibility, polarization, and assimilation are each associated with particular interaction dynamics that in turn generate typical token responses. These dynamics are similar regardless of the category from which the token comes, although the token's social type and history of relationships with dominants shape the content of specific interactions. Visibility creates performance pressures on the token. Polarization leads to group boundary heightening and isolation of the token. And assimilation results in the token's role entrapment.

PERFORMANCE PRESSURES

The women in the sales force I studied were highly visible, much more so than their male peers. Managers commonly reported that they were the subject of conversation, questioning, gossip, and careful scrutiny. Their placements were known and observed throughout the sales unit, while those of men typically were not. Such visibility created a set of performance pressures: characteristics and standards true for tokens alone. Tokens typically perform under conditions different from those of dominants.

1. Public Performance
It was difficult for the women to do anything in training programs or in the field that did not attract public notice. The women found that they did not have to go out of their way to be noticed or to get the attention of management at sales meetings. One woman reported, "I've been at sales meetings where all the trainees were going up to the managers – 'Hi, Mr. So-and-So' – trying to make that impression, wearing a strawberry tie, whatever, something that they could be remembered by. Whereas there were three of us [women] in a group of 50, and all we had to do was walk in, and everyone recognized us."

Automatic notice meant that women could not remain anonymous or hide in the crowd; all their actions were public. Their mistakes and their relationships were known as readily as any other information. It was impossible for them to have any privacy within the company. The women were always viewed by an audience, leading several to complain of "overobservation."

2. Extension of Consequences
The women were visible as category members, and as such their acts tended to have added symbolic consequences. Some women were told that their performance could affect the prospects for other women in the company. They were thus not acting for themselves alone but carrying the burden of representing their category. In informal conversations, they were often measured by two yardsticks: how *as women* they carried out the sales role and how *as salesworkers*

they lived up to images of womanhood. In short, every act tended to be evaluated beyond its meaning for the organization and taken as a sign of "how women do in sales." The women were aware of the extra symbolic consequences attached to their acts.

3. Attention to a Token's Discrepant Characteristics

A token's visibility stems from characteristics – attributes of a master status – that threaten to blot out other aspects of the token's performance. While the token captures attention, it is often for discrepant characteristics, for the auxiliary traits that provide token status. No token in the study had to work hard to have her presence noticed, but she did have to work hard to have her achievements noticed. In the sales force, the women found that their technical abilities were likely to be eclipsed by their physical appearance, and thus an additional performance pressure was created. The women had to put in extra effort to make their technical skills known, to work twice as hard to prove their competence. Both male peers and customers would tend to forget information women provided about their experiences and credentials, while noticing and remembering such secondary attributes as style of dress.

4. Fear of Retaliation

The women were also aware of another performance pressure: to avoid making the dominants look bad. Tokenism sets up a dynamic that makes tokens afraid of outstanding performance in group events and tasks. When a token does well enough to show up a dominant, it cannot be kept a secret, because all eyes are on the token. Therefore it is difficult in such a situation to avoid the public humiliation of a dominant. Thus, paradoxically, while the token women felt they had to do better than anyone else in order to be seen as competent and allowed to continue, they also felt in some cases that their successes would not be rewarded and should be kept secret. One woman had trouble understanding this and complained of her treatment by managers. They had fired another woman for not being aggressive enough, she reported; yet she, who succeeded in doing all they asked and had brought in the largest amount of new business during the past year, was criticized for being too aggressive, too much of a hustler.

RESPONSES OF TOKENS TO PERFORMANCE PRESSURES

There are two typical ways tokens respond to these performance pressures. The first involves overachievement. Aware of the performance pressures, several of the saleswomen put in extra effort, promoted themselves and their work at every opportunity, and let those around them know how well they were doing. These women evoked threats of retaliation. On the gossip circuit, they were known to be doing well but aspiring too high too fast; a common prediction was that they would be cut down to size soon.

The second response is more common and is typical of findings of other investigators. It involves attempts to limit visibility, to become socially invisible. This strategy characterizes women who try to minimize their sexual attributes so as to blend unnoticeably into the predominant male culture, perhaps by adopting "mannish dress" (Hennig 1970, chap. 6). Or it can include avoidance of public events and occasions for performance – staying away from meetings, working at home rather than in the office, keeping silent at meetings. Several of the saleswomen deliberately kept such a low profile, unlike male peers who tended to seize every opportunity to make themselves noticed. They avoided conflict, risks, and controversial situations. Those women preferring social invisibility also made little attempt to make their achievements publicly known or to get credit for their own contributions to problem solving or other organizational tasks. They are like other women in the research literature who have let others assume visible leadership (Megaree 1969) or take credit for their accomplishments (Lynch 1973; Cussler 1958). These women did blend into the background, but they also limited recognition of their competence.

This analysis suggests a reexamination of the "fear of success in women" hypothesis. Perhaps what has been called fear of success is really the token woman's fear of visibility. The original research identifying this concept created a hypothethical situation in which a woman was at the top of her class in medical school – a token woman in a male peer group. Such a situation puts pressure on a woman to make herself and her achievements invisible, to deny success. Attempts to replicate the initial findings using settings in which women were not so clearly tokens produced very different results. And in other studies (e.g., Levine and Crumrine 1975), the hypothesis that fear of success is a female-linked trait has not been confirmed. (See Sarason {1973} for a discussion of fear of visibility among minorities.)

BOUNDARY HEIGHTENING

Polarization or exaggeration of the token's attributes in contrast to those of the dominants sets a second set of dynamics in motion. The presence of a token makes dominants more aware of what they have in common at the same time that it threatens that commonality. Indeed it is often at those moments when a collectivity is threatened with change that its culture and bonds become evident to it; only when an obvious outsider appears do group members suddenly realize their common bond as insiders. Dominants thus tend to exaggerate both their commonality and the token's difference, moving to heighten boundaries of which previously they might not even have been aware.[4]

1. Exaggeration of Dominants' Culture

Majority members assert or reclaim group solidarity and reaffirm shared in-group understandings by emphasizing and exaggerating those cultural elements which they share in contrast to the token. The token becomes both occasion and audience for the highlighting and dramatization of those themes that differentiate the token as outsider from the insider. Ironically, tokens (unlike people of their type represented in greater proportion) are thus instruments for underlining rather than undermining majority culture. In the sales-force case, this phenomenon was most clearly in operation in training programs and at dinner and cocktail parties during meetings. Here the camaraderie of men, as in other work and social settings (Tiger 1969), was based in part on tales of sexual adventures, ability with respect to "hunting" and capturing women, and off-color jokes. Secondary themes involved work prowess and sports. The capacity for and enjoyment of drinking provided the context for displays of these themes. According to male informants' reports, they were dramatized more fervently in the presence of token women than when only men were present. When the men introduced these themes in much milder form and were just as likely to share company gossip or talk of domestic matters (such as a house being built), as to discuss any of the themes mentioned above, this was also in contrast to the situation in more equally mixed male-female groups, in which there were a sufficient number of women to influence and change group culture in such a way that a new hybrid based on shared male-female concerns was introduced. (See Aries [1973] for supportive laboratory evidence.)

In the presence of token women, then, men exaggerated displays of aggression and potency: instances of sexual innuendo, aggressive sexual teasing, and prowess-oriented "war stories." When one or two women were present, the men's behavior involved showing off, telling stories in which masculine prowess accounted for personal, sexual, or business success. The men highlighted what they could do, as men, in contrast to women. In a set of training situations, these themes were even acted out overtly in role plays in which participants were asked to prepare and perform demonstrations of sales situations. In every case involving a woman, men played the primary, effective roles, and women were objects of sexual attention. In one, a woman was introduced as president of a company selling robots; she turned out to be one of the female robots, run by the male company sales manager.

The women themselves reported other examples of testing to see how they would respond to the "male" culture. They said that many sexual innuendos or displays of locker-room humor were put on for their benefit, especially by the younger men. (The older men tended to parade their business successes.) One woman was a team leader and the only woman at a workshop when her team, looking at her for a reaction, decided to use as its slogan "The [obscenity] of the week." By raising the issue and forcing the woman to choose not to participate in the workshop, the men in the group created an occasion for uniting against the outsider and asserting dominant-group solidarity.

2. Interruptions as Reminders of "Difference"

Members of the numerically dominant category underscore and reinforce differences between tokens and themselves, insuring that the former recognize their outsider status by making the token the occasion for interruptions in the flow of group events. Dominants preface acts with apologies or questions about appropriateness directed at the token; they then invariably go ahead with the act, having placed the token in the position of interrupter or interloper. This happened often in the presence of the saleswomen. Men's questions or apologies were a way of asking whether the old or expected cultural rules were still operative — the words and expressions permitted, the pleasures and forms of release indulged in. (Can we still swear? Toss a football? Use technical jargon? Go drinking? Tell in jokes? See Greenbaum [1971, p. 65] for other examples.) By posing these questions overtly, dominants make their culture clear to tokens and state the terms under which tokens interact with the group.

The answers almost invariably affirm the understandings of the dominants, first because of the power of sheer numbers. An individual rarely feels comfortable preventing a larger number of peers from engaging in an activity they consider normal. Second, the tokens have been put on notice that interaction will not be "natural," that dominants will be holding back unless the tokens agree to acknowledge, permit, and even encourage majority cultural expressions in their presence. (It is important that this be stated, of course, for one never knows that another is holding back unless the other lets a piece of the suppressed material slip out.) At the same time, tokens have also been given the implicit message that majority members do *not* expect those forms of expression to be natural to the tokens' home culture; otherwise majority members would not need to raise the question. (This is a function of what Laws [1975] calls the "double deviance" of tokens: deviant first because they are women in a man's world and second because they aspire inappropriately to the privileges of the dominants.) Thus the saleswomen were often in the odd position of reassuring peers and customers that they could go ahead and do something in the women's presence, such as swearing, that they themselves would not be permitted to do. They listened to dirty jokes, for example, but reported that they would not dare tell one themselves. Via difference-reminding interruptions, then, dominants both affirm their own shared understandings and draw the cultural boundary between themselves and tokens. The tokens learned that they caused interruptions in "normal" communication and that their appropriate position was more like that of audience than full participant.

3. Overt Inhibition: Informal Isolation

In some cases, dominants do not wish to carry out certain activities in the presence of a token: they have secrets to preserve. They thus move the locus of some activities and expressions away from public settings to which tokens have access to more private settings from which they can be excluded. When information potentially embarrassing or damaging to dominants is being exchanged, an outsider audience is not desirable because dominants do not know how far they can trust tokens. As Hughes (1944, 1958) pointed out, colleagues who rely on unspoken understandings may feel uncomfortable in the presence of "odd kinds of fellows" who cannot be trusted to interpret information in just the same way or to engage in the same relationships of trust and reciprocity (see also Lorber 1975). The result is often quarantine – keeping tokens away from some occasions. Thus some topics of discussion were never raised by men in the presence of many of the saleswomen, even though they discussed these topics among themselves: admissions of low commitment to the company or concerns about job performance, ways of getting around formal rules, political plotting for mutual advantage, strategies for impressing certain corporate executives. As researchers have also found in other settings, women did not tend to be included in the networks by which informal socialization occurred and politics behind the formal system were exposed (Wolman and Frank 1975; O'Farrell 1973; Hennig 1970; Epstein 1970). In a few cases, managers even avoided giving women information about their performance as trainees, so that they did not know they were the subject of criticism in the company until they were told to find jobs outside the sales force; those women were simply not part of the informal occasions on which the men discussed their performances with each other. (Several male managers also reported their "fear" of criticizing a woman because of uncertainty about how she would receive it.)

4. Loyalty Tests

At the same time that tokens are often kept on the periphery of colleague interaction, they may also be expected to demonstrate loyalty to the dominant group. Failure to do so results in further isolation; signs of loyalty permit the token to come closer and be included in more activities. Through loyalty tests, the group seeks reassurance that tokens will not turn against them or use any of the information gained through their viewing of the dominants' world to do harm to the group. They get this assurance by asking a token to join or identify with the majority against those others who represent competing membership or reference groups; in short, dominants pressure tokens to turn against members of the latter's own category. If tokens collude, they make themselves psychological hostages of the majority group. For token women, the price of being "one of the boys" is a willingness to turn occasionally against "the girls."

There are two ways by which tokens can demonstrate loyalty and qualify for closer relationships with dominants. First, they can let slide or even participate in statements prejudicial to other members of their category. They can allow themselves to be viewed as exceptions to the general rule that others of their category have a variety of undesirable or unsuitable characteristics. Hughes (1944) recognized this as one of the deals token blacks might make for

membership in white groups. Saleswomen who did well were told they were exceptions and were not typical women. At meetings and training sessions,
women were often the subjects of ridicule or joking remarks about their incompetence. Some women who were insulted by such innuendos found it easier
to appear to agree than to start an argument. A few accepted the dominant view
fully. One of the first saleswomen denied in interviews having any special problems because she was a woman, calling herself skilled at coping with a man's
world, and said the company was right not to hire more women. Women, she
said, were unreliable and likely to quit; furthermore, young women might marry
men who would not allow them to work. In this case, a token woman was taking
over "gate-keeping" functions for dominants (Laws 1975), letting them preserve
their illusion of lack of prejudice while she acted to exclude other women.

Tokens can also demonstrate loyalty by allowing themselves and their
category to provide a source of humor for the group. Laughing with others, as
Coser (1960) indicated, is a sign of a common definition of the situation; to allow
oneself or one's kind to be the object of laughter signals a further willingness to
accept others' culture on their terms. Just as Hughes (1946, p. 115) found that
the initiation of blacks into white groups might involve accepting the role of com-
ic inferior, the saleswomen faced constant pressures to allow jokes at women's
expense, to accept kidding from the men around them. When a woman objected,
men denied any hostility or unfriendly intention, instead accusing the woman by
inference of lacking a sense of humor. In order to cope, one woman reported,
"you learn to laugh when they try to insult you with jokes, to let it roll off your
back." Tokens thus find themselves colluding with dominants through shared
laughter.

Responses of Tokens to Boundary Heightening

Numerical skewing and polarized perceptions leave tokens with little choice
about whether to accept the culture of dominants. There are too few other people of the token's kind to generate a counterculture or to develop a shared in-
tergroup culture. Tokens have two general response possibilities. They can accept isolation, remaining an audience for certain expressive acts of dominants, in
which case they risk exclusion from occasions on which informal socialization
and political activity take place. Or they can try to become insiders, proving
their loyalty by defining themselves as exceptions and turning against their own
social category.

The occurrence of the second response on the part of tokens suggests a reexamination of the popularized "women-prejudiced-against-women" hypothesis or
the "queen bee syndrome" for possible structural (numerical) rather than sexual
origins. Not only has this hypothesis not been confirmed in a variety of settings
(e.g., Ferber and Huber 1975); but the analysis offered here of the social
psychological pressures on tokens to side with the majority also provides a compelling explanation for the kinds of situations most likely to produce this effect,
when it does occur.

ROLE ENTRAPMENT

The third set of interaction dynamics centering around tokens stems from the perceptual tendency toward assimilation: the distortion of the characteristics of tokens to fit preexisting generalizations about their category. Stereotypical assumptions and mistaken attributions made about tokens tend to force them into playing limited and caricatured roles in the system.

1. Status Leveling

Tokens are often misperceived initially as a result of their statistical rarity: "statistical discrimination" (U.S. Council of Economic Advisers 1973, p. 106) as distinguished from prejudice. That is, an unusual woman may be treated as though she resembles women on the average. People make judgments about the role played by others on the basis of probabilistic reasoning about the likelihood of what a particular kind of person does. Thus the saleswomen like other tokens encountered many instances of mistaken identity. In the office, they were often taken for secretaries; on the road, especially when they traveled with male colleagues, they were often taken for wives or mistresses; with customers, they were usually assumed to be substituting for men or, when with a male peer, to be assistants; when entertaining customers, they were assumed to be wives or dates.

Such mistaken first impressions can be corrected. They require tokens to spend time untangling awkward exchanges and establishing accurate and appropriate role relations, but they do permit status leveling to occur. Status leveling involves making adjustments in perception of the token's professional role to fit the expected position of the token's category—that is, bringing situational status in line with master status, the token's social type. Even when others knew that the token saleswomen were not secretaries, for example, there was still a tendency to treat them like secretaries or to make demands of them appropriate to secretaries. In the most blatant case, a woman was a sales trainee along with three men; all four were to be given positions as summer replacements. The men were all assigned to replace salesmen; the woman was asked to replace a secretary—and only after a long, heated discussion with the manager was she given a more professional assignment. Similarly, when having professional contacts with customers and managers, the women felt themselves to be treated in more wifelike or datelike ways than a man would be treated by another man, even though the situation was clearly professional. It was easier for others to make their perception of the token women fit their preexisting generalizations about women than to change the category; numerical rarity provided too few examples to contradict the generalization. Instances of status leveling have also been noted with regard to other kinds of tokens such as male nurses (Segal 1962); in the case of tokens whose master status is higher than their situational status, leveling can work to their advantage, as when male nurses are called "Dr."

2. Stereotyped Role Induction

The dominant group can incorporate tokens and still preserve their generalizations about the tokens' kind by inducting them into stereotypical roles; these roles preserve the familiar form of interaction between the kinds of people represented by the token and the dominants. In the case of token women in the sales force, four role traps were observed, all of which encapsulated the women in a category the men could respond to and understand. Each centered on one behavioral tendency of the token, building upon this tendency an image of her place in the group and forcing her to continue to live up to the image; each defined for dominants a single response to her sexuality. Two of the roles are classics in Freudian theory: the mother and the seductress. Freud wrote of the need of men to handle women's sexuality by envisioning them as either madonnas or whores—as either asexual mothers or overly sexual, debased seductresses. (This was perhaps a function of Victorian family patterns, which encouraged separation of idealistic adoration of the mother and animalistic eroticism [Reiff 1963; Strong 1973].) The other roles, termed the pet and the iron maiden, also have family counterparts in the kid sister and the virgin aunt.

A. Mother. A token woman sometimes finds that she has become a mother to a group of men. They bring her their troubles, and she comforts them. The assumption that women are sympathetic, good listeners, and can be talked to about one's problems is common in male-dominated organizations. One saleswoman was constantly approached by her all-male peers to listen to their domestic problems. In a variety of residential-sales-training groups, token women were observed acting out other parts of the traditional nurturant-maternal role: cooking for men, doing their laundry, sewing on buttons.

The mother role is a comparatively safe one. She is not necessarily vulnerable to sexual pursuit (for Freud it was the very idealization of the madonna that was in part responsible for men's ambivalence toward women), nor do men need to compete for her favors, because these are available to everyone. However, the typecasting of women as nurturers has three negative consequences for a woman's task performance: (1) the mother is rewarded by her male colleagues primarily for service to them and not for independent action. (2) The mother is expected to keep her place as a noncritical, accepting, good mother or lose her rewards because the dominant, powerful aspects of the maternal image may be feared by men. Since the ability to differentiate and be critical is often an indicator of competence in work groups, the mother is prohibited from exhibiting this skill. (3) The mother becomes an emotional specialist. This provides her with a place in the life of the group and its members. Yet at the same time, one of the traditionally feminine characteristics men in positions of authority in industry most often criticize in women (see Lynch 1973) is excess emotionality. Although the mother herself might not ever indulge in emotional outbursts in the group, she remains identified with emotional matters. As long as she is in the minority, it is unlikely that nurturance, support, and expressivity will be valued or that a mother can demonstrate and be rewarded for critical, independent, task-oriented behaviors.

B. *Seductress.* The role of seductress or sexual object is fraught with more tension than the maternal role, for it introduces an element of sexual competition and jealousy. The mother can have many sons; it is more difficult for a sex object to have many lovers. Should a woman be cast as sex object, that is, seen as sexually desirable and potentially available ("seductress" is a perception, and the woman herself may not be consciously behaving seductively), share her attention widely, she risks the debasement of the whore. Yet should she form a close alliance with any man in particular, she arouses resentment, particularly because she represents a scarce resource; there are just not enough women to go around.

In several situations observed, a high-status male allied himself with a seductress and acted as her "protector," not only because of his promise to rescue her from the sex-charged overtures of the rest of the men but also because of his high status per se. The powerful male (staff member, manager, sponsor, etc.) can easily become the protector of the still "virgin" seductress, gaining through masking his own sexual interest what other men could not gain by declaring theirs. However, the removal of the seductress from the sexual marketplace contains its own problems. Other men may resent a high-status male for winning the prize and resent the woman for her ability to get an in with the high-status male that they themselves could not obtain as men. While the seductress is rewarded for her femaleness and insured attention from the group, then, she is also the source of considerable tension; and needless to say, her perceived sexuality blots out all other characteristics.

Men may adopt the role of protector toward an attractive woman, regardless of her collusion, and by implication cast her as a sex object, reminding her and the rest of the group of her sexual status. In the guise of helping her, protectors may actually put up further barriers to a solitary woman's full acceptance by inserting themselves, figuratively speaking, between the woman and the rest of a group. A male sales trainer typically offered token women in training groups extra help and sympathetically attended to the problems their male counterparts might cause, taking them out alone for drinks at the end of daily sessions.

C. *Pet.* The pet is adopted by the male group as a cute, amusing little thing and taken along on group events as symbolic mascot—a cheerleader for the shows of male prowess that follow. Humor is often a characteristic of the pet. She is expected to admire the male displays but not to enter into them; she cheers from the sidelines. Shows of competence on her part are treated as extraordinary and complimented just because they are unexpected (and the compliments themselves can be seen as reminders of the expected rarity of such behavior). One woman reported that, when she was alone in a group of men and spoke at length on an issue, comments to her by men after the meeting often referred to her speech-making ability rather than to what she said (e.g., "You talk so fluently"), whereas comments the men made to one another were almost invariably content or issue oriented. Competent acts that were taken for granted when performed by males were often unduly fussed over when performed by saleswomen, who were considered precocious or precious at such times. Such attitudes on the part of men in a group encourage self-effacing, girlish responses on the part of solitary women (who after all may be genuinely relieved to be included) and prevent them from realizing or demonstrating their own power and competence.

D. *Iron maiden.* The iron maiden is a contemporary variation of the stereotypical roles into which strong women are placed. Women who fail to fall into any of the first three roles and in fact resist overtures that would trap them in such roles (like flirtation) might consequently be responded to as though tough or dangerous. (One saleswoman developed just such a reputation in company branches throughout the country.) If a token insisted on full rights in the group, if she displayed competence in a forthright manner, or if she cut off sexual innuendos, she was typically asked, "You're not one of those women's libbers are you?" Regardless of the answer, she was henceforth viewed with suspicion, treated with undue and exaggerated politeness (by references to women inserted into conversations, by elaborate rituals of *not* opening doors), and kept at a distance; for she was demanding treatment as an equal in a setting in which no person of her kind had previously been an equal. Women inducted into the iron maiden role are stereotyped as tougher than they are (hence the name) and trapped in a more militant stance than they might otherwise take.

Responses of Tokens to Role Entrapment

The dynamics of role entrapment tend to lead to a variety of conservative and low-risk responses on the part of tokens. The time and awkwardness involved in correcting mistaken impressions often lead them to a preference for already-established relationships, for minimizing change and stranger contact in the work situation. It is also often easier to accept stereotyped roles than to fight them, even if their acceptance means limiting a token's range of expressions or demonstrations of task competence, because acceptance offers a comfortable and certain position. The personal consequence for tokens, of course, is a certain degree of self-distortion. Athanassiades (1974), though not taking into account the effects of numerical representation, found that women, especially those with low risk-taking propensity, tended to distort upward communication more than men and argued that many observed work behaviors of women may be the result of such distortion and acceptance of organizational images. Submissiveness, frivolity, or other attributes may be feigned by people who feel these are prescribed for them by the dominant organizational culture. This suggests that accurate conclusions about work attitudes and behavior cannot be reached by studying people in the token position, since there may always be an element of compensation or distortion involved. Thus many studies of professional and managerial women should be reexamined in order to remove the effects of numbers from the effects of sex roles.

IMPLICATIONS

This paper has developed a framework for understanding the social perceptions and interaction dynamics that center on tokens, using the example of women in an industrial sales force dominated numerically by men. Visibility generates performance pressures, polarization generates group boundary heightening, and assimilation generates role entrapment. All of the phenomena asociated with tokens are exaggerated ones: the token stands out vividly, group culture is dramatized, boundaries become highlighted, and token roles are larger-than-life caricatures.

The concepts identified here are also applicable to other kinds of tokens who face similar interaction contexts. Hughes's (1944, 1946, 1958) discussions of the problems encountered by blacks in white male work groups are highly congruent with the framework presented here. Taylor and Fiske's (1976) laboratory research demonstrates the perceptual phenomena mentioned above in the black-white context. Segal (1962) also provides confirming evidence that, when men are tokens in a group of women, the same concepts apply. He studied a hospital in which 22 out of 101 nurses were men. He found that male nurses were isolates in the hospital social structure, not because the men disassociated themselves from their women peers but because the women felt the men were out of place and should not be nurses. Male and female nurses had the same objective rank, but people of both sexes felt that the men's subjective status was a lower one. The women placed the men in stereotypical positions, expecting them to do the jobs the women found distasteful or considered men's work. During a personal interview, a male nursing student reported that he thought he would enjoy being the only man in a group of women until he found that he engendered a great deal of hostility and that he was teased every time he failed to live up to the manly image, for example, if he was vague or subjective in speech. And "token men" working in child-care centers were found to play minor roles, become social isolates, and bear special burdens in interaction, which they handled like the saleswomen, by defining themselves as "exceptional" men (Seifert 1973). Similarly, a blind informant indicated to me that, when he was the only blind person among sighted people, he often felt conspicuous and more attended to than he liked. This in turn created pressure for him to work harder in order to prove himself. In the solo situation, he was never sure that he was getting the same treatment as other members of the group (first, fellow students; later, fellow members of an academic institution), and he suspected that people tended to protect him. When he was the only one of his kind, as opposed to situations in which other blind people were present, sighted people felt free to grab his arm and pull him along and were more likely to apologize for references to visual matters, reinforcing his sense of being different and cast in the role of someone more helpless than he in fact perceived himself to be.

If the token's master status is higher that that of the situational dominants, some of the content of the interaction may change while the dynamics remain the same. A high-status token, for example, might find that the difference-reminding interruptions involve deference and opinion seeking rather than patronizing apology; a high-status token might be allowed to dominate formal colleague discussion while still being excluded from informal, expressive occasions. Such a token might be trapped in roles that distort competence in a favorable rather than an unfavorable direction; but distortion is involved nonetheless. Further research can uncover appropriate modifications of the framework which will allow its complete extension to cases in the category just discussed.

The analysis undertaken here also suggests the importance of intermediate-level structural and social psychological variables in affecting male-female interaction and the roles of women in work groups and organizations. Some phenomena that have been labeled sex related but have not been replicated under all circumstances might be responses to tokenism, that is, reflections of responses to situational pressures rather than to sex differences. "Fear of success" might be more fruitfully viewed as the fear of visibility of members of minority groups in token statuses. The modesty and lack of self-aggrandizement characteristic of some professional and managerial women might be accounted for in similar ways, as situational responses rather than sex-linked traits. The prejudice of some women against others might be placed in the context of majority-culture loyalty tests. The unwillingness of some professional and managerial women to take certain risks involving a change in relationships might be explained as a reasonable response to the length of time it may take a token to establish competence-based working relationships and to the ever-present threat of mistaken identity in new relationships.

The examination of numerical effects leads to the additional question of tipping points: how many of a category are enough to change a person's status from token to full group member? When does a group move from skewed to tilted to balanced? Quantitative analyses are called for in order to provide precise documentation of the points at which interaction shifts because enough people of the "other kind" have become members of a group. This is especially relevant to research on school desegregation and its effects or changing neighborhood composition as well as occupational segregation by sex. Howe and Widick (1949, pp. 211–12) found that industrial plants with a small proportion of blacks in their work force had racial clashes, whereas those plants in which blacks constituted a large proportion had good race relations.

Exact tipping points should be investigated. Observations from the present study make it clear that even in small groups two of a kind are *not* enough. Data were collected in several situations in which two women rather than one were found among male peers but still constituted less than 20% of the group. Despite Asch's (1960) laboratory finding that one potential ally is enough to reduce the power of the majority to secure conformity, in the two-token situation in organizations dominants were nearly always able to defeat an alliance between two women by setting up invidious comparisons. By the exaggeration of traits in both cases, one woman was identified as a success, the other as a failure. The one given the positive label felt relieved to be accepted and praised. She recognized that alliance with the identified failure would jeopardize her accep-tance. The consequence in one sales office was that the identified success stayed away from the other woman, did not give her any help with her performance, and withheld criticism she had heard that might have been useful. The second woman soon left the organization. In another case, dominants defeated an alliance, paradoxically by trying to promote it. Two women in a training group of 12 were treated as though they were an automatic pair, and other group members felt that they were relieved of responsibility for interacting with or supporting the women. The women reacted to this forced pairing by trying to create differences between themselves and becoming extremely competitive Thus structural circumstances and pressures from the majority can produce what appear to be prejudicial responses of women to each other. Yet these responses are best seen as the effects of limited numbers. Two (or less than 20% in any particular situation) is not always a large enough number to overcome the problems of tokenism and develop supportive alliances, unless the tokens are highly identified with their own social category.

Tokens appear to operate under a number of handicaps in work settings Their possible social isolation may exclude them from situations in which impor tant learning about a task is taking place and may also prevent them from bein in a position to look good in the organization. Performance pressures make i more dangerous for tokens to fumble and thus give them less room for error. Re sponding to their position, they often either underachieve or overachieve, an they are likely to accept distorting roles which permit them to disclose onl limited parts of themselves. For all these reasons, in situations like industri; sales in which informal interaction provides a key to success tokens are not ver likely to do well compared with members of the majority category, at least whil in the token position.

These consequences of token status also indicate that tokens may undergo great deal of personal stress and may need to expend extra energy to maintain satisfactory relationship in the work situation. This fact is reflected in their con mon statements that they must work twice as hard as dominants or spend mo:

time resolving problematic interactions. They face partially conflicting and often completely contradictory expectations. Such a situation has been found to be a source of mental stress for people with inconsistent statuses and in some cases to reinforce punitive self-images. In addition, turning against others of one's kind may be intimately connected with self-hatred. Finally, tokens must inhibit some forms of self-expression and often are unable to join the group in its characteristic form of tension release. They may be asked to side with the group in its assaults-through-humor but often cannot easily join the group in its play. They potentially face the stresses of social isolation and self-distortion.[5]

Thus social-policy formulations might consider the effects of proportions in understanding the sources of behavior, causes of stress, and possibilities for change. The analysis of tokenism suggests, for example, that merely adding a few women at a time to an organization is likely to give rise to the consequences of token status. Despite the contemporary controversy over affirmative action quotas (Glazer 1976), numbers do appear to be important in shaping outcomes for disadvantaged individuals. Women (or members of any other under-represented category) need to be added to total group of organization membership in sufficient proportion to counteract the effects of tokenism. Even if tokens do well, they do so at a cost, overcoming social handicaps, expending extra effort, and facing stresses not present for members of the numerically dominant group. The dynamics of tokenism also operate in such a way as to perpetuate the system that keeps members of the token's category in short supply; the presence of a few tokens does not necessarily pave the way for others – in many cases, it has the opposite effect.

Investigation of the effects of proportions on group life and social interaction appears to be fruitful both for social psychological theory and for understanding male-female interaction. It is a step toward identifying the structural and situational variables that intervene between global cultural definitions of social type and individual responses – that shape the context for face-to-face interactions among different kinds of people. Relative as well as absolute numbers can be important for social life and social relations.

NOTES

1. Thanks are due to the staff of "Industrial Supply Corporation," the pseudonymous corporation which invited and provided support for this research along with permission for use of the data in this paper. The research was part of a larger project on social structural factors in organizational behavior reported in Kanter (in press). An early version of this article was prepared for the Center for Research on Women in Higher Education and the Professions, Wellesley College, which provided some additional financial support. Barry Stein's colleagueship was especially valuable. This article was completed while the author held a Guggenheim fellowship.

2. As an anonymous reviewer pointed out, newness is more easily distinguished from rarity conceptually than it may be empirically, and further research should make this distinction. It should also specify the conditions under which "accidental loneness" (or small relative numbers) does not have the extreme effects noted here: when the difference is noted but not considered very important, as in the case of baseball teams that may have only one or two black members but lack token dynamics because of the large number of teams with many black members.

3. The 17 least active subjects (out of a total of 144) were dropped from the analysis; their sex is not mentioned in published reports. Those 17 might have skewed the sex distribution even further.

4. This awareness often seemed to be resented by the men interviewed in this study, who expressed a preference for less self-consciousness and less attention to taken-for-granted operating assumptions. They wanted to "get on with business," and questioning definitions of what is "normal" and "appropriate" was seen as a deflection from the task at hand. The culture in the managerial/technical ranks of this large corporation, like that in many others, devalued introspection and emphasized rapid communication and ease of interaction. Thus, although group solidarity is often based on the development of strong in-group boundaries (Kanter 1972), the stranger or outsider who makes it necessary for the group to pay attention to its boundaries may be resented not only for being different but also for giving the group extra work.

5. The argument that tokens face more personal stress than majority group members can be supported by studies of the psychosocial difficulties confronting people with inconsistent statuses. Among the stresses identified in the literature on class and race are unsatisfactory social relationships, unstable self-images, frustration over rewards, and social ambiguity (Hughes 1944, 1958; Lenski 1956; Fenchel, Monderer, and Hartley 1951; Jakson 1962). Token women must also inhibit self-expression and self-disclosure, as the examples in this paper and the discussion below indicate; yet Jourard (1964) considers the ability to self-disclose a requisite for psychological well-being.

REFERENCES

Aries, Elizabeth (1973) "Interaction Patterns and Themes of Male, Female, and Mixed Groups." Ph.D. dissertation, Harvard University.

Asch, Solomon E. (1960) "Effects of Group Pressure upon the Modification and Distortion of Judgments." Pp. 189–200 in *Group Dynamics*, edited by Dorwin Cartwright and Alvin Zander, 2d ed. Evanston, Ill.: Row, Peterson.

Athanassiades, John C. (1974) "An Investigation of Some Communication Patterns of Female Subordinates in Hierarchical Organizations." *Human Relations* 27 (March): 195–209.

Coser, Rose Laub (1960) "Laughter among Colleagues: A Study of the Social Functions of Humor among the Staff of a Mental Hospital." *Psychiatry* 23 (February): 81–95.

Cussler, Margaret (1958) *The Woman Executive*. New York: Harcourt Brace.

Epstein, Cynthia Fuchs (1970) *Woman's Place: Options and Limits on Professional Careers*. Berkeley: University of California Press.

Fenchel, G. H., J. H. Monderer, and E. L. Hartley (1951) "Subjective Status and the Equilibrium Hypothesis." *Journal of Abnormal and Social Psychology* 46 (October): 476–79.

Ferber, Marianne Abeles, and Joan Althaus Huber (1975) "Sex of Student and Instructor: A Study of Student Bias." *American Journal of Sociology* 80 (January): 949–63.

Glazer, Nathan (1976) *Affirmative Discrimination*. New York: Basic.

Greenbaum, Marcia (1971) "Adding 'Kenntnis' to 'Kirche, Kuche, and Kinder.'" *Issues in Industrial Society* 2(2): 61–68.

Hennig, Margaret (1970) "Career Development for Women Executives." Ph.D. dissertation. Harvard University.

Howe, Irving, and B. J. Widick (1949) *The UAW and Walter Reuther*. New York: Random House.

Hughes, Everett C. (1944) "Dilemmas and Contradictions of Status." *American Journal of Sociology* 50 (March): 353–59.

——— (1946) "Race Relations in Industry." Pp. 107–22 in *Industry and Society*, edited by W. F. Whyte. New York: McGraw-Hill.

——— (1958) *Men and Their Work*. Glencoe, Ill.: Free Press.

Jackson, Elton F. (1962) "Status Inconsistency and Symptoms of Stress." *American Sociological Review* 27 (August): 469–80.

Jourard, Sidney M. (1964) *The Transparent Self: Self-Disclosure and Well-Being*. Princeton, N.J.: Van Nostrand.

Kanter, Rosabeth Moss (1972) *Commitment and Community*. Cambridge, Mass.: Harvard University Press.

——— (1975) "Women and the Structure of Organizations: Explorations in Theory and Behavior." Pp. 34–74 in *Another Voice: Feminist Perspectives on Social Life and Social Science*, edited by M. Millman and R. M. Kanter. New York: Doubleday Anchor.

——— (1976a) "The Impact of Hierarchical Structures on the Work Behavior of Women and Men." *Social Problems* 23 (April): 415–30.

——— (1976b) "Interpreting the Results of a Social Experiment." *Science* 192 (May 14): 662–63.

——— (1976c) "The Policy Issues: Presentation VI." *Signs: Journal of Women in Culture and Society* 1 (Spring, part 2): 282–91.

——— (1976d) "Women and Organizations: Sex Roles, Group Dynamics, and Change Strategies." In *Beyond Sex Roles*, edited by A. Sargent, St. Paul: West.

——— (1977) *Men and Women of the Corporation*. New York: Basic.

Laws, Judith Long (1975) "The Psychology of Tokenism: An Analysis." *Sex Roles* 1 (March): 51–67.

Lenski, Gerhard (1956) "Social Participation and the Crystallization of Status." *American Sociological Review* 21 (August): 458–64.

Levine, Adeline, and Janice Crumrine (1975) "Women and the Fear of Success: A Problem in Replication." *American Journal of Sociology* 80 (January): 964–74.

Lorber, Judith (1975) "Trust, Loyalty, and the Place of Women in the Informal Organization of Work." Paper presented at the annual meeting of the American Sociological Association, San Francisco.

Lynch, Edith M. (1973) *The Executive Suite: Feminine Style*. New York: AMACOM.

Megaree, Edwin I. (1969) "Influence of Sex Roles on the Manifestation of Leadership." *Journal of Applied Psychology* 53 (October): 377–82.

O'Farrell, Brigid (1973) "Affirmative Action and Skilled Craft Work." Xeroxed. Center for Research on Women, Wellesley College.

Rieff, Philip, ed. (1963) Freud: Sexuality and the Psychology of Love. New York: Collier.

Sarason, Seymour B. (1973) "Jewishness, Blackness, and the Nature-Nurture Controversy." American Psychologist 28 (November): 961–71.

Segal, Bernard E. (1962) "Male Nurses: A Case Study in Status Contradiction and Prestige Loss." Social Forces 41 (October): 31–38.

Seifert, Kelvin (1973) "Some Problems of Men in Child Care Center Work." Pp. 69–73 in Men and Masculinity, edited by Joseph H. Pleck and Jack Sawyer. Englewood Cliffs, N.J.: Prentice-Hall, 1974.

Simmel, Georg (1950) The Sociology of Georg Simmel. Translated by Kurt H. Wolff. Glencoe, Ill.: Free Press.

Strodtbeck, Fred L., Rita M. James, and Charles Hawkins (1957) "Social Status in Jury Deliberations." American Sociological Review 22 (December): 713–19.

Strodtbeck, Fred L., and Richard D. Mann (1956) "Sex Role Differentiation in Jury Deliberations." Sociometry 19 (March): 3–11.

Strong, Bryan (1973) "Toward a History of the Experiential Family: Sex and Incest in the Nineteenth Century Family." Journal of Marriage and the Family 35 (August): 457–66.

Taylor, Shelley E. (1975) "The Token in a Small Group." Xeroxed. Harvard University Department of Psychology.

Taylor, Shelley E., and Susan T. Fiske (1976) "The Token in the Small Group: Research Findings and Theoretical Implications." In Psychology and Politics: Collected Papers, edited by J. Sweeney. New Haven, Conn.: Yale University Press.

Tiger, Lionel (1969) Men in Groups. New York: Random House.

Tiger, Lionel, and Joseph Shepher (1975) Women in the Kibbutz. New York: Harcourt Brace Jovanovich.

U.S. Council of Economic Advisers (1973) Annual Report of the Council of Economic Advisers. Washington, D.C.: Government Printing Office.

Wolman, Carol, and Hal Frank (1975) "The Solo Woman in a Professional Peer Group." American Journal of Orthopsychiatry 45 (January): 164–71.

Zaleznick, Abraham, C. R. Christensen, and F. J. Roethlisberger (1958) The Motivation, Productivity, and Satisfaction of Workers: A Prediction Study. Boston: Harvard Business School Division of Research.

Chapter 17

Sexual Politics in the Workplace: The Interactional World of Policewomen

Susan E. Martin
American University

This paper examines the dynamics of male-female interaction in one work setting – the backstage region of a police department – and explores the variety of ways that policewomen are pressured to "stay in their place" by male coworkers. Policewomen face interpersonal dilemmas because as police officers they are expected to behave like colleagues (i.e. as status equals); as women they are expected to behave as status subordinates. This paper investigates a number of the techniques by which female officers' gender is made salient and male officers assert dominance over female officers. The verbal techniques employed include the use of euphemisms, affectionate terms of address, cursing, joking and putdowns, and gossip. Non-verbal messages are transmitted by the use of personal space, touch, and chivalrous ceremonies. In addition the problems posed by sexuality and sexual harassment in the workplace are discussed. Data are based on nine months of participant observation and 55 interviews with officers in one police district in Washington, D.C.

I n a discussion of "the sexual politics of interpersonal behavior," Henley and Freeman (1975:391) observed:

Social interaction is the battlefield where the daily war between the sexes is fought. It is here that women are constantly reminded where their "place" is and here that they are put back in their place, should they venture out. Thus social interaction is the most common means of social control employed against women. By being continually reminded of their inferior status by their interactions with others, and continually compelled to acknowledge that status in their own patterns of behavior, women learn to internalize society's definition of them as inferior so thoroughly that they are often unaware of what their status is. Inferiority becomes habitual.

Source: Susan E. Martin, "Sexual Politics in the Workplace: The Interactional World of Policewomen." *Symbolic Interaction* 1 (1978): 44-60. Reprinted by permission of JAI Press, Inc., Greenwich, Conn.

This paper examines the dynamics of such interaction in one setting: the back-stage regions of police work. It explores the microlevel dilemmas faced by policewomen which have wider ramifications for occupational performance among peers by scrutinizing how female officers are hindered in effective job performance by the "trivia" of interpersonal interaction with male supervisors and fellow officers.

Although some studies have examined women's problems in non-traditional occupations at the professional level (Cussler, 1958; Bernard, 1964; Rossi, 1965; Astin, 1969; Epstein, 1971; Perrucci, 1970; Theodore, 1971; Wolman and Frank, 1975), little attention has been paid to the growing number of women moving into non-traditional blue collar jobs (See Roby, 1975). Some of the problems of women in non-traditional work roles are shared across occupations; others are rooted in the particular work environment. By focusing on the interactional dilemmas of policewomen in relating to their coworkers, this paper will elucidate one facet of the work experience of a group of blue collar women.

The data come from a larger study of policewomen's problems in gaining acceptance as officers, and the coping strategies they adopt in meshing their sex role and occupational role on the job. This paper concentrates on one particular barrier, the sexual politics of interpersonal interaction. Kanter (1977a and 1977b) noted the importance of relative numbers, opportunity, and power in understanding organizational behavior of men and women. While some of the patterns to be described in this paper are related to those factors, other aspects of the policewomen's situation are rooted in cultural patterns of male-female interaction and power relations and thus are separate from the effect of relative power and numbers within the work organization alone. Because male-female relations where sex ratios are skewed exaggerate the cultural norms pertaining to such interaction, the stationhouse provides a fruitful locus for the examination of the way culturally prescribed (male-female) behavior affects situationally prescribed work relations and behavior.

THE FIELD STUDY

Although policewomen have served as sworn officers in the U.S. since 1910, until quite recently their numbers were insignificant and their roles sharply limited.[1] Only in the past few years has there been a significant increase in the number of female officers, some of whom now are being assigned to patrol duties.[2] To understand better the problems and coping strategies of this new group of women in a non-traditional occupation I undertook a study of patrol officers in a single patrol district in Washington, D.C., to which approximately thirty policewomen out of 400 officers were assigned. The research findings are based on both participant observation and interview data. I joined the Metropolitan Police Reserve Corps,[3] a volunteer citizens' organization, received limited training and a uniform barely distinguishable from that of a sworn officer, was assigned to a district of my choice, and was able to patrol with officers who did not have a partner for their tour of duty. I had access to many of the back-stage regions of the police station including the women's lockerroom and roll call. The department was informed of my research but neither sponsored nor assisted me. During nine months I worked all three shifts on all days of the week with ap-proximately fifty officers including eight women. During the last three months I interviewed twenty-eight policewomen, twenty-seven male officers, and fifteen officials from the observation district as well as a number of key informants in a variety of positions related to the department's policewomen program. The inter-view averaged one and a half to two hours in length (for further details see Mar-tin, 1977).

THEORETICAL ISSUES

Policewomen face interactional dilemmas because they are both police of-ficers, expected to behave according to the norms governing relations among peers, and women who are expected to adhere to the norms governing male-female interaction. The former norms call for symmetrical interaction among status equals, the latter for asymmetrical relations between superordinate (males) and subordinate (females) with the additional complications posed by sexuality.

While all individuals simultaneously hold several statuses, certain statuses tend to cluster and it is felt appropriate that they do so. Hughes (1944:355) observed that among work colleagues "expectations concerning appropriate aux-iliary characteristics . . . become . . . the basis of the colleague group's definition of its common interests, of its informal code, and of selection of those who will become the inner fraternity." The consequence for those who have a "wrong" auxiliary status is that their irrelevant characteristics, which have associated with them a set of assumptions about people of their type, become the focus of others' attention. Thus the irrelevant auxiliary status becomes the salient status in interaction and minority or token[4] individuals become a representative of their ascribed category to the majority group whether they choose to do so or not. In the case of women in non-traditional occupations, their "female" status is ac-tivated, interferes with their ability to work effectively, and poses interactional dilemmas.[5]

Kanter (1977a) observed that in such situations, due to the skewed ratios, tokens face a number of problems. These include increased performance pressures which arise from their greater visibility, boundary heightening and isolation as a result of the tendency to exaggerate the tokens' attributes in con-trast to those of the dominants, and entrapment in stereotypic roles arising from the frequent distortion of tokens' characteristics to fit preexisting generalizations about their category.

While they have the characteristic problems of tokens in an organization, policewomen also must cope with particular norms that put them at a disadvantage in male-female interaction. In examining interaction ritual, Goffman (1956) distinguished between the substantive and ceremonial orders. Ceremonial activities were defined as matters not significant in their own right, but a conventionalized means of communication by which people express their character or convey appreciation of the other participants in the situation through displays of deference and demeanor.[6] He noted that in certain instances the ceremonial component of activity had substantive value.[7] In fact, that the ceremonial level of male-female interaction is guided by asymmetrical rules of conduct[8] has great substantive significance for the interaction between male and female police officers because the rules governing interactions among work peers are different from those guiding male-female interaction. As a result, male officers frequently engage in interaction rituals and ceremonies calculated to convey male dominance and sexualize the work environment to keep interaction on a(n) (asymmetrical) male-female level with negative consequences for the female officers' occupational self-image and behavior. The male officers enforce the "handicap rule"[9] (Spradley and Mann, 1975) which dictates that in such interaction females must play with an arbitrarily imposed handicap which affects occupational role performance.

Many of the dilemmas men and women experience in working together revolve around their sexuality (i.e. how each sees herself or himself as a sexual being and responds to the sexuality of a coworker of the other sex) because "being influenced and responding either consciously or unconsciously to the sexuality of the other is the primary way men and women have learned to relate to each other" (Bradford *et al.* 1975:46). Even when sexual attraction is not involved, the expectation of a male, as a man, that he will "protect" a woman gets carried into the workplace. The result is a set of reciprocal roles that are particularly dysfunctional for policewomen's occupational role performance.

A variety of cues in social interaction maintain women's handicap, sexualize the workplace, and assure their subordinate status. These include verbal cues conveyed by the use of language, terms of address, swearing and joking behavior, and gossip. Non-verbal techniques of control include touch, eye contact, "door ceremonies," and other rituals. In addition, messages are transmitted by general environmental indicators of place and status. The remainder of this paper examines the way these cues are activated, affect the behavior of police officers, and hinder the job performance of policewomen.

ENVIRONMENTAL CUES

"Environmental cues set the stage on which the power relationships of the sexes are acted out and the assigned status of each sex is reinforced" (Henley and Freeman, 1975:392). Territorial arrangements reflect the basic definitions of gender roles. There are male places and female places. When women enter "male turf" they find they attract attention and are regarded either as deviant or having a special (i.e. service or sexual) function. While the streets are common territory by day, at night they "belong" to men and policewomen are reminded that they are "out of place" by the near absence of women at certain hours. Police are expected to make "business checks" into many "male" establishments such as bars, barber shops, and pool halls. When a policewoman enters, the attention she attracts may cause her great discomfort. She must learn how to act in places with which many men are familiar and how to direct attention away from her sex to function as an officer.

Police stations are male sanctuaries. Several stations do not have adequate lockerroom or lavatory facilities for women and even in the newer stations with women's lockerrooms that include shower facilities, such rooms are significantly smaller than the male facilities. This reflects not only the current low numbers of policewomen but departmental expectations of limited future recruitment.

VERBAL CUES

Language and Women

The terms of address and language employed to describe people are important in conveying messages regarding their status and the behavior others expect of them. Lakoff (1975) observed that when a word is associated with something embarrassing or unpleasant, people substitute euphemisms for it to avoid their discomfort. "Woman" is such a word and is frequently replaced by "lady," "broad," "girl," and "bitch," each of which by connotation denies equality or full humanity to women. Associated with these terms are stereotypic roles into which women are cast and counterroles assumed by men.

A "lady" is expected to be dainty, demure and proper in language, manners and sexual behavior. Put on a pedestal (i.e. sexually unavailable and also removed from "the action"), a lady is given deference and displays of respect. She is permitted to exercise moral power in return for which she abdicates responsibility for herself and control of her destiny. She is dominated and protected by men who expect little of her.

"Broads" are sexual objects, since the term removes the connotation of the affective aspect of male-female relations, thus making the user less uncomfortable with the dehumanizing aspects of the relationship with such a woman. Broads, too, are denied full control of their life and fate, since they cannot be treated as peers or equals. They are pursued sexually but subject to scorn and abuse when they attempt to be taken seriously.

"Girl" removes the sexual connotation in woman by stressing the idea of youth but implies frivolity and irresponsibility. A girl is teased affectionately, not taken very seriously, and given little power, since one can hardly expect a "girl" to do a woman's job. The women who do not fit into these categories get labeled "lesbian" or "bitch," particularly when they are unresponsive to sexual invitations. Upset at their inability to control these women, the men assume there is something wrong – with the women – and express this through the labels they apply to them.

The policemen's use of language reminds the women how they are perceived by peers and supervisors, indicates that female officers are offered a limited range of role behavior which denies a central aspect of themselves, and keeps them subordinate to the men. One male spoke of supervising women in this manner:

> Treat them differently? Nope, I put them *broads* in the worst assignments. I put them anywhere I put a *man* . . . As far as the street is concerned, there isn't a *woman* in thirty who is worth her salt as a street *policeman,* er . . . *woman* . . . . I have one in my squad and I have no problems with that *girl.* I come in contact with the other *gals* only occasionally.

Another sergeant said:

> I give the *girls* in this district credit. Those *girls* earn their pay . . . although they're not doing the job a *man* would do. Ask the *men,* deep down they're looking out for the *girls* . . . . There's one *woman* we've come down hard on (by strong discipline). She's been *woman* enough to take her lumps.

The latter official makes clear the distinction in his expectations of a "woman" and a "girl." The former found it virtually impossible to speak about policewomen in any but euphemistic terms.

The terms by which an individual is addressed indicate status. A superior can first name the status inferior in situations where the latter must use the superior's title and last name. Superiors may initiate or increase intimacy in the relationship, giving them greater control. Policemen sometimes keep policewomen "in their place" with the use of terms of endearment or first names. One policewoman remarked that she had quickly acquired a reputation as "stuck up" because when one officer said to her, "Hey, baby, how ya doing?" she replied,

> "Are you talking to me?" He replied, "Yeah" and I said, "You don't know me that well. When I tell you my name is 'baby' and ask you to address me that way, o.k. Until then my name is Officer –."

I observed that policemen that I had never met addressed me as "sweetheart" and "dear." By the end of one tour of duty one officer was calling me "hon" and others called me "Suzie" although I had introduced myself as Susan.

In a heterosexual work environment among peers, both men and women face "the language dilemma." Men among males are permitted to express the full range of feelings through cursing, an art highly refined among policemen. They tell raunchy stories and tales of sexual prowess which strengthen the bonds of male solidarity. Such language is considered inappropriate for female ears. The presence of women thus disrupts group solidarity and leads the men either to resentfully act like "gentlemen," inhibiting their expressiveness, or to curse loud-ly and make pointedly sexual remarks which make clear to the women that they are uninvited "guests" in the men's world who must tolerate the men's behavior. The women face problems dealing with the men's language as well as their own. When women curse like men, many of the latter are offended and withdraw the deference they give to "ladies." Other women avoid cursing. This often results in the woman making less forceful statements which are taken less seriously and in the need for an alternative outlet for strong feelings. Some women turn these feelings in on themselves; others express them in a traditionally feminine manner by crying, which reduces them to the implicit status of an impotent child. Several female officers reported that they had left the room when the men per-sisted in cursing despite their requests that they stop. Others take a more tolerant approach. One woman said:

> I let them talk gross; it shows their immaturity but I stop it before it gets to the point of upsetting me . . . . They're like schoolboys who try to dip the girls' braids in the inkwell to get a reaction.

Joking and Verbal Putdowns

In structured relationships where there is tension the conflict may be par-tially resolved by an institutionalized behavior known as a joking relationship in which one person by custom is permitted (and in some instances required) to tease or make fun of the other who, in turn, must take no offense. It is a relation-ship of "permitted disrespect" (Radcliffe-Brown, 1965:90-1) which is restricted to certain participants in limited settings, involves ritual insults and sexual topics, and is a public encounter. It is asymmetrical in that men are permitted to joke about a woman's anatomical features which have sexual connotations but women do not conversely joke about men since it would be seen as "crude."

Such joking can frequently be observed among police officers. A male and female officer who do not generally work together had been assigned together for a tour of duty. Throughout the tour the male told his partner to walk three paces behind him. He told the lieutenant about the "joke" as well.

One policewoman told of her anguish when as a trainee she and several other students were assigned to protect a visiting foreign dignitary's hotel. A sergeant, in front of the other trainees, said to her, "Come on, I have a room. I want a header." She was shocked, less at the proposition than that it was made in front of others and was calculated to humiliate her. She added, "He was just pulling my leg and not at all serious but no matter what I said I looked worse and worse!"

One female officer reported that at check off (signing out) several officials looked at her chestline and remarked, "How long do you think she can float?" as others stood chuckling. She noted:

> I know this is sexism and I try to put them in their place but if I get snippy they'll get me for insubordination.

Other women are less concerned with reprisals. One woman was greeted as a newcomer to the district by the comment,

> Officer, I don't mean any harm but I just want you to know that you have the biggest breasts I've ever seen on a policewoman.

She reports that she replied:

> Officer, I don't mean any harm but I just want you to know that you don't comment on my anatomy in any shape, form, or manner unless I comment on yours . . . . When you see me coming just act like you don't see anything. Don't speak to me and I won't speak to you.

The result was that he was humiliated in front of his peers and she acquired a reputation for being "stuck up, snotty and evil; even being a lesbian." But, she added, "I preferred it that way. Then they'd leave me alone."

In roll call and in the scout car policewomen are reminded that they are viewed as females and should stay in their place. In roll call one day the captain read a letter from a female citizen who complained about police service, then invited officers to drop by any time after 6 p.m. The captain added, "I won't make any further comments since there are ladies present" amid the snickers of the men. At another roll call, following an airing of officers' gripes about supporting services including helicopters and dispatchers one male piped up, "That female dispatcher is not designed for what she's being used for either."

Two women work together infrequently. In one roll call my request to work with a particular female officer led to the sergeant's comment, "Put two females together? I can't allow that . . . no way." He quickly added that he was joking but it occurred at the expense of the women.

Although these are three seemingly minor incidents, if one were to substitute black or Negro for female or lady the tone of disparagement becomes clear. Such racial expressions would not be tolerated; sexist remarks, however, still produce laughter and serve as a public form of embarrassment to the women.

Even on duty in scout cars women are subjected to reminders of their female status and to sexual invitation. When I banged my knee on the edge of the car radio, resulting in a large bruise, and reacted with an "ouch," my partner replied, "What did you do, dear, break a fingernail?" In another instance, my partner and I had hiked down and up a steep hill in pursuit of a pursesnatcher or the aban-doned purse. When I observed that the man, who smoked heavily, was panting and "out of shape" he replied, "Too bad I can't see your shape with that raincoat on."

Gossip

Another form of verbal interaction that affects policewomen's behavior is gossip. In all work settings workers gossip about each other, the supervisors, and the work. This has several functions. It is a key mechanism of group control over the behavior of members, provides feedback on performance, limits competition, is a source of vital information about work related matters, and is a medium of exchange among the workers. Gossip makes the police work environment closely resemble a fishbowl. The struggle to be "in the know" and maintain one's privacy affects all officers but poses particular problems for policewomen because they are excluded from much of the information exchange and, at the same time, are a primary subject of the gossip.

Workers' gossip controls other workers' behavior, thereby reducing produc-tion pressures and unpredictability. When work is a matter of life and death, as it is for the patrol officer, the need to know if one can rely on a colleague is in-tense and the grapevine becomes an important social institution of worker con-trol. An important norm among police is that one officer does not complain about or "squeal" on another officer to an official. When a partner fails to provide ade-quate back-up it is generally dealt with through whispers among the officers or by direct confrontation. When two men have a disagreement or one is highly critical of the other's performance they have a "man to man" talk or even, on rare occasions, physically fight. When the men have complaints about a woman they whisper among themselves or complain to a sergeant, who is left to handle the problem without revealing names, rather than directly confronting her as they might if she were male. Thus the policewomen are deprived of an important source of feedback which, particularly for a new officer, serves as a form of infor-mal socialization.

Police officers are in fierce competition for the system's limited rewards but this competition must be tempered due to the need for teamwork. Gossip serves to sanction those who would compete "unfairly" and thereby gain control over their behavior by ostracism and ridicule. The men fear that women will gain ex-emptions and favorable assignments by taking "unfair advantage" of their sex (i.e. using something that men cannot use to gain favor, thus changing the rules of competition). They also are afraid of being outdone by a woman who plays by the rules. The ambitious woman and those who gain good assignments are sub-ject to much gossip and pressure. One policewoman was asked by a former academy classmate, "Who'd you sleep with to get Sunday and Monday off?"

Several others noted defensively that despite what "they" may say, they had *earned* their high ratings and/or good assignments. A number of the women are probably deterred in their mobility aspirations by fear of rumor and reprisals for competing strenuously with the men.

Often the few openings in desirable units are not well publicized. The grapevine is an important source of information, enabling an officer to be "in the right place at the right time." To gain access to valuable data, however, an officer must be tied into the gossip exchange network through friendships and alliances and be willing to play by the rules. Information may be traded for favors between patrol officers and others in strategic positions. "Insiders" with ties to those with information are better able to exchange gossip with others. Thus close ties to powerful individuals are vital in gaining information and assignments. While these ties may develop merely through working together, they are generally cultivated through informal socializing. One policeman caught the eye of the district inspector when they both participated in the intradistrict softball league. Another was told that to gain a promotion he should get into the habit of coming into the station well before roll call, "hanging around," chatting with the officials, and making himself visible. Women are excluded from playing on the men's teams and often are self-conscious about "hanging around" because their presence may be misinterpreted. One woman noted that while men often seek to be friendly with officials:

> I don't talk to them. I don't know what to say and don't want them to know my personal business. If . . . I'm friendly, being female, they'll approach me for a date, taking what I do or say the wrong way . . . . To avoid any problems I just don't act too friendly with them and take my chances about assignments.

Thus, excluded from access to "inside" information and lacking personal ties to influential members of the department, women remain outsiders in the informal exchange network.

The police have the time and hospitable settings which facilitate gossip. In court and the scout car, like housewives "with nothing to do but gossip," they pass the time talking. Twice daily, workers in one section meet in the lockerroom away from the public, officials and members of the other sex. The women's lockerroom is quiet and relatively empty with only two to seven occupants at any time. The men's lockerroom buzzes with tales of exploits, gripes about officials, and gossip about officers whose work or interpersonal behavior does not conform with group norms. Women miss out on this informal social interaction which is an important source of both socialization and sociability.

The policewomen who enter the police social system are both excluded from much of the talk and subject of much discussion since they are highly visible outsiders, feared competitors and desired sexual objects. They cannot act freely as

the men since they are concerned with how their words or acts will be inter-
preted. Many avoid interactions with officials that might be viewed as having
sexual connotations and so fail to build close interpersonal ties or gain sponsors.
The threat of gossip and the discomfort of being a woman among a group of
men also inhibits women's informal socializing off duty with fellow officers.
While many of the men go drinking together after work, women seldom go along.
Usually they are not invited because the men feel inhibited by their presence.
Some said they declined invitations due to domestic responsibilities or fear of
rumor. Contributing to the separation of the sexes are working class attitudes
regarding sexuality and human nature found among officers. A former
policewoman from middle class origins observed:

> One thing that made me uncomfortable in police work is that the average policeman
> doesn't have very many categories to put women into. You're either having an affair
> with someone or you've no relationship whatsoever. I found it very difficult just to
> develop friendships with the men I worked with. . . . (Going out for a drink after
> work) was awkward with the guys I worked with because most policemen don't have
> friends who are women.

By their voluntary withdrawal the women miss out on an important source of information and feedback, and on the opportunity to make contacts, cultivate
sponsors, and build alliances necessary for occupational success. Their limited interaction with coworkers is interpreted by the men as a sign of the women's
disinterest, lack of dedication to the job, and inappropriateness as patrol officers.
Most policewomen do not feel that there are more "goings on" in the police
department than other work organizations; it is just that their coworkers talk
more and focus on the women. This appears to be related both to high visibility
of the few "token" women and to the nature of the work and work organization.

NON-VERBAL MESSAGES

Non-verbal cues of dominance and deference include the use of personal
space and such simple interactions as "door ceremonies." The higher the status,
the greater the personal space permitted to the person. Willis (1966) found that
in conversational settings the personal space of women is more likely to be
breached than that of men. One such breach is touching, which implies privileged access to another person. Higher status people are more likely to touch
subordinates, since the reverse is considered presumptuous.
Henley (1970) observed that men interpreted a touch by a woman as conveying sexual intent. Because a touch is an indication of either power or intimacy, and women are status inferiors who are not supposed to have power

over men, it was inconceivable for woman to be exerting power. If their behavior could not be given a sexual interpretation, it was assumed that the woman was deviant (i.e. unfeminine and castrating).

In police work a touch is an important line of demarcation and an indication of superior-subordinate status vis-a-vis citizens. While police today are expected to tolerate verbal insult, a touch, taken to mean an assertion of another's power, is not tolerated and frequently results in criminal charges.[10]

Policewomen are kept in place by the men's breaches of their person. A female officer in a new assignment for less than a week responded angrily when one of her sergeants put his arm around her, saying, "If you want to put your hands on me, put me under arrest; otherwise, keep your hands off." He interpreted her response as racially motivated.

Conversely, a policewoman reported being told by a sergeant that he thought she was "fresh" because she touches people. She insisted that she was simply friendly and had no sexual intent, but her behavior was not correctly interpreted by her male superior.

While working to complete a complicated arrest form, a policewoman sat typing in the station. There were other officers and her prisoner present when a male officer swept in and gave her a playful kiss on the back of the neck. His behavior was a reminder not only to her but to the man she had arrested that even though she had police powers which she had just exercised, she was still treated as a woman. Further undermining her authority, the prisoner addressed her by her first name (which I had made the mistake of using in his presence) rather than Officer−. His breach went uncorrected.

In another instance a policewoman called for back up. Several cars arrived and broke up an impending group fight. The woman was angered by the men's handling of the incident and at the end of the tour of duty, outside the station, discussed the incident with several of the men. While they were talking, another policeman started playfully nipping at her ear. His message was clear: I don't want to hear what you have to say about work. I will treat you as a woman to be played with instead.

Off duty, the boundaries of male-female relationships are also problematic. One policewoman who had struggled for acceptance noted that she had become a regular member of the group from her squad that went out for beer after work. One evening sitting with the others in the park where they usually went, one officer put his arm around her. Although the men immediately told him to "stop acting like an ass" and leave her alone, the damage was done. She dejectedly reported:

> We were all buddies but I happen to be a girl and have to pay the price of having people make passes at me.

It was probably more a friendly gesture than a pass but it singled her out as "different," since the men would not have done the same thing with a male officer.

Thus, men's attempts to assert power over women by touch undermine the women's attempts to gain equal status as a peer. Through non-verbal cues women are reminded that they are both sex objects and subordinates who must accept the limitations imposed by the handicap rule. Similarly, chivalrous ceremonies and rituals remind women of their subordinate status. One policewoman remarked that when she lit her partner's cigarette while he was driving the scout car, he got upset and insisted that it took away from her femininity. "He wants to treat me like a lady, but I'm not," the woman exclaimed. If she is not permitted to light his cigarette, how much of the police work is she permitted to do?

SEXUALITY AND SEXUAL HARASSMENT

Sexuality[11] and sexual harassment pose problems for policewomen. These issues have rarely been discussed in the literature on occupations (see Roy, 1974; Kanter, 1974; Bradford, et al. 1975; and Reimer, 1976). In interaction on the job, policemen cast female officers into several stereotypic roles which closely reflect their linguistic categories for dealing with women (Kanter, 1974) and place themselves in parallel counter-roles (Bradford, et al., 1975), all of which have a "semi-sexual basis," limit participants' behavioral options, and are particularly harmful for policewomen's occupational role performance. These role pairs include the seductress and the macho, the helpless maiden and the chivalrous knight, the pet and protective father, and the nurturant mother and the tough warrior. Women are pressed to choose among the sexually available seductress ("broad") and the sexually inactive maiden, mother ("lady") and pet ("girl") or be labeled an "iron maiden" (lesbian, bitch or deviant) for their failure to flirt, foster the men's sense of masculinity, or acknowledge men's superiority. The seductress, mother, maiden, and pet are not expected to fulfill occupational role norms and often are encouraged not to do so by the men who "protect" them on the job. The men's sense of protectiveness makes the men's work more difficult but affirms their sense of masculinity. It puts the women in a bind because they are criticized for failing to carry their share of the work load at the same time that they are pressured not to develop occupational skills and may be prevented from doing so. Both men and women are trapped in these reciprocal roles which severely limit the women's ability to function effectively as police officers. Several women who noted that they were struggling to move beyond stereotypic or traditional female behavior said they sometimes found themselves unconsciously reverting to interaction patterns established in their childhood out of habit.

Sexual propositions and harassment also present difficulties for female officers. Harassment, as distinguished from a proposition, occurs when a man in a position to control, hamper or affect the job or career of a woman who refuses his offer, uses his authority or power to coerce the woman into sexual relations or punishes her rejection. For policewomen, handling sexual approaches is particularly problematic because of the openness and persistence of the men, the need for a sponsor and the good will of others in doing the work, and the social attitudes of the predominantly working class officers.

A new policewoman faces a particularly difficult situation:

> They all tried to hit on us when we arrived, to see who could be the first to get one of us. When we had the — detail (and had to remain at a fixed post), they'd line up their cars trying to get our phone numbers.

This was upsetting because she was painfully conspicuous and because many of the men were married. She observed that some of the policewomen did date the men but they got a "reputation"; those that refused invitations had to find a way of saying "no" firmly without being insulting. In a number of instances it required unladylike bluntness and/or threats of public exposure, tape recordings or telephone calls to wives to make clear their unavailability. Bluntness and coldness, however, make many women uncomfortable. They had to unlearn the lessons of childhood when they found that a tactful refusal was ignored or taken as a sign of encouragement. One single woman pointedly talked endlessly about her boyfriend; another began wearing a wedding ring. A third woman said:

> If I'm unfriendly I get labeled a snob . . . which you can't be. If I'm friendly some of them think "she's looking at me." If I act as I generally am (warm and friendly) there are some who figure "she's an easy catch." What you have to do is catch it on the first remark and let them know where you stand. If you laugh it off, it doesn't do any good. . . . They take it as encouragement.

One officer, comparing her situation with that of two female friends who experience little sexual teasing in their middle class jobs lamented, "No matter how well they know you, they think the only thing a woman's good for is to have relations with men."

The power of the officials to punish makes the women's situation difficult. A new woman can be assigned to a scout car with a friendly partner or to a footbeat with one who will teach her nothing; she can be protected from minor disciplinary action or face full enforcement of the rules. When there is no relationship she can be embarrassed by the appearance of one. A woman noted that one sergeant rode in on all of her assignments and frequently called for her location, singling her out for unwanted attention. Several other incidents illustrate the power of the official to put sexual pressure on the women. Two former high school classmates, a male and a female, found that they were in the same class at the police academy. They were talking before class when a sergeant sought to gain the attention of the woman who ignored him. Within fifteen minutes both the officers had dereliction notices in their personnel jackets. Although they were destroyed at the end of the training period, it was a quick demonstration of the power of the sergeant who made clear the priority of his "hunting rights."

Another female officer complained that when she went into a special unit and the officers were able to choose partners, she was told that she could not work with a particular unmarried male. Her sergeant assigned her instead to work with a different man because he said he wanted to minimize her chances of becoming pregnant!

A policeman found that when he was assigned to work with a particular policewoman who had been in his class at the academy, one sergeant was frequently "on his back." The sergeant, who was sexually interested in the female officer, thought the officer was dating her. The officer requested not to work with the female since he "could feel a dereliction coming." Thus it was the woman who paid the price in isolation from others by being unavailable to the sergeant.

A factor that adds to the burden of the women is the strong feeling among both male and female officers that the woman who gets sexually harassed "asked for it" and thus is responsible for what occurs. According to many policewomen, "It all depends on how a woman carries herself." While it may be true that some women act seductively and then turn around and shout "foul play," such a view puts all of the responsibility for interaction on the women. One policewoman, upset at the behavior of several female officers, said:

> If a person cannot deal with their own sexuality, they have no business having a gun, arresting people or making serious decisions about other people.

She did not apply this standard, however, to the men. Her anger and that of many policewomen was directed at the women who are available and/or those who complain of harassment rather than at the men or at the sex role ideology that keeps both men and women in stereotypic roles and women in subordinate yet "responsible" positions.

IMPLICATIONS AND CONCLUSIONS

The compounding of the handicap of status inferiority as a female and the problems resulting from token status lead to a difficult interactional environment for policewomen. Although officially they are expected to fulfill the substantive role obligations of an officer and adhere to the ceremonial norms of interaction among peers, as women they are subject to pressures to "stay in their place" by a variety of verbal and non-verbal cues. The terms by which they are addressed and/or described, the "language dilemma," the joking relationship, gossip, touch and door ceremonies, sex role stereotyping, and sexual harassment all remind policewomen that they are not "just another officer." Highly visible and much talked about, they are excluded from the information exchange network and the informal social life which is so important in the competition among officers for better assignments and high efficiency ratings. Their occupational role behavior is circumscribed by the sex stereotyped roles into which they are cast. Adding to the discomforts in the work environment is the sexual atmosphere of the police station, which reminds women that as females they are sex objects, vulnerable to harassment yet held responsible for the outcome of the interaction.

This study suggests the need for further examination of sexuality and heterosexual interaction in the workplace and their implications for workers' behavior. A variety of work settings that differ with respect to the nature of the work tasks, the structure of the work organization, the relative numbers and power of male and female workers, and the social class origins of the participants ought to be explored to pinpoint the effects of these factors alone and in combination on work behavior.

Since the policewomen's presence in only token numbers exacerbates the interactional problems by heightening the visibility of their salient status, an increase in the representation of women in policing would diminish some of their interactional dilemmas. It would not, however, eliminate them. Many interactional rituals, although part of the ceremonial order, have an impact on substantive behavior in the workplace. These rituals are rooted in the cultural patterns of male-female *power* relations and reflect the substantive disparities in power. Thus a change in the cultural values and social order on which the interactional ceremonies rest must occur as well before female officers can be free to enact their occupational role as individuals and function as peers of their male coworkers. In the words of one policewoman, "We need to learn to treat people like people instead of treating women like women or like men."

NOTES

1. For many years policewomen constituted about 1 percent of all sworn police personnel. They faced higher educational requirements than male officers, height and weight standards that limited 90 percent of all women from eligibility, quotas, restrictions on promotion, and an absolute prohibition from patrol. As officers their work was an extension of women's traditional domestic and service roles. They served as "preventive-protection officers" assigned to work with women and children and as clerical workers. Many urban departments assigned female officers to separate Women's Bureaus within the department.

2. The 1960 Census reported 5617 publicly employed policewomen comprising about 2 per cent of the total of publicly employed police and detectives. By 1970 the number of female officers had doubled but their representation among police remained the same. Since 1972 and the passage of the 1972 Amendments to the 1964 Civil Rights Act the number of policewomen has increased. In 1975 policewomen made up just over 2 per cent of all sworn city police personnel; 4 percent of suburban agencies' officers; and 8.1 per cent of sheriffs' department's sworn personnel (Uniform Crime Reports – 1975).

The assignments of female officers also underwent change. The first city department to use a substantial number of female officers on patrol was Washington, D.C. In late 1971, 25 women were assigned to patrol division and in 1972 approximately 100 new female officers were hired for patrol assignments. By late 1975 there were 330 policewomen out of a department of about 4600 officers. Women thus comprised 7 per cent of the department's sworn personnel. Two hundred of these women were assigned to the patrol division. Other departments have been more reluctant to assign women to patrol. Horne (1974) estimated that there were about 1000 women on patrol in 1974 throughout the U.S. This number has surely increased in the intervening years although no statistics for women's current assignments are available.

3. The Metropolitan Police Reserve Corps of Washington, D.C. was founded twenty-five years ago to guard fireboxes on Halloween. Currently, the approximately 400 police officers assist sworn police with crowd control and traffic direction at special events such as parades and football games, sponsor a number of crime prevention and public education programs, and work alongside sworn police officers on patrol in each of the city's seven police districts.

4. Kanter (1977a:968) uses the term "token" for minority members who not only dif- fer from other group members along any single dimension but also are "people identified by ascribed characteristics (master statuses such as sex, race, religion, ethnic group, age, etc.) or other characteristics that carry with them a set of assumptions about culture, status, and behavior highly salient for majority category members." They do not differ from others in their ability to do the work or in acceptance of work norms but in terms of the informal assumptions others make about them. The significance of their auxiliary traits is increased if majority members have a history of interacting with members of token's category in ways different from the requirements of interaction in the current work situation.

5. Hughes (1944) illustrated the dilemma with the case of the woman engineer who, after designing a new plane wing, was expected to go on its maiden flight and give a (stag) dinner for co-workers. She was urged by fellow workers not to go (i.e. act like a lady rather than as an engineer). She chose to take the flight and give the party like an engineer. After the food and one round of drinks she left the party like a lady.

6. Goffman (1956:56 and 67) distinguished between deference and demeanor as follows: deference is "that component of activity which functions as a symbolic means by which appreciation is regularly conveyed to a recipient of this recipient, or of something of which this recipient it taken as a symbol, extension or agent." Demeanor refers to "that element of the individual's ceremonial behavior typically conveyed through deportment, dress, and bearing, which serves to express to those in his immediate presence that he is a person of certain desirable or undesirable qualities."

7. Goffman (1956:54) cites as an instance in which the symbolic value of a ceremonial act has substantive value the phenomenon of gallantry, as when a man permits a lady to precede him into a lifeboat or faces actual danger rather than permitting her to do so. Such a situation can frequently arise in police work.

8. In examining rules of conduct Goffman (1956:52-53) distinguished two classes: symmetrical and asymmetrical. The former "leads an individual to have obligations or ex- pectations regarding others that these others have in regard to him." An asymmetrical rule is "one that leads others to treat and be treated by an individual differently from the way he treats and is treated by them."

9. Normally games are played according to rules which have equal application to all players. If they decide to substitute a handicap (i.e. a rule that places some players at a

SEXUAL POLITICS IN THE WORKPLACE

disadvantage), it is usually determined by the nature of the game and the players' ability rather than some arbitrary criterion. In most games the handicap is explicit; hidden advantages are considered cheating. In male-female interaction, however, females are required to play with an arbitrarily imposed handicap. Spradley and Mann (1975:37) note that "it is as if all the players in the game made a tacit agreement that women must play by different rules than men. Even a suggestion to make these rules the same arouses male anger."

10. Technically it constitutes assault on a police officer. Since that charge is difficult to prosecute, officers generally charge disorderly conduct unless they are seriously injured.

11. Bradford, et al., (1975) distinguished four aspects of sexuality in the workplace: sexual messages underlying male-female interactions; the way men measure their masculinity and women measure their femininity and the relation of these self images to work success; the likelihood that the introduction of women into a male work environment will disrupt male ways of interrelating; and the matter of mutual attraction leading to sexual intercourse.

REFERENCES

Astin, Helen   1969   The Woman Doctorate in America. New York: Russell Sage.

Bernard, Jessie   1964   Academic Women. University Park: Pennsylvania State Press.

Bradford, David L., Alice Sargent and Melinda Sprague   1975   "The executive man and woman: The issue of sexuality." Pp. 39–58 in Francine E. Gordon and Myra H. Strober (eds.), Bringing Women into Management. New York: McGraw-Hill.

Cussler, Margaret   1958   The Woman Executive. New York: Harcourt Brace.

Epstein, Cynthia F.   1971   Woman's Place: Options and Limits in Professional Careers. Berkeley: University of California Press.

Goffman, Erving   1956   "The nature of deference and demeanor" American Anthropologist 58:473–502. Reprinted in E. Goffman, Interaction Ritual. New York: Anchor, 1967, pp. 47–95.

Henley, Nancy   1970   "The politics of touch." Paper presented at American Psychological Association. Reprinted in P. Brown (ed.) Radical Psychology. New York: Harper and Row, 1973.

Henley, Nancy and Jo Freeman   1975   "The sexual politics of interpersonal behavior." Pp. 391–401 in Jo Freeman (ed.) Women: A Feminist Perspective. Palo Alto, Calif.: Mayfield.

Horne, Peter   1974   Women in Law Enforcement. Springfield, Ill.: Charles Thomas.

Hughes, Everett C.   1944   "Dilemmas and contradictions of status." American Journal of Sociology 50:353–59.

Kanter, Rosabeth Moss   1974   "Women in organizations: Change agent skills." Paper presented at the National Training Laboratory Conference on New Technology in Organizational Development. Printed in Conference Proceedings.

1977a   "Skewed sex ratios and responses to token women." American Journal of Sociology, 82:965–90.

1977b   Men and Women of the Corporation. New York: Basic Books.

Lakoff, Robin   1975   Language and Women's Place. New York: Harper Colophon Books.

Martin, Susan E. 1977 "Breaking and Entering": Policewomen in the Police World. Unpublished Doctoral Dissertation, American University, Washington, D.C.

Perrucci, Carolyn C. 1970 "Minority status and the pursuit of professional careers: Women in science and engineering." Social Forces 49:245–58.

Radcliffe-Brown, A.R. 1965 Structure and Function in Primitive Society. New York: The Free Press.

Reimer, Jeffrey W. 1976 "'Deviance' as fun–a case of building construction workers at work." Paper presented at 71st Annual Meeting of American Sociological Association.

Roby, Pamela 1975 "Sociology and women in working class jobs," Millman, M. and R.M. Kanter, Another Voice. New York: Anchor.

Rossi, Alice 1965 "Barriers to the career choices of engineering, medicine or science among American women." Pp. 51–127 in Macquelyn Mattfield and Carol Van Aken (eds.) Women and the Scientific Professions. Cambridge: MIT Press.

Roy, Donald 1974 "Sex in the factory: Informal heterosexual relations between supervisors and work groups." Pp. 44–66 in Clifton Bryant (ed.), Deviant Behavior. Chicago: Rand McNally.

Spradley, James P. and Brenda J. Mann 1975 The Cocktail Waitress: Women's Work in a Man's World. New York: Wiley.

Theodore, Athana (ed.) 1971 The Professional Woman. Cambridge, Mass.: Schenkman.

1976 Uniform Crime Reports–1975. Washington, D.C.: Federal Bureau of Investigation.

Willis, F.N. Jr. 1966 "Initial speaking distance as a function of speakers' relationship." Psychonomic Science 5:221–22.

Wolman, Carol and Hal Frank 1975 "The solo woman in a professional peer group." American Journal of Orthopsychiatry 45:164–71.

Chapter 18 ———————————————————————————

Race, Sex, and Class: Black Female Tobacco Workers in Durham, North Carolina, 1920-1940, and the Development of Female Consciousness

Beverly W. Jones

T his article examines how race, sex, and class affected the lives and
consciousness of black female tobacco workers in Durham, North
Carolina, and how they conceptualized work and its meaning in their lives. The
research was based on fifteen interviews. The interviewees fall into three broad
age categories: five were born before 1908, seven between 1908 and 1916, and
three between 1916 and 1930. All were born in the rural South. The majority
migrated to Durham in the 1920s, subsequently entering the labor force.

Historically, black labor of both females and males has been critical to the
tobacco manufacturing industry. As cigarette manufacture became mechanized,
blacks were hired as stemmers, sorters, hangers, and pullers. These "dirty" jobs
were seen as an extension of field labor and therefore as "Negro work" for which
whites would not compete.[1] The rapidly expanding number of tobacco factories
employed the thousands of black females and males migrating from the rural
South. The pull of better paying jobs and the push of falling farm prices, peren-
nial pests, and hazardous weather induced a substantial number of black
sharecroppers, renters, and landowners to seek refuge in Durham.

Charlie Necoda Mack, the father of three future female tobacco workers,
remembered the difficulties of making an adequate living out of farming in Manning, South Carolina. "I was a big cotton farmer; I made nine bales of cotton one
year. Next year I made, I think one or two, and the next year I didn't make none.
I left in July, I had to leave. I borrowed money to get up here – Durham. I had six
children and I know no jobs available. Well, then I came up here in July in 1922
and got a job at the factory. And by Christmas I had all my children with clothes

Source: Beverly W. Jones, "Race, Sex, and Class: Black Female Tobacco Workers in Durham,
North Carolina, 1920-1940, and the Development of Female Consciousness." This article is
reprinted from FEMINIST STUDIES, Volume 10, No. 3 (1984):441–451, by permission of the
publisher FEMINIST STUDIES, INC., c/o Women's Studies Program, University of Maryland,
College Park, MD 20742.

and everything." Unlike the Mack family who were pushed out of South Carolina, others were pulled into the city. Dora Miller, after marrying in 1925, left Apex, North Carolina, because she heard of the "better paying jobs in Durham." Mary Dove, at age ten and accompanied by her family, left Roxboro, North Carolina, because a "Duke agent told us that a job in the factory at Liggett Myers was waiting for my daddy." Rosetta Branch, age eighteen and single, left Wilmington, North Carolina, because her mother had died and "there were no other kinfolks."[2]

Thus, Durham's gainfully employed black population swelled from 6,869 in 1910 to 12,402 in 1930. (The city's total black population in 1930 was 23,481.) According to the census, the number of black female tobacco workers in 1930 was 1,979 out of a total black female population of 12, 388. (See Table 18.1) Durham and Winston Salem tobacco factories employed more black females than other cities: one-half of the number of women employed in tobacco factories in 1930 in these cities were black compared with the 19.7 in Petersburg and Richmond in Virginia.[3]

Upon disembarking the central train station, the newly arrived southern migrants were immediately faced with race restrictions. Rigidly segregated communities were the dominant feature of Durham's black life. Many of the migrants settled in the dilapidated housing in the larger communities of East End and Hayti, a bustling commercial district of black businesses, and in the smaller areas of Buggy Bottom and Hickstown. Almost all black workers rented either from the company and white landlords or from black real estate agents. The comments of Annie Barbee, the daughter of Necoda Mack, reflect her first impressions of Durham.

> We were renting in the Southern part of Durham–the Negro section–on Popular Street, second house from the corner, across the railroad tracks. The house was small, two rooms, but somehow we managed. The street was not paved and when it rained it got muddy and in the fall, the wind blew all the dust into your eyes and face. There were no private family bathrooms. But it was an exciting life. See, in the country things were so dull–no movie houses. . . . Up here people were always fighting and going on all the time.[4]

Despite the exploitive living conditions described by Barbee, urban employment did have some liberating consequences for rural daughters.

Race restricted the black population to segregated neighborhoods and also determined the kinds of jobs black females could get. Black female tobacco workers also faced discrimination as poor people and as females. Although class and sex restraints punctuated the lives of white female tobacco workers, their impact was reinforced by management policies. Although white females' wages were a fraction of white males' and inadequate to support a family, black females' wages were even lower. According to some black female tobacco workers, the wage inequity led many white women to consider black women inferior. This in

TABLE 18.1
Tobacco Industry Employment by Race and Gender

Durham County: 1930

White		Negro	
Male	Female	Male	Female
2,511	2,932	1,336	1,979

North Carolina: 1940

White		Negro	
Male	Female	Male	Female
6,517	3,175	5,899	5,898

Source: U.S. Bureau of the Census. *Population: 1930* (Washington, D.C.: GPO), vol. 3, pt. 2, pp. 355, 378; *Labor Force: 1940* (Washington, D.C.: GPO, 1940), vol. 3, pt. 4, p. 566.

turn led to an atmosphere of mistrust between black and white females. Management strengthened racial and class inequities in hiring practices, working conditions, and spatial organization of the factory, and therefore impeded the formation of gender bonds among working-class women.

Black females were usually hired as if they were on an auction block. "Foremen lined us up against the walls," one worker stated, "and chose the sturdy and robust ones." Mary Dove recalled that she had "to hold up one leg at a time and then bend each backwards and forwards."[5] Once hired, black and white women were separated on different floors at the American Tobacco Company and in entirely different buildings at the Liggett Myers Tobacco Company. In the 1920s and 1930s, according to a report by the Women's Bureau (the federal agency created in 1920), and confirmed by my interviews, 98 percent of these black females were confined to the prefabrication department where they performed the "dirty" jobs – sorting, cleaning, and stemming tobacco.[6] White females had the "cleaner" jobs in the manufacturing department as they caught, inspected, and packed the tobacco. However, both jobs were defined by the sex division of labor – jobs to be performed by women. Black men moved between the areas pushing 500-lb. hogsheads of tobacco while white men worked as inspectors, safeguarding the sanctity of class and sex segregation.[7]

Reflecting on these blatant differences in the working conditions, some fifty years later, many black women expressed anger at their injustice. Annie Barbee recalled: "You're over here doing all the nasty dirty work. And over there on the cigarette side white women over there wore white uniforms. . . . You're over here handling all the old sweaty tobacco. There is a large difference. It ain't right!" Rosetta Branch spoke of her experience with anger. "They did not treat us Black folks right. They worked us like dogs. Put us in separate buildings . . . thinking maybe we were going to hurt those white women. Dirty work, dirty work we had to do. Them white women think they something working, doing the lighter jobs."[8] These comments reflect both the effectiveness of management policies to aggravate racial and sexual differences in order to preclude any possible bonds of gender, but also illustrate the unhealthy working conditions to which black women were exposed.

In fact, interviews indicate that the health of some black women suffered in the factories. Pansy Cheatham, another daughter of Necoda Mack, maintained that the Georgia leaf-tobacco "was so dusty that I had to go to the tub every night after work. There was only one window and it got so hot that some women just fainted. The heat and the smell was quite potent." Mary Dove recounted one of her fainting spells. "You know on the floor there was a salt dispenser, because it would get so hot. I did not feel so well when I came to work but I had to work. After about two hours standing on my feet, I got so dizzy – I fell out. My clothes was soaking wet from my head to my feet. When I woke up I was in the dispensary."[9]

Blanche Scott and another worker were forced to quit for health reasons. Scott, who began working for Liggett Myers in 1919, quit four years later. "When I left the factory, it became difficult for me to breathe. The dust and fumes of the burly tobacco made me cough. The burly tobacco from Georgia had chicken feathers and even manure in it. Sometimes I would put an orange in my mouth to keep me from throwing up. I knew some women who died of TB." The other worker had miscarried twice. Pregnant again, she decided not to return to the American Tobacco Company. "I felt that all that standing while I stemmed tobacco," she stated, "was the reason I lost my two children." Some women found momentary relief from the dust by retreating outside the confines of the factory complex to breathe the fresh air while sitting under the trees or on the sidewalk during lunch.[10]

These comments on the poor, unhealthy, working conditions were verified by research on Durham's death records between 1911 and 1930. In many instances, the records were imprecise and failed to provide information about race and occupation. Of the 105 certificates that identified black women as tobacco workers, who died between 1911 and 1920, 48 (about 46 percent) died of tuberculosis, sometimes listed as phthisis and consumption. Of the 134 recorded deaths of black female tobacco workers between 1920 and 1930, 86 (64.5 percent) died of tuberculosis. Because tuberculosis is a bacteria that can be transmitted by a tubercular person through the cough, it is likely that poorly ventilated rooms and incessant coughing by workers, possibly by a carrier, made some workers susceptible to the disease, although deplorable living conditions of workers cannot be dismissed as a contributing factor.[11]

As studies have found in other cities, black females in Durham were more likely to work than white females.[12] Black females also earned lower wages than white females. In the early 1900s, wages for black tobacco workers, both female and male, ranked the lowest in the nation. In 1930, 45.5 percent of native-born white women in Durham were gainfully employed – 27.7 percent in tobacco. While 44 percent of black women were working, 36.2 percent were employed in tobacco. From 1920 to 1930, Durham's white female tobacco workers averaged about 29 cents per hour, while black female hand stemmers earned about 11.9 cents and hour. However, black men, as well as black women who stemmed tobacco by machine, averaged about 27 cents an hour, still less than white women.[13]

Wage differential continued and worsened throughout the 1930s. By the eve of the New Deal, A Women's Bureau survey reported figures for North Carolina which revealed an even higher wage discrepancy. White women working in the making and packing departments reported a median weekly wage of $15.35. Wages ranged from $14.10 earned as catchers to $20.50 on older packing machines. On the newest packing machines, the median wage was $18.15. Black women, working in the leaf department, reported a median weekly wage of $7.95. Hand stemmers earned a median wage of $6.50.[14]

The low wage was itself demeaning to black female workers. But the inadequate wages also forced many into the labor force at an early age. Black women thus worked for a longer part of their lives, and henceforth were more vulnerable to diseases and other health problems. Blanche Scott, for example, began working at the age of twelve. "Since my mother stayed so sick, I had to go to work. I worked at Liggett Myers after school got out. I attended West End School. I'd normally get out at 1:30 and worked from two o'clock to 6 p.m. I was just twelve years old. In the summer, they're let children come and work all day until four o'clock." Pansy Cheatham began working at age thirteen. "My father talked to the foreman," she stated, "I worked because my sisters Mae and Annie worked; I stemmed tobacco by hand. But Papa did collect the money and use it for food and clothing." Cheatham's statement would indicate that the gender hierarchy of the black family resided in the father who controlled the daughter's wages.[15]

Many women saw their employment as a means of "helping out the family." Better stated in the words of Margaret Turner, "that's what a family is all about, when we – the children – can help out our parents."[16] Out of the fifteen interviewees, the ten women who entered the work force at an early age all conceptualized the central meaning of their work in relation to their families.

By the late 1920s and early 1930s, the enforcement of the Child Labor Law of 1917 arrested the practice of employing children under the age of sixteen. "They began to ask for your birth certificate," one worker stated. A study done by Hugh Penn Brinton substantiated the decrease of child labor employment in Durham's factories. Brinton found that from 1919 to 1930 the percentage of black laboring-class households sending children into the labor force had decreased from 35 to 14 percent.[17]

However, the legislation against child labor did not force the wages up for black tobacco workers, and the constant low earning power of both female and male breadwinners continued to affect the lives of black female workers psychologically. Many women submitted to the demands of the foreman and other company officials. Viewed as short-term cheap labor, some females submit-

ted to physical and verbal harassment, because in many instances defiance
would have certainly resulted in the loss of jobs. Dora Miller asserted that "since
the foreman knew you needed the job, you obeyed all of his demands without
question. He called you dirty names and used foul language but you took it."
Mary Dove recalled what it was like to work under one "of the toughest bosses."
"Our foreman was a one-eyed fella named George Hill. He was tight! He was out
of South Carolina, and he was tight. I mean tight! He'd get on top of them
machines – they had a machine that altered the tobacco – he'd get on top of that
machine and watch you, see if you was working all right and holler down and
curse. Holler down and say, "GD . . . get to work! GD . . . go to work there you
ain' doin' nothin." Janie Mae Lyons remembered one who walked in on her
while she "was in the sitting position on the stool" and told her "that if you ain't
finished then you can pack up and leave. I was so embarrassed and that's what I
did."[18]

Lyons's departure from the factory represented a form of militancy – a
definitive stance against further harassment. Other women resisted verbally.
Annie Barber publicly castigated "women who allowed the foreman to fumble
their behind" and further stated that if "one did that to me he would be six feet
under." She indicated no one ever did. Once worker resisted "by playing the
fool." "The foreman thought I was crazy and left me alone."[19]

Constantly resisting physical and verbal abuse and trying to maintain their
jobs, the workers were further threatened by increased mechanization. "I don't
think it is right," one woman stated, "to put them machines to take away from us
poor people." "Because of the strain we work under," another maintained, "they
don't care nothing for us." One woman recalled crying at the machines because
she could not quit in the face of high unemployment. "With them machines you
have to thread the tobacco in. Them machines run so fast that after you put in
one leaf you got to be ready to thread the other. If you can't keep pace the
foreman will fire you right on the spot. Sometimes I get so nervous but I keep on
goin'."[20]

The increased mechanization of the tobacco factories resulting in physical
hardships of female workers can to some degree be attributed to Franklin D.
Roosevelt's National Industrial Recovery Acts of 1933 and 1934. On the one
hand, President Roosevelt's New Deal measure fostered economic stability for
many black families by establishing standard minimum wages and maximum
hours. On the other hand, this standardization exacerbated the job insecurity of
black workers by indirectly catalyzing many companies to maximize profits by
replacing hand labor with technology. During the latter part of the 1930s, Liggett Myers closed its green leaf department that had employed the majority of
black women.[21]

The long-term insecurities of their jobs led black female stemmers to
organize Local 194. The limited success of the union was reflected in the decline
of its membership of two thousand in January 1935 to less than two hundred by

May 1935. Black female union members found little support from either Local 208, black controlled, or Local 176, white controlled. In the eyes of the male unionists, the temporary nature of women's jobs excluded them from any serious consideration by the locals.[22] Conscious of their auxiliary position and the lack of support from male-led unions, black females chose not to support the April 16, 1939, strike at Liggett Myers. Reporting for work on that day, they were turned away as management had no other recourse but to close the factory. Dora Miller recalled that the black stemmery workers "were never involved in the strike because demands for wage increases did not include us."[23] On April 26, 1939, the company capitulated. The contract indeed reaffirmed Miller's assessment because the stemmery workers were not mentioned.[24]

The factory policies of hiring, wages, working conditions, and spatial segregation, inherently reinforced by racism, the "cult of true white womanhood," and the inadvertent effect of New Deal governmental measures, all came together to touch the lives of black women tobacco workers, with sex, race, and class exploitation. These practices further dissipated any possible gender bonds between black women and white women workers. As a race, black female tobacco workers were confined to unhealthy segregated areas either in separate buildings or on separate floors. As a working class, they were paid inadequate wages. As a sex they were relegated to the worst, lowest paid, black women's jobs.

Black females conceptualized work as a means of "helping out the family." Denied self-respect and dignity in the factory, black female tobacco workers felt a need to validate themselves in other spheres. Victimized by their working conditions, female tobacco workers looked to the home as a preferred if not powerful arena. The home became the inner world that countered the factory control over their physical well-being. The duality of their lives – workers of production and nurturers of the family – could be assessed as a form of double jeopardy. But it was their role as nurturers, despite the hardship of work, that provided them with a sense of purpose and "joy." As Pansy Cheatham described her daily routine, "I get up at 5:30 a.m. I feed, clothe, and kiss my children. They stay with my sister while I work. At 7 a.m. I am on the job. A half-hour for lunch at about twelve noon. At 4 p.m. I quit work. At home about 4:30 then I cook, sometimes mend and wash clothes before I retire. About 11:30 I go to bed with joy in my heart for my children are safe and I love them so."[25]

Black females who worked together in the tobacco factories also had the positive experience of creating networks of solidarity. Viewing their plight as one, black females referred to one another as "sisters." This sisterhood was displayed in the collection of money during sickness and death and celebration of birthdays. The networks established in the factory overlapped into the community and church. Many of these workers belonged to the same churches – Mount Vernon, Mt. Gilead, and White Rock Baptist Church – and functioned as leaders of the usher boards, missionary circles, and Sunday School programs.

These bonds were enhanced in the community by the development of clubs. these church groups and female's clubs overlapped the factory support networks and functioned in similar ways.

Finally, the resistance to the physical and verbal abuse that was a constant in the work lives of black women fostered among some a sense of autonomy, strength, and self-respect. Annie Barbee was one of those women. The assertiveness, dignity, and strength she developed through work became an intricate part of her private life. At age forty and pregnant, she decided to obtain private medical assistance despite her husband's resistance. "When you know things ain't right God gave you a head and some sense. That's my body. I knew I wasn't going to Duke Clinic. And I was working and making my own money, I went where I wanted to go. You see, being married don't mean that your husband controls your life. That was my life and I was carrying his child, it's true, but I was going to look after myself."[26]

Although the work experience of black women tobacco workers was one of racial, sex, and class oppression, the early advent into the labor force, the resistance to exploitation, and the longevity of work created a consciousness that fostered a sense of strength and dignity among some women in this working class. Management tactics of wage inequity, hiring practices, and racial-sexual division of labor pitted black women against white women economically as workers, and made the formation of gender bonds across race lines all but impossible. Yet among black women, the linkages of sisterhood engendered a consciousness of female strength, if not feminism.

NOTES

I am deeply grateful to North Carolina Central University for a Faculty Research Grant and for the excellent editorial comments of the *Feminist Studies* editors.

1. For discussion of the historical involvement of black labor in tobacco manufacturing, see Joseph C. Robert, *The Tobacco Kingdom* (North Carolina: Duke University Press, 1938).

2. Charlie Necoda Mack, interview with author, 22 May 1979, on file in the Southern Oral History Program, University of North Carolina. Chapel Hill, hereafter cited as SOHP/UNC. Dora Miller, interview with author, 6 June 1979, SOHP/UNC; Mary Dove, interview with author, 7 July 1979, SOHP/UNC; Rosetta Branch, interview with author, 15 Aug. 1981.

3. The 1940 labor force figures do not include information for Durham County. U.S. Bureau of the Census, *Population: 1930* (Washington, D.C.: GPO, 1930), 3:341. In 1900, the major tobacco industries in the South were the American Tobacco Company and Liggett Myers in Durham; R.J. Reynolds in Winston Salem; and P. Lorillard in Richmond, Virginia.

4. Annie Barbee, interview, 28 May 1979, SOHP/UNC.

5. Interview, 30 May 1981; Mary Dove, interview.

6. Women's Bureau, *The Effects of Changing Conditions in the Cigar and Cigarette Industries*, Bulletin no. 110 (Washington, D.C.: GPO, 1932), 774–75. The Women's Bureau was established by Congress in 1920 under the aegis of the United States Department of Labor. Its purpose was to gather information and to provide advice to working women.

7. Mary Dove, interview; interviews, 15 and 28 Aug. 1981.

8. Annie Barbee and Rosetta Branch, interviews.

9. Pansy Cheatham, interview with author, 9 July 1979, SOHP/UNC; Mary Dove interview.

10. Blanche Scott, interview with author, 11 July 1979, SOHP/UNC; interviews, 8, 13 June, 1981; Mary Dove, Annie Barbee interviews.

11. Death Certificates, 1911–1930, Durham County Health Department, Vital Records, Durham, North Carolina. I was also interested in the correlation of working conditions and female-related maladies such as stillbirths, miscarriages, and uterine disorders. Further perusal of death certificates of stillbirths were less valuable for there were no indications of mothers' occupations. Even hospital statistics lacked occupational data. This area of inquiry as it relates to the health of black female workers and working conditions needs further research. Further questions that will have to be explored include: Was there a higher percentage of female tobacco workers dying of tuberculosis than non-female tobacco workers? How long were stricken female workers employed in the factory? How much weight must be given to the working environment over that of the home environs? Despite the lack of solid data on these questions, the interviews and death records clearly indicate that racial division of labor negatively impacted upon the health of many black female tobacco workers.

12. Elizabeth H. Pleck, "A Mother's Wage: Income Earning among Married Italian and Black Women, 1896–1911," in *The American Family in Social-Historical Perspective*, 2d ed. Michael Gordon (New York: St. Martin's Press, 1978), 490–510; "Culture, Class, and Family Life among Low-income Urban Negroes," in *Employment, Race, and Poverty*, ed. Arthur M. Ross and Herbert Hill (New York: Harcourt, Brace and World, 1967), 149–72; "The Kindred of Veola Jackson: Residence and Family Organization of an Urban Black American Family," in *Afro-American Anthropology: Contemporary Perspective*, ed. Norman E. Whitten, Jr., and John F. Szwed (New York: Free Press, 1970), chapt. 16.

13. U.S. Bureau of the Census, *Population: 1930*, vols. 3 and 4; U.S. Department of Labor, Women's Bureau, *Hours and Earning in Tobacco Stemmeries*, Bulletin no. 127 (Washington, D.C.: GPO, 1934).

14. Women's Bureau, *Effects of Changing Conditions*, 172–75.

15. Blanche Scott and Pansy Cheatham, interviews.

16. Margaret Turner, interview with author, 25 Sept. 1979, SOHP/UNC.

17. Interview, 8 June 1981; Hugh Penn Brinton, "The Negro in Durham: A Study in Adjustment to Town Life" (Ph.D. diss., University of North Carolina, Chapel Hill, 1930).

18. Dora Miller, and Mary Dove, interviews; Janie Mae Lyons, interview with author, 4 Aug. 1981.

19. Annie Barbee, interview; interview, 10 July 1981.

20. Interviews, 4 and 15 June 1981.

21. For the best discussions of the National Industrial Recovery Acts' impact on blacks, see Raymond Wolters, *Negroes and the Great Depression: The Problem of Economic Recovery*, ed. Stanley E. Kutler (Westport, Conn.: Greenwood Publishing Co., 1970); and Bernard Stemsher, ed., *The Negro in the Depression and War: Prelude to Revolution,*

1930–45 (Chicago, Ill.: Quadrangle Books, 1969). Also see Dolores Janiewski, "From Field to Factory: Race, Class, and Sex and the Woman Worker in Durham, 1880–1940" (Ph.D. diss., Duke University, Durham, North Carolina, 1979).

    22. *Durham* (N.C.) *Morning Herald*, 17, 18 Apr. 1939, p. 1; Janiewski.

    23. Dora Miller, interview.

    24. For terms of contract, see *Durham* (N.C.) *Morning Herald* and *Durham* (N.C.) *Sun*, 27 Apr. 1939, pp. 1, 2; Janiewski.

    25. Pansy Cheatham, interview.

    26. Annie Barbee, interview.

Chapter 19 ―――――――――――――――――――――

The Making of a Female Researcher: Role Problems in Field Work

Lois Easterday
Diana Papademas
Laura Schorr
Catherine Valentine

S ocial scientists do research in hopes of discovering how society works. Years are spent in graduate training learning how to gather, record, and analyze data. Courses are not segregated by sex, and we are told that research is research, regardless of one's gender. Our experiences have led us to believe differently.

Being single females doing field work, we discovered there were research problems related to that status. The methodological literature (e.g., Adams and Preiss, 1960; Bogdan and Taylor, 1975; Bruyn, 1966; Junker, 1960; McCall and Simmons, 1969) and the women studies literature (e.g., Bernard, 1966; Epstein and Goode, 1971; Huber, 1973; Rossi, 1965) do not mention the effects of sex on research relationships or how these can be dealt with in field work. A few sociologists comment on female observers (Douglas, 1976; Riesman, 1954; Stein, 1954; Wax, 1960), and others consider more general problems, such as the participant observer as a human being (Gans, 1968), or friendships and personal feelings (Johnson, 1975). Also, some anthropologists have described their status as women in other cultures (Bowen, 1954; Gold, 1974; Powdermaker, 1967) that are suggestive of some of the issues of this paper.

We focus on specific problems of being a female field researcher in relation to general methodological issues such as the establishment and maintenance of rapport and research relationships. We do this by extracting observations from our twelve research studies. These include an art museum, an embalming school, a funeral parlor, a medical team in a nursing home, a military photography program, a morgue, a newspaper, two social service agencies, a stock brokerage of-

Authors' Note: A version of this paper was presented at the annual meetings of the New York State Sociological Association, October 1976.

Source: Lois Easterday, Diana Papademas, Laura Schorr, and Catherine Valentine, "The Making of a Female Researcher: Role Problems in Field Work," Urban Life Vol. 6 (October 1977), pp. 333–348. Copyright ©1977 by Urban Life. Reprinted by permission of Sage Publications, Inc.

fice, a television station, and a university film-making program. We additionally present a typology of sex roles and power. We then discuss varieties of sex role relationships in those settings, showing disadvantages and advantages. Our conclusions offer suggestions on how young women researchers can minimize the liabilities of their sex status in field work.

TYPOLOGY OF SETTINGS AND SEX ROLES

While being young and being female represent two ascribed criteria influencing social interaction in any setting, the configuration of social relationships in a particular organizational setting further defines our opportunities and limitations as researchers. As Kanter (1975: 55) indicates, "In addition to sexual and cultural issues, there are also status and power issues when men and women interact, a function of the structural positions and organizational class membership of the sexes."

A simple typology characterizes the research settings in terms of sex roles and power: primarily male (those dominated both in number and power by men), traditional male-female (those dominated in power but not in number by men), nontraditional male-female (those in which women occupy some positions of power).

Primarily male settings include a morgue, a military photography program, and a university film-making program. Traditional male-female settings include an embalming school, two social service agencies, a medical team, and a stock brokerage office. Nontraditional male-female settings include an art museum, a funeral parlor, a newspaper, and a television station.

The morgue is primarily a male setting of doctors and attendants, so sex role differentiation is not customarily part of their definition of work. The perspective of the morgue director toward women is expressed in the absence of female attendants; as he says, "there are no sleeping facilities to accomodate them," and bodies are "too heavy" for women to carry when they are retrieved at great distances. The attendants have no objections to hiring female attendants, but the authoritative dominance of the director prevents their presence. Also women who come to the morgue to identify bodies of relatives are defined as more emotional than men and are in need of protective handling. The female researcher is subject to similar paternalistic treatment.

The military-photographer training program is exclusively male. Like the morgue, establishing rapport was easier with subordinates in the setting than with directors, who upheld traditional attitudes toward women. Their authority defined the work situations for all participants, to the exclusion of females as employees and researchers. Dissimilarly, the university film-making program, while predominantly male, encouraged female students (and the researcher) to participate. The director's encouragement was not a perspective shared by male students, who saw females in the setting as "coeds" playing at a male occupation.

In traditional male-female settings, our general status liability was compounded by specific role expectations attached to women in the organization. For lack of female authority models, we often found ourselves lumped together with other female subordinates in the sexual stratification system of the setting. And we were treated accordingly.

> A short two-day study was designed to observe medical teams of doctors, social workers and nurses while they conducted an evaluation study of health care facilities. As a group of observers studying several teams, we found common situations in the relationships among the team members. Among the team members it was expected that the doctor would "take charge" over the team as the male member of an all-female team. As a young female observer, I found the passive role to be an accepted role among the other team members during the formal part of the health care study. At lunch I seemed to be one of the "women" on the team, referred to by first name while the doctor was deferred to and called by title.

In the brokerage office, largely male-dominated (one female broker among ten, and a customer population of retired men), young single females were not present. The researcher in this setting was defined as "cute" and "the girl" or "the young lady here."

Our sex status often caused us to be "channeled" into particular activities, thus potentially curtailing the range of our data collection.

> Although not rigid, the division of labor in television newswork follows male-female roles. As a female observer, I was expected to be more interested in the features and human interest stories than the political or crime news. One woman reporter looked deflated the day I decided to go with a reporter covering a presidential candidate rather than with her to do a feature on a magician.

Traditional male-female settings are sometimes sexually segregated, creating difficulties for the researcher in establishing rapport with all persons.

> A sharp characteristic of the gatherings at the brokerage office was sex role separation among customers. Women talked with women and men with men. Female customers identified the female broker as "theirs" although her customers were male as well. Early in the field work, I found it easier to approach the women informally rather than the men. Later in the field after developing an informant relationship with one of the customers, a male university professor who was amused by my being there, I was introduced to other customers as "the girl from the university" or simply "this young lady" who wants to learn more about the stock market and why people are here.

MAKING OF A FEMALE RESEARCHER

In certain organizational settings, the professional power of male administrators is intertwined with and enhanced by their personal, sexual dominance as men. The male director of a predominantly female-staffed social service agency allegedly employed his personal attractiveness as a means of increasing allegiance to his administration by acting seductively toward some of the women – including the researcher. The charisma attached to his position as effective leader of the organization, as well as his legitimate authority over the professional activity and conduct of his staff, enchanced his status. Although the agency publicly encouraged autonomy and administrative participation on the part of female group leaders, it was clear that the chief administrator had the final word on important decisions and policies. In addition, the administrator was regarded by many as being skillful at political interaction with regional superordinates and staff members alike. The nature of one of our encounters as a young female researcher with him reflected this institutionalized pattern of relationships in which women are professionally, personally, and politically subject to male authority.

Nontraditional male-female settings included the art museum, the funeral parlor, the television station, and the newspaper. While women occupy positions as directors, assistant directors, museum curators, reporters, and photographers, they do not dominate the work situation. In these settings relationships can become a problem of "overrapport," where coupling-off and male-female pairing are the practice among members, or where the researcher finds herself more attracted to "feminist" men and women. Tensions among nonfeminists and feminists in such settings are problematic; the researcher may find herself typed as a "female libber" and tested for "where she stands" – as either friend or enemy, but clearly as female.

As can be seen, our typology is fluid enough to include a variety of sex role relationships. We will further discuss some of these.

VARIETIES OF SEX ROLE RELATIONSHIPS

The Fraternity
On entering male-dominated settings, female researchers often have difficulty gaining access to the setting itself. One of us established rapport with the photographers of a special military program by being a photographer and knowing their language. The relationship was sustained by insisting that the researcher not be photographed as a model, but rather that she be "one of the boys" on the other side of the lens. In an attempt to gain approval for the study from the program's director, the researcher was denied full access with the statement, "It won't work. The men in the program are a close bunch, and the talk is rough. They wouldn't be themselves if you are there."

Once a female researcher gains entree to a setting, she may find it necessary to break into female groups similar to the male fraternity. Among the client population of a social service agency were parent groups composed primarily of poor, divorced women in their twenties and thirties. Since the contact was infrequent over two years, rapport among them in some cases took that long to establish. Stereotyped observations of the researcher went something like, "How can you [single, childless] understand what it's like for us?" We felt the best way to counter this was to show genuine interest in things of importance to them, like children, the absence of stable marriages and partners, and having a good time. Over time, while we recognized our different situations, close relationships emerged on the basis of "we women" having similar problems of loneliness, being "stuck here," not finding work that pays enough or is interesting, and other common plights.

Hustling

One of the problems a young single female researcher has to deal with is "hustling." Particularly in male-dominated settings where the observer is talking to one male at a time, the male-female games come early to the fore. Two researchers observing the same setting (the morgue) at different times (one year apart) experienced very similar problems in this regard.

> I was in the midst of industriously questioning the attendant about his job at the morgue and he came back with, "Are you married?"
>
> OBSERVER: "No. How long have you worked here?"
> ATTENDANT: "Three years. Do you have a steady boyfriend?"
> OBSERVER: "No. Do you find this work difficult?"
> ATTENDANT: "No. Do you date?"
> OBSERVER: "Yes. Why isn't this work difficult for you?"
> ATTENDANT: "You get used to it. What do you do in your spare time?"
>
> And so our interview went on for over an hour, each of us working at our separate purposes. I doubt whether either of us got any "usable data."

In instances such as these, the researchers either had to avoid the informant or avoid letting him talk about other subjects he was interested in. In the one instance, in the morgue, the researcher avoided visiting the setting when one particular male was there. She was unable to discuss anything without the conversation being overshadowed by discussions of dating, marriage, or "getting together." However, it is not always possible to avoid such problems. At the funeral home run by a black husband/wife team, the wife became increasingly hostile toward the researcher.

I increasingly became aware of his wife's coolness toward me, although I tried in my dress and in my demeanor to be as professional as possible. When I raised this prob- lem to the husband, asking if it would be advisable for me to leave the site, he brushed off the wife's hostility toward me, with "Oh, you know women, they get jealous. But we know there's nothing between us, right?" About a month after my entree at the site, the husband called me at home on three occasions, apparently on the pretext of assuring me that I would not be thrown off the site by his wife. At the conclusion of two of these calls, he reminded me not to mention to his wife he had telephoned me.

The source(s) of the wife's hostility can only be hypothesized. Perhaps it was a combination of sexual jealousy, racial hostility, or professional protectiveness. In any case, the hostility became so intense that the researcher terminated observa- tions at the funeral home.

She told me in a friendly tone of voice that she thought I had accumulated enough observations, and that if I needed more data, I should interview her instead of her husband. She claimed my presence at the funeral services, as the sole white presence, was conspicuous and disturbing to the mourners (an observation which I wholeheartedly agreed with). I told her I thought it would be better if I left the site.

At the social service agency, the story was different. Staffed by fifty women and three men, one of whom was the top administrator, multiple female-female rela- tionships were problematic, since these were defined in relationship to the male director. Frequently "on the make," the man used his position in the authority structure of the agency to assert himself as boss, commanding deference.

It often appears that the researcher has only two options. She can totally re- ject the advances of the hustler and risk his feeling that he has been rejected, or she can welcome his advances and allow the female-male relationship to develop. However, either can have detrimental effects on the research. An informant who feels rejected as a person is not likely to be a wealth of information and cooperation. In some instances he can disrupt her relationship with other infor- mants, and possibly even have her ejected from the setting. This would be especially true if the male happened to be in a supervisory position.

To establish rapport with the females in the situation, I adamantly refused the ap- proaches of the director. The other consequence of that "no" response on my part was a reciprocal denial in the way of avoiding me personally, and delaying and deny- ing, covertly, important information about the project.

Similar pressures occurred at another social service agency.

During my first week at the agency, the male administrator and a group of outside consultants held an "in-service" meeting to improve staff rapport. The day after this session, the administrator approached me while I was helping a child, took my hand in his, and said to me, "Any time you want, we can have our private little in-service." The same week, I saw him in the parking lot, and he asked me, "When are you inviting me over to your place for dinner?" On another occasion, when I went into his office to request some information, he said kiddingly, "Bribe me." . . . Every encounter became a balancing act between cordiality and distance.

The young single female researcher must be careful that her behavior, when designed to discourage hustling, does not backfire. This might result in stimulating the desire of the "hustler" to conquer the woman, whose behavior is (mis)interpreted as elusive; thus she becomes a real trophy to possess.

On the other hand, "getting involved" with an informant could also result in termination of the field work. It could result in bad feelings among the other informants, jealousy, or exclusivity. A relationship such as this could also color the data and make it unusable or very "skewed" and inaccurate. For some researchers, there are great ethical dilemmas over these sorts of involvements, both professionally and personally. Few want to "use" persons and relationships to get data. Therefore, the researcher often finds herself walking a tightrope between rejection and involvement.

It seems that each situation of this nature must be evaluated and dealt with carefully. There are some men who, as hustlers, never give up. It is probably best to avoid extended interaction with them. Other situations can be handled honestly, by emphasizing one's research role. One of us simply told a man she was interviewing that her role could not permit her to respond to his insistent overtures. Other men are not serious about or committed to "scoring" and can be discouraged with no hard feelings.

The "Go-fer"

In some settings the female researcher may be cast in the role of "go-fer," a typical role for the young woman, to which men can easily relate.

In a social service agency, the male staff member I was assigned to observe continuously devised clerical errands for me to do—partly, it seemed, to keep me from observing him, but also to provide secretarial assistance. On more than one occasion I politely protested that I was employed to observe him rather than be his assistant, but he curtly informed me that I could not observe him unless I provided this kind of aid.

The Mascot

Unlike the "go-fer," who is expected to do things, the mascot is accepted simply for her "being."

In a peer setting [university students in a film-making program], efforts were made to characterize my participation at times as "mascot" with statements like: "We like your company" and "It looks good to have a pretty girl along."

I asked to observe some visiting professionals at work in the morgue. One of the attendants introduced me and conveyed my request. The response was, "Of course. Who wouldn't want a pretty girl watching them work?" There were no questions about the purpose of my observations. In a similar instance, I requested access to a particular procedure, but this request was turned down, due to legal restrictions. In reporting the refusal, one man stated, "He said you can't watch this time, but some other time. But don't worry, he still loves you."

Father-Daughter

Older males in a setting may interact with a young female researcher in a manner we describe as paternalistic. Given the legitimacy of traditional sex role relationships, the father daughter relationship offers older males – threatened by young women or unable to interact with young women as peers – a safe, predefined interactional context. At a morgue, one of us experienced such a relationship with an older and powerful male in that setting.

The Medical Examiner (M.E.) treated me very paternalistically. When I was to observe an autopsy, he took me in hand, protectively.

M.E.: Have you ever seen a dead person?
OBSERVER: Yes, once before while I was here.
M.E.: Well, you know, all nurses have to attend autopsies. For some, it takes two or three, others are not bothered at all. . . . Now, if you feel you need to leave, do so.

He also protected me by discouraging attendants from showing me "bad cases."

Experiences with males in a social service agency and at the funeral home were also, at times, paternalistic, despite efforts to emphasize the research role.

ADVANTAGES

Although the thrust of our paper concerns the liabilities connected with being a female field researcher, we and others have found definite advantages. The previously mentioned problem of not being taken seriously can work to one's benefit.

If a researcher is not taken seriously because she is a young female, this can facilitate entree into an otherwise difficult or inaccessible setting. In one instance, one of us was granted access to a school of mortuary science to which an older, well known female researcher had been denied access. The young researcher was taken in on a "mascot" basis by one of the male faculty members. The researcher's position and work were fully described to the "gatekeeper," the dean of the school. In a rather offhand way – "oh sure, come on in" – he granted the access. His only concern was that the researcher dress appropriately for the setting.

Also, if the researcher is not taken seriously, people in a setting may confide in the researcher or let her hear things because they perceive her as powerless and nonthreatening. Lofland (1971: 100–101) writes of the observer as accept-able incompetent, "Or the observer may be a woman of any age, and 'everybody knows' that women don't know anything about much of anything that is impor-tant." Elsewhere, Douglas (1976: 185) has written similarly that the "boob ploy" benefits women researchers, sometimes unintentionally. Women in research teams were thought by people in settings (e.g., a drug rehabilitation center) to be ineffective enough to be harmless.

Personal interest in the researcher can also work to the researcher's advan-tage after she is in the setting. An informant who is attempting to "hustle" an observer may, at times, reveal more than he otherwise would in an attempt to show how friendly, cooperative, and accommodating he is. Stein (1954: 265–266), in Gouldner's work on industrial bureaucracy, talks about how a young woman was taken into the field, and how, despite the concern of other male team members, she was well-received by men in the gypsum plant: "Actual-ly she got along wonderfully with the men, who in an effort to impress her, would often give her more revealing data than they might to a male interviewer."

One may, if skillful and if willing to take the risks involved, use one's femininity and desirability to manipulate males in a setting for information. As Wax (1960: 97) notes, "a coquette is in a much better situation to learn about men than a nun." Complications can arise, however, leading to over-rapport problems. And one is not advised to adopt views or practices one does not ac-cept. One's values may undergo changes as a result of field experiences, which may be beneficial if one sees them as broadening experiences.

There is also a component to being a marginal person, an outsider, "the other" throughout one's life, which can contribute to the perceptiveness a woman brings to field research. In a personal correspondence to one of us, Blanche Geer writes, "The most handicapped observer is the one doing people and situations he/she is closest to. Hence, women are in luck in a male-run world. They can see how few clothes the emperor has on, question the accepted, what is taken for granted."

SUGGESTIONS FOR FIELD TACTICS

People experience their relations with one another problematically: it is not necessary to conduct field research to learn that. While there are no set pro-cedures that would anticipate all potential problems, there are certain tactics we suggest to minimize the liabilities and enhance the benefits of being a female researcher. Improved research reliability suggests appropriate behavioral guidelines for those doing field work.

A general rule we have followed has been to avoid personal involvement with subjects as intimate friends. Ethical and practical problems such as over-rapport (Miller, 1969) suggest reasons for this rule. Generally, problems include researcher bias, data distortion and limitation, reactivity, and observer effects. As we encountered these potential problems in our researches, we developed tactics in our relationships and guided our orientations toward the research enterprise. For example, we tried to manage potential over-rapport problems by equalizing time with all people in the field situation, by not discussing details of the research with the informant/friend, and by checking comments and behavior of others in the field as a way to verify observer perceptions. Other suggestions are to emphasize the research role in gaining entree and to develop a "spiel," choosing and accepting roles (as participant and observer) that facilitate observations, avoiding participants who monopolize research time and activity, fabricating information about oneself (e.g., the boyfriend back home), and recording and evaluating with honesty and rigor all observations, including feelings about participants during the research process.

Our discussion of sex role problems in a variety of field settings reflects both the disadvantages and advantages of being a young woman, as we have experienced them. Research courses and methodological texts only teach students how research ought to go, rather than how it does go in the real world. As social scientists, we have an obligation to share experiences with other researchers in order to develop our research skills and enterprise.

We do not feel that admitting the effects of an observer's ascribed statuses sacrifices objectivity. Rather, we feel that "No observation can become objective unless the observer is also observed objectively" (Mitroff, 1974: 238). Sharing our analysis with others is a step in that direction. Thus, the statuses of young, single females acting as field workers emphasizes a set of problems. It would be beneficial to all field researchers to take a look at the problems and benefits their status characteristics present.

What is it like to be a young, single male or an older, married male field researcher in a female-dominated setting? What about being a black researcher in a white setting? Or what happens if one is an older, married female in a male-dominated setting? When teams of researchers enter a setting, are there differences between the experiences of men and women, young and old, single and married, and so forth? Most important, how do these differences affect reality perspectives in any setting? Further study may suggest the extent to which ascribed status affects the research process.

Continued discussion of these and related problems will further our understandings not only of field methods, but also of theoretical areas such as sex role theory, minority group study, and the sociology of knowledge. By looking at sociologists, at ourselves as participants in a society in which we are both defining and being defined by others, we can recognize our part in the social drama and perhaps achieve our hopes for discovering how society works.

REFERENCES

Adams, R. N. and J. J. Preiss [eds.] (1960) Human Organization Research. Homewood, IL: Dorsey.

Bernard, J. (1966) Acadmic Women. Cleveland: World.

Bogdan, R. and S. J. Taylor (1975) Introduction to Qualitative Research Methods. New York: Wiley-Interscience.

Bowen, E. S. (1954) Return to Laughter. Garden City, NY: Doubleday.

Bruyn, S. T. (1966) The Human Perspective in Sociology – The Methodology of Participant Observation. Englewood Cliffs, NJ: Prentice-Hall.

Daniels, A. K. (1975) "Feminist perspectives in sociological research," pp. 340–380 in M. Millman and R. M. Kanter (eds.) Another Voice: Feminist Perspectives on Social Life and Social Science. New York: Doubleday.

Douglas, J. D. (1976) Investigative Social Research. Beverly Hills, CA: Sage.

Epstein, C. F. and W. J. Goode [eds.] (1971) The Other Half: Roads to Women's Equality. Englewood Cliffs, NJ: Prentice-Hall.

Gans, H. J. (1968) "The participant-observer as a human being: observations on the personal aspects of field work," pp. 300–317 in H. S. Becker, B. Geer, D. Riesman, and R. S. Weiss (eds.) Institutions and the Person. Chicago: Aldine.

Gold, P. [ed.] (1974) Women in the Field. Chicago: Aldine.

Gornick, V. (1971) "Woman as an outsider," pp. 117–139 in V. Gornick and B. K. Moran (eds.) Woman in Sexist Society: Studies in Power and Powerlessness. New York: Basic Books.

Huber, J. [ed.] (1973) Changing Women in a Changing Society. Chicago: Univ. of Chicago Press.

Johnson, J. M. (1975) Doing Field Research. New York: Free Press.

Junker, B. H. (1960) Field Work – An Introduction to the Social Sciences. Chicago: Univ. of Chicago Press.

Kanter, R. M. (1975) "Women and the structure of organizations: explorations in theory and behavior," pp. 34–74 in M. Millman and R. M. Kanter (eds.) Another Voice: Feminist Perspectives on Social Life and Social Science. New York: Doubleday.

Lofland, J. (1971) Analyzing Social Settings. Belmont, CA: Wadsworth.

McCall, G. J. and J. L. Simmons [eds.] (1969) Issues in Participant Observation. Reading, MA: Addison-Wesley.

Miller, S. M. (1969) "The participant observer and 'over-rapport'," pp. 87–89 in G. J. McCall and J. L. Simmons (eds.) Issues in Participant Observation. Reading, MA: Addison-Wesley.

Mitroff, I. I. (1974) The Subjective Side of Science: A Philosophical Inquiry into the Psychology of the Apollo Moon Scientists. Amsterdam: Elsevier.

Powdermaker, H. (1967) "A woman alone in the field," pp. 198–214 in Stranger and Friend. London: Secker & Warburg.

Riesman, D. (1954) "Foreward," pp. ix–xviii in E. S. Bowen, Return to Laughter. Garden City, NY: Doubleday.

Rossi, A. A. (1965) "Women in science: Why so few?" Science 148 (May 28): 1196–1202.

9

9

3 Stein, M. (1954) "Field work procedures: The social organization of a student research team," pp. 247–269 in A. W. Gouldner, Patterns of Industrial Bureaucracy. New York: Free Press.

Wax, R. H. (1971) Doing Field Work. Chicago: Univ. of Chicago Press.

——— (1960) "Reciprocity in field work," pp. 90–98 in R. N. Admas and J. J. Preiss (eds.) Human Organization Research. Homewood, IL: Dorsey.

Section VIII

Working Hypotheses as Problematic "Solutions"

Chapter 20 ———————————————————————————

Collective Protest and the Meritocracy: Faculty Women and Sex Discrimination Lawsuits

Emily Abel

INTRODUCTION

T he pursuit of sex discrimination grievances by faculty women in institutions of higher education involves a conflict between two competing
images of society: the individualism that underlies both the legal and the educational systems, and the collectivism inherent in any political protest. In order to
assert that they have suffered discrimination on the basis of gender, women
must recognize the commonality of their interests with those of other women.
Moreover, their chances of success are greater and the significance of their action is enhanced if their protest is waged collectively. Such a strategy, however,
is inconsistent with the meritocratic ideal of the educational selection system,
according to which rewards are distributed solely on the basis of individual
talent and effort. Women who have derived real benefits from this system are
often reluctant to question its basic tenets. Collective aims are also undermined
by the grievance process itself. Complainants are often forced to couch their
cases in individualistic terms, focusing more on their own personal and professional qualities than on systemic patterns of discrimination.

These themes will be explored in the following paper, which is based on interviews with twenty faculty women who filed charges of sex discrimination
against colleges and universities.[1] These women relied on laws and regulations
passed during the late sixties and early seventies which promised a significant
improvement in the status of women in academia. The first federal measure to
prohibit sex discrimination in higher education was Executive Order 11246,
which requires all colleges and universities receiving at least $10,000 in federal
contracts to implement an affirmative action plan in hiring.[2] The Equal Pay Act

Source: Emily Abel, "Collective Protest and the Meritocracy: Faculty Women and Sex
Discrimination Lawsuits." This article is reprinted from FEMINIST STUDIES, Volume 7, no. 3
(1981):505–538, by permission of the publisher FEMINIST STUDIES, Inc., c/o Women's Studies
Program, University of Maryland, College Park, MD 20742.

of 1963, which mandates equal pay for equal work, was extended to cover executive, administrative, and professional employees in 1972.[3] Title IX of the Education Amendments Act of 1972 prohibits sex discrimination in eduational activities in all federally assisted programs.[4] The most significant law for faculty women, however, is Title VII of the Civil Rights Act of 1964, prohibiting discrimination in hiring and establishing the Equal Employment Opportunities Commission (EEOC) to enforce its provisions.[5] This act is often heralded as one of the first tangible victories of the women's movement. True, the insertion of the word "sex" in the original bill was not just a result of pressure by feminist legislators and lobbyists, but also a consequence of the misguided machinations of conservative southerners, intent on dealing a deathblow to the entire bill. Nevertheless, women's groups could claim responsibility for the fact that sex as well as race discrimination subsequently came to be considered by the EEOC as a legitimate area of concern. Moreover, it was largely as a result of pressure from feminists, joining with civil rights advocates, that amendments were passed in 1972 strengthening the enforcement powers of the EEOC and including educational institutions as well as governmental bodies within its jurisdiction.[6] Although a few of the women interviewed for this study also asserted rights under several other laws, all relied primarily on Title VII.

Many academic women viewed Title VII as a powerful weapon with which to attack institutional sexism, and they began to take advantage of this measure almost immediately. Within the first year after passage of the 1972 amendments, two hundred and fifty cases were filed against educational institutions.[7] But other women were more skeptical. Looking at the experience of the civil rights movement, they questioned the ability of laws to alter ingrained attitudes and patterns of behavior. Moreover, they pointed to aspects of Title VII that made it an ineffective agent for the redress of past injustice. First, the initiative for investigating discrimination has to come from an individual, who is then vulnerable to harassment and retaliation. Second, the law upholds the traditional liberal goal of fair cooperation, but leaves unchallenged the structural sources of unequal opportunity.[8]

As previous studies have demonstrated, Title VII has not proven to be an effective mechanism for eliminating sexism in academic employment. For one thing, faculty women have won only a small proportion of cases decided since Title VII was extended to educational institutions.[9] Furthermore, the condition of women in colleges and universities has not improved since 1972;[10] as we will see, women continue to be concentrated in low-status and low-paying positions.

This study seeks to assess the effectiveness of Title VII as a vehicle for redressing injustice by examining how women who have suffered discrimination experience the complaint process from the point at which they first recognize that they are victims of discrimination until their cases are concluded.[11] I will first discuss the position of faculty women in colleges and universities, the responses of the interviewees to the incidents of discrimination, and the factors involved in their decisions to protest. I will then trace the complaint process, including campus grievance mechanisms, governmental enforcement agencies, and litigation. Next I will discuss the role of lawyers, and the extent to which the grievants were successful in gaining the support of other women. Finally, the costs and benefits of filing a sex discrimination charge will be assessed.

To understand the significance of Title VII in the lives of women who protest, we can not limit ourselves to that relatively small percentage whose cases are resolved by judicial decisions. Most cases are dropped at a relatively early stage or settled out of court.[12] Of the twenty women interviewed for this study, only two have been through court trials. Four accepted out-of-court settlements, and the remainder were interviewed while their cases were still pending.

The unfavorable precedents that have been accumulating in academic Title VII cases affect women at every stage in the grievance process, increasing their difficulties in obtaining both legal services and financial support from outside groups, and often weakening their determination to proceed with litigation. But an analysis of the entire complaint process permits us to answer the following questions: To what extent are the victims of sex discrimination in academia victimized by the very law that purports to help them? How has the feminist movement influenced women who decide to challenge sexism in universities? Conversely, to what extent do these cases foster some of the aims of the women's movement, such as raising the consciousness of other women and men on campus, providing the basis for ongoing organization, and effecting institutional change? Above all, how do various women reconcile the contradiction between their individual aim of personal academic success and the collective goals of women as a group?

DISCRIMINATION IN THE IVORY TOWER

Although most of the interviewees filed charges as individuals, they were all challenging patterns of discrimination that have become the concern of a growing number of academic women. The position of women academics in four-year colleges and universities has not changed since the passage of the 1972 amendments to Title VII: women continue to constitute only 24 percent of the full-time faculty, and they remain clustered in the lower levels of the academic hierarchy.[13] In all institutions, women hold a larger proportion of the part-time than of the full-time positions;[14] part-time teachers are typically paid significantly less than the prorated full-time salary; they are denied security of employment, opportunity for advancement, research support, fringe benefits, and access to the departmental decision-making process. Even full-time women faculty are more likely than their male counterparts to hold nonladder appointments; women represent 37 percent of the lecturers and 49 percent of the instructors, as opposed to 18 percent of professors in the tenure track.[15] The proportion of women at each level within the tenure track also is inversely related to the status of that position: women constitute 28 percent of the assistant professors, 16 percent of the associate professors, and 8 percent of the full professors.[16]

The major problem, then, is not entry but advancement, and this is the issue raised by many of the women in the present study. One woman alleged discrimination in promotion after receiving tenure, and two challenged the termination of their contracts at the stage of a pretenure review. Seven other women claimed that unfair practices had adversely affected their tenure decisions. Certainly in this era of retrenchment in higher education, advancement is extremely difficult for men as well as for women. Although the promise of regular promotions and tenure is often implicit in initial appointments, increasing numbers of junior faculty are forced to recognize that there is no longer any room for them at the top. Nevertheless, as the previous statistics suggest, promotion is especially difficult for women, and they receive tenure far less frequently than their male counterparts.[17]

These figures also show that an additional hurdle is placed in the path of many women: a disproportionate number begin their careers in part-time or temporary positions, not in the tenure track.[18] In fact, the only significant gains for women have been in such slots.[19] Because most part-time faculty are ineligible for promotions and they lack access to grievance procedures, the issues raised in this study do not pertain to them. Hence, none of the interviewees were employed solely on a part-time basis.

Women who accept temporary, full-time appointments often expect to advance rapidly to regular positions. In some cases they are virtually guaranteed promotions; in others, they are assured of priority when a tenure-track position becomes available. But they are gradually made aware that their expectations are unfounded. Either funding for the promised position disappears, the job description is written so as to exclude them, or they are informed that they are disqualified by virtue of poor recommendations or unsatisfactory performance. As we will see, the women's movement has helped to demystify this process, encouraging women to blame institutionalized sexism for their blocked careers rather than their own deficiencies. Seven of the claimants in this study alleged that discriminatory treatment had prevented their promotion from a nonladder position to a regular appointment; a job they had initially viewed as the first rung of the academic ladder was in fact a revolving door.

Wage differentials in higher education constitute a second major concern of faculty women. In 1972, women faculty members earned an average of $1,700 less each year than their male counterparts; by 1977 the gap had widened to $2,316.[20] One woman interviewed for this study based her claim entirely on an allegation of discrimination in pay, and two women filed a charge on this count as well as on others.

Another feature that many interviewees shared was involvement in women's studies. Eight women (more than one-third) reported that they had either taught some of the first women's studies courses at their schools or had played instrumental roles in establishing women's studies programs on their campuses. These figures can be explained in two ways. On the one hand, women's studies faculty and supporters might be particularly prone to view an injustice as discrimination and to recognize the necessity of confronting men in positions of power. But on the other hand, many women argued that their mistreatment was a direct consequence of their participation in women's studies. By insisting that the study of women had a legitimate place in a university curriculum, they had lessened their own chances of career advancement.[21]

The interviewees uniformly agreed that the discriminatory practices they were challenging were qualitatively different from any sexism they had encountered as graduate students.[22] Some women did report that, since acquiring a feminist consciousness, they had begun to reinterpret their graduate school experiences: "I didn't recognize the anti-feminist problem when I was a graduate student but in retrospect I realize that . . . all the supervisory little things within the Teaching Assistant system . . . were all given to men. So male graduate students would come and judge my classes, never a woman. I never went to their classes and judged them. It didn't hit me then." Nevertheless, even allowing for an increased feminist awareness, the discrimination these women were protesting seemed to them far more blatant than any earlier mistreatment. Their testimony lends support to studies demonstrating that the more status and authority a woman seeks, the greater the discrimination she encounters.[23]

RESPONSE TO DISCRIMINATION

The experience of discrimination was extremely painful for most of the interviewees.[24] Those women who were denied tenure typically had to sever their connections with institutions to which they had devoted a great deal of energy and where they had spent critical years of their lives. More seriously, they realized that, in a tight job market, the termination of their appointments could signal the end of their days as academics. Five of the interviewees were unemployed for at least one year after they were fired, and six others took jobs outside of higher education, many after a futile search for another teaching position. Many had tried to "play by the rules" and had expected that diligence would be rewarded, as it had been in the past. Some also feared that they would be diminished in the eyes of others: "I didn't want anyone to think that what happened to me happened because of my inadequacies."

The traumatic effects of sex discrimination were intensified by the tendency of many women to blame their own deficiencies. Such a response is natural in a society that stresses individual achievement and propagates the dream of universally attainable upward mobility. These women, moreover, had previously achieved a high level of success through the educational system, the chief

mechanism for disseminating this ideology. Although students are often channeled into predetermined slots in the social hierarchy, they are taught that there
is a close correlation between reward and merit. The socialization of women also
contributes to their tendency to blame themselves for any setback; women are
taught to look to others for approval and affirmation.[25] Even successful women
often carry within themselves a fear that they are in fact frauds, that momentarily they will be "found out."[26] A rejection thus reinforces their own sense of unworthiness.

This psychological composite is particularly important because the first step
in filing a sex discrimination charge was recognition that an injustice had occurred. The women had to believe that they had been judged not as individuals,
but rather as members of a group that is generally accorded a lesser value.
Although a number of grievants claimed that they had long been conscious of
sexism at their colleges or universities, others described the painful process of
discovering the existence of institutionalized discrimination. In a few instances,
the women's awareness of discrimination crystallized only after their appointments were terminated. One woman's testimony provides an exceptional example of how an understanding of the operation of discrimination can transform
feelings of unworthiness into anger and a determination to seek redress:

> When I was fired, I went into a complete and total depression. Much of my trouble
> was that I needed a definition of my case. All I knew was that there was unfairness
> but I didn't know what had happened or why. I wasn't involved in women's groups,
> but if I had been, that might have helped me perceive at an earlier time what was go-
> ing on.
>
> But then someone told me to go to EEOC and when I got there, they asked me
> questions about my salary, my working conditions, and how many other women
> were on the faculty. Then they said, "You've got a sex discrimination suit; you're just
> one of the others."
>
> Then NOW contacted me, and people began calling me who also had problems
> at the university and I began to realize it wasn't just me. Now I have strength both
> physically and emotionally. I know what took place and so I can defend myself.

This woman's discovery that her personal problems originated in the structure of the university made her determined to challenge her treatment and gave
her the courage to do so. Nevertheless, it is often difficult for academics to question the fairness of the educational system. Accustomed to succeeding in school,
they have a stake in believing that the brightest and most talented rise naturally
to the top. Any suggestion that their present failure is caused by systemic forces
casts doubt on the validity of their past successes and the possibility of future
ones. Moreover, an important part of their own jobs is evaluating the work of
others, and they want to believe that they can do so without being influenced
by subjective factors.

Some women academics may be particularly resistant to perceiving themselves as victims of social and economic forces.[27] Although many faculty women have formed active support networks, others cling to the illusion that they, as individuals, can transcend collective social constraints. Even when they owe their positions to pressure from the women's movement, such women persist in believing that they have "made it" on merit alone. They take pride in being "special" and "exceptionally deserving," and focus on elements that separate them from other women on campus, whether students, secretaries, research assistants, librarians, or teachers. The discovery that they share problems with other women threatens this sense of uniqueness.[28]

Women with these views are caught in a bind. Self-respect may depend on recognizing the systemic causes of their present plight, but challenging the meritocracy calls into question a system that rewarded them in the past. In fact, many of the women never completely resolved the issue of whether their problems originated in personal failure or social forces. They were forced to reconsider this question at many stages during the grievance process. In turn, this ambiguity affected both their goals and their strategies.

THE DECISION TO PROTEST

Although the women's movement has stressed the significance of protest and confrontation, the act of filing a grievance is difficult for many women. The very qualities that women are encouraged to develop—dependence, conformity, and passivity—tend to discourage many from asserting their rights. It is possible that some academic women believe they achieved their past success only by being "good" students and exhibiting deference toward their male professors.[29] Ambivalence about pursuing a high-level career presents another barrier to confrontation.[30] Finally, to the extent that women take pride in their professional status, they might feel it unbecoming to complain or even to admit publicly that they have suffered from discrimination.

Nevertheless, the women reported a variety of motives for filing grievances. Several had been involved in the civil rights and antiwar movements and they viewed the present protest as a natural extension of their earlier social activism. Many women described themselves as having a "combative personality" or being unable "to pass up a good fight," although these qualities are not considered "feminine." A black interviewee stated: "All Blacks learn that they have to keep fighting for what's rightfully theirs." Significantly, almost one-half of the plaintiffs turned to the example of a female relative—an aunt, a mother, or a grandmother—whom they characterized as a fighter. In addition, a number of women stated that they had been aware of the psychic costs of taking no corrective action; had they done nothing, they would have internalized the judgments against them. Finally, at least four women mentioned that they were strongly impelled by revenge, "a much underrated emotion," according to one.

But above all, when asked why they had decided to protest, the women stressed the goals they hoped to accomplish. In fact, the interviewees can be divided into two groups on the basis of their aims. A few women claimed that personal considerations were primary. One woman, for example, insisted: "Initially I was concerned with my own particular oppression, my particular instance. My grievance was filed because of my own situation, not because of any principle. I didn't think about other women." A second woman similarly denied the link between the details of her case and larger patterns of discrimination: "I saw my case as a personal thing. If it had had some social benefits that would have been all right, but essentially it was a personal fight. There were a lot of unique factors." Women such as these will be characterized as "apolitical." They emphasized the idiosyncratic or accidental aspects of their own cases, and they confined their vision to their own specific concerns. Furthermore, they generally wanted to attain greater power or higher status within the university without necessarily questioning traditional methods of operation or calling into doubt any of the assumptions underlying the educational system.

The majority of women interviewed dwelled on the larger purposes of their individual protests. Although only one-quarter of the women defined themselves as committed activists, many claimed that they were motivated largely by idealistic concerns. While seeking personal vindication and professional advancement, they stressed the political significance of their action. They were "working for other women," "fighting for the principle," or "showing the university that it couldn't do whatever it wanted to women." In some instances, their cases had become moot by the time they were resolved. Three women who were contesting the termination of their contracts insisted that they did not want their jobs back. But most were motivated by an amalgam of personal and political aims and viewed these two goals as inseparable. Thus one woman, who spoke of her need to convince herself that, as she put it, "my case, my battle was worth fighting for," assumed that her search for personal vindication was related to the shared experience of women as a group. Moreover, many of the women whom I define as "political" sought to alter fundamental patterns in the university. For example, one woman explained: "My aim was not just back pay or promotion. My aim was to transform the entire system, to redistribute power, to change the status quo so that women could participate equally."

In sum, the grievants divided along the same lines as supporters of the women's movement in general. Some feminists emphasize the attainment of individual self-fulfillment and authenticity; others stress social change to improve the position of women as a group. Decisions these grievants made throughout the course of the complaint process reflected these different outlooks.[31]

What did most of the women believe would happen if they charged a university or college with discrimination? Both groups of women approached the grievance process with high expectations about the outcome.[32] One woman "truly believed that the law would work," and she noted how difficult it was to abandon the illusion of an early or easy victory: "At each stage what kept me going was the naive belief that at the next stage it would all be settled." Some of these women had filed their cases soon after the passage of the 1972 amendments to Title VII, and they shared the general excitement surrounding that event. But the high expectations of the grievants also can be viewed as a consequence of their class position. Just as many academics have a stake in upholding the educational system that has rewarded them in the past, so most members of the middle class assume that the legal system will be responsive to any rights they assert; in the past, when they put forward a claim, they generally were rewarded.[33] Part of the outrage many grievants felt as their cases progressed stemmed from the disjunction between the privileges they had previously received and the poor treatment they experienced when protesting sex discrimination. But their class position also gave them confidence. Their heightened, even unrealistic expectations were vital in sustaining them during the long, tedious frustrating, and degrading grievance process.

THE COMPLAINT PROCESS

Few women had definite notions about how to proceed when they decided to seek redress. Despite the prevalence of discrimination against women in academia, some faculty women are not connected to any networks that might furnish them with information about possible remedial action. Moreover, the grievants were naturally unable to obtain advice from university officials about how to file a sex discrimination charge. University rules of confidentiality also impeded initial attempts to fight back. Many women reported that they were unable to obtain information about either the procedures that had been followed in their cases or the criteria on which an unfavorable decision had been based. One woman stated: "One of the most difficult things about these decisions is that no one will tell what the vote was and who had been involved. It took me a year and a half just to find out what had happened."

Many women first appealed to various administrators, including the campus president and system-wide chancellor. Although these officials routinely expressed interest and concern, in no instance did they intervene on a grievant's behalf. Some administrators counseled the woman "not to make waves," warning that her career would be ruined irreparably if she proceeded to lodge any complaint. Affirmative action officers were similarly unhelpful. Despite the promise inherent in that title, these officers generally report to personnel committees or deans and are frequently criticized for contributing to a false appearance of equal opportunity that obscures the facts.[34] The verdict of most of the interviewees was that these administrators were "ineffective" or "useless."

Most women also requested an internal grievance hearing. They reported, however, that the campus grievance committees were dominated by male senior professors; thus, their appeal was decided by those who either were responsible for the initial discrimination or who had a strong interest in refusing to acknowledge the existence of sexism on campus. Moreover, these committees typically had jurisdiction only over procedural irregularities and were unable to consider issues of racism or sexism. A few of the women who held nonladder appointments were shocked to discover that they lacked grievance rights entirely. Only two women reported that grievance committees had found in their favor, and in both cases these decisions were reversed by the administration.[35]

The next stage was equally frustrating. Most of the complainants filed a grievance with EEOC, the regulatory agency established by Title VII.[36] Whenever there is a state agency, the case is automatically deferred to that agency for sixty days; however, over 85 percent of the cases revert back to EEOC after this period has elapsed because the state agency has not resolved them.[37] EEOC investigates the charges and decides whether there is "reasonable cause" to believe that discrimination has occurred. If so, the commission seeks a settlement between the aggrieved party and the employer.

Since the passage of Title VII, women have criticized both state and federal enforcement agencies for unnecessary delays, ineptitude, and lack of diligence in pursuing sex discrimination cases.[38] The experiences of most of the women interviewed substantiate these charges. One woman concluded that EEOC "did nothing but push papers." Another characterized the commission as "very stuffy, very bureaucratic, very against rocking the boat." The main criticism was the length of time the investigation took. Since its inception, EEOC has been plagued by enormous backlogs and inadequate staffing. By 1974, the commission had 90,000 unresolved cases;[39] three years later, the backlog had grown to 126,000.[40] Thus, although the commission is supposed to settle cases within 120 days, most women reported that their complaints took at least two or three years. The inadequate qualifications of the investigators were another cause of complaint. Two women did report that their cases were handled expeditiously by dedicated and diligent investigators, but most grievants were convinced that their complaints were processed by investigators who knew little about academic employment practices and did not consider allegations of sex discrimination very significant.

Whether or not EEOC has taken action on a particular case, it will routinely issue a "right to sue" letter after 180 days if requested.[41] Five of the women chose to go into court without waiting for a determination by EEOC. The others were advised by their attorneys to exhaust administrative remedies before proceeding with litigation.

In all but one of the seven cases in which EEOC rendered a decision, the finding was favorable to the complainant. In other words, the agency discovered that there was "reasonable cause" to believe discrimination had occurred. Nevertheless, the outcome was disappointing to the grievants. Although conciliation proceedings are supposed to follow a ruling by EEOC, the agency has no power to compel a university to participate. One woman remarked: "I received my certified letter from EEOC stating that they found in my favor. It all seemed so promising. But then the university refused to conciliate and that was the end." Then, too, the conciliation process tended to focus exclusively on the issues in the specific case under consideration.[42] Thus, despite the desire of a significant number of grievants to alter campus policies and practices, institutional reforms were never part of the final agreement. One woman did design a new tenure-review procedure which was then written into the agreement, but the university was only required to follow it in her case. Moreover, the most common form of relief was a cash settlement. Women who were seeking goals other than pecuniary compensation were outraged: "They tried to buy me off," was one woman's reaction. Even the less political women had sought moral satisfaction or personal vindication, but this was often explicitly denied. In one instance, a grievant was asked to sign a statement that the university had never discriminated against her. In another, the university refused to sign the final agreement if it contained a statement asserting that the claimant was competent. Finally, none of the women thought that the award was adequate compensation for the pay she had lost or the damage to her career.[43]

When conciliation attempts fail, the Civil Rights Division of the Justice Department can take cases to court. However, the Department chooses to handle only a few such cases every year and, as of late 1980, it had not yet intervened in an academic suit. Two interviewees reported that the division had "flirted" with their cases, but then decided against intervention. Since 1972, EEOC has also had the power to file suit in federal court against intransigent private institutions. But EEOC, like the Department of Justice, will litigate only landmark cases. Hence the burden of filing a suit generally falls on the individual complainant.

The decision to litigate represented a critical juncture in the complaint process. Two women decided not to persevere after considering the time and energy that would be required and the slim likelihood of success.

The first step in litigation was often to seek to obtain class certification. In order to do this, a plaintiff must demonstrate that her case is typical and that it adequately represents the class. Once a class is certified, the case has a greater potential to confer benefits on other women and to effect structural change. In other words, an individual claim is transformed into a collective action.[44]

One type of evidence used in litigation also underlines the collective aspect of Title VII cases: statistical proof of a pattern of discrimination. The use of statistics illustrates the tensions inherent in this law between equal opportunity for individuals and the enhancement of the position of disadvantaged groups as a whole. In fact, even women who have not sought class certification generally rely at least partially on statistics. In such cases, evidence of group discrimination is used to prove an individual claim.

Nevertheless, faculty women, like professional women generally, have been notoriously unsuccessful in resting their cases on statistics. Instead, they are forced to rely on evidence of procedural irregularities or of their personal characteristics. The latter type of evidence is most commonly used, but from the plaintiff's point of view, it has severe disadvantages. For one thing, the trial is diverted from the real issue at stake. Although the grievant went to court to protest a university's discriminatory practices and policies, the trial focuses on her own qualifications.[45] Moreover, she is even less likely to receive a fair hearing than she did at her original review for promotion. She carefully produces evidence of her academic accomplishments, but the university summons all its power to prove that she is inadequate as a teacher, scholar, and human being. As many interviewees remarked, the process of taking depositions and answering interrogatories in the pretrial stage revived questions about individual worth that arose at the inception of the case. One woman noted:

> The interrogatories were even worse than the initial denial of a promotion. . . . I began to question my own worth and wonder, well, maybe the college is right, look what they're saying. It's very hard to have people that you think highly of saying these things. I could hardly bear to read the answers to the interrogatories in the beginning because I took it so personally.

A woman whose case did go to trial recalled:

> It was very unpleasant when my own academic reputation was being scrutinized. I wasn't just a statistic. They couldn't say, "she's terrible," because then it would have been clear that interviewing me at all was a sham. But there was always a sense that I wasn't quite good enough and that was very hard and it took me a long time to overcome that. And I of course had to say that I was wonderful. That was hard too, because you're taught to be terribly modest.

Of the ten women who undertook litigation, only one obtained a resolution that she considered satisfactory. In an out-of court settlement, she was granted tenure; furthermore, the university agreed to institute a far-reaching plan of affirmative action. Two women lost their cases after trials. One other negotiated an out-of-court settlement that fell short of her original goals. The other women, still awaiting a court hearing, tended to be less than sanguine about achieving their original expectations.

LAWYERS

Most of the claimants first sought legal counsel when they appealed to an enforcement agency, although two women hired attorneys as soon as they filed charges with university grievance committees, and two others waited until they undertook litigation. As professionals, they often had better access than most women to information about legal services. Many had friends or relatives who were lawyers or could furnish the names of attorneys. In addition, the women's movement has served as an important source for disseminating such information. Four of the women were either referred to lawyers by an organization such as the National Organization for Women (NOW) or followed the recommendation of other women who had filed similar cases. Of the remaining interviewees who consulted lawyers, one received a referral from the campus chapter of a faculty union, and two others were advised by the EEOC investigators who handled their cases.

The major problem was not locating a lawyer, but convincing that lawyer to handle the case. For many women, the difficulty of obtaining legal counsel presented the first indication that suing a university would be a far more difficult and frustrating process than they had originally assumed. From the point of view of lawyers, Title VII cases have a number of disadvantages. Because most individuals lack large amounts of capital to invest in paying a retainer, the only workable arrangement is a contingent fee. Thus, lawyers are forced to invest their own money in the cases. Moreover, Title VII cases typcially last a long time, and lawyers can not expect to obtain any return on their investment for several years. Should the cases lose, the lawyers are paid nothing. All Title VII cases are difficult to win, but academic sex discrimination suits face unusually unfavorable odds. Thus, even lawyers who specialize in Title VII litigation refrain from taking such cases. Persuading a lawyer to accept a retainer requires a showing that success is not just likely, but is highly probable. Such success turns not on a showing of discrimination, but on whether or not the individual is unusual. One of the few attorneys who continues to represent a sizable number of academic plaintiffs explained the criterion of selection she uses: potential clients must demonstrate an academic record "of clearly outstanding excellence."

What did the women look for in their lawyers? The "apolitical" women were largely indifferent to the political orientations of their attorneys. They wanted a specialist whose legal competence inspired confidence. Moreover, they tended to be pleased if their attorneys could relate to university officials and opposing counsel on terms of easy familiarity. Thus, one woman expressed satisfaction with her lawyer because he was "brash, aggressive, flirtatious and loud, just like the men at the college and the other lawyers, and so he could deal with them." She explained why it was essential for grievants to obtain legal counsel: "Government agencies must protect a whole class action, while a lawyer will work just for you as an individual."

The other group of women sought lawyers who shared their concern with the principled as well as the tactical aspects of litigation and who were willing to raise political issues in the trial. Moreover, they were suspicious of the relationship between their lawyers and the legal community:

My lawyers are feminists and one is known as a civil rights attorney but they do first name [sic] the lawyers of the university system and they work with them and against them on different kinds of issues and cases and it sometimes makes me wonder.

These lawyers kept saying, "we can't antagonize the judge too much, because he'll screw us in another case." I would say, "well, you have to ask this." "We can't, it would upset him, we can't upset him," and on and on. So how I fit into their relationship to that judge – that was the most important thing for them.

As these quotes suggest, conflicts between lawyers and clients were built into their relationship.[46] Regardless of how strongly lawyers believed in the principles raised by particular cases, their primary allegiance was apt to remain with the legal community and they were likely to avoid action that could undermine their standing with the judge or opposing counsel. Feminist lawyers, moreover, face the same dilemmas as the complainants; their own desire for professional success compels them to seek acceptance from other attorneys, even at the expense of the political purpose of the legal suit. Lawyers and clients were divided by other factors as well. For example, although many of the women worked closely with their lawyers, providing the latter with evidence and even discussing legal issues, at some point they had to reliquish control of their cases to experts whose judgment they could not question. One woman spoke of her difficulty in relying on someone else to "choreograph" her case in court. Financial arrangements also opposed the interests of lawyers and clients. As in most Title VII litigation, the lawyers in these cases ususally worked on a contingent fee basis. This arrangement had clear advantages for the plaintiffs, most of whom lacked the resources to pay legal fees in advance of or during the proceedings. But lawyers who were not reimbursed for each hour of work were strongly motivated to conclude the cases as quickly as possible.[47] Thus, the grievants' relationships with their lawyers tended to replicate their experiences with the enforcement agency to which they had appealed. They found themselves under pressure to accept whatever the university officials offered, without regard to the principles that originally stimulated them to protest:

The university pressed me very hard to accept their offer and my lawyers said, "take the money settlement, take the money settlement," and I said, "My job, the principle," but they didn't listen. The whole fight I had been fighting on principle seemed to be restructured entirely and I was helpless. It was done with me standing outside and flailing and shrieking, "You can't do that to me, I've fought this fight for three or four years." The principle was lost entirely and this is what really caused my breakdown. After all that fighting the fight was being taken away from me and made into a sort of commodity for the lawyers and for that legal system of ours. That was too much.

SUPPORT

> Feminist consciousness begins with self-consciousness, an awareness of our
> separate needs as women: then comes the awareness of female collectivity – the
> reaching out toward other women, first for mutual support and then to improve our
> condition.[48]

We might assume that an academic woman engaged in a sex discrimination
case would be strongly motivated to enlist the support of other women. Before a
teacher could protest her situation, it was first necessary that she recognize that
she was oppressed as a woman, not simply mistreated as an individual.
Moreover, the grievants faced overwhelming odds. Their opponent was an institution accustomed to litigation, which could not be hurt by delays and harassment, and which had enormous financial resources at its disposal.[49] Most
significantly, the women were fighting not simply against the actions of individual male professors and administrators, but also against university policies
and practices that systematically discriminated against women. When the
grievants took their cases beyond the confines of the university, to government
agencies and courts, they discovered that these institutions also were controlled
by men and that they enforced male dominance. Efforts to seek redress were
continually hampered by informal bonds among men who could have furnished
assistance. As the women's movement has constantly asserted, women cannot
fight as individuals if they want to overcome the forces that oppress them as a
group.

Nevertheless, asking for support runs counter to the individualism inherent
in the educational system. Although this system serves to allocate people to
prescribed slots in the social hierarchy, it also holds out the promise of upward
mobility based on individual merit. Just as the "apolitical" woman viewed her
prior academic success as a personal achievement, so now she was determined to
continue to "make it" on her own. Moreover, she considered it inappropriate
to ask others for help because she was fighting to rectify a personal injustice, not
to further a cause. One woman explained how perceiving her case in highly
individualistic terms inhibited her from seeking support from other women:

> My case was primarily personal and I suppose that might account for why it wasn't
> easy or necessary for me to feel that I should go out and find other people to give me
> money or to support it. Wives of friends [who taught at a nearby university] said, "let
> us know if there's anything we can do," and I found that sort of embarrassing. To ask
> somebody for help is a rather personally involving thing. I would have been in the
> position of saying to people, "take me on as your case."

She could not ask for assistance, then, because she did not believe her case had
implications for others.

In addition, the primary loyalty of the apolitical woman was to the university, not the women's movement. Thus, she sought to placate the colleagues whom the protest might have offended and carefully avoided any connection with organizations that might be considered radical. One woman considered approaching the American Civil Liberties Union or NOW, but then decided that it would be unwise to consult "any of those propaganda groups." A second woman stated:

> I didn't connect myself with groups like NOW or something simply because this college doesn't like publicity, they do not like being hounded by groups. I wanted to protest, but I wanted to do it in the most civilized, quiet way that I could, meaning maintaining everyone's dignity if possible.

As this quote illustrates, it was extremely important to many women to retain an image of themselves as professionals; they regarded any form of collective activity as unbecoming to a faculty member. One woman explained why she did not discuss her case with students or colleagues: "I wanted very much to be completely professional these last weeks of school." Thus, these women sought to present themselves as embodying an ideal toward which others could aspire; they did not wish to work as one among a group of equals. When asked about her association with the women's movement, a woman responded:

> I considered myself one of the people who was helping the women's movement in the best way I knew how which was doing my work, teaching, publishing, simply being the first woman at this university, but I wasn't doing it by being a banner waver.

Occasionally, the less political women rejected the few offers of help that were forthcoming, but several expressed bitterness about the isolation they had experienced once they filed complaints. When they had been most in need of friendship and affirmation, no women had come forward. Although they did not actively seek to organize support, they were hurt when others did not rally around them.

The more political women were generally determined that their protests not remain isolated events. Viewing their grievances as social in origin, not individual, they looked to group action for a remedy. Moreover, many of these women were accustomed to operating within a collective context and had a strong sense of solidarity with others. One woman described herself as someone who "goes from group to group, taking care never to be isolated." She used her own experience to make the point that all support must actively be solicited: "I worked for my support, I earned it. . . . I put myself on the line for a lot of people. I defended people when I did not have tenure and I took strong stands. So I didn't just come forward saying, support me because I've been treated badly. . . . I did a lot for other people and in return I got support."

Like the less political grievants, they spoke of the anxiety they experienced when they had to ask others for help or when their cases formed the focuses for fund-raising activities. However, they coped with such anxiety by recognizing that it had a social base, just like the adverse decisions by their departments. Thus, one woman recalled the rallies organized on her behalf as initially painful: "As women, we are not socialized to be the center of our own rallies. I had to learn to say what was true about myself, even if it sounded like boasting."

These women were strongly motivated by the goal of politicizing other women on campus. One said she was "gratified" when some of her colleagues "started a Title VII fund" and used it "as a focal point for general organizing of other women." A second noted with pleasure that the women who helped her collect data "turned into conscious feminists." In a third instance, women faculty organized discussion groups in which they examined "the familiar but largely unexplored words like 'merit' and 'excellence.'" Thus, a primary function of these cases was to furnish a catalyst for the formation of new groups on campus.

Nevertheless, even the more political grievants were not very successful in securing support from other women. Many did speak gratefully of the activities of their former students and of secretaries. In a few instances, the interviewees were helped and sustained by the efforts of other women faculty. The following comment is representative: "Many of the people – some at the college and some who have left the college – have turned out to be just amazingly supportive, at the risk of their own careers, and that has made all the difference to me." However, such testimonials were relatively rare. Although women often mildly protested the injustice that had occurred, they generally stopped short of offer-ing such help as providing financial assistance, speaking to administrators and other faculty members on the grievants' behalf, soliciting off-campus support, or furnishing necessary information.

Of course, in no case were there many women in a position to supply assistance. One interviewee was the first female professor at her university. Others were part of the small numbers of women in predominantly male faculties. It is easy to understand why untenured women might be reluctant to support a colleague who alleges sex discrimination; as the job crisis intensifies, many junior faculty refrain from taking action that could jeopardize their careers. From the security of their tenured jobs, senior faculty women have less to fear from championing the cause of an aggrieved sister. Nevertheless, these women have the greatest stake in maintaining belief in meritocracy. Even if they owe their positions to pressure from the women's movement, they tend to perceive themselves as uniquely deserving. Thus, they view women who file sex discrimination charges as failures in the academic race, rather than as victims of a biased selection system.[50] In sum, the very factors that inhibited many inter-viewees from acknowledging sexism at their own universities or subsequently organizing support networks operated to deter other women from rallying around them.

The failure of most of the grievants to elicit support from their female colleagues can be explained in other ways as well. Grievants who had held only short-term temporary appointments had had no opportunity to develop collegial relations with other faculty members. Those few interviewees who did succeed in mobilizing others when they first filed a grievance found this support slowly waning as their cases dragged on. Many of their supporters left the university when their own appointments ended, or they found employment elsewhere. Others lost interest in the case as it slowly meandered through the labyrinth of government agencies and courts without producing any perceptible results.

When the grievants turned to off-campus groups and individuals, they were even less successful in generating support:

> I wrote to a large number of women off campus and only heard from one. This one woman was very nice, she sent about $10. But that was it. I wrote to about thirty women's groups, including women's caucuses and women's professional groups, and to the unions—A.F.T., N.E.A., and A.A.U.P.—and I didn't hear from any of them.

Two women did report that the Women's Equity Action League had provided some assistance in raising funds, and another stated that this association would write an amicus brief when her case went to trial.[51] In general, however, whatever support comes from outside sources tends to be sporadic and unorganized.

A few women did manage to wage a collective fight by filing their complaints together. One woman asserted that "we all became stronger working with each other." In addition, they were able to aggregate their financial resources, collaborate in the work of accumulating data, and share a lawyer. They were also less vulnerable to harassment and reprisals: "Nobody has been a martyr. There are just too many of us to try to pick off, and if someone did try, the pattern would be very clear." Moreover, group action permitted women to broaden the scope of their protest:

> Our suit is massive. . . . It differs from the kind of case where only one person comes forward with a grievance. We are attacking many different causes—election of chairpeople, who's eligible to vote for the chairperson, initial appointment, rank, pensions; maternity benefits. We can cover so many areas, we're really moving to change the system.

These women, then, represented an important exception to the portrait of the isolated Title VII litigant. But few fought as a group.[52] For most, protesting sex discrimination in academia remained a lonely pursuit.

COSTS

Women typically found themselves subjected to ridicule and disparagement as soon as their cases became public knowledge.[53] Many were surprised by the rapidity with which rumors began to circulate, discrediting them as scholars, teachers, and colleagues. One woman was known as "the crazy lady on campus," a second as "a liar and hysterical," and a third as "a bitch, a terrible woman, all-powerful, evil, and wicked." Others simply described themselves as "tainted."

Some women considered themselves fortunate to be able to leave their institutions shortly after filing charges. Those who remained often found themselves isolated from their former colleagues: "Last year I walked through the halls as if I were wearing a red star." "I expected to be challenged, I didn't expect nothing. The people I had most counted on acted as though I didn't exist, and it was really eerie." It is easy to understand why labeling and ostracism would be difficult for any woman with lingering doubts about whether her career had been ruined by systemic forces or by her own inadequacies. One woman described the way personal charges affected her:

> I have begun to wonder: if six or seven or ten male people in my department say that I am this kind of person, is it possible that I really am? When they say that I said or did something which I do not believe I said or did but they all agree, is it possible I did? The self-doubt is enormous and you begin to think you're probably crazy.

But retaliation also took more serious forms.[54] A number of women cited instances of blacklisting. One woman heard reports that she "was being smeared." Another stated:

> I applied for jobs for many years without getting any and I had indications that I was blacklisted. For example, people told me that they couldn't get me through their administration because I was a troublemaker. The clearest indication of this was when I went to a university for an interview and I gave a seminar talk and it all went very well, and the chairman walked me back to my hotel and he said to me, "Well, I'm certainly glad to meet you, I really pictured you with claws."

Why do women elicit such extreme hostility and retaliation when they complain about sex discrimination? One reason is undoubtedly that women traditionally have been punished for stepping out of line, and these women were deviating from prescribed conduct in two ways: they were demonstrating serious professional commitment, and they were confronting men in positions of power. As one woman recalled, "It was as if I had done the unthinkable. I had clearly transgressed." Moreover, it is definitely in the interest of the men on campus to deflect the charge from the institution by blaming the individual, proving that she is clearly unworthy of the job or promotion she is claiming; they insist that discrimination never occurs in the university. Some male administrators may also have feelings of guilt which they allay by exaggerating or even manufacturing faults of the plaintiffs. Specific instances of retaliation must also be viewed within the broader context of the white male backlash in academia, which takes such forms as resistance to mandatory affirmative action

and charges of reverse discrimination and which undoubtedly will intensify during the Reagan administration.[55] But the frequency and extent of the reprisals
also serve to remind us just how threatening these cases are to the members of a
university community. Any complaint of bias challenges fundamental assumptions underlying the educational selection system. Indeed, as we have seen,
some of the grievants themselves stopped short of recognizing that sexist
behavior pervades academia.

There are a number of other costs entailed in filing a sex discrimination
charge against an institution of higher education. Almost all the women spoke of
the enormous amounts of time and money required and of the strains on both
themselves and their personal relationships. Each step took much longer than
the complainant originally anticipated, and years often elapsed between the initial filing of a grievance and the final resolution of a case.[56] Much of this
slowness can be explained by factors previously discussed: the inefficiency and
inertia of government bureaucracies and the accumulated backlog of EEOC in
particular. But a persistent complaint was that the university had purposely
tried to delay the proceedings in the hope that the plaintiff would grow
discouraged and give up.[57] In a few instances, university officials pressured the
woman to refrain from filing a charge with EEOC while her case was under
review by a campus grievance committee; the university proceedings then
dragged on for months without any resolution. Once cases went beyond the confines of the university, employers resorted to such delaying tactics as refusing to
relinquish critical documents or requesting endless postponements of hearings.

Women also complained about the amount of time they had to spend preparing for trial. One litigant who was coordinating a large class action reported:

> I have lost almost entirely any personal life. If I were married or if I had children or if I
> had any personal obligations, I couldn't do what I do. It's only possible because I'm
> single and my only obligation is to a cat. There are times when I work literally day
> and night, six and seven days a week.

More frequently, women spoke about the incursions on their work time. After
all, academic reputations must be made early, and the worth of an article is often
gauged by the age of its author.[58] Thus, many of the women assumed that their
value in the job market had diminished as years passed without any entry added
to their curricula vitae. Revealingly, they often measured the amount of time
spent on the case in terms of scholarship they might have produced. To two
women, legal action represented lost articles; two others equated their cases
with books. Nevertheless, it would be wrong to overstate the costs to these
women of investing so many hours preparing their cases for trial. As a few of the
interviewees noted, the ability to arrange their work schedules and to allocate
time to a court case was one of the substantial privileges they enjoyed as
members of the middle class.

The financial costs for women who undertook litigation were "unending and staggering." Although lawyers were typically paid on a contingent fee basis, other costs mounted rapidly. One group involved in a massive class action against a major university spent $20,000 a year exclusive of attorneys' fees. A woman fighting an individual lawsuit estimated that she spent $7,000 for xeroxing, depositions, computer time, and statistical analysis during the pretrial period. Some women noted that their ability to pay legal costs was "a luxury" made possible by a spouse's earnings or by savings. But it is important to note that the greater resources the employers could muster totally dwarfed the advantages of these litigants as middle-class women. The individual grievants were pitted against institutions that could easily spend huge sums of money fighting the allegation of sex discrimination.[59]

Finally, there are subjective costs of fighting a university.[60] A number of women spoke of "becoming the case," as they invested so much time and energy in it: "Your sense of who and what you are becomes eroded." A few also described physical ailments that they attributed to the tension of litigation. One discovered that she had become so anxious that her handwriting had altered.[61] Protest also takes its toll on personal relationships. The great majority of women spoke of the critical support they had received from husbands and lovers: "If there is one hero in the case it is my husband," said one. But they also acknowledged that they found themselves venting their rage and frustration on the people closest to them.

GAINS

Despite the many costs of protest, most of the interviewees claimed they were glad they had decided to assert their rights. They pointed to the substantial gains their protest had achieved for other women. Although it is clearly impossible to measure precisely the impact of a particular case on the position of women faculty on that campus, the grievants were frequently convinced that their struggles had been responsible for major improvements in the position of other women.[62] In some instances, they pointed to an increase in the number of women who were appointed or promoted. One woman contended:

Because I went to court, things changed on that campus, even though I lost. They've become more careful. Women were promoted and their salaries were raised. I know that where I am now my department was famous for being abominable to women and many people suffered but I felt absolutely none of that because I came after someone else had sued the college. So I think things are changing and that we're changing them for each other.

New policies and practices were also adopted:

> Because of my questioning of things, there have already been many changes in the
> tenure process. There have been new procedures established for promotion and
> tenure.
>
> I'm sure that Title VII changes an institution even if women lose the case.
> . . . At the very least, this university knows that it can't just do anything it wants,
> that it is accountable. The university knows that it has to watch itself, that its power
> it limited, that there are definite constraints.

Ironically, then, despite the individualistic nature of the cases, institutional
changes often resulted, and the individual complainants were led to assess their
cases in collectivist terms.

There were also benefits for the claimants themselves. For one thing, during
the course of their protests, most of the women acquired information that had
previously been withheld, and thus they understood exactly why they had been
denied promotions or salary increases. In many instances, they were permitted
to see their personnel files for the first time. Two women discovered that
negative evaluations of their work had been solicited, another that positive letters of recommendation had been removed from her file, and still another that
the letters on file had all been written by friends of the male colleague who was
her competitor for the one tenured position in her department. Others were
heartened to learn that the letters from outside referees were better than they
had been led to believe:

> I had been told that the letters were marginal and that was one reason why I couldn't
> get tenure. But they had lied. I had to fight to see the letters, and when I finally did, I
> found that there were very good; in fact, they were embarrassingly good.

Some women also gained access to correspondence between department
members. As a result, one woman learned that her family responsibilities had
been used to justify her department's continual refusal to promote her The
revelations of another were far more dramatic:

> My lawyer asked if there was any private correspondence dealing with the case.
> . . . The judge finally ruled on this and people had to divulge this. Of course there
> was a lot of faculty resistance and the chairman grumbled about the time it took. But
> through that I got hold of a set of letters from the chairman and the person who is
> now chairman with very good comments, nasty sexist comments about me. It was
> terrific evidence. There had been a conspiracy between these two men to get me
> denied tenure on the basis of incredibly personalistic and sexist criteria. There were a
> lot of machinations back and forth.

Thus, the information acquired often removed any lingering suspicions that lack
of advancement resulted from personal inadequacies.

In addition, university procedures were demystified:

> We forced the university to open up their confidential files, . . . and now we know what a dreadful shape these files are in. We know now that academic judgment is all too often a cover. . . . There is no way you could make an academic judgement in large numbers of files we saw. It's done with whispers and in deals.

Another woman deepened her understanding of the meaning of sexism:

> I just didn't realize the dimensions of discrimination, and the connection between discrimination and power. . . . The lawsuit has given me a chance to step back and look at my culture as though from the outside. It's been difficult to do because it's like looking at the air. I've had these moments when suddenly the air has color and I can see it. I have found out that sex discrimination permeates just about everything and that it has so many more dimensions than I thought it did.

When the grievants had to decide how to make use of this information, they divided along familiar lines. The more political women were committed to sharing the information as broadly as possible. As we have seen, they regarded the education of others as a crucial aspect of their protest. In many instances, their lawyers advised them to refrain from writing or speaking publicly about the development of their cases. Nevertheless, they publicized their cases as much as they could and encouraged other women to attend any hearings that were conducted. To the "apolitical" women, however, publicity had a more limited value. Less concerned about politicizing others, they spoke about publicity as a "weapon" they could employ strategically. Thus, one woman agreed with a university request that the grievance committee hearing be closed. She then informed university officials that she intended to issue a press release if she did not obtain satisfaction at this level: "I think that the university settled because of their fear of publicity. This was my trump card." When a second grievant gave her letter of determination from EEOC to university officials, she agreed to avoid publicity if the university acted quickly in accordance with the agency's findings. Her decided preference was to refrain from "making a fuss out of my case. I didn't want a turmoil in the newspapers. I did not want the university to be publicly charged with discrimination."

When interviewees testified that the gains of protest outweighed the costs, they referred above all to their heightened self-respect. Despite the charges that had been leveled against them at various times, they gained a sense of their own power as a result of fighting on their own behalf. A number of women who had never before challenged injustice expressed pride in their new-found ability to assert their rights. One stated: "This case has made a fighter out of me. Now I make trouble when I find myself abused." Others described their growth in self-confidence. For example, one woman said:

I know I'm a lot stronger now. People out there can no longer define me. I think women have been defined so long by roles, by husbands, by parents, by society, by other women often. I think this case has freed me from a lot of that. It's almost intangible, but I have a sense of who I am. There's just some core that I recognize and know and no one can touch me at that core. They can't knock it down. They can't crumble it.

CONCLUSION

The effectiveness of Title VII as a vehicle for remedying sex discrimination in university hiring and promotion is undermined both by the contradictory position of the grievants and by the individualism of the legal process. Women who pursue grievances under this law must first recognize the existence of sexism in academia and the way in which they, along with all other women on campus, are victimized by institutionalized discrimination. However, they are often reluctant to acknowledge the extent to which their cases challenge the ideology of the educational selection system. This system is simultaneously the mechanism for sorting students into predetermined slots in the social hierarchy and the means of legitimating professional status. All academic women have reaped substantial benefits from this system as it currently operates. Furthermore, one of their tasks as professors is to judge and rank their students and colleagues, and in this way they participate in the channeling process. Thus, the grievants do not want to cast doubt on their past academic successes or to question their current roles.

As we have seen, some of the women interviewed for this study insisted that they were primarily interested in rectifying personal injustices and in advancing their own careers. True, the majority did hope to change fundamental patterns in the university. To further this goal, they sought the support of women's groups, both on and off campus, tried to find lawyers who were willing to raise political issues, and they publicized their cases widely. Nevertheless, even these women found themselves caught in a double bind.

Moreover, the grievance process itself undermined collectivist ideals. All the women were forced to couch their cases in individualistic terms, focusing on their own merit and achievements, rather than on systematic patterns of discrimination. University grievance committees restricted themselves to procedural matters and ignored larger issues of racism and sexism. Similarly, government agencies often limited their investigations to the specifics of each case, rather than looking for patterns of institutional behavior. Even ostensibly feminist lawyers frequently pressured the women to accept settlements that benefitted only the particular grievants. In addition, the structure of academic institutions and the widespread acceptance of meritocratic ideology militated against the formation of women's support networks; hence, few of the women succeeded in waging a collective protest.

Nevertheless, the protests did promote some collective goals. As a result of filing grievances, many women overcame feelings of personal inadequacy. Access to closed personnel files demystified university procedures, revealing the means by which men in positions of power succeed in excluding large numbers of women from university faculties. Despite the limited scope of support networks, female students and faculty frequently were politicized by the publicity surrounding the grievances. Finally, the cases often led to substantial improvement in the status of campus women other than the grievants themselves.

Both the positive and negative experiences of the interviewees provide lessons for the faculty women who are likely to encounter discrimination during the eighties. The large number of women who received initial appointments in the mid-seventies will come up for tenure during the next few years, in a period of university retrenchment and in an environment increasingly hostile to the goals of affirmative action. This paper suggests that personal, professional, and political gains may result from more conscious and effective work to create collective forms of protest.

But it is equally important for complainants to work in conjunction with other campus struggles that demonstrate a greater potential for eliciting collective action and furthering political aims. Two examples are campaigns to establish and defend women's studies and ethnic studies programs, and organizing drives for unions of both faculty and clerical and maintenance workers. Certainly the prospects for fulfilling broad-based political goals on campuses are gloomy at present. Assaults on both women's studies and ethnic studies programs and attempts to undermine academic unions suggest that progressives on campuses will be devoting their energies primarily to defensive battles. But these trends also make apparent the necessity for links between different campus groups committed to the redistribution of power and privilege within institutions of higher education.

NOTES

I wish to thank the following people for their help: Richard Abel, Grace Blumberg, Gloria DeSole, Nancy Gertner, Sherna Gluck, Annette Kolodny, Carrie Mendel-Meadow, Ruth Milkman, Margaret Nelson, Ros Petchesky, Deborah Rosenfelt, Linda Shaw, Joan Smith, and Judith Stacey.

1. One-half the women lived in California. Of the remaining, two-thirds lived on the East Coast. The interviews were semistructured, lasting on an average of between one and two hours. They were tape recorded, except in the case of four women who voiced objections.

All the women had filed charges of sex discrimination against four-year colleges and universities in which they had held full-time appointments. In addition, two women alleged discrimination on the basis of national origin, one on the basis of religion, and three others on the basis of race.

I have accepted at face value the accounts of what the women experienced and have not tried to assess whether or not they were "deserving" of the jobs and promotions they were seeking. It would have been impossible to assess the qualifications of the women, compared with those of their male colleagues. Moreover, statistics about the position of women in academia suggest that, although individual women may well be unqualified, discrimination is pervasive.

2. As amended by Executive Order 11375, effective October 1968.

3. Public Law 88-38, 1963.

4. Public Law 92-318, 1972.

5. Public Law 88-352, 1964; the courts have not yet determined whether or not Title IX applies to employment in education.

6. Public Law 92-261, 1972; see Barbara Sinclair Deckard, *The Women's Movement: Political, Socioeconomic, and Psychological Issues*, 2nd Ed. (New York: Harper and Row, 1979), p. 410; Mary Eastwood, "Legal Protection against Sex Discrimination," in *Working Women*, ed. Shirley Harkess and Ann Stromberg (Palo Alto, Calif.: Mayfield Publishing Company, 1978), pp. 113-17; Jo Freeman, *The Politics of Women's Liberation* (New York: Longman, 1975), pp. 53, 188; and Donald Allen Robinson, "Two Movements in Pursuit of Equal Opportunity," *Signs* 4, no. 3 (Spring 1979): 413-33.

7. Bernice Sandler, "Sex Discrimination, Educational Institutions, and the Law: A New Issue on Campus," *Journal of Law and Education* 2 (1973): 613. By 1974, 1,500 complaints against colleges and universities had been filed with EEOC (Thomas M. Divine, "Women in the Academy: Sex Discrimination in University Faculty Hiring and Promotion," *Journal of Law and Education* 5 [1976]: 434, n.)

8. Ruth B. Cowan, "Legal Barriers to Social Change: The Case of Higher Education," in *Impact ERA: Limitations and Possibilities*, ed. California Commission on the Status of Women (Millbrae, Calif.: Les Femmes, 1976), pp. 158-83; Arlene Kaplan Daniels "A Survey of Research Concerns on Women's Issues" (Washington, D.C.: Association of American Colleges, 1975), pp. 4, 15; and Sara Evans, *Personal Politics: The Roots of Women's Liberation in the Civil Rights Movement and the New Left* (New York: Alfred A. Knopf, 1979), pp. 212-32.

9. Judith P. Vladeck and Margaret M. Young, "Sex Discrimination in Higher Education: It's Not Academic," *Women's Rights Law Reporter* 4 (1978): 59-78. There have, however, been recent victories at Muhlenberg College, Keene State College, Georgia Southwestern College, and the University of Minnesota.

10. Divine, "Women in the Academy," p. 431; Suzanne Howard, *But We Will Persist: A Comparatie Research Report on the Status of Women in Academe* (Washington, D.C.: American Association of University Women, 1978).

11. Studies that discuss the human impact of filing charges of sex discrimination against universities include Joan Abramson, *The Invisible Woman: Discrimination in the Academic Profession* (San Francisco: Jossey-Bass, 1975); Joan Abramson, *Old Boys, New Women* (New York: Praeger Publishers, 1979); and Athena Theodore, "Academic Women in Protest," unpublished paper, January 1974.

12. Divine, "Women in the Academy," p. 434, n.

13. Howard, *But We Will Persist*, p. 8.

14. Ibid.

15. Ibid., p. 57.

16. Ibid., p. 22.

17. In their classic study, "Sex Discrimination in Academe," Helen S. Astin and Alan E. Bayer concluded that women are promoted more slowly than men, "*independent of individual background characteristics, professional activities, and work settings*" (in *Academic Women on the Move*, ed. Alice S. Rossi and Ann Calderwood [New York: Russell Sage Foundation, 1973], pp. 333–56).

18. Howard, *But We Will Persist*, p. 23. See also Carnegie Council on Policy Studies in Higher Education, *Making Affirmative Action Work in Higher Education* (San Francisco: Jossey-Bass, 1975), p. 89; and Lora H. Robinson, "Institutional Variation in the Status of Academic Women," in *Academic Women on the Move*, pp. 212–14.

19. During the 1959–60 academic year, women constituted 9.0 percent of the full professors, 17.5 percent of the associate professors, 21.7 percent of the assistant professors, and 29.3 percent of the instructors (Lionel Lewis, *Scaling the Ivory Tower: Merit and Its Limits in Academic Careers* [Baltimore: Johns Hopkins University Press, 1975], pp. 129–30). See also Marion Kilson, "The Status of Women in Higher Education," *Signs* 1 (1976): 937–38; and Bernice Sandler, "Backlash in Academe," *Teachers College Record* 76, no. 3 (February 1975): 403.

20. Women's Equity Action League, "Facts about Women in Higher Education," (1977), p. 8. During the academic year 1978–79, the salaries of male faculty increased 6.4 percent, while women received an increase of 5.6 percent (U.S. Department of Health, Education and Welfare, National Center for Education Statistics, news release, "Selected Statistics on the Salaries, Tenure and Fringe Benefits of Full-Time Instructional Faculty for the 1978–79 Academic Year," 27 February 1979, p. 1.)

21. Florence Howe and Carol Ahlum, "Women's Studies and Social Change," in *Academic Women on the Move*, p. 403, n.

22. A study comparing the perceptions of male and female graduate students about sex discrimination found that the men tended to "see" more discrimination than the women reported having experienced (Joyce Mitchell and Rachel R. Starr, "A Regional Approach for Analyzing the Recruitment of Academic Women," in *Women in the Professions: What's All the Fuss About?*, ed. Linda S. Fidell and John DeLamater [Beverly Hills: Sage Publications, 1971], pp. 39–40).

23. Cynthia Fuchs Epstein, *Woman's Place: Options and Limits in Professional Careers* (Berkeley: University of California Press, 1970); and Constantina Safilios Rothschild, "Women and Work: Policy Implications and Prospects," in *Working Women*, p. 429.

24. One of the women interviewed for this study was the leader of a campus women's group which filed a charge on behalf of other individuals. She had no personal complaint herself. This section of the paper is based on the experiences of the other interviewees, all of whom did have personal claims.

25. See, for example, Sandra Bem and Daryl Bem, "Case Study of a Nonconscious Ideology: Training the Woman to Know Her Place," in *Female Psychology: The Emerging Self*, ed. Sue Cox (Palo Alto: Science Research Associates, 1976), pp. 180–91; Leonore Weitzman, "Sex Role Socialization," in *Women: A Feminist Perspective*, 2nd ed. edited by Jo Freeman (Palo Alto: Mayfield, 1979), pp. 153–216.

26. Jane Flax, "The Conflict Between Nurturance and Autonomy in Mother Daughter Relationships and Within Feminism," *Feminist Studies* 4, no. 2 (June 1978): 181; cf. Saul Feldman, *Escape from the Doll's House* (New York: McGraw-Hill, 1974), pp. 95–98.

27. A number of studies of grievance behavior have concluded that Americans are inhibited about complaining because of the fear of appearing to have been "taken"–or even acknowledging it to oneself–in a society that prizes autonomy and competence. See, for example, Arthur Best and Alan R. Andreasen, "Consumer Response to Unsatisfactory Purchases: A Survey of Perceiving Defects, Voicing Complaints and Obtaining Redress," *Law and Society Review* 11, no. 4 (1977): 701–42; Barbara A. Curran, *The Legal Needs of the Public* (Chicago: American Bar Foundation, 1977); and Carrie Menkel-Meadow, *The American Bar Association Legal Clinic Experiment: An Evaluation of the 19th Street Legal Clinic, Inc.* (Chicago: American Bar Association, 1979). We can assume that these fears are particularly pronounced for victims of discrimination because those who are discriminating invariably explain their behavior in terms of the inadequacies of the victim.

28. For example, Marianne Githens and Jewel L. Prestage, "Introduction," in *A Portrait of Marginality: The Political Behavior of the American Woman*, eds. Githen and Prestage (New York: David McKay, 1977), pp. 6–9; Carolyn G. Heilbrun, *Reinventing Womanhood* (New York: W.W. Norton and Co., 1979), pp. 37–70; Arlie Russell Hochachild, "Making It: Marginality and Obstacles to Minority Consciousness," in *Women and Success: The Anatomy of Achievement*, ed. Ruth B. Knudsin (New York: William Morrow, 1974), pp. 194–99; Dorothy Richardson Mandelbaum, "Women in Medicine," *Signs* 4, no. 1 (Autumn 1978): 138; Mitchell and Starr, "Regional Approach," p. 40; Adrienne Rich, "Toward a Woman-Centered University," in *Women and the Power to Change*, ed. Florence Howe (New York: McGraw-Hill, 1975), p. 2; and G. Staines, C. Tavris, and T. E. Jayaratne, "The Queen Bee Syndrome," *Psychology Today* 7, no. 7 (1974): 55–60.

29. Rich, "Woman-Centered University," pp. 26–28.

30. Patricia Albjerg Graham, "Status Transitions of Women Students, Faculty and Administrators," p. 167, and Joan Huber, "From Sugar and Spice to Professor," pp. 125–35, both articles in *Academic Women on the Move*.

31. It was not possible to explain the women's political orientations by differences in individual background.

32. Curran, *Legal Needs*; Austin Sarat, "Studying American Legal Culture: An Assessment of Survey Evidence," *Law and Society Review* 11, no. 3 (1977): 427–88; and Adam Podgorecki et al., *Knowledge and Opinion about Law* (London: Martin Robertson, 1973).

33. Best and Andreasen, "Consumer Response"; H. Laurence Ross and Neil O. Littlefield, "Complaint Problem-Solving Mechanism," *Law and Society Review*, 12, no. 2 (1978): 199–216; Sarat, "Studying American"; and Patricia Ward Crowe, "Complainant Reactions to the Massachusetts Commission Against Discrimination," *Law and Society Review* 12, no. 2 (1978): 217–36.

34. Nuala McGann Drescher, "Affirmative Action: Outlook Not Sunny at SUNY," *Universitas* 1, no. 2 (1979): 10; Florence Howe, "Introduction," in *Women and the Power to Change*, p. 9; and Deborah S. Rosenfelt, "Affirmative Action: The Verdict is Still Out," *Radical Teacher*, no. 11, p. 5.

35. The exhaustion of internal remedies can be viewed as a means of "cooling out." Although most of the women interviewed for this study went on to file a charge with a government agency, large numbers of women grow discouraged after appealing to campus administrators and grievance committees and decide not to proceed with any further protest (cf. Laura Nader, "Complainer Beware," *Psychology Today* 13, no. 7 1979): 60.

36. In this section, I am discussing only the agencies that enforce Title VII because all
of the women relied primarily on this law. Five women also brought charges under Ex-
ecutive Order 11246, which was administered by the Office for Civil Rights, Health,
Education and Welfare until 1978. This agency also had authority to enforce Title IX.
HEW has been particularly unresponsive to allegations of discrimination and in 1974, a
number of women's groups sued it for failure to enforce antidiscrimination laws. Women's
Equity Action League et al., v Califano, F., Ray Marshall, et al., United States District
Court for the District of Columbia, filed 11-26-74; see also Abramson, *Invisible Woman*,
pp. 169-85; Sandler, "Backlash," p. 407; Women's Equity Action League, "Facts about
Women in Higher Education," p. 11. Since the reorganization of civil rights agencies in
1978, all individual cases filed under the Executive Order are referred automatically to
EEOC. Before 1978, the Equal Pay Act was enforced by the Wage and Hour Division of
the Employment Standards Administration of the Department of Labor; one interviewee
filed a complaint with this agency. In 1978, EEOC was given responsibility for administer-
ing the Equal Pay Act; administration of the Executive Order was transferred to the Office of Federal Contract Compliance Programs. What follows is an account of the experiences of the women interviewed for this study, not an analysis of the actual operation
of state and federal agencies.

37. Joel F. Handler, "Public Interest Law and Employment Discrimination," in *Public
Interest Law*, ed. Burton A. Weisbrod, Joel F. Handler, and Neil K. Komesar (Berkeley:
University of California Press, 1978), p. 264.

38. Abramson, *Invisible Woman*, pp. 186-97; Cowan, "Legal Barriers," p. 171; New
Jersey Advisory Commission on the Status of Women, "Report on Sex Discrimination
Cases in Higher Education Filed with the New Jersey Division on Civil Rights," (1978);
Norma K. Raffel, "The Enforcement of Federal Laws and Regulations, A Report and
Recommendations for the U.S. National Commission on the Observance of International
Women's Year," (Washington, D.C.: Women's Equity Action League, 1975); see also
U.S. Commission on Civil Rights, *The Federal Civil Rights Enforcement Effort — 1974:
Volume V: To Eliminate Employment Discrimination*, pp. 500-541.

39. Freeman, *Politics of Women's Liberation*, p. 35.

40. Deckard. *Women's Movement*, p. 411. Under the administration of Eleanor
Holmes Norton, appointed Commissioner of EEOC in 1977, this backlog has been
substantially reduced, and cases are concluded more quickly than before (*Newsweek* [24
December 1979], p. 15).

41. If EEOC intends to litigate the case, the agency may refuse to issue such a letter.

42. Theodore, "Academic Women in Protest," p. 35; Leonore Weitzman, "Affirmative Action Plans for Eliminating Sex Discrimination in Academe," in *Academic Women
On the Move*, p. 502; but see "Proceedings of the Symposium on Equal Employment Opportunity and Affirmative Action," April 28-29, 1977, Wellesley College, pp. 20-21; Raffel, "Employment," p. 10; cf. Leon H. Mayhew, *Law and Equal Opportunity: A Study of the
Massachusetts Commission Against Discrimination* (Cambridge, Mass.: Harvard University Press, 1968), pp. 234-35, 253-56.

43. Even after an agreement is reached, many complainants remain dissatisfied.
Unlike almost all other agencies, EEOC lacks the power to enforce its conciliation
agreements except by initiating litigation.

44. Numerosity is a third requirement for class action suits: the plaintiff must
demonstrate that the class she/he is representing is so large that it would be impossible for

all members to join the suit. In some instances, academic women have been successful in claiming that they represent all past, present, and future women employees and applicants. (Vladeck and Young, "Sex Discrimination," pp. 68–9). Nevertheless, the paucity of female professors has occasionally been used as grounds for refusing to certify the class of academic plaintiffs. In other words, women are penalized precisely because most academic departments are white male bastions.

45. Abramson, Old Boys, New Women, p. 91.

46. These conflicts have been analyzed in other substantive areas of legal practice, such as personal injury (Douglas E. Rosenthal, Lawyer and Client: Who's in Charge? [New York: Russell Sage Foundation, 1974] and criminal defense (e.g., Abraham Blumberg, "The Practice of Law as a Confidence Game," Law and Society Review 1, no. 1 (1967): 15. See generally "Plea Bargaining," Law and Society Review (Special Issue) 13, no. 2 (1979).

47. Rosenthal, Lawyer and Client, chap. 4.

48. Gerda Lerner, The Majority Finds Its Past: Placing Women in History (New York: Oxford University Press, 1979), p. xxxii.

49. On the importance of collective rather than individual action in litigation, see Marc Galanter, "Why the 'Haves' Come Out Ahead: Speculations on the Limits of Legal Change," Law and Society Review 9, no. 9 (1973): 95–160; Stuart A. Scheingold, The Politics of Rights: Lawyers, Public Policy and Political Change (New Haven: Yale University Press, 1974); Joel F. Handler, Social Movements and the Legal System: A Theory of Law Reform and Social Change (New York: Academic Press, 1978); and Stephen Wexler, "Practicing Law for Poor People," Yale Law Journal 79 (1970): 1049.

50. See Abramson, Invisible Woman, pp. 111–25; and A. Leffler, D. L. Gillespie, and E. Lerner Ratner, "Academic Feminists and the Women's Movement," Insurgent Sociologist, 4 (1973): 45–56.

51. See Women's Equity Action League, "What WEAL Fund Can Do" (Washington, D.C.: 1979).

52. The coordinator of a local chapter of the National Organization for Women, who had organized a "Title VII Hotline," noted that, of all the women she aided, academics were the most resistant to the strategy of filing charges of sex discrimination with other women: "Each woman wanted to believe that her case was worse than that of anyone else." Similarly, although I informed all of the interviewees that I was speaking to a large number of women in similar situations, many told me that their cases were "unbelievable" or "too incredible for words." Their determination to consider themselves unusual inhibited them from taking group action.

53. Abramson, Invisible Woman, pp. 105–8; and Theodore, "Academic Women in Protest," p. 24.

54. Retaliation can be the source of a new complaint. One of the women in this study did file such a charge with EEOC.

55. See, for example, Leigh Bienen, Alicia Ostriker, and J. P. Ostriker, "Sex Discrimination in the Universities: Faculty Problems and No Solutions," Women's Rights Law Reporter 2, no. 3 (1975): 3–12; Cowan, "Legal Barriers," pp. 173–74; and Sandler, "Backlash in Academe."

56. A primary source of dissatisfaction among litigants is the endless delay they must endure, see Curran, Legal Needs; and Sarat, "Studying American."

57. See also H. Laurence Ross, Settled Out of Court: The Social Process of Insurance Claims Adjustment (Chicago: Aldine, 1970).

58. Arlie Russell Hochschild, "Inside the Clockwork of Male Careers," in *Women and the Power to Change*, p. 61.

59. Many public institutions are particularly advantaged because they are not re-quired to pay legal fees out of their institutional budgets. A study conducted in New Jersey discovered that, as a consequence, private colleges and universities settled sex discrimination cases sooner than did public institutions (New Jersey Advisory Commis-sion on the Status of Women, p. 6).

60. Phyllis Z. Boring, "Filing a Faculty Grievance" (Washington, D.C.: Women's Equity Action League, 1978), p. 4.

61. The extraordinary difficulty of isolating the impact of law upon social change is revealed in many studies, see, for example, Theodore Becker and Malcolm Feeley, eds., *The Impact of Supreme Court Decisions* 2nd ed. (New York: Oxford University Press, 1973); and Stephen Wasby, *The Impact of the United States Supreme Court: Some Perspec-tives* (Homewood, Ill.: Dorsey Press, 1970).

62. However, because reforms occurred only as a by-product of legal action, they were often used to reinforce the myth that universities are dedicated to eradicating ine-quities. It is easy to understand why university officials would deny a causal relationship between protest and reform. By demonstrating that improvements in the status of women result solely from their long-standing commitment to equal opportunity, officials can prove that both pressure from outside groups and intervention from the government are unnecessary. Even those women who gain indirectly from a Title VII case have a stake in ignoring the impact of the litigation on their campuses and attributing their promotions or salary increases to their individual merit and achievements. Thus, many groups on campus are intent on denying the impact of the sex discrimination suit. As long as the role of legal action remains invisible, however, the academic process is legitimized, and future protest is discouraged.

Chapter 21 ⸻

Negotiating Trouble in a
Battered Women's Shelter

Kathleen J. Ferraro

The treatment of battered women is discussed by examining the micro- and macropolitical forces impinging on the operation of a battered women's shelter. Funding agencies, other social services, and interpretive frameworks of staff members formed the organizational context of the micropolitical context. The women's troubles were negotiated at three major stages – intake, processing, and return to the shelter – and the major micropolitical features of this negotiation were a therapeutic ideology, the need for social control, interpersonal conflicts, and personal feelings. Criteria for evaluating and controlling the troubles of women were established in light of self work, the primary objective of shelter residence. Professional expertise was the justification for imposing staff's definitions. Women who rejected the demands of staff were labeled failures and held responsible for the problems they encountered as battered women.

S ociologists of the labeling school, despite a general appreciation of the relevance of macropolitical processes for the creation of deviant categories and statuses, have rarely systematically examined the impact of macropolitical forces upon the micro-level interactional processes whereby deviants are defined and processed in specific situations of social control. In this article, I will describe how decision making in a battered women's shelter is shaped at the micro-level of interaction within a context of macropolitical forces. The analysis will begin by looking at the macropolitical factors that gave rise to and shaped the current operation of a shelter of this sort. It will then turn to a consideration of the actual ongoing functioning of this institution, analyzing the micropolitics of trouble in this particular context.

Author's note: I would like to thank Robert M. Emerson, John M. Johnson, and Carol A. B. Warren for their helpful comments on earlier versions of this article.

Kathleen J. Ferraro is on the faculty of the Center for the Study of Justice at Arizona State University, Tempe, Arizona. She has published articles on battered women and battered women's shelters, and is currently working on a theoretical formulation of the process of victimization.

Source: Kathleen J. Ferraro, "Negotiating Trouble in a Battered Women's Shelter," Urban Life, Vol. 12 (October 1983), pp. 287–306. Copyright © 1983 by Urban Life. Reprinted by permission of Sage Publications, Inc.

METHOD

Data for this analysis were collected over a two-year period of participant observation of a shelter for battered women.[1] The shelter consisted of two three-bedroom homes located in a middle-class suburb of a large, southwestern metropolitan area. Its staff included a director, MSW consultant, three advocate counselors, a secretary, housemother, and myself as a part-time researcher. It accommodated 16 women and children at a time, and placed a maximum six-week limit on residence. All women who entered the shelter agreed to stay at least one week, to abide by house rules, and to participate in counseling, both group and individual. Funding for the shelter was provided by a matching funds grant from the state which monitored its functions through an umbrella agency.

As staff researcher, I had access to all aspects of life and decision making in the shelter. I gave particularly close attention to the staffing sessions held weekly to discuss and evaluate the cases of all women in the shelter at that time. I sat in on and tape recorded all such sessions during the 14-month period I worked at the shelter.

THE MACROPOLITICS OF TROUBLE

The very existence of this shelter, and others like it, reflects a number of macropolitical factors, beginning with the social movement that redefined woman-battering as illegitimate. This movement drew upon several different social sources, particularly the feminist movement and mental health practitioners, each committed to somewhat different philosophies.[2] Feminists view woman-battering as an extension of the patriarchal structure of society. As such, the proper response is restructuring the social order and providing support to battered women. Battering is conceived as a political problem with political solutions. Help to battered individuals should assume the forms of advocacy and sisterhood as opposed to therapy. Mental health professionals are also involved in the movement, but bring a professional therapeutic framework to bear on an understanding of woman-battering. From this perspective, battering is only one form of a larger problem – domestic violence – which is the consequence of family dysfunction. The appropriate response is to provide research and therapeutic treatment to such dysfunctional families. Thus, there are several competing approaches to the redefinition of this previously acceptable behavior, woman-battering.

Economic and Political Factors

While there is no longer widespread explicit support for the use of violence to control wives, other macro-level conditions and ideologies perpetuate an environment in which escape from a violent marriage is difficult for women. Patriarchal structures remain the basis for all major institutions. The majority of women of working age are employed, but the vast majority remain in traditional, low-paying female occupations. The poverty rate among single women heads of households is 34.6% (U.S. Bureau of the Census, 1982). Males are still expected to be the major breadwinner, and when wives work it is often to supplement husbands' incomes. When that supplement becomes the sole means of support, it is usually inadequate.

In addition, the moral concern with the rights of individuals is accompanied by a belief in individualism. Social agencies and programs are provided to people on a short-term basis to overcome temporary problems. Implicit in the provision of services is an assumption that recipients will strive to become independent of public support. Shelters in the United States limit stays to four to six weeks. Upon leaving shelters, women are expected to enter independent or familial living situations and to support their families, often with the help of government programs. In contrast, many shelters in the United Kingdom have no limit on length of stay and formerly battered women commonly set up communal living situations (Pizzey, 1974).

Therapeutic Ideology

Some of the earliest shelters were founded by feminists who advocated a "self help" model of women helping women (Leghorn, 1978). According to Leghorn, a long-term activist in the battered women's movement,

> grassroots groups, in their very structure and the nature of their services, have said clearly to battered women: It is not you that is sick. It is our society which is responsible, in its structure of sexual domination, for condoning and perpetuating this behavior and the institutions that sustain it [1978: 447].

In practice, however, the majority of existing shelters have rejected the self-help model and have adopted some version of a professional therapeutic model. Emotional counseling conducted by degree professionals prevails; democratic, collective decision making is a rarity in shelters (cf. Colorado Association for Aid to Battered Women, 1978; see also Ferraro, 1981b). To a large extent, shelters have been coopted into the traditional welfare, social service bureaucracy (Johnson, 1981). Therapeutic intervention is an integral aspect of this bureaucracy at an ideological level and a major technique of social control within specific agencies (Rieff, 1968).

In summary, economic dependence on violent husbands leads women to seek public support in creating a safer environment for themselves and their children. Such public support is offered to battered women through shelter services. However, like all helping agencies, shelters are structured on the assumptions of both the therapeutic ideology and individualism. Shelters must demonstrate the ability to make changes in clients so that the need for social services will be short- rather than long-term. As extensions of the traditional welfare network, shelters do not alter existing institutions but try to help battered women fit in as autonomous individuals.

THE JUNCTURE OF MACRO- AND MICROPOLITICS

The economic, political, and ideological forces just described were translated into the structure of the shelter where this research was conducted through its dependence on existing social agencies and their influence on the interpretative framework staff brought to their work.

From its beginnings in 1978, the shelter depended upon state financial support, and staff continued to believe that continued funding by the state depended on widespread community support which could only be gained through favorable impressions on existing service providers. These social agencies then came to exert great power over the life of the shelter through control of resources. The view these agencies held of battered women thus played an important role in the ideology and practices of the shelter.

The umbrella agency that oversaw the shelter operations had been primarily concerned with providing thereapeutic counselling for those with drug and alcohol abuse problems. Having no conception of clients without mental health problems, they equated battering with the victim's emotional disturbance and saw any effort to provide only material aid as irresponsible. Furthermore, they evaluated the work of the shelter through periodic reviews of counselors' case files and occasional observation of staff meetings, stressing concrete therapeutic treatment plans with specific goals and methods of treatment. Efforts to counter this emphasis early in the shelter's existence were met with condescending rebuttals. Agency auditors had authority and money behind their directives, so staff soon conformed to the traditional mental health model.

When the shelter was formed, there were initially unarticulated differences in philosophy among staff and board members that soon erupted into open, bitter conflict. Six months after opening, several board members decided to reorganize the shelter and professionalize it by firing the director and hiring a full-time MSW to conduct all counseling. Current counselors were told that because they lacked professional training or degrees, they were incompetent to counsel and would be restricted to household and advocacy duties. These conflicts resulted in high staff turnover and an ongoing concern for job security. Practical constraints prohibited implementation of the proposed plan. One person could simply not accomplish all the counseling. But the board's expressed preference encouraged all staff members to more fully embrace the therapeutic role (see Ferraro, 1981b, for a fuller discussion of this conflict). Thus, the therapeutic framework became the predominant context for defining battered women's problems and approaches to solving them.

Staff members, lacking professional degrees but aspiring to a professional image, felt highly vulnerable to charges of unprofessionalism by other agencies. The director's exhortation not to become "rescuers" — as evidenced in the following example — shows how perceptions of other agencies impacted directly on the provision of services to women:

I got some feedback (from another agency) that sometimes we have a tendency, instead of being counselors to our clients, sometimes, almost starting to be mother. We start getting involved with our clients, and we start doing more for them than we really should for all practical purposes.

Staff was thus deterred from crossing the boundaries of a "therapeutic relationship," at least in part by the need to create a professional image in the community.

Practical space consideratioins as well as the interorganizational context in which the shelter operated affected internal policies and practices. There was a strong belief that space at the shelter was at a premium and that those who utilized it had a moral responsibility to "work on themselves." The high demand for admittance to the shelter gave staff the flexibility to set their own standards of acceptability. Numbers meant money, and if the shelter wasn't kept full, it would not be fully paid each month. Other agencies (e.g., those dealing with the mentally ill) could not afford to be so choosey. But as the shelter always got more requests than it could fill, so staff could turn away those who did not fit their criteria. Women who did come in were expected to utilize their residency to make substantial efforts to change themselves and their situations. Those who were defined as "not working" would justifiably be asked to leave.

> DENISE (Director): She's using this space, and I know this sounds cold and hard-hearted, but she's using this space that someone else could be using who is willing to change.
> LAUREN: I agree. I think we should be able to say there are clients we can't do it for. They come in, and they are just not prepared to work, to look at themselves, and they "exit stage left," and . . .
> DENISE: We need, rather than them, we need to direct them, and we rather than them, need to "exit stage left," very clearly stating our concern and care for them, and why we are exiting them.

Those women who did not meet the staff's expectations knew they were not fitting in and usually left of their own accord. The staff definitions of such departures will be discussed below.

The micropolitics of trouble at this shelter involved the ways in which staff defined shelter policies and the troubles of individual women. Social, political, and interorganizational factors were translated at the level of the shelter in order to maintain control and develop feelings of professional competence.

THE MICROPOLITICS OF TROUBLE

The negotiation of trouble within the shelter revolved around staff's efforts to keep out troublemakers, which included inappropriate (nonbattered) clients and disruptive clients, and to minimize disorder and trouble within the shelter. Formal rules and counseling sessions were tools for controlling trouble, but the interpretation of troublesome behavior was never straightforward (Emerson and Messinger, 1977); defining behavior as trouble was subject to the ideological, interpersonal, and personal forces operating between and within staff members.

The Psychotherapeutic Framework
Defining both the troubles that brought women to the shelter as well as their behavior in the shelter was carried out within an interpretive theory of the mental health problems of women. Numerous psychological characteristics were used to describe women in defining the source of their troubles, such as "immature," "passive/aggressive," "depressed," "rebellious," and "self-destructive." Staffing sessions were arenas for accomplishing therapeutic diagnoses of client behaviors. Diagnoses were rarely straightforward but were forged through negotiations between staff members. Similar behaviors were defined differently for different women and the same woman was sometimes defined differently by different staff members.

Interpersonal Factors: Conflicts and Coalitions
There were often strong feelings of hostility and competition between staff members which resulted in the formation of coalitions. The definition of clients' troubles reflected the problems staff had with one another. Clients who were friendly with a staff member's enemies were generally perceived as troublemakers while the actions of clients close to the staff member were seldom perceived negatively. On occasion, there were overt efforts by staff members to discredit one another by pointing out the consistency with which the clients of one staff member caused trouble.

Fusions of Perceptions, Feelings, and Values
How an abused woman's trouble was interpreted by shelter staff combined perceptions, values, and feelings in complex ways which staff members found hard to articulate. The feeling that a client invoked in a staff member was often very important for understanding how a case was interpreted and what action occurred. Sometimes staff members "clicked" with a client and a positive evaluation of that client was practically insured. On other occasions there were women who irritated counselors by their style and manner. Such women were commonly seen as troublemakers. There was little consensus about formal definitions or criteria concerning abused women, so the gut-level feelings of staff were seen as important by them. However, these feelings were not entirely personal, idiosyncratic, or irrational. They combined immediate perception with commonsense, cultural (or normative) knowledge. An individual's cognitive and affective responses changed in an evolutionary manner as her experience changed and evolved. These determined interactional levels between client and counselor and thus mediated the content of a counselor's knowledge about the women. In a

typical case, Nikki, a counselor, reported that she had a hard time relating to Bonnie, an ex-junkie rock groupie with tattoos:

> She made it a day-time obsession to follow me around and let me know, minute by minute, where she was at, what was happening, what had happened in her life, and she was driving me crazy. And I did, several times, tell her that we were going to have to restrict it to counseling sessions, and that we should keep it social out here . . . I told her at one point that I really needed my space, and that I was busy. . . . You try to sympathize, but after a while, it's like, get out, leave me alone!

Not only did Nikki's dislike of interacting with Bonnie limit their interactions, it also provided a context in which Bonnie's communication patterns became "trouble."

These four factors – the need for social control, the therapeutic ideology, interpersonal conflicts, and personal feelings – were the micropolitical context in which trouble was negotiated at the shelter. Trouble was negotiated at three stages: intake, processing, and returning. I will now describe each of these stages in terms of the factors outlined above.

SPOTTING TROUBLE AT INTAKE

Women come to these shelters with a broad range of abusive experiences. When women present themselves at the shelter, they are thereby making certain claims about their past lives and current living circumstances. The typical claim would be that a woman had been beaten or abused by a violent partner. Coming to the shelter is additionally taken as an indication that they want to get away from this violence. Shelter staff may come to question and even to invalidate such claims, however, in the process of reinterpreting the trouble presented by the woman.

This reinterpretation began with intake screening which revolved around staff evaluation of commitment to self work. Were potential clients able and willing to get involved in counseling and make personal changes? A "good client" was one who demonstrated, through her situation and demeanor, a commitment to get help. By contrast, a client might be defined as "trouble" (for the shelter or staff) if her (putative) behaviors might upset the equilibrium of the house or if her demeanor was judged inappropriate for the situation. We have two distinct kinds of "trouble" here. On the one hand there are "troubles" which bring the woman to the shelter in the first place. These are subject to some amount of definition, negotiation, and redefinition. And on the other hand there are actions by the women that constitute "trouble" for the shelter and staff, actual or potential dilemmas in the ongoing management of the smooth flow of case processing. We discuss several of these kinds of trouble below.

Potential residents exhibiting signs of "severe pathology" or drug or alcohol problems were rejected at intake (or "referred out" shortly after arrival). This informal policy was discussed in staffing:

> NIKKI: Generally, there's been a tremendous amount of instability that comes through with the client where it turns out they're much more seriously ill than we're prepared to deal with here.
>
> LAUREN: Ok, something you can learn from, the last client I brought in like that was Jean.
>
> NIKKI: Yeah, but, that, Jean was somewhat workable, she . . .
>
> LAUREN: No she wasn't, not in this shelter, not at all.
>
> NIKKI: Yeah, she was very sick, yeah (laugh).
>
> LAUREN: She was a very sick, sick girl, and she had people paranoid within 24 hours of being in this place, and that's your message that they're not appropriate. What half of these women, when you start to hear things like, all these things like the VA hospital, all these mixed messages, no clear thing that's going on, the drinking, they all have this . . . with somebody that's got that much going on, with so many godawful things, they are just not appropriate for this place.

This screening process had very practical benefits in terms of protecting both staff and clients. It allowed staff to maintain control over the composition of clients, and thus potential trouble. Another local women's shelter accepted all "women in crisis," without focusing on battering. They housed exinmates, drug addicts, the mentally ill, and the transient. Women who came to our shelter from this crisis house expressed terror at the situation there. They did not feel safe and were afraid for their children.

Staff held certain assumptions regarding the appropriate demeanor of a woman coming into the shelter. Women were expected to be emotionally upset. Individual manifestations could vary, but would include indications that the woman felt overwhelmed and helpless. Women who did not seem emotionally distraught or who appeared confident or enthusiastic did not convince the staff that they were worthy and sincere applicants for help. Consider the following staff discussion of Dorothy, a problematic case because she had not actually been battered, but she and her children had been threatened with abuse:

> MARIA: And she said she's not going back anymore. She sounded really determined. She sounds like she really doesn't wanna go back, she's afraid that he will hurt the kids.
>
> JILL (MSW consultant): Does anybody else know anything about this scene?
>
> MARY (student intern): Well, I brought her in, and she seemed to be in pretty good condition when I met her at the 7-11 at 56th and State with the Crisis Intervention team. She was asking me a lot of questions about the shelter, and what we could do for her, and that she wanted an apartment. She's very interested in what we can do for her. I thought it was kind of a different type of client. She's very determined. But she seemed to be in pretty good condition that night.

LAUREN: Determined in what way?

MARY: Just to get out, to get an apartment, she kept saying over and over, "I wanna get an apartment, I wanna get an apartment, can you help me. I only make $66 a week."

SOPHIE: Did she seem scared?

JILL: I don't know why you're smiling. Was she, was she . . . did it seem like you would be in that situation?

MARY: (laugh) I wouldn't think so, I don't think I would be like that. That's what I mean, she seems like she's kind of a different client.

MARIA: Yeah, she's really, I mean she's really determined.

Note the dilemma here, reflected in different staff reactions: On the one hand, Dorothy showed determination to make changes. On the other, she appeared overly confident and concerned with what the shelter could offer her. Ambivalent feelings about her at intake set the stage for later interpretations of her behavior as disruptive and uncooperative. Dorothy had an argument with another client and left within a week after her arrival. She was working and had found her own apartment. However, she was viewed negatively because she accomplished these things without "working on herself" and without integrating into the shelter.

Women were referred to the shelter through a variety of sources. Many were self referred, responding to a public service announcement or the advice of a friend. Others were referred by social service, law enforcement, or medical agencies. In almost all cases, women who were referred by hospitals were considered "really battered" and appropriate for residency. Hospital referrals meant that there was physical injury severe enough to require emergency room treatment or hospitalization. This level of injury, immediately prior to a request for admittance, was dramatic enough to override concerns with commitment and sincerity. Women referred by hospitals were never denied admittance.

Concern with community relations influenced the response to other referrals. Counselors explicitly expressed in staffings their belief that referrals from certain agencies should never be rejected. The local crisis intervention unit and the community service agency which supplied the shelter with a free office were two agencies with which good relations were crucial. Rejection of their referrals implied rejection of their professional judgments. So clients were refused from these agencies only if staff held strong reservations and with the knowledge that rejection would create more work and trouble for them in dealing with these agencies.

Another important consideration in screening was the woman's reported history of prior attempts to escape violence. Almost all women who came to the shelter had made other efforts to leave their husbands. Most of these ended when husbands begged them to return. A history of such aborted attempts was viewed as typical and, in and of itself, neither a positive nor negative indicator of a woman's commitment to leave. However, there were a number of women whose escape efforts involved dramatic stories and heroic efforts. Women who traveled from other states to escape, often with very few possessions and little money, were seen as highly motivated and deserving. Also, women who had escaped to other states in the past only to be forced to return home were viewed as limited in their choices by husbands' drastic actions. Mary, for example, had moved to two different states on the other side of the country, and both times had been tracked by a private detective. Her husband appeared at her new homes and threatened her and her son with death if they did not accompany him home. Her account of these incidences at intake resulted in unanimous opinion that she sincerely wanted to get out of her situation and should be accepted into the shelter.

Women who had never left their husbands before (unless referred by another agency) or who expressed uncertainty about their decision to leave their husbands were evaluated more cautiously. First-timers were sometimes seen as using the shelter as a temporary weapon to punish or get back at their husbands rather than as a means for making significant changes. Callers who expressed strong feelings of ambivalence often failed to appear even if they were accepted or they called back and said they had decided not to leave home. Each woman who decided in favor of staying home after being accepted to the shelter reinforced staff's tendency to reject ambivalent cases.

PROCESSING TROUBLE

The intake process just described involved a tentative, provisional assessment of the woman's appropriateness for residency. A fuller evaluation emerged in the process of interaction on a daily basis at the shelter. As mentioned above, the main consideration in evaluating clients was their commitment to engage in "self work" — that is, to make substantial efforts to change the factors resulting in their abuse. Evaluations of clients' sincerity in self work were discussed in staff meetings. If staff concluded that a woman was not "working on herself," her prior actions became subject to reinterpretation as trouble. Evaluations of self work acted as a technique of control because women who were not "working" could legitimately be asked to leave. Negative personal feelings toward a client who failed to participate in counseling contributed to the negotiational process which labeled her a failure.[3]

By way of illustration, consider the following discussion of Donna, a professional woman who had lived with and fully supported a man 10 years her junior who had killed one of her children by abuse and who severely beat Donna and her remaining child.

> NIKKI: I've sort of come to the conclusion that the shelter's providing some service to her, and that it is a place for her to sleep and bring the baby. I'm not sure how ef-

fective the counseling is to date, because I think, I think, that she is seeing her boyfriend regularly, I really do.

SOPHIE: How many counseling sessions have you had with her? Just two, isn't it?

NIKKI: Can't get ahold of her. I had to stay one night 'til 8:30, I was on call, and she came in at 7:30 because her boyfriend had intercepted her.

SOPHIE: Let me ask you something, she's been here three weeks? And she's had two counseling sessions with you, one with you, one with you, she's actually had two sessions.

LAUREN: You might want to put this in (her case file). I told her about an apartment the first day she came in, $150 including utilities, down on [street], and she said she couldn't take it because her boyfriend lived there.

SOPHIE: She sounds like she's just full of shit. She's just doing a con job. She's using the services here as just a sleeping place. She has not participated in any counseling, she's avoided you, and I think it's time we just lay our cards on the table. One, we're not really equipped to help her. Two, she's not letting us do what we can do. And, three, she's taking up a bed, wasting our time. You're wasting your time. Now that I think of it, she's hopeless, and she's just fallen by the wayside. I think we have to admit defeat.

Donna was asked to leave on the grounds that she failed to demonstrate sincerity in her "self work." Exaggerated emphasis on self work meant that women who actually used the shelter as it was designed were perceived as "con artists."

Participation in Counseling

Staff evaluations were tied to the kinds of feelings evoked through interaction with clients. Staff and clients represented a broad range of social types, some attracting and others repelling each other. Women who appealed to a counselor could exhibit behavior that would be defined negatively if performed by a less attractive woman and still be positively evaluated. Conversely, women who were personally unattractive to a counselor had a hard time doing anything right. In this way, identical behaviors took on different meanings (see also Warren, this volume). These differences were exacerbated by conflicts among staff members. Clients were sometimes caught in shelter politics, and were unable to establish positive relationships (and thus evaluations) with counselors in conflict with one another.

Two examples of divergent evaluations of similar behaviors are Ruby and Sue. Ruby was considered by all staff members to be a very good client:

LAUREN: Ruby started out this whole thing by being very open and confronting, she was a very good therapeutic person to have around, she was just straight down the line. If something irritated her, she'd say, "hey, I don't like what you're doing," and the other person would go (pause) and then you'd go on from there, but it was really good.

Ruby was also helpful around the shelter. She cooked and cleaned without being asked and listened to other women's problems. She was a nice person who people enjoyed being around.

Sue was also open and helpful but she was defined by several staff members as "a pain in the ass."

> LAUREN: She was still a disruptive person, I mean you can say all these good things about Sue, she was still a highly disruptive person to the other clients staying here, there was a lot of interference, and it, it affected, it definitely had a tremendous effect on [other client], the stuff that she was feeding her, she was very strong, very good at taking over, and she took over to such a point that she'd interfere with other people's treatment.

Lauren's aversion to Sue was related to Sue's dislike of Lauren. Two former staff members had described Lauren's shortcomings at length to the clients, and Sue had been particularly close to these staff members. Lauren felt Sue had turned against her, and her "interference" involved voicing her disapproval to other clients.

> LAUREN: Sue had a definite problem with me because of [counselor] and [housemother] – they were closeted in there doing a number on me, that was how they relieved their anxiety about me was telling the clients how they all hated me, and the clients, I'd walk in and I'd see the clients look at me, I'd see Sue look at me like this, and then go (gasp) and I'd leave the room in horror.

Lauren's negative evaluation of Sue was based largely on her own feelings of rejection and of resentment toward the former staff members. Sue did not like Lauren and did not respond to her, so Sue's helping behavior was described as disruptive, while that of Ruby was "therapeutic."

Diligence

Commitment to self work was also demonstrated by diligent efforts at locating a job and housing. Success in these endeavors would enable the client to move out of the shelter and build a life separate from an abuser or at least free of total dependence on him. Staff put considerable effort into helping women with these tasks, and were naturally upset when women failed to follow through. Grievances were aired in staff sessions regarding such failures, and clients were consistently blamed for lack of initiative.

A positive evaluation of a woman, then, rested on three major factors: her participation in counseling, her diligence in seeking work and housing, and her relationship with counselors. The ideology of the shelter stressed the importance of involvement in activities that would resolve the emotional and practical problems that kept them in violent situations. These factors could even override considerations of physical safety in evaluating women's acceptability as continued residents. They were also reflexively related to the feelings women evoked in particular counselors. Counselors responded to clients on the basis of preferences which emerged from commitment to the therapeutic ideology and relationships among staff members.

These criteria for evaluation were negotiable, resulting in different analyses of similar behaviors and even of the same client. On several occasions shelter staff were confronted with the necessity for deciding whether to readmit a client a second or third time. When this occurred, there were further evaluations and negotiations over whether a client had been or was now "sincere," "committed," and so on.

CONCLUSION:
EVERYDAY CONTROL OF TROUBLE

The cases that have been described demonstrate that a variety of interpretations can be applied to similar actions, and that determination of a particular definition of trouble depends on shifting, ambiguous criteria, such as staff's feelings and interpersonal conflicts. Battered women's troubles did not exist as objective facts but were negotiated by staff through their discussions in staffing sessions. This analysis has detailed the political process through which definitions of battered women's troubles were negotiated by shelter staff. The organizational account of these negotiations glossed over the political aspects of decision making through invocation of professional expertise. However, the decision-making process here was not simply a matter of applying clinical norms but was the manifestation of political negotiation.

From the variety of perspectives on which to base a program for battered women, this shelter chose the therapeutic ideology. The therapeutic ideology provides an account of the source of women's troubles that focuses on their own emotional problems rather than on their husbands' behaviors. Staff then evaluated women in terms of their commitment to self work to overcome these problems. Women who did not feel the need or desire for emotional counseling or who were ambivalent about leaving their husbands did not evidence commitment to self work and were therefore negatively evaluated and sometimes denied access to shelter services. In some cases, this meant that women in physical danger were denied protection.

These are very concrete, practical consequences of defining and responding to "battered women" from a therapeutic ideology. The first consequence was projecting a professional image to outsiders and other staff. As mentioned earlier, the umbrella agency that monitored the shelter assumed that serious counseling would occur at the shelter. Staff felt pressure to demonstrate to umbrella personnel that they were competent counselors who persuasively encouraged their clients to become immersed in analysis. Clients who were uncooperative in this process did nothing to build a case file that reflected the counselor's ability to counsel or to manage her clients.

Staff members experienced pressures to act and feel "professional." There was a tremendous amount of conflict between staff and board of the shelter, and people often worried about losing their jobs. Thus, adherence to the therapeutic ideology provided a vehicle for demonstrating competence to other staff members and especially to the MSW supervisor. The use of "presenting problems," diagnoses, and case files listing therapeutic interventions were techniques for establishing a claim to professionalism.

A second consequence of adhering to a therapeutic ideology was the provision of an explanation for the problems encountered by staff at the shelter. Given the belief that women who came to the shelter had to participate in psychological therapy, there were many instances in which the counselors felt both they and the women failed. The therapeutic ideology (which imposed these expectations initially) provided a built in rationale for the failure of women to respond to therapy.

> JILL: I think a lot of the reason why it's hard to get an effective program is a lot of the people have very long-term problems, and they have fixed personality structures, and really, given even three months, that would be a very radical kind of thing for them to be able to grow and develop that much, for them to be able to go out on their own. . . . A lot of adults are walking around, and they're missing some very critical ingredients that they need to be able to function well, at any kind of a mature level . . . I think that it's limited in some ways to what you can do.

The counselors could feel better about their work if they believed that women who did not "work on themselves" at the shelter did so because of problems in their childhood rather than a failure of the counselor to help them. For every woman, a social and family history was taken and were always discussed in staffing. If a woman came from a broken or violent home, that was evidence enough that she would be very difficult to reach. If she did do well at the shelter, that did not bring the issue of deeply rooted psychological problems into question but served as a validation of a counselor's outstanding skills.

Finally, the therapeutic ideology was a basis for establishing that the staff, not the residents, were in control of the shelter. In a shelter that rejected the therapeutic ideology and focused on egalitarian treatment of women, actions of the shelter staff would be open to challenge and change. When staff is empowered to interpret women's actions from a therapeutic perspective, however, such challenges can be dismissed as evidence of psychological disturbance and used as grounds for negative evaluations of self work. Lisa, for example, was described as exhibiting "super passive-aggressive behavior."

> LAUREN: She hasn't followed through. This is total self-defeating behavior. She sets herself up to be helped, and then takes the help away with the same stroke. She gets a lot of attention. This is self-defeating. She had an appointment to see a social worker and did not follow through. She has avoided all sessions, we never see her. She's gone when we get here.

DENISE (Director): If she's avoiding, you do some insisting. . . . Rather than them controlling the system, we do have the power to control. We need to look at that because we're having people that don't want to work, who are taking up bed space, who are just using us as a dumping ground, in essence what they're doing is getting in the way of other people, because other people don't need the stress. You're gonna get a lot less fighting if you establish that you're in control. They know the rules when they come in, they make a couple mistakes, that's ok, they make a couple of major mistakes, that's it.

The staff was encouraged to define trouble in a way that clearly established their authority within the shelter. Women who had valid, principled complaints about the shelter rules and structure were defined as demonstrating hostility and were negatively defined by the staff. Such women had no power to change the opinion of staff and so left the shelter. Control of the shelter was established and maintained through a priori rejection of clients' ability to legitimately challenge the decisions of staff. All women were expected to follow rules, but assessment of compliance was filtered through counselors' perceptions of individual cases.

The therapeutic ideology has commonly produced definitions of troubles that "blame the victim" for their circumstances (Ryan, 1971). Rape victims have been accused of unconscious desires to be raped, incest victims have been described as active participants in "family pathology," and battered women have been portrayed as masochists. In each case, the contextual, situational, and political nature of defining people's troubles from the therapeutic framework has been ignored. By adhering to the therapeutic ideology, staff in this shelter for battered women focused almost exclusively on the emotional problems of individual women. Decisions and policies favored women who acquiesced to staff's insistence on self work and discriminated against those who refused to "accept responsibility" for their situations. That is, women who tried to use the shelter only as a refuge and support system without becoming immersed in self work were defined as "con artists."

Operating on the basis of the therapeutic ideology permitted staff to maintain control of residents by discrediting challenges to authority as manifestations of psychological disturbance. It also allowed staff to portray their decisions as rational, clinical judgments founded on professional expertise. Examination of the decision-making process reveals the political nature of these decisions and demystifies the therapeutic justifications. The response to battered women in this shelter was a political one, and one that tended to place the blame on the battered victim for involvement in a violent situation.

NOTES

1. More details and analyses of the research can be found in Ferraro, 1981a and 1981b, and in Ferraro and Johnson, 1983.

2. Social scientists have been involved in the battered women's movement providing analyses of incidence and social structural variables (Straus et al., 1980), psychological aspects of the problem (Walker, 1979), and political analyses (Dobash and Dobash, 1979; Johnson, 1981).

3. Using factors that stressed the behavior of the woman in the shelter rather than more practical considerations created the potential for rejecting a woman in serious danger. Such a rejection did occur in the case of Jessie. Jessie was asked to leave after two days in the shelter because she was viewed as insincere and a troublemaker. She changed the story of her problems each time she told it, and the staff finally concluded that her "real" problem was not having enough money to keep the electricity turned on. She talked to her husband daily and planned a "date" with him. So, she was asked to leave. Several days later, the local police crisis intervention unit called and informed the shelter staff that Jessie had been beaten by her husband and was taken by them to the hospital for treatment of lacerations and two broken ribs. The staff was embarrassed by this situation, but still maintained that Jessie was a con artist and had probably exaggerated her injuries to gain sympathy. Ideological and personal assessments took precedence over serious injury in evaluating this woman's right to receive help.

REFERENCES

Colorado Association for Aid to Battered Women (1978) Services to Battered Women. Washington, DC: Office of Domestic Violence, Department of Health, Education, and Welfare.

Dobash, R. and R. Dobash (1979) Violence Against Wives. New York: Free Press.

Emerson, R. and S. Messinger (1977) "The micro-politics of trouble." Social Problems 25: 121–134.

Ferraro, K. (1981a) "Processing battered women," J. of Family Issues 2: 415–438.

———(1981b) Battered Women and the Shelter Movement. Ph.D. dissertation, Arizona State University.

———and J. Johnson (1983) "How women experience battering," Social Problems 30: 325–339.

Johnson, J. (1981) "Program enterprise and cooptation of the battered women's shelter movement." Amer. Behavioral Scientist 24: 827–842.

Leghorn, L. (1978) "Grassroots services for battered women: a model for long term change," pp. 444–463 in Battered Women: Issues of Public Policy. U.S. Commission on Civil Rights.

Pizzey, E. (1974) Scream Quietly or the Neighbours Will Hear. Baltimore, MD: Viking.

Rieff, P. (1968) The Triumph of the Therapeutic. New York: Harper & Row.

Ryan, W. (1971) Blaming the Victim. New York: Vintage.

Straus, M., R. Gelles, and S. Steinmetz (1980) Behind Closed Doors: Violence in the American Family. Garden City, NY: Doubleday.

U.S. Bureau of the Census (1982) Current Population Reports, Series P-60, #133, Characteristics of the Population Below Poverty Level: 1980. Washington, DC: U.S. Government Printing Office.

Walker, L. (1970) The Battered Woman. New York: Harper & Row.

Feminism and the Mass Media: A Case Study of *The Women's Room* as Novel and Television Film *

Linda M. Blum

INTRODUCTION

A s more and more women enter the paid labor force, the divorce rate rises, and the number of single parent households continues to grow,[1] it becomes clear that family life in contemporary American society is undergoing fundamental changes. Such changes are becoming central political issues as well, as in fact, only 17% of us now live in the "ideal" nuclear family of husband, wife and two children,[2] and out of all two parent households with two or more children, only 13.5% consist of families in which the husband is the sole wage earner.[3] While these empirical indicators, and the intensity of the political debates,[4] tell us that the traditional system of gender roles and the organization of family life is changing, it is unclear what meaning this has for people in their day to day life experiences, and the understandings or interpretations they construct from these experiences to make them coherent and intelligible. One way of getting at these constructed understandings of the world is to look at popular and mass cultural products. Such products would not find an audience unless the understandings of the world which they express resonate with large numbers of people. Members of an audience respond to fictional characters with whom they can, or wish they could, identify. Furthermore, mass culture itself influences people's interpretations of the meaning of their lived experience at the same time as it expresses popular conceptions. Therefore, in attempting to decipher the understandings people have of the changing sex/gender system an important place to look is at mass media images of men and women.[5]

*I would like to thank Tom Long for his helpful comments, and Vicki Smith for the time and care she put into editing several drafts of this article. Also, thanks are due to several other members of the BJS editorial board for goading me on. [Editor's Note: This article was the 1982 winner of the University of California's Gertrude Jaeger Prize.]

Source: Linda M. Blum, Feminism and the Mass Media: A Case Study of *The Women's Room* as Novel and Television Film." *Berkeley Journal of Sociology* – 27 (1982): 1–24. Reprinted by permission of the *Berkeley Journal of Sociology*.

In this paper we will look at one example of such a mass media image, a television film, which was based on a novel that had been specifically written and marketed as an indictment of the current, male dominated sex/gender system. *The Women's Room* written by Marilyn French, published in 1977, became a bestseller, and as the cover of the latest paperback edition boasts, it sold over three million copies. The fact that the book was so widely read is significant for our purposes of understanding changing cultural norms surrounding gender arrangements. This popular novel was subsequently made into a special television production, which appeared in September of 1980. It is the central focus of this paper to detail the crucial changes made in the transformation of the novel to the television version. We argue that the more radical, or far-reaching indictment of contemporary gender arrangements of the novel was undercut, and transformed into a liberal statement for TV, in order to have the broadest possible audience appeal. In addition, we would pose the case of *The Women's Room* as an illustrative example of a more general tendency of the mass media to present feminism and feminist themes, critical of the existing male dominated sex/gender system, in a liberal frame.

Liberal theory forms the basis of American political institutions, and many of our most sacred cultural values as well. As such, it provides the terms by which we evaluate social reality and the terms within which political debates occur. Stemming from the tradition of Hobbes, Locke, Bentham and Smith, liberal thought stresses the autonomy of the individual as a rational, utility maximizing actor for whom forms of association are mere means to the furthering of individual ends. As the view of human nature is of the rational individual, liberalism stresses equality before the law and equality of opportunity, while at the same time, legitimating inequality of outcomes as the just reward for individual merit or achievement. Liberalism thus arose as the legitimation of rising capitalism and the bourgeois democratic state. Its stress on voluntarism, as individuals are seen to freely participate in exchange relations, serves to obscure oppressive aspects of market based societies. The liberal conception of freedom of choice, within the economy and within the political realm, obscures the fact that choices are made within structured limits.

As women have struggled for equality in the workplace and the political arena, this has most often occurred within the vocabulary provided by liberalism. Struggles for the vote, for the ERA, and for equal pay can be cast as the simple extension of liberal rights to women as a previously excluded group. Political struggles seen in this way do not pose a threat to the social structure itself – they become calls to include women in the existing institutional structures rather than demands to transform the social order itself.

On an individual level, the inability to successfully compete for economic resources within these institutional structures tends to be experienced as personal failure. The hypothesis of this paper is that feminist critiques which are more radical, in the sense of seeing the male dominated sex/gender system as deeply rooted in the existing social order such that radical change is required to uproot it, are recast by the mass media in liberal terms. Thus, contemporary concerns of men and women regarding changes in the family and workplace are expressed, but in forms in which they are less threatening or disturbing. We are most often presented with images that tend to depict sexism or gender asymmetry as an individual problem, lingering from the past, a problem of faulty socialization or lack of adequate role models, a problem which can be easily overcome.

The transformation of *The Women's Room* from novel to the television production provides an excellent case for the illustration of this hypothesis. While many criticisms have been leveled against Marilyn French's novel for its conventional narrative form, contending that it reads like a soap opera or deals with stereotypical situations, we will be more interested in the fact that, as a social commentary, it does depict the problem of gender asymmetry as deeply embedded. Furthermore, the conventional form and stylistic problems which flaw the novel's literary or artistic value, and may perhaps flaw the novel's critical thrust, at the same time lend the book an accessibility it might not otherwise have had. Consequently, were it not for this accessibility as a book, it would certainly have never been considered as a possible television production.

The novel, nearly seven hundred pages long, documents the life of Mira, a middle class, white woman, through the interplay and juxtaposition of three different periods of her life. We begin and end with Mira in her late forties. This Mira leads us through the other two major periods of her life, speaking of her former "selves" in the third person. In the first period, in the suburbs of New Jersey in the 1950's, Mira lives out the American dream. Leaving college to marry a medical student, she raises two children while her husband climbs up the ladder of economic success. The circle of order of her life is shattered when, after fifteen years of marriage, her husband asks for a divorce. Freedom is thrust upon her, and she struggles painfully to deal with it. In the second major period, Mira has gone back to school. Having done well and received tremendous praise, at the age of thirty-eight, she has moved to Cambridge to enter graduate school at Harvard. It is 1968. In this period Mira struggles to realize new parts of herself, to find fulfillment in a world where she is less constrained.

How does it end? Mira endures, but her struggle against a male dominated society does not bring her success, nor does it bring her happiness. We leave Mira bitter, sad and alone: a middle-aged woman who made choices, had high merit, and yet, did not receive the rewards promised by liberal society. Through a consideration of two central issues in Mira's life, and women's lives in general – women's domestic work and the possibility of egalitarian love relationships – we will examine the complex manner in which the television film has reframed the feminist critique presented in the novel. Specifically, while painting over much of the critical content with images of individual success, the film at the same time attempts to retain aspects of the original themes of the novel, which apparently had considerable market appeal. Therefore, we will focus on the various levels by which the feminist critique in the novel is both revealed and obscured in the film narrative. On one level, aspects of women's lives in male dominated society are simply made visible. Visibility itself can expose stereotypical notions, unmasking the illusion of "naturalness" and revealing ex-periences as socially constituted. Beyond the simplest level of exposure, other aspects of women's lives are revealed as problematic. We will therefore look at conflicts depicted in the television film, examining carefully how painful or prob-lematic they are shown to become, and what options are represented for resolu-tion of the conflict. Lastly, we will be interested in the interpretations of these conflicts put forth, and the general ambiguity created for the evaluation or judg-ment of choices in women's lives.[6]

I. DOMESTIC WORK

In the television production of *The Women's Room* many problematic aspects of women's lives in the suburbs are exposed quite clearly. One example of this is the representation of the separateness of the world of women and children from the world of men. We see images of women with their children at the park, women sitting in Mira's kitchen with children surrounding them (and climbing on top of them, and interrupting them), women in their yards waiting for school buses—over and over, the women and their children. The men are not in these scenes, and we are not shown images of men relating with children. We are shown scenes which point out the work involved in caring for children, that which is so often not thought of as work.[7] As one character, pregnant with her sixth child, comments: "My husband says nursery schools are for lazy women who want to play bridge all day." We, as an audience, can see how untrue this statement is right along with the characters. We see Mira, waking in the middle of the night, running from room to room, grabbing a crying infant in one arm and soothing it, while putting its bottle on the stove to warm; then she grabs her other crying baby with her free arm, setting the infant down while she changes the baby's diapers; and then carrying both to the kitchen table, she hands the bottle to the infant and gets a cookie for the baby, all the while remaining calm, and clucking and talking softly to them. Meanwhile, her husband Norm, yells at her to be quiet, finally getting up and stumbling angrily into the kitchen himself. After one feeble attempt to hold the infant's bottle, which he quickly gives up, Norm just stands there complaining about Mira's "over indulgent" attitude towards the children. Even as he does this, Mira is still calm, clucking and coo-ing at her babies, moving back and forth between them. And Norm stands there, demanding, like one more child.

Although the work of childcare is made quite visible in the television film, the work of keeping house, the other work women do in the home is strangely invisible. In the novel form of *The Women's Room*, Marilyn French, the author, told us that Mira spent hours everyday of her marriage making beds, cleaning dishes, washing toilets, doing laundry, mending, polishing, dusting, straightening. After her children were in school, she even made a file, listing all the big tasks on cards, and rotating the cards, noting the date each time she completed a task. And every morning over coffee, which Mira stumbled downstairs to make, Norm gave her the chores for the day. Marilyn French describes Mira's reflections on housework in the following manner:

> . . . She felt that the three others lived their lives and she went around after them cleaning up their mess. She was an unpaid servant, expected to do a superlative job. In return, she was permitted to call this house hers. But so did they. (213)

Furthermore, the unacknowledged nature of women's domestic work is stressed in the novel. For example, at the end of a typical day during her married life, Norm says to Mira:

> "And what about you? What did you do all day?"

To which Mira replies:

> "I cleaned – in here. Doesn't it look shiny?"
> He looked around. "I didn't really notice." (233)

Thus in the novel Mira knows that her domestic work, in addition to being repetitive and boring, is not really recognized as work. And she thinks about this, and has a great deal of suppressed anger and resentment due to it. This is erased for television. In fact, it is made so completely invisible that we do not even see Mira doing *any* housework.

On television we see Mira depicted as a busy suburban mother, and the amount of work her mothering role requires is clearly made visible, while the housecleaning work, perhaps the most unpleasant and least rewarding aspect of the housewife's "job," is concealed. However, moving beyond the level of what is merely made visible, we need to ask how Mira the television character appears to feel about her position in the family, i.e., how is her character's subjective experience of the gender division of labor in the home, portrayed on TV?

Amazingly enough, all negative feelings about the gender division of labor, so prominent in the novel as a part of Mira's experience, are expressed in the television production *solely* by discredited characters. We do not see Mira feeling or expressing hostility over the work she does for her family. This would be too much of a direct threat to the audience, as Mira is the central character, with whom we are supposed to sympathize and identify. Rather, the feminist critique of the gender division of labor enters in solely through the feelings and expressions of the characters from whom we, as members of the audience, would tend to distance ourselves. It is Lily, the mad woman, victim of a nervous breakdown, who expresses hostility over the housework she performs for her family. Lily exclaims to Mira in one scene in particular in which this is expressed:

> He (Lily's husband) asks me, "Lily, why aren't the dishes dried?" But I ask you, *what is the point* of drying dishes? They dry themselves! But then I have to run and dry them, or else I'll have to argue with him; and I'm *always* wrong.

> He didn't have a pair of dark socks. I didn't have a full load of dark and I didn't want to put them in with the whites, so I didn't wash them. And I said: "Wear white socks, or wear dirty socks." Is that crazy? So I washed them by hand, and he's in a hurry, so I put them in the oven to dry. But then I forgot them, and oh (beginning to laugh), did they smell awful! Is that crazy Mira?

This scene which expresses the anger of a housewife is very ambiguous as it is rendered for television viewing; it is subject to very different interpretations. Do we, as members of the audience, view Lily's expression of rage as a psychological or as a political problem? Does she appear to be simply an hysterical woman, or do we see her madness as a response to an extremely oppressive situation, a response we can understand?

Writers such as Phyllis Chesler have pointed out that historically women's individual rejection of, or resistance to, assigned roles has been categorized as an individual, psychological problem; in the extreme case – insanity. This madness may have been viewed as a religious or moral problem prior to the twentieth century; since, it is commonly typed as a medical or scientific problem, i.e., mental "illness". Yet in either frame of reference, madness is a problem attributed to the individual woman, and is not recognized as related to the social context of her life, or the limits and expectations placed upon her within a male dominated society. In a similar vein, Peter Lyman has written that making a problem appear to be one of an individual personality conceals oppression by blaming the victims for their symptoms (1981: 58–59). This process of interpretation turns forms of resistance and opposition into non-political acts such that "symptoms" are not perceived as challenges to the legitimacy of the existing social order.

In the novel of *The Women's Room* Lily's madness is presented sympathetically, and as existing in a social context. We can understand why Lily is enraged – and her madness seems to make sense. Her situation is so extremely oppressive it requires an extreme response. The narrator's voice, the middle-aged Mira looking back at herself realizes this. The Mira she is looking back at, the Mira presented in the third person, was not able to make the connection between Lily's breakdown and its social or political context. The connection would have led her to reconsider her own life, something she maintained a fierce resistance towards at that time in her life. Mira's marriage was not as extreme as

Lily's, so she could adjust to its terms and conditions, accepting its limits by con‑
structing herself and her conception of herself in the world. For Lily this was too
much; she failed to adjust. At the time Mira simply had too much at stake to
make any conscious connection between Lily and herself, or to see that they
faced similar conditions. Mira struggled to believe that her life and her marriage
were different. But the narrator's voice forces us to make the connection, point‑
ing out that adjustment and madness are simply different forms of expression of
the same oppression.

> She is still there, Lily. Mira hasn't seen her in years. I haven't either. It's not because
> I don't care about her, it's that I sometimes get confused about who is who, I think
> I'm Lily, or that she's me, and when I'm there I'm never sure which of us is supposed
> to get up and bend and kiss the other and walk down the stone paths to the gate and
> go out into the parking lot with all the other people who look just the same as the
> ones inside who get into cars and drive away. And even when I'm in the car I'm not
> sure I'm supposed to be, I don't feel as if I'm in my body . . . .
>
> Actually, Lily and I aren't so different: she's inside those gates, I'm inside these.
> We're both insane, both running on and on over the same track, around and around
> hopelessly. Only I have a job and I have an apartment and I have to clean my own
> place and cook my own meals and I don't get to have electric shocks twice a week.
> It's strange how they think that giving electric shocks will make you forget the truths
> you know. Maybe what they really think is that if they punish you enough, you'll
> pretend to forget the truths you know, you'll be good and do your housework
> (332–333).

In the ambiguity of the television production, the narrator's voice, the voice
of Mira reflecting back and telling us that she is like Lily, is missing. Mira in the
novel makes it clear how we must interpret Lily's story. However, the TV au‑
dience is left to interpret Lily's madness as is consonant with their own
understandings of the world, and they hear no voice which forces the painful
and threatening connection of Lily with themselves. The audience is encouraged
to identify with Mira, but whether Mira identifies with Lily is ambiguous. In
the film for television, after Mira visits Lily for the last time,[8] she comments in
voice‑over narration:

> I grew bitter at the injustice of the way the world treats women. I drank brandy and
> blamed men; I watched my bitterness eat away at what was left of my life. And I
> began to realize that there was no justice. There was only life. And life I still had. I
> went back to college . . . .

This statement can be read in a critical manner to mean that society is un‑
just; that women are oppressed; that men have more power; that women's anger
or "madness" makes sense; that every woman is somewhat like Lily. On the
other hand, the critical thrust which questions an unjust society and
acknowledges the validity of resistance is undercut by the universalizing

language in which the critique is expressed. The language implies that injustice is an inherent part of life, universal, nature-like, and unchanging. This obscures the fact of human agency, of social institutions as results of past human collective activity, and of the potential of collective action to transform an unjust society. This rendering of the narration therefore leads to a message of acceptance of subordination and injustice as inevitable. Individual survival and sanity depend on a *renunciation* of the desire to resist injustice. Mira must stop blaming men and go back to college; she must forget about the social context and think only of her individual interests. In political terms, this can be seen as a message about the futility of opposition. Mira will survive only if she goes on her individual path. If she thinks of Lily, allowing herself to see and feel their common oppression, her life will only be eaten away.

These lines are pulled, out of context, from a different episode in the novel. There is a subtle, but crucially different meaning conveyed. Mira has already begun graduate school at Harvard, and these lines represent an inner dialogue in which she realizes that, in spite of the painfulness of her divorce, her life has progressed. In this moment she *transcends* her anger, seeing that it was a necessary step, but also a movement of simple negation which kept her trapped within the same limited set of terms, i.e., Norm's wife – Norm's ex-wife. The subtle difference from the television version consists in that she realizes the anger, the moment of negation, was necessary, and was not to be simply denied or avoided. In fact, it is even to be appreciated, for without it one does not reach the point of progressing to something new. Here is one of the lines crucially omitted for TV: "And suddenly it was all right, the past, even if it was all wrong, because it had freed her, it had placed her here, still alive . . ." (342). In other words, rather than *renouncing* her anger and bitterness, Mira moves through it and beyond it.

To summarize briefly, the television production of *The Woman's Room* has reframed the critique of women's domestic work presented in the novel in such a way as to undercut its strength, effectively delegitimizing it. This is accomplished subtley. The work involved in childrearing is exposed through the depiction of the protagonist's life. However, the work of housekeeping, the other, more menial part of women's unpaid domestic labor so prominent in the novel, is concealed on television by making it an invisible aspect of the protagonist's life. The subjective experience of the oppressiveness of the gender division of labor in the home is exposed to us only through the discredited character, Lily, who unlike Mira, is "mad". In other words, only Lily seems to directly feel the oppressiveness of her role in the family; she is the sole character in the television production who expresses anger and hostility about her position. Yet she suffers a nervous breakdown, which frames the expression of anger as hysteria, and therefore invalid. In the novel the breakdown was used as a symbolic device to voice the critique of the socially constructed position of women. Thus, the liberal reframing of domestic work effectively renders a social problem as an individual problem within a fixed, universalized context.

II. EGALITARIAN LOVE RELATIONSHIPS

In both the novel and television versions of *The Women's Room*, after Mira's divorce and move to Cambridge, she develops a new relationship with a male graduate student, Ben. For both versions, Mira's relationship with Ben represents the hope for, or the possibility of, a new kind of love relationship be-tween men and women.[9] Mira and Ben symbolize the attempt to form equal rela-tionships, relationships characterized by intimacy *and* freedom, allowing in-dependence for each as an individual while providing the security of a deep mutual commitment to the relationship. As Mira says on T.V.: ". . . it was a vi-sion of what could be – a family in which people love each other without oppress-ing each other." And in the novel Marilyn French, the author, had written:

> If anyone ever had a chance for a good mutual life, it was Mira and Ben. They had enough intelligence, experience, goodwill, and enough room in the world – whether you call that opportunity or privilege – to figure out what they wanted and to achieve it. So what happened in their relationship ought to be paradigmatic somehow. It seemed so at the time. It seemed to glow with the divinity of the ideal. They had the secret, keeping both intimacy and spontaneity, security and freedom. And they were able, somehow to keep it up. (464)

But then, ultimately, they are not able to – it falls apart. Both the novel and film of *The Women's Room*, while they end very differently, end with Mira alone, without Ben; the relationship could not be sustained. If their relationship is, as Marilyn French writes, paradigmatic, a vision of what could be, what meaning can we infer from such an ending? What does this mean about our collective vi-sions and truths? Before giving a theoretical interpretation of the failure of Mira and Ben's relationship we will first examine the differences between the novel and the television version's presentation of this episode.

On television Mira and Ben's relationship cannot survive the demands of each for fulfilling work; Ben must return to Africa to complete his thesis research, while Mira's work is in Cambridge. And unlike the novel, in the televi-sion production of *The Women's Room*, there is really no negotiation of the con-flict; both Mira and Ben accept the situation as completely irresolvable. They part sadly, but they part nevertheless.

This presents a curious switch from the novel in which Mira and Ben en-gaged in a real struggle over whose needs would be met in the relationship. In the novel, Ben tried to convince Mira to leave Cambridge, to accompany him to Africa, and to have a baby as well. Mira was outraged by his insensitivity to her needs, and by his ability to fall back so quickly into very traditional gender role expectations. As a forty year old woman who had already raised two sons, she had no desire to have additional children. And feeling as excited as she did about her research, she was gravely affronted by Ben's presumption that she subor-dinate her work to his career needs. Moreover, Mira felt that Ben was willing to "eradicate" her as an individual in order to obtain his desires. In the novel, Mira tells this to Ben in the following speech:

> "You wanted to go, and it would hurt you to go without me, and so you simply assumed I would go with you because that was the simplest solution to the problem. And you never, never once", she rose and her voice rose, "never thought about me! About my needs, my life, my desires! You *eradicated* me, me as a person apart from you, as successfully as Norm did!" (663–664)

Furthermore, in the novel we realize very clearly, as does Mira, that Ben is leaving her to live out his traditional male identity, to claim his male "rights". Mira would not let him dominate her life; she would not have his children nor accompany him to Africa, and it is clear that he wants a woman who would. After Ben leaves her we are told that:

> Mira never heard from him again, but she heard about him through the grapevine. He stayed in Africa for a year and a half . . . and came back to a cushioned chair at a large state university. He is a consultant to a number of foundations and to the federal government, and is considered the world's expert on [specific African nation]. At thirty-eight, he is a high success. He married the woman who was his secretary in [Africa], and they have two babies. She takes care of the babies and the house and him because he is very busy, very successful. They live in a large house in a good neighborhood, and people think they are a model couple. They are invited everywhere and women everywhere are attracted to him. His wife shows signs of whiny clinginess. Yes.
>
> So, you see, the story had no ending. They go on; . . . (682–683)

In the television production of *The Women's Room* much of the struggle between Mira and Ben is erased, simply made invisible. There are two scenes in which Ben brings up the issue of having a baby, but the conflict does not seem to be as fundamental a problem, and it appears as separable from the issue which ends the relationship. The linkage is not made explicit between Ben's desire to dominate Mira in one sphere of life, i.e., the family, with his need to dominate her in another, i.e., his career taking precedence over hers. The conflict is also muted and made less problematic because on T.V., Ben does not ask Mira to accompany him to Africa. He simply assumes that they will be ending their relationship. This creates ambiguity in our reaction to the ending of the relationship which did not exist in the novel.

The aspect of ambiguity is introduced in that Ben seems to be a more sympathetic character, and Mira less so, than in the novel. Because he does not even pose the possibility of Mira's coming to Africa, Ben appears less dominant; he does not seem to be imposing any unfair demands on Mira to surrender parts of herself or her autonomy. He appears merely to be operating as an equal – his work is in Africa, hers is in Cambridge – and that's that! And on T.V., Ben appears to understand this; therefore there is no point in discussing it: he simply leaves.

Another aspect adding to the ambiguity of the relationship's end is introduced by the fact that Ben's age is lowered by several years from the novel. It is lowered from thirty-two to twenty-eight, making Mira a full ten years older than Ben, rather than six. This has several possible effects on audience interpretations. One might be simply that a ten year age difference makes the relationship appear improbable from the start, and unlikely to be a lasting relationship. If it ends at this particular point, one cannot feel too badly, knowing an end was rather inevitable. In addition, considering cultural norms and conventions which regard older woman-younger man relationships in a pejorative light, audiences may not have felt overly sympathetic to the relationship. Obviously, this is only heightened by exaggerating the age difference. Furthermore, lowering Ben's age makes his desire for children a more reasonable feeling – one which actually seems commendable, even altruistic. Mira's obstinate refusal to even consider having a baby appears overly selfish and unreasonable. This, of course, adds even more to the effect of making Ben a more sympathetic character while Mira seems less admirable. We like Mira less for her shrill and strident tone when discussing the issue of having a child with Ben, and thus we can begin to understand why Ben would leave her with so little resistance or inner conflict when his grant money is approved.

Further ambiguity surrounding the relationship's end is introduced by the construction of this part of the film, or the form of the scenes. Visual and verbal images conflict as arguments quickly close into images of embraces and kisses, or dissolve into images of Mira and Ben making love.

In the first scene, in which Ben first brings up the issue of having a baby, they clearly disagree. In fact, in the discussion Mira makes a slip and calls Ben by the name of her ex-husband Norm. This ends the conflict for the scene. Mira becomes completely apologetic. They embrace. It is as if, in apologizing for her slip, Mira has said she is *wrong* to unconsciously identify Ben as being like Norm. In other words, it is as if Mira was, on some level, thinking that if she had another child, she would be in a similar position with Ben as she had been with Norm, or that the problems might be the same. If she had another child she might again have to sacrifice her desire for autonomy and the pursuit of her career, becoming again subordinate to a husband, a man, who has a place in the outer world. However, in becoming so apologetic, Mira is presented as regretting having these thoughts. She takes them back; she takes her anger back. She embraces Ben, and the scene ends on this harmonious image.

In the next scene Ben brings up the issue of having a baby again, this time with the added proviso that he does not expect Mira to give up her career. He says "I can change diapers with the best of them." At this point, Mira brings up the fact of her age, and that she has already reared two children. Now the situation appears more conflictual than in the previous scene. Ben responds to Mira's statements by saying that Mira must not love him enough. This angers Mira, who raises a claim of the inequality inherent in his demand that she have a child. In other words, all she asks out of the relationship is that Ben love her. Ben, on the other hand, is asking for something far more than Mira's love. He asks that she prove her love by having another child at the age of thirty-eight. Ben laughes at Mira's anger. This undercuts the truth of the inequality she has uncovered and angrily denounced. He cannot take the claim of inequality seriously. He chuckles as if her anger is cute, commenting: "I love getting diatribes on every zit in our relationship." This comment succeeds in reducing the problem of gender asymmetry in the relationship to "a zit", thereby making Mira's anger, and her needs, seem trivial, laughable. After Ben's comment Mira completely drops her anger and kisses Ben, and the scene dissolves to an image of Mira and Ben making love. At this point, whether we even interpret the episode as presenting a conflict becomes ambiguous. Musical and visual images are used to create a sense of harmony, a feeling of resolution of any trivial differences. The additional fact that these images are a repetition from the previous scene adds to the ambiguity. It is unclear whether the issue has been resolved; verbally it has not been, but musical and visual clues leads us to think it has been. Also, we have seen Mira concede in each scene, giving up her anger. We might think therefore that she will, or *ought to*, concede to Ben's demand to have a baby.

In the next scene, however, Ben is telling Mira that his grant has been renewed, and that he is going back to Africa for two years. And then he says, in a completely opposite manner from the novel: "I know that your work is here. Your future is here. I can't even ask you to go with me." They embrace in the rain, the music swells up, Ben walks away, and we know this relationship is over. This relationship, which embodied our vision of what could be, of the perfect balance of dependence and autonomy, is over. But why exactly is unclear from this juxtaposition of scenes. If Mira had wanted to have Ben's baby would this have made a difference? Would he have given up his grant and his chance at success to have a family with Mira? Or might they have been able to reach some compromise with a child to hold them together? If the issue of the baby was the decisive one for Ben, then we can interpret these scenes as meaning that it was Mira's choice which ended the relationship. Immediately prior to Ben's receiving the grant, as he left Mira to go to the meeting in which they would inform him of the news, Ben said: "It would help if I knew your answer." And Mira said: "Just love me." This is evidence that it was her decision, by denying him a baby, to end the relationship. On the other hand, we might see the two issues as more separable. Perhaps Ben simply feels that this opportunity is too good to be missed, that his career ambitions must take precedence over his desire to have a family. After all, he is still quite young. If this is the interpretation we arrive at, then it seems to be Ben's choice to end the relationship.

What is represented abstractly in the fact that the relationship between Mira and Ben ends is the conflict between the human need for independence, to be autonomous, and the need to be dependent, or related to another.[10] Individual autonomy becomes symbolized as a career, as in our society the job and the paycheck are the arbiters of individual value and self-worth. The need for dependence is symbolized by the family, or the male-female couple, that realm in our society in which people let their individualities merge, surrendering some autonomy for the feeling of relatedness. The conflict for Mira between the realization of her needs for autonomy and for dependence are a central theme in the novel as well as in the television production of *The Women's Room*. Can she have a love relationship, i.e., experience relatedness, and yet create and retain a sense of individual autonomy by going out in the world to achieve her own goals, to accomplish her own work? The answer seems to be no, she cannot.

While Mira is, of course, only a fictional character, we can find much evidence that this conflict is increasingly echoed in the lives of real women. Recent socialist feminist analyses on the rise of anti-feminism[11] conclude that striking demographic changes in family and household structures over the past fifteen years have led to real fears over the seeming loss of intimacy and commitment between the sexes, identified with the increase in women's labor force participation, and supposedly advocated by the feminist movement. In other words, for many women, the move beyond traditional roles of wife and mother, with entry into the paid labor force, has become identified as the cause of the "breakdown" of the family; this invokes deeply embedded fears about the loss of relatedness or dependence in personal life. Many see this loss as endorsed by the feminist movement, which unfortunately, has tended to stress a liberal notion of equality based on individual autonomy. Therefore, the need for autonomy and the need for dependence come to be experienced as they were for Mira, in an opposition, and for women this becomes like a zero-sum game. In other words, what one gains in autonomy, one gives up in relatedness. It becomes a question for many women of whether they will give up part of their selfhood for a relationship or family, or whether they will give up the need to be in relationship or to have a family in order to realize a sense of autonomous selfhood.[12]

Social theorists such as Jessica Benjamin, Nancy Chodorow and Dorothy Dinnerstein have pointed out how the conflict between the human needs for autonomy and for dependence become more problematic for women in contemporary society. Because women mother, providing care and nurturance for dependent infants and children, they become the cultural expression of the need for dependence. In addition, because females mother, female children develop weaker ego boundaries, never separating as completely as male children from the mother, such that merging and feelings of relatedness are more central to adult female personality. Males on the other hand, develop with stronger ego boundaries, stressing their difference from the female mother. Therefore adult male personality has a far greater stress on autonomy than the female sense of self-in-relation. The interpenetration, or dialectic, of these two essential human needs is broken, and rather than each individual maintaining a tension between the two tendencies, they become split or dichotomized by gender. As women push for greater equality, using the vocabulary of liberalism dominating our political culture, this comes to mean that women must become like men – autonomous individuals, rational utility maximizers oriented towards instrumental action in the world, i.e., the mastery and control of objects in the world, as opposed to be-ing in relation to other subjects in the world. As women have been both the symbols and providers of non-instrumental action, it is women who most clearly feel this conflict as family structure changes. Men have always had the benefit of both autonomy and dependence in the family; they were not the ones assigned to surrender their individuality to create and maintain family life. Women pro-vided this for them. If women cease to provide this because they desire equality, one wonders who will.

In addition to the film version of *The Women's Room*, the conflict between autonomy and dependence can be found as a theme in many mass media depic-tions of modern or "liberated" women. This may again testify to how widespread and deeply felt a problem this conflict is in the lives of actual women today. These fictional portrayals which have found great popularity are clearly reso-nant with the experience of many, many women. It is obvious that an audience exists for whom these media depictions have a tremendous appeal.

III. THE ENDING: LIBERAL EQUALITY VS. A RADICAL VISION

After Ben leaves Mira, only two scenes remain in the television production of *The Women's Room*. Neither of these are a part of the novel's closing section, which has been entirely eliminated from the film. In this section the two final T.V. scenes will be examined in detail, and then compared to the novel's closing portion, in order to both clarify the ambiguity regarding the end of the "ideal" relationship and to answer the question of what a woman ought to expect in a relationship with a man. This clarification returns us to the question of the balance of autonomy and dependence, freedom and commitment, and to the issue of individualistic versus collective solutions to the inequities of the current sex/gender system.

In the first television scene following Ben's departure, we see an image of a glass breaking against a wall, right on a poster of Golda Meier, the former Israeli prime minister, symbolic of a powerful woman. And then we hear Mira scream-ing: "I hate men! I hate them all!" Next we see that she is at her woman friend, Val's apartment. Val appears to be older than Mira, although in the novel they are the same age. She appears controlled and calm, even amused, as she sweeps up the broken glass resulting from Mira's outburst. Val then gives Mira her words of worldly wisdom. She begins by countering Mira's rage with the lusty com-ment that she, Val, loves men. Val continues by advising Mira that she must stop looking for men to be like gods who will make her life make sense, that she must make her own life, that it is her own responsibility. Mira counters that she has needs. To this Val responds in a half mocking, half wise woman tone:

> "Needs! Women are *awash* in needs! . . . What about man's needs? . . . They have no choices, they can only work, to be manly, to make money, to be a good daddy, to mow the lawn, to fix the plumbing, to satisfy us sexually. And never, *never* cry! Is that freedom? What choice do they have? At least with Ben, he wanted one thing and you wanted another – you both made choices."

Mira responds to this, saying, "And I'm miserable," admitting the pain of the zero-sum game for women, admitting that this is a "choice" which hurts. This is a painful truth for women, to know that the pursuit of their ambitions may mean being alone. In addition, we should notice that in this dialogue any claim of inequality, acknowledging the asymmetry of the choices for women as compared to men, has dropped out. If anything, Val's speech makes it seem that it is *men* who suffer most from current gender arrangements.

In the television production of *The Women's Room* the painfulness of the zero-sum choices is quickly muted. Immediately after Mira says that she is miserable, letting us see her pain, Val retorts:

> "No you're not! Not really. It isn't the end of the world. Pick up the pieces Mira and get on with it. It's your life! Make something out of it!"

Suddenly Mira is transformed. The moment of pain is gone. She cries: "Yes, I will, yes!" And then she jumps up, smiling and hugging Val. There is no pain or anger if one simply chooses to "get on with it"; after all, it's "not the end of the world." This sudden transformation reminds us that in the mass media women do not get angry, not unless they are "mad".

The television version of *The Women's Room* cuts immediately from the scene described above to the concluding scene of the film. It opens with shots of spires and towers, the visual image of a very prestigious academy, a very old, tradition-bound university. Next we see Mira, speaking to an auditorium full of students. Panning shots indicate there may be several hundred, mainly women, with a few scattered males among them. Mira is giving an inspirational speech, quite similar in feeling to the speech Val has just made to her in the previous scene. This juxtaposition of scenes creates the impression of women passing their worldly wisdom down, from one generation to the next. Val has given it to Mira, and now Mira passes it on to these young students. And what is the message? As Val has said to Mira, that she has made *her choice* when Ben left, now Mira tells the auditorium of students: "A woman is a person who makes choices." She repeats this over and over; it seems to be every other sentence in the speech; it is like the gospel. She also claims that things have changed:

> Today women *do* have choices . . . If she has a child she has the choice to take it to work, to class, on the campaign trail. A woman is a person who makes choices.

Mira closes this inspirational address by challenging her audience, asking:

> Will you choose change? Will you choose to become the vanguard of the new world?

This is followed by great applause, and then a standing ovation – all for Mira. Now she has her hair pinned up and a professional suit on. She smiles, flushed with accomplishment, and turns to leave. The camera freezes, and on this image the film ends.

In interpreting the meaning of this last scene, we, first of all, note the images of impressive spires and the full auditorium creating the impression that Mira has become a huge success, obviously on the way to a very prestigious career. However, at the same time, we know she is alone, that she has made her *choice* for change, for autonomy, and she has paid the price by losing Ben.

Mira in this final scene is depicted as an example of a woman who has "chosen change", who has "chosen to become the vanguard of the new world," as she challenges others in her speech. As she followed Val, we ought to follow Mira. If she represents change, or the new world, we can therefore ask what this new world looks like. If the choice between autonomy and dependence is a zero-sum decision, and Mira is an example of the vanguard of change, this leads to a rather frightening image of a new world of totally atomized individuals, a world in which women – who had represented dependence, relatedness and nurturance in the old world – become like men, autonomous, self-contained, strong and unemotional. It is an image of a world without mothers. It is a world in which no enduring relationships between men and women are possible, in which freedom and equality mean that only fleeting or transient connections are possible. It is a world in which women have given up dependence on men, and it is no longer valid for anyone to expect, or to desire, to be taken care of.

On television Mira seems to be content with her set of choices, and with this vision of a world of autonomous individuals. Indeed, she had said she was miserable when Ben left, but when Val had retorted: "No you're not! Not really," that had been enough. She no longer was hurt or angry; the pain and loneliness immediately vanished. To emphasize this even more, in the closing shots, Mira is practically beaming, flushed with happiness at her success. It seems very significant that the film ends on such a shot. Comments were made that an "upbeat" ending was required for TV, and that the novel was too negative. Yet, one must look behind this to see what upbeat means, and why one vision is less painful than another. Let us look at the close of the novel to examine this issue.

In the novel there are two fundamental differences in the ending. First, Mira is *not* a success in her career. She does complete her dissertation, but instead of an academic job, teaching at a major university and writing literary criticism, the best she can get is a job at a "third rate community college" in an isolated area in Maine, where she teaches composition courses, and "Grammar

12" (14). ". . . Nobody wanted to hire a woman over forty even if she had a Harvard degree . . ." (683). Thus, in the novel, institutional structures get in the
way of Mira simply "making choices", and constrain her ability as a woman to
simply "pick up the pieces" or to "get on with her life." The emphasis in the film,
was, as we have discussed, extremely voluntaristic. Following a liberal framework, we saw Mira succeed by her own merits and actions, i.e., her own talents
and efforts brought her a just reward.[13] The notion that despite her individual
merits and rational calculations, social structure might place severe limits on her
"choices" is absent. That patriarchy or male domination is patterned into the existing social order, such that the life chances of all women are negatively affected, is a predominant theme in the novel. We read of many women other than
Mira, tales of her friends, and of their friends, which forces us to face the reality
of these patterns. Marilyn French wrote, speaking through the narrator's voice
of the middle-aged Mira:

> I only know the women are all middle-aged and poor as shit . . . (293).

For television, framing the problem in a liberal perspective, Mira's decisions and
her successes become individual rather than social. While women's choices may
have been limited in the past, the message is repeated again and again, today
they are not. (Furthermore, as Val told Mira, men had no choices either, in the
old world.) It seems not to be appealing or marketable for the mass media to end
the film with the point that social, political and economic equality for women is
still, today, very far from being realized, and that the choices women can make are
still more limited than men's. As Marilyn French wrote in the novel: ". . . the
women I know have gotten fucked, literally and figuratively . . ." (288) In the
novel, Mira endures, she survives and becomes stronger. While she is bitter at
the story's close, she tells us that her life is not over yet. For TV, Mira must be
made a more "upbeat" character; her pain is muted, and her conflicts are resolved,
and resolved *within* the existing social structure. And so Mira on TV is "a person who made choices," an individual who successfully made her own life, free of
the impediment of a commitment to another.

The second fundamental change in the ending of The Women's Room concerns the vision of the world that could be, the world we can choose to be in the
vanguard of. On TV, Mira has chosen autonomy and work over dependence
and love. And, as we have said, she is depicted as being happy with this choice,
as well as with this set or grid of choices. There is no criticism presented of the
zero-sum grid, leaving us to conclude that equality for women will mean a world
in which women give up nurturance, motherhood, and dependence and become
like men, rational and autonomous. In the novel, Mira is very alone at the end of
the story, yet she is also aware that she has been forced into the zero-sum
choices of being alone as opposed to, and exclusive of, surrendering part of her
self. Mira in the novel had realized since the days of her marriage, that, for

women, to break the rules of the traditional gender system meant that "forever and forever you would be alone." (269) Mira, in the novel, is not satisfied with this grid of choices; this is not enough and she will say it aloud. She is bitter, lonely and sad, and she knows no answers. However, she will continue to resist and reject the world as it is, this limited set of choices, and the world as the TV film would paint it. Mira of the novel is willing to reveal the truth in order to hopefully, someday, push beyond it. This critique, and this attempt to push beyond what is already known, is crucially eliminated from the film version of *The Women's Room* in order to create an attractive "upbeat" ending.

In the novel we are presented with probing and insightful discussions concerning the possibility of personal relationships with true equality for males and females, in which equality does not have to mean that women become like men. Most of the relationships fail, and Marilyn French is willing to address, through her protagonist, that thorniest of questions asked of feminists, namely, does Mira hate men?

> You think I hate men. I guess I do, although some of my best friends . . . I don't like this position. I mistrust generalized hatred. . . . That's no answer, is it? . . .
> Well, answers I leave to others, to a newer generation perhaps, lacking the deformities mine suffered. My feelings about men are the result of my experience . . . The stone in my stomach is like an oyster's pearl – it is the accumulation of defense against an irritation. My pearl is my hatred; my hatred is learned from experience . . . (289–291).
> What holds people together? And why do we hate each other so much? I ask this not to have you shake your head piously and pronounce that we must certainly not hate, not hate our fellowman. We do. What I want to know is why? . . . Why do we love and hate? How in hell do we manage to live together? I don't know. I already told you: I live alone.
> It's easy to blame men for the rotten things they do to women, but it makes me a little uncomfortable. It's too close to the stuff I read in the fifties and sixties when everything that went wrong in a person's life was Mother's fault. (463)

All of this heartfelt discussion of a painful truth – the real anger women can come to feel against men, men for whom they surrender their autonomy, men who benefit from the existing gender system – is exaggerated into absurdity in the television film, and then quickly dismissed. Rather than a presentation of the wrenching problems women feel in their relationships with men, and the real anger they experience, we see Mira, on TV, throwing a glass against the wall as she shrieks: "I hate men!" This is such an overdrawn gesture that the image becomes ridiculous, especially when the glass hits the wall exactly on a poster of Golda Meier. At this moment, Mira becomes a caricature, and we cannot recognize, nor would we want to, any part of ourselves in her. This is not real pain, nor does it appear to be a real woman. We can only laugh at this stick figure, rather than seeing the truth of anyone's experience in this. Also, the moment itself of Mira's anger does not last. It seems in the context of the scene, to be only a fleeting loss of control. The pain of the limited choices women face is thus denied any actual legitimacy. The decision Mira makes to be autonomous and alone, which in the novel is forced upon her, appears on TV as voluntary and desirable: a course of action arrived upon by free choice, and from a set of reasonable options. Mira *has* achieved her equality on TV, the equality to be like a man. This is an upbeat ending.

CONCLUSION

This paper has been centered on a close comparison of the book and television film versions of *The Women's Room*. The comparison of the two afforded an excellent view as a case study of how feminism and feminist critiques are presented in the mass media. Because the novel, a radical indictment of the existing sex/gender system, became on television a liberal statement about individual choices made within existing social arrangements, much about the relationship of feminism to popular culture in contemporary society could be illustrated.

The major point made throughout this paper, on each topic discussed, was that the force of the feminist critique within the novel, exposing our society as oppressive to women, was muted and undercut for television. The threat, or the painfulness, of the brutal force of the novel had to be made more palatable, and therefore, easier for a mass audience to watch. However, and this introduces much of the complexity, at the same time as the forcefulness is muted, the critique of gender asymmetry is also present and emerges to a limited extent, although couched in ambiguity and re-framed in a liberal perspective. The fact that the novel sold three million copies seems to signal that its truth must have resonated with the experiences of many, and that it was desirable to retain this in the television production. The end result is therefore a contradictory production in which verbal and visual images conflict, and in which messages about existing gender roles are rendered ambiguous, becoming subject to competing interpretations. Finally, what critique emerges becomes, as stated above, a statement that gender equality is achievable within the existing social structure. And this notion of equality, is as we have shown, an inherently limited one – the equality of atomized, instrumental individuals.

In closing, it should be pointed out that it is precisely the liberal vision of equality, which has been illustrated as the presentation of equality in the television production of *The Women's Room*, which frightens people, and actually leads them to reject feminism. If equality means that women must renounce their needs for a sense of relatedness, and for committed love relationships, in order to obtain a sense of an autonomous self in the world, we can expect that many women will be willing to sacrifice that sense of independent selfhood. If entering the "man's world" means one has to become like a man, many women will continue to be attracted by those, such as Phyllis Shlafly, who defend a traditional notion of femininity and the patriarchal family. Furthermore, men are also frightened by an image of a world in which women renounce expressivity and nurturance. While the home may no longer be a "haven in a heartless world" it is still the primary location in which men and women expect to have their non-instrumental needs fulfilled. In fact, it is the last remaining institution in our society which provides this. Men look to women, as wives and mothers, to provide them with a sense of connectedness, a sense of merging out of their lonely autonomy. While much social theory has been written about the problem of society without the father, it appears that it is the vision of a society without the mother which is the most truly frightening to men and women.

NOTES

1. By 1977, 75% of all married women were in the paid labor force. Divorce rates have doubled since the 1960's. Today, one out of three marriages will end in divorce. The number of female-headed households has also doubled since the 1960's. By 1977 one out of seven households was headed by a single woman. See Petchesky 1981: 235.

2. Eisenstein 1981: 202.

3. Petchesky, 1981: 235.

4. I am specifically referring to the current anti-feminist backlash and the so-called pro-family politics of the New Right. See Eisenstein 1981, English 1981, Oliker 1981, Petchesky 1981.

5. The way I have described popular and mass culture is analogous to the term ideology, but I use the term extremely cautiously. The notion of ideology should not refer to some unified body of ideas which are simply false, or simply the ideas of ruling groups. This results in a view which sees most people as therefore duped, suffering from "false consciousness." Ideology is most usefully conceived of as an ensemble of elements – ideas, values, symbols, and practices – existing in particular combinations in specific historical conjunctures. Furthermore, the elements of an ideological ensemble may conflict and exist in a contradictory unity, as the awareness people have of their lived experience can be very complicated and multi-layered; it is never simply false. Thus while ideology serves to generate consent to oppressive social relations, it both obscures and reveals those relations, and the consent itself is always problematic. See Gramsci 1971, Poulantzas 1973. For a summary, Kellner 1978.

6. A group of feminist film critics discussing the mass media contended that the creation of ambiguity is a primary mechanism by which feminist critiques can be expressed, but in less threatening ways, so as to speak to the broadest possible audience. "[The film industry] wants to let everybody have their ideological cake and eat it, too." Therefore, what most often results is a deliberate ambiguity structured into the film such that critical or radical moments exist, but are coopted within a less critical frame. See Citron, et al., 1978: 91. This notion is very similar to my hypothesis, except that I wish to argue for a particular, liberal manner of reframing radical moments.

7. Of course, I do not mean to argue that childrearing is the same kind of work as work which involves production of objects or things. Obviously, the "production of people" involves a fundamentally different orientation to action, or form of rationality,

from the "production of things." What I mean to say is that mothering does involve the expenditure of great amounts of physical and mental effort, at least as much, if not more, than that required in any paid job. The difference is that while in the "production of things" humans act instrumentally to control and transform non-human objects to their, human, ends, in the "production of people" there is a purely non-instrumental moment of mutual recognition – a recognition of the child's human subjectivity, a subjectivity which is similar yet distinct from one's self, which cannot be controlled as a mere object for the parent's purposes. See Benjamin (1978) and Chodorow (1978), for important discussions of mothering and instrumental rationality.

8. This is after Mira herself is divorced. It is the same scene from which the monologue Lily delivered on housework was excerpted.

9. Relationships *between women* are presented as crucial aspects of the female characters' lives in the novel *The Women's Room*. The analysis of how these relationships among women were portrayed in the television production represented a major focus in an extended version of this paper. In my analysis, I maintained that the television version made both the female friendship networks and the lesbian relationships appear as far less significant, and far less positive aspects of the lives of the women characters than they had been in the novel. Therefore, women characters who were seen as fundamentally linked in their daily lives to a community or social network of women became, on TV, atomized individuals. As suggested earlier, this portrayal points towards a liberal view of human nature based on a notion of instrumental, autonomous individuality. In this section I discuss the issue of individual autonomy in terms of its import for heterosexual relationships, but this should not suggest that women's connections to men are the only alternative to the problem of atomization.

10. See Long 1980.

11. See Eisenstein 1981, English 1981 and Petchesky 1981.

12. The New Right has accentuated this opposition by stressing that feminists are narcissistic, or excessively *self-interested*. This has an unfortunate convergence with the position of some so-called Leftists, most notably Christopher Lasch.

13. While Mira is a greater success in the film, her ambitions have been lowered. In the novel Mira goes to Harvard seeking a Ph.D. in literature, but on television she is only working towards an M.A. in education. Perhaps this conveys a subtle message that women do better when they are careful not to aim too high.

BIBLIOGRAPHY

Applebaum, R. P. and H. Chotiner, 1979, "Science, Critique, and Praxis in Marxist Method," *Socialist Review*, No. 46, July–August.

Benjamin, Jessica, 1978, "Authority and The Family Revisited: or, A World Without Fathers?" *New German Critique*, No. 13, Winter.

"Internalization and Instrumental Culture: A Reinterpretation of Psychoanalysis and Social Theory," Ph.D. Diss. Unpublished. NYU, 1978.

Blum, Linda M., "Beyond the Limits of Hartmann's Vision of Family Life," Unpublished seminar paper, Berkeley, 1982.

Chesler, Phyllis, 1972, *Women and Madness*. Garden City, N.Y.: Doubleday.

Chodorow, Nancy (1978) *The Reproduction of Mothering: Psychoanalysis and the Sociology of Gender*. Berkeley: University of California Press.

Citron, M., *et al* (1978) "Women and Film: A Discussion of Feminist Aesthetics," *New German Critique*, No. 13, Winter.

Dinnerstein, Dorothy (1976) *The Mermaid and The Minotaur: Sexual Arrangements and Human Malaise*. New York: Harper and Row.

Eisenstein, Zillah (1981) "Antifeminism in the Politics and Election of 1980," *Feminist Studies*, Vol. 7, No. 2, Summer.

English, Diedre (1981) "The War Against Choice," *Mother Jones*, Vol. VI, No. 11, Feb.-March.

Foucault, Michel (1980) *The History of Sexuality, Volume I: An Introduction*. New York: Vintage Books.

French, Marilyn (1977) *The Women's Room*, New York: Harcourt, Brace, Jovanovich.

Freud, Sigmund (1925) "Some Psychical Consequences of the Anatomical Distinction Between the Sexes," in Philip Rieff, ed., *Sexuality and the Psychology of Love*, New York: Collier Books, 1963.

Giddis, Diane (1977) "The Divided Woman: Bree Daniels in 'Klute' " in K. Kay and G. Peary, ed., *Woman and the Cinema: A Critical Anthology*. New York: E.P. Dutton.

Gramsci, Antonio (1971) *Selections From The Prison Notebooks*. New York: International Publishers.

Hartmann, Heidi I. (1981) "The Family as a Locus of Gender, Class and Political Struggle: The Example of Housework," *Signs*. Vol. 6, No. 31.

Haskell, Molly (1974) *From Reverence to Rape: The Treatment of Women in the Movies*. Baltimore: Penguin Books.

———— (1977) "Liv Ullman: The Goddess as Ordinary Woman," in K. Kay and G. Peary, ed., *Women and the Cinema: A Critical Anthology*. New York: E.P. Dutton.

Himmelstein, Jerome L. (1981) "God, Gilder, and Capitalism," *Society*, Vol. 18, No. 6, Sept.-October.

Hobbes, Thomas (1958) *Leviathan*, Parts One and Two. Indianapolis: Bobbs-Merrill.

Horkheimer, Max. "Authority and the Family". (1936), trans. J. Cummings, in *Critical Theory*, New York: Herder & Herder, 1972.

Kellner, Douglas (1978) "Ideology, Marxism, and Advanced Capitalism," *Socialist Review*, No. 42, Nov.-December.

———— (1979) "TV, Ideology, and Emancipatory Popular Culture," *Socialist Review*, No. 45, May-June.

Kolodny, Annette (1980) "Dancing Through the Minefield: Some Observations on the Theory, Practice and Politics of a Feminist Literary Criticism," *Feminist Studies*, Vol. 6, No. 1, Spring.

Lasch, Christopher (1977) *Haven in a Heartless World*. New York: Basic Books.

Locke, John (1952) *The Second Treatise of Government*. Indianapolis: Bobbs-Merrill.

Long, Tom (1980) "Marx and Western Marxism in the 1970's," *Berkeley Journal of Sociology*, Vol. XXV.

Lyman, Peter (1981) "The Politics of Anger: On Silence, Ressentiment, and Political Speech," *Socialist Review*, No. 57, May-June.

Oliker, Stacey (1981) "Abortion and the Left: The Limits of a Pro-Family Politics," *Socialist Review*, No. 56, March-April.

Petchesky, Rosalind Pollock (1981) "Antiabortion, Antifeminism, and the Rise of the New Right," *Feminist Studies*, Vol. 7, No. 2, Summer.

Poulantzas, Nicos (1973) *Political Power and Social Classes*. London: NLB Verso.

Rosen, Marjorie (1973) *Popcorn Venus: Women, Movies and the American Dream*. New York: Avon Books.

Rubin, Gayle (1975) "The Traffic in Women: Notes on the 'Political Economy' of Sex," in Rayna Rapp Reiter, ed., *Towards an Anthropology of Women*. New York: Monthly Review Press.

Tuchman, Gaye and Arlene Kaplan Daniels and James Bennet (1978) *Hearth and Home: Images of Women in the Mass Media*. New York: Oxford University Press.

Wright, Charles R. (1975) *Mass Communications: A Sociological Perspective*. New York: Random House.

Chapter 23 ───────────────────────────────

Sexuality, Class, and Conflict in a Lesbian Workplace

Kathleen M. Weston
Lisa B. Rofel

L esbian-feminist discussions of class and conflict have defined class almost exclusively in liberal terms by reducing it to a matter of individual background.[1] "Liberal" in this sense describes not a position on the political spectrum from left to right but a conception of society as a collection of individual actors who make independent choices based on free will alone. These liberal assumptions are not unique to lesbian feminism; indeed, they underlie the dominant world view in American society, with intellectual antecedents far back in the Western tradition.[2] As lesbians concerned about recent conflicts in lesbian institutions, we have found that liberal interpretations leave too many questions unanswered about how class affects the way power and privilege are structured in those institutions. Socialist-feminist and Marxist analyses offer valuable criticism of individualistic approaches to class theory but are of limited use insofar as they ignore debates about sexuality and sexual identity or assume that sexuality and class constitute discrete levels of oppression.[3] Our intention in this article is to move toward an integrated theory of class and sexuality that views class as the ongoing production of social relations structured through the division of labor, rather than simply as class background, and that also comprehends the significance of lesbian identity as a historical construct affecting social relations in lesbian institutions.

In order to examine these issues in a specific context, we undertook a case study of a recent strike at a lesbian auto-repair shop in a metropolitan area with a sizable lesbian community. The study was based on in-depth interviews with eight of the ten women who worked in the shop at the time of the strike, in-

Our thanks to the women of Amazon for their willingness to relive their experiences of the conflict with us; and to Jane Atkinson, Akhil Gupta, Nancy Hartsock, Rebecca Mark, Sabina Mayo-Smith, Kathy Phillips, Renato Rosaldo, the San Francisco Lesbian and Gay History Project, and Anna Tsing for their insights and support.

Source: Kathleen M. Weston and Lisa B. Rofel, "Sexuality, Class, and Conflict in a Lesbian Workplace," Signs, Vol. 9 (Summer 1984): 623–646. Copyright 1984 by The University of Chicago. All rights reserved. Reprinted by permission of the publisher, The University of Chicago Press, and the authors.

cluding the two owners.⁴ Although this is just one example of the conflicts that have emerged in lesbian institutions in recent years, its dynamics clarify cultural constructs and material relations that operate in larger social processes.

The women we interviewed constitute a fairly diverse group of self-identified lesbians. The different conceptions they have of their lesbian identity are reflected in the labels they choose to describe themselves – "queer," "gay," "dyke," or "lesbian." Some consider themselves feminists; others do not. Some are in long-term relationships with lovers; some are not. Two co-parent children. They range in age from mid-twenties to late thirties. They locate their class backgrounds along a continuum from working class to upper middle class, with both workers and owners at each end of the spectrum. Everyone is white; two of the women are Jewish. For reasons of space, we are unable in this analysis to explore the interconnections among race, ethnicity, class, and sexuality, a topic we believe is crucial for any comprehensive theory of conflict in lesbian institutions.

Although all the women interviewed were willing to be quoted by name, we have chosen to alter their names as well as the name of the business. This strike has generated a certain amount of controversy, and we want to be able to explore the theoretical issues it raises without reducing those issues to the sum of the personalities involved.

HISTORY OF THE CONFLICT

Amazon Auto Repair was founded in 1978 by two lesbian auto mechanics, Carol and Lauren, with $1,400 in capital from personal savings. Within the first two years, their financial success led them to hire several more mechanics, who were paid on a commission basis of 50 percent. In the summer of 1981, the owners embarked on a major expansion, raising the total number of employees to eleven. When their clerical worker left in August of that year, both owners went into the office, discontinuing the practice of one owner's supervising on the shop floor at all times.

The first overt incident in the conflict occurred about this time when Mary, the parts runner at the bottom of the job hierarchy, refused to stop working on a car in order to get lunch for everyone, as had been her custom. The owners not only insisted that this task was one of her job responsibilities but also added office filing to her duties, a change she resisted. In Mary's view, they also reneged on their earlier promise to make her an apprentice.

When the owners responded to new problems and pressures associated with expansion by tightening shop discipline, conflicts with other employees seemed to escalate as well. Tensions erupted at Christmas when the owners gave each employee a small gift that included a nailbrush and chocolate-covered almonds. The workers, insulted by what they regarded as insignificant gifts in place of bonuses, presented the owners with a list of issues and demands calling for continued commission with a guaranteed base pay of $200 per week, paid sick leave and a paid vacation, and a salaried shop manager. On February 2, 1982, the owners distributed statements rejecting the employees' demands, accompanied by nonnegotiable job descriptions that put everyone on an hourly wage effective the following week. That Friday, the workers asked the owners to postpone implementation of the descriptions and to meet with them in order to discuss salaries, the apprenticeship promised Mary, and other issues.

At this meeting the owners informed their employees they could no longer work at Amazon if they did not sign the job descriptions by 8 A.M. that day. Employees refused and, claiming they felt sick, left the shop. While the owners insist the employees walked out on their jobs, the workers say they were essentially locked out. The workers promptly filed charges of unfair labor practices with the National Labor Relations Board and set up a picket line, successfully turning away much of Amazon's business.

On February 24, the owners offered immediate and unconditional reinstatement under the old working conditions if the workers would drop all charges. But contrary to their stated intentions, the owners instituted speedups, set up procedures for signing in and out, and fired Mary for refusing to do filing. Two days later, the workers went on strike. After picketing for several weeks with no sign of negotiations resuming, the workers reluctantly decided to join the Machinists Union and sought other employment. The owners continue to operate the business with a reduced staff of new employees. Technically the Amazon conflict still has not been resolved, but a year after the strike workers have given up hope of reaching a settlement.

BRIDGING THE PUBLIC AND PRIVATE

The establishment of Amazon as a lesbian workplace challenged one of the deepest cultural divisions in American society: the split between private and public life. The very categories "lesbian" and "work" mirror this dichotomy, since lesbian identity has historically been defined in terms of the sexual and the personal,[5] whereas wage work in a capitalist context constitutes the public activity par excellence. In a homophobic society, any attempt to establish an institution that links lesbian identity and productive activity entails – not as a matter of ideological principle but by definition – a renegotiation of the culturally constructed boundary that differentiates public and private spheres. To the degree that Amazon integrated these spheres by hiring lesbians and bringing them into an environment that encouraged them to be "out" on the job, it not only provided a space sheltered from the heterosexism of the wider society but also undermined the compartmentalization of lives and self characteristic of most workplaces. Out of this radical potential to create a nonalienating work environment emerged an atmosphere of involvement, excitement, and commitment at

Amazon during its early years. An analysis of the reconciliation of private and public inherent in the project of a lesbian workplace cannot explain Amazon's ultimate failure to realize this radical potential. But because sexual and class politics meet at the boundary between personal and public life,[6] such an analysis is crucial for understanding aspects of the Amazon case that resemble conflicts in other lesbian institutions and that distinguish it from more traditional labor disputes.

The measure of what made Amazon a specifically lesbian workplace was not the sexuality of individual employees or the women's music played on the shop floor but the extent to which sexual identity received public affirmation in a place where being a lesbian was the rule rather than the exception.[7] Being out at Amazon was different from "coming out" at a straight workplace because, as one mechanic put it, workers "didn't *have* to talk about being dykes. It was pretty obvious!" Yet, as another woman said, "You could go in and when you're sitting around having lunch you could talk about your family, you could talk about your lover, you could talk about what you did last night. It's real nice to get that out and share that." Conversations at work led to friendships that carried over into the evenings and weekends. Women went to flea markets together, carpooled to work, cooked dinner for one another and attended each other's sporting events. Lovers were treated as members of the extended Amazon "family" and welcomed into the shop during business hours. One woman's lover acknowledged: "There's nothing like walking into a women's[8] business and being able to walk right up to my lover and kiss her and have lunch with her and have my kids behind me, our kids. But you can't do that in the straight world, you know? It was a real valuable place to be." Friendships spanned all levels of the job hierarchy, weaving together employees' lives inside and outside work.

In a sense, Amazon resembled other small and alternative businesses that foster the development of multiplex ties among employees. Although such businesses often promote an integration of personal and work relationships, the size of an enterprise does not necessarily contribute to a breakdown of the private/public split within the self. The compartmentalization of life in Western industrial societies often leads individuals in public situations to withhold full expression of their feelings, sexuality, and other central aspects of identity regarded as private.[9] One decisive difference between Amazon and the "straight" businesses employees mentioned in contrast was the way public and private aspects of the self were united once lesbian identity became linked to productive activity. In attempting to elucidate how lesbian identity shaped social relations at Amazon, we are not asserting that the reconciliation of the cultural dichotomy between public and private is characteristic of lesbian institutions alone. A similar integration may occur in any organization of an oppressed group that explicitly invokes racial, ethnic, gender, or sexual identity to set the institution and its members apart from the dominant society. At the same time, we believe there are factors unique to lesbian institutions that affect the way conflicts are generated and negotiated but that cannot be explored here. These include the effect of same-sex romantic and sexual involvements on work relationships; the possibility that lesbian institutions foster what Audre Lorde calls "the power of the erotic," which may contribute to the transformation of alienated labor;[10] and the ways in which lesbian-feminist ideology, the organization of production, and systems of meaning originating in the wider lesbian community interact in the formation of lesbian workplace culture.

A principle effect of structuring Amazon so that lesbians could "be themselves" at work was the integration of emotions into workplace dynamics. "There was far more feeling than there ever is when it's just a cold business situation with men," remembered one owner. The reason was not simply, as she surmised, that women are socialized to express their feelings more freely than are men. Most former Amazon employees emphasized that their present work situations in straight businesses are not as emotional for them. But as a lesbian-identified workplace, Amazon encouraged the women who worked there to bring with them onto the shop floor the entire range of emotions and personal attributes associated with identity in American culture.[11]

Despite the lesbian-feminist principles of Amazon's owners, it is important to remember that this integration of public and private was not the product of a shared ideology. The commitment workers felt to Amazon was developed on the job, not brought to the workplace from other contexts. Some started their jobs with a nine-to-five attitude, only to find themselves becoming increasingly involved in what happened during business hours. It would therefore be a mistake to portray the Amazon conflict as a case in which women's unrealistically high expectations for an alternative institution led to disappointment when those expectations could not be met.

When she first came to Amazon from her job in a straight repair shop, one woman said, "I didn't *have* different expectations." But within a month, she was "like a kid in a candy store." It was precisely because working at Amazon had been such a positive, fulfilling experience, said another, that the rift between owners and workers came as such a shock and a loss: "That's why [leaving Amazon] feels like death. It was a part of my life – it was a part of our [family's] life – that would have gone on and on." By December 1981 the excitement of earlier years had given way to feelings of anger and betrayal, feelings so intense that the women involved in the dispute still dream about Amazon a year after the strike. "It hurts more with lesbians," concluded one mechanic, recalling that it had felt as though her whole being were under attack. The hurt was as much a product of the integration of private and public as the fulfillment that preceded it. In most work situations, the compartmentalization of life and self that accompanies alienation also protects individuals from the destructive effects of fixed power inequities.[12] Without that protection, the women at Amazon found themselves particularly vulnerable as tensions began to explode.

When Mary refused to get the mechanics' lunches, her intention was to defend herself against what she regarded as the owners' arbitrary exercise of power. Because she refused on the grounds that this task was a personal favor rather than a job duty, she tacitly reinvoked the private/public split. As the conflict deepened, attempts to reaffirm this distinction assumed a key position in the strategies of both parties. Workers called for a "businesslike" handling of affairs and tried to put their emotions aside. The owners took steps to distance themselves from workers by curtailing friendships and adopting written rules. By the time women were called back to work the employee phone had been disconnected, giving symbolic emphasis to the new segregation of work from personal life.

Even as Amazon's radical potential to provide a nonalienating work environment was being undermined, its distinctive characteristics as a lesbian workplace continued to shape the course of the conflict by focusing the struggle on the division between the private and the public. But with the reaffirmation of the private/public split, many of the special qualities that distinguished Amazon from straight repair shops seemed to disappear. "I'm not in business to be a machine, to be a man, to be something I don't want to be," protested one owner. "This wasn't what we wanted to create," insisted the other. Both sides were left wondering how the conflict could have escalated so quickly, destroying relationships of trust and cooperation built up over three and one-half years.

THE POLITICS OF TRUST

In the eyes of everyone who worked there, Amazon was built on trust. The owners trace this trust to their political commitment to lesbian feminism, which fostered a sense that a common lesbian identity would override other differences.[13] Before the February 8 walkout/lockout, neither seriously believed a strike could occur at Amazon. They displayed a similar degree of confidence in each other when they elected to go into business without a partnership agreement. For the workers, trust was not so much an outgrowth of ideology as a consequence of the multiplex ties that developed in the workplace. Not all employees identified strongly as feminists or saw themselves engaged in the project of creating a feminist business. But for workers and owners alike, trust was underpinned by friendships and the support Amazon provided for being openly and proudly lesbian.

From the beginning Lauren and Carol stressed that they were the owners, that Amazon was not a collective, and that they reserved the right to make all business decisions. Beyond these ground rules, however, they assumed a basic compatibility between their needs and those of their employees. In accordance with a feminist ideology that valued being "nurturing" and "supportive," the owners installed a separate phone for employees' use and agreed to flexible scheduling around women's extra-work commitments. The lack of set policy and formalized rules, combined with the owners' efforts not to "act like bosses," made it easy to believe that everyone was equal at Amazon and that trust grounded in the integration of public and private life would constitute a sufficiently radical solution to the problems of oppression women face in other workplaces. But in the absence of a clearly defined business structure, this trust became politicized when owners and workers had to rely on interpersonal relationships to negotiate labor relations from day to day. The emergence of a politics of trust at Amazon points to a conclusion the owners never reached and the workers only gradually realized: the personal can be political, even among lesbians, whenever the personalization of work relations obscures power differentials structured through property relations and the division of labor.

As managers, the owners had the authority to define and evaluate others' needs, transforming what would otherwise have been examples of mutual agreement into instances of benevolence. Even if they had been able to satisfy every request or concede every point raised by employees, control of the business altered the meaning of their actions. What the owners perceived as gifts or favors the workers often saw as customs or rights. It is not surprising, then, that the owners began to get angry when workers stopped asking permission for routine procedures such as leaving early when work was finished for the day. Conversely, the workers' mistrust for the owners developed when Lauren and Carol chose to assert their covert power – for example, when they forced Mary to get lunches or do filing. For some workers the strike came to be seen as a fight to create a work environment in which the owners "would not have the power to say one thing and do another thing and change things around" when their decisions could have a major impact on employees' livelihoods.

It was not coincidental that the politics of trust fragmented along class lines, pitting owners/managers against workers. But because such a politics was grounded in interpersonal relationships it tended to personalize the issues for the women involved, leading them away from a relationally defined class analysis. The politics of trust, rooted in the liberal conception of autonomous selves interacting on a basis of equality, supported interpretations that reduced the conflict to a matter of individual actions, intentions, and capabilities.

The analysis of the conflict favored by the owners was built on a personality/provocateur theory, which held that the strike was instigated either by chronically dissatisfied workers or by someone in league with outside forces interested in destroying a "growing, thriving lesbian business." The owners alternately portrayed the workers as lazy, irresponsible, resentful because of unrequited love, or consciously determined to undermine the business. Power enters into this analysis only in the owners' focus on the individual psychology of certain employees who allegedly were not comfortable accepting authority and so created a strike situation in order to feel some measure of control.[14]

Explanations that ascribe the conflict to static personality traits fail to account for the workers' movement from enthusiasm to anger over time. The provocateur theory provides no better explanation, since it discounts the solidarity maintained by the workers throughout the struggle.[15] To speak of the "mob mentality" that held workers together, or the weakness of character that prevented individuals from standing apart from the group, implies that the workers followed one another like sheep, without legitimate grievances and a clear understanding of their own actions. The owners' preoccupation with the personality/provocateur theory also draws attention away from the possibility that they too might be implicated in the conflict.

The workers were less inclined to reduce the conflict to personalities, insisting instead that "nobody [at Amazon] was a good guy or a bad guy." They learned to distinguish between an individual's particular attitudes or competencies and her standing in the job hierarchy. Rather than defending Mary's actions, they identified broader problems with training and apprenticeship. Rather than attacking Carol's decision to side with Lauren about the lunches, they criticized the division of labor that induced the owners to take the same position. However, this growing awareness of structural factors underlying the conflict existed alongside, and in contradiction with, a set of liberal presuppositions evident in the workers' two most popular explanations for the dispute: the miscommunication theory and the mismanagement theory.

The miscommunication theory represents the women of Amazon as equal, rational, independent individuals who came into conflict only because they misunderstood one another. Individual interviews clearly show, however, that both sides in the dispute can accurately reproduce the other's point of view. In addition, the premises of this theory are invalidated by the power differential that allowed the owners to set the terms for communication and to refuse to negotiate with their employees.

The mismanagement theory depicts the owners as incompetent managers; presumably, if Lauren and Carol had taken a few business courses or had acquired more experience running a shop, the conflict could have been avoided. Although this analysis recognizes the power differential at Amazon, it does not call for a redistribution or redefinition of power because it shares the owners' basic assumption that the needs of employers and employees can always be reconciled. But if we consider needs as historical products tied to a changing division of labor,[16] it becomes apparent that merely substituting more competent actors or rectifying individual "mistakes" would not have been sufficient to prevent these needs from coming into conflict.

We believe that a class analysis is essential for comprehending the social, historical, and structural factors shaping the conflict that these theories ignore. By class we mean the relations of property and production mediated by the division of labor that separated the women of Amazon into owners/managers and workers, adding a dimension of power to personal relationships that politicized bonds of mutual trust. In our view, material factors like ownership, the division of labor, and the organization of production are dynamically interrelated with the production of needs, culture, perceptions, and feelings. Obviously, then, we disagree with those who interpret class in a narrowly economistic or deterministic sense. The way in which the public/private split is bridged by linking lesbian identity to productive activity demonstrates that class relations alone cannot explain events at Amazon. But without an understanding of class relations, lesbian feminism remains grounded in the same liberal, individualistic assumptions that orginally led the women of Amazon to expect the bonds of trust to prevail over any dissension that could arise.

CLASS RELATIONS AND THE ORGANIZATION OF PRODUCTION

Class relations at Amazon, based on a hierarchical division of labor that enabled two individuals to own the business and maintain the power to define the conditions under which the others would work, shaped the tensions that eventually led to the strike. From the beginning, these tensions were inherent in the organization of production at Amazon, particularly in four key areas: the commission system, job allocations, apprenticeships, and informal job definitions.[17] They surfaced and became the focus of overt conflict only after the owners decided to expand the business and work in the office, creating a dichotomy between mental and manual labor that sharply distinguished owners from workers. In the face of these charges, Lauren and Carol found themselves struggling to defend their prerogatives as owners as their needs increasingly came into contradiction with the needs of their employees.

Carol and Lauren certainly never aspired to be bosses. In establishing Amazon they were motivated not by the desire for profit or the will to exercise power for power's sake but by the vision of working independently and determining the conditions of their own labor. Like many entrepreneurs who open small businesses, they initially hoped to escape the alienation[18] they had experienced in other work situations: "Do we want to work for those creepy lawyers and doctors for the rest of our lives? [Or] do we want to try to set up something that's ours? It may be a lot of things, but it will at least be ours." The connection Lauren and Carol drew between ownership and self-determination lay behind their insistence on maintaining control as tensions heightened during the months prior to the strike.

When Carol and Lauren first began to hire mechanics to work under them, they decided to pay them by commission rather than salary to ensure that the fledgling business would not go in the red. The commission system allowed mechanics a degree of control over their work, an arrangement that neither owner initially regarded as problematic but that later became a key issue in the struggle. Because mechanics were paid not by the hour but for jobs actually completed, they came to feel, as one mechanic phrased it, that "the time we worked there was our time." Some saw themselves more as subcontractors than employees, insisting, "All we were doing, really, is using [the owners'] space and giving them half the money we made." Workers felt not so much a time obligation to Amazon as an obligation to get the work done.

The commission system also tended to give employees a clearer picture of how Amazon made its profit and how much of that profit came from their labor: "We could see how much money they made off of our labor. . . . You doubled everyone's wages and they got it, plus the money they made on parts." This perception of the relation between their work and the business's prosperity fed the workers' sense of outrage when the owners refused to negotiate the terms of the February job descriptions.

The owners' control of job allocations constituted another potential source of conflict. A mechanic's commission-based income was contingent on the availability of work and on whether or not she received time-efficient jobs that matched her skill level. Several workers recalled being the "star" or the "fave" when they first arrived at Amazon only to become the recipients of time-consuming "shit jobs" as newer employees were given preferred assignments. Although not all the mechanics at Amazon experienced favoritism, concentration of the power to allocate jobs in the hands of the owners made the workers equally dependent on Carol and Lauren's continued good will.

Training and apprenticeship were vital under commission, since specialization in only a few tasks left an apprentice-level mechanic particularly vulnerable to job-allocation decisions. Without adequate supervision and opportunities to learn new skills, a novice assigned an unfamiliar task – and the more experienced mechanics she turned to for help – lost time and money. At Amazon apprenticeship was not a formal program but a loosely structured arrangement in which employees were told an owner would be available to assist them when necessary. After the owners moved into the office, apprentices were largely left to fend for themselves in what became an increasingly untenable position.

Finally, the informality of job definitions under the politics of trust highlighted the inconsistencies between the owners' feminist ideals and Amazon's actual business structure. The owners promised their parts runner, Mary, that she could become an apprentice as part of their commitment to helping women enter the auto-repair trade. At the same time, however, the owners expected her to continue to make herself generally available to meet their needs because she was the only salaried worker below them in the job hierarchy. Without reorganizing the division of labor, the owners never provided the conditions that would have made it possible for Mary to become a mechanic. Nor were the owners willing to relinquish their control over defining the content of workers' jobs, as Mary discovered when she confronted them on this issue.

Because capitalist culture values conceptual work over the "mere" execution of ideas,[19] the mental/manual division between owners and employees that arose in the late summer of 1981 reinforced the owners' power to set the terms for the other women's labor. In practice, this separation meant that the two owners' needs and perceptions became more congruent and more opposed to those of their employees. One owner noted, "There's always been a kind of 'us' and a 'them' between the office and the shop," a division that separated even the two owners when they worked in different spheres. "You're in the shop and you see everything from the mechanics' side. You're in the office and you see everything from the customers' side." For Carol, "the one thing that was a big pull for me about both of us being in [the office] was that we were going to be on the same side."

The way the owners chose to expand the shop and the creation of a mental/ manual split deepened class divisions at Amazon and brought underlying tensions to the fore. A heavier work load, tighter scheduling, and a greater number of mechanics meant an increase in work pressures and a decrease in the time available to resolve conflicts as they emerged. As the owners perceived a need to cut overhead and raise productivity, they began to contest accustomed areas of worker self-determination in a general move to tighten up the shop.

Control over mechanics' hours became a matter of controversy once the owners decided to adhere to a strict 8:30 to 5:30 rule. When workers resisted rigid scheduling by arguing that their time was their own under commission, the owners interpreted their defiance as laziness and a lack of commitment to Amazon's success. In their proposed job descriptions, the owners finally decided to replace the commission system with salaries "because that was the only way . . . we could know we were going to get eight hours of work from people." Many mechanics opposed the change because their new salaries were based on individual averages of their previous year's wages, which meant that they would receive the same amount of money annually for working longer hours.

Meanwhile, the owners' preoccupation with office work meant a decline in income for apprentice-level mechanics, who lacked regular supervision. Although the more experienced mechanics were willing to offer their assistance, they nonetheless resented these costly intrusions on their time. The owners rebuffed the workers' suggestion to pay a mechanic to be a lead worker or supervisor, even though the owners previously had compensated themselves for the same responsibility. Problems involving novice mechanics' limited training and narrow specialization were compounded when the owners allocated simple but moneymaking jobs to a new employee hired in the fall of 1981, who turned out to be on an apprentice level. The other less-experienced mechanic in the shop promptly witnessed a sharp drop in her weekly paycheck as she lost most of the jobs she knew how to do well. Such actions incensed many workers, ultimately leading to their demand for a steady base pay.

Carol and Lauren found themselves in the middle of yet another struggle when what they saw as a need for greater efficiency with expansion led them to oppose Mary's efforts to renegotiate the definition of her job to meet her need for an apprenticeship. By insisting Mary get the lunches and do the filing, the owners invoked tasks especially symbolic of female subordination. The other workers, disturbed by the way the owners were "jerking Mary around," made her right to an apprenticeship a major issue as the strike developed.

With tensions mounting, workers saw their Christmas presents as the "last straw." The owners still find it incomprehensible that the workers organized over such a seemingly trivial issue because they fail to recognize the symbolic meaning of those presents. Since Christmas bonuses traditionally serve as a statement of evaluation from employers, these token gifts were taken as a "slap in the face" of the workers' commitment to Amazon. The gifts had economic as well as ideological significance, since they were associated with the owners' decision to close the shop for a week, leaving the workers with no income, no Christmas bonus, and, according to employees, no respect. Because the owners were now so clearly treating the other women not as friends and equals but as employees, the Christmas presents symbolized the demise of the politics of trust by marking the class division that later would separate the two sides in the dispute.

PARADIGM SHIFTING: FROM THE POLITICS OF TRUST TO THE POLITICS OF CONTRACT

As the politics of trust began to disintegrate, the women of Amazon adopted an opposing symbolic paradigm, what we term the politics of contract. It represented an alternative mode of negotiating labor relations in which owners and workers ideally would bargain to agree on a business structure made explicit through written job descriptions and set policies. Although this formulation appears neutral from the standpoint of gender and sexual identity, the women at Amazon came to favor it precisely because the two paradigms of contract and trust were relationally defined by incorporating popular – and opposed – notions of male and female.[20] Although the women at Amazon did not consciously define themselves in relation to men, their understanding of a lesbian business as an "all-giving, all-nurturing, endlessly supportive" institution carried an implicit contrast with the "cold, unfeeling" world of heterosexual male businesses where decisions were held to be determined legalistically without regard for workers' needs.[21] Becuase the categories female and male exhaust the range of possible gender attributes in American society, the link between these categories and the two contrasting paradigms made those paradigms appear to be the only conceivable options for conducting labor relations. When the politics of trust proved inadequate, the politics of contract provided a readily available model sanctioned by the dominant society for attempting to settle the growing differences between workers and owners.

Both paradigms obscured class relations within Amazon. Under the politics of trust, the owners had asserted that Amazon was a nonoppressive environment by definition because it provided a haven from the "real world" where women have to "put up with crap from men." This belief allowed them to argue that any woman dissatisfied with working conditions should "go be with the boys," which had the double effect of augmenting their power and suppressing worker initiatives for change. At the same time, industry standards implicit in the contrast between Amazon and the straight male business world could be selectively invoked to justify practices such as paying the parts runner a minimal salary.

The owners' shift toward a politics of contract came in the wake of expansion. In light of their new concern with raising productivity and decreasing overhead, the owners began to perceive their employees as taking advantage of Amazon's loose structure. The institution of a written policy in October marked the owners' first attempt to establish a more structured work environment. To the owners, this deliberate decision to "act like bosses" meant abandoning the ideals of nurturance and sensitivity they associated with lesbian-feminist entrepreneurs to assume the straight male-identified role of a "wrist-slapping disciplinarian." By the time they handed out job descriptions in the form of ultimatums, they had come to see themselves as "behaving maybe the way the boys do when . . . they say, 'This is it. Either you do it or you're not here.' "

The workers also came to accept the framework of the politics of contract in their interactions with the owners, but for very different reasons. Workers began to press for job descriptions, monthly shop meetings, and more specific policies in order to protect themselves against what they regarded as arbitrary assertions of managerial power. The formal presentation of a list of issues and demands represented their attempt to "depersonalize [the situation at Amazon] and make it a business thing."

Because the politics of contract was identified with a combination of formality and male gender attributes, the women of Amazon began to belittle emotional reactions to the growing conflict as responses typical of women but inappropriate to businesslike conduct. In the process, they unknowingly rejected one of the most positive aspects of lesbian workplace culture: the integration of public and private that encourages bringing the whole self, including feelings, into work. Workers criticized the owners for responding "on this real emotional level to our demands, about how we were insulting their intelligence and honor." Meanwhile, the owners dismissed the strike as lacking substantive issues by referring to the emotional weight behind workers' actions. Maintaining the bridge between the private and public would have allowed both sides to acknowledge the intensity of feeling surrounding the dispute without separating emotions from more tangible bread-and-butter issues. Instead, the women at Amazon redrew the private/public boundary by shifting to a paradigm identified solely with the public sphere.

No one at Amazon was satisfied with the character of labor relations under the politics of contract, but the dualistic definition of the two paradigms made contractual relations seem to be the only possible substitute for relations based on friendship and trust. Since both sides viewed the loose structure and informal managerial style associated with the politics of trust as the source of the conflicts at Amazon, both initially expected a shift to a more formalized business structure to solve their differences. While some workers continued to hope for a consensual settlement, others began to understand the conflict as a power struggle rooted in the division of labor that would not be resolved by the establishment of a set policy. Implicit in the struggle over job descriptions was the recognition that measures intended to protect workers could also be used by the owners to maintain control. Workers who once had argued against the commission system opposed conversion to salary on the grounds that an hourly wage would "give [the owners] too much power" by allowing them to regulate employees' hours and subject workers to arbitrary requests.

Despite their growing awareness of the implications of the power differential at Amazon, workers believed the dispute could be resolved within the existing class structure. Yet the issues they raised posed a tacit challenge to relations of production that concentrated decision-making power in the owners' hands. This seeming paradox rests on the fact that, to the degree the workers' stand encompassed a claim to self-determination, their concerns could not have been adequately addressed while class relations at Amazon remained unaltered. Ownership never became an articulated issue largely because the workers were tactically and philosophically committed to a politics of contract that limited their proposals to discrete, point-by-point demands.

Frustration with the restrictions of a bargaining procedure derived from male trade unionism led the workers to search for a "different way" to approach the owners, but their efforts to break through the paradigms that framed their struggle were unsuccessful. They failed in part because the shift from a politics of trust to a politics of contract focused discussions on questions of work discipline and managerial style. The deeper questions concerning ownership and the division of labor at Amazon, which were not mediated by notions of gender and sexual identity, could not be addressed within the terms of either paradigm. The final irony was that the configuration of class relations at the heart of the Amazon conflict was never questioned as being incongruous in a lesbian institution but was instead uncritically adopted from the straight male world.

LESBIAN IDENTITY IN THE FORMATION OF A WORKERS' ALLIANCE

The radical potential created with the bridging of the private and public was not completely destroyed by the elaboration of class relations and the emergence of open conflict at Amazon. The commitment that accompanied the integration of personal and work life had the radicalizing effect of motivating workers to struggle against what they perceived to be unfair labor practices. The unusually high degree of solidarity maintained by the workers throughout this struggle also had its roots in the kind of workplace Amazon was before the strike. Solidarity among workers was not a deterministic consequence of their being lesbians per se, but an outgrowth of a social context that allowed them to be out on the job in a lesbian-identified institution. Any analysis that reduced events at Amazon to a class conflict without taking these distinguishing features into consideration would miss the dynamics that turned a situation of contention and contradiction into a full-blown labor dispute.

The workers' radicalization was gradual. In the beginning, one mechanic commented, "We weren't a political force; we were just a bunch of women working." Concern about working conditions led them to meet as a group, but class and politics were not explicit topics at these initial meetings. At first women simply compared their reactions to incidents at work, breaking through the silence surrounding grievances that had kept individuals believing they were the only ones angered and confused by the owners' actions. As workers found their personal experiences confirmed by the experiences of others, they began to discuss the possibility of collective action.

Paradoxically, the same bonds of trust and friendship that made it difficult for many workers to break with the owners also stimulated their willingness to challenge the owners' position. Because the politics of trust masked power inequalities at Amazon, it had encouraged workers to consider all points negotiable and to believe they could ask for whatever seemed "fair" and "reasonable" according to their own needs. When the owners met their list of issues with a set of nonnegotiable job descriptions, the workers' fundamental point of unity became an agreement not to accept the job descriptions in the form of ultimatums.

The workers' ability to achieve and maintain such solidarity is all the more remarkable given the diversity of the group and the differences in their politics. But the foundation for the collective structure that enabled them to mediate their disagreements had already been laid by the patterns of cooperation and strong emotional ties the women had developed working together in the shop. Workers referred to this sense of camaraderie and closeness to explain what differentiated Amazon from a shop employing straight women, suggesting that these patterns were a product of lesbian workplace culture rather than a composite of individuated ties: "Everybody was a tight group at Amazon. . . . You've got all these dykes! [The owners] used to be a part of that when we were smaller, but then we started getting bigger and everybody had different needs, and so it was 'us' and 'them.' Unfortunately, it had to come to that. But we were all pretty grouped emotionally before this stuff came up, so that we were all grouped in battle."

The workers' alliance was based on the synthesis of lesbian identity and a growing awareness of class divisions tied to the division of labor. On the one hand, the women clearly interpreted the conflict as a labor dispute and took a stand based on their needs as workers. On the other hand, they directed their appeals primarily to other lesbians and selected their tactics with the aim of keeping the struggle within the lesbian community.

Sensitivity to stereotypes about lesbians' pugnacity and women's alleged incompetence in business affairs made the workers deliberately protective of Amazon at the gay/straight boundary. Workers consistently refused to address the general public or what they considered the "straight media." They turned to the National Labor Relations Board as a last resort in order to keep the owners' job proposals from taking effect as contracts. Workers reluctantly agreed to bring in the "big boys" from the union only after they felt they had exhausted alternatives within the lesbian community and faced the possibility of having to abandon the strike effort altogether. Today, the union's failure to make progress toward a settlement seems to confirm the workers' original skepticism about the union's commitment to the Amazon struggle and its ability to comprehend the concerns of a lesbian shop.

Stanley Aronowitz has argued that the most significant innovations in recent social theory have come from movements like feminism that have grown up outside the traditional boundaries of Marxist and trade unionist politics. Because strictly economic disputes appear to have lost their subversive potential under advanced capitalist conditions, Aronowitz predicts that questions raised by what he calls "cultural movements" will become the new focus of historical change.[22] Events at Amazon seem to corroborate both hypotheses. However, Aronowitz's thesis is qualified by the fact that lesbian workplaces represent a historically unprecedented form of organizing productive relations that cannot be adequately comprehended by a notion of culture set apart from economic factors. The culture that has emerged in institutions like Amazon is not a simple reflection of lesbian-feminist principles but results in part from the bridge between the public and private spheres created by bringing together in practice the hitherto ideologically opposed categories of labor and sexuality. In the Amazon case, the development of a lesbian workplace culture united workers in a struggle that encompassed both economic and cultural concerns. In this sense the Amazon conflict challenges socialist-feminist theory to grapple with issues of sexuality, and urges lesbian-feminist theory to move beyond its focus on sexuality and its legacy of liberal assumptions, in order to develop an analysis of class relations in the lesbian context.

CONCLUSION: CLASS AND SEXUALITY

Why has a dialogue about class comparable to the current discussion of race and racism failed to emerge within lesbian feminism? The Amazon case draws attention to several contributing factors: (1) the limited interpretation of class as class background favored by lesbian feminists; (2) liberal strains in lesbian-feminist theory that discourage a relational analysis of class focusing on social structure; (3) the institutional hegemony of an entrepreneurial and professional stratum within the lesbian community; and (4) the heterosexual bias of socialist and socialist-feminist approaches to class theory, which limits their applicability to lesbians.

Information on individuals' class backgrounds clearly cannot explain events at Amazon, for women from both middle-class and working-class backgrounds allied on opposite sides of the dispute. "It would be so much easier, in a way," observed the owner who grew up in a working-class household, "if Lauren and I were both upper class and my father gave me $50,000 and her father gave her $60,000, and we plunked it into a bank and started the business. . . . But it's not that simple." To claim that class background does not determine present behavior does not mean it did not influence decisions made and strategies adopted during the conflict. For example, the limited resources available to workers from certain class backgrounds made it more difficult for them to remain out on strike. In general, however, Amazon's employees had a clear sense that their current position in the relations of production outweighed their varied class backgrounds: "We all knew where we came from, but we all were working, and we knew how hard we worked, and we knew how we were getting treated. When you're a worker, you're a worker."

A background interpretation of class has led most lesbian feminists to define class according to individualized criteria like occupation, income level, education, values, attitudes, and other indicators of socioeconomic status. While these at-tributes may be linked to class, they do not define class, unless one accepts the liberal view of society as an amalgam of autonomous actors fixed in absolute class positions. On the basis of occupation, all the women at Amazon could be labeled working class because of their blue-collar trade. If a combination of income and educational attainment were used as a gauge, some workers might be assigned a higher class position than the owners. Aside from the mutual inconsistency of these evaluations, neither offers any insight into the relations of class and power that actively shaped the Amazon conflict.[23] In contrast, placing the owners within the context of the job hierarchy at Amazon and the division of labor that structures ownership in society at large allowed us to explore the power dif-ferential that put Lauren and Carol in a position of dominance over other women working in the shop.

A relational analysis of events at Amazon supports the conclusion that since property relations and the division of labor continuously generate class divisions, tactics of consciousness raising and moral exhortations to eliminate classism will be insufficient to keep conflicts from emerging in lesbian and feminist institu-tions. The expectation that "feminist morality" or a principled politics can mitigate class differences rests on a notion of politics as an individualized, ideological stance adopted at will, independent of material circumstances and capable of transcending them. But at Amazon, differences in the values and political commitments of the owners did not prevent them from taking the same side in the dispute once lines were drawn. Lauren felt "morally justified" in presenting the workers with nonnegotiable job descriptions, never realizing the extent to which she defined morality and "responsible action" with regard to the needs of the business. Carol, on the other hand, found it "bizarre to be on the side of the owner. It's much easier for me to think of it from the workers' stand-point." Yet she held to her position.

The owners both supported the principle of solving Amazon's problems through dialogue rather than firing dissenting employees, yet in the end their power as owners and managers allowed them to abandon this ideal. In Carol's words, "Somebody reached the point where they put their foot down and said, 'That's it.' And you can only do that when you are in the powered position, which we were." Both owners admitted having discussed strategy about the possibility of an employee walkout in response to their job descriptions: "We did discuss it. We said, 'If that happens, the two of us built this from nothing. Now we have the books, we have the diagnostic equipment, we have the customers, we got the building, we're way ahead.'"

In the workers' eyes, control of the property associated with the business gave the owners a decisive advantage during the struggle. When economic necessity forced the workers to drop the picket line to look for other jobs, the prospect of negotiation receded as the owners continued production in the building all ten women had shared before the strike. Since the owners established Amazon with minimal capital investment and took out few loans in succeeding years, the property and equipment that helped them win the struggle actually came from surplus value created by the combined efforts of Amazon's employees and nonpartisan support from the women's community. The owners' exclusive claim to this property was based solely on a legal concept of ownership backed by a patriarchal state. The same principle of ownership underpinned the dominant class position that structured the owners' moral stance, neutralized their well-meaning intentions, and superseded their lesbian-feminist politics at the point of conflict.

It is true that Amazon is "not Bechtel"—a major multinational corporation—as the owners were quick to point out, but this fact obviously did not prevent class relations and a class-linked conflict from emerging in the shop. Although the lesbian community lies well outside the mainstream of American capitalism, it does include a stratum of entrepreneurs, professionals, and small capitalists like Carol and Lauren who own or control many of the institutions serving and symbolizing that community. We suggest that in practice such control allows this group of women to maintain an institutional hegemony[24] that mediates the relation of lesbian identity to community in ways that alternately support and oppress lesbians who stand in different relations to the social division of labor.[25]

The concern with self-reliance and independence that originally led Carol and Lauren to become entrepreneurs also informed their argument that dissatisfied workers should open their own enterprises rather than challenge the owners' right to make unilateral decisions in matters affecting employees.[26] Yet what might otherwise be dismissed as regressive, petty-bourgeois values in the tradition of nineteenth-century entrepreneurial capitalism has a different meaning, origin, and political significance in this lesbian context. For Lauren and Carol, self-sufficiency represented a liberating ideology that signified autonomy from men in the area of skills, training, and the ability to earn an equitable income. The same ideology became oppressive only when, as owners and employers, they confused self-determination with the need to control the labor of women they hired.

The coincidence of entrepreneurial values with aspects of lesbian identity in the ideology of self-sufficiency is one more example of the recurrent theme in this study: there is no justification at the level of concrete analysis for abstracting class from sexuality or for treating heterosexism and class hegemony as two distinct types of oppression operating along separate axes. The strike at Amazon cannot be analyzed as a textbook labor conflict precisely because the male and heterosexist bias of most scholarly texts renders them incapable of grasping this integration. While a critique of the bias in class theory is beyond the scope of this paper, the Amazon case indicates why such an integration is necessary.

Lesbians are not simply exceptions to the rule who defy categorization as "nonattached" or "single" (but presumably self-supporting) women or as women residing in households with men.[27] Since self-identified lesbians in American society share an ideology of self-sufficiency rather than the ideological expectation not to work traditionally held by many heterosexual women, the question of derived class becomes largely irrelevant in speaking of lesbian relationships.[28] None of the women in the Amazon study even suggested the possibility of defining her class position through her lover, though several were in relationships of long standing. Lesbians also fall outside the theoretical focus of most debates in socialist feminism, which tend to center on the sexual division of labor.[29] Although the sexual division of labor and job segregation by sex influence all women's experience, for most lesbians gender distinctions do not coincide with the split between home and work life or with the allocation of tasks within the home. When the split between personal and work life is linked to sexuality with the bridging of the private/public split in lesbian workplaces, socialist feminism proffers no theory capable of grasping the significance of what happens once lesbian identity is joined to productive activity.

At Amazon we saw how the reconciliation of the public and private created the potential for a nonalienating work environment where women were able to develop close ties with co-workers as well as to bring into the shop emotions and other ostensibly personal aspects of the self. After the walkout/lockout this integration shaped the dispute by placing emotions at the center of the struggle so that at various points the struggle itself involved drawing and redrawing the boundary between elements of public and private life. While the bridging of the private/public split could not defuse class relations at Amazon, it generated the conditions for overcoming class divisions by fostering a lesbian workplace culture that promoted solidarity among the workers and motivated them to defend their needs in a situation where the owners held the balance of power.

One of Amazon's owners ended her interview with a plea that lesbians learn to "put aside personal feelings and vested interests" or risk the destruction of community institutions. A careful analysis of the Amazon dispute points to the importance of taking personal feelings into account rather than putting them aside and remaining within the limitations of the contrasting paradigms of trust and contract. The effect of suppressing or ignoring the personal will be to rein-voke the division between the private and public, when the ability to bridge that gap constitutes one of the greatest strengths of lesbian institutions. In this sense, the experience of the women of Amazon Auto Repair challenges both lesbian feminism and socialist feminism to break through old paradigms, to recognize that separating sexuality and class in theory merely replicates the segregation of the private from the public, and the personal from the political, in the realm of every-day life.

As for vested interests, they cannot simply be discarded at will, since they have material roots in socially constructed needs mediated by property relations and the division of labor. Yet there exist options for restructuring lesbian workplaces that reject ownership while providing leadership roles, job rotation, procedures for delegating responsibility, shared decision-making processes, and a division of labor that does not rest on a fixed power differential. The radical potential for nonalienated labor created in lesbian workplaces invites us to ex-plore these alternatives as a means of redefining power as energy, skill, and capacity rather than as domination.[30] By drawing attention to the ongoing reproduction of class relations within the lesbian community, the struggle at Amazon advances the possibility of self-determination inside and outside the labor process for all lesbians, not just for the few who formally or informally con-trol lesbian institutions.

NOTES

1. For examples of the interpretation of class as background within the lesbian-feminist movement, see Charlotte Bunch and Nancy Myron, eds., *Class and Feminism* (Baltimore: Diana Press, 1974); Joan Gibbs and Sara Bennett, eds., *Top Ranking: A Collection of Articles on Racism and Classism in the Lesbian Community* (New York: Come! Unity Press, 1980).

2. See Zillah R. Eisenstein, *The Radical Future of Liberal Feminism* (New York: Longman, Inc., 1981).

3. Christine Riddiough, "Socialism, Feminism, and Gay/Lesbian Liberation," in *Women and Revolution*, ed. Lydia Sargent (Boston: South End Press, 1981).

4. One woman had moved out of the area, and we were unable to contact the remaining mechanic.

5. Regardless of where one stands in the definitional debate on lesbian identity (see Ann Ferguson et al., "On 'Compulsory Heterosexuality and Lesbian Existence': Defining the Issues," *Signs: Journal of Women in Culture and Society* 7, no. 1 [Autumn 1981]: 158–99), it is clear that competing usages of the term "lesbian" all rest on criteria such as friendship, sexuality, and feeling, which historically have been assigned to the realm of the personal.

6. See Annete Kuhn and Ann Marie Wolpe, eds., *Feminism and Materialism: Women and Modes of Production* (London: Routledge and Kegan Paul, 1978); Iris Young, "Beyond the Unhappy Marriage: A Critique of Dual Systems Theory," in Sargent, ed. (n. 3 above), pp. 43–69.

7. Lesbian identity then becomes a defining element of a distinctive type of workplace culture, making Amazon something more than an aggregation of isolated employees who "happened" to be lesbians or a repository for the piecemeal importation of artifacts from lesbian feminism.

8. In our heterosexist society, "woman" and "feminist" often function as code words among lesbians for "lesbian" and "lesbian feminist," in much the same way as sexism encourages the substitution of "people" or "men" as generic terms for "women."

9. Nancy Harsock, "Political Change: Two Perspectives on Power," in *Building Feminist Theory*, ed. Quest Staff (New York: Longman, Inc. 1981), pp. 3–19.

10. Audre Lorde, *Uses of the Erotic: The Erotic as Power* (New York: Out & Out Books, 1978).

11. The bridging of the private/public split provides a mechanism to explain the high levels of commitment often noted as characteristic of lesbian institutions. See Barbara Ponse, *Identities in the Lesbian World: The Social Construction of Self* (Westport, Conn: Greenwood Press, 1978). Contrary to Ponse's findings, no significant association between commitment and conformity appeared in the Amazon case.

12. Hartsock.

13. An assumption widely criticized in recent years in the discussion on race and difference within the women's community. See Cherrie Moraga and Gloria Anzaldúa, eds., *This Bridge Called My Back: Writings by Radical Women of Color* (Watertown, Mass.: Persephone Press, 1981).

14. Compare Sherry McCoy and Maureen Hicks, "A Psychological Retrospective on Power in the Contemporary Lesbian-Feminist Community," *Frontiers: A Journal of Women Studies* 4, no. 3 (1979): 65–69. Their exclusively personal conception of power ignores the possibility that both power and needs may be shaped by social relations like class that divide the lesbian community.

15. We do not mean to imply that the owners' fears for the survival of lesbian businesses are groundless; we do question the allegation that the workers acted as agents of reactionary forces.

16. Agnes Heller, *The Theory of Need in Marx* (London: Allison & Busby, 1976), p. 25.

17. On the links between the changing organization of production and class relations under industrial capitalism, see Harry Braverman, *Labor and Monopoly Capital* (New York: Monthly Review Press, 1974); Richard Edwards, *Contested Terrain: The Transformation of the Workplace in the Twentieth Century* (New York: Basic Books, 1979).

18. Bertell Ollman, *Alienation* (London: Cambridge University Press, 1971), pp. 133–34. Following Ollman, we take alienation to mean a separation of the individual from her life activity, the products of her labor, and other human beings within the labor process.

19. Karl Marx and Frederick Engels, *The German Ideology* (New York: International Publishers, 1978), pp. 51–52.

20. For cross-cultural discussions of relationally defined gender constructs, see Carol MacCormack and Marilyn Strathern, eds., *Nature, Culture and Gender* (London: Cambridge University Press, 1980); Sherry B. Ortner and Harriet Whitehead, eds., *Sexual*

Meanings: The Cultural Construction of Gender and Sexuality (New York: Cambridge University Press, 1981).

21. On the owners' side this understanding reflected lesbian-feminist ideology, but for most workers it developed through an appeal to notions of gender and sexuality to explain differences in their work experiences at Amazon and at other businesses.

22. Stanley Aronowitz, *The Crisis in Historical Materialism* (New York: Praeger Publishers, 1981), pp. 105–6, 133.

23. Anthony Giddens, "Class Structuration and Class Consciousness," in *Classes, Power, and Conflict,* ed. Anthony Giddens and David Held (Berkeley and Los Angeles: University of California Press, 1982), p. 158.

24. On the concept of hegemony, see Antonio Gramsci, *Selections from the Prison Notebooks* (New York: International Publishers, 1980), p. 12; Raymond Williams, *Marxism and Literature* (Oxford: Oxford University Press, 1977), pp. 108–14.

25. Introducing power as a variable challenges Susan Krieger's static view of lesbian communities as either supportive or coercive to individuals ("Lesbian Identity and Community: Recent Social Science Literature," *Signs* 8, no. 1 [Autumn 1982]: 91–108).

26. Clearly it would be impractical for every lesbian auto mechanic to open her own repair shop. This admonition also avoids dealing with the source of divisions in the lesbian community by deprecating worker struggles and initiatives.

27. Elizabeth Garnsey advances these categories in an attempt to correct the androcentrism of such theories ("Women's Work and Theories of Class and Stratification," *Sociology* 12, no. 2 [1978]: 223–43.).

28. Jackie West, "Women, Sex, and Class," in Kuhn and Wolpe, eds. (n. 6 above), pp. 220–53.

29. The isolated attempts to apply socialist-feminist analysis to lesbians ignore class relations within the lesbian community, directing their attention instead to the origins of women's oppression or to relations at the gay/straight boundary. In addition to Riddiough (n. 3 above), see Susan Williams, "Lesbianism: A Socialist Feminist Perspective," in *Pink Triangles: Radical Perspectives on Gay Liberation,* ed. Pam Mitchell (Boston: Alyson Publications, 1980), pp. 107–16.

30. Hartsock (n. 9 above) draws a useful distinction between power understood as domination and power understood as energy, capacity, and initiative.

Section IX

Concluding and Beginning

Chapter 24 ────────────────────────────

Working Hypotheses for Women and Social Change

Mary Jo Deegan

───────────────────────────────────────

INTRODUCTION

The early founders of symbolic interaction, particularly G. H. Mead and Jane Addams, envisioned a new society based on their theory of social behavior. They assumed people were capable of collectively shaping their own fates, and social scientists played a unique role in this process. The latter group, stating a problem, collecting data concerning it, devising a solution based on that information, and then modifying that solution based on its success or failure, generated knowledge that could be used by others making democratic choices. Their theory was designed to organize and plan social action, but its political potential has been dormant for decades. This impetus was lost, for several reasons, but the particular failure to study women's issues is linked systematically to the quiescent women's movement after 1920. As a result of the second wave of feminism, beginning around the mid-1960s, a second wave of symbolic interactionism has emerged.

This book has advanced a number of hypotheses for improving women's social status. Mead called such solutions to social problems "working hypotheses" because they required constant reconsideration and reevaluation in light of changing conditions. He explained:

> It is always the unexpected that happens, for we have to recognize, not only the immediate change that is to take place, but also the reaction back upon this of the whole world within which the change takes place, and no human foresight is equal to this. In the social world we must recognize the working hypothesis as the form into which all theories must be cast as completely as in the natural sciences. (Mead, 1899: 369)

The authors' "working hypotheses" found in the chapters included here are restated now to emphasize their common orientation to change.

I present their working agenda in the full knowledge that women form a diverse group with varied definitions of what it means to be a woman. Class,

───────────────────────────────────────

Source: This chapter was written for inclusion in this volume.

race, age, sexual preference, disability, weight, attractiveness, language, and religion provide patterned dimensions for defining women and women's behavior. A portion of these patterns provide overlapping definitions of the meaning of women's rights; other patterns are quite distinct from, if not at odds with, each other. Symbolic interaction, as a theoretical perspective, provides a tool for articulating these intersections and incongruities. It does more, however. It also provides a set of pragmatic assumptions to create and maintain desired social behaviors.

WORKING HYPOTHESES FOR WOMEN'S LIBERATION

Concepts to Guide the Changes

Taft (chapter 2; hereafter, chapters are referred to by #) stresses the need for a women's movement whose members are guided by a broad social conscience. The home and the working place must not be defined *a priori* as conflicting sex-linked choices. Defining responsibilities in the home and the marketplace as adult questions, not gendered ones, places women firmly in both worlds. The schisms between family and social claims are created by people and can be changed by them.

Goffman (#3) shows that sex is the underlying code for social action. A pervasive set of gendered social rules guides the daily paths of inequality. The prevalence of gender divisions, however, is severely underperceived; thus, explicating the rules for traditional gender roles is an excellent mechanism for consciousness raising. Goffman provides a language for discussing the arrangement between the sexes in a manner that helps restore the political potential of symbolic interactionism.

Changing the Way We Acquire Gender in Early Childhood

Cahill (#4) shows the systematic way children are perceived as gendered. Adult caretakers can be encouraged and trained to monitor their behavior toward children and thereby become aware of their role in creating sexual divisions. Revising stereotyped interaction patterns affects both the child and the adult because symbolic interactionists assume that both are capable of learning and changing.

Reeves and Boyette (#5) suggest that children's art tells adults what children think about gender. Art work provides empirical data through which changes in attitudes and behavior can be gauged. Such data can be used to evaluate the effectiveness of sex desegregation programs in the schools and can provide indicators of life cycle changes in gender differentiation. In similar ways, many more gender indicators can be discovered in our daily interactions, thereby providing a concrete method to implement new ideas about sex/class rules.

Changing the Way We Acquire and Negotiate Adult Gender

Risman (#6) demonstrates that gender identity is more flexible and adaptable than many social and behavioral theorists believe. This finding has important ramifications for adult choices concerning sexuality and sexual behavior. By analyzing the linkages between identity, gender, and anatomy, she shows that these factors are not identical and do not need to be congruent for a person to achieve normality.

Risman (#6) also reveals how sororities structure traditional sex roles on contemporary university campuses. I have found this chapter to be highly charged and controversial in the classroom. It is a powerful and challenging reading for college women: women in sororities do not believe they are willingly participating in a group that is not progressive toward women's rights. Women not in sororities have rarely had the opportunity to tell "sorority girls" openly that the latter exhibit conservative gender roles. Women in sororities state openly in the classroom that they are individually egalitarian but that "other sisters" are not. They do not like to choose "sisters" on the basis of looks and money, but they "have to do it." I have always had at least one (if not two or three) students in a class of approximately fifty students drop the course after reading Risman's article! This particular article dramatically shows college women the commonplace nature of discrimination in which they themselves may participate. More researchers need to explore women's participation in traditional gender roles in everyday life.

Hammond (#8) reveals that "biography building" for women medical students is one way to unite family and social claims. These women justify their entrance into this traditionally male work by claiming that women have unique skills as physicians. Hammond does not find that this legitimation of female virtues resolves the women's problem but merely postpones its confrontation. Despite this justifiable criticism, female medical students mentioned in the article articulated a pragmatic philosophy enabling them to survive their training. A longitudinal study of these women during their medical careers could show if professional women continue to support these kinds of motives for action or if they find them as problematic as Hammond suggests.

Dill (#9) stresses the vital need to understand the wide range of women's views and experiences. Her pluralistic approach recognizes these objective differences. Working in coalitions to support specific shared interests is an important way to move toward a more egalitarian society. The recognition of the common roots of oppression is part of coalition building and uses group differences as strengths instead of barriers.

Understanding and Changing the Conflicting Demands of the Family Claim on Wives

Andersen (#10) finds that the material conditions of upper-middle-class women make traditional sex roles comfortable for this elite group. These wives define their dependence on their husbands as nonproblematic because these women have control over or access to capital earned by their husbands. Because Andersen listened to these women's accounts of their lives, she shows some of the distinctions in experience noted by Dill. These dramatically different class perspectives explain why the problems of working class and poor women appear to be nothing more than simple individual failures if defined from the perspective of women of privilege.

Gillespie (#11) suggests that public wives should have the option to be individuals instead of being mere extensions of their husbands. The recent and increasing presence of public husbands provides an opportunity to build new, nongendered partner roles for public figures. Reading and analyzing newspaper and magazine accounts of public spouses are effective everyday techniques for understanding self-preservation, gender, and power.

Gross's (#12) study of commuting couples provides concrete evidence that individuals can change institutions, in this case the institution of marriage as a social pattern. Such changes are difficult to maintain, however, and considerable emotional work is required to make these new arrangements successful. Intentional commitment provides motivation to establish and support new everyday patterns until they become more widely accepted as "normal."

Understanding and Changing the Conflicting Demands of the Family Claim on Mothers

Reinharz (#13) points to miscarriage as an experience shared by many women but discussed by few. The failure to respond to the women who miscarry and the lack of study of this major social event poignantly reveal how women's pain is denied. For some women, miscarriage is a deeply traumatic issue of being human, a mother, and physically capable of bearing a child. Sharing, discussing, and understanding this process are involved in this major women's issue, and this chapter is part of that new vision.

Horowitz (#14) reveals the innovative behavior of unmarried mothers who establish moral identity and sexuality in a community holding traditional views on appropriate behavior for women. She shows that individual women in a community can draw on a variety of resources to create new situations and legitimation. These creative solutions are not guided by an overall vision of "correct action" but emerge out of the strength of women who must survive painful, conflicting definitions of "proper behavior."

Shaul, Dowling, and Laden (#15) reveal that many people assume that disabled women are asexual and incompetent. Mothers with disabilities must fight to legitimate their adult roles as caretakers. As successful mothers, they develop new, specific rules of obedience, physical aids, and a supportive environment in which they are expected to be loving and nurturing. They are generating new ways of being mothers, radicals, and change agents.

Understanding and Changing the Conflicting Demands of Social Claims

Kanter (#16) stresses the need to increase the number of women in organizations in order to increase their power. Behavior often attributed to gender may reflect instead the organizational situation of being a numerical minority. Understanding the structural effects of relative numbers of minorities in given positions or situations pinpoints barriers to women's equality and full participation in the marketplace.

Martin (#17) extends Kanter's work on token women by looking at the traditionally masculine job of being a police officer. In addition to the low numbers of women officers, language and nonverbal dilemmas make this work gendered so it becomes nearly impossible to be a female and a competent officer. New nongendered definitions of police work are needed to eliminate the paradoxes faced by women officers.

Easterday, Papademas, Schorr, and Valentine (#19) provide detailed information on the alteration of scientific research procedures as a function of the researcher's gender. By revealing the gendered definitions of the research setting, these authors show that the process of doing research, interpreting it, and learning how to engage in it is gendered work.

Jones (#18) reminds us that women's lives are historically based, dependent on individual people, and often require the ability to survive multiple oppressions. Concrete daily acts of caring knit communities together to create female consciousness. The power to demand respect successfully and to resist exploitation. Symbolic interactionism stresses that the world is created through language, interaction, and behavior. The black women tobacco workers analyzed by Jones changed themselves, their communities, and their consciousness.

Revising Working Hypotheses

Abel (#20) powerfully documents a liberal flaw in our legal system. Women encountering job discrimination in academia discover that it is an individual problem. They are pitted against the power of a bureaucracy and colleagues with vested interests in the academy. Not only radical women are subjected to job discrimination; all women share this fate. The process of discovering the group basis for discrimination instead of defining it as an individual problem makes women who sue more radical about their rights. Changes in the marketplace must apply to all workers, and organized workers have the greatest probability of victory over discriminatory employers and colleagues.

Ferraro (#21) examines a feminist working hypothesis for aiding battered women. Shelters designed to remove women from the immediate abuse situation were intended to help eliminate battering. Such agencies, however, operate within a context of other social agencies, growing bureaucratization and specialization, and ideologies that blame the victims for their problems. Despite the original feminist agenda for battered women, these shelters were redefined by their staff in response to the larger community's expectations and training for such work. Because of similar problems with other shelters, feminists are suggesting new working hypotheses, such as removing the batterer instead of the victim from the home. Ferraro's critique is part of the process of improving working hypotheses as they are enacted in everyday life.

Blum (#22) also traces the power of the liberal vision to destroy more radical possibilities. The transformation of radical ideas in novels into liberalized, simplified, and popularized versions in movies neither challenges the everyday world nor creates a viable alternative to it. Again, family and social claims appear at odds, but the liberal version suggests these can be individually resolved whereas the radical version points to inherent contradictions that cannot be resolved for large numbers of women without institutional restructuring.

Weston and Rofel (#23) show that public and private lives need to be integrated. Cooperative goals and strong emotional ties provided a situation of solidarity that helped lesbian workers to survive class conflicts. This lesbian community, like many others, assumed that cultural or individual perspectives were able to define and resolve problems. The issue of power and control over resources appeared to be inconsequential. They soon discovered that class relations were more important than they had expected, however. They also learned that their definitions of themselves and others were stereotypical and restrictive. Despite their strengths in bridging the gaps between the public and private in the lesbian workplace, they were unable to forge similar strengths in their class relations. The authors note that the workers' failure to connect their cultural and material worlds does not negate the significant changes that were made. Once more, the power of coalitions and recognizing the strength in differences are advocated.

WORKING HYPOTHESES FOR THE FUTURE

As a group, these authors suggest a systematic approach to change every aspect of life. They emphasize that each person in every situation needs to alter gender rules. This individual action must be co-ordinated in larger groups, however, to become institutionalized. The failure to integrate changes in women's roles perpetuates inequality over many situations. The number of people involved in these changes is an important factor here. So far, only token numbers of feminists have struggled for integrated change embracing the public and private, family and social claims. The dominant patriarchal definitions of society remain fundamentally the same. The range of situations in which feminists act must be encompassing, and their language and vision must be shared.

Resolving the conflicts between family and social claims requires new definitions of work in the family and emotional bonds outside of the family. These redefinitions of situations are social changes beyond any one individual's free choices. Public rules and spaces segregate the sexes in the worlds of finance, politics, the military, education, and the streets. Similarly, public rules keep behavior in the home hidden, including beating and raping of women and children. Only public solutions to public problems will provide equality for both sexes.

We need to be daring in our experiments, while we are critical of our plans and results. Only such an open mind toward action will provide hypotheses that work for the good of all people. The liberation of women means the liberation of both sexes, but it will occur only after many bitter struggles. To call oneself liberated is easy; to become liberated is difficult. It is the task of a people, and not merely individuals, to be free.

REFERENCE

Mead, George H. 1899 "The Working Hypothesis in Social Reform." *American Journal of Sociology* 5 (March): 369–71.

For Product Safety Concerns and Information please contact our EU
representative GPSR@taylorandfrancis.com
Taylor & Francis Verlag GmbH, Kaufingerstraße 24, 80331 München, Germany